A Brush With The Real

Figurative Painting Today

Marc Valli & Margherita Dessanay

An Elephant Book
Laurence King Publishing

Introduction

For Slower Images: The Rebirth of Painting

At the inception of this book were questions such as, 'why do we *still* have painting?' or, 'does painting still have a role to play in contemporary culture?' Paradoxically, I believe, in order to start replying to those questions it may be helpful to compare the role the art form plays today, in the age of mass media and digital communication, to the one it performed at the outset of our modern Western tradition of painting, whether in fourteenth century Florence or in fifteenth century Flanders.

The world has never been so full of images: those on our mobile phones and computer screens, on newsstands and book covers, in films and on TV, on packaging and billboards and in shop windows. We walk, work and rest amid throngs of vivid, avidly attention-seeking images, every space and every moment of our lives crammed full of them. You couldn't imagine a more different environment from the late Middle Ages when the world would grow pitch black as night fell. Not only were images rare the very medium allowing us to see them – light – was severely rationed. Every night, you would be plunged into long (or, depending on the season, slightly less long) periods of darkness. Imagine, as Johan Huizinga once suggested, the effect of a candle-lit window on the weary traveller as he made his way through an almost pitch black landscape.[1] Now imagine the effect of a fresco in a chapel on that same traveller. In those days, images didn't have to work so hard to portray miraculous deeds: every image was in and of itself already a small miracle.

But if the environment in which painters live and work today could not be more different from that of their early Renaissance counterparts, surprisingly, the language and the way in which they practise their trade (an over-reliance on Google Images aside) are not so different: canvases, brushes, meticulously primed surfaces, carefully chosen and attentively studied subjects – not to mention rich patrons (with the museum having replaced the church as the awe-inspiring institution of choice). After more than a century in which artists were obsessed with effecting radical breaks from older forms of making art, a new generation of painters is by no means indifferent to this continuity present in their chosen art form, even to the earliest days of human history. For example, Cynthia Daignault tells us that she feels that 'one of the best things about being a painter is being on a continuum with a long, unbroken history of human production that stretches back thousands of years'. Similarly, Wilhelm Sasnal remarked outside the interview included in this book that 'there are so many images around these days, but most of them are not "real", as in they only exist on the Internet.... On the other hand, painting is based on a very prima technique (you're almost back to the Lascaux caves). You have these real tools there in your hands and you are trying to depict something....'

Just as surprising is the thought of how the primary role of painters has remained largely unchanged. Like their Renaissance counterparts, painters today are still responsible for creating *unique* images. And, as we shall argue throughout this book, this role has never been of such vital importance to the culture.

Rescuing Subjects from the Flood

Today, in the world of mass media, a world where everything is being instantly, infinitely and indefinitely reproduced, a world of low-quality images, a world in which a blurry snapshot can find itself on millions of screens, in which 'visual culture has been reduced to imaginary spam'[2]... painting has rediscovered its own uniqueness. A carefully chosen image, an image made out of accurate, thoughtful brushstrokes (or any other carefully considered technique for that matter), an image that carries the weight of human touch – of human presence, of repeated

[1] Johan Huizinga, *The Autumn of the Middle Ages* (London, 1924).

[2] Franco 'Biffo' Berardi, in his introduction to Hito Steyerl's *The Wretched of the Screen* (New York, e-flux journal, 2012).

analysis, of intense gazing – a *full*-resolution image, life-size, and in real time – the apparition of such an image today can be just as miraculous as that of the fresco in a remote late medieval chapel.

Painter and graffiti artist Dan Witz told us how, in his lifetime (Witz was born in 1957), 'there's been a revolution in representational capabilities comparable to the switch from tempera to oil paint in the fifteenth century. The opportunities today are just unbelievably exciting,' only to add that painting is still the 'perfect antidote to that kind of noise [image proliferation] ... paintings are handmade, one-of-a-kind, extremely fragile objects. They're absurd. Extravagant. Intrinsically worthless. And seeing paintings is an experience you absolutely must have in person – in real life. Direct human contact is the point.'

Part of a new wave of painters working firmly within a Realist tradition, artist Caroline Walker speaks of how her generation lives in 'an image-saturated culture where we consume and discard images with little pause for thought, and this seems to have given painting a new agency as a slower medium. It can ask a viewer to reassess how they look at the world in a very direct and personal way.' Faced with what artist Andy Denzler calls 'the hegemony and the aesthetic of the jpeg, which we now almost exclusively read as source' and which he describes as 'a compromised image that is reduced to a hand-held format', painting has recovered its semi-miraculous status, its wow factor.

Clearly, the 'slow' images created through painting have assumed a new meaning for the jpeg generation. Sigrid Holmwood likens her 'Slow Painting' to the 'Slow Food' movement, highlighting contemporary 'anxieties about the alienated existence of post-industrial life'. The stillness inherent in the works of Kevin Cosgrove or Zhang Enli demonstrates how the medium of painting can add to an image of the everyday. But there are also more practical aspects to the relationship between contemporary image-makers and painting. For example, Tomishitsu Baba (whose practice is largely based on updating traditional Japanese techniques) tells us how figurative painting can still play an important role 'when it comes to transmitting an accurate and precise image'. He explains that 'drawing with a computer means that the image is first input, then the information is transferred to the printer, and the image is printed out on the support medium. During this process the images fall apart. In order for me to carry down the image directly, from my mind to the support (I wish I could do that with technology!), I have to rely on my hand skills.' For Toshimitsu and others like him, painting is still ahead of technology in transmitting the artist's vision in two dimensions.

The camera and the computer have been comfortably assimilated into the practices of most contemporary painters, no longer representing either a threat or an obsession. Liberated by image-making technologies from affectations such as those of Pop and Op, the tricks of hyperrealism and Colour Field painting (that kind of thing now looks as if it has come out of a computer, an iPad or even an iPhone), artists are again free to develop the ample and supple medium that is figurative painting. Through its physicality and its malleability, it is a medium perhaps most suited to and capable of capturing the complexity and intensity of contemporary life. When asked about the appeal of painting Dan Witz explains how 'back in my early 20s, as my brief career as a punk rocker was closing down, I knew that I'd really miss the physical intensity of performing. But I began to discover in my museum wanderings that painting actually had plenty of potential for the intensity I needed.'

Humanizing the Feel of Now

Is it still possible for someone to sit down in front of an easel and paint something? Is this basically late medieval method still capable of producing interesting results in a world in constant acceleration and in which images are endlessly being captured and stored away? Possibly more than ever: in a world in which most image capturing and storing is indiscriminate, inattentive and even automated, the painter's intent and minute attention to life and the rhythms of life has become a radical position.

Painting offers an option – it is almost a lifestyle option – to the contemporary artist. 'Painting is a strange occupation: I lock myself in my studio for 14 hours a day, not talking to anyone and not answering the phone', says Nicholas McLeod. Its slower rhythms allow for a more intimate connection to human perception (which is true both from the point of view of the artist and the viewer). But it also allows the depiction of an imaginary realm, an investigation into what connects human beings to places and space.

David Brian Smith's dreamy pastoral landscapes often start with a photograph, but then 'the painting begins and often the initial composition will be painted out.' The infusion of elements from his own childhood on a farm – 'memory plays a role in it, in the sense that you can't stop it' – and the addition of text and texture, allow his painting 'to transcend its specificity and relate to an audience'. This is not nostalgia, but a deep reconnection to nature. The equally dream-like work of Simon Willems has a futuristic feel, despite often drawing on historical images; he is also influenced by cinema. Painters can do this, mixing periods in time, the real and the invented, to make a wider point. 'I guess my most direct reference to films is *Star Wars*, but even then it was more to do with the idea of humanizing fictitious icons to force real emotions in the viewer than it was specifically about *Star Wars*.'

This humanizing eye, recapturing the presence of the present moment, is a recurring theme in this book. The sheer superfluity of imagery makes us dulled to the impact of the visual information that surrounds us. But a painting that reimagines an act of war may be far more effective and affecting than a piece of digital photojournalism; a painted portrait may have more subtlety and nuance than a social-media 'selfie'.

In less extreme and more domestic circumstances, the need for models connects paintings to the intricacy of human relationships, or what connects human beings to places and space. It is interesting the way expressions such as 'baby sitting' and 'cat or dog sitting' recur in our interviews with painters.

There is still something incontrovertibly fertile and wholesome in the relationship between a painter and a canvas on an easel (or any other similar method). Eduardo Berliner moved from being a professional graphic designer and typographer to become a painter because painting provided a space where he could combine all his interests. He describes the experience of painting in revealing terms: 'I am interested in the vigour of the brushstroke: patches of colour that can be evaluated in an autonomous way as a pictorial event, which at the same time describe a very sophisticated visual experience on the surface of the canvas, as though by way of our sense of sight we could understand the change in temperature from a patch of shade to a sunlit area, the humidity of the air on an overcast day, or the glimmer in an animal's eyes.'

At this point, let us return to Johan Huizinga, writing in 1919: 'the modern city hardly knows pure darkness or true silence'.[3] Painting still does. And it knows

[3] *The Autumn of the Middle Ages*, op. cit.

many things more – things that remain invisible to lenses and software. Painting knows texture. It can still render the idea of touch (whereas the world of digital and virtual imaging has been completely desensitized to these, becoming a 'textural wasteland').[4] Painters manage to entertain an intimate relationship with accident, without having to give up on purposeful action and method. Painting is not indifferent to meaning. Painting is attentive to singularity. While images are constantly flying around, being digitalized, re-used, cropped, intercut, blown, shrunk, lit, printed, projected, edited, Photoshopped, etc., and all the time fading, losing their original meaning, poignancy and context – painters keep going back to their studios and slowly, patiently, trying to hold back the flood.

Figurative painters cut curious figures in the world of visual communication, and even in that of contemporary art. Conceptual artists, for example, are trained to think (in all kinds of ways and all possible directions) – to question, to plan, to foresee; they are attuned to the frantic pace of contemporary culture. Like molecules in a solution in ebullition, the thoughts of the Conceptual artist bubble with the culture, and their often topical works will regularly create media sensations. A painter is a different animal. Painters tend to spend more time in the studio, working with their hands and their eyes as much as with their brains, avoiding making big statements, focusing on small decisions, often on almost imperceptible shifts and slides, rhythms and textures, stepping backwards and forwards, like a chef tasting Slow Food, helping it on its way, spicing it up every now and then. The daily practice of their art allows painters to give their creative impulses both time and space.

Imagine a battle in a sci-fi movie: a titanic struggle to save the notion of Time from that of 'saving time' or 'being in tune with the times'. Our hero, the painter, is dressed in a lab coat (already paint-bespattered) and instead of leaning over a microscope or typing frantically into a computer, chooses instead to light a cigarette and play some music before starting to apply dabs of fresh paint to a glistening surface.

When a painter like Ulrich Lamsfuß selects an image from a magazine or newspaper clipping and works on it for weeks, if not months, he is like a scientist studying the DNA of that image, tracking back the convoluted story of that image, its path through the world of mass media, from the original event to the position it occupies in our consciousness, re-examining the intensity of the original moment or act, as well as the incongruity of the whole situation. Anna Bjerger, who paints almost exclusively from found photographs, describes this process as 'deciphering an image'. Like archaeologists analysing the remains of an ancient civilization, appropriation masters such as Sasnal and Marcin Maciejowski interpret and reimagine discarded printed matter, thereby making poignant existential statements about the contemporary experience.

Real-res

Now more than ever, paintings have something to offer us: we the digitally, distractedly desperate, we the culturally shipwrecked, adrift in a sea of information. Paintings don't flash, they don't glow, they aren't backlit, they don't move. Stubbornly, they resist taking their place in modern mass media's daily line-up, standing out as anomalies when they do. Just to take one example, despite being reproduced endlessly, and despite the fact that his work has been among the most influential in the twentieth century, the paintings of Lucian Freud never fail to look odd and out of place, his obstinate brushstrokes refusing to conform or blend into the general media landscape. One cannot help being struck by the differences when comparing the paintings of Freud with the depictions of contemporary human life in advertising, fashion, photography, television and film.

To quote Philippe Sollers (writing about Cézanne), a 'painting is not an image'.[5] A painting is a fact. It *exists* and invites us to share in that experience: the miracle of presence, of meaning, of touch, of communion with another human being through the same physical medium. And in that sense painting has never been so vital (in the literal sense of the term), so important and necessary to our culture. And that is why, despite the exponential growth in the number of images and ways in which they can be produced and reproduced, painting will continue to fascinate, intrigue and enthral viewers across generations, dragging them away from their screens to stare at those incongruous rectangles hanging on walls.

Editorial Note

I should say a few words about the book's structure and our selection process. Those expecting rigour and precision will be disappointed. I have come to believe that no set of criteria could have proved watertight – and ours was always going to be on the leaky side.

We wanted to create a book about the renewed excitement around figurative painting. But defining figurative painting is already in itself problematic. When does a painting stop being figurative and become abstract? When does a shape lose contact with the thing it is supposed to represent? When does a circle stop being a head and become just a geometrical shape? The relationship between signifier and signified is always a temporary arrangement – and never more so than in painting. Since Modernism this ever-shifting border between figuration and abstraction has been a fertile ground for painters. But this was not what we wanted to talk about, and therefore we decided to keep our distance from the discussion – and from the more recent (and less realistic) works of brilliant artists such as Peter Doig, Luc Tuymans, Chris Ofili and even Tala Madani (to mention only a few of the most illustrious names who have been associated with figurative painting) – moving our focus on to painters operating within a largely figurative, Realist mode of representation.

But then.... The notion of the 'realistic' proved contentious too. Where do you draw the line? How do you define Realism? Is it in the accuracy of the rendering, or the connection between the subject matter and a certain reality outside the painting? Is a carefully rendered picture of a dream 'realistic'? How about a rougher sketch representing a factual subject (in the case of Madani, for example)? In the end, we opted for a definition that balances style, methodology and subject matter, the key question being: how much of the grain of contemporary reality (and contemporary unreality) is contained in these paintings? Needless to say, there was no precise criteria.

That still left a lot of open ground ahead of us – and a lot of painters. So how did we decide who went in and who didn't? Why this painter and not that one? Again, no clear-cut rule was applied: no distinctions of age (or generation), curriculum vitae or movement. We wanted the works we chose for the book to feel as contemporary as possible. And – haha! – now how do you define that? Well... it had to feel fresh, like a new attempt to define the role of the contemporary painter; or present a different way of applying paint to a surface in figuration, come to a certain kind of painting from a new angle. I must add that even a certain naïve clumsiness was preferred to masterful skill, provided it was related to an attempt at doing something new. Our choices were made with complete disregard for

[4] Nicola Bozzi, 'News From The Textural Wasteland', in *Elephant* 14 (2013)

[5] Philippe Sollers, *Eloge de l'infini* (Paris, 2001)

trends or art-world status. In a way, our selection process was not so different from that of making a painting itself: lots of trial and error, juxtapositions, some arguing, some reflection, a lot of contemplation and time-wasting, before going for what still felt right at the end of all that.

Then came the issue of structuring the book. After much discussion, during which all kinds of categories were introduced and then dropped and ridiculed, we divided the book into three parts. The first looks at the 'mediated image', examining the work of painters who actively engage with the contemporary visual (often digital) landscape: painters working with appropriation (taking images from the Internet, found photographs, discarded printed matter, etc.) and painters whose style and content is inspired or influenced by film, TV and journalism. The second looks at artists trying to circumvent the mass-media circus in order to find unmediated images (even if they will also occasionally source material from the Internet – hey, who doesn't?); those painters aiming to reach their subjects from a fresh and more directly painterly angle, to reinstate the humanity in experience, in presence. Finally, the third part looks at works of the imagination: artists examining the past (Neo-traditionalism, Pastoralism) or the future; painters creating a landscape of thought systems or imaginary scenarios, employing Utopias or dreams as their subject matter.

Contemporary painting is a vast field and, as our editor at Laurence King pointed out when we were once again questioning the categories in the book, a large part of the fun of such a project is finding flaws and picking holes in its selection criteria or its curatorial stance. And in that sense I am sure this particular one will provide readers with a rich source of material.

— Marc Valli

The ubiquity of the camera, the influence of cinema and film language, the attraction and the uses of the mediated image, an engagement with the contemporary visual landscape, appropriation found images, modern myths

Part 1

Life and Death in the Labyrinth of Images

'I'm an eye. A mechanical eye. I, the machine, show you the world the way only I can see it.' For Dziga Vertov, writing in 1923, and referring to the movie camera, this 'mechanical eye' was an alien vision; today, it is omnipresent. It has radically transformed our perception of reality. Memories and fantasies take the visual semblance of camera-framed shots. In our minds, we can give a holiday destination a panoramic bird's-eye view. We can approach a beloved face in close-up. We can project a scary scenario as witnessed from a diagonal high-angle shot. We can figure emotional experiences not as seen by our eyes, but by the 'mechanical eye'.

In contemporary painting, we see how some painters have developed what we might call a 'cinematic style', making use of visual tools and tricks inherited from the camera: blurring images, framing their subjects as if seen through a wide-angle lens, or 'shooting' them in close-ups or deep focus. Jeremy Geddes's work imagines Photorealist scenes of suspended animation we are more used to seeing in the most recent technological advances of cinema. But the moving image holds an evocative dimension of narrative and mood released over time and through movement, in carefully planned sequences. By contrast, a painting is a still object, with a static image, in which the painter aims to translate that same evocative capacity. A sapient brushstroke can recreate an out-of-focus image or a low-quality still from a CCTV camera, but the medium adds time in its own long-drawn 'pause mode', rather than movement. The canvas develops itself in depth, through the accumulation and the overlapping of layers. Through such painterly means the venerable tradition of painting is in dialogue with the more recent tradition of the digital image. This conversation is sometimes made explicit, for example in the dramatically lit urban compositions of Guillaume Bresson, who refers to the influence of Caravaggio and Tintoretto in the same breath as film directors including Godard and Kassovitz.

Not surprisingly, most of the artists included in Part 1 do not paint from life. Rather, they are incessant gatherers of visual material from modern mass media: from the Internet, the screen, discarded printed matter. This means that, most frequently, they work from photographs, from the commercial portraits on which Harding Meyer stages his interventions, to the medical directories and photojournalistic records of war used by Justin Mortimer. The canvas becomes a screen, a board, on which to transpose a still and reflect upon our unbelievably complex contemporary visual landscape. Their paintings are thus 'the mediation of an already mediated image'. These painters use the intrinsic qualities of painting – stillness, texture; and in particular size and staying power – to examine our relationship to a world in which these types of images are prevalent.

When Marcin Maciejowski appropriates images from the old film programmes he found at his parents' home (in rural Poland) for his paintings – making use of their genre descriptions ('comedy', 'thriller', 'romantic comedy') and even the screening times – his process is not so dissimilar from what Renaissance painters did when they chose mythological or sacred subjects. He examines the myths that envelop our lives, questioning their reality, both for us (the mortals living in small Polish villages, for example) and their protagonists (existing up in the Hollywood pantheon).

Artists working with appropriation employ images taken from the media maelstrom to try to understand how the contemporary world works, how the contemporary psyche functions (or dysfunctions), holding up their ingrained codes for analysis, exploring the ambiguity at the heart of human nature and the contemporary experience.

Woman with Dog
2009, oil on canvas, 200 × 150 cm
(79 × 59 in).

Eduardo Berliner
Born: 1978, Rio de Janeiro
Lives: Rio de Janeiro

While studying industrial design, the Brazilian artist Eduardo Berliner started drawing and making notations in a series of notebooks, and his college work was soon influenced by this process, which thus gave rise to his first personal works. This interdisciplinary posture, floating between different media, has stayed with him through the construction of sculptures and the creation of photographs, drawings, videos, texts and watercolours. He combines a career as an artist with teaching typography. His paintings often combine animal and human subjects in surreal versions of everyday situations.

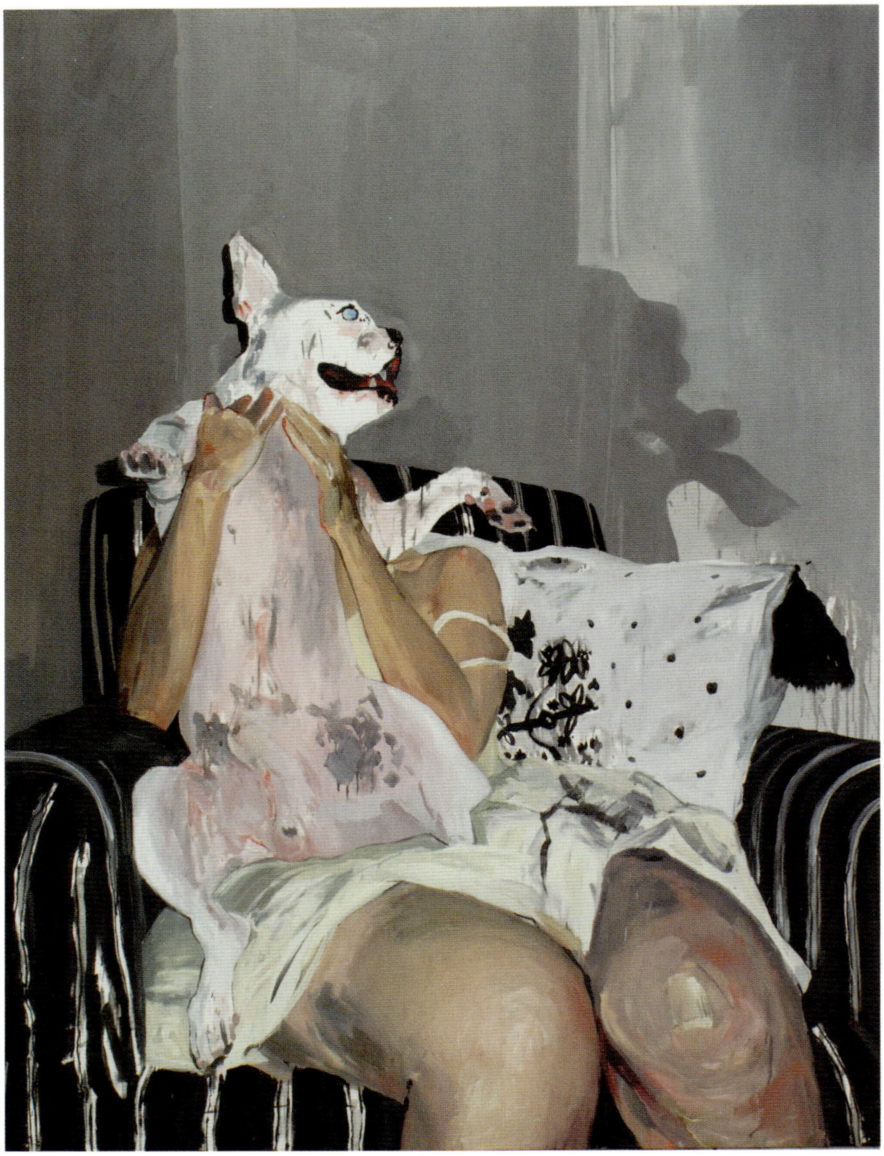

Background

I had my first experience with oil painting on canvas only in 2002. Until then I had not considered the possibility of painting on canvas; I think I felt discouraged by the weight of the history of painting. Soon, however, this weight was replaced by curiosity and a desire to continue painting [previously Berliner had painted in TK acrylics on board] – the medium started to make sense to me. It became a place where I could combine all my interests. Painting offered the possibility to work in a direct way without any separation between thought and the act of doing. I did a master's degree in typographic design in England; when I came back to Brazil I taught and worked as a freelance designer, and began to work regularly with oil painting. Gradually I managed to direct more time and energy towards my painting, until the situation inverted itself. Today, I give classes in typographic design once a week, because I know that there are not many teachers in this discipline in my country, and in this way I think I can help young people.

Process

A painting begins long before one applies paint to canvas. For about 14 years I have maintained the daily practice of making notations in notebooks. For the most part these are drawings. Some of them are made from memory, others from observation, and still others can arise from a simple mark on the paper. These drawings spring from the act of drawing itself, and sometimes I look at them and don't quite understand where they came from. But once they are in the world, I must live with them.

I take my camera wherever I go. Some of the pictures I take are based on ephemeral situations, others record objects – photographs of people, animals, architecture, changes of lighting. Each month I choose a large number of photographs, which I print and leave around the studio, and use them as a basis to begin to draw and make small watercolours. Sometimes I mix parts of different photographs in the same drawing and complete it with a drawing from memory. At other moments I become aware that an image has started recurring. When it arises from a mental image, I feel the need to find something in the world that serves as a visual reference to begin a painting or take it forwards: I perceive a great power that arises from the borderline territory between what I see and what I imagine; between what the things are and how they function as a mirror of what lives in my thoughts and my memory. But a moment comes during the process when I begin to be guided by the material information on the canvas and by the relationship between my body and the support.

I believe that throughout the painting process something unforeseeable needs to happen: it is at these moments that a painting comes into its own. I never know how much time the process of painting a canvas will take.

Drawing

When I make a drawing of something, the information becomes intensified in my memory. Drawing helps me understand what I think and feel; for this reason, when I am confused, I draw to help myself get back on my feet. It makes me aware that through the encounter with my own limitations and vulnerability, an immense power can arise.

Painting from life

The construction of a two-dimensional space based on the observation of something outdoors is different from the experience of painting the same thing based on a photograph, which is itself a two-dimensional representation. When I look at a photograph, the space is already mapped out. Outdoors, you make contact with characteristic smells, climate and noises, and I believe that these influence the painting. Just as in the studio I can make contact with the randomness inherent in the very process of painting, when painting outdoors you are subject to another sort of randomness. Observing the same place one hour later, you perceive that it has changed; new points of interest have arisen because the lighting is different or because a dog has lain down nearby, and this offers the possibility of quick changes in relation to the subject you are working on. I am interested in the vigour of the brushstroke: patches of colour that can be evaluated in an autonomous way as a pictorial event, which at the same time describe a very sophisticated visual experience on the surface of the canvas, as though by way of our sense of sight we can understand the change in temperature from a patch of shade to a sunlit area, the humidity of the air on an overcast day, or the glimmer in an animal's eyes.

Narratives

When experiences of a different nature are connected through memory, a narrative emerges. In the attempt to transform my initial motivations or mental images into drawings or paintings, new questions of a practical order arise; and the process of evaluation and reflection on what I am seeing begins to guide the work. The narrative is determined by the process itself. Associative processes are important for me. When I come across something that affects me, my memory often produces complex associations with recent or very distant events. When I look at the work once it is finished I perceive the presence, even if residual, of both events, except that they are now fused.

On the role of painting

To look at something truly is an act that involves more than the eyes. Looking with intensity demands an entire lifetime of accumulated sensory memory: each noise, smell, change of lighting.... Painting and drawing remind us of the possibility of transcendence through the act of looking. Beyond this, for me, painting is a way of being in constant contact with my own vulnerability, my limitations. It is necessary to live with error and chance,

CPR
2010, oil on canvas, 200 × 200 cm
(79 × 79 in).

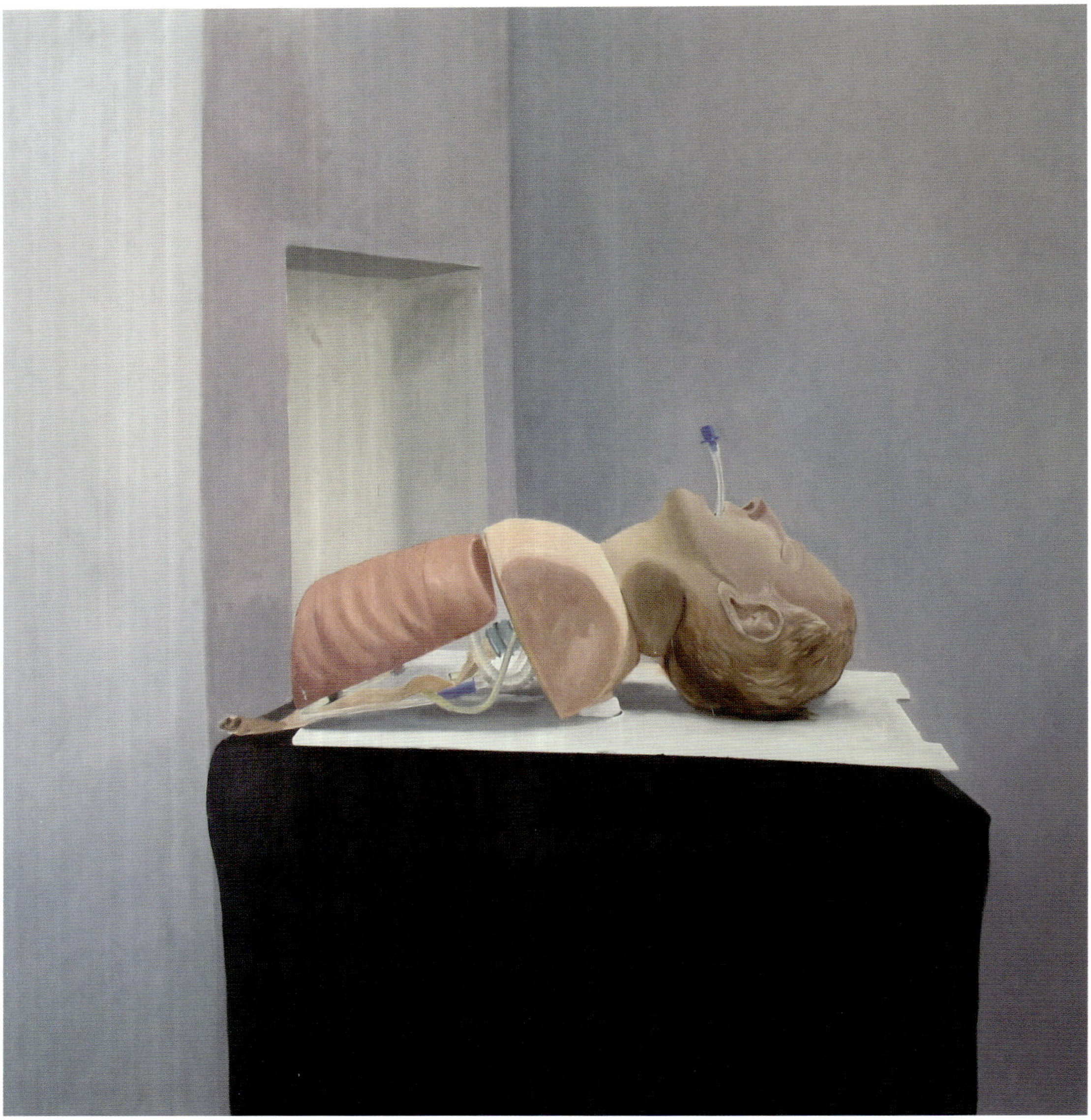

Little Pig
2012, oil on canvas, 200 × 110 cm
(79 × 43 in).

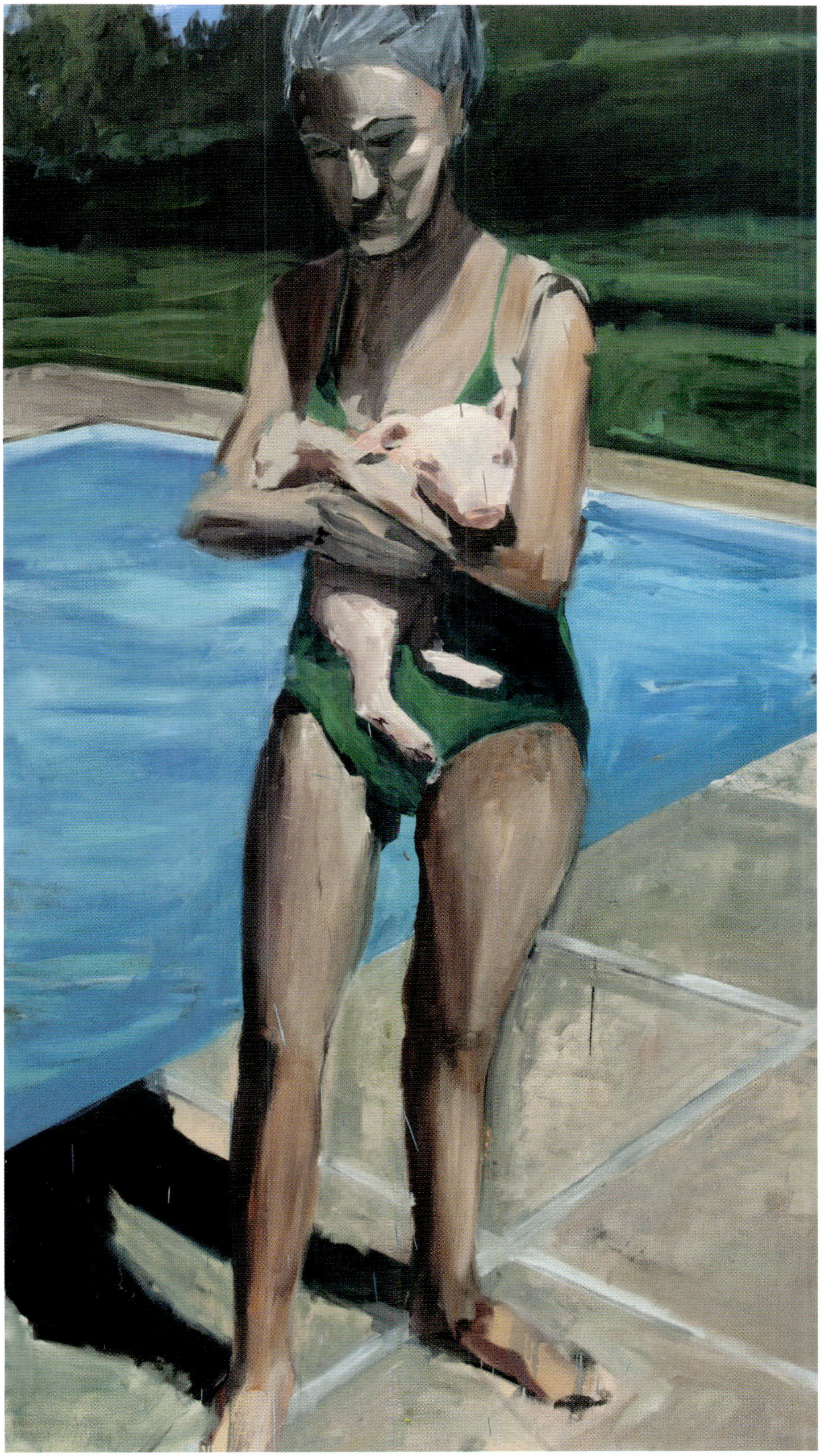

Handsaw
2009, oil on canvas, 214 × 170 cm
(84 × 67 in).

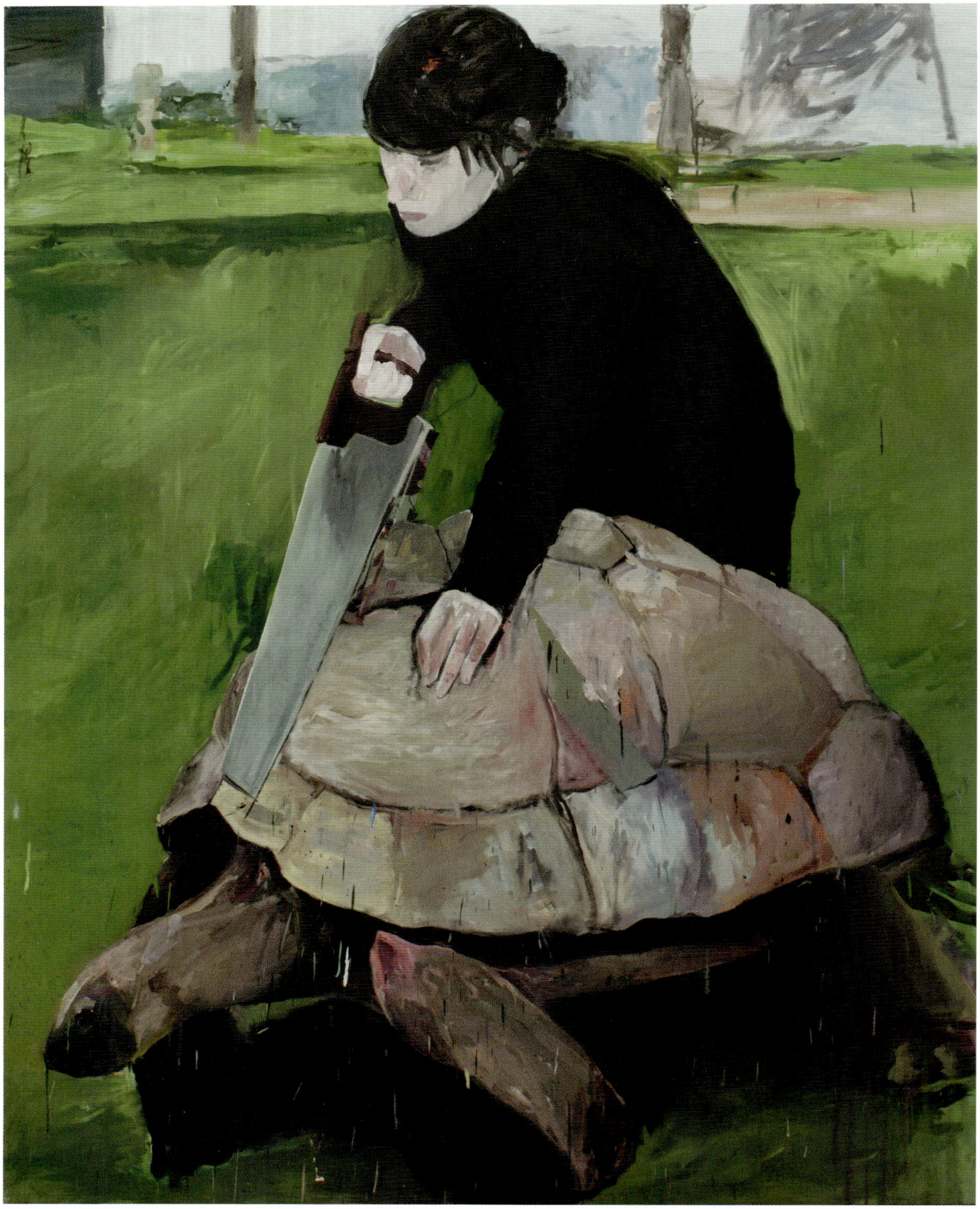

Tubing
2012, oil on canvas, 188 × 150 cm
(74 × 59 in).

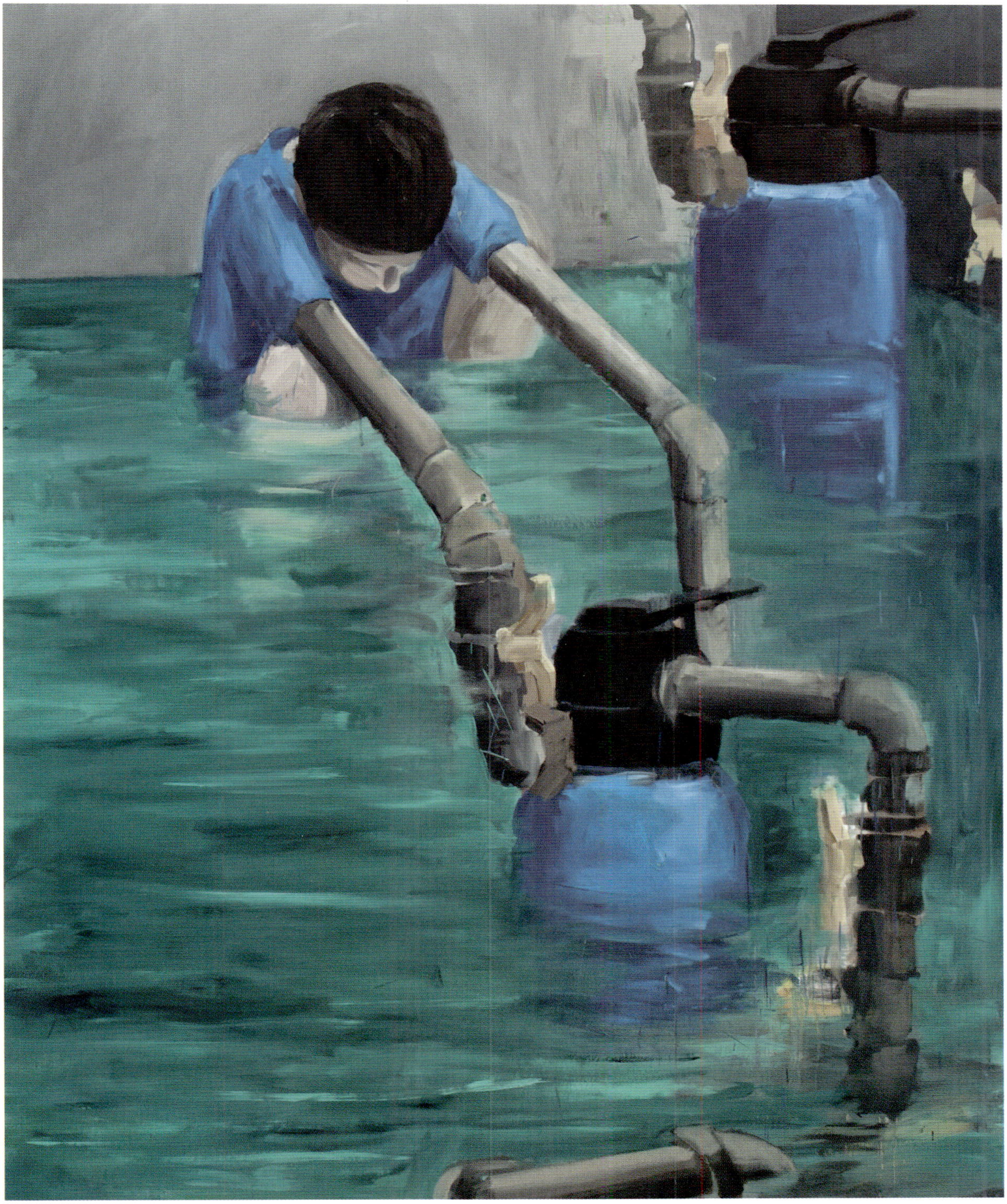

Anna Bjerger
Born: 1973, Skallsjö (Sweden)
Lives: Småland (Sweden)

Anna Bjerger's pictures are painted from photographs rather than life, their subjects derived from out-of-date reference books, instruction manuals, gardening books and magazines. Familiar, anonymous, intimate, yet curiously disconnected, these are unsettling narratives, the meanings becoming slippery and ambiguous (she has described photographs as containing 'a certain ambiguity'). The resulting paintings also call attention to the physicality of their medium. Paint is applied wet-on-wet in broad brushstrokes over aluminium panels. The speed with which the works have been painted seems to strive for the instantaneous quality of photography, while at the same time asserting the transformative nature of painting. Like a key passage in a novel (the description of a scene, a moment or a mood), every Anna Bjerger picture seems to depict a moment of transition, of change, when something shifts, somewhere, at some level.

Background
For as long as I can remember I have wanted to be an artist in a romantic sense. I was 19 and went to Germany with my lithography course to look at 'Art' and I was confronted with German Expressionism, Georg Baselitz and also Marlene Dumas. And there are so many other artists – Edvard Munch, Pierre-Auguste Renoir, Alex Katz, Francis Bacon, Piero della Francesca, Edouard Manet, Vija Celmins, Vera Nilsson, Hannah Höch, Lovis Corinth, to mention a few.

References
I mainly use found imagery that makes no artistic claim; occasionally a personal photograph will find its way into the studio. Photographs contain a certain ambiguity and are instantaneous objects of the past. Sometimes there is reference to a particular painting when selecting and painting a certain image. I search for painterly qualities in the images; sometimes it is the subject matter and other times formal elements that hold my interest.

Process
The process of collecting photographic material (from out-of-date reference books and magazines, for example), looking through images, finding arbitrary connections and making a selection of what to paint, is a big part of my work.

I think of this process – painting a photograph – as a way of deciphering an image. I want it to be an intuitive and almost subconscious act, which is why I like to start a painting in the morning first thing when I get into the studio. I don't think of it either as an original, or a copy – the painting is a hybrid. When I paint the photograph I don't change the composition or the framing, but I might exaggerate certain areas.

The process of collecting photographic material and looking through images is meditative and allows me to think about my practice in a constructive way. Spending time with images, reversing them, imagining scale and becoming familiar with the details, the colour, the light – to me they are a great inspiration. If I were thinking in terms of painting 'live', I would find it daunting to consider the boundaries of the space I am depicting [to frame the image].

Workplace
My studio is in an old school situated in the forest in the south of Sweden. It is a red wooden building from the turn of the last century [early twentieth], the only source of heating is a log fire.

Painting
Painting should get under your skin. It is a balancing act between control and the accidental. Painting is the subject of my work: everything around it is just a way of making sense of it.

Brushwork
I am using the paint and the brush-marks to clarify the depicted image. I hope the painting exudes confidence, meaning it could have been executed no other way. The texture of oil paint, colour, light and surface – it never ceases to engage me.

Man with Light
2011, oil on aluminium, 90 × 75 cm
(35½ × 29½ in).

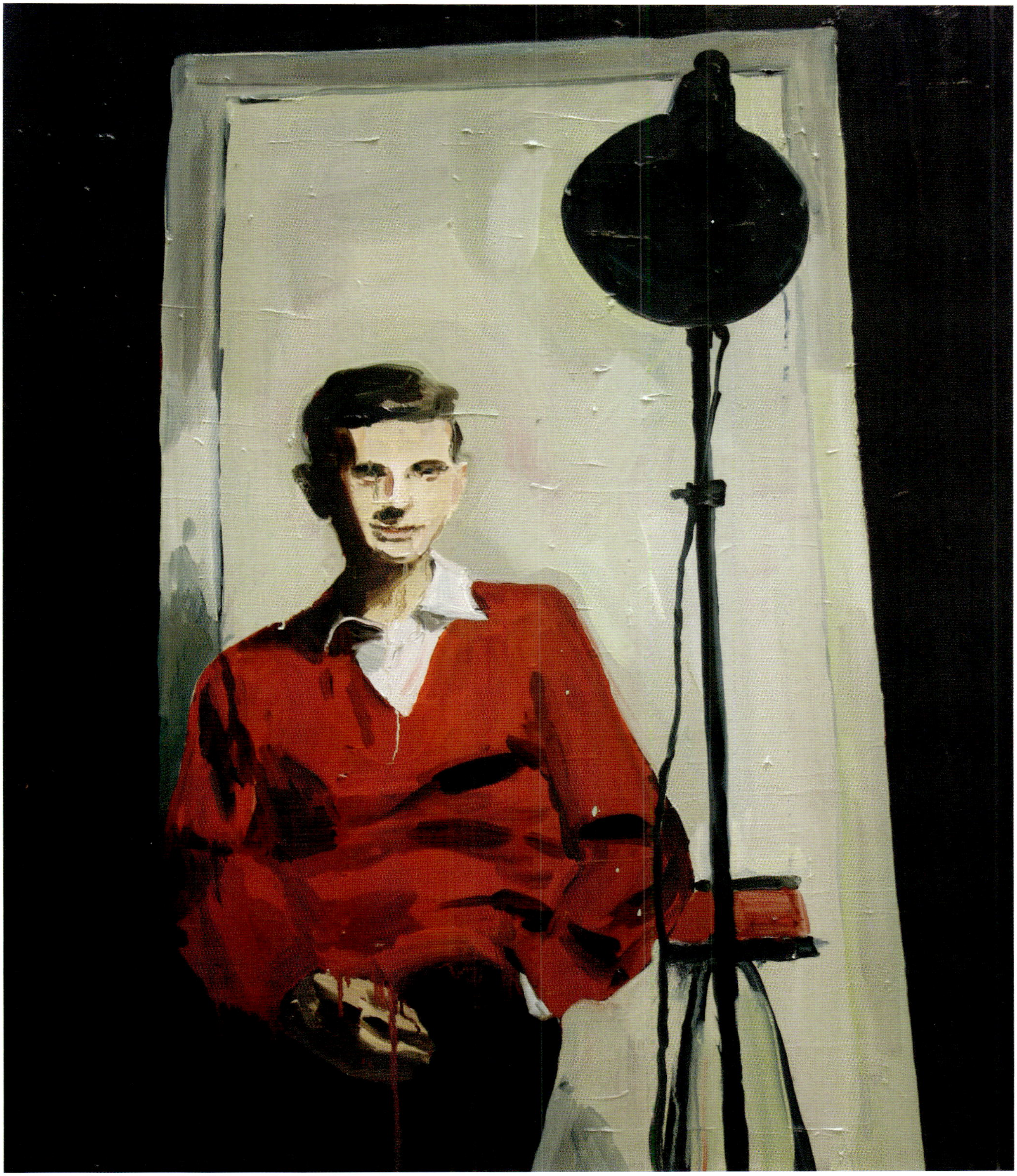

Film Still
2012, oil on aluminium, 120 × 120 cm
(47 × 47 in).

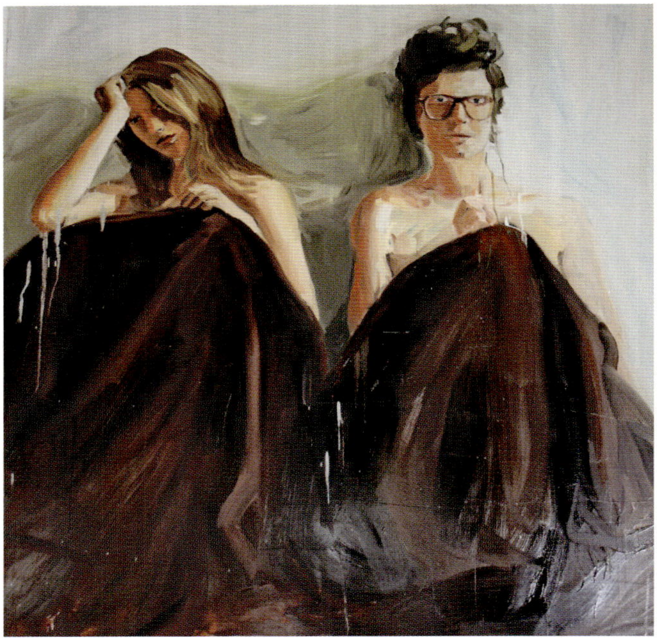

Swimmers
2010, oil on aluminium, 90 × 90 cm
(35½ × 35½ in).

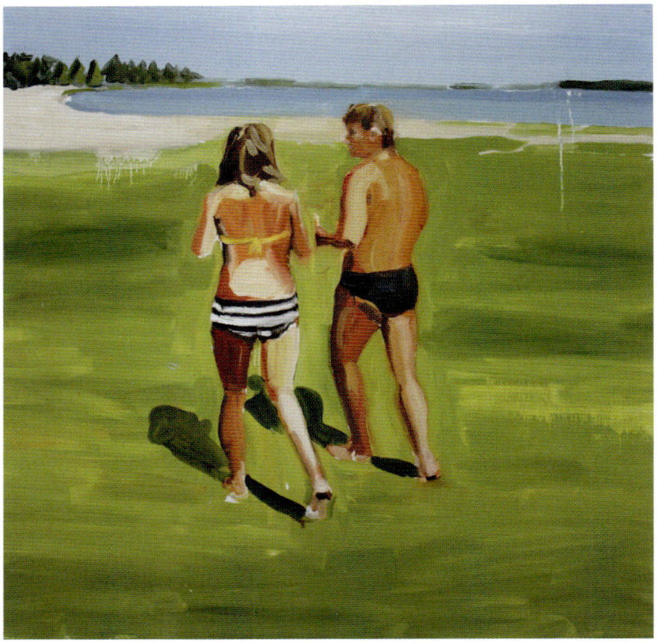

Abyss
2012, oil on aluminium, 120 × 90 cm
(47 × 35½ in).

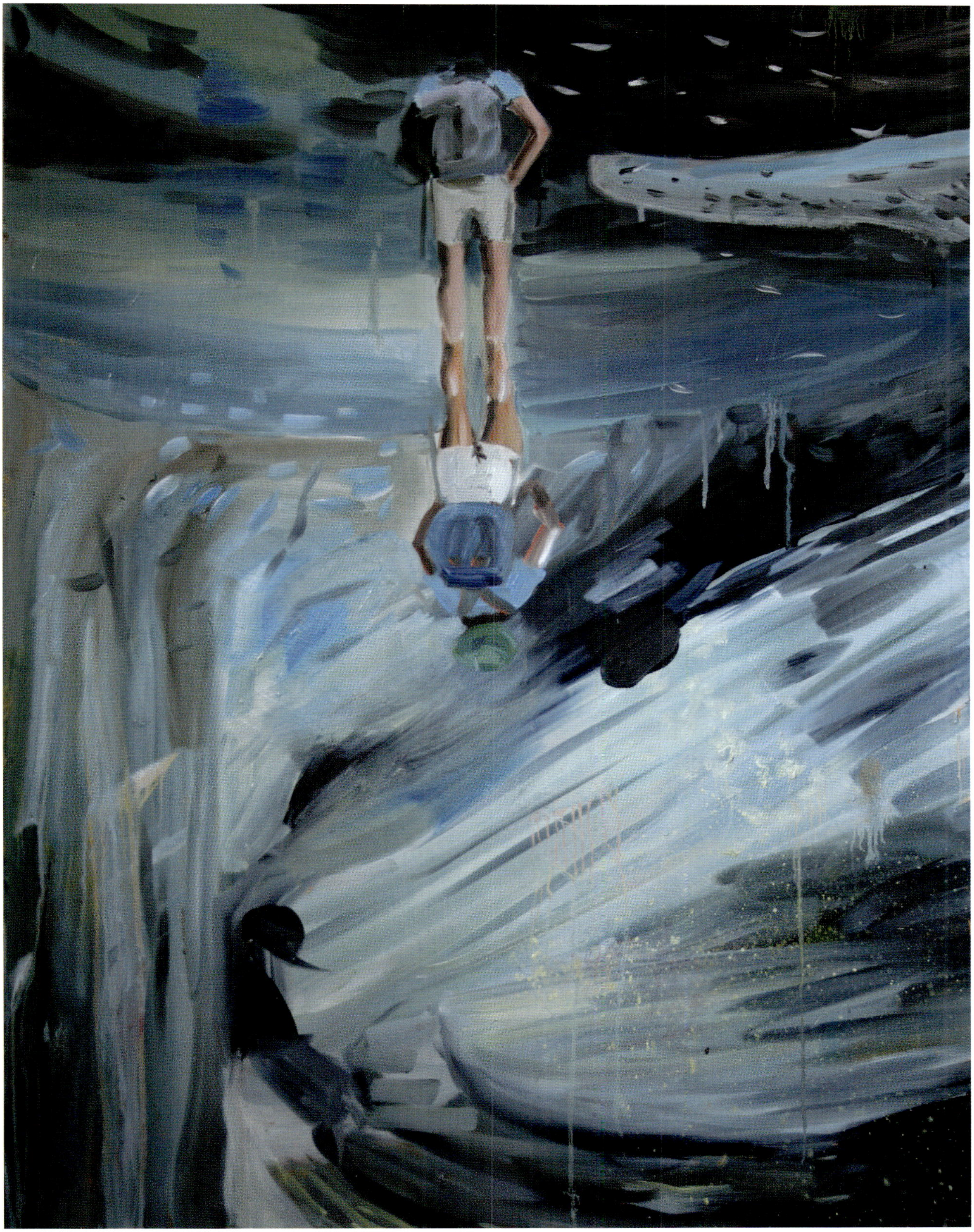

Camouflage
2012, oil on aluminium, 50 × 40 cm
(19¾ × 15¾ in).

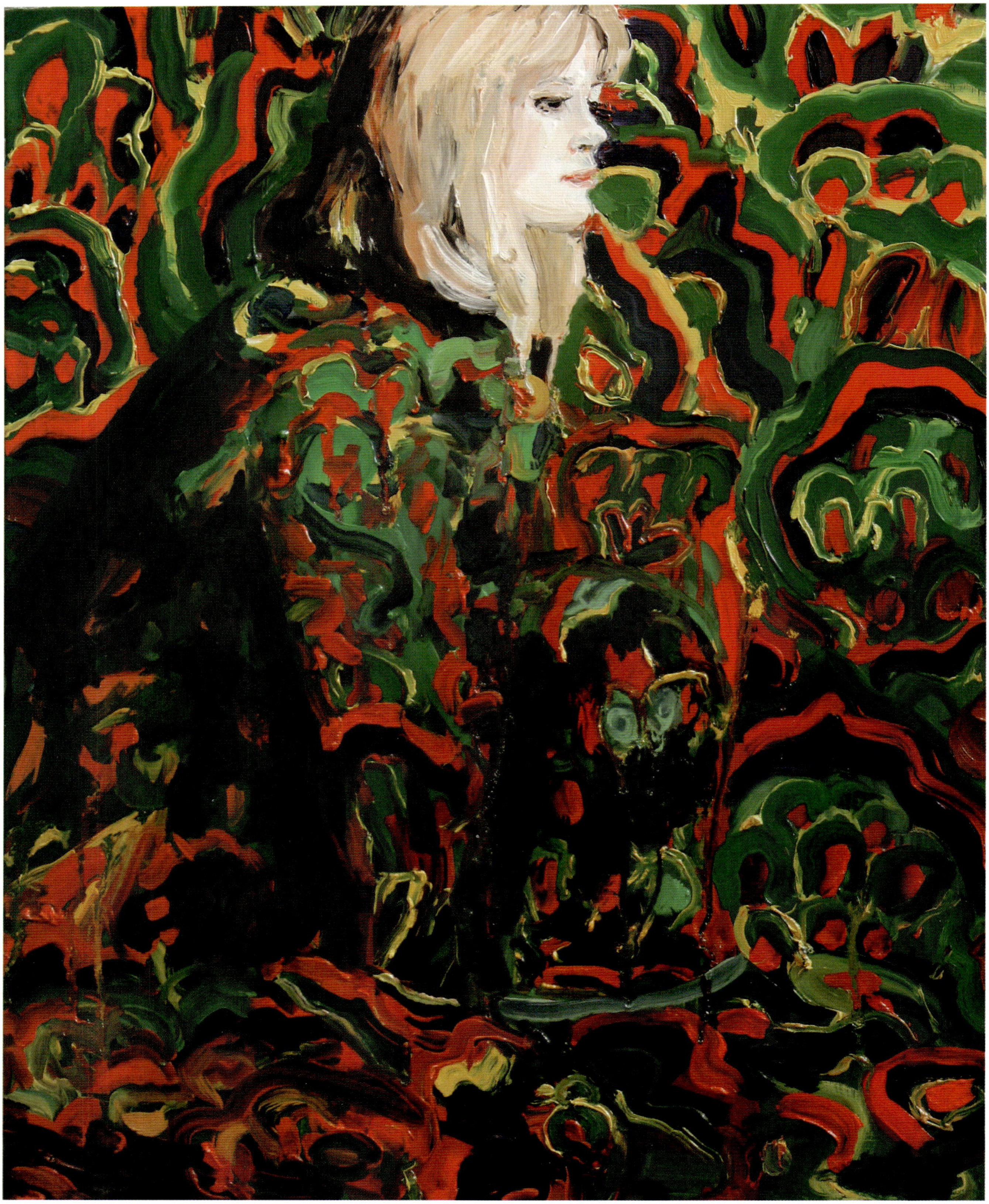

Wood Anemones
2012, oil on aluminium, 90 × 100 cm
(35½ × 39 in).

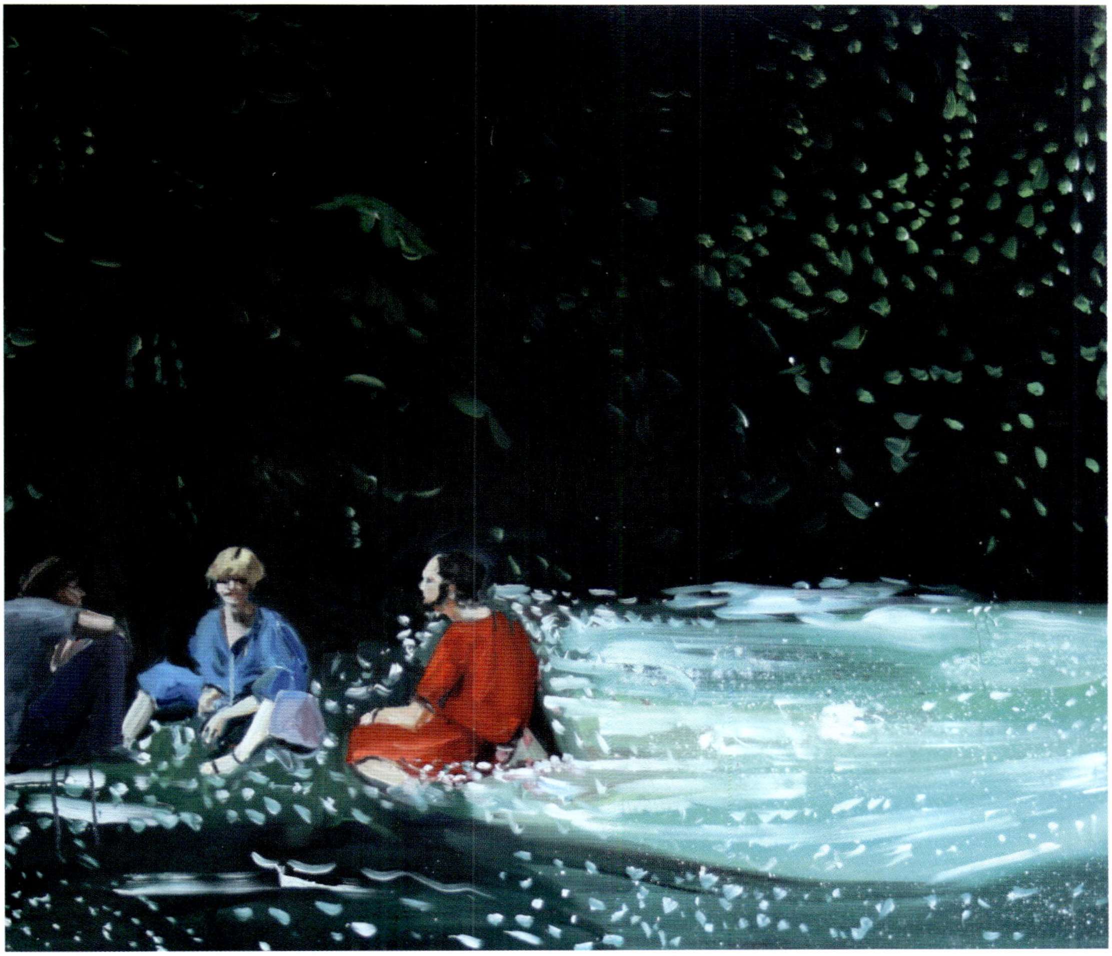

Sans titre/Untitled (detail of a triptych)
2007, oil on canvas, 130 × 97 cm (51 × 38 in).

Guillaume Bresson
Born: 1982, Toulouse (France)
Lives: Paris

Guillaume Bresson's first contact with painting was through graffiti as a teenager. It was his first experience of the notion of painterly composition. After that, he attended the École nationale supérieure des Beaux-Arts in Paris and graduated in 2007. He draws from sculptures, paintings and from life. When asked to distinguish visual influences, he points to the Renaissance, to Tintoretto and to Alberti's 'Historia'; to Cézanne; and to the Baroque as expressed in Caravaggio and Poussin's work. Then he adds the work of film directors – Godard, Eisenstein, Lucas, Rohmer, Kassovitz (in particular *La Haine*), Dumont and Lynch. Describing the relationship between painting and contemporary media, he says that today painting is just one medium among others and that 'it no longer has a central role in art'.

Process
I go through different preparatory stages. I start with sketches from my imagination in which the situations and the gestures are defined. From these, I then realize photographic sequences with models. The attitude, the facial expression, the movements and the clothes all are planned in detail according to the role of each model. Afterwards, I cut and recompose the pictures and, finally, with the help of computer graphics, I reinsert that *mise-en-scène* into a set. It is when one of these photomontages looks interesting to me that I start work on a canvas.

Screening
The choice of the point of view determines the relationship between the painting and the viewer. Whenever possible I take the exhibition space into account when I am deciding the dimensions of the canvases and working out the parameters for the perspective. Usually I realize the virtual space of my canvases with a relatively rigorous linear perspective, which enhances the scenic aspect of the whole composition, of set and characters. The horizon line is placed at the level of the characters' heads and the painting is hung in such a way that this horizon line is level with the spectator's eye. In this way the space of the painting is a sort of prolongation of the space of the exhibition.

Lighting
I don't want to depend on natural light and on weather conditions. I transfer a particular lighting atmosphere (daylight, neon...) into my paintings according to the subject.

Narrative
All the compositional elements conduct the viewer's attention from one moment to the next. There are numerous possible moments represented in one painting, so the viewer's attention has the time to get around the composition in order to understand the whole story. A series of paintings can constitute a sequence: a more cinematographic narrative develops alongside them, as in different sequence shots. In these cases every painting represents a moment of a broader story.

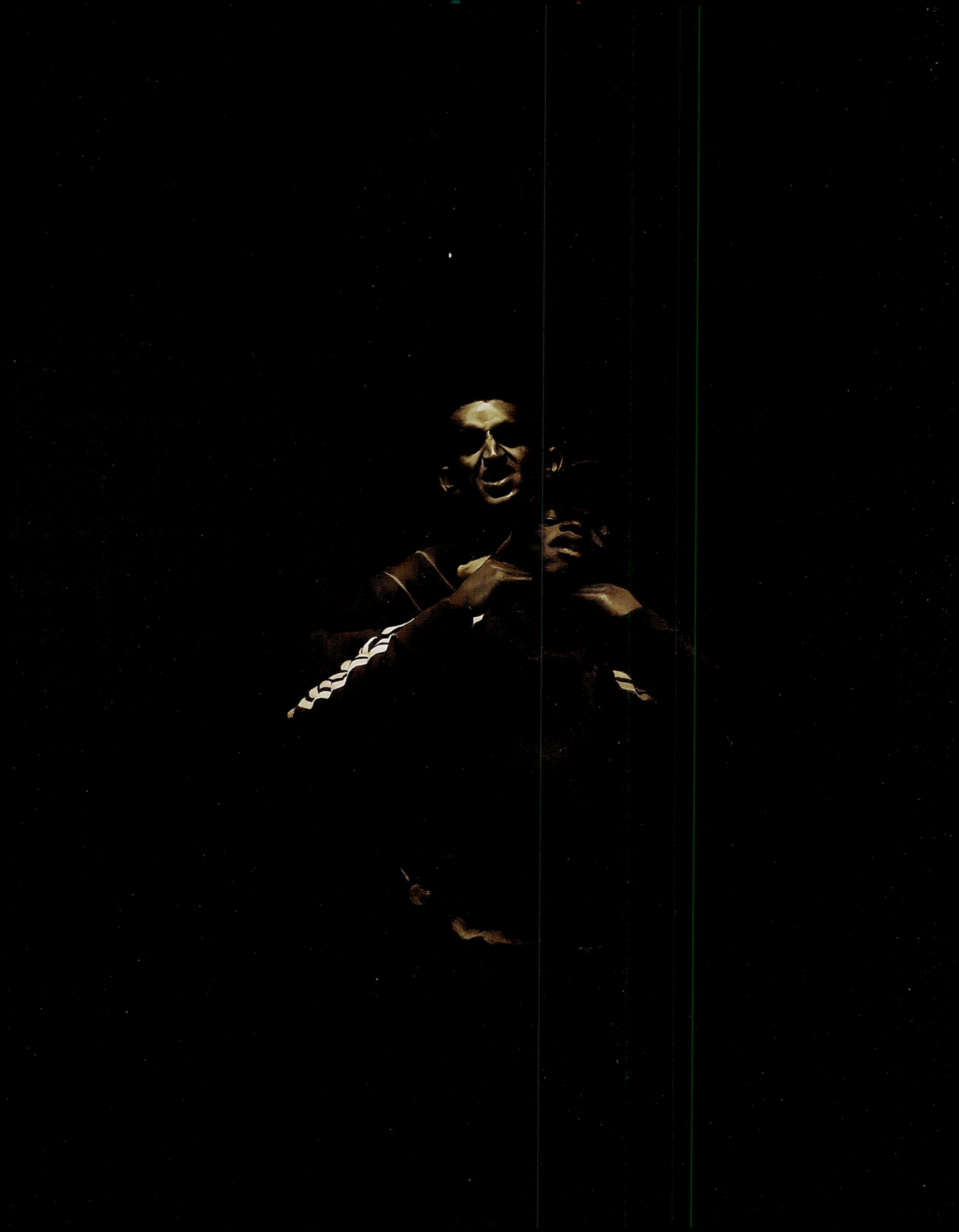

Sans titre/Untitled
2008, oil on canvas, 170 × 300 cm
(67 × 118 in).

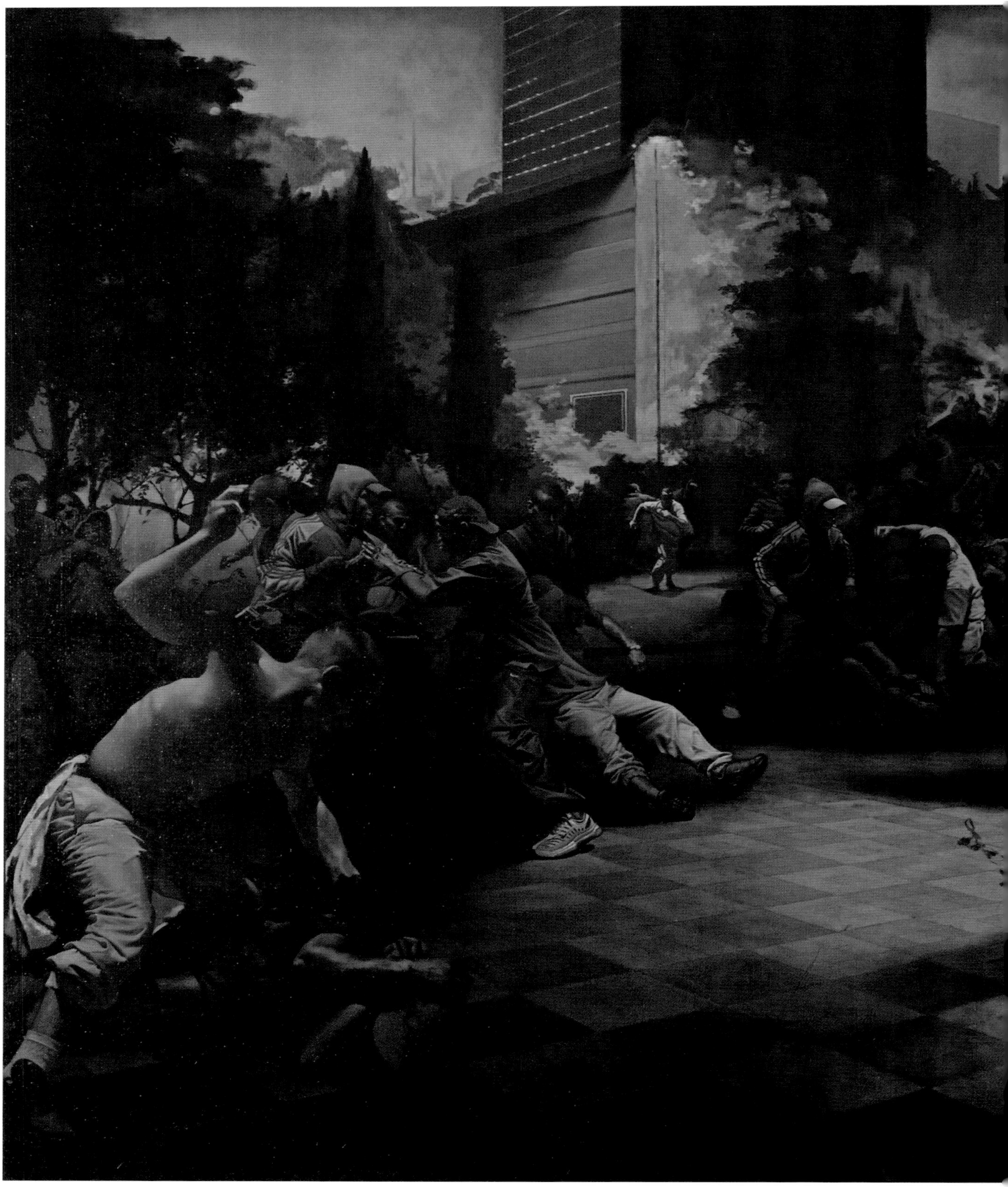

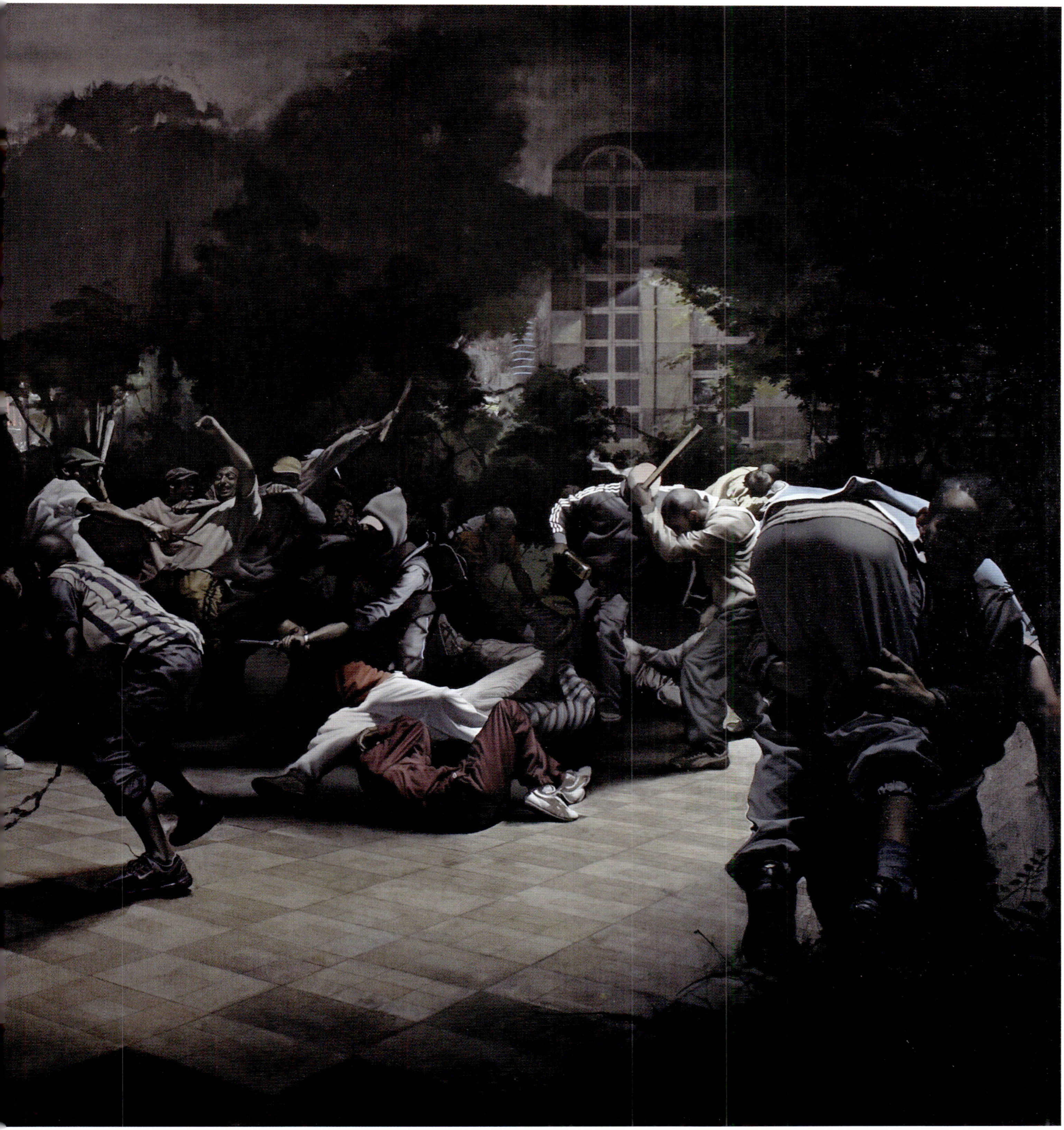

Below: Sans titre/Untitled
(detail of a triptych)
2007, oil on canvas, 130 × 160 cm
(51 × 63 in).

Bottom: Sans titre/Untitled
(detail of a triptych)
2007, oil on canvas, 130 × 160 cm
(51 × 63 in).

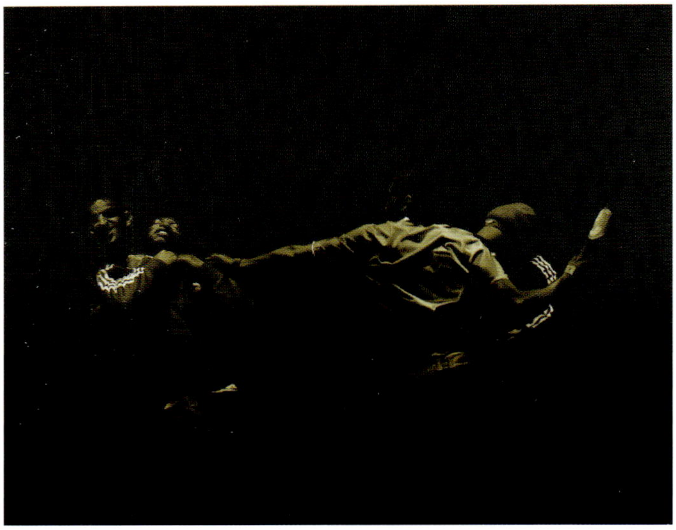

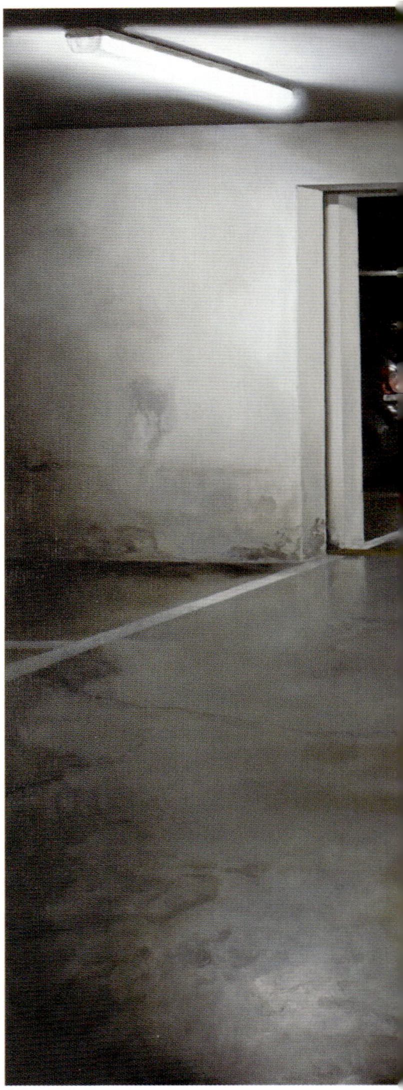

Sans titre/Untitled
2008, oil on canvas, 170 × 200 cm
(67 × 79 in).

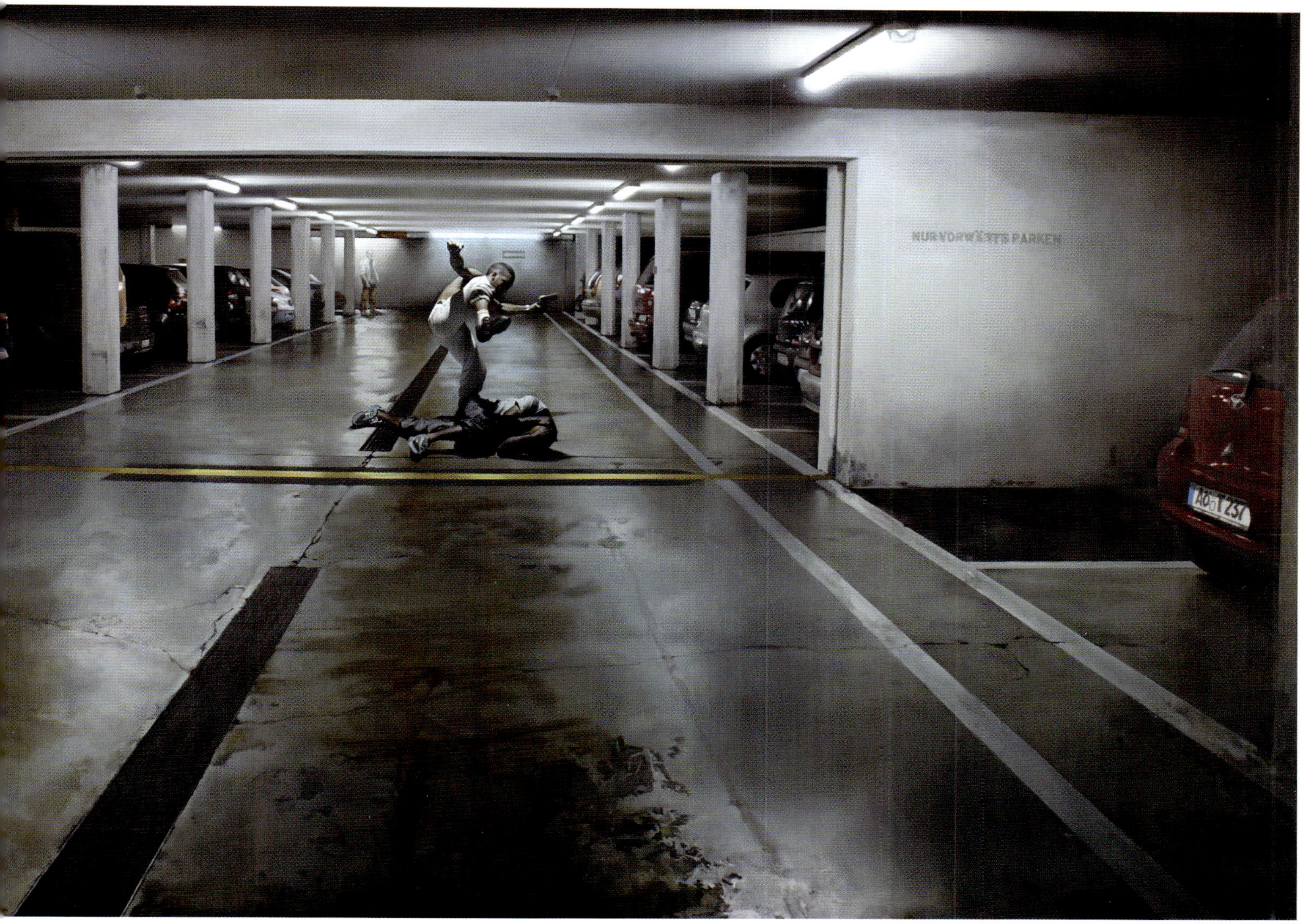

Body & Faces Study 4
2010, oil on cardboard, 47 × 37 cm
(18⅜ × 14⅜ in).

Andy Denzler
Born: 1965, Zurich
Lives: Zurich

According to Andy Denzler, painting has the unique ability to sustain and destroy the tradition of representation simultaneously. This challenge to tradition leads to a confrontation between painting and contemporary media, a reinterpretation, and this challenges us to re-educate our ways of seeing. His work seems to hover and shift constantly between abstraction and figuration, and the influence of contemporary media is latent, a mutant virus constantly affecting and troubling our relationship with traditional visual representation.

Inspiration
Mostly I paint conceptually for a certain project or show. It can be a political or critical social theme. I start with a topic and do some research or use my own photography and found images from the newspaper or the Internet.

The 'disturbed screen' effect
When I was 20, as a photographer and graphic designer, I had the opportunity to work with all different kinds of audio-visual equipment, like video recorders and photographic material. I was interested in experimenting with different techniques. For more than a decade I painted non-figuratively, and my abstract work had a reference to nature. Photographic or filmic colourfields began to appear. They had a vague connotation of something hidden – one could sense something lying below the surface – like a long exposure time. These elements started to become stronger in 2000 and I tried to develop a method to make it possible to transport my abstract vocabulary into figurative motif, like black-and-white sepia portraits painted from my own photography and film screenshots.

The canvas and the screen
The hegemony and the aesthetic of the jpeg, which we now read almost exclusively as source, is problematic. We are viewing a compromised image that is reduced to a hand-held format and backlit by a light source emitting from a terminal; an aesthetic that translates poorly from screen to painting and vice versa.

Suggestive vs. narrative
I am not really after a narrative. As much as I am concerned with movement, I prefer to be suggestive at most, implying only a mood or feeling. Any type of moralizing or story-telling is intended to be frozen, inert, non-revealing to the viewer. I am generally after an expressive documentation of situations plausible enough, but aloof and distanced, in which the viewer must not be distracted by narrative, so that they may engage themselves in the expression, material and execution of the work.

Painting as a subversive hybrid
Painting today is perhaps in a hybridization period, giving the artist a way to slow down the mass media's accelerated production/consumption rate of images, [which are seen as] past their expiry date even before the issue illustrated has saturated the public psyche. By subverting the mass media, the painter can refresh a 'dead' image, reanimating it in the way that Lucian Freud painted the flesh, providing it with an extended shelf life.

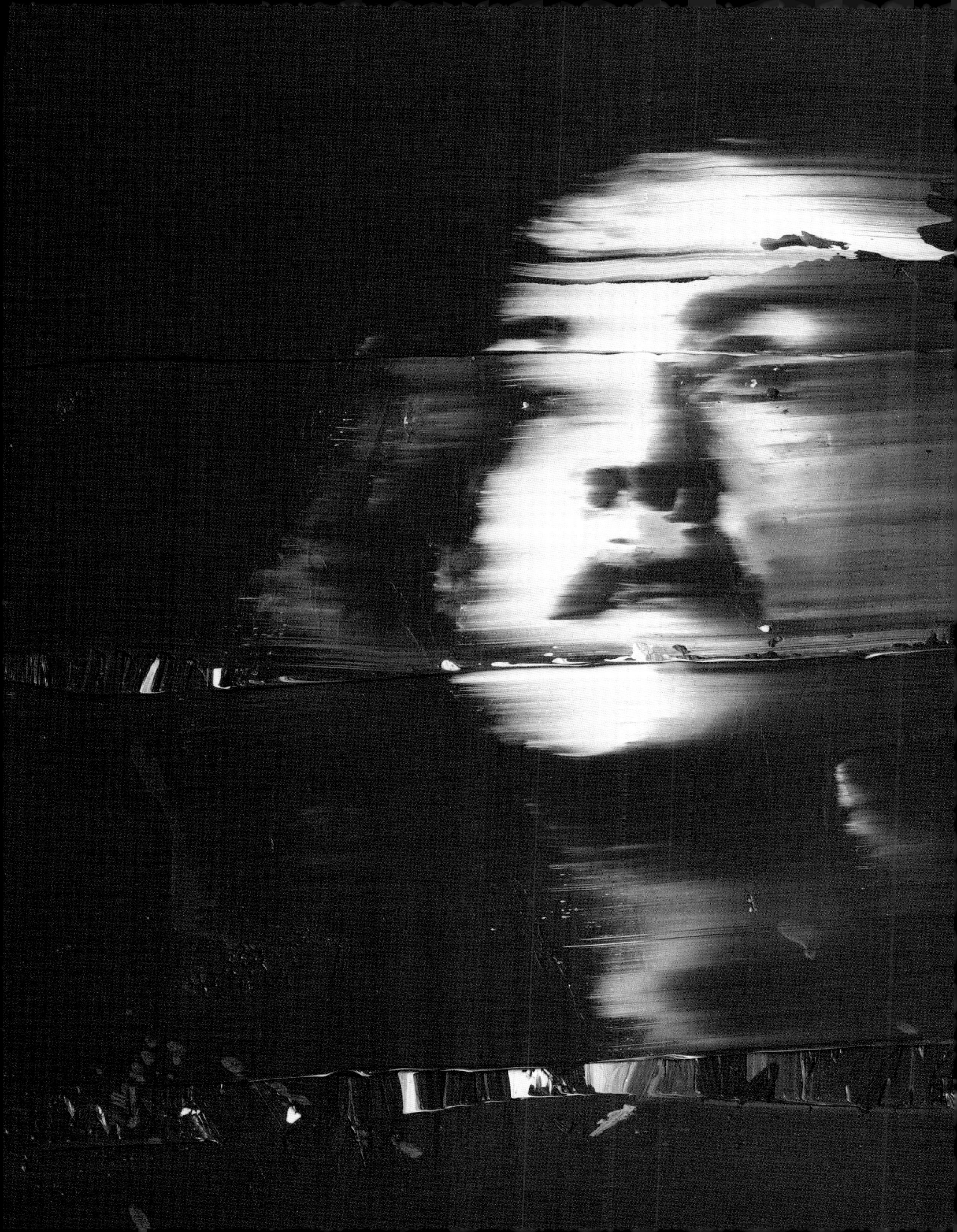

The Goddess of Imaginary Light
2012, oil on canvas, 190 × 160 cm
(75 × 63 in).

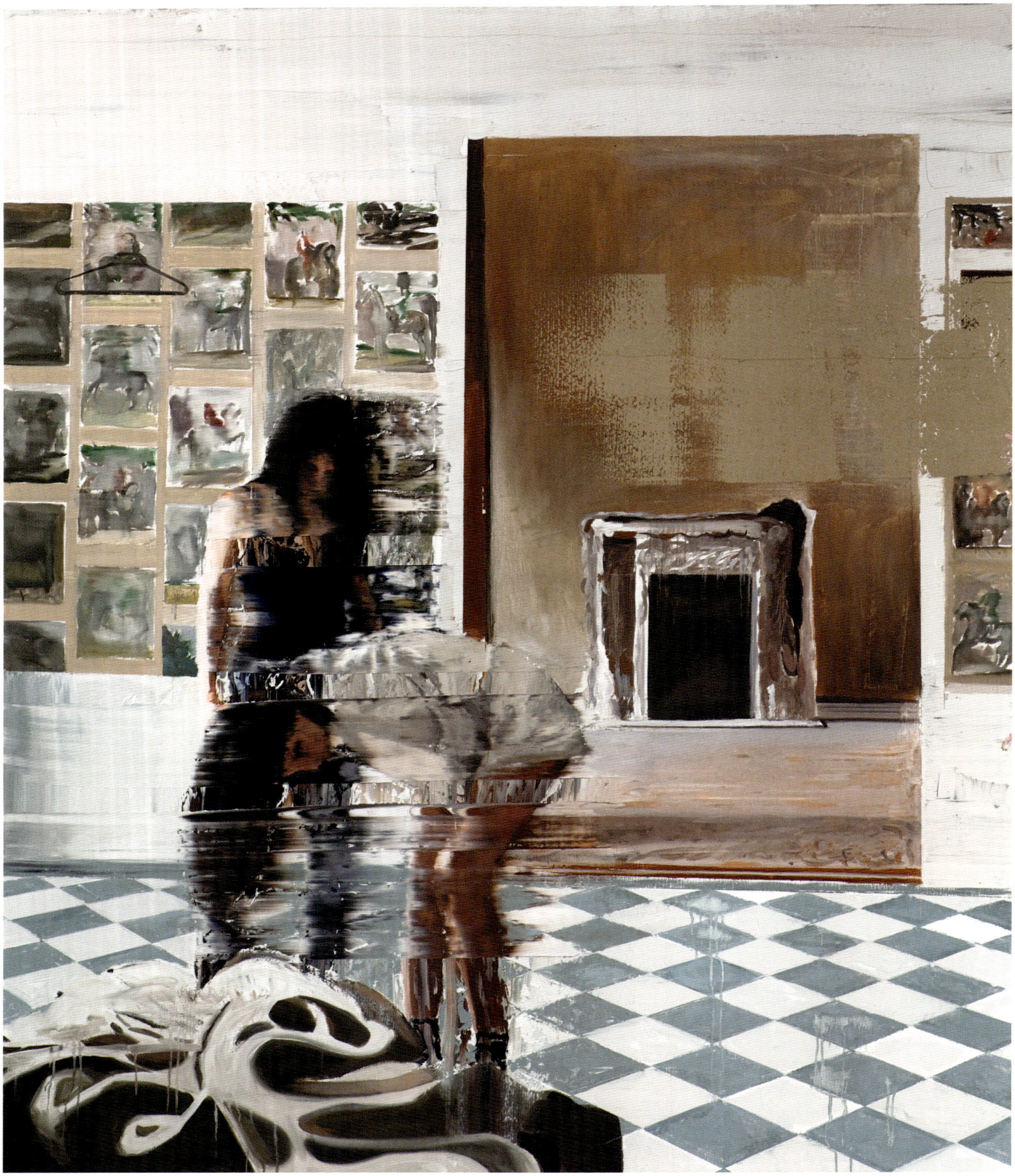

Couple Sharing Bed
2010, oil on canvas, 120 × 140 cm
(47 × 55 in).

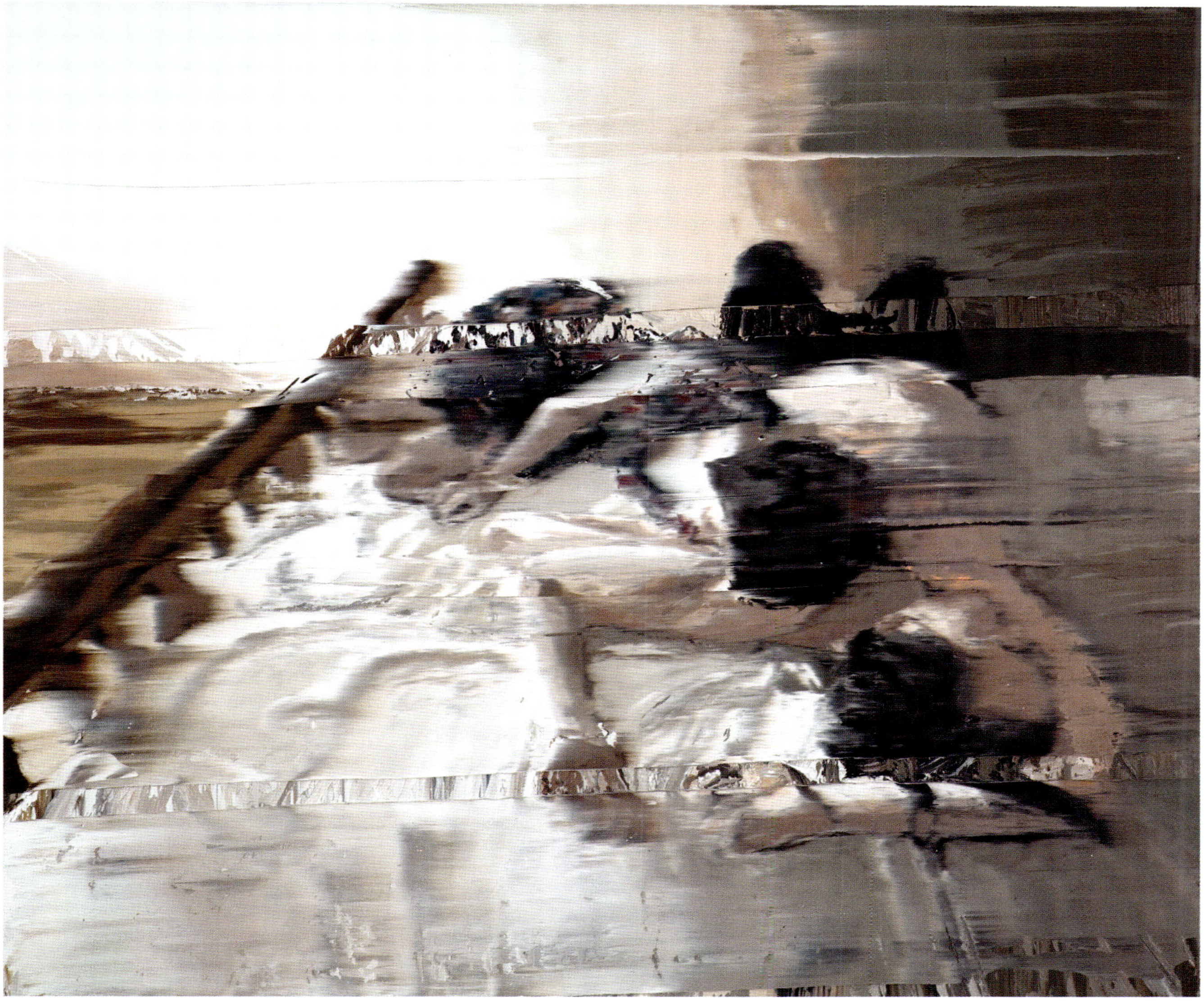

Jeremy Geddes
Born: 1974, Melbourne (Australia)
Lives: Melbourne

Before becoming a painter full-time, Jeremy Geddes spent a few years in video and online game development, following art school in Melbourne, Australia. He says he had been painting in one form or another since he was a teenager and that it has been with him for long enough to feel totally natural. Geddes applies a Photorealist style to surreal moments of suspended animation. When asked about the role of painting in today's visually saturated world, he replies that, 'Yeah, painting can be seen as a weird anachronism. My only response is really a painter's response that, in the flesh, there's nothing quite like brush-marks, glazes and a beautiful varnish!'

Influences
Both painting and film have had a large impact on me. Film has been the most influential visual art form for a few generations (perhaps now beginning to be superseded by games), and has given Western populations a very specific visual vocabulary. It would be foolish to ignore it, but obviously painting is more relevant to me. Painters all deal with the same strengths and limitations of the medium, and so understanding how they have approached ideas or solved problems is directly applicable to my own efforts.

Film directors
Some of the best compositional set-ups come out of film, specifically directors like Kubrick, Fincher and Malick. These are the kind of directors who make me itch to get back to work when I see their films.

The canvas and the screen
Obviously I, along with (I assume) most other painters, think that standing in front of the physical painting is the only real way to view that work properly, but the vast majority of people will only see the image on a screen, and I will only see most other painters' work through the same medium. It can be both a blessing and a curse, it can hide areas of dodgy paintings, or tighten sloppy brushwork, but it can't possibly reproduce the optical quality of paint or glazes.

Movement
I'm very aware of the inherent limitations of the medium I work in, and hopefully I am able to use these factors as strengths. Movement, or lack of, can be implied through the static image. This is both a limitation and a strength, depending on the skill of the painter.

Process
I go through a lot of preparation before I begin a painting; I often paint multiple studies trying to resolve issues. As my paintings have become more complex, I've found that this preparatory stage becomes longer and more involved as I try to resolve all the issues before I begin the large-scale piece. Painting from life isn't practical with the type of imagery I'm interested in, so I take a bunch of photos. I almost never find exactly what I'm after from a single reference, so usually I end up stitching figures together from a bunch of sources and try to resolve any issues this brings up during the painting process.

Red Cosmonaut
2009, oil on board, 66 × 69 cm
(26 × 27 in).

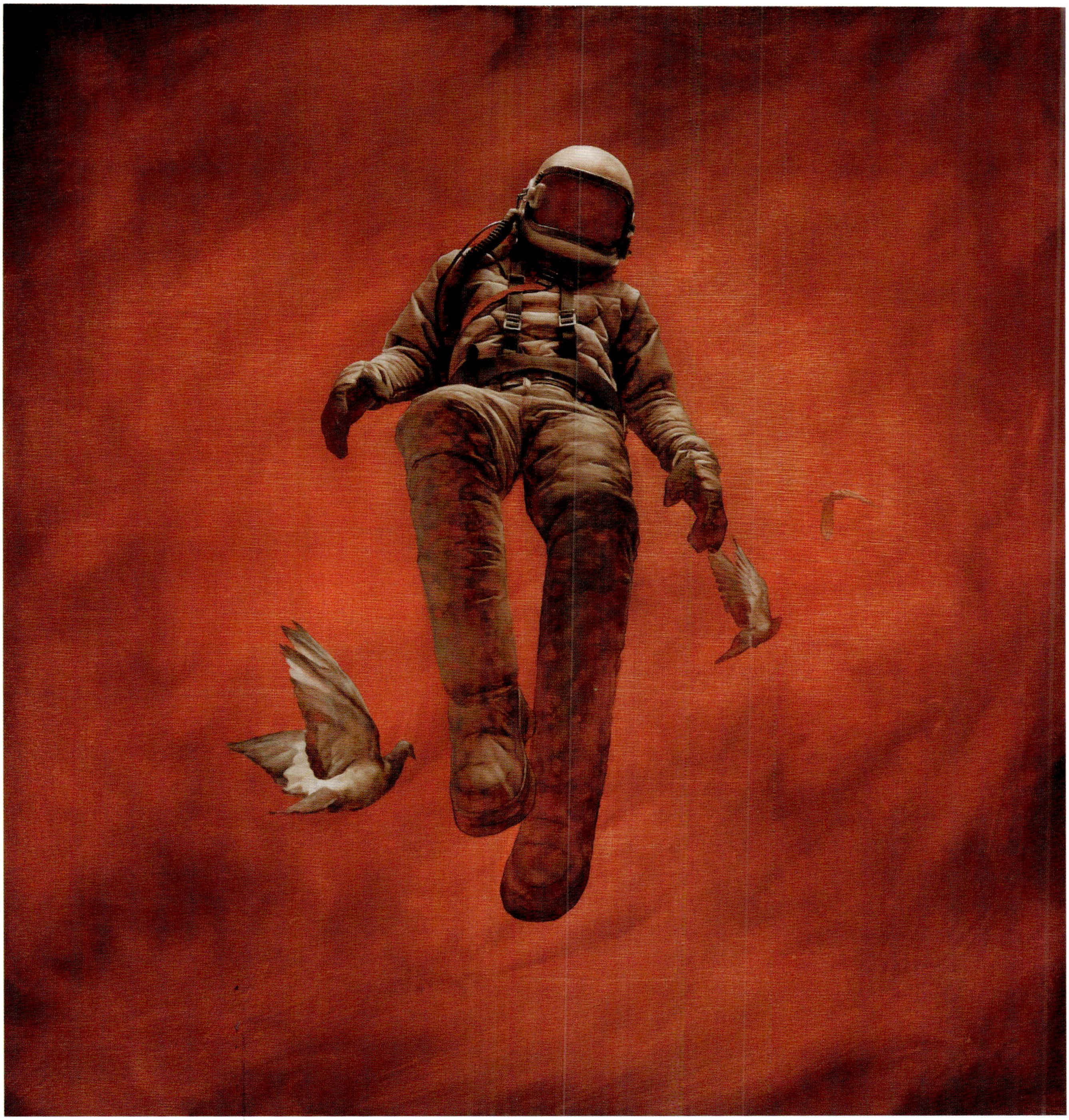

The Street
2010, oil on board, 86 × 63 cm
(34 × 25 in).

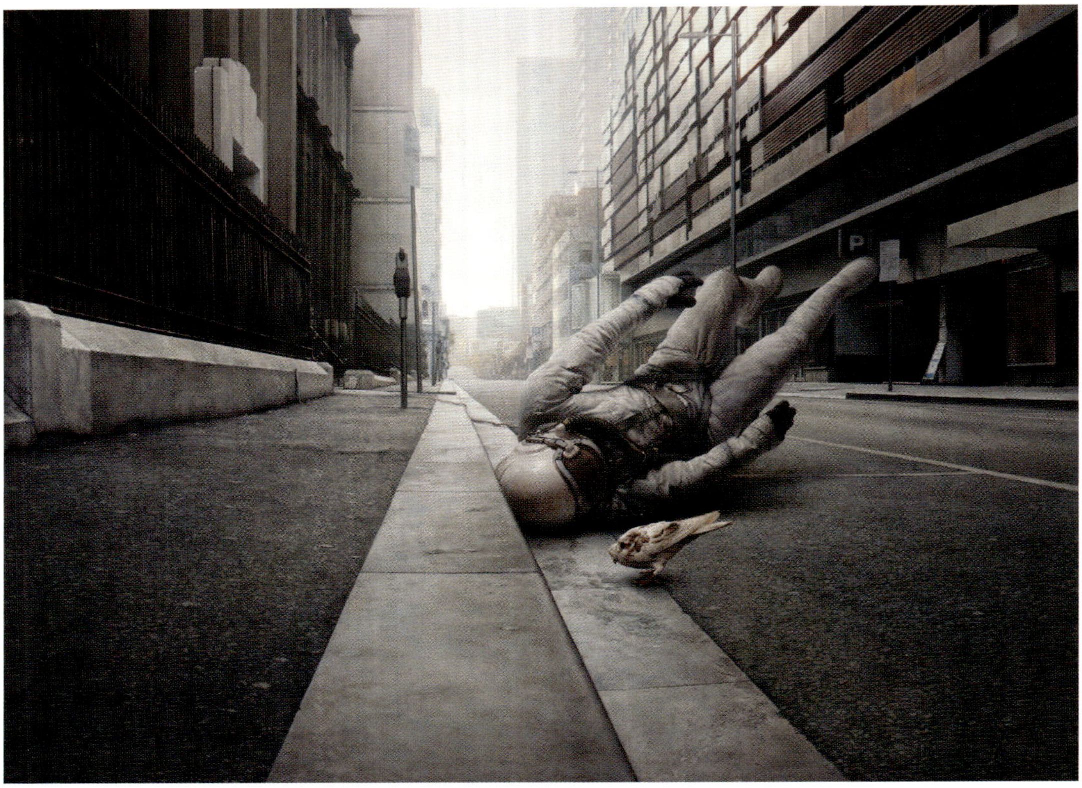

Heat Death
2008, oil on linen, 41 × 96 cm
(16 × 38 in).

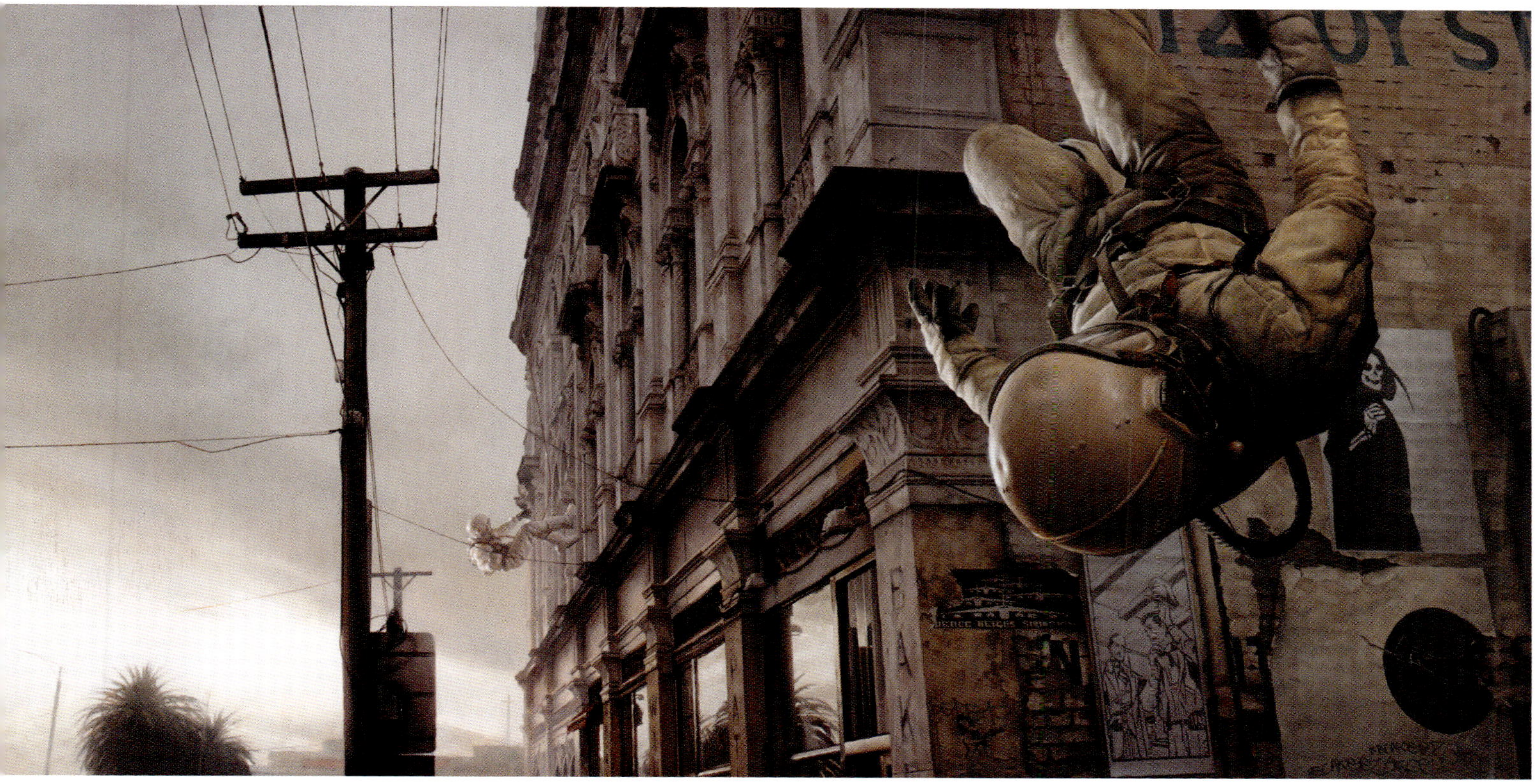

There is Glory in Our Failure
2007, oil on linen, 152 × 91 cm
(60 × 35⅞ in).

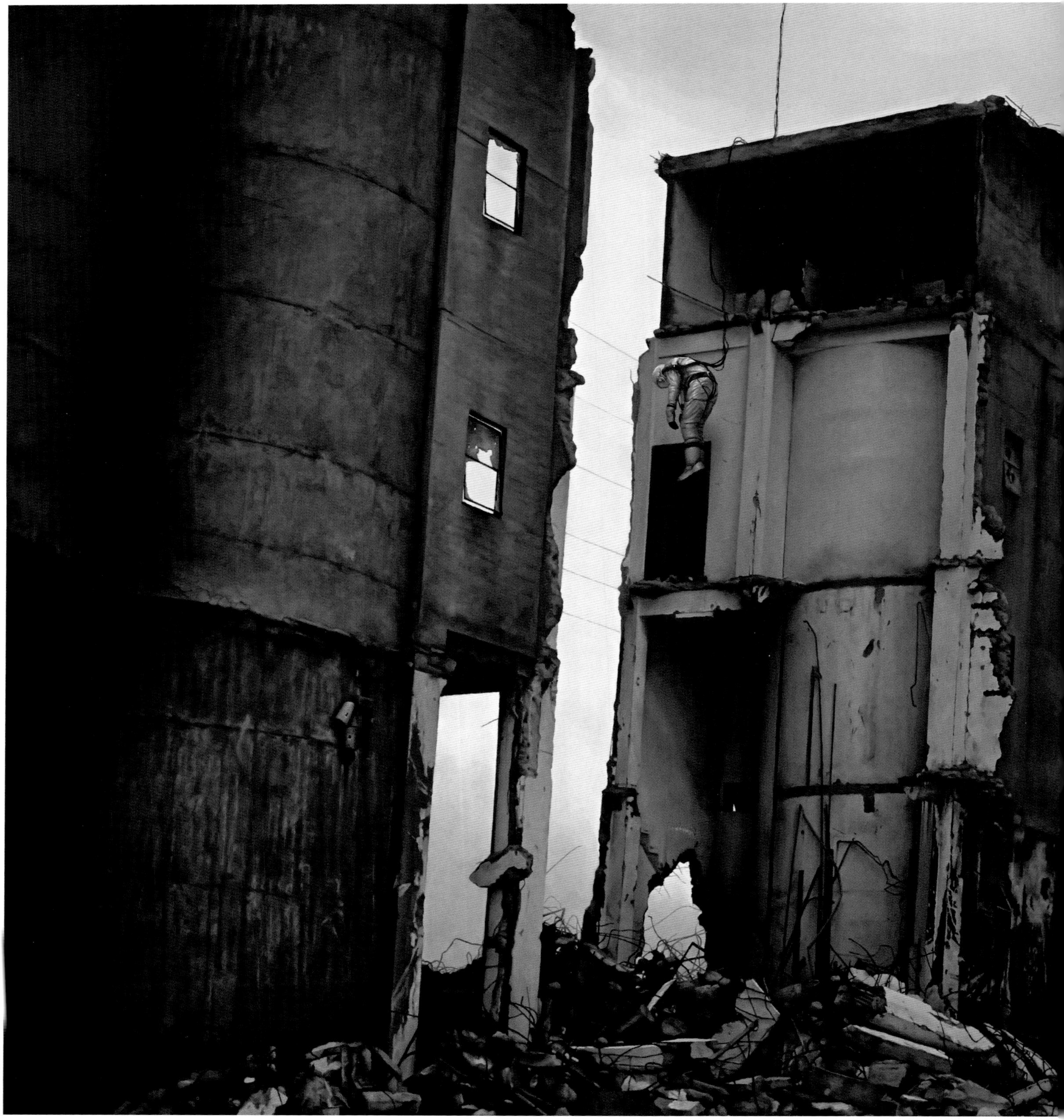

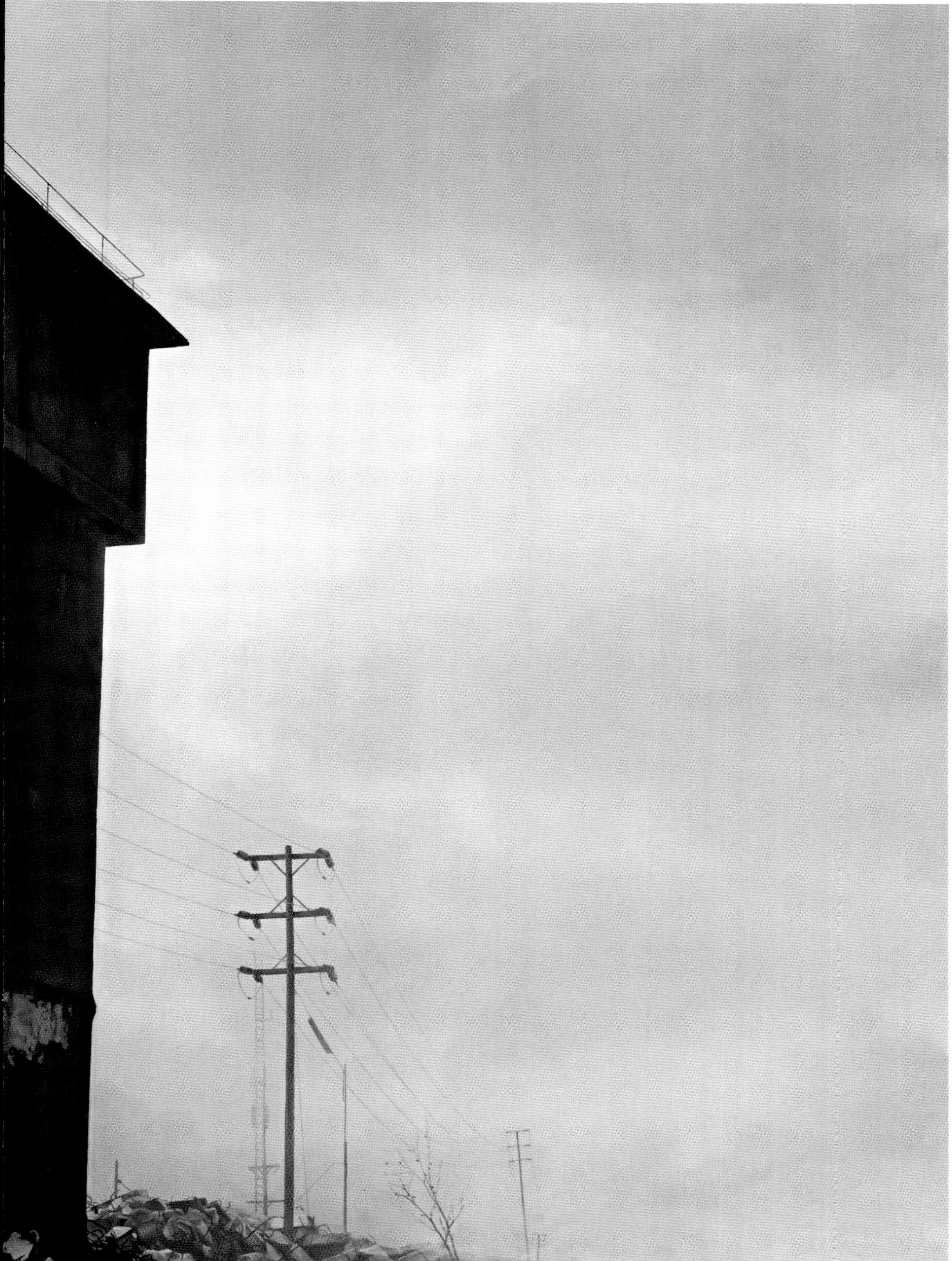

Luka Kurashvili
Born: Tbilisi (Georgia), 1985
Lives: Düsseldorf

The youngest painter featured in the current volume, Luka Kurashvili was 22 when he left his native Georgia for Germany. He was accepted into the prestigious Kunstakademie in Düsseldorf, which has played an important part in the development of figurative painting in and around Germany. He still studies (he is in his last year) under Peter Doig, who he describes as 'one of the best professors in the world'. Though clearly influenced by the older painter, Kurashvili has developed a distinctive personal style, a fresh and youthful mix of folk and poetic elements combined with global politics and his own background. The dictators in his 'The Damned and Our Leaders' series appear almost as a child would see them: enormous, gaudy, whimsical, and yet at the same time very real, with a profound sadness visible in all their pomp and glory.

Background
I was born in Tbilisi, the capital of Georgia, into a family of artists. My mother is a ceramicist and my father is a cinematographer. Georgia, as a post-Soviet country, was still under the influence of Communism [when I was growing up] and this affected almost all areas of society, including the arts. There was the so-called 'Classic School' at the Tbilisi State Academy of Arts, which I had to go through. As I never liked this 'system', I left the Academy and my home country. I do like Georgian culture, but the methodology of the art education system was not appropriate [for me].

Technique
Mainly I use oil and canvas, but I'm working with other media as well – creating art movies. When I get an idea, the first thing I do is to think about what technique would be best to realize and present it. Sometimes the concepts I'm thinking of using to create paintings end up transforming themselves into a screenplay, or vice versa.

My most recent works are based on my imagination and fantasies. I make sketches at the beginning, then imagine how these will look as a completed painting. I never come to the canvas unprepared.

The dictators series ['The Damned and Our Leaders']
I became interested in politics in art at an early age, maybe because that played such an important role in my home country. Politics and politicians were the most popular figures, as leaders, or enemies. That was a period when there was almost no space for art: political broadcasts and news took up most of the time in people's lives.

Often I make works based on something important that happens in my life, but also I choose subjects directly related to the latest news broadcasted. I believe that showing works about current issues is interesting to the public. And I also believe that the artist's work should be defined by and engaged with society: this is the main role of the artist.

Film influences
Cinematography has played an important role in my life since childhood, and has influenced my art very much, though I can't pinpoint a particular movie. In general I think that the spirit of my works is cinematographic and my compositions avant-gardist and poetic – sometimes they look like images from Surrealist movies. And they tell stories.

The role of painting
Every now and then I think that painting is almost exhausted. But the 'New Painting Art' exists. It might be invisible today, but tomorrow it will show up. What I do is not only for or about my personality. I consider art [to have a role] as a poetry, history, interest, communication, intelligence, fear, war, and so on. I try to make art in a way that means I can add something to the world's culture and history, no matter at what level.

Portrait of Muammar Gaddafi
2012, oil on canvas, 120 × 120 cm
(47 × 47 in).

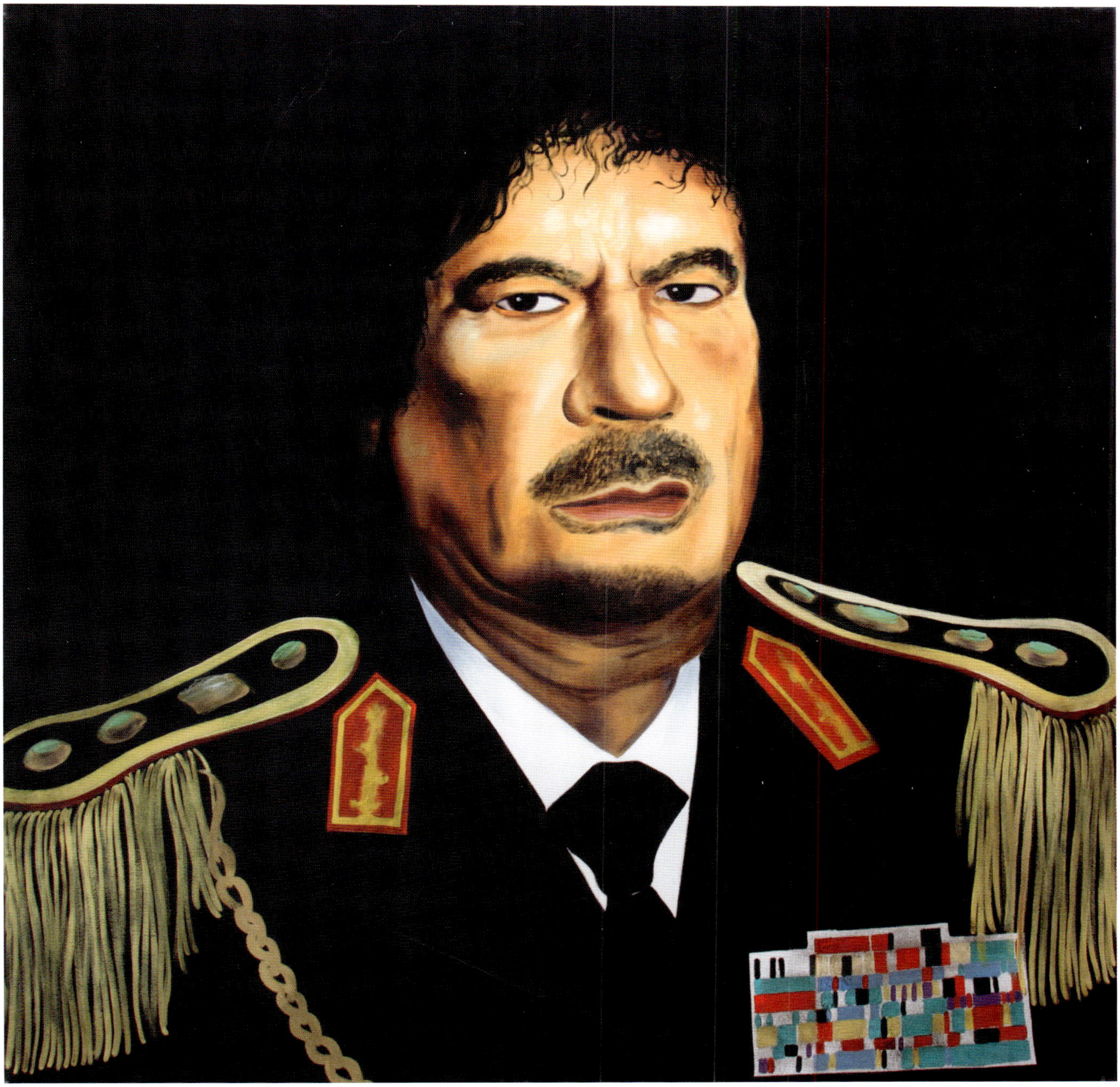

Portrait of Osama bin Laden
2012, oil on canvas, 120 × 120 cm
(47 × 47 in).

Portrait of George W. Bush
2011, oil on canvas, 120 × 120 cm
(47 × 47 in).

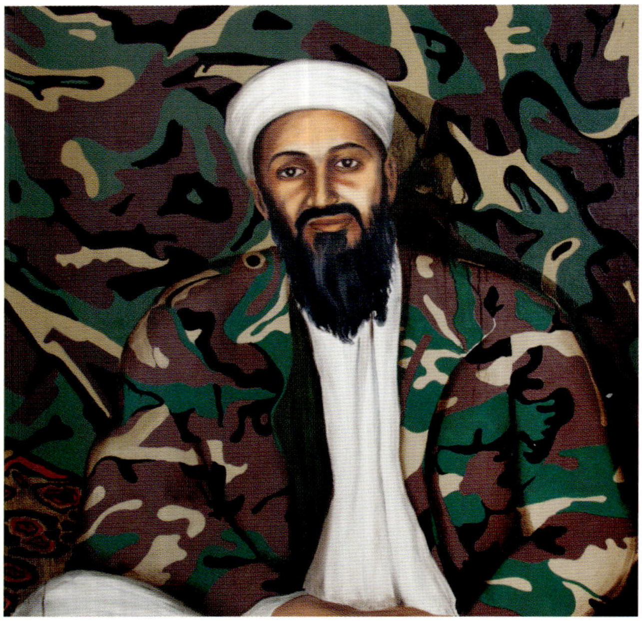

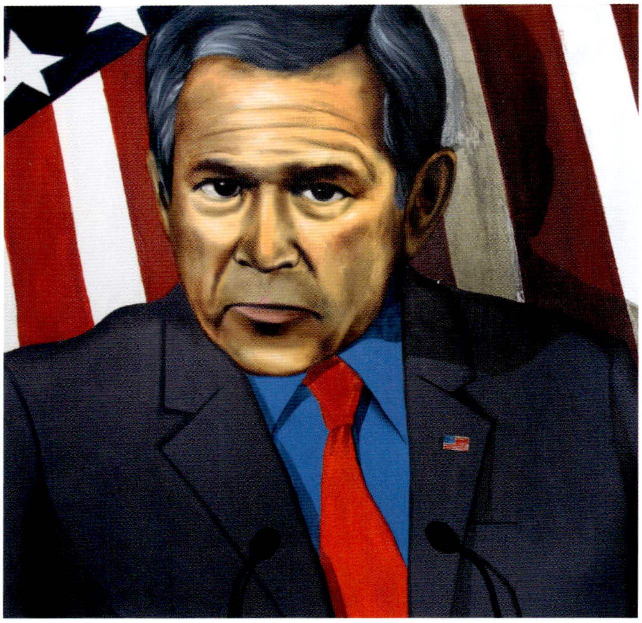

9/11
2013, oil on canvas, 180 × 180 cm
(71 × 71 in).

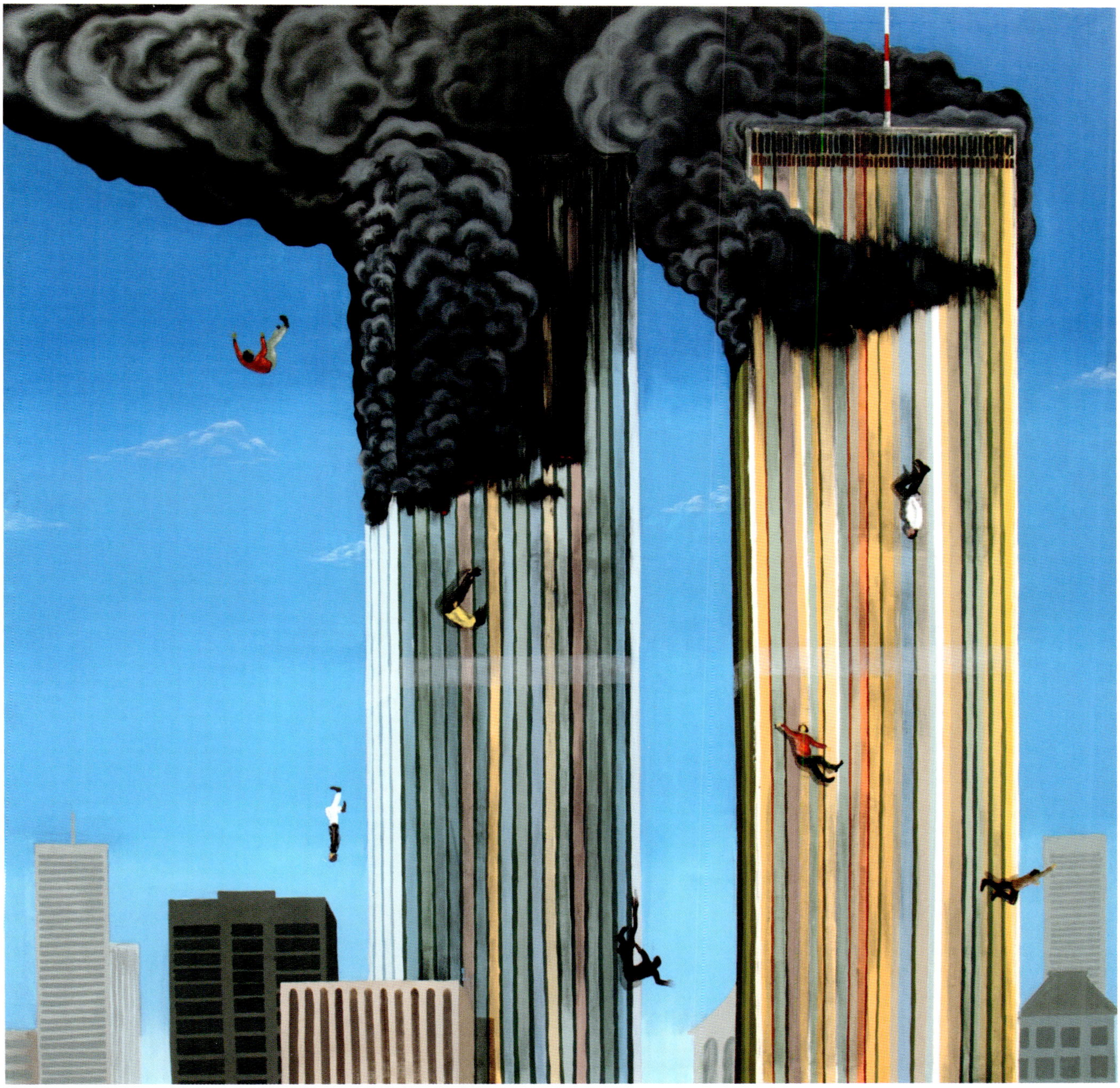

Wounded Boxer #2
2007 (diptych), oil on canvas,
150 × 300 cm (59 × 118 in).

Jérôme Lagarrigue
Born: 1973, Paris
Lives: New York

Boxing has been the subject of many great works of literature and film, but with a few notable exceptions (George Bellows comes to mind) it has not been a focal point for painters. Born in Paris, but now living in Brooklyn (he studied at Rhode Island School of Design, where he discovered his vocation as a painter), Jérôme Lagarrigue has developed a particularly close relationship with the sport; and an equally visceral relationship with most of his subjects. His paintings are highly successful in capturing, through dynamic brushstrokes, the vivid and bustling complexity of reality, from the smell of sweat in a gym, or the focus in the eye of a boxer, to the palpable tension of a riot or the defiance of a shantytown perched on a Brazilian hillside.

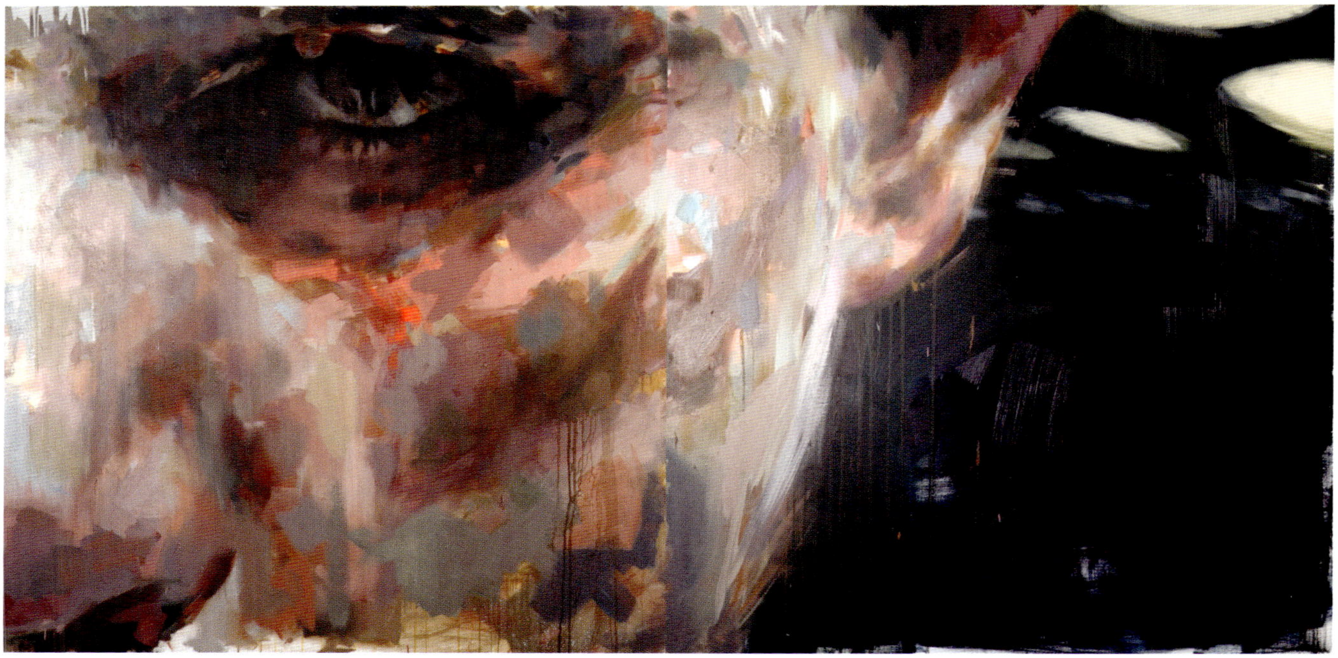

Technique
I attended life-drawing classes in the past and sometimes miss it now. Having an understanding of drawing is imperative and unavoidable in the field of figurative painting. Drawing is the spine behind any representational painting, to some degree. Drawing is observing. I don't see or understand technique. I work instinctively, doing what I can. Somehow mistakes become part of my means of expression. Achieving a technique is perhaps more suitable for illustrators. I mostly paint from photographs that I shoot myself or find randomly in prints or online.

Moving images
Film influences my work because I am sensitive to moving imagery. When watching a film or looking at photography, I am always on the look-out for interesting new compositions, new ways of lighting a subject. I find myself pausing and rewinding certain movie scenes in appreciation of an actor's placement within the picture frame, for example, or the direction in which he tilts his head (Stanley Kubrick is one of my favourite artists of all time!). I decide to delve into a subject when I feel all the elements are there to produce an interesting film, metaphorically speaking.

Subjects
My love for boxing started when I entered the legendary Gleason's Gym [where Robert De Niro researched his role in *Raging Bull*] in Brooklyn in 1995. From the smell of sweat, the sound of fists landing on punching bags, the light hitting a boxer in front of a decaying red wall, to the notion of the enclosed, still arena, in which fighters are in a state of collision – I just knew it had to be documented. I will paint boxers for the rest of my life.

I don't have favourite subjects. But these days my work deals with collisions. I am painting riot scenes and devoting a series of paintings to one boxer in particular. The notion of series is helpful to me, because the paintings start to interact with each other as you're working on them, therefore making it easier to take bold decisions.

Secret cities
I visited a favela in Salvador de Bahia in Brazil. A friend took me to the studio of a very affluent percussionist in Bahia The idea came to me that I did not want to paint favelas from the inside but rather from the outside looking in, as a place into which you are not invited. I like the concept of forbidden, secret cities within cities. That is the case with Rocinha in Rio de Janeiro, the largest, most iconic and popular favela, media-wise at least. I used available imagery online, satellite and Google Earth pictures to paint these. I purposely decided to focus only on the architecture of the shantytowns as opposed to their populations, consequently reinforcing the notion that I am just an outsider (a 'gringo') looking in.

Influences
Many painters inspire me, mostly European: from Byzantine triptychs to Francis Bacon, Velázquez, Rembrandt, Lucian Freud, Jenny Saville, Van Gogh, Corot, etc. .. I seem to be more interested in blurriness: I am perhaps from the school of blurry painters....

Painting today
If, as some people claim, painting is dead, why was there a two-hour wait with hundreds of people in line at any given time during the Edward Hopper exhibition at the Grand Palais in Paris? There is a lot of painting being shown these days, in museums, at art fairs and in galleries. It never went away, [though] sometimes it fades. What is the only medium that cannot be turned into an MP3, MPEG or AVI file, and still remain interactively interesting? Painting. Only the original piece is the true experience and, as a means of expression, it is here to stay, like forks and knives.

Figurative art will always have a role (the same fascinating role it has always played, giving the viewer an opportunity to dive temporarily into someone's intimate world through his or her work), even in the age of Photoshop, in the same way food plays a role in our survival. We need it. We also need a little Photoshop here and there.

Collision Sequence #1
(detail of a triptych)
2007, oil on canvas, 25 × 50 cm
(9⅞ × 19¾).

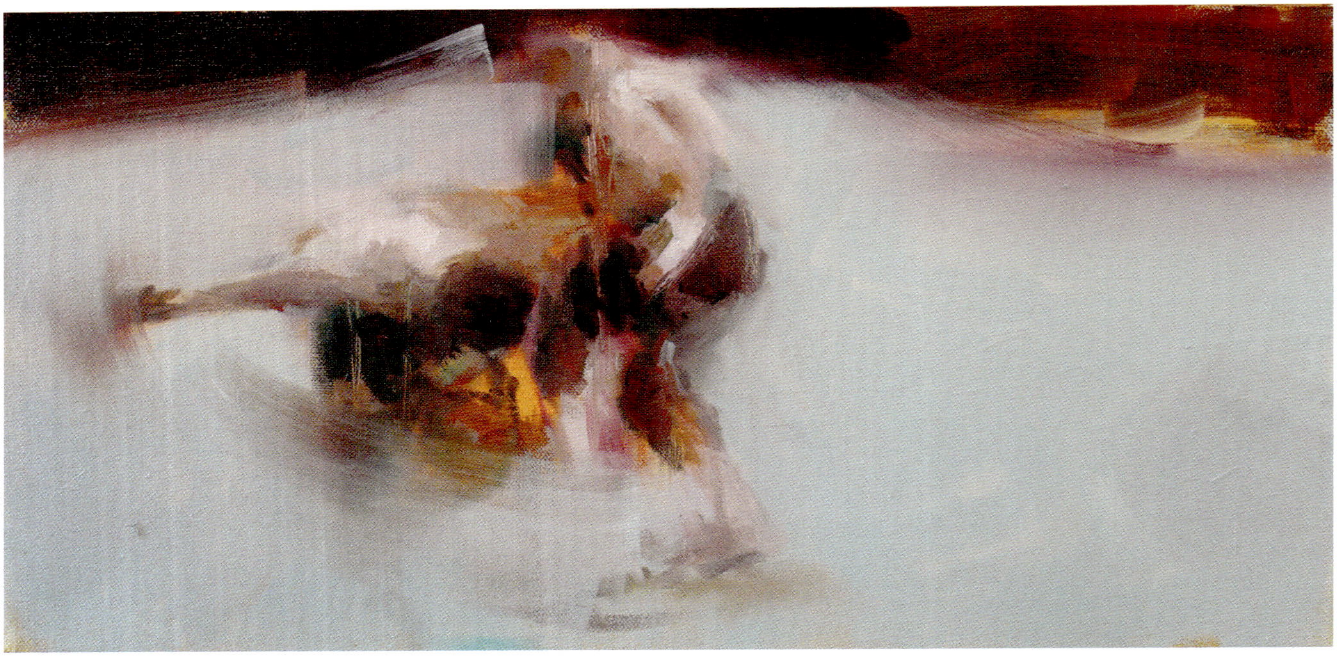

Collision Sequence #1
(detail of a triptych)
2007, oil on canvas, 25 × 50 cm
(9⅞ × 19¾ in).

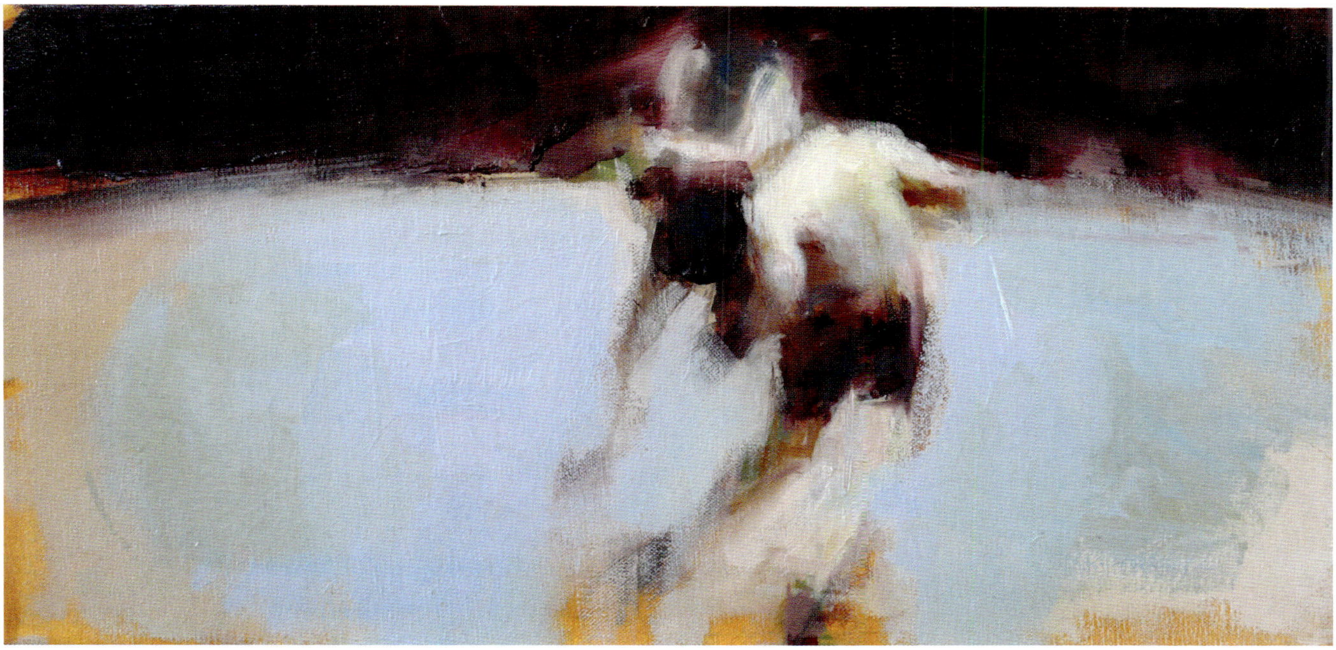

Blue Headgear
2007, oil on canvas, 200 × 200 cm
(79 × 79 in).

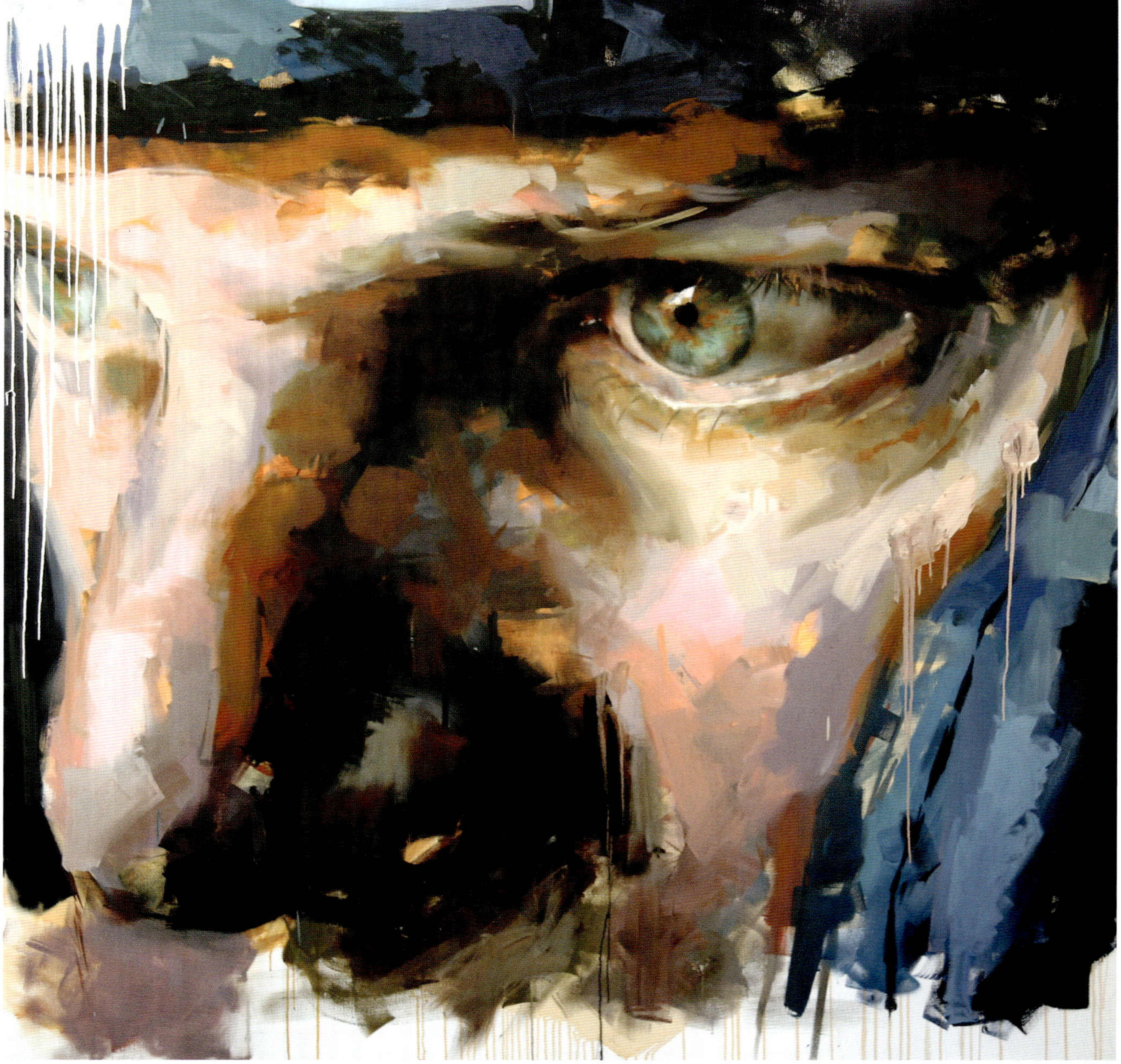

Boxer Wearing Towel
2007, oil on canvas, 250 × 200 cm
(98 × 79 in).

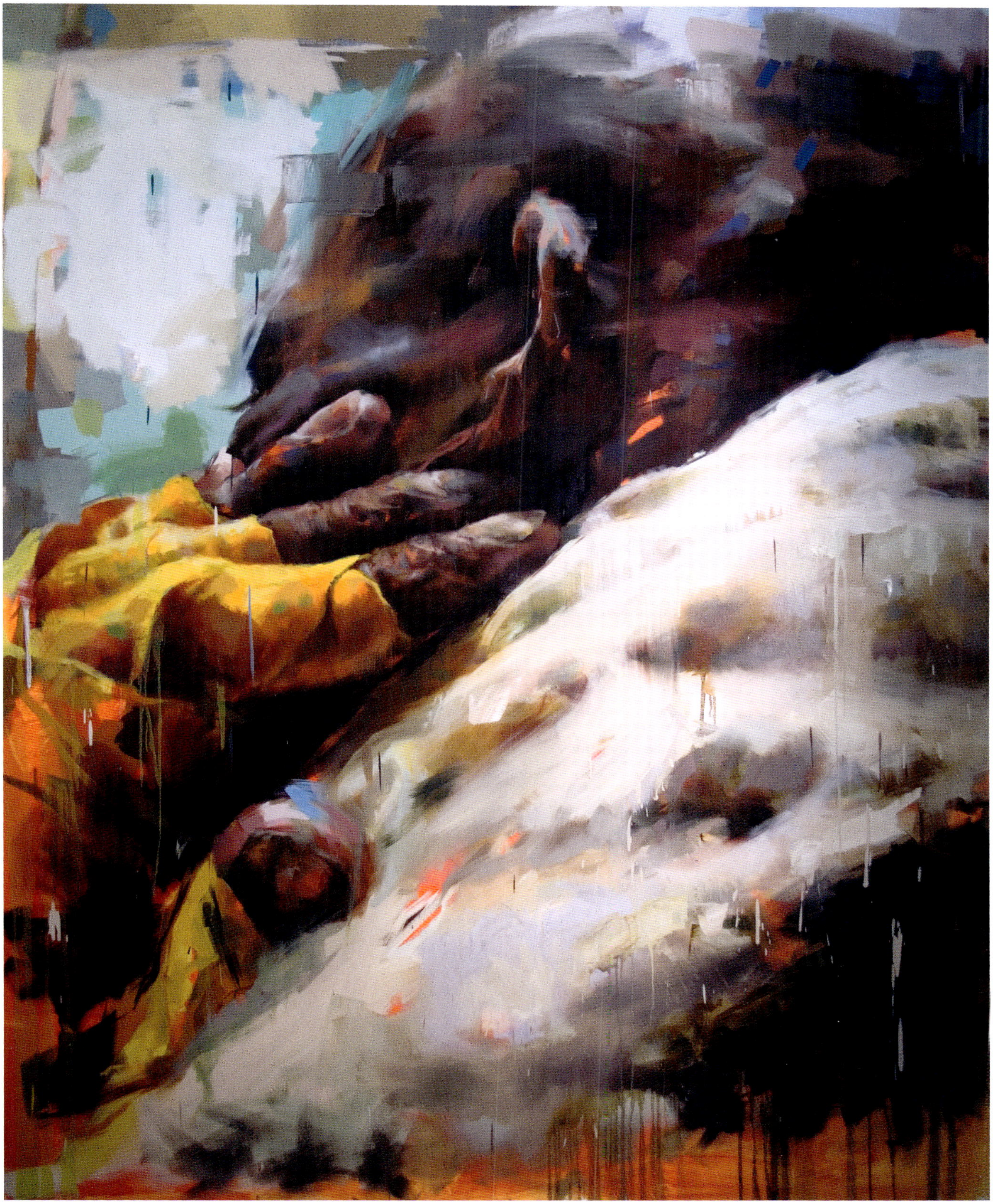

Nikolas Weise/Ulrich Lamsfuß
Pinocchio
2006, oil on canvas, 60 × 70 cm
(23⅝ × 27⅝ in).

Ulrich Lamsfuß
Born: 1971, Bonn (Germany)
Lives: Berlin

Reality, representation, originality and appropriation are constant themes running through the work of Berlin-based painter Ulrich Lamsfuß. The subjects for his paintings come from disparate sources (often magazines and newspapers).
He reworks these images with meticulous and heavy brushstrokes in an attempt to recapture the intensity of the original material and the complex drama of its reproduction through mass media, as well as the incongruity of its depiction in paint. The physical quality of his canvases and the slow rhythm of painting create an intriguing paradox between the ephemerality of the original material and its artistic transposition. Thus famous and anonymous people alike when portrayed by Lamsfuß are rapidly elevated to an illusory yet mythical status, their images reaching stability only through painting.

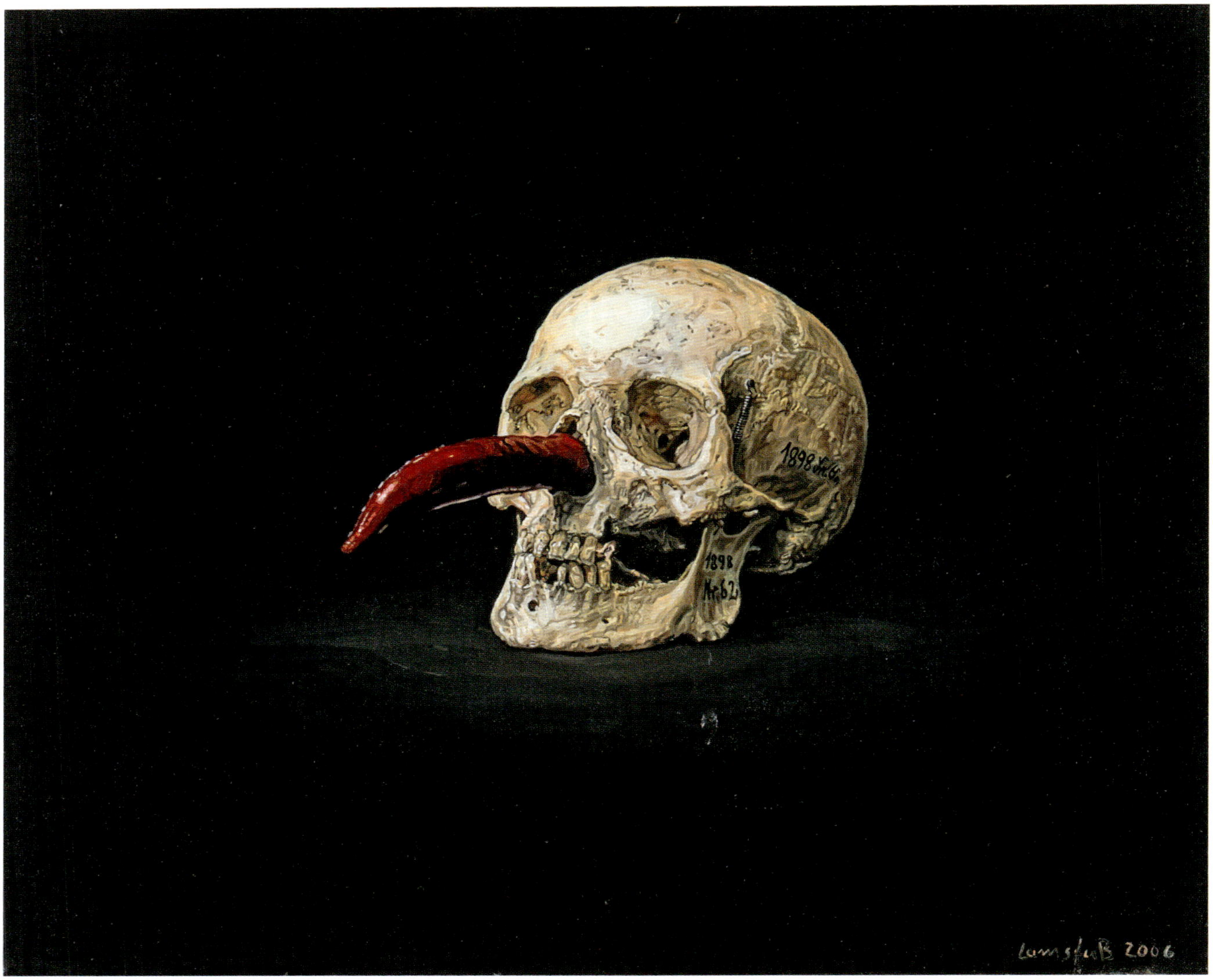

Background
My parents are teachers and active '68ers' [the post-war generation that as students took part in Europe-wide demonstrations, which reached a peak in 1968], who have made it pretty clear to me that words are just words and that the power of pictures is much more relevant. I really love the fact that pictures don't talk. It seems to me that I always thought that the world was in bad shape and always wanted to belong to those trying to bring some light and beauty in.

Art school
I went to a few academies: [Willem de Kooning Academie] Rotterdam, [Kunstakademie] Düsseldorf and finally UdK Berlin [Universität der Künste] in the masterclass of Georg Baselitz, but I was not really able to learn much. I was looking for a type of relevance and evidence that I did not find at school.

Technique
My painting technique is basically non-existent. It's just about putting the right colour directly on the canvas exactly where I find it on the original. It is more about plotting. I want to have a straight, non-artistic, dry, honest and evident surface. You can follow every brushstroke, you can see and understand how it is done. No tricky tricks. So my artistic development is just about getting more exact. My drawing technique is the opposite. It is more spontaneous and juicy and faulty: it is therapy.

It took a lot of willpower to 'keep on keeping on'. It took a while for me to understand that what I am doing is shifting from showing to seeing, and that this makes sense to me.

Authenticity
Wherever I go somebody has been there before and everything has been said. I am interested in mirroring this situation. And I choose to create confusion. A subject can be anything as long as I have the feeling that it makes for a proper painting – which means it has the potential to be a good fetish, something you want to have. It should be entertaining, interesting, confusing It can be right or wrong, true or false ... anything goes (note that the source is interesting too: what it was intended for, where it was published, who did the piece, its history, etc.).

I think what is called authenticity is something pretty idealized (and a good selling point) and I am sick of looking at it. My art should not be more intelligent than the spectator. The only way of being authentic is by admitting that one cannot be so (and cannot really be different).

On the choice of subject matter
It is more about themes, about *zeitgeist*. I am more interested in subtext than in the story and in the end everything is media. I can read everything, but the point is that the painting does not talk. Actually, the contradiction and diversity of the subjects is meant to make them stop talking. The *zeitgeist* is defined by attention deficit disorder and that really makes me want to move slowly and with exactitude. So I slow it down to a maximum of ten images a year – in the end, my dream would be to keep on painting just one image over and over again. It is a little bit like DJ-ing. I always like to have images that make it easy for an audience to connect, and then come up with more queer stuff.

Influences
Actually I do not feel so very much like a painter. First there is an artistic attitude and then one chooses the medium because of personal preference. It should be about content, attitudes and ideas, and not about media or techniques. I am mainly inspired by all appropriation artists, from Duchamp and Picabia via Warhol and Sturtevant to Sherrie Levine, Richard Prince, Robert Longo, Franz Gertsch, etc. I also like people working on misunderstandings, mistakes, fakes or similar transgressions of appropriation.

On the condition of the contemporary painter
Contemporary culture is entropy. It is complex, ignorant. Maybe there is something like 'swarm intelligence'. I have no idea how to influence or shape up these times. But every time gets the culture it deserves, and this is probably a time that will be named after its economic system and not after its art. It is for sure the capitalist era – art does not matter much, be it painting or any other media.

I try to make my way in the ruins of Modernism, and hope this is a visible effort. I am working on the Utopia of a motivated life. I try to give my best and to avoid being too stupid. I hope to bring my confusion to a higher level and in the end I try to entertain.

Dirk Hasskarl, Michel Houellebecq (Qvest Sept./Okt. 2006) 2010, oil on canvas, 90 × 90 cm (35½ × 35½ in).

Fergus Greer, Leigh Bowery, (14/ August 1990), Session III (Looks) 2008, oil on canvas, 200 × 140 cm (79 × 55 in).

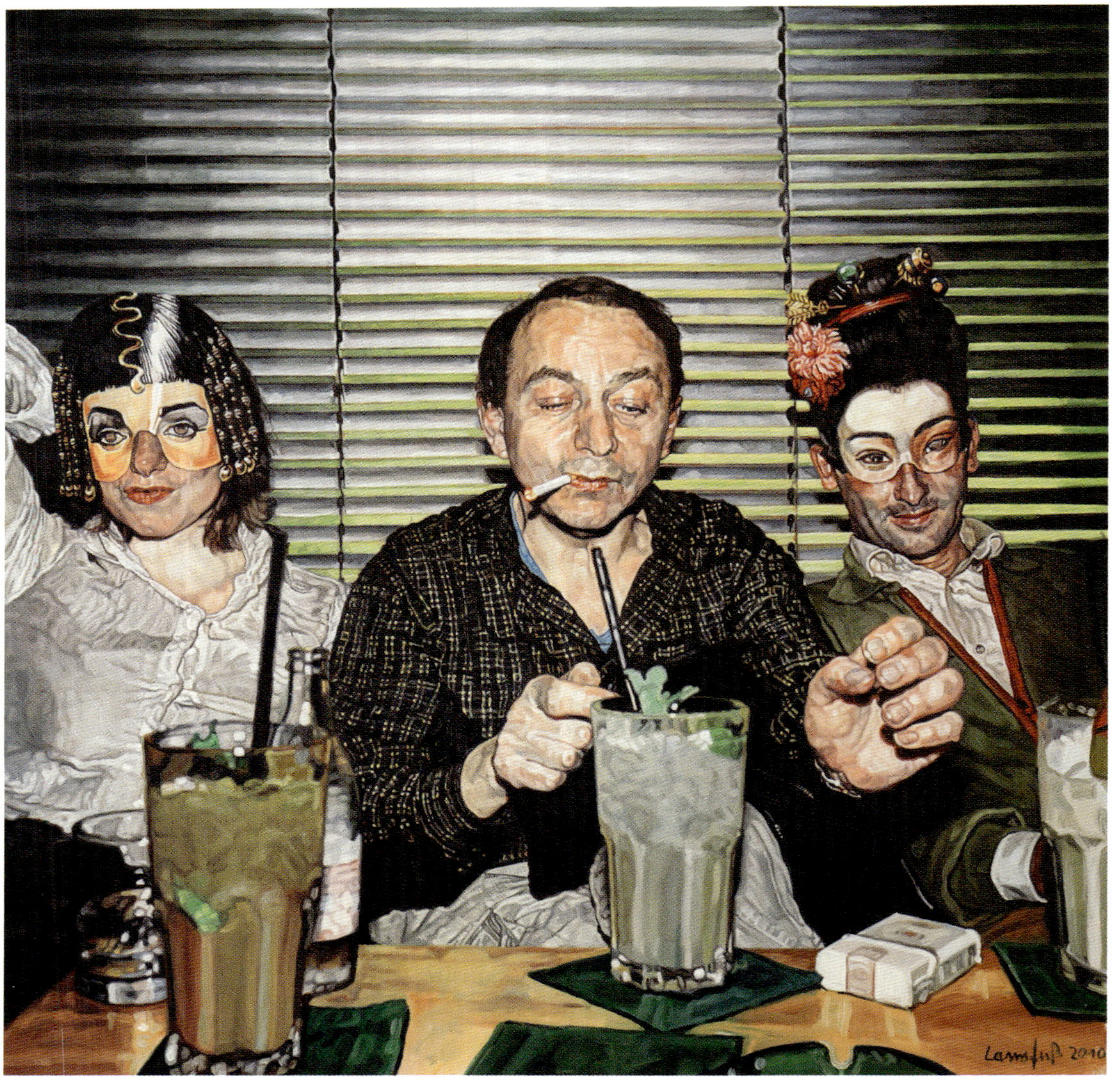

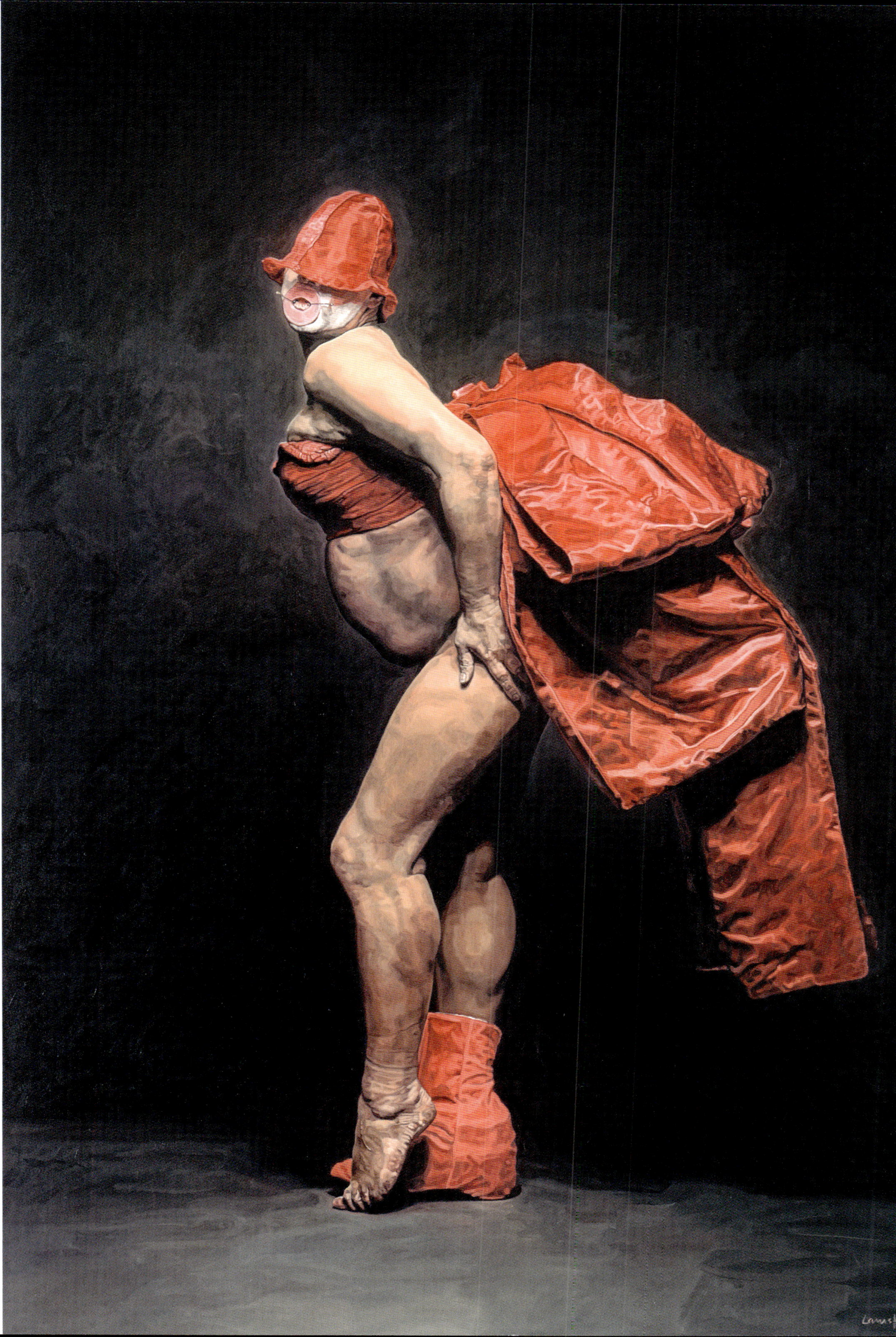

Holger Niehaus/Ulrich Lamsfuß,
Arbeiterbild, Fließbandarbeiterin
(Sophie Rois)
2008, oil on canvas, 100 × 80 cm
(39 × 31½ in).

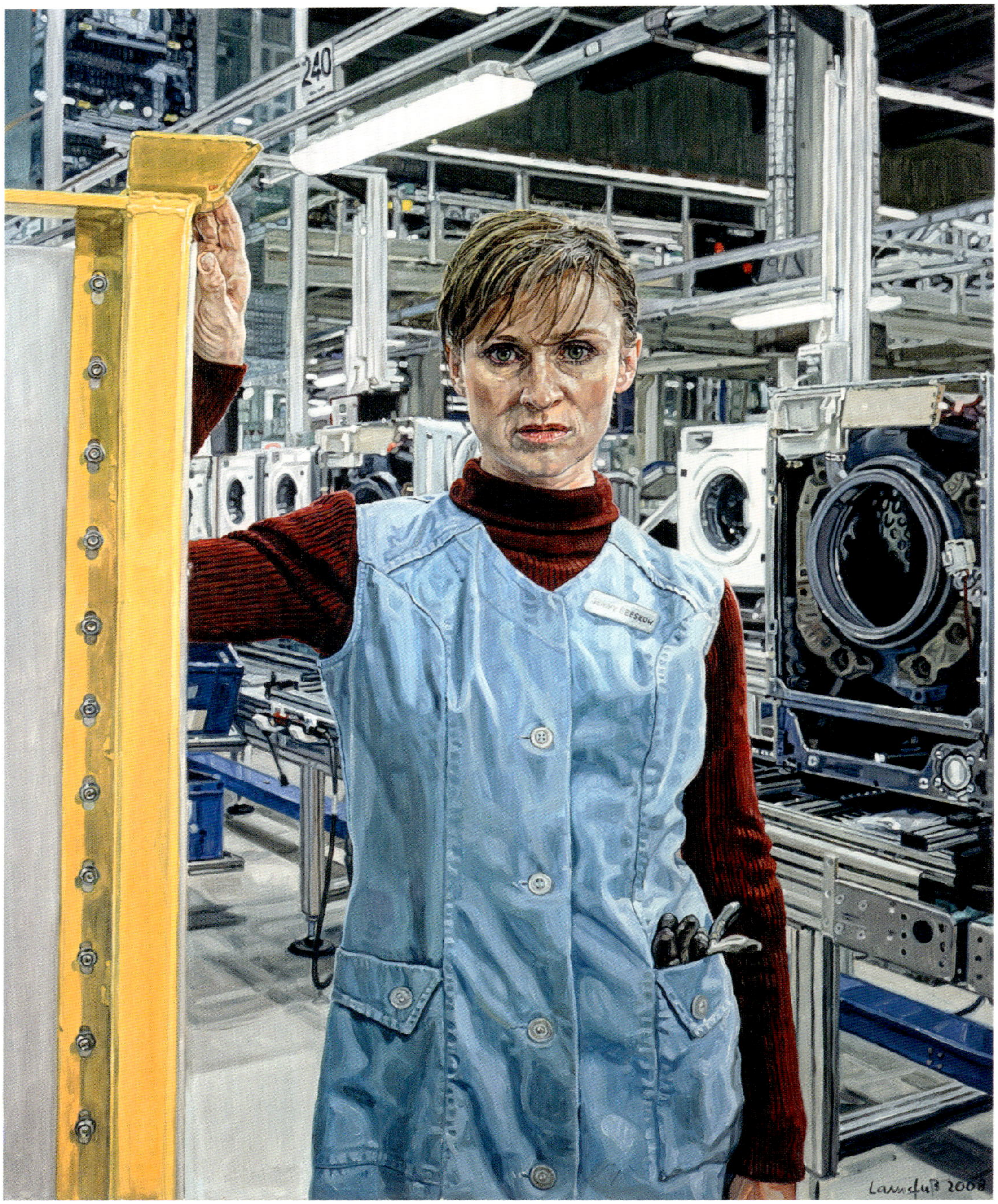

Heike Ollerz/Ulrich Lamsfuß, African Torso, Dual Sex (3B scientific, Made in Germany III) 2011, oil on canvas, 140 × 110 cm (55 × 43 in).

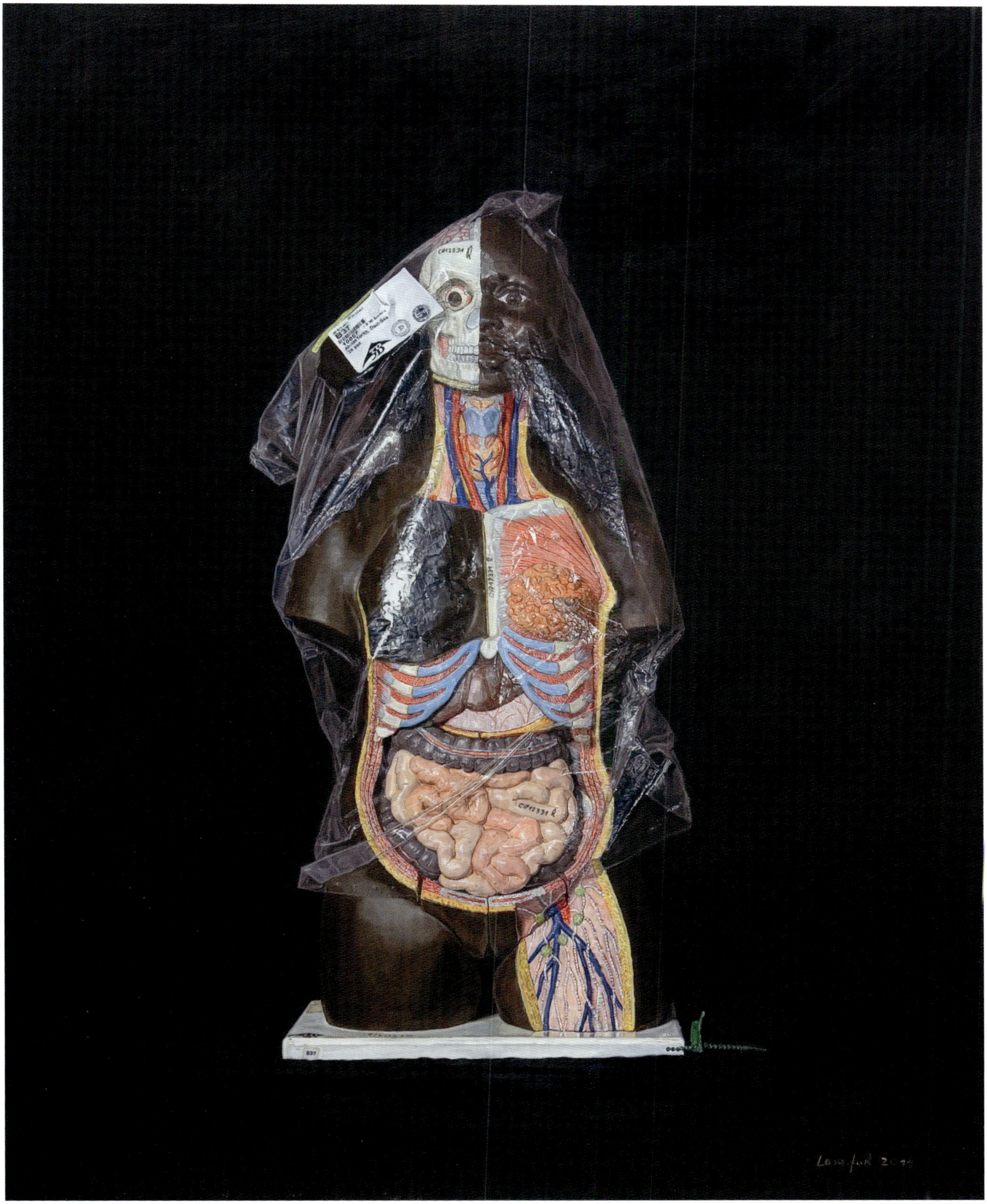

Lucecita wyznaje Gustawowi
(*Lucecita Confessing to Gustaw*)
2000, oil on canvas, 119 × 118 cm
(47 × 46⅜ in).

Marcin Maciejowski
Born: 1974, Babice (Poland)
Lives: Cracow

Marcin Maciejowski grew up in the countryside (Babice, near Krakow) in a worker-peasant family. His father was a coal-miner and farmed the family smallholding. It was an 'idyllic' and 'boring' setting in which he spent a lot of his free time practising long-distance running. He remembers being very intrigued by the youth newspaper *Polish Soldier*, which his father bought for him every Friday. He remembers the pictures in them (full of propaganda during the 1980s, when Poland was still under the Communist rule of the USSR). Later, his first 'serious' paintings were based on newspapers such as this. He has kept a certain distance from nature as a subject: 'I grew up in the countryside where I had a glut of landscapes. I painted views of the mountains, but it was a background for a girl who was my model. I strongly prefer the urban landscape. In the landscape of the country, there is a lot of greenery, and green oil colour is difficult to paint. Using green paint is technically difficult.'

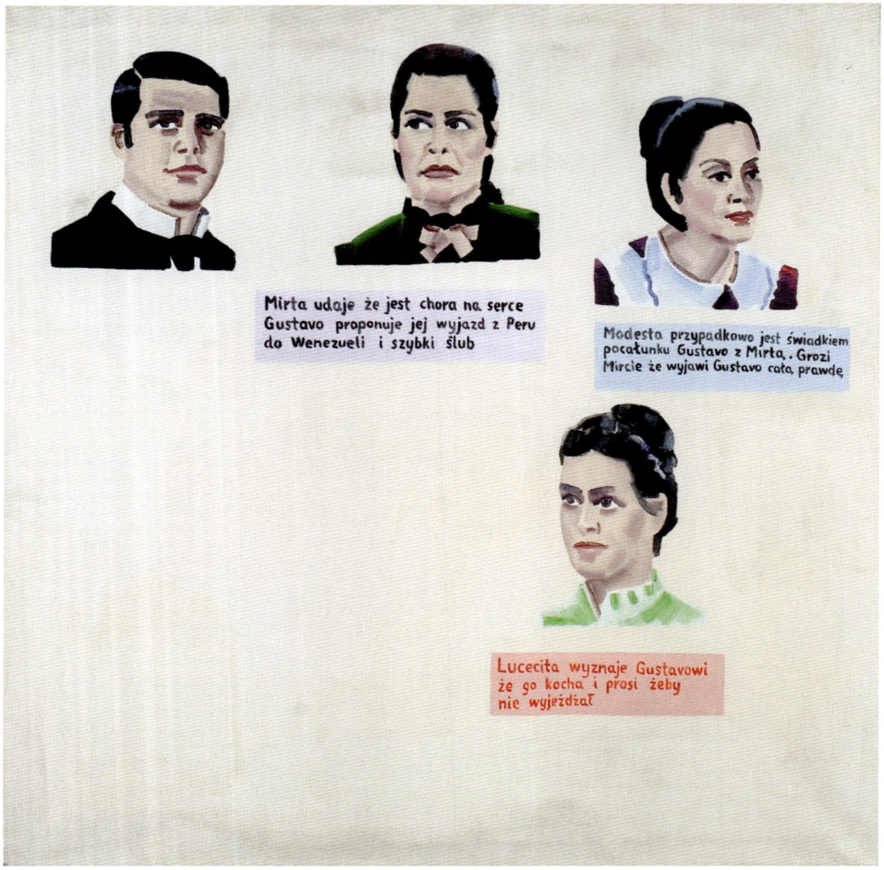

Background

I was first an architecture student, but after three years I left it to start at the Jan Matejko Academy of Fine Arts in Krakow, where we were told to paint some rotten still lifes and older models. A student had to stand at some distance from a model and it was impossible to take a closer look and paint their faces. But I could look closely at Lidka (who is my wife now) and I paint her the most frequently to this day. Thanks to her I learned how to paint in a realistic mode, how to paint faces and character. I also remember finding a pile of newspapers next to the trash skip at my house. I began to list the interesting things in them (titles, captions) and paste clippings into sketchbooks. I brought these to school for my lessons – news about football and boxing – and painted these instead.

At college, I signed up for architectural drawing but it was more like friends meetings and drinking beer together. There I met Rafał Bujnowski, Wilhelm Sasnal, Marek Firek and Jósef Tomczyk Kurosawa (who was modelling) and we founded 'Grupa Ładnie'. I do not know if such classes in drawing were profitable. I made a note of the dialogues between fellow students and models that I heard during classes; I started to draw comics about friends and stories about what happened in our student flat. I could catch really good texts, and those were more important than the correctness of the figures I was drawing. Then I turned photocopies of these drawings into an art-zine together with my friends from Grupa Ładnie; the title was *Famous Letter on Tuesday* – because we made the photocopies on a Tuesday.

Process

I didn't think I could be a painter so I entered the graphics department. Later I realized that I preferred paint and brushes and started painting after school. No one was showing me how to use colours, how to put paint on the canvas and make brush-marks. I never used an easel, I had everything spread out on the floor and I painted crouching or kneeling. I still do it like this.

A few people posed for me, but it was tiring and stressful for them. It was also too 'arty'. Now I prefer to sketch a picture. I'm interested in stories from newspapers, books. Mostly I paint from photographs, though not in a hyperreal way. I look at the photograph as if I were looking at a live model or real situation. I use a projector and pencils to draw shapes and proportions on canvas. Previously, I used a grid for transferring pictures to canvas in proportion, but I noticed that when I drew without it or painted immediately on canvas the results were more expressive and that maybe that was an advantage.

I paint at night. I need two or three nights for a bigger painting, sometimes longer. It depends on how many hours I dedicate to painting. When I start to paint a picture I have to finish it while it is wet. When it is dry I don't change anything.

Paintings based on film subjects

My first such paintings were actually based on newspapers with TV programme listings, which were bought by my parents. In those newspapers there was always a 3 × 4-centimetre (1 × 1½-inch) photograph of a movie with a brief description, projection time, year of production and genre. I treated the images as base material and included these details as additional content (telling us, for example, that the image was also psychological, from a comedy, thriller, or that it was played at 20:05). I made paintings like *Roman and Magda*, *One Flew Over the Cuckoo's Nest*, *Easy Rider*. I also used episode descriptions from newspaper programme listings to build the story that forms 'Lucecita's Confessions to Gustav', based on a Peruvian soap opera titled *Luz Maria*, which my mother liked to watch. In each of the four portraits was a description of what the person was doing, feeling and planning.

I often watch movies with the sound off, or listen to the sound of the movie without looking at the screen. Suddenly a single scene interests me, the colours of the film, the composition of the scene on the screen or the dialogue. Then I make a note.

Discipline

Regularity and diligence are important in painting. There should be no day without a visit to the studio. I think about painting even at dinner or in the pub. Using good-quality brushes, colours and canvases also had an influence on the development of my painting.

Art and politics

The sincerity of political involvement in the arts is not always so strong. When Picasso created one of the most political paintings, *Guernica*, he was abusing, mentally bombing his women, and maybe *Guernica* is about himself – not about the war. Picasso declared he was a Communist while on the Côte d'Azur ... I really like this commitment!

Lidia (like Danaë)
2006, oil on canvas, 120 × 135 cm
(47 × 53 in).

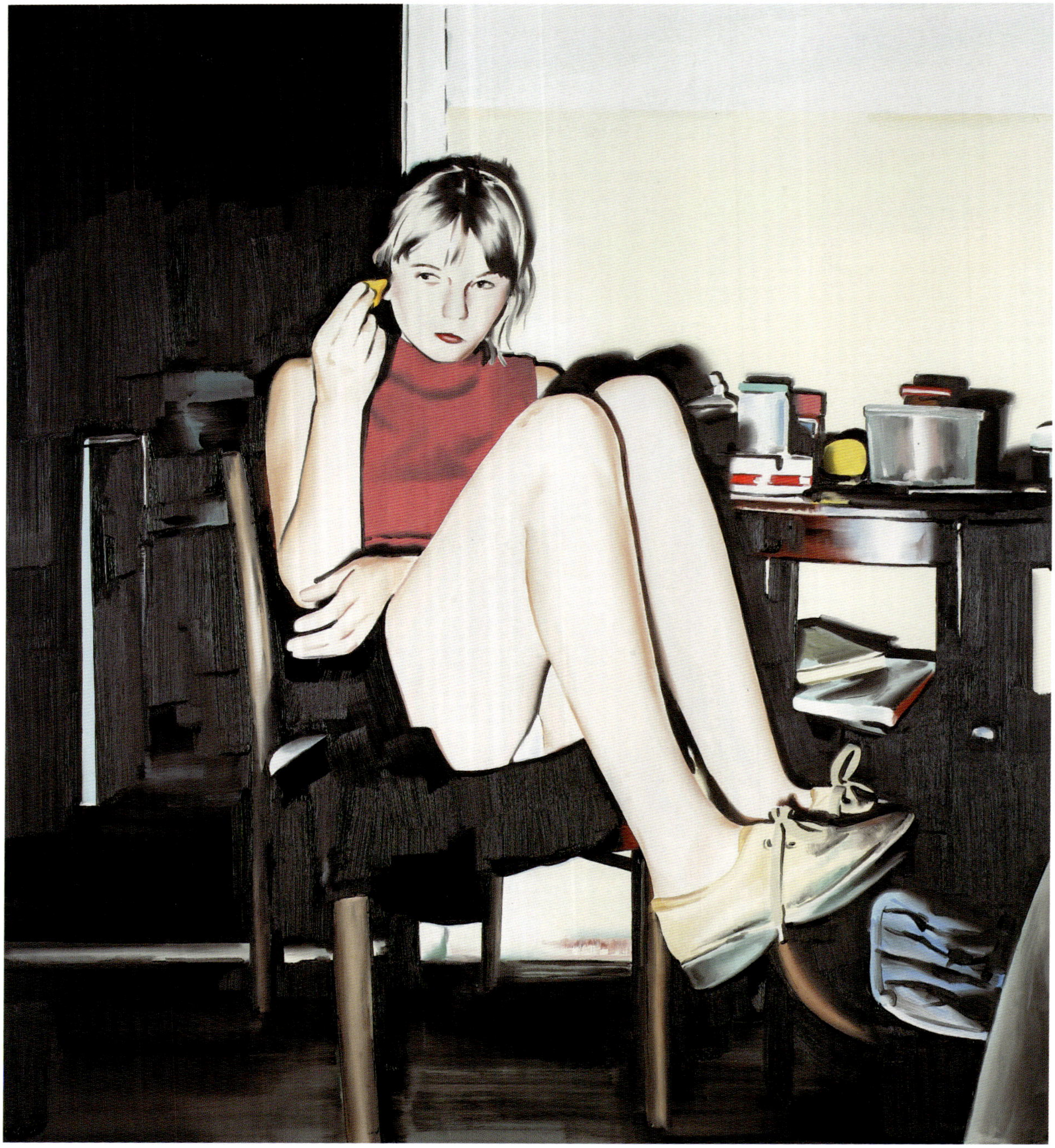

Nude and a Fuse Box
2009, oil on canvas, 110 × 80 cm
(43 × 31½ in).

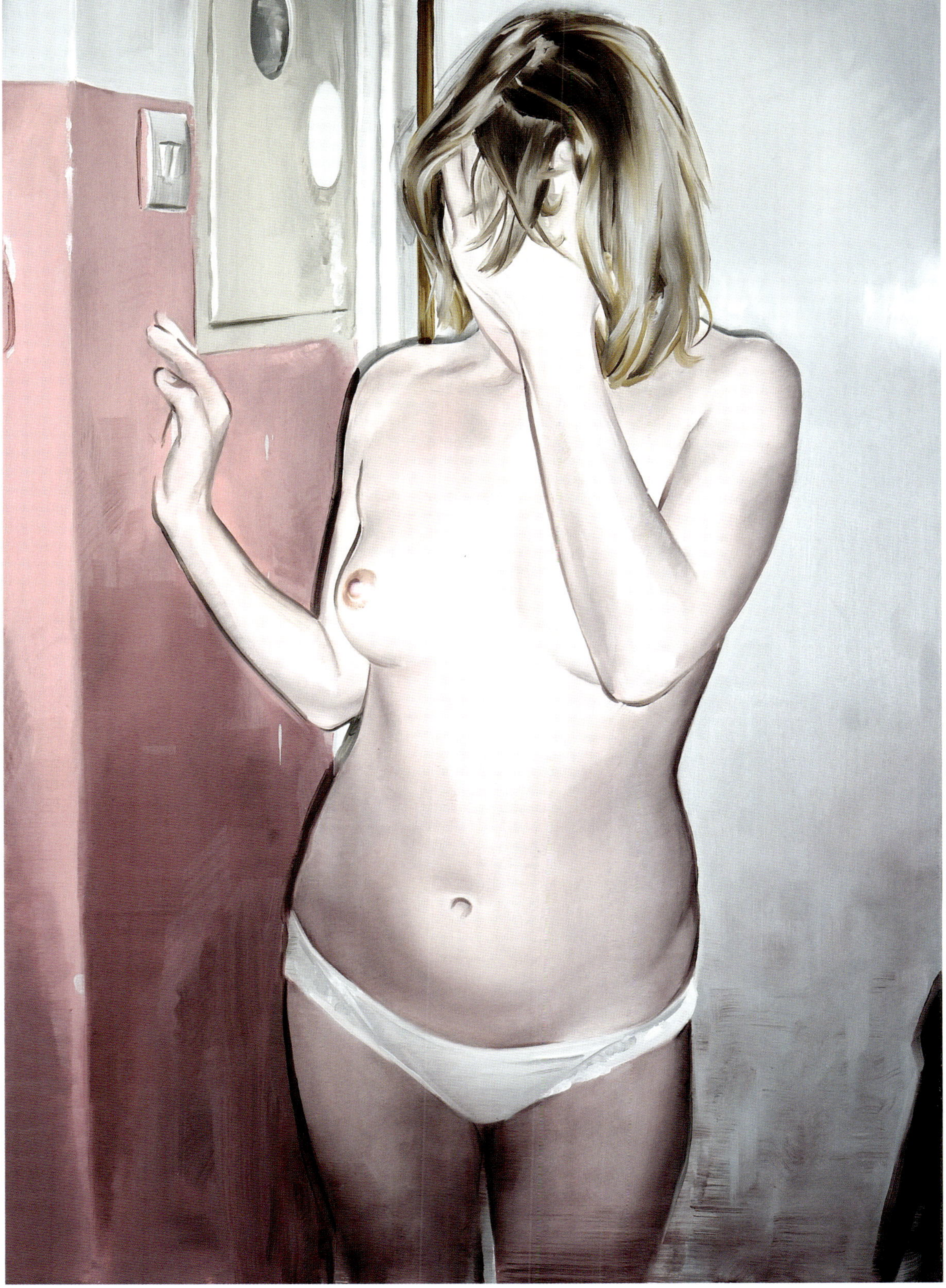

Roman i Magda
2008, oil on canvas, 30 × 36 cm
(11⅞ × 14¼ in).

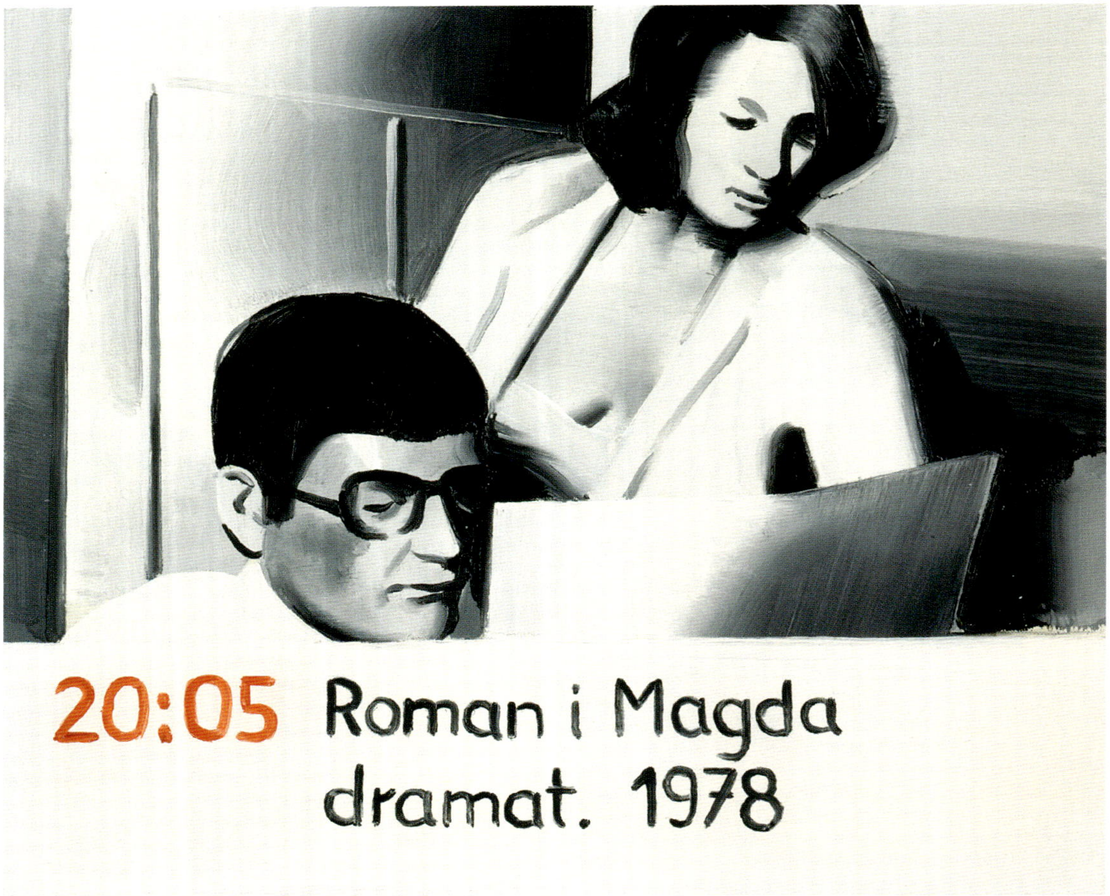

(Roman Polanski)
2008, oil on canvas, 27 × 27 cm
(10⅝ × 10⅝ in).

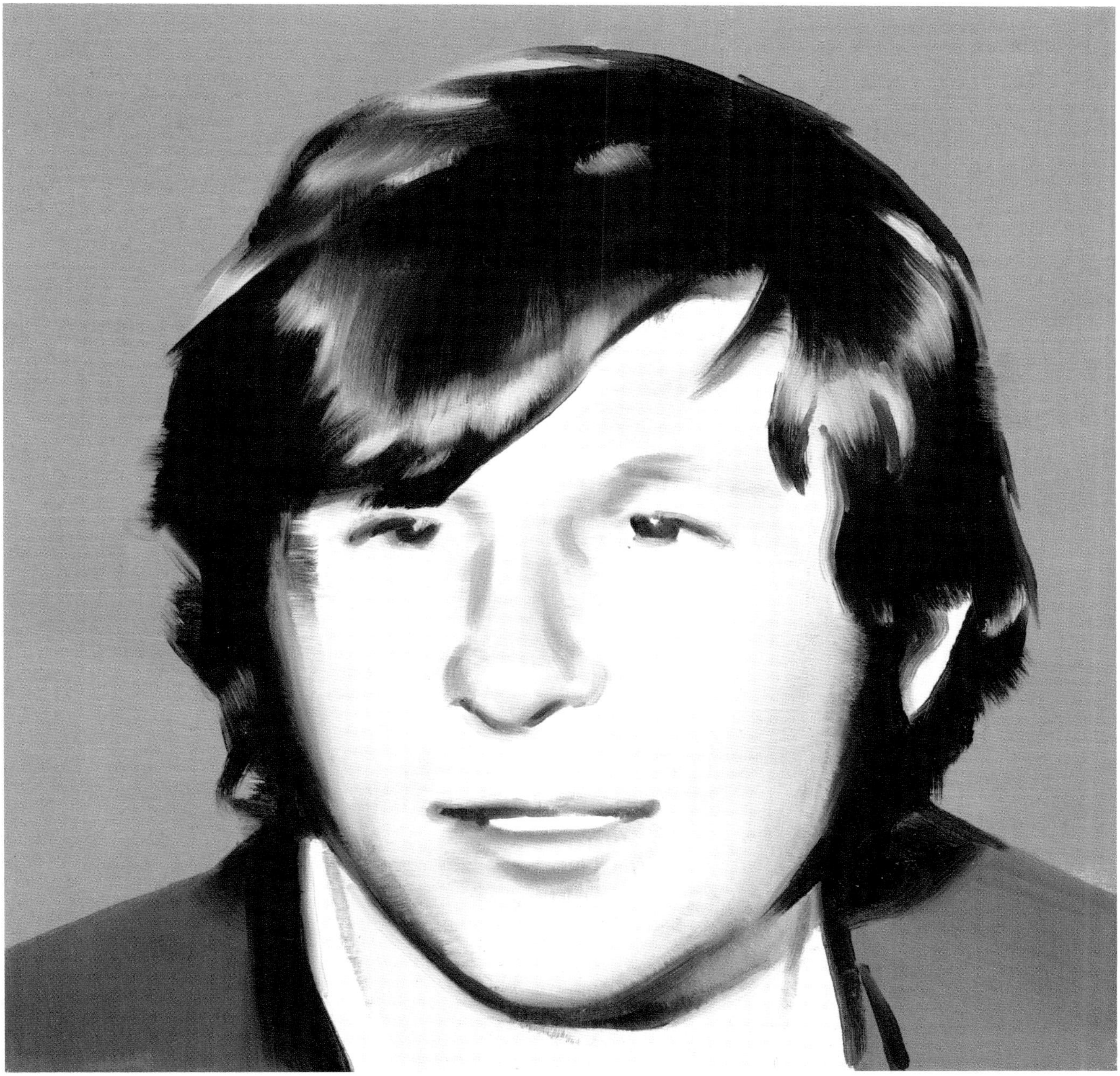

Harding Meyer
Born: 1964, Porto Alegre (Brazil)
Lives: Karlsruhe (Germany)

The Brazilian-born painter Harding Meyer, who lives and works in Germany, has been studying and scrutinizing the human face for over 15 years. Rarely has a painter engaged so intensely with the idea of portraiture. But these are not 'portraits' so much as the crystallization of a collective perception – portraits of portraiture. They explore not just the nature of the sitter and his or her gaze, but also our cultural assumptions about the subject. Scavenging from the vast maze of faces that float around us daily (from TV screens to the covers of magazines), Meyer isolates certain traits, certain looks, removing them from their initial context before rebuilding their auras, brushstroke by brushstroke, making them alive again through depth, texture and light. Each work has at least six layers of paint and, by the end of this process, none of the original subjects or models are identifiable. This could be described as the painterly equivalent of the work of replicant 'maker' Eldon Tyrell in Ridley Scott's *Blade Runner*, but with the difference that the painter is careful to insert self-doubt from the word go, cutting these smooth surfaces with his knife as soon as a face reaches completion. Meyer agrees, 'they are like a cyborg of a painting, and a face'.

It might be tempting to invoke Meyer's Brazilian origins and that country's love affair with plastic surgery, but the painter resists that idea, arguing that his 'Brazilian roots are unfortunately unimportant for my work. I grew up in Europe, so the main influences are European.' The surgery in this case is cultural and conceptual, slashing and digging into ideas, both public and intimate, of the nature of the self and what a face can represent.

Background
My paintings developed from the abstract paintings I was doing in the 1990s and small watercolour heads I produced at the same time. When I tried to paint these fictional small heads in oils on a big canvas, I noticed that I needed photographs as a template for giving them more density. In the beginning I used photographs of friends, but then I starting using pictures from fashion magazines and, in the late 1990s, I tried stills from TV. That's the reason I use horizontal formats. I have been using these until now. These stills were very blurred and fragmented, which is also a characteristic of my paintings. My personal style developed over a long period of time and is changing still today.

Process
Creating one of these paintings takes about three months, sometimes longer. It depends on how long each layer of paint takes to dry. And I proceed through a lengthy approximation towards the finished painting. At first I'm painting the motif in a relatively realistic fashion, but after that I add layer upon layer of paint to give it more density and to create doubt at the same time. It isn't a straight process, it includes a lot of wrong turns and mistakes. I find my faces in other, more restless, kinds of media and then I try to slow them down.

Living matter
I reduce my 'portrait' to the face, because it's the part of the human I'm interested in the most. I'm aware that they are real humans, but normally I'm not interested in their life or in their personality, that's the reason why I avoid painting famous people. I was never interested in traditional portrait painting, but in faces. You can see my work on faces as one long line.

The role of painting in contemporary culture
As an artist you have the possibility to design reality in a way that is more personal and extraordinary than in any other media. My job description is 'painting with the eyes'.

o.T (4-2013)
2013, oil on canvas, 190 × 150 cm
(75 × 59 in).

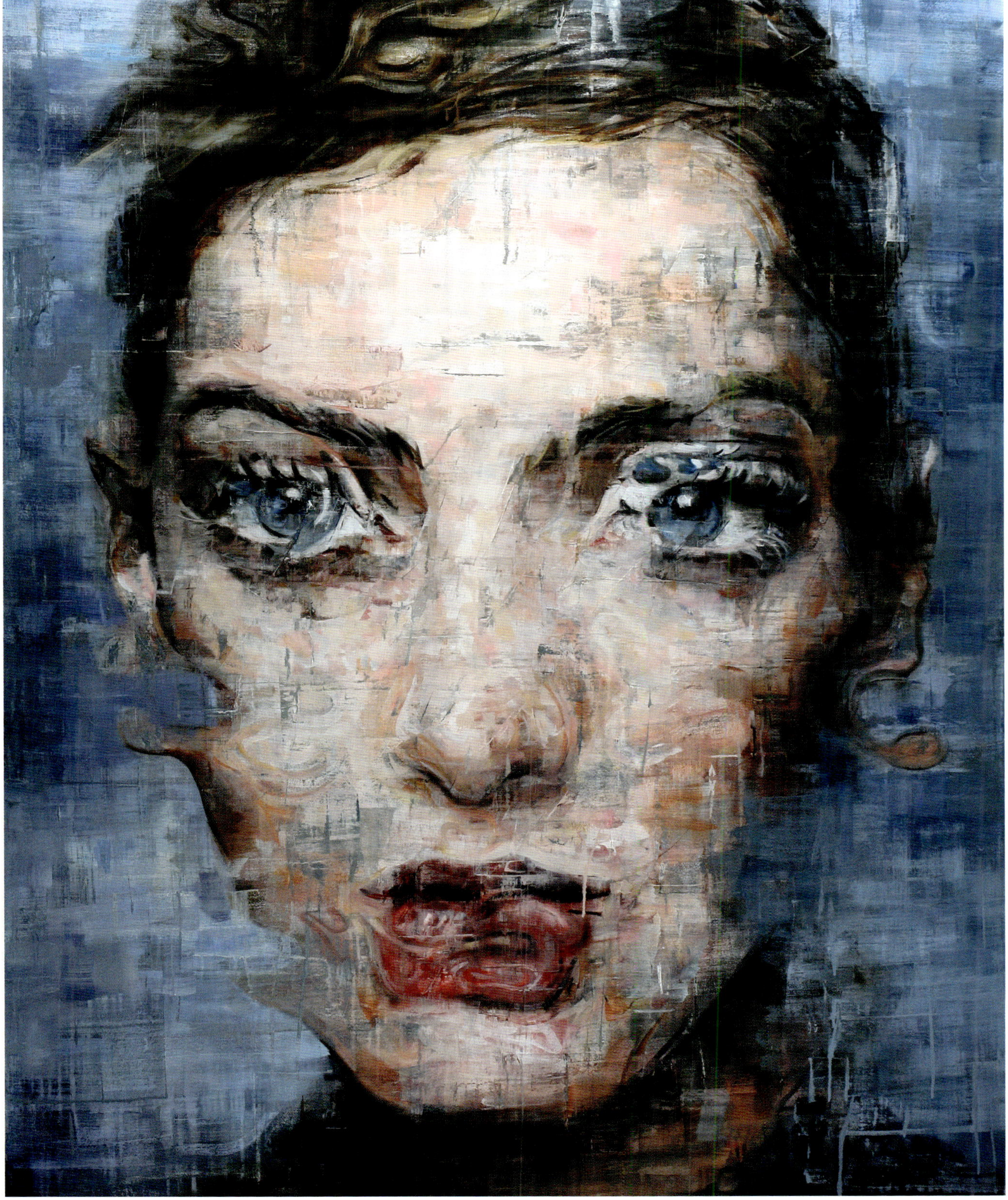

o.T. (16-2012)
2012, oil on canvas, 190 × 260 cm
(75 × 102 in).

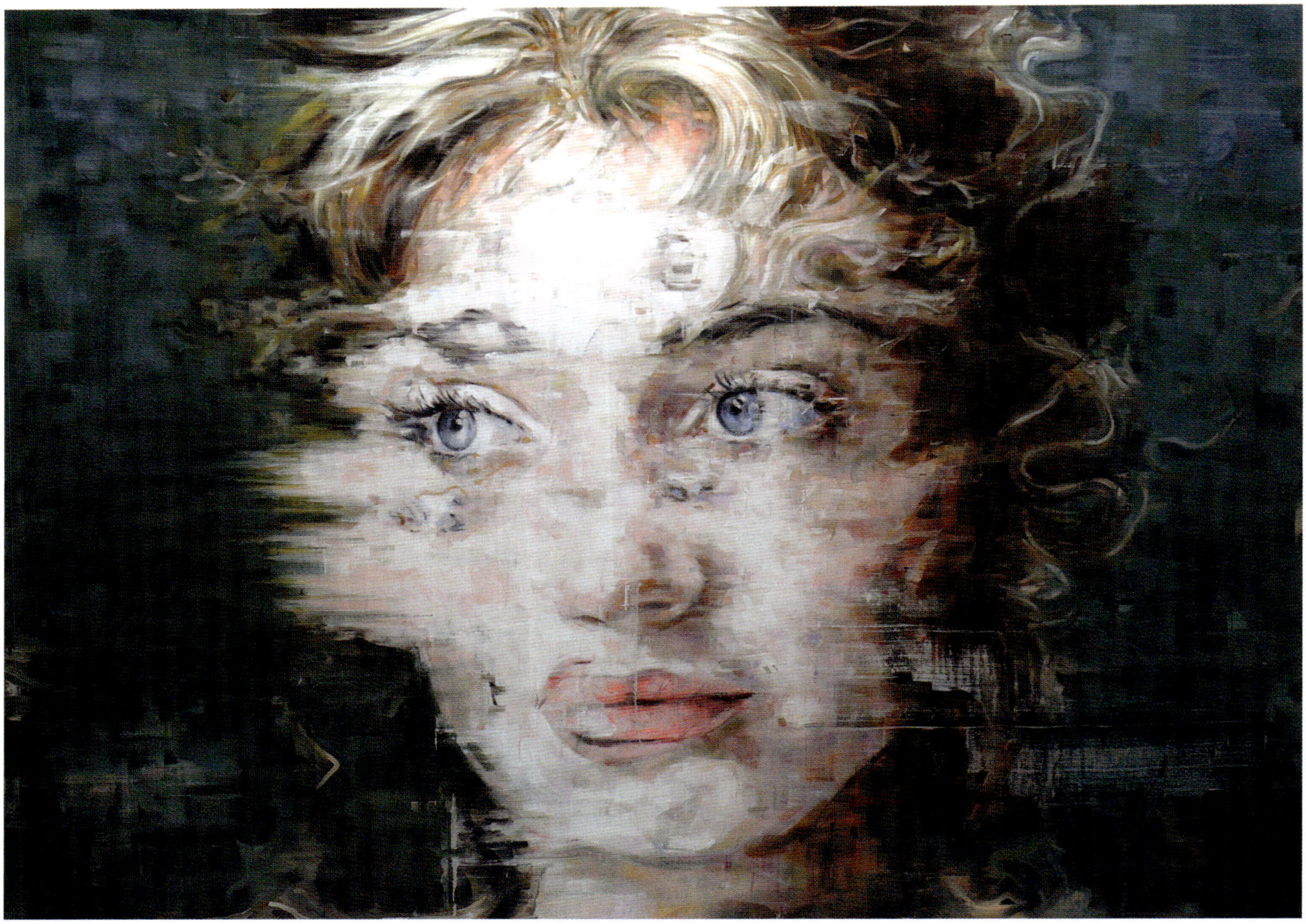

o.T. (11-2011)
2011, oil on canvas, 150 × 190 cm
(59 × 75 in).

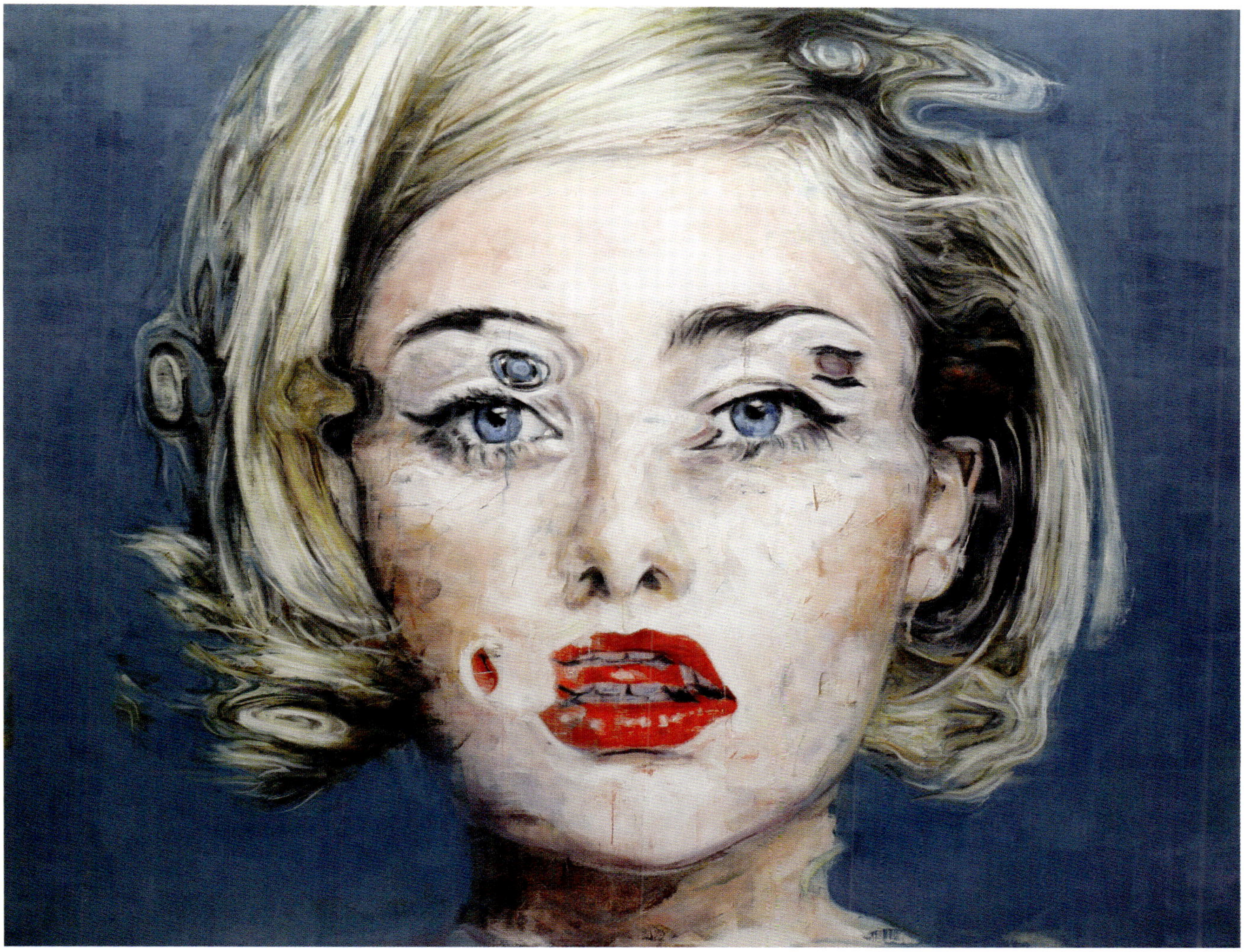

Depot
2009, oil on panel, 80 × 60 cm
(31½ × 23⅝ in).

Justin Mortimer
Born: 1970, Cosford (UK)
Lives: London

Justin Mortimer has been a member of London's Colony Club for about 20 years and has commented that 'Bacon's ghost walks the carpet there'. The ghost of Francis Bacon also haunts Mortimer's pictures. It is almost as if the younger artist were trying to update the master's project and bring it into the world of CNN, Google Images and mass media. Mortimer has always collected images of war and medicine and recently he has incorporated these explicitly (though anonymously) into his own pictures. Moving through these subjects, often gathered from the Internet, his canvases continue to grow darker emotionally. As he gets older, he says, he feels more able to deal with his preoccupations with the outsider, the victimized and the vulnerable.

Setting up a scene
Preparation is a large part of what I do in the studio. Unless I am working from life, each painting will involve first making a series of crude digital collages. These are my references to which I'll return continually, making adjustments in response to issues thrown up during the process of painting.

Angles
The only conscious decision about viewpoint I would make would be if I wanted the viewer to be the protagonist, or witness to the events unfolding in the image. Apart from that all angles would be decided by instinctive abstract and compositional tensions.

Narrative
There are clear narrative dimensions in my work, although it is sometimes hard to identify these being so close to and involved in it. Certainly there are a small number of themes I return to constantly and I am aware that when making my paintings I am constructing a narrative, which can be interpreted by others. When preparing works for a show I do make editorial choices so that a stream or storyline can be discerned among the pieces.

Portraying the threat of violence
It's often down to the shoe or the telephone – the everyday objects of a violent person. A violent person might have an Oyster card in their pocket but will still kick the shit out of you.

On the relationship between painting and contemporary media
I'm one of those artists forever snapping my half-finished pictures on my mobile phone, and many of my recent paintings wouldn't have been realized if certain online image libraries didn't exist. Before digital imagery and online exposure it was a total bore (and expensive) to distribute images of your work.

The epic dimension
With the ubiquity and homogeny of digital witness photography/film, painting (like music, or poetry) is reinstating its power to cut through to the marrow of experience. Painting can still capture the epic, but rarely – just as good painting is rare. I make 'history' paintings in the sense that [these works] are testimony to conflict and war in recent times. I want the people in my pictures to be stand-ins for emotional, psychological elements of humanity.

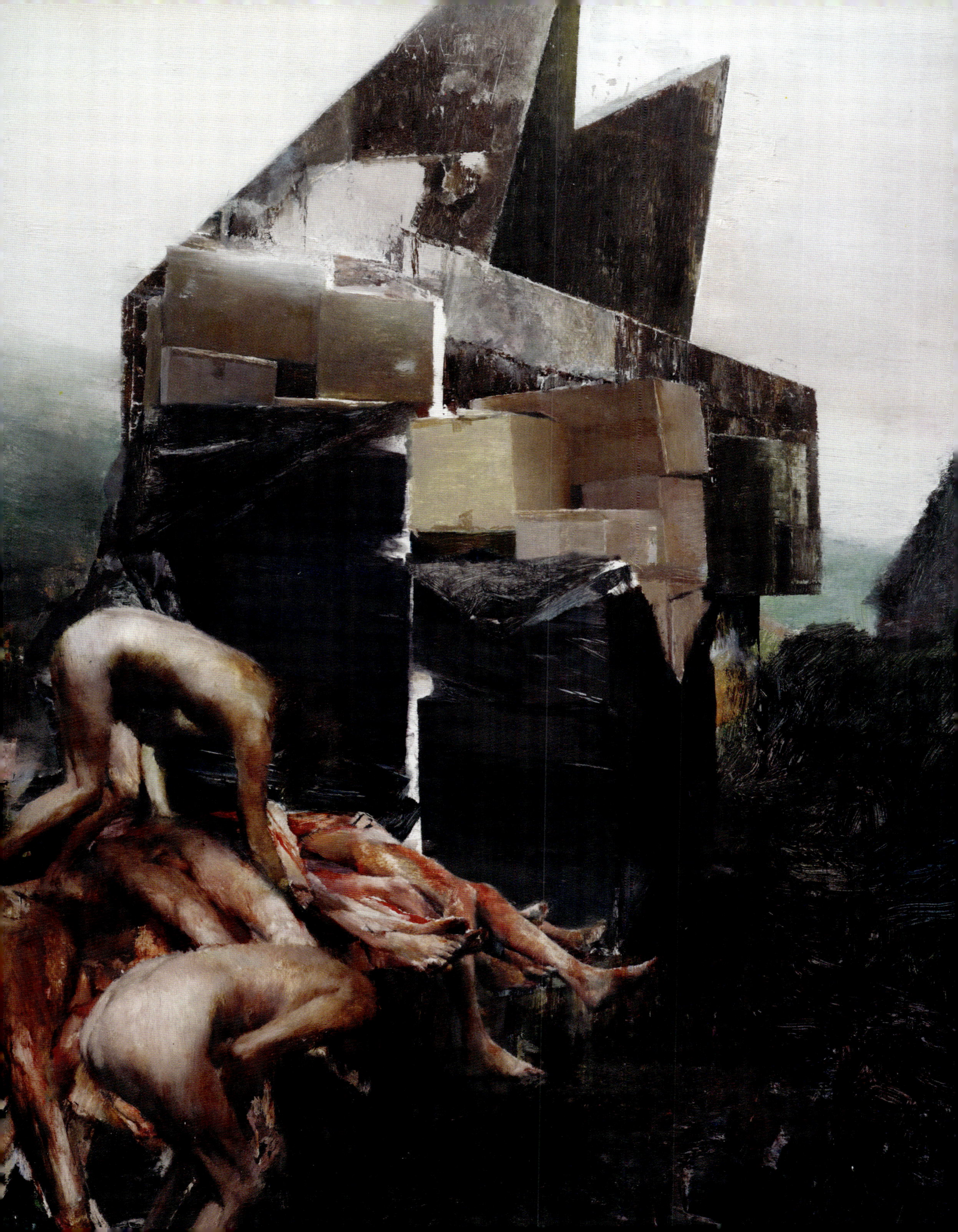

Chamber
2011–12, oil on panel, 240 × 180 cm
(95 × 71 in).

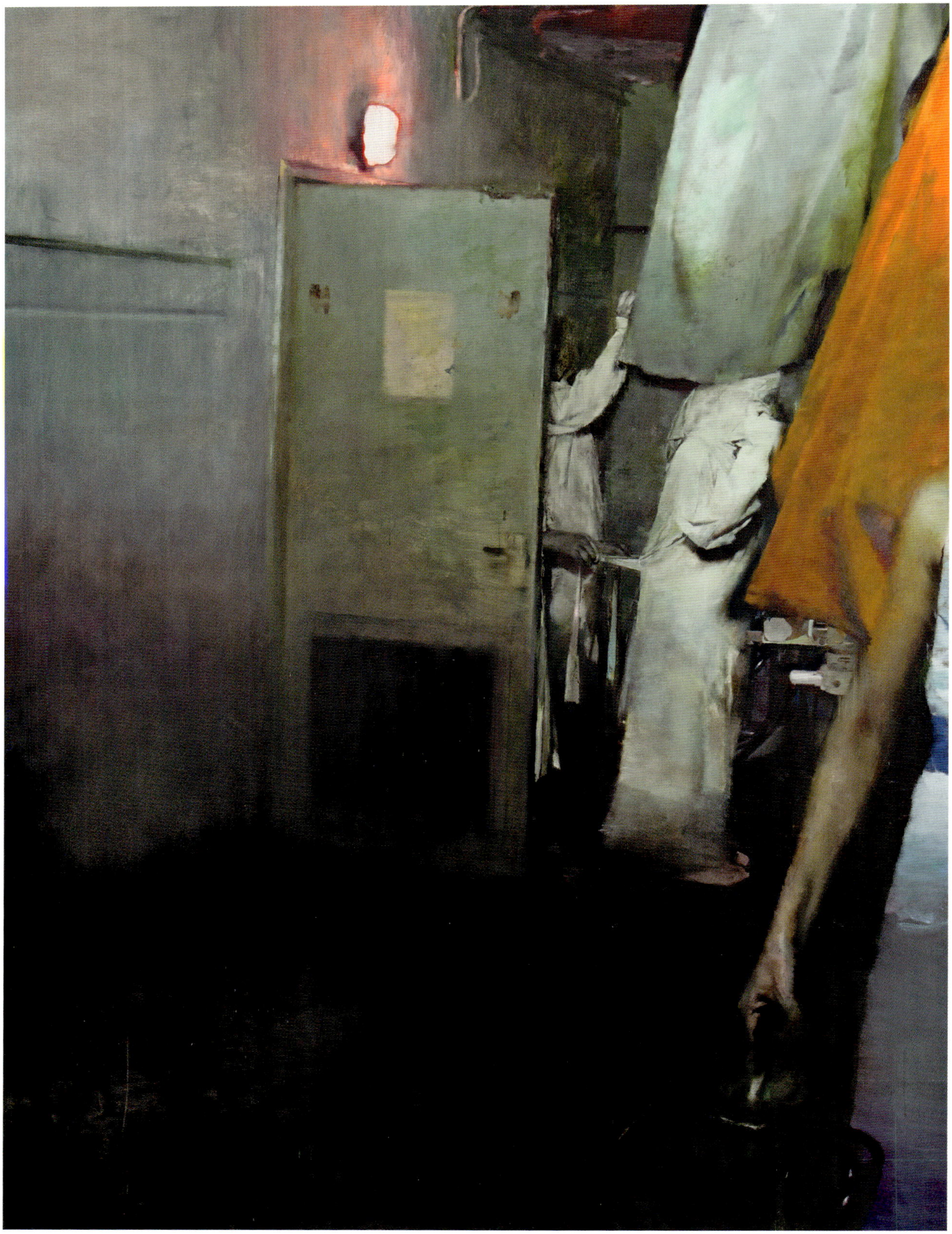

Perimeter
2011, oil on panel, 183 × 183 cm
(72 × 72 in).

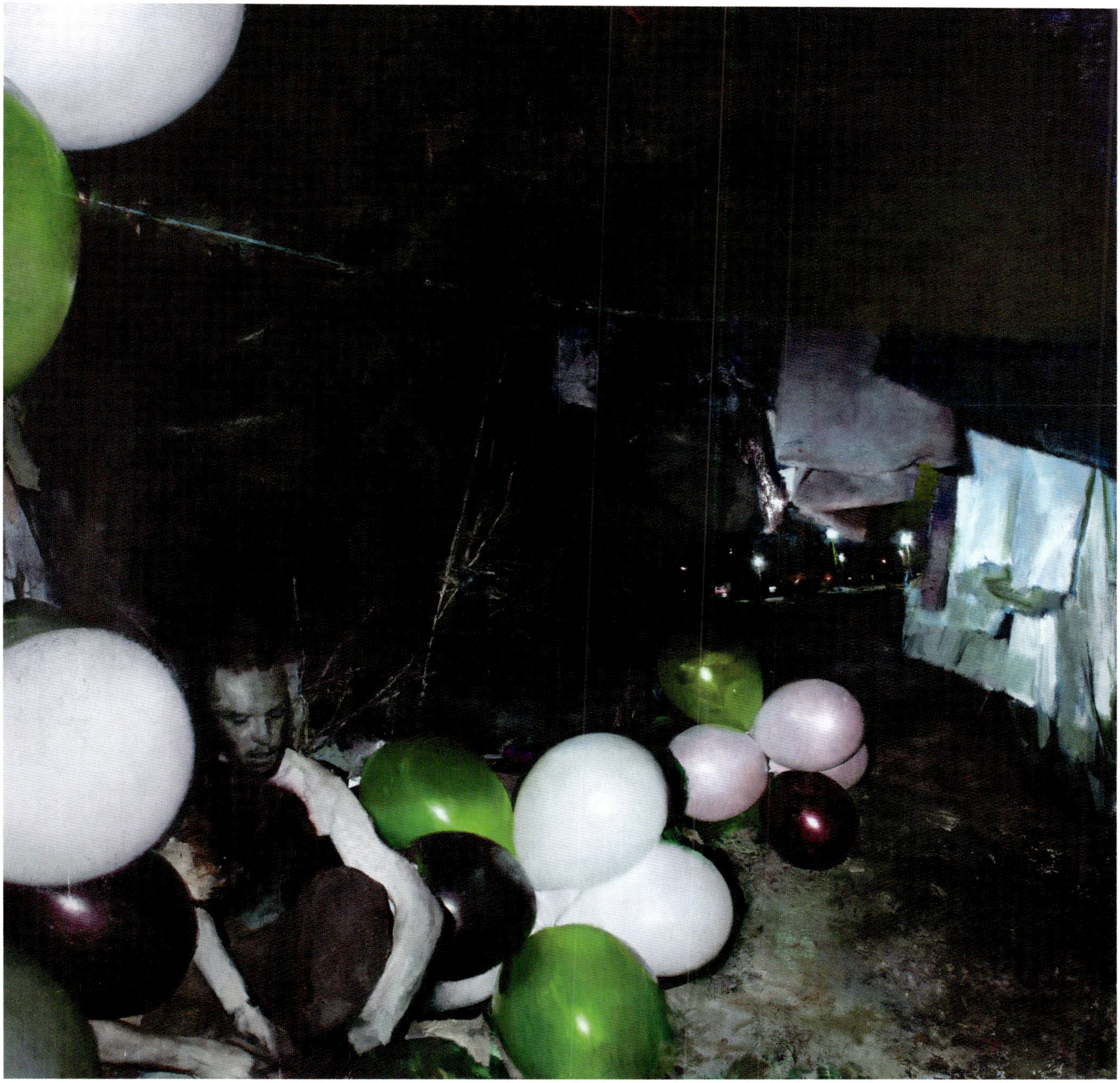

Untitled (Perhaps Only People Who Are ...)
2012, oil on canvas, 92 × 69 cm (36¼ × 27⅛ in).

Muntean and Rosenblum
Born: Muntean, 1962, Graz (Austria); Rosenblum, 1962, Haifa (Israel).
Live: Vienna and London

Since they first met at art school in Vienna in 1992, Austro-Israeli artistic duo Markus Muntean and Adi Rosenblum have focused their work on translating in painterly terms the sense of existential boredom affecting Western contemporary life. They construct scenes using subjects from digital photographs of the kind that appear in fashion and lifestyle magazines, but they completely reinterpret this visual material in compositions typical of traditional figurative painting.

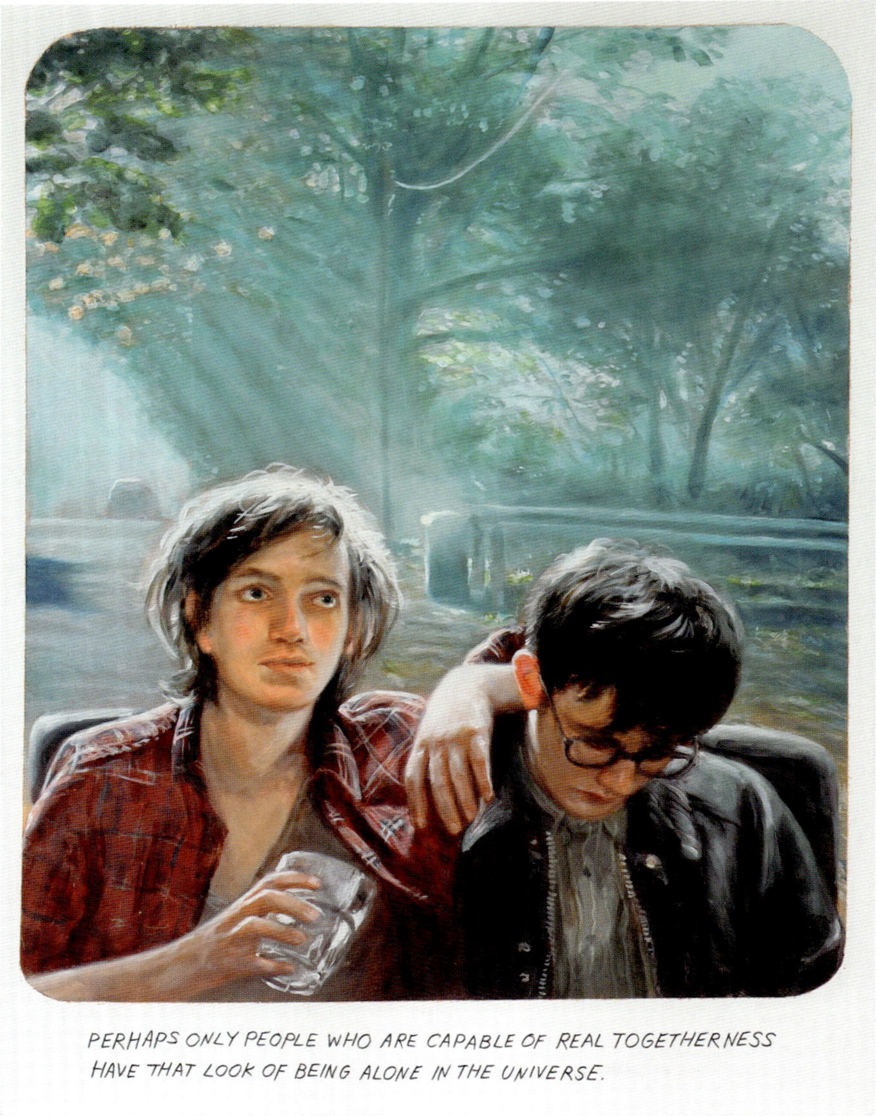

No painting is an island
In our paintings we always maintain a white border area on the canvas, which creates an opening toward the surrounding space. In this way the image becomes embedded in the environment we prepare. We do not think of our paintings as self-sufficient islands, they are always part of a more complex ensemble of practices that are staged in a precise manner. The whole concept of a painting as a self-sufficient entity is a relatively new phenomenon in the arts. Paintings in churches were always part of an architectural ensemble and an intricate set of choreographies with a shared focus and site-specificity. Our work revolves around the contemporary absence of such clear belief systems, but in order to make this visible we adopt traditional strategies of representation.

The aesthetics of new media
Since [digital, social] media has become a constituent part of how we stage our lives and of our perception of events, we seem to be forever collecting experiences that are framed by pre-existing aesthetic formations. Everybody has to ask themselves whether they have done enough interesting things lately, nobody wants to be caught leading a boring life. This leads to a frenzy of collecting seemingly extraordinary experiences that also have to be proved to others – through, for example, all the travel photographs shared on social networks. Sometimes it seems that making and sharing such photographs replaces the actual events; this accumulation does not leave an individual enough time to make sense of what has really happened. The resulting lack of personal meaning leads to feelings of satiety and emptiness. Most experiences and products appear to be charged with a special magic that should somehow make us more individual and interesting. However, they deliver precisely the opposite [effect] because they are fully scripted and prepared by specialists and thus allow us no breathing space to leave a personal trace. This form of existential boredom and pain is what we depict.

Pathos
In our paintings, the characters are arranged in groups of isolated individuals, all of them like islands. There is no real communication between them, they only share the prescribed consumer environments with which we are all familiar. The paintings question whether or not there is still a coherent structure to the self and ask, if there is, how can we recapture it?

The principal goal of our art is to come up with a contemporary solution for what we still consider the basic function of art: to revolve around death, entrusting people with little bits of transience. We were convinced that we had to choose figurative painting precisely because it seemed to be an 'impossible' medium. We saw that the image universe of advertising had made it highly dubious for artists to use figurative images to trigger emotional states. Forms of pathos seemed to have been entirely lost to art and had been relocated to the domains of popular entertainment and advertising. We rejected this logic because we are convinced that human beings are condemned to experience affect and emotion. After all, beyond the explosion of means of communication, what we really share is the pain that is inextricably part of human existence. Yet the experience of pain remains somehow private and words cannot easily transfer it between individuals. The fact that images operate on a slightly different perceptual plane makes them ideologically problematic when co-opted into the political or economic arena yet too important to be altogether avoided. Thus the gambit is to work towards a 'de-co-opting' of pathos.

Digital/pictorial
Our work exists in between two poles. One is painting in reference to technological optical devices, like the camera obscura and the camera eye, and photographic effects. The other pole is the potential of the surreal, that is, the point at which painting develops its own logical universe beyond the representational 'correctness' of optical devices, central perspective and any kind of photographic realism. We use elements from both approaches, but we try to develop our own position in this field of possibilities.

The medium also allows us to create images that present spatial relations beyond the dominance of the photographic paradigm. By working with figurative painting, we are engaging in the long tradition of painting, aided and influenced by optical devices and technologies; but we don't singularly transpose each picture, we construct a new homogenous pictorial space. All our paintings adhere to the laws of central perspective, but you could never recreate them with a camera, because the painted spaces become too heterogeneous and flexible. Perspectives can be much more stretched in painting.

Craft
In a very personal sense, to work as an artist is an attempt to create something meaningful. Yet, often this meaning is not only the content of the work, it also concerns the aspect of trying to become better at what you do through acts of repetition and variation. While the pride of the craftsperson is sometimes sneered at as obsolete and conservative in contemporary art, we know that it is an important element for us. Making art then becomes a ritual of self-transformation: to paint every day and to try to get better at it is an attempt to generate personal meaning.

Untitled (We Were Afraid ...)
2012, oil on canvas, 181 × 221 cm
(71 × 87 in).

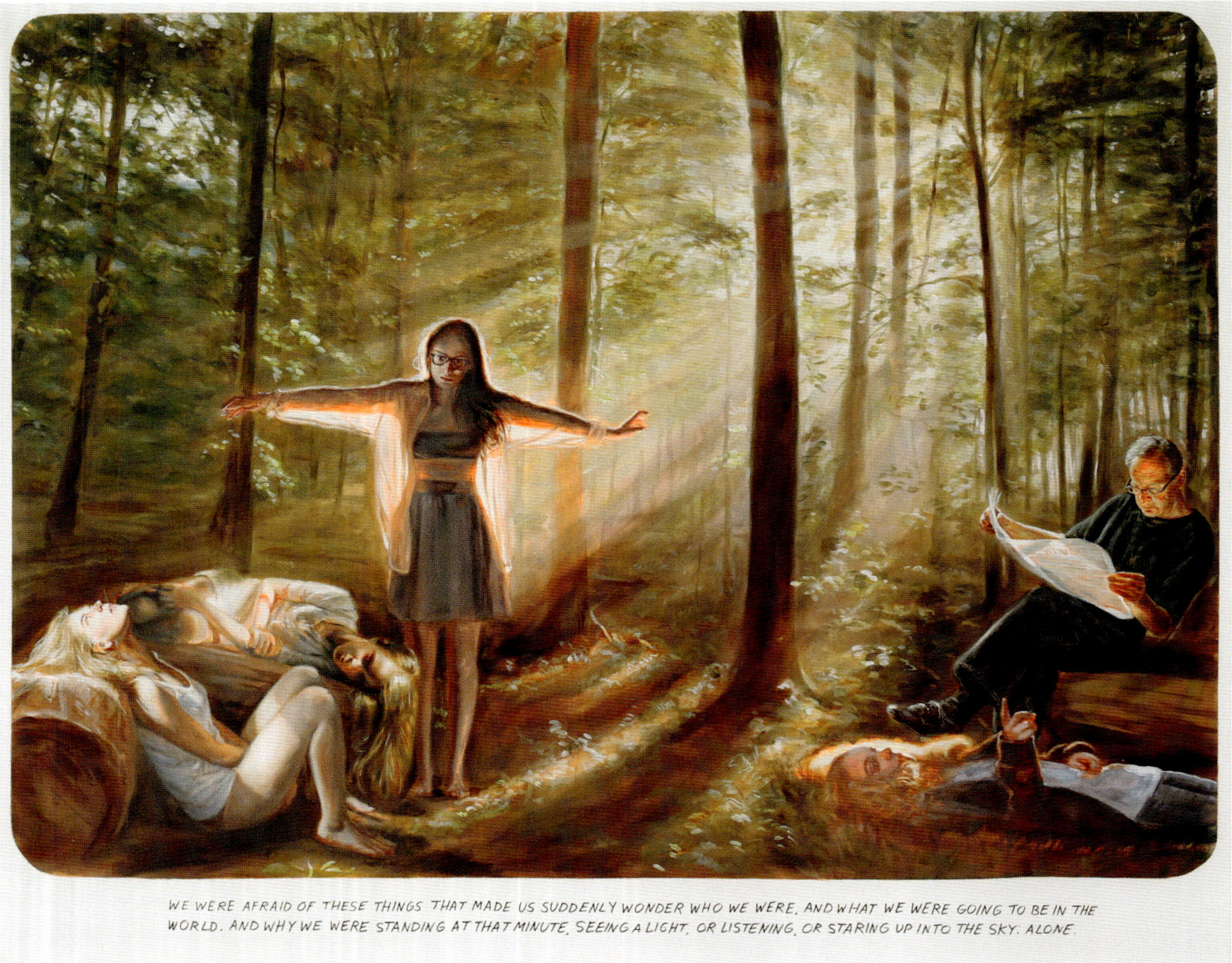

Untitled (Unexpected Instructions
of Beauty ...)
2012, oil on canvas, 63 × 81 cm
(25 × 32 in).

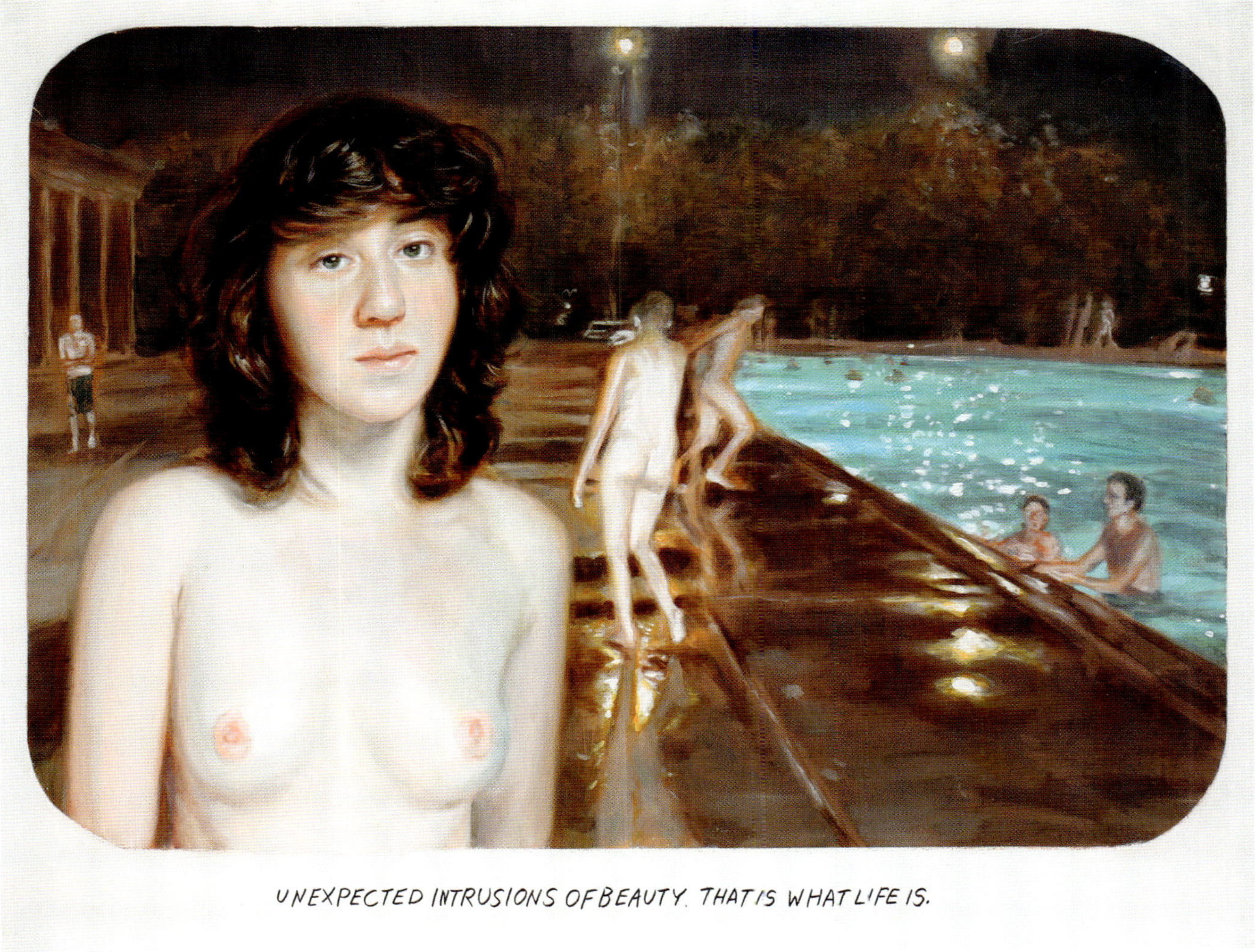

Untitled (It is Better ...)
2010, oil on canvas, 75 × 80 cm
(29½ × 31½ in).

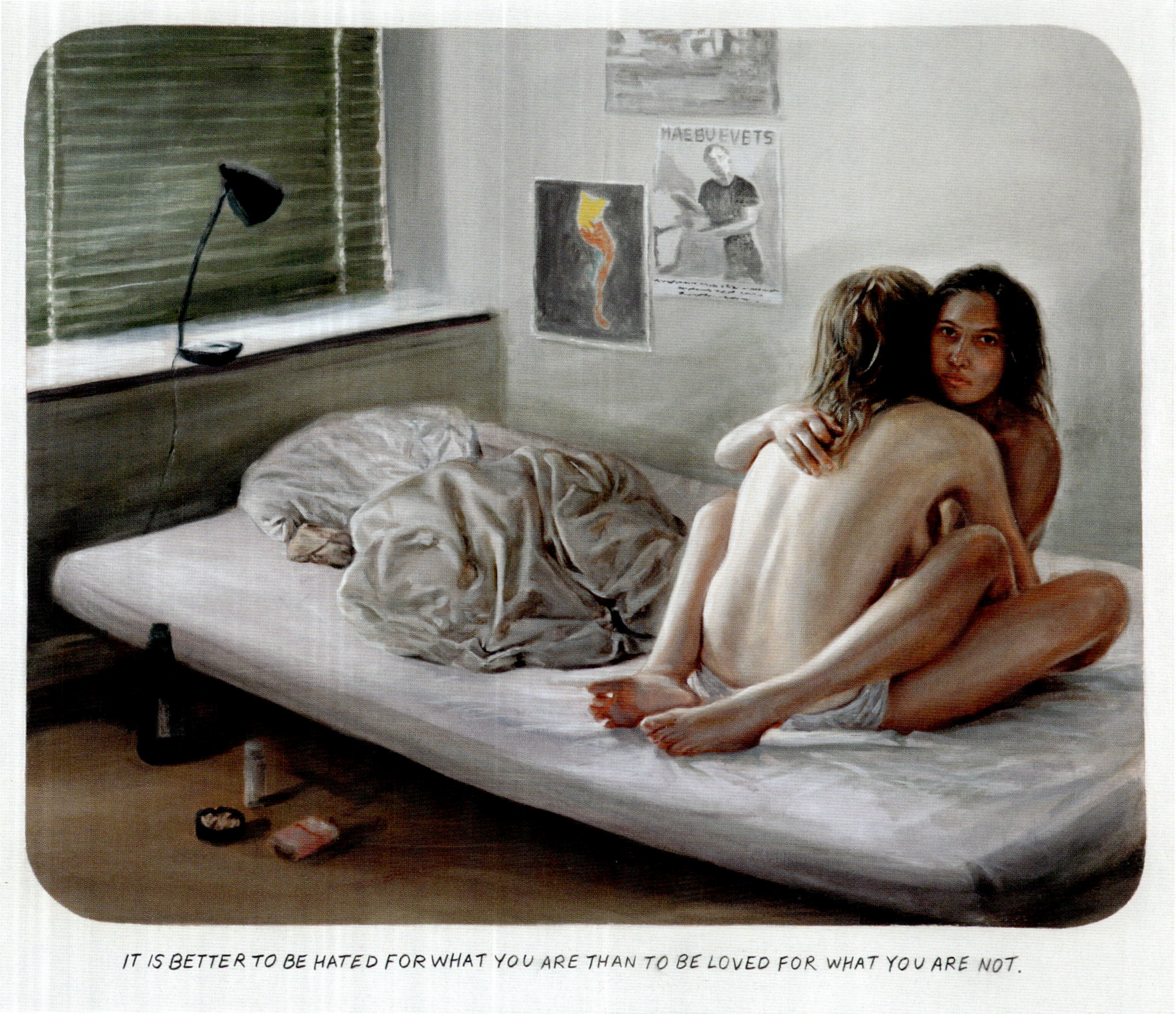

Untitled (Nothing Fixes a Thing ...)
2010, oil on canvas, 62 × 60 cm
($24\frac{1}{2}$ × $23\frac{5}{8}$ in).

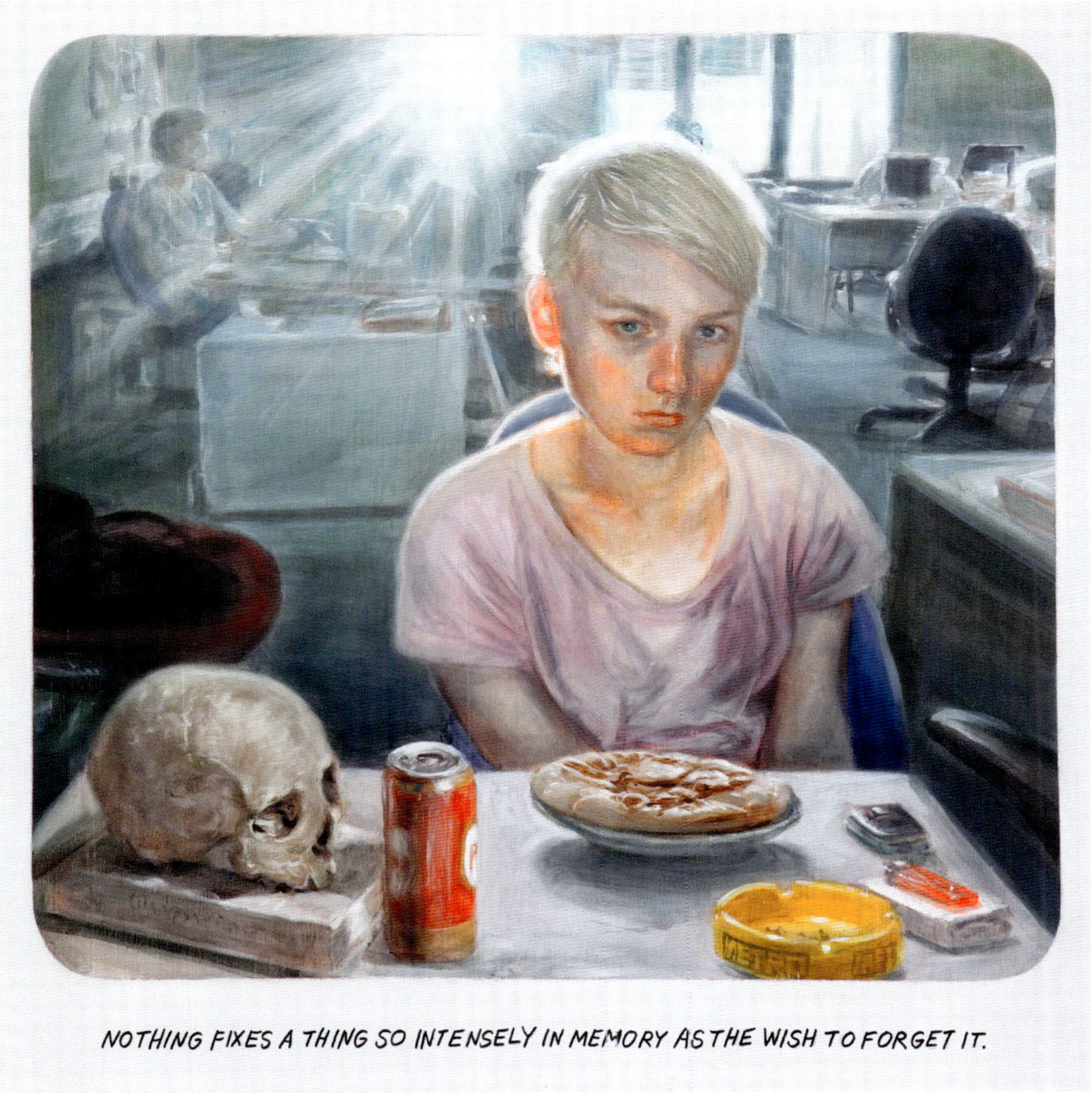

Search Party
2008, oil on canvas, 100 cm x 175 cm
(39 × 69 in).

Benjamin Rubloff
Born: 1975, New York
Lives: Berlin

American painter Benjamin Rubloff lives in Berlin. His haunting paintings explore how, in our media- and image-saturated world, notions of place and presence and the distinction between private and public have shifted to become more complex and ambiguous than ever before.

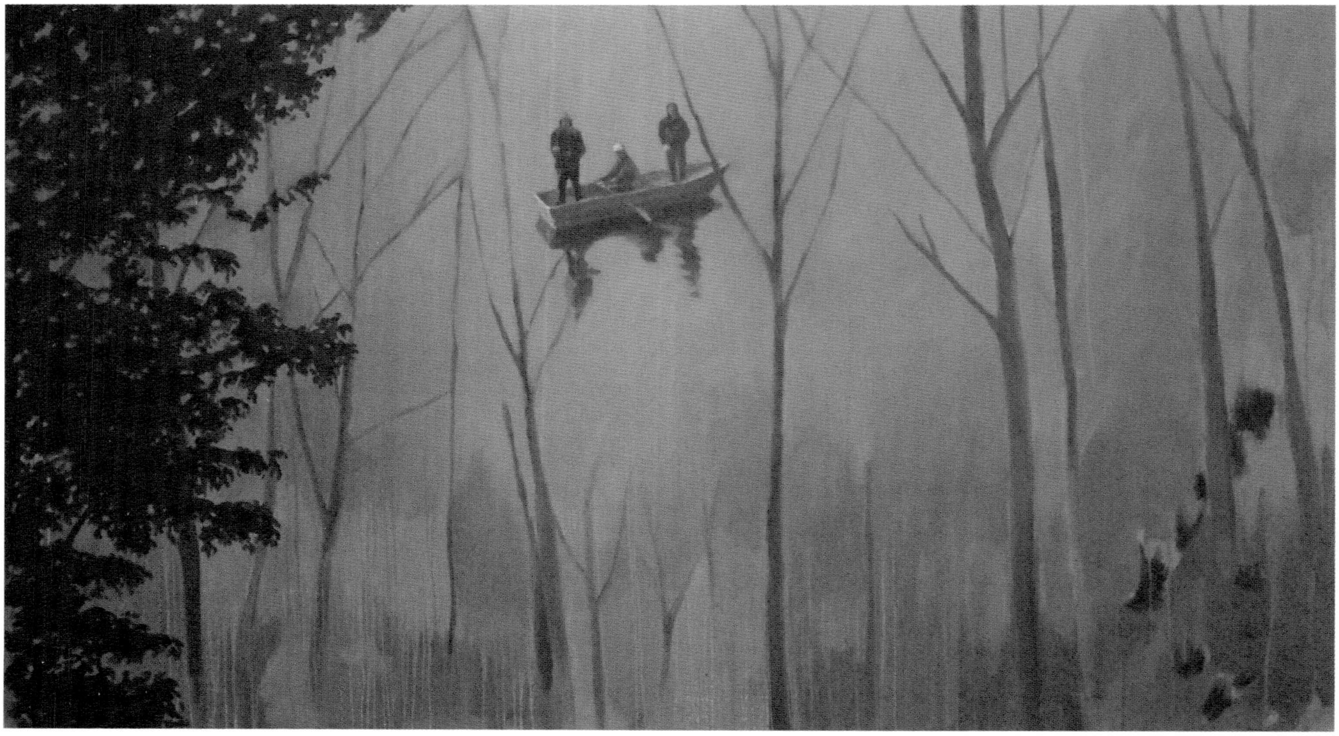

Technique
For me, the imperative is to get at a particular behaviour that each painting has, that is rooted in the image and in my relationship to the image. I work from photographs, but the paintings are not straight translations of the image; they are responses to the images, in which I work at bringing forth what attracts me to an image in the first place.

I do work directly with photographs, but the set of correspondences that I seek out in the process are more rooted in memory, in my remembered experience of things. I suppose that is where the question of atmosphere comes in: how does one find a way to present things in their original context? I am interested in how practices of recall overlap, where photographic images and memories and the visceral experience of direct observation become intertwined, like the way one confuses a personal memory with a photograph, or a lived experience with a movie. There is an uncanny kind of slippage that strikes me as an important way that paintings resonate; they are part of the world and they also reference our experience of the world.

Cinematic painting
Atmosphere is a primary concern. I am particularly interested in how a commonplace image assumes an uncommon presence. The paintings are based on a fragmentary collection of images; they are pretty thin, the structure of the surfaces is understated, and so I rely quite heavily on atmosphere to energize the space. The relationship to cinema is an interesting question because I think that film [also] relies so heavily on atmosphere to create a context for meaning. The relationship between film and paintings is certainly in that space, where the presentation of a detail, an interior or a landscape ignites a particular kind of response.

Other media
I am intrigued by the strange effects photographs produce that we accept as reality. In the popular imagination, the photographic and the real are intertwined, but it's really the case only insofar as photographs have become our way of qualifying reality.

I am influenced by new photographic technologies, especially those that are used for surveillance, mapping and virtual imaging. As a lot of my work has to do with ideas of secrecy and concealment, I have explored the language of these new technologies and ways of seeing quite a bit to try and get a handle on how they function and how we relate to these kinds of images. It's broadening the language and changing our behaviour in relationship to images. Everything has become an image, but images remain rather mysterious and complex and, for me, there is always something secretive in them.

Favourite subjects
I am drawn to images and subjects that hold tightly to their façades and do not give themselves up easily. This has led me to work with a lot of architectural subjects – allotment gardens, suburbs, apartment buildings – places where the social and the private overlap. I am interested in how the necessity of privacy demands a certain degree of refusal, of limited access. This kind of refusal fascinates me because it provokes an anxiety about what is inside. I think it's a primary anxiety of our times, this fear and suspicion about what might be hidden or ulterior. That anxiety was also the starting point for the 'Captive' series, which is based on images of suspected militants being apprehended in the Middle East. There is a staging going on in those kinds of media images. I wanted to bring that to the fore, to explore the ways in which we might experience an image differently when we see the shell of the figure – the clothing – which conceals identities through its banality, but also manages to communicate something about the violence that one sees in the figure. What is drawing me back to figurative painting is this aspect of biopolitics: in the post-9/11 era, the body is increasingly subject to surveillance and suspicion. It's a significant way in which our view of the figure is shifting.

The realist mode
In my mind, the prevalence of reality TV, social networking technology and surveillance points to a visual culture that is increasingly concerned with surfaces and appearances, all in a language that normalizes this engagement through a vernacular that is informal, casual and unstaged. The visual language of contemporary media creates an interesting set of problems for the realist mode in painting.

Through painting, I seek to shift the relationship between a viewer and an image. For me, painting is a way of destabilizing things, of creating a slippage that is productive in terms of how we grapple with images and their contexts.

Captive #3
2012, oil on canvas, 60cm × 90 cm
(23⅝ × 35½ in).

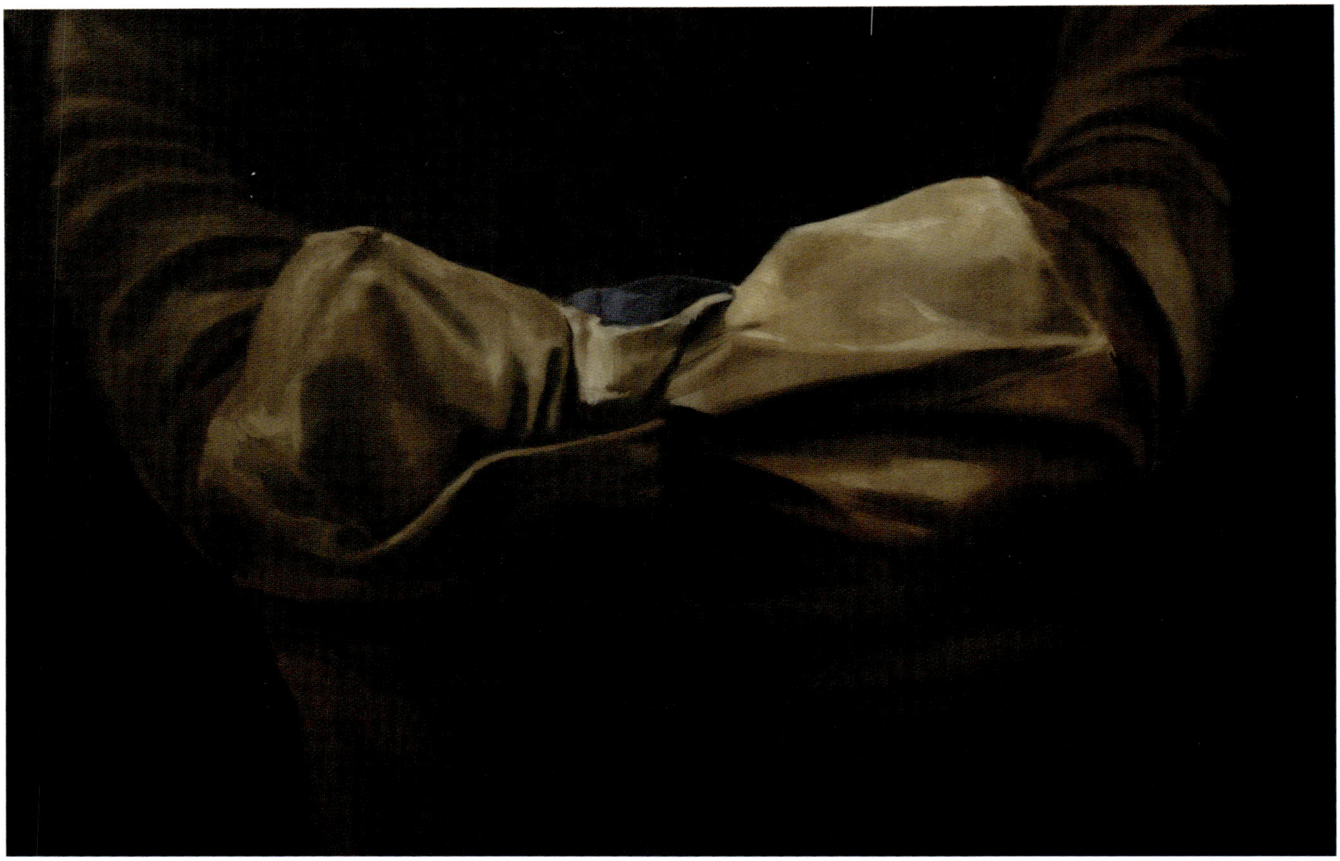

Captive #4
2012, oil on canvas, 90cm × 60 cm
(35½ × 23⅝ in).

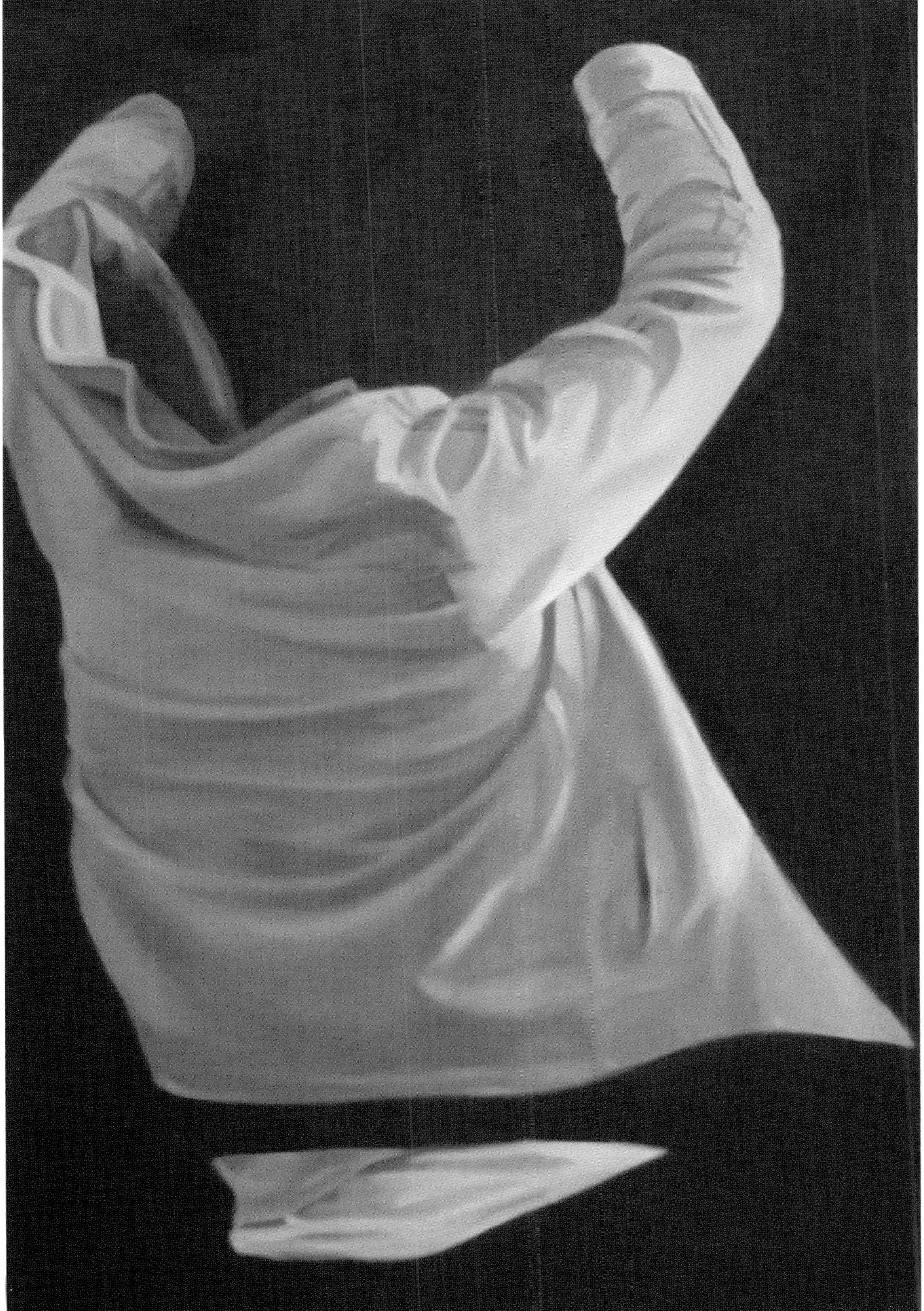

Talk
2011, oil on paper, 127cm × 98 cm
(50 × 38½ in).

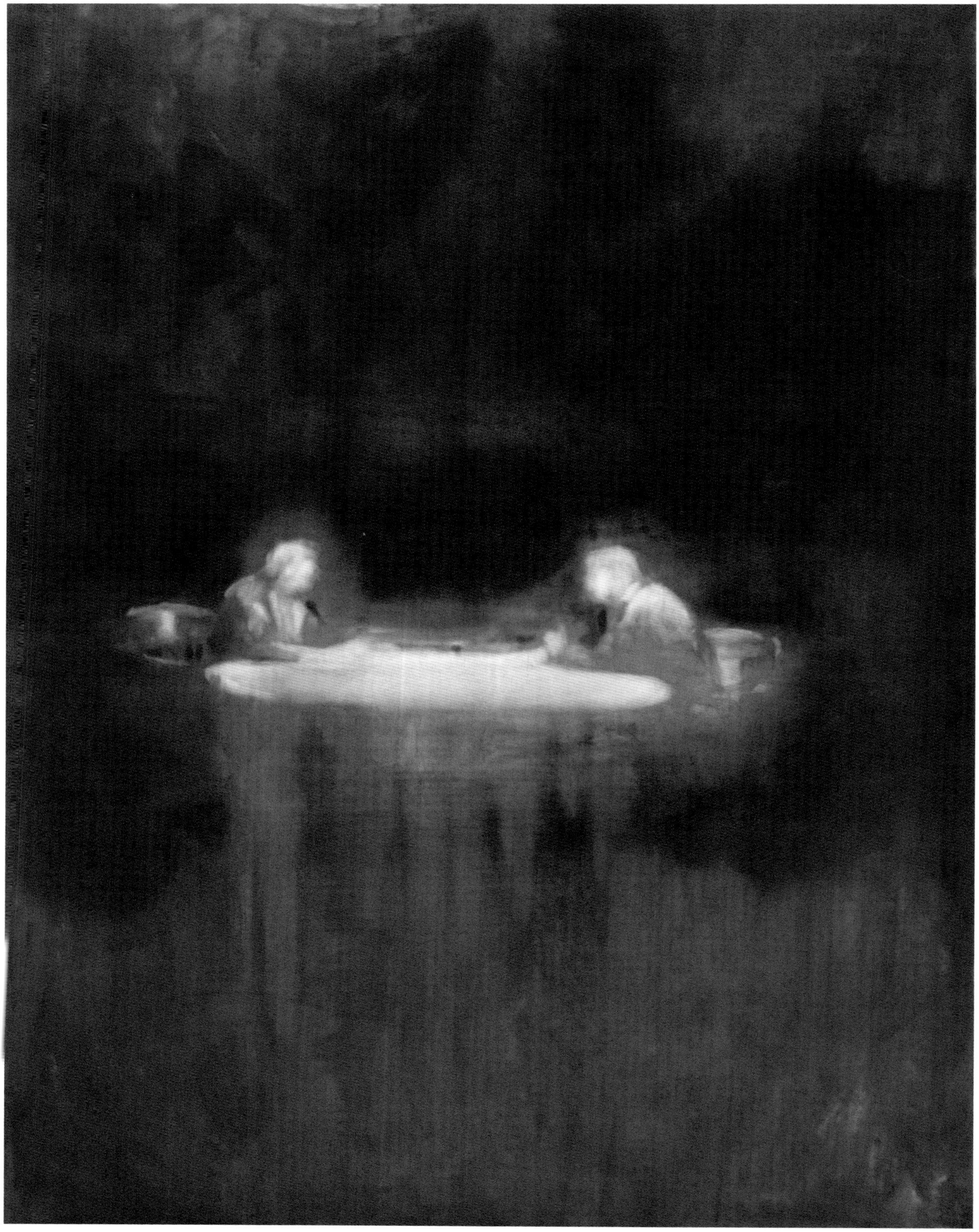

The Wait
2011, oil on canvas, 40cm × 30 cm
(15¾ × 11¾ in).

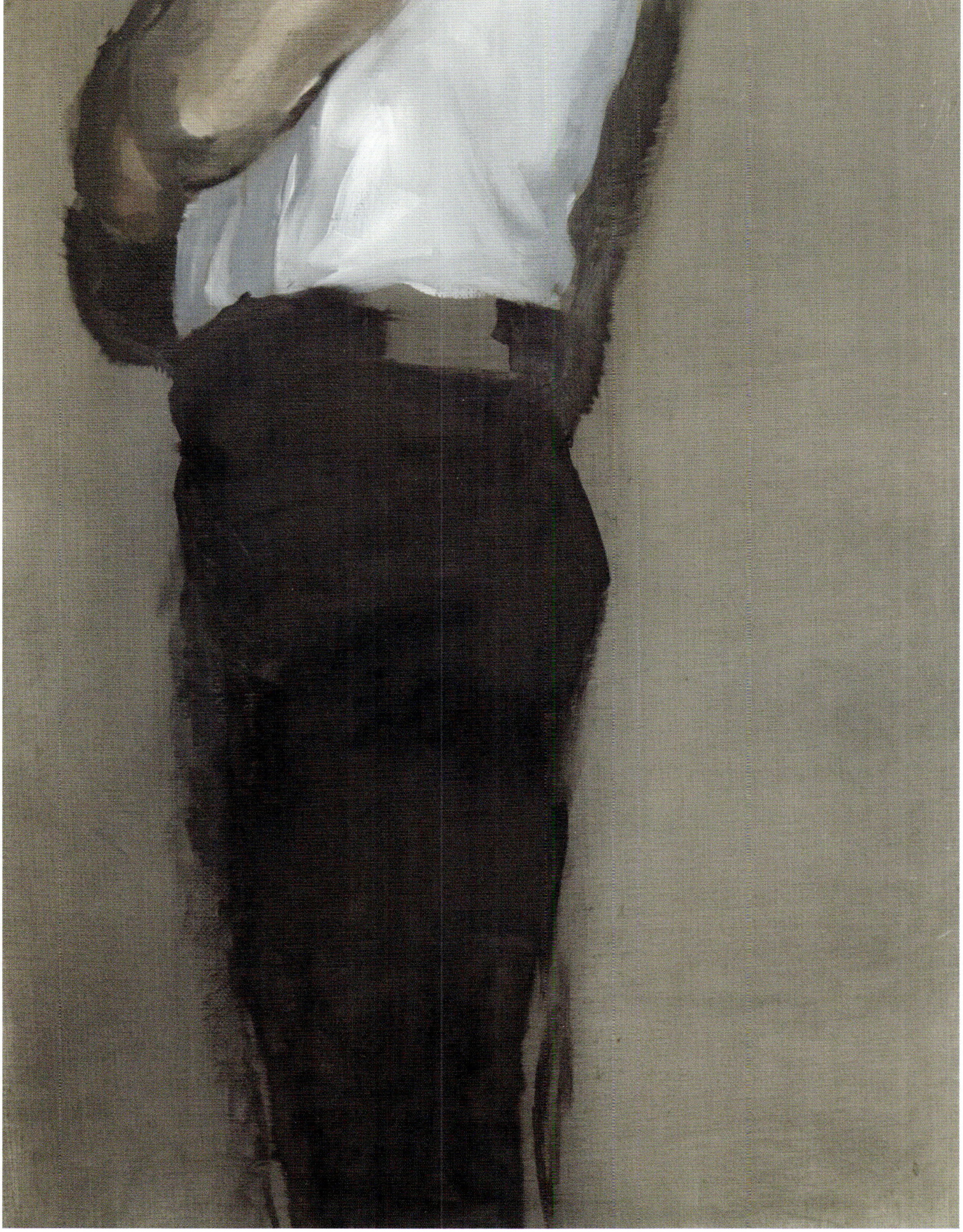

Roy Orbison 1
2007, oil on canvas, 35 × 30 cm
(13¾ × 11⅞ in).

Wilhelm Sasnal
Born: 1972, Tarnow (Poland)
Lives: Tarnow

Wilhelm Sasnal is one of the most significant figurative painters of his generation. Like almost every figurative painter today, he has clearly been marked by Gerhard Richter; but he differs tellingly from the German painter. He is more playful (as comfortable talking about his favourite bands as he is talking about Poland in World War II) and has a more spontaneous, sensual and instinctive relationship to paint. Crucially, Sasnal's work is also more committed to representation. The same could be said when comparing his work to that of Luc Tuymans or Peter Doig – two key influences from the generation preceding his. With deceptively 'easy' and free-flowing brushwork, Sasnal's canvases are engrossed in the excitement of the encounter between the medium of painting (with its tendency towards texture and abstraction) and an array of very contemporary subjects. The Polish painter will often start with an image he has stumbled upon in a book or a magazine, then use his dextrous and unpredictable brushwork to weave in complex layers of narrative, rhythm and perception, so that the final painting retains a relatively clear subject or thrust, while at the same time constantly eluding the viewer.

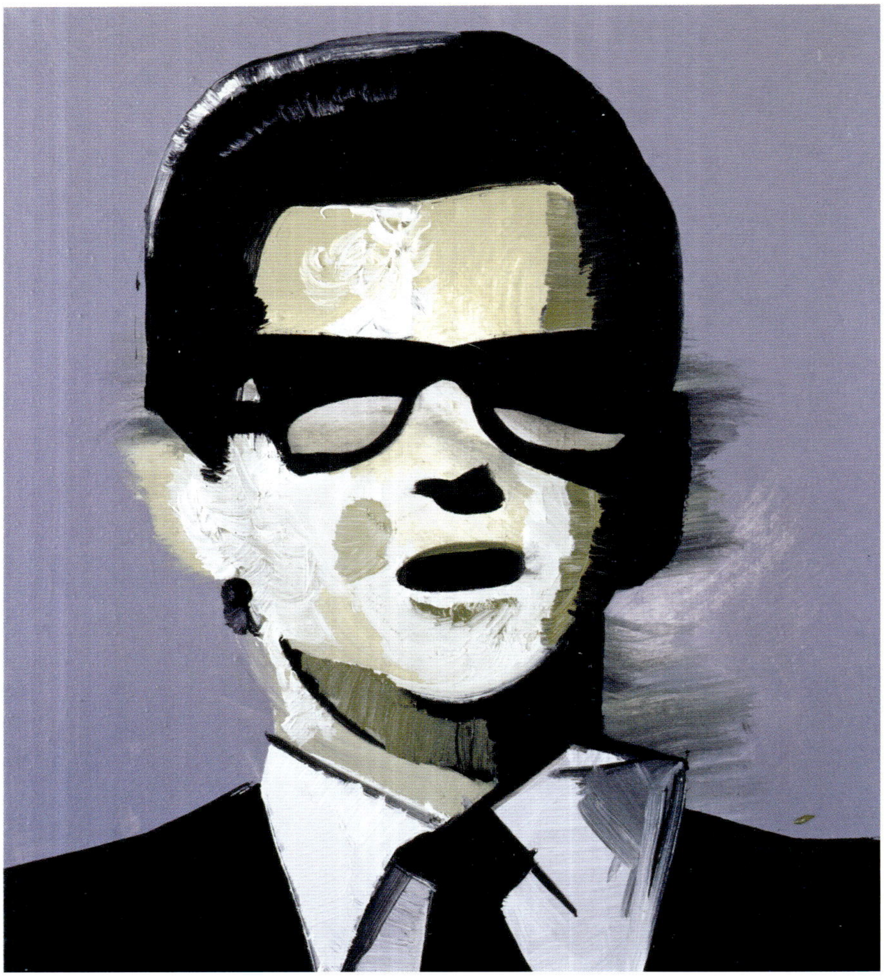

Background
My interest in art came largely through music. For example, I started listening to Bauhaus (the band) when I didn't know what 'Bauhaus' [the school of design] was – so all these music references and influences (and the artwork for the sleeves) were introductions to art for me. I realized that I had skills in drawing and it was easy to copy these sleeves. I remember The Smiths' album cover with a torso, which only later I realized was a still from an Andy Warhol film [*Flesh*], even if I listened mostly to Metal and these covers were rather cheesy.

Art school
My secondary school was a technical one, and after that it was too difficult to get straight into the [Jan Matejko] Academy of Fine Arts [in Krakow], so I tried to be realistic and studied architecture first, though I was already more interested in art than architecture and gave that up after two years to apply.

At the beginning art school was quite interesting: I worked a lot and was so excited I was studying there. But it was a very conservative school within a conservative city [Krakow]. I didn't have any illusions; I knew that most of the teachers there were not on my side. I didn't believe in certain things that some students believe in: the big topics, such as 'truth', 'life', or 'God'. I am not denying that these are important subjects, but they are not necessarily crucial for someone in their mid-twenties. When I finished at the Academy of Fine Arts I couldn't walk into a museum as I felt they were too connected to the Academy. Now I appreciate them, but then I had something like a hangover. I now realize that many of the things I did were done against school and against this rigid system. We always did still lifes and in the afternoons we drew nudes. Up to a point that was OK, but for how long can you practise subjects that have nothing to do with your life?

Once you believe in your tutors you are lost! Or you will become lost. You will be just a clone. Painting is too individual. On a very basic level teaching can help: a bit like learning the alphabet. It is better to kill your master than follow him.

Process

When I am not travelling or on holiday, I go to the studio every day. Not every day is fruitful. There are days when I just erase what I did the previous one and start again.

When I start I don't know if a painting is going to be more or less realistic. I don't paint the paintings: they paint themselves. When something is enough, it's enough. It doesn't matter if I control it. I don't exclude mistakes, they are refreshing. I am afraid of being in the position of a painter who thinks he knows everything and is just copying his own style. There are so many paths you can take which you wouldn't find if you were not lost at some point.

Subject matter

I usually begin a painting over something very banal. Then as I start painting I discover so many connections and associations, all loaded with stories and context. But I don't want to disclose them, nor do I reject the stories created by the viewer.

My paintings are mostly based on photographs – some of them are my own, some I have found on the Internet. Occasionally, I work from drawings. In this, again, there are no rules. I use Google Images, but I would rather not start with Google. I prefer coming across images by chance in books and newspapers. But when I need to get deeper into a subject then I go to Google.

The paintings drawn from Art Spiegelman's *Maus*

When I made these paintings it was a very topical subject in Poland, as we began to regard ourselves as the victims of World War II, which we hadn't always. When you ask if a painting can cope with current issues, I think this is an interesting example. I asked myself how painting might cope with a comic strip like Spiegelman's – it is only a comic strip, but it is such a comic strip! It was so important that it transcended the medium. So I was interested in how much could still be conveyed through paintings based on it – nearly abstract paintings, without speech bubbles or text or narrative.

The life of a painter

Everything went so smoothly.... There was a big departure point in my career in 2002 [Sasnal first participated in big museum shows – in Basel and Paris – which lead to the artist being taken on by international galleries in New York and London], but I just went back home and painted. I didn't get seduced by other things. I was living in my hometown, which is completely detached from the art world. And that did protect me from going crazy, or believing in something more than what you get in your small, provincial town. I am not looking for a place with an art scene. I am too involved with my private life.

But then is it better to be aware of what is going on with your paintings, or not to know? I think it is better not to be naïve and pretend that some calculations don't exist. They do exist, though you shouldn't try to play with them. I don't flatter collectors to sell better. I just do my work. And as long as I can do that, I don't mind that the art world is the way it is. I know some collectors well; some of them I like better than others; some are wiser and have more interesting observations than others. What is most important is to have galleries with whom you can talk about your work, and not just in terms of whether it can sell, but on all levels.

Gerhard Richter's ambiguity

Gerhard Richter has been influential for everybody, whether you like him or not. I was particularly interested in his ambiguity. He was always hidden behind the paintings. I find that very powerful. Painting works better within that area of ambiguity. Painters don't speak aloud, they don't use words – and that's important. I think that this is very puzzling, the mystery of the author – what is in fact his or her opinion?

Why paint?

I like painting. I like this practice: sitting in the studio listening to music and painting. It's a very privileged activity. Painting is a very good field for being irresponsible and making mistakes. It is an activity that allows you to be selfish. Your level of responsibility is very low: you can spoil the painting, you can start all over again – you won't hurt anyone. Provided you don't cheat yourself.

Kodak
2012, oil on canvas, 50 × 40 cm
(19¾ × 15¾ in).

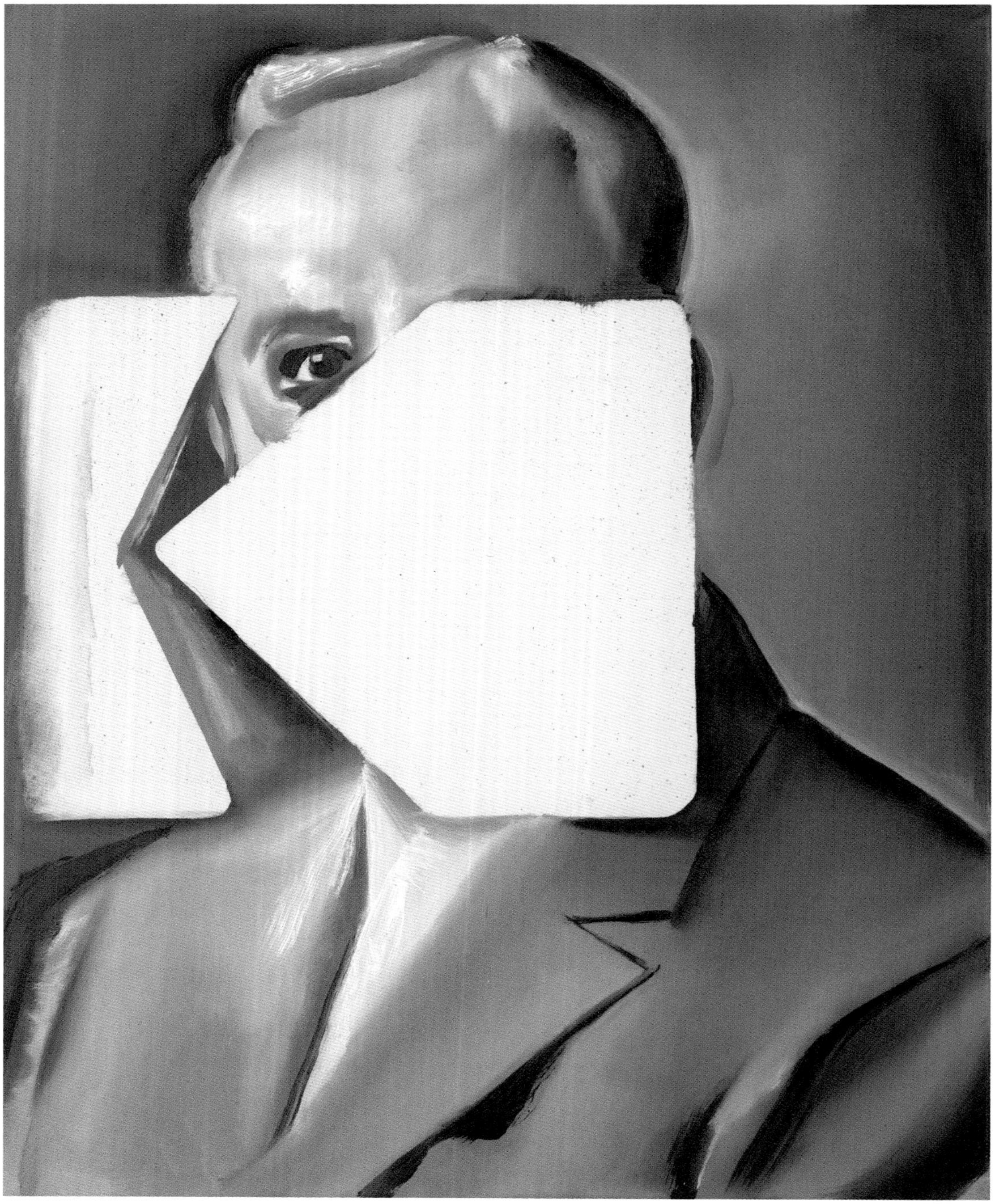

Kacper
2010, oil on canvas, 40 × 50 cm
(15¾ in × 19¾).

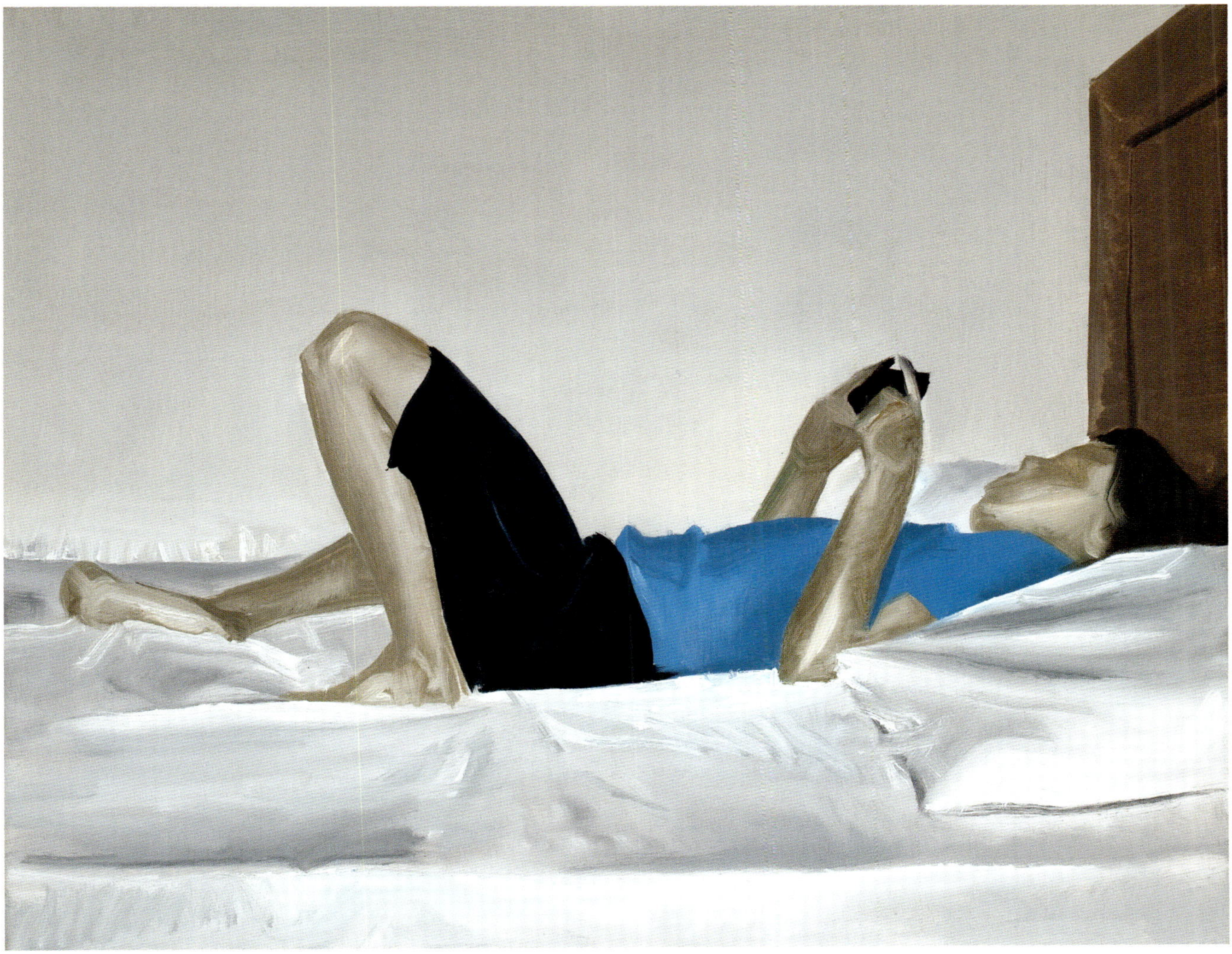

Untitled
2010, oil on canvas, 200 × 220 cm
(79 × 87 in).

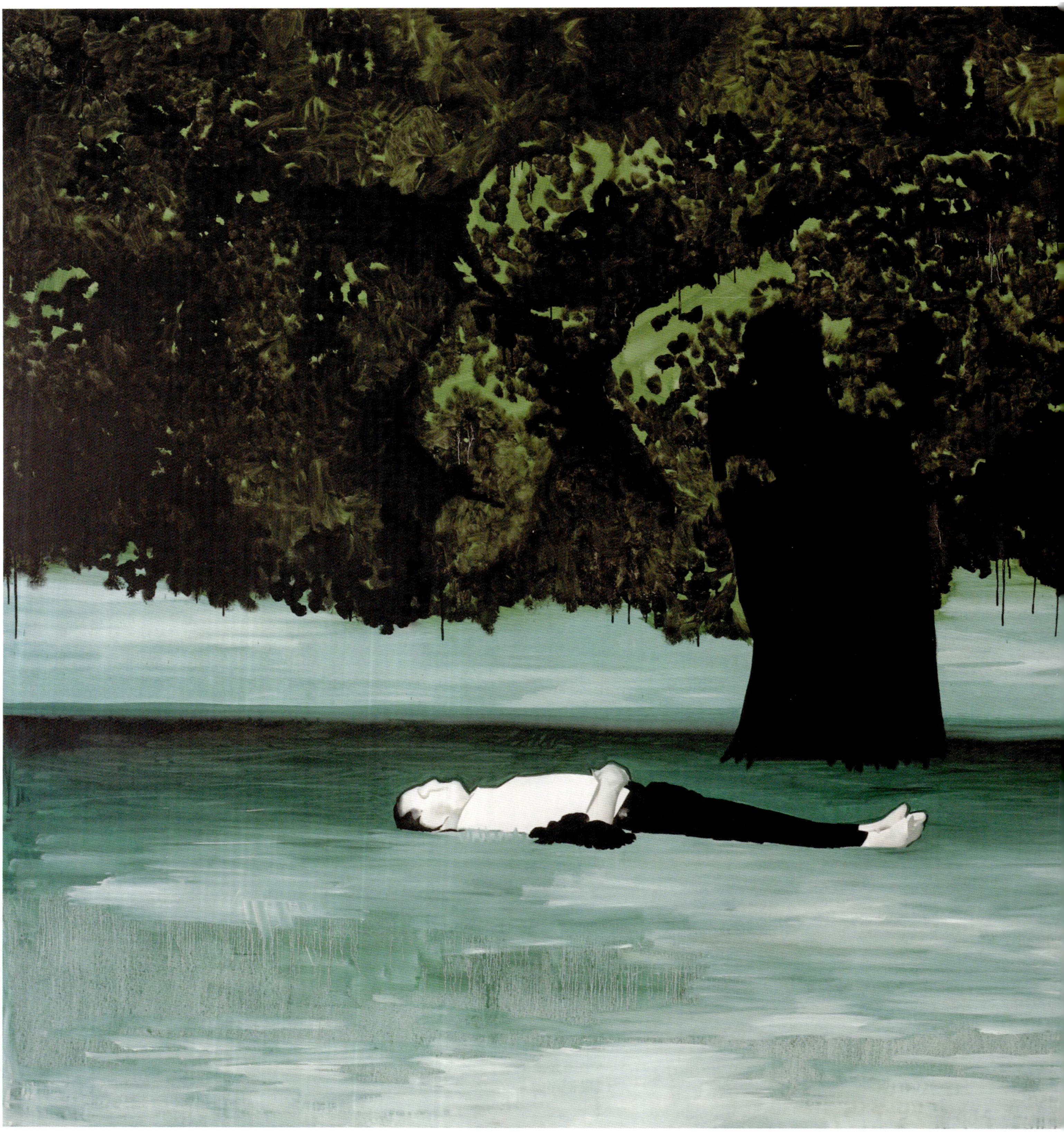

Untitled
2012, oil on canvas, 200 × 220 cm
(79 × 87 in).

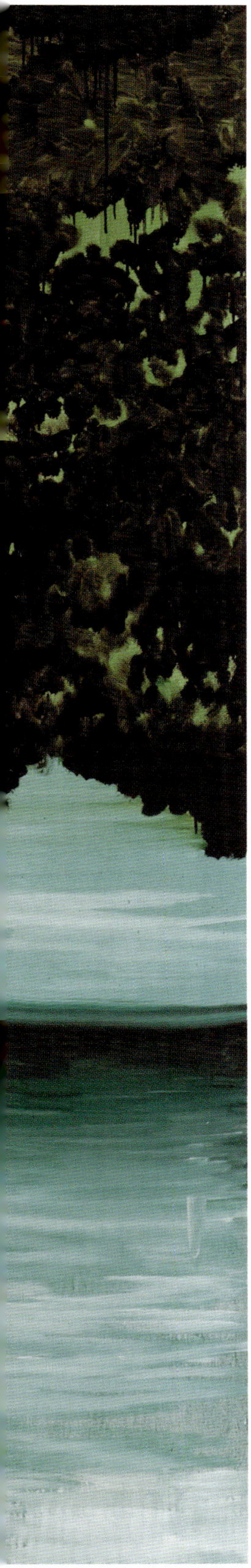

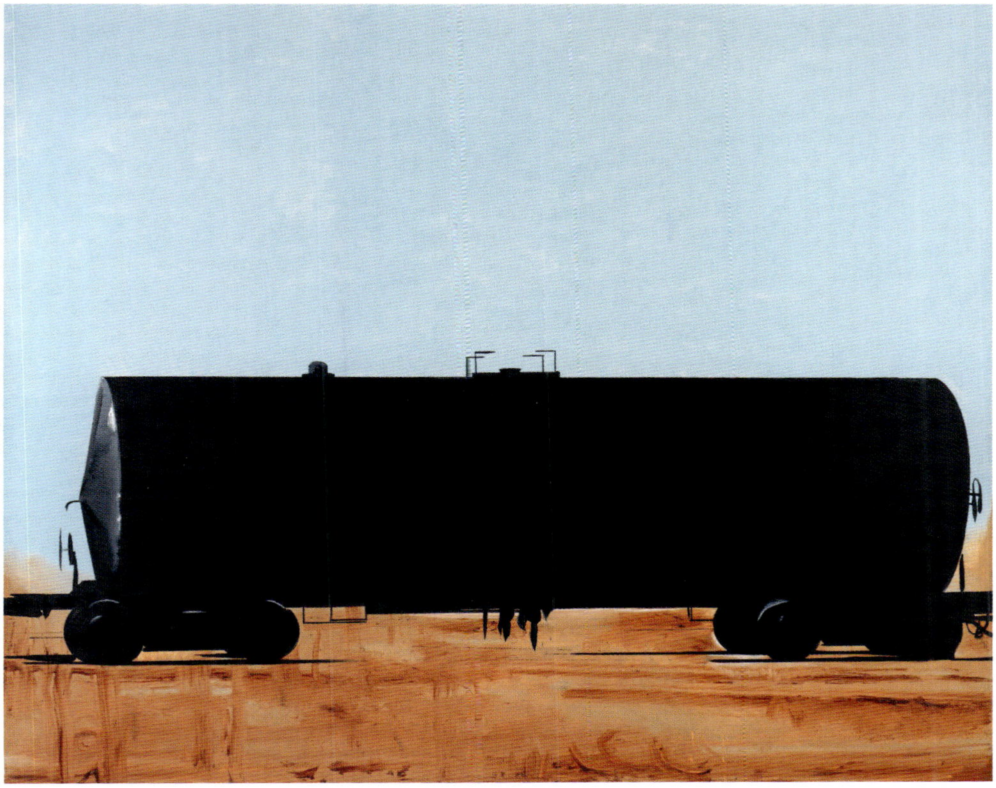

Untitled (Andrzej and Adam)
2009, oil on canvas, 120 × 160 cm
(47 × 63 in).

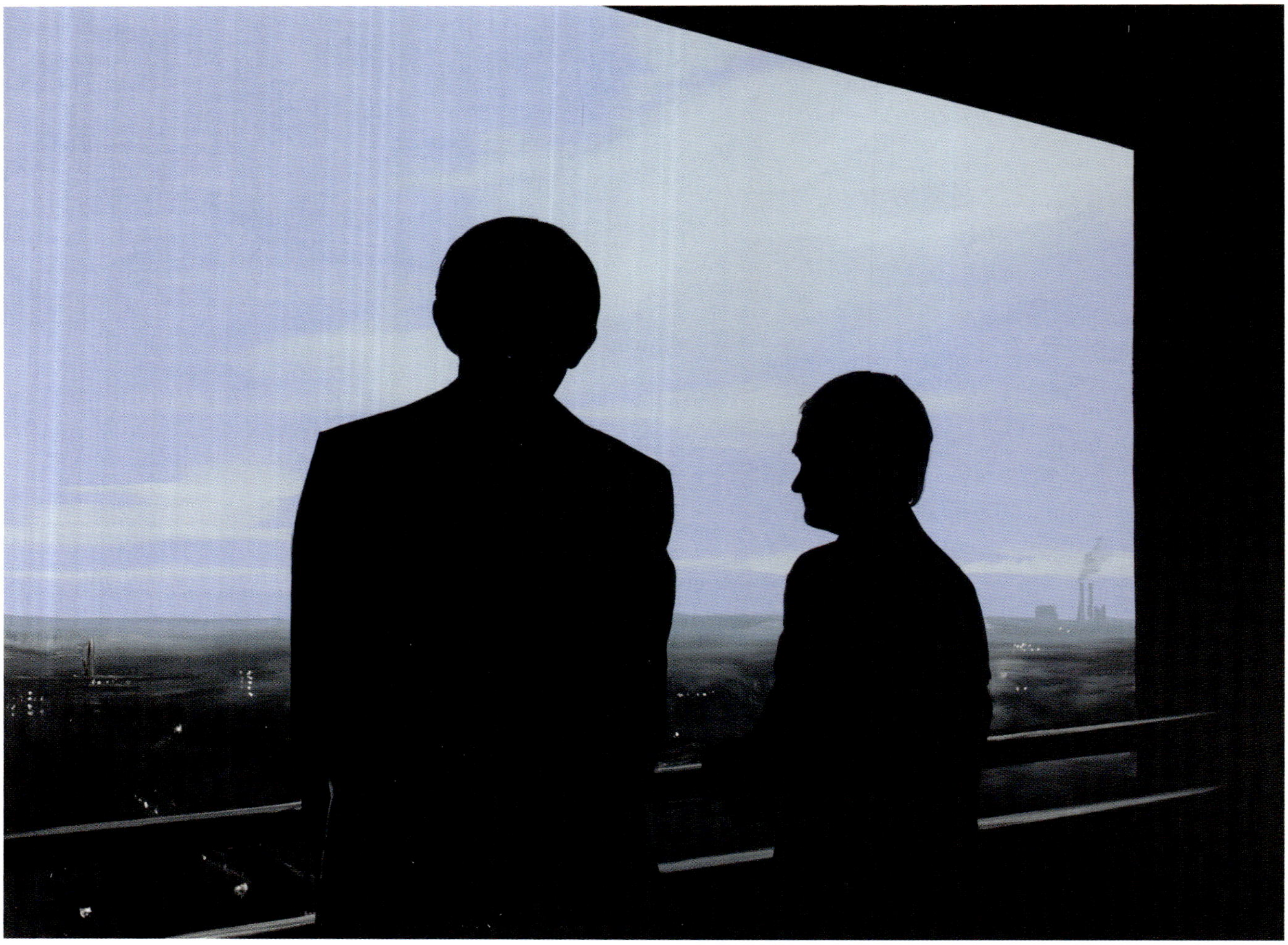

Untitled (Anka)
2010, oil on canvas, 70 × 90 cm
($27\frac{5}{8}$ × $35\frac{1}{2}$ in).

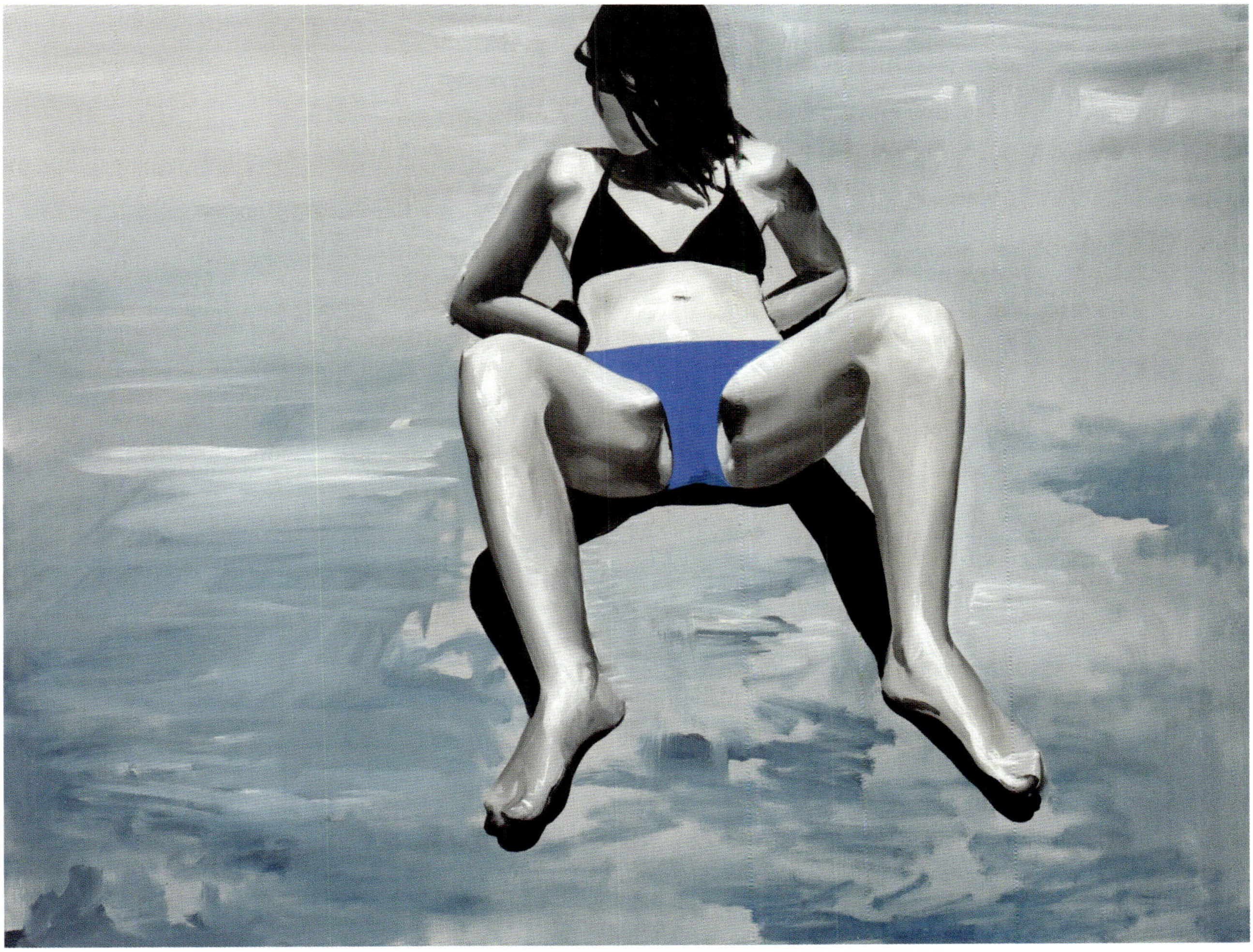

Li Songsong

Born: 1973, Beijing
Lives: Beijing

Chinese Li Songsong is a laconic man. An artist of facts and action rather than of words, he entrusts his paintings with the task of conveying his view of recent history and life in general through the physicality of the pictorial gesture. In an introductory essay for the catalogue *Li Songsong: Hypogenesis*, curator Jeff Kelley wrote: 'Li paints like a farmer who is tilling and tending a field of varied crops. Just so, his paintings are divided into square and rectangular patches, a kind of aesthetic acreage, each of which is a section of the larger historical scene.' The comparison with the work of a farmer beautifully summarizes the central role of the brushstroke in Songsong's art. The artist works with the large format of historical painting, drawing his subjects from archive images (from newspapers and newsreels) of China after the Cultural Revolution, but he completely dissects and alters them. Once covered with layers of thick, coloured paint, the original images of official events and everyday life seem to fade and disappear, losing their powers of persuasion as propaganda, and gaining a new and opposite meaning. The powerful gesture of the artist removes those events and situations from a narrative context that no longer exists, if it ever existed: that official façade of grandeur at political events, and of happiness in simplicity for common people, is recast as a secondary background. We have become accustomed to learning history through images, through photojournalism and video journalism. Songsong uses those images to rethink the meaning of history with purely pictorial means, through the strong traces of his gesture, the sensuous mellowness of the pigments and his excellent workmanship. In recent times Li Songsong has also worked with installation and he is now developing his painting towards abstraction.

Background

My father was a soldier, my mother was an editor, and both are retired. I was not born into an artistic family. I attended both high school and college at the Central Academy of Fine Arts in Beijing. In comparison, the high school period was more interesting.

Painting from photographs

Photographs are only the source for my [process of] creating, rather than a source of artistic inspiration.

Method

Work every day, if this can count as developing. I don't believe that there is something that you can get quickly, also I don't really think there are wrong turns during working.

On the painting *I Saw National Socialism*

I Saw National Socialism (2012) is from a news photograph. It's about Hitler visiting the injured after the failed assassination attempt in 1944. This fading history reminds us that when the realization of an individual ambition is attached to a group, it provides a nutritious environment for the growth of autocracy, and the formation process of this situation must be accompanied by the loss of freedom and dignity of human beings. And today, we are still able to see these examples of this kind of thing.

Actors
2011, oil on canvas, 290 × 360cm
(114 × 142 in).

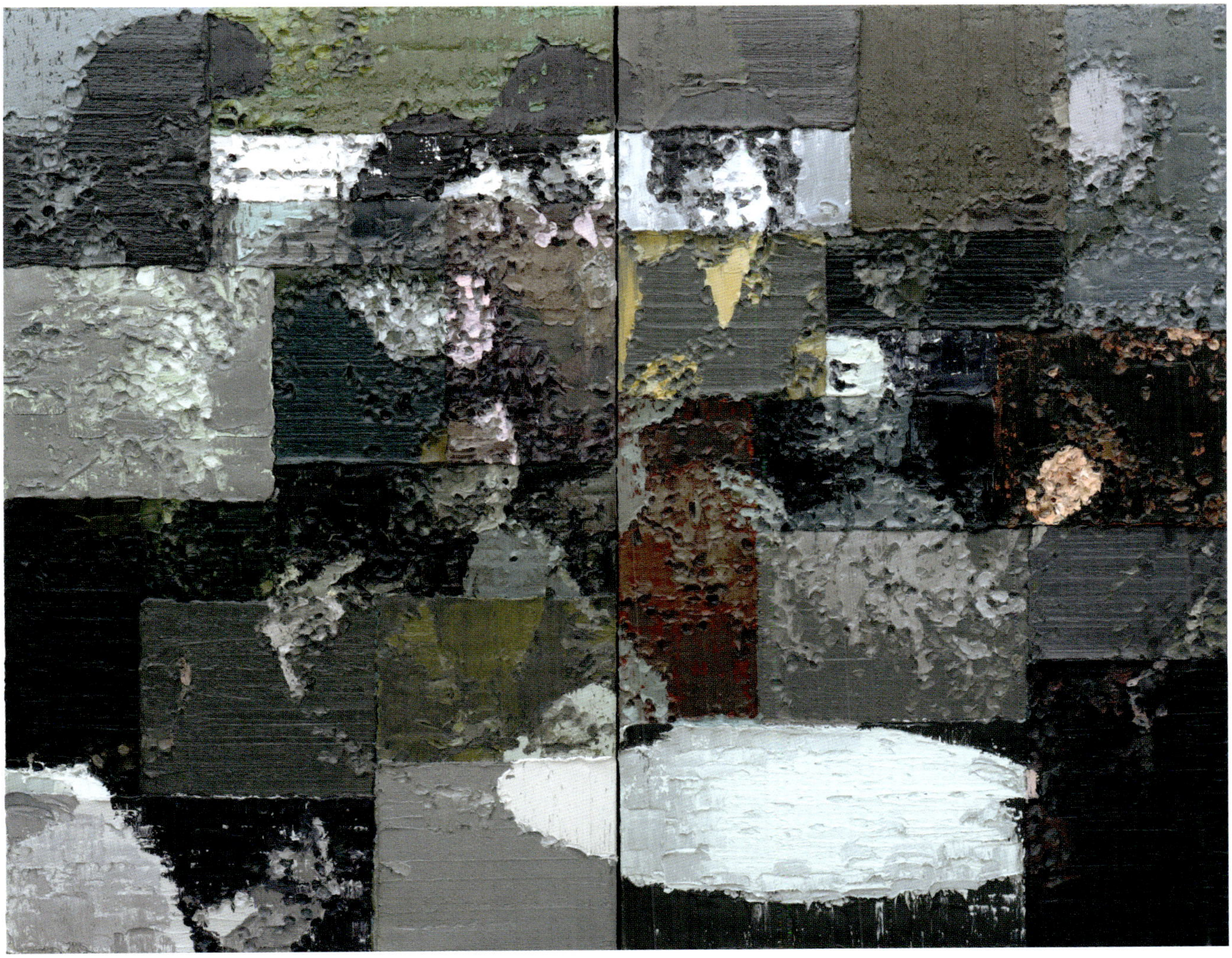

Making the Coffin
2010, oil on board, 244 × 244cm
(96 × 96 in).

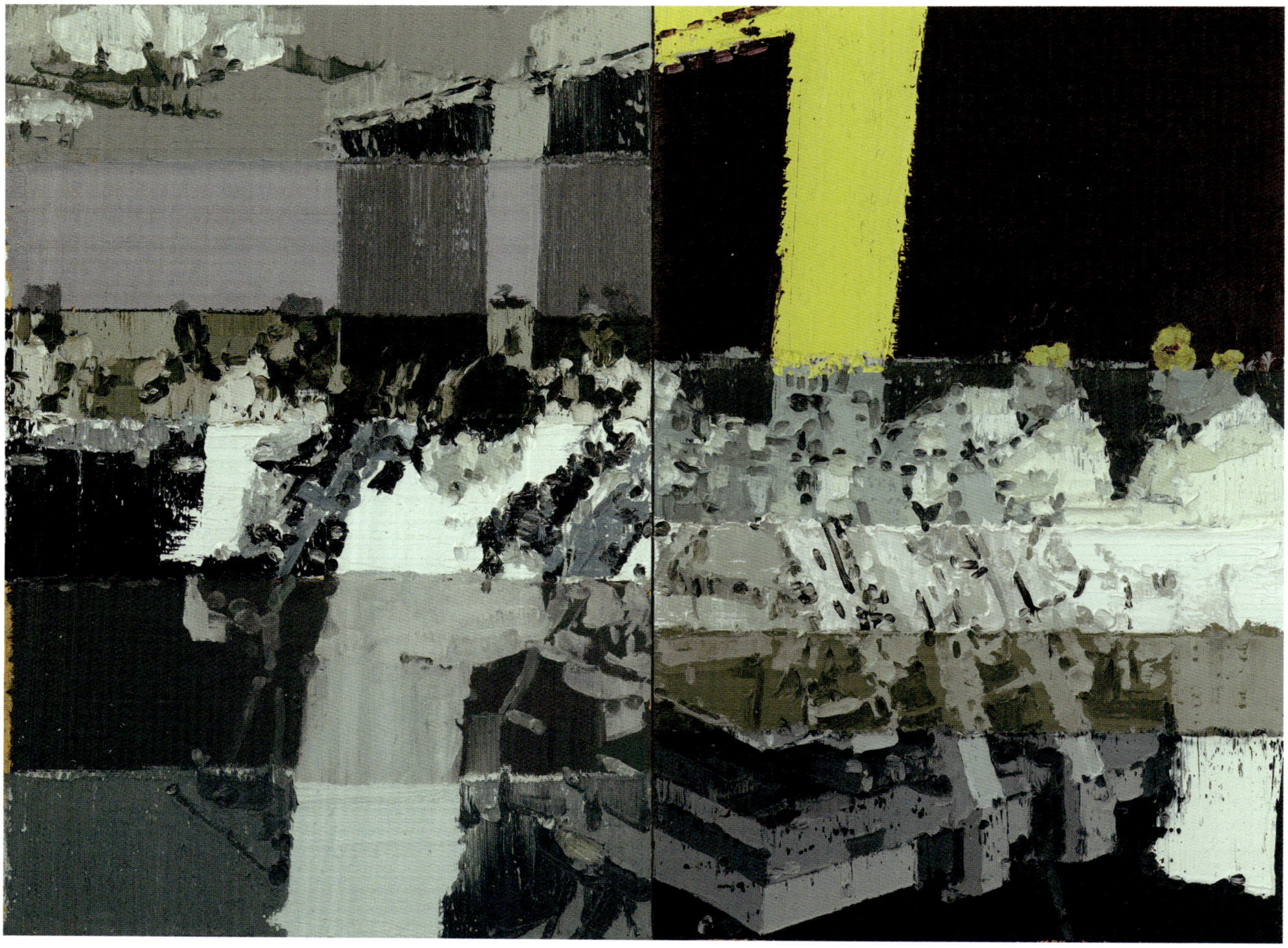

Craving and Flaws
2011, oil on canvas, 200 cm × 260 cm
(79 × 102 in).

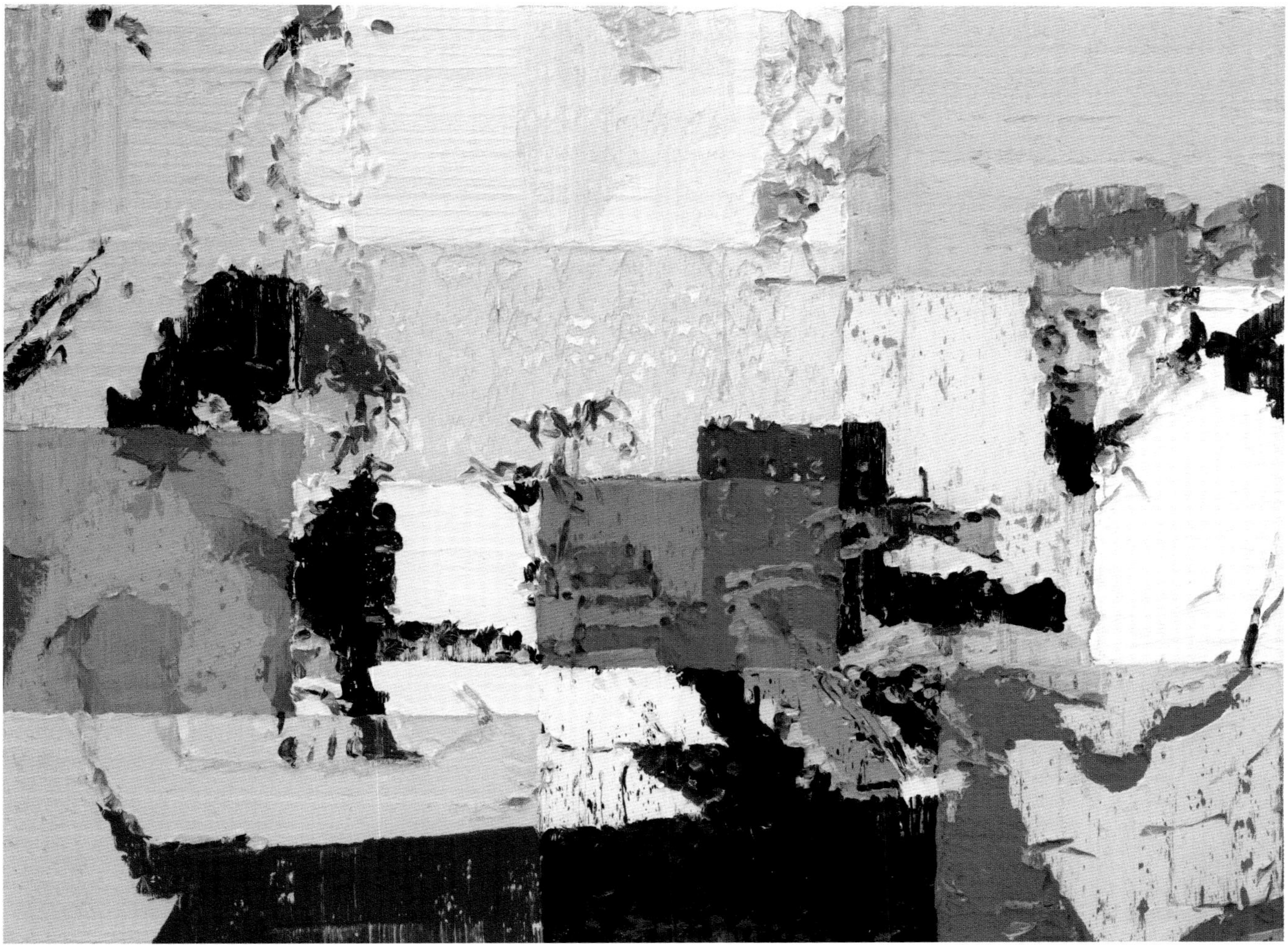

Sodium Vapor #2
2010, oil on canvas, 91 × 122 cm
(35⅞ × 48 in).

Wayne Toepp
Born: 1954, New York
Lives: New York

Through both his fine art degrees, American artist Wayne Toepp spent a good deal of time wrestling with the somewhat quixotic problem of maintaining a long-term investigation into the viability of painting. But he also mentions cinema as a primary influence, especially Italian neo-realism, film noir and, to a lesser degree, Hitchcock. Muybridge is a visual touchstone.

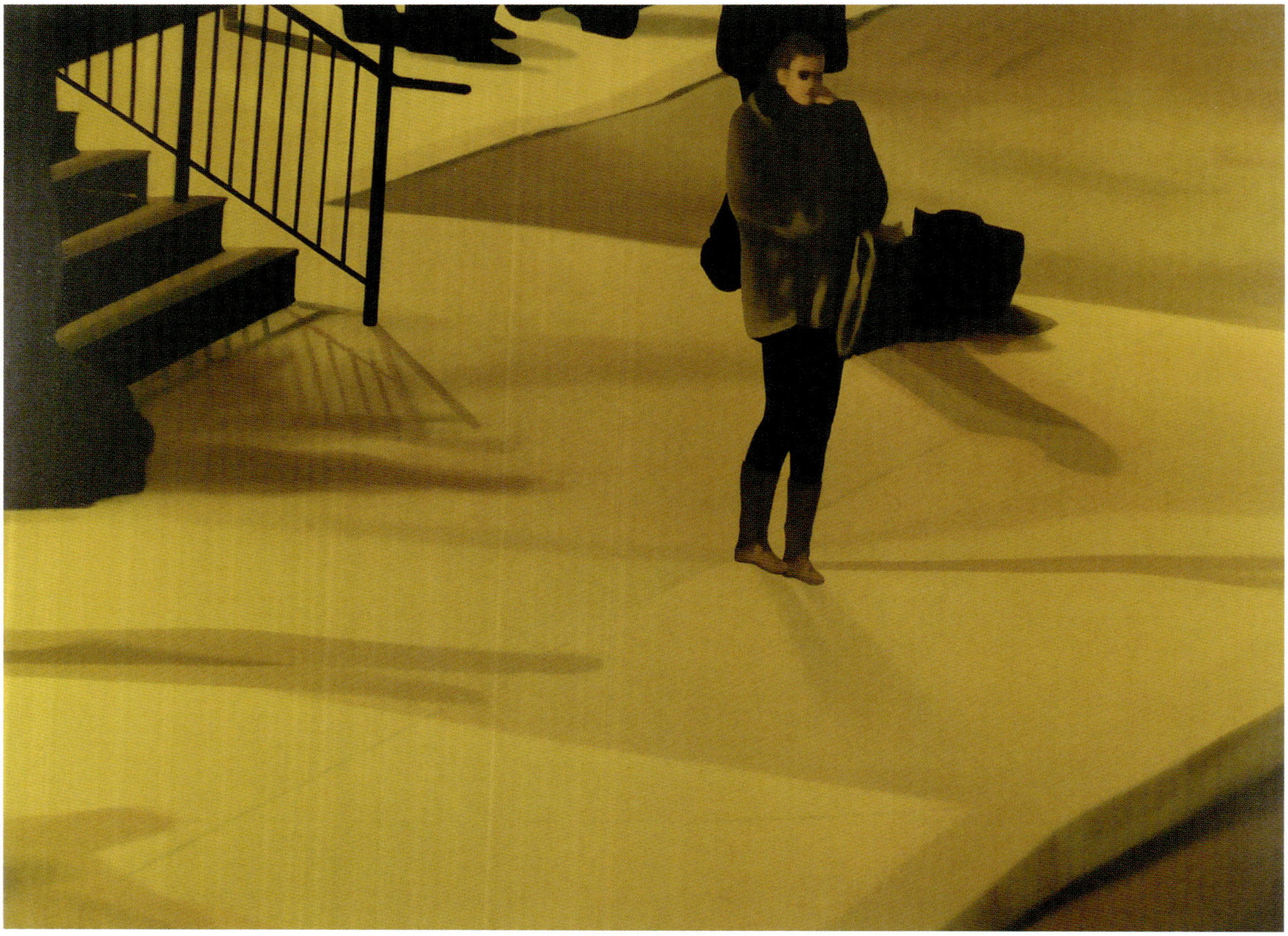

The canvas and the screen

The screen has, in my view, come to occupy the space that was traditionally thought of in painting as the fourth wall – the portal through which we experience and process our ideas and perceptions. But the simple act of moving the image from the LCD screen to an analogous surface in real space causes the registration of the image to shift in slight but important ways.

The pleasure of technology

I do find intense visual pleasure in technology – in its visual apparatus and the manner in which it renders the world. I have an equivalent experience watching a Rossellini film to what I might experience in a museum or, more to the point, in looking at an analogue surveillance monitor screen.

Process

Selecting the specific still that I'm going to work with from my inventory of files is in some ways the most difficult part. The source images I'm working from are generally pretty low resolution – so I end up paying a great deal of attention to the optical structure of the image, how it's actually articulated in scan lines [the alternating coloured and black rows] on the analogue screen or pixels on digital interfaces. One odd aspect to the working process is that the painting's orientation on the wall is usually rotated 90 degrees clockwise or counter-clockwise from its normal orientation, because of the actual mechanics of the paint application.

I try to select images that are legible though it interests me if the actual spatial configuration in the camera view isn't easy to decipher. Most surveillance video is shot from a pretty high point of view, and often with a wide-angle lens, both qualities that I like and that also have particular connotations of power and control.

Movement

As much as I love film, my particular fascination with freeze-frame video images is largely tied to the notion of the interstice and its inherent reference to an implied but unavailable (to the viewer) relationship to time. In working with static images that reference time, perceptions that relay my understanding of Henri Bergson's *duration* and Deleuze's *time-image*, can be activated by the painted image. What I'm doing with regard to time in these paintings relates to the idea of the surgical slice, in the sense that a cross-section might relate to the larger tissue from which it's removed.

I don't see a way through the problem of the integration of sequential moments within the painted image that isn't a sort of reprise of the Futurist notion of multiple tails wagging on the little dachshund. Having said that, I do feel that Francis Bacon succeeded in incorporating something of that in his smeared and blurred 'stills'. The only thing that I have done with this idea occurs within the connected time-thread from painting to painting as opposed to within the same frame. The three *Capella Medici* paintings present the visual incidents of elongated shadows cast on the security camera view of the piazza directly in front of the Medici Chapels Museum over a span of less than a minute – the three paintings together providing a summary of the single camera view over that span of time.

The role of painting today

Painting has always been about mediating reality. What I find most interesting now is the movement of painting towards mediating already mediated images. In an environment saturated with a continual stream of image-producing technology, the critical function of working with that as source material in painting continues to pose interesting questions and challenges.

Below: Cell Still #2
2011, oil on canvas, 91 × 122 cm
(36 × 48 in).
Bottom: Cell Still #6
2012, oil on canvas, 91 × 122 cm
(36 × 48 in).

Below: Cell Still #3
2011, oil on canvas, 91 × 122 cm
(36 × 48 in).
Bottom: Cell Still #4
2011, oil on canvas, 91 × 122 cm
(36 × 48 in).

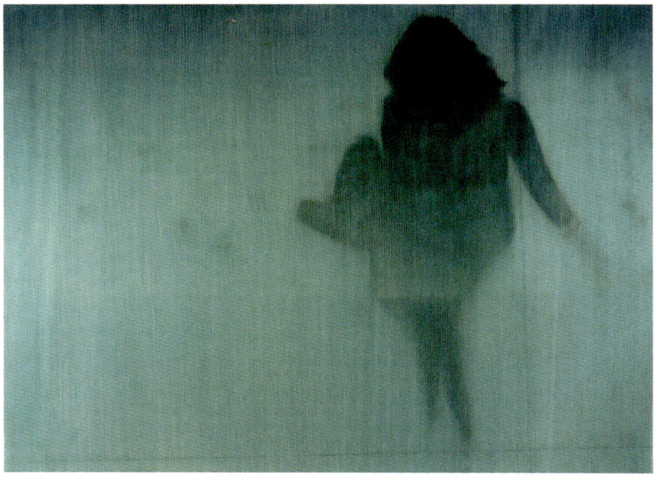

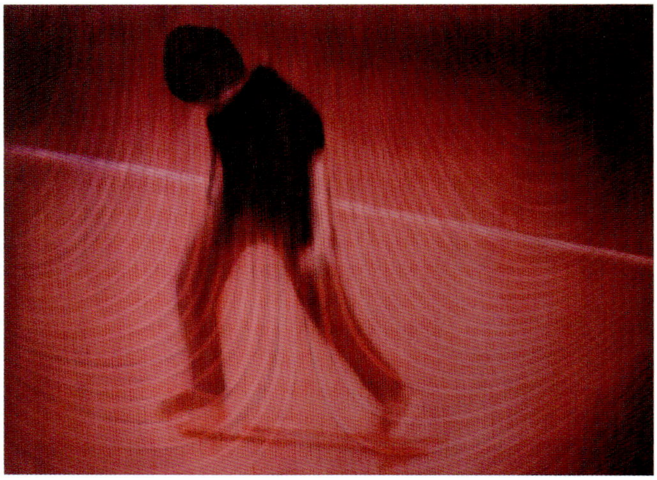

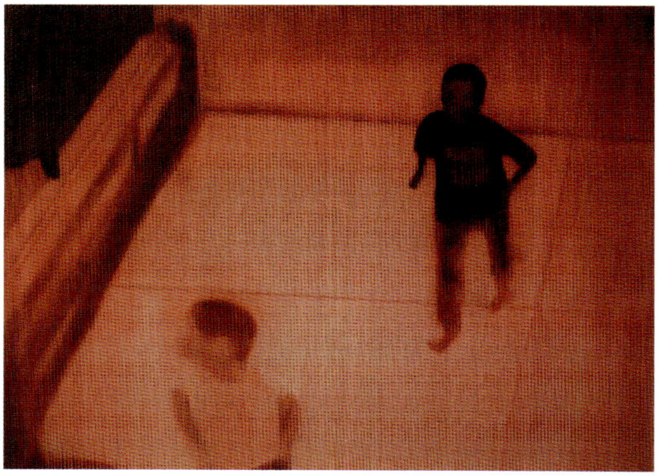

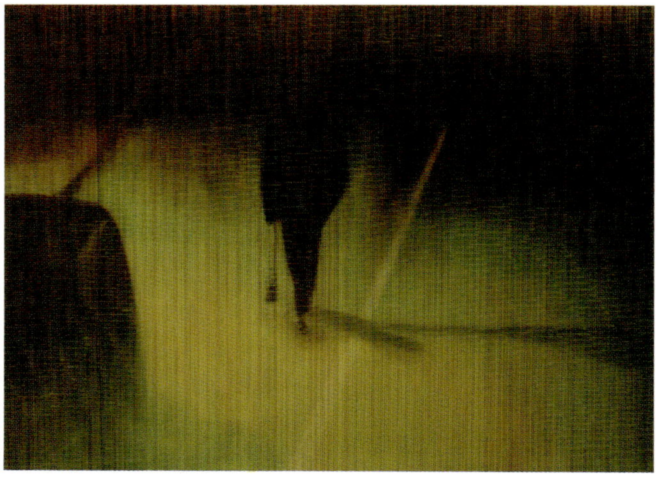

Station Building Hall 15:06:40
– 07/23/2007
2008, oil on canvas, 91 × 122 cm
(36 × 48 in).

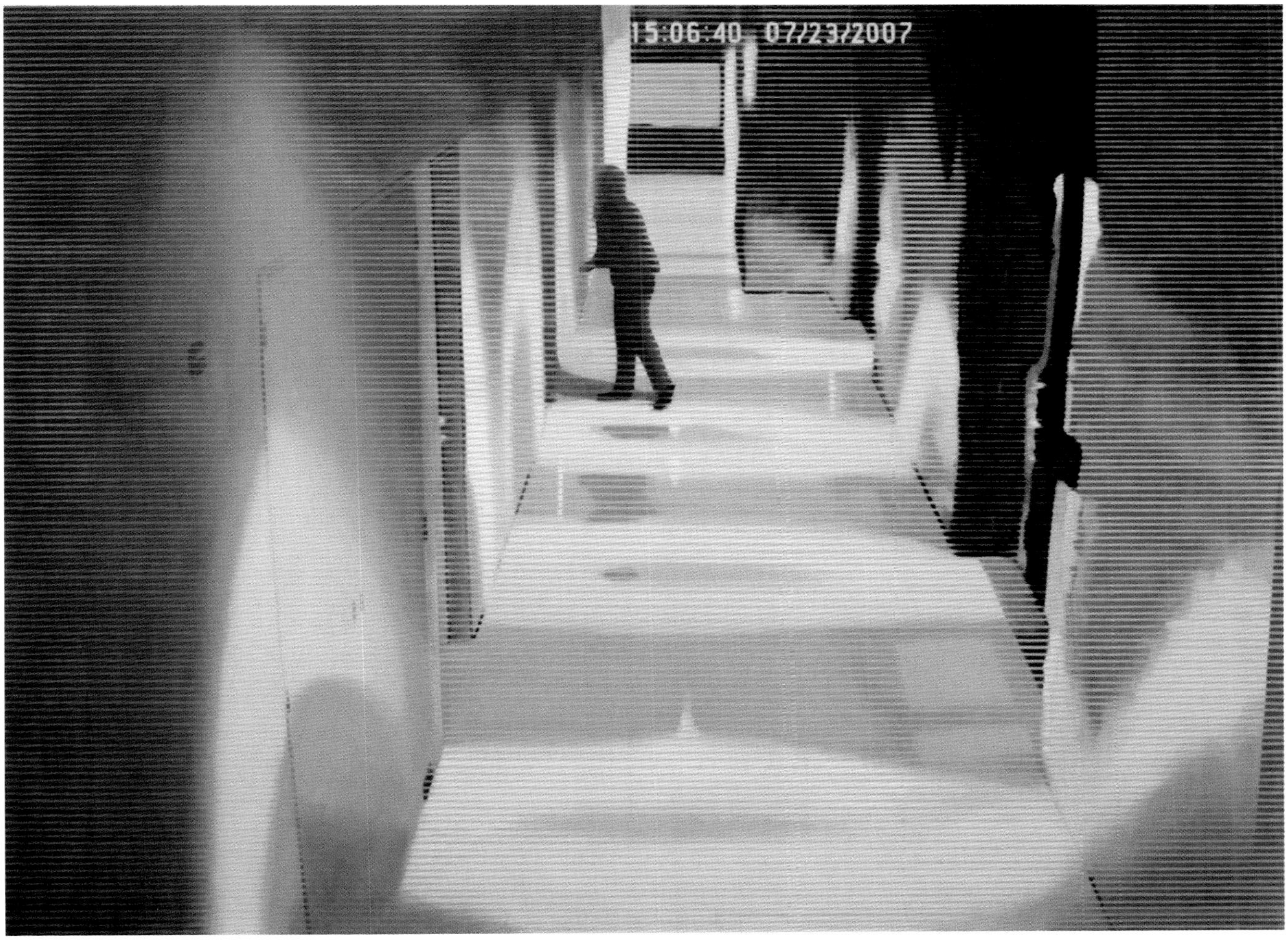

Inter
2012, oil on linen, 75 × 116 cm
(29½ × 46 in).

Jonathan Wateridge
Born: 1972, Zambia
Lives: London

Since 2006, Jonathan Wateridge has embraced painting as his medium of choice, and his work has gone through many changes. His body of work is concerned with Realism and ideas of the real, but all the images are derived from situations set up in the studio. Over the last few years, Wateridge's practice has focused increasingly on the structural aspects of painting. 'Any ideas have to be expressed formally. Depiction and form need to cohere', he says. Rather than being based exclusively on subject matter, his artistic explorations around 'the real' and 'the constructed' are developed via experimentation with the ways a painting can be made.

Embracing painting
I was very committed to painting from the age of 14 or 15 but stopped a year after I got to art school [Glasgow School of Art] in 1990. Despite an instinctive love for the medium, I feared that it was effectively an anachronism without relevance to contemporary culture. I didn't make paintings for nearly 15 years, thinking I should be pursuing a much more conceptually driven practice. It's taken a very long time but I'm now comfortable with the obsolescence of painting and, ironically, I now find its 'out-of-dateness' liberating.

Realism v. Photorealism
If I had to define myself, I'm most likely a Realist painter as opposed to a Photorealist. I have to make the point here that this is often the unfortunate result of seeing the paintings via reproduction rather than in the flesh, which reduces them to imagery alone at the expense of their materiality. It forces a painting to be seen via the prism of a photograph, which inevitably renders it more 'photographic'. Photography allows the possibility of the cinematic to enter the paintings but their rendering has to be about exploring the materiality of paint rather than denying it. In retrospect, that may have been one of the reasons I've increasingly emptied the frame in my paintings, placing more emphasis on the formal aspects of the paint itself.

Source material and subject matter
By virtue of building sets and using actors, all my images become elaborately crafted 'non-events' that merely have the trappings of a real occurrence but actually do not exist outside the studio. Everything you see in the pictures is rendered false. Regardless of the source, the painting is a fiction. This process has itself become a point of inspiration as many paintings now come about as a result of incidents that have happened in the studio during the shoots and that would have been impossible to predetermine. Source material is therefore only a starting point, while a crucial one.

A central element of my process is the physical reconstruction or reconfiguring of the initial source. Regardless of what that source is, I'm always trying to apply a sense of remove from any idea of a 'true' origin or referent. Any image one makes, however unique or idiosyncratic, joins this chain of pre-existing cultural imagery and it's important as an artist to question one's place in relation to that.

Transitions
One of the big problems I had with 'Another Place' [the series, from 2010, presents scenes from an imaginary film set] was that by making another medium the subject of the paintings, it unfortunately rendered the work far more illustrational than I would have liked. In dealing so explicitly with cinema and a specific genre, I probably shouldn't have been too surprised by the fact that the aesthetic of that genre then pervaded the paintings and left them far more dramatic, overwrought and narrative-laden than I would like.

The works I made in around 2011 were an attempt to pare back that aesthetic, subdue the palette and minimize the events within the frame. I wanted to shift towards quieter and more prosaic imagery. I wanted the paintings to have an anonymous, suburban feel. I tried to depict things in a very incidental and modest way, but still on an epic scale. This was my

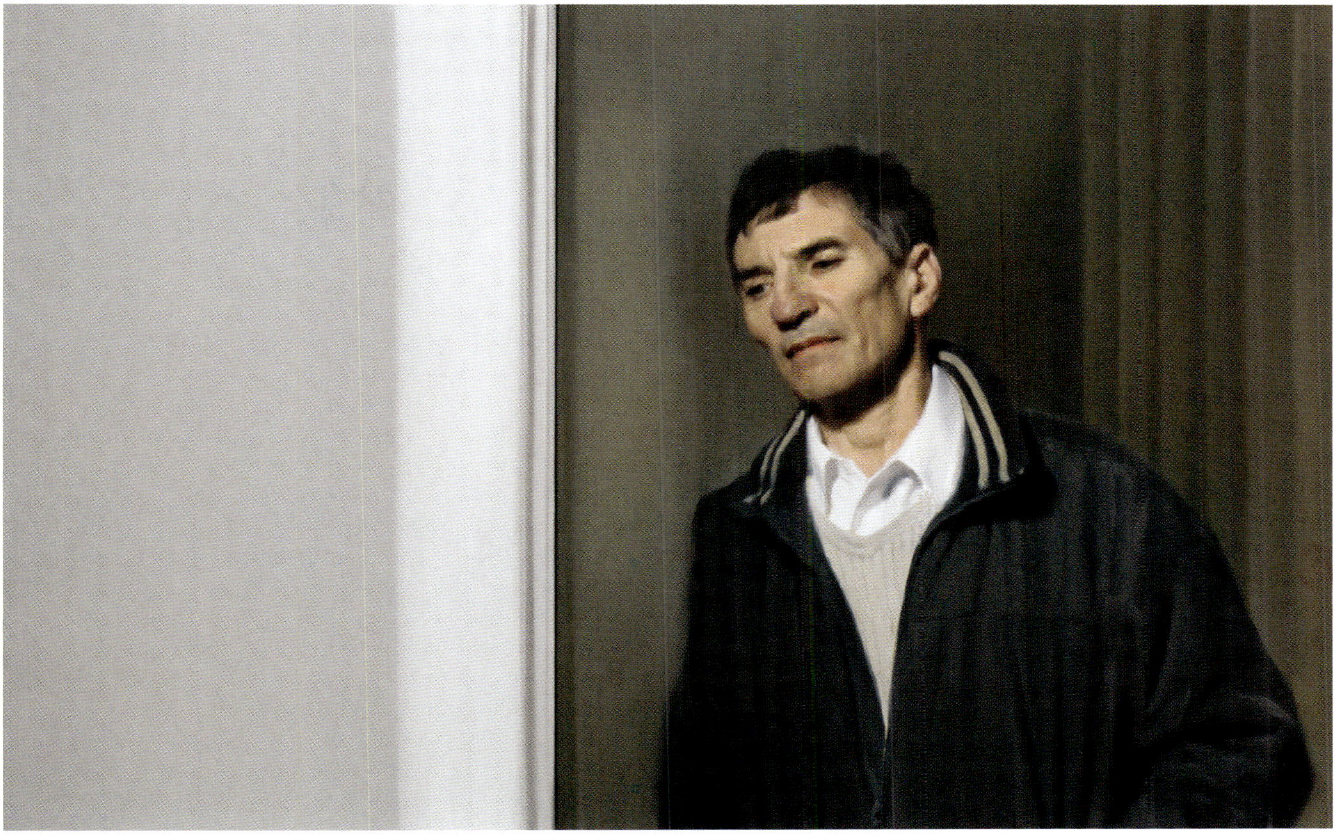

first opportunity to build life-sized sets, which became very immersive for the performers; they could just 'behave'. Subsequently, instead of setting out to do something documentary, the world [I wanted to create] was brought back into the studio, and instead of looking for the fixed or the monumental, I tried to find fleeting, incidental and quietly captured moments – but in an incredibly controlled context.

All of these paintings are very much about structure. There are lots of lines, lots of intersections; the infrastructure underpinning each picture is key. The fact that they were sets meant that I didn't feel the need to tag on any notions of fiction as part of the subject matter, as it's all right there in the way that the paintings are constructed.

All for the painting

While making these paintings [in 2010 and 2011], a couple of things became very clear to me. Firstly, the amount of work involved in preparing and building the sets seemed disproportionate to the fact that it was all for one painting. It occurred to me that I needed to start planning sets in order to allow for the possibility of [making] multiple works off the back of them. This would afford greater flexibility and, more importantly, the opportunity to also make smaller work.

That was the second issue – the problem of working in the large-scale tableau format, which increasingly felt very restrictive. I missed a sense of play in the painting process and that could only really come about by varying the sizes of canvas and types of images that I was making.

A new direction

Having turned the volume down, I wanted to take that even further by making the subsequent subject matter more intimate and ambivalent, and the surrounding environments for the figures increasingly spare. I did everything I could to empty most of the paintings of event, and tried to avoid pinning anything down in terms of meaning, but the pictures shared certain themes of obfuscation; with figures obscured by fog or glass doors; a sense of distance or removal in viewing the subject, and of boundary or containment, such as lifts or the barrier in *Vista* (2012). Any movement depicted was minimal and the settings were banal and nondescript. Effectively the paintings depicted action without action.

The palette was even more limited than previously. In fact, the only colours I used were two whites (titanium and lead), yellow ochre, Venetian red, green earth and two blacks (ivory and lamp). Crucially though, the paintings were all very different sizes and some canvases were entirely devoid of figures, bordering on the abstract. This created a much more open sense of rhythm throughout the space and for me that was like breathing lungfuls of fresh air. It's completely freed my approach to making upcoming paintings.

Glass Doors
2012, oil on linen, 200 × 290 cm
(79 × 114 in).

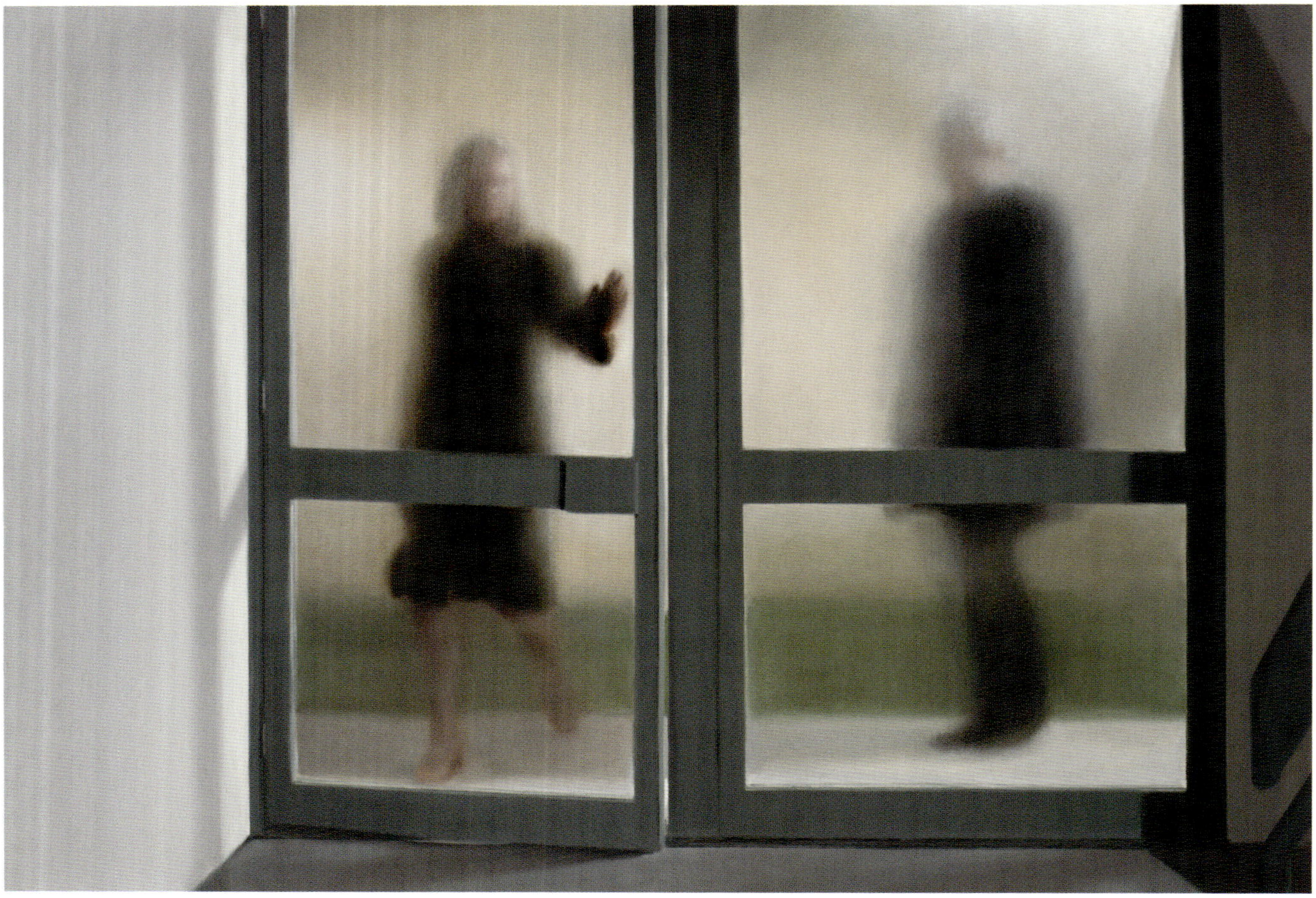

Boy on Wall
2012, oil on linen, 282 × 400 cm
(111 × 158 in).

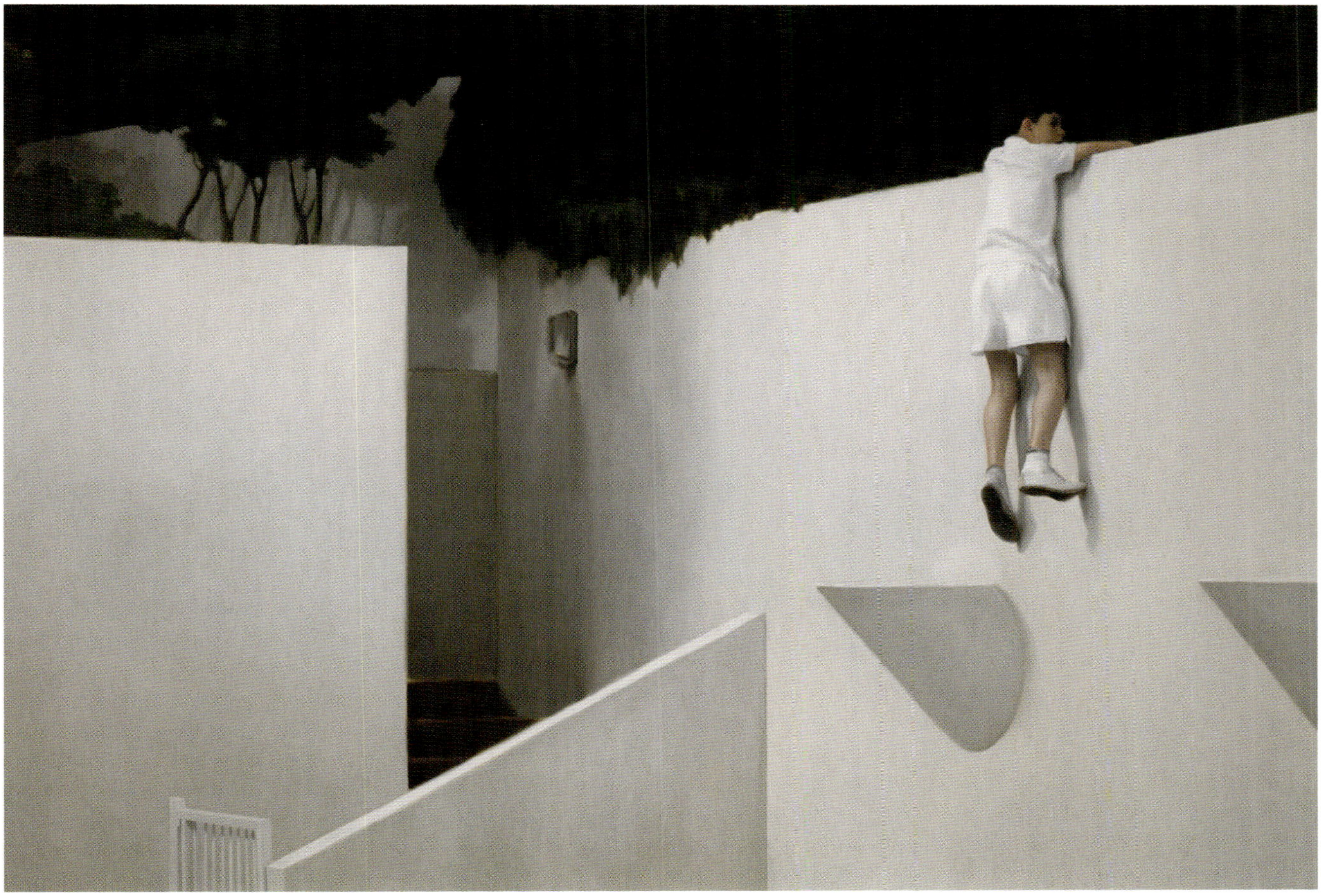

Matinee
2011, oil on linen, 282 × 400 cm
(111 × 158 in).

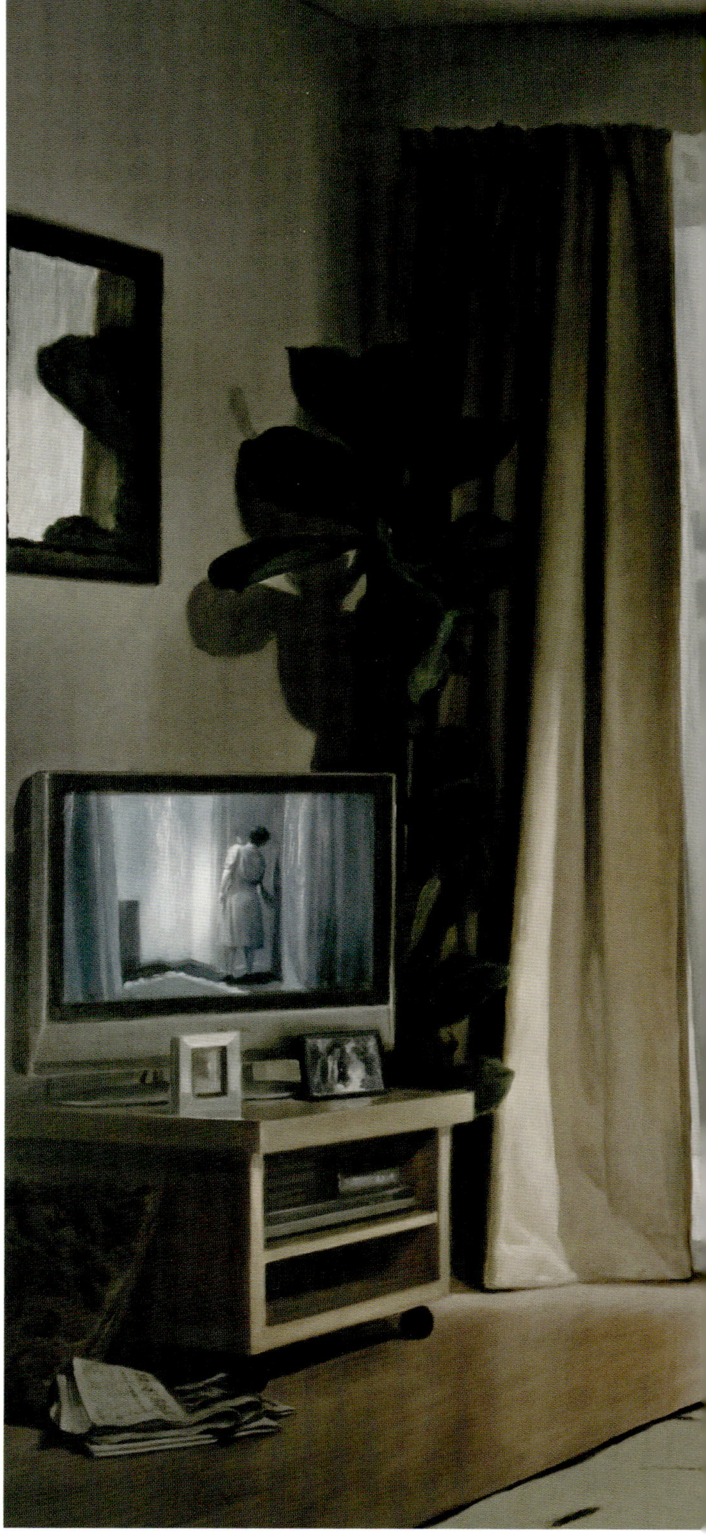

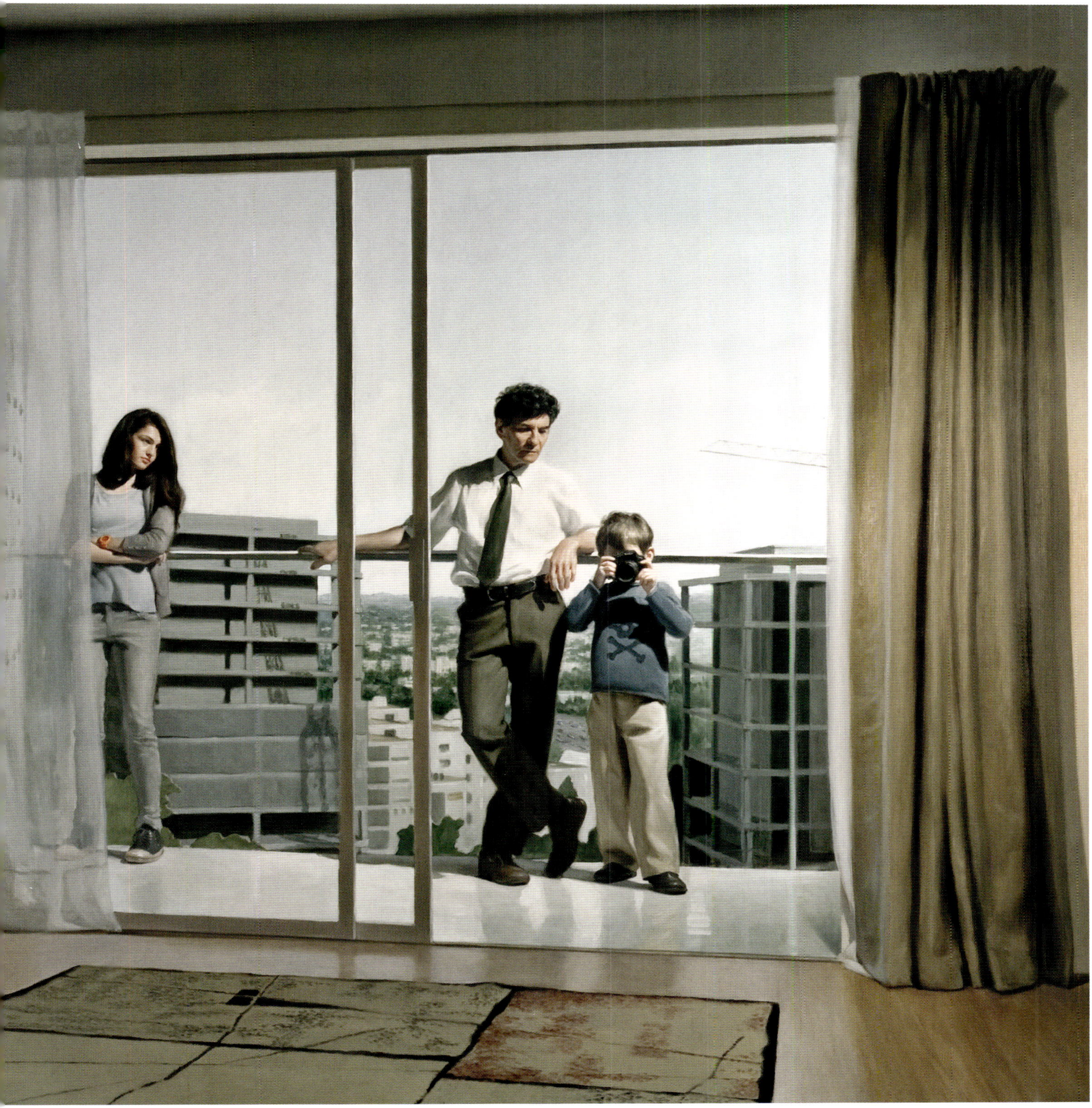

Swimming Hole
2011, oil on linen, 282 × 400 cm
(111 × 158 in).

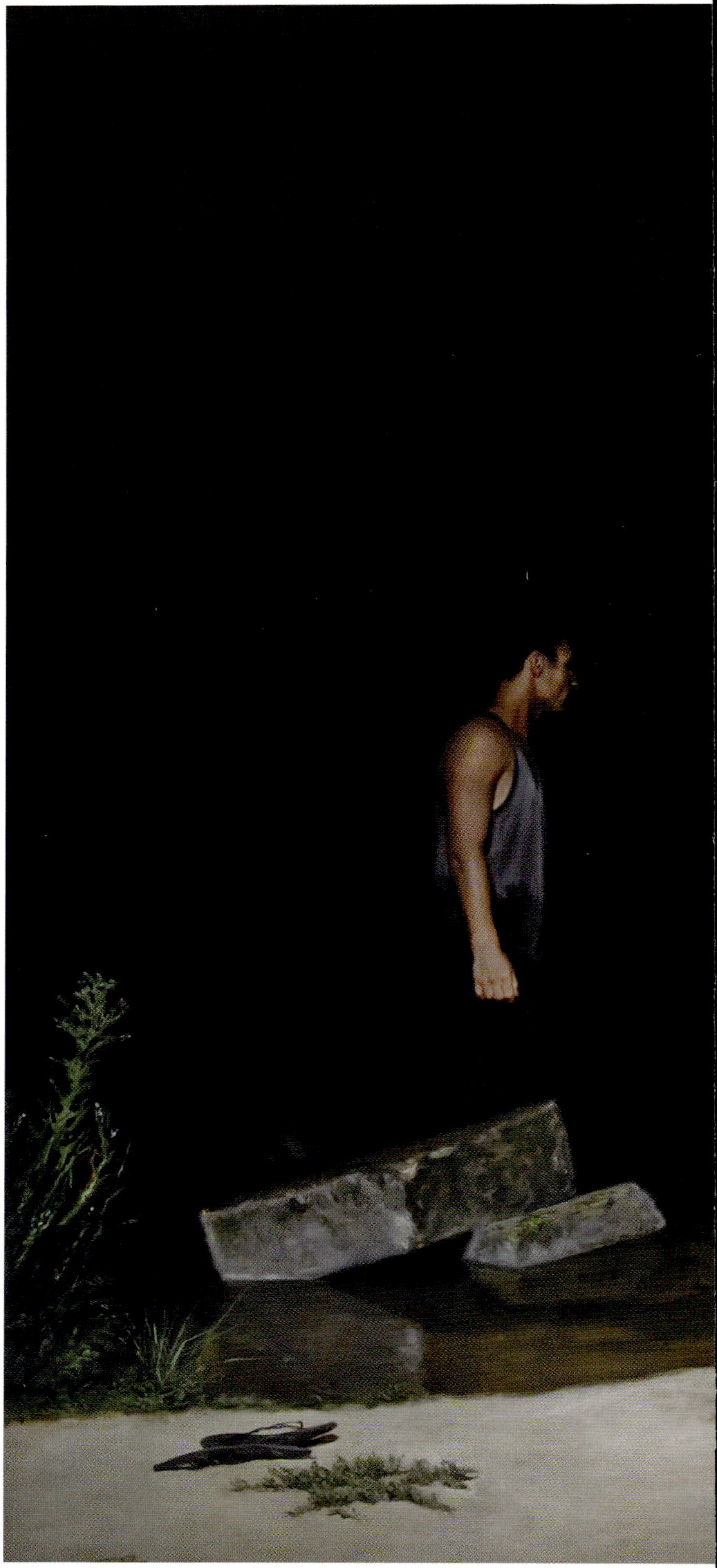

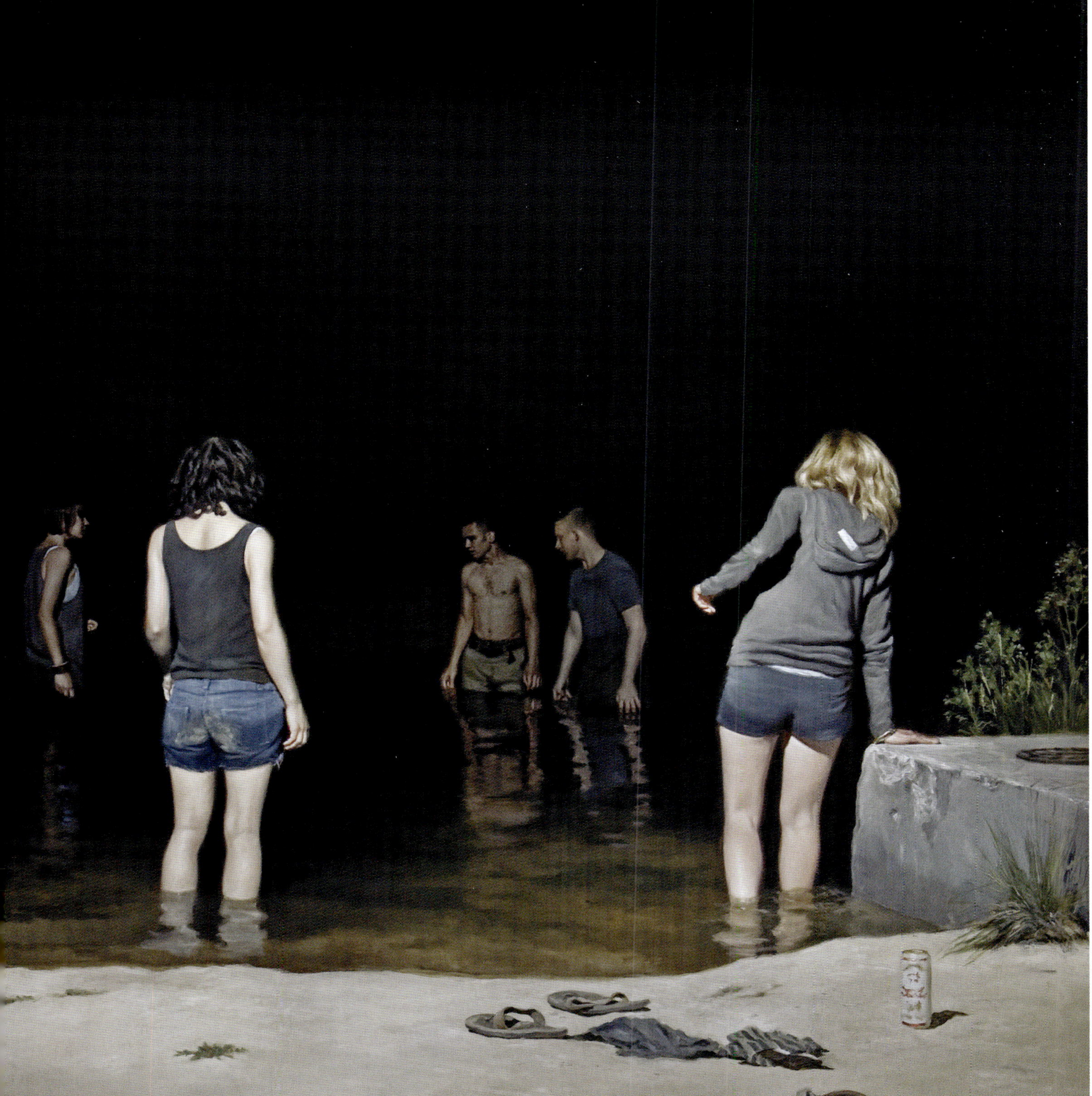

Lift I
2012, oil on linen, 100 × 150 cm
(39 × 59 in).

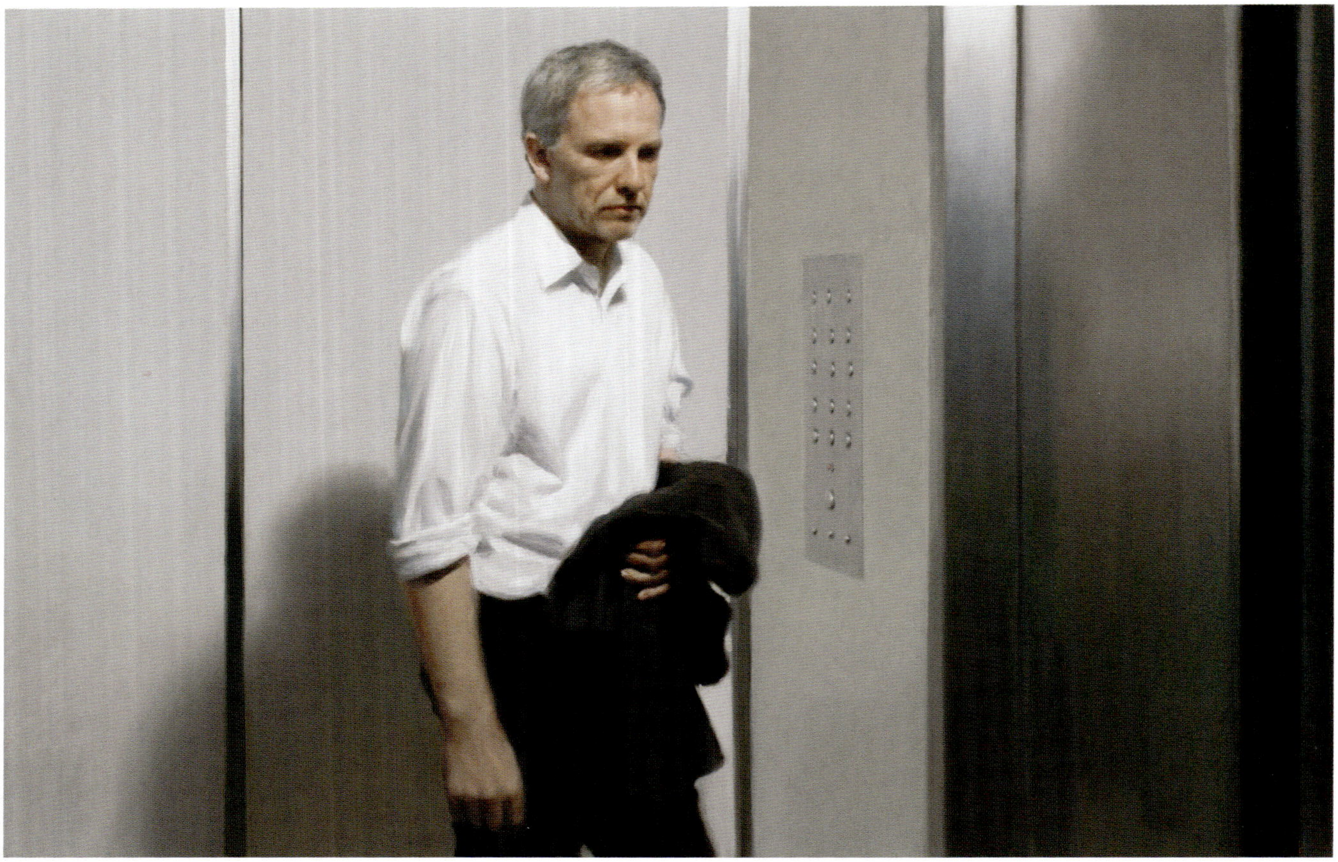

Lift II
2012, oil on linen, 100 × 150 cm
(39 × 59 in).

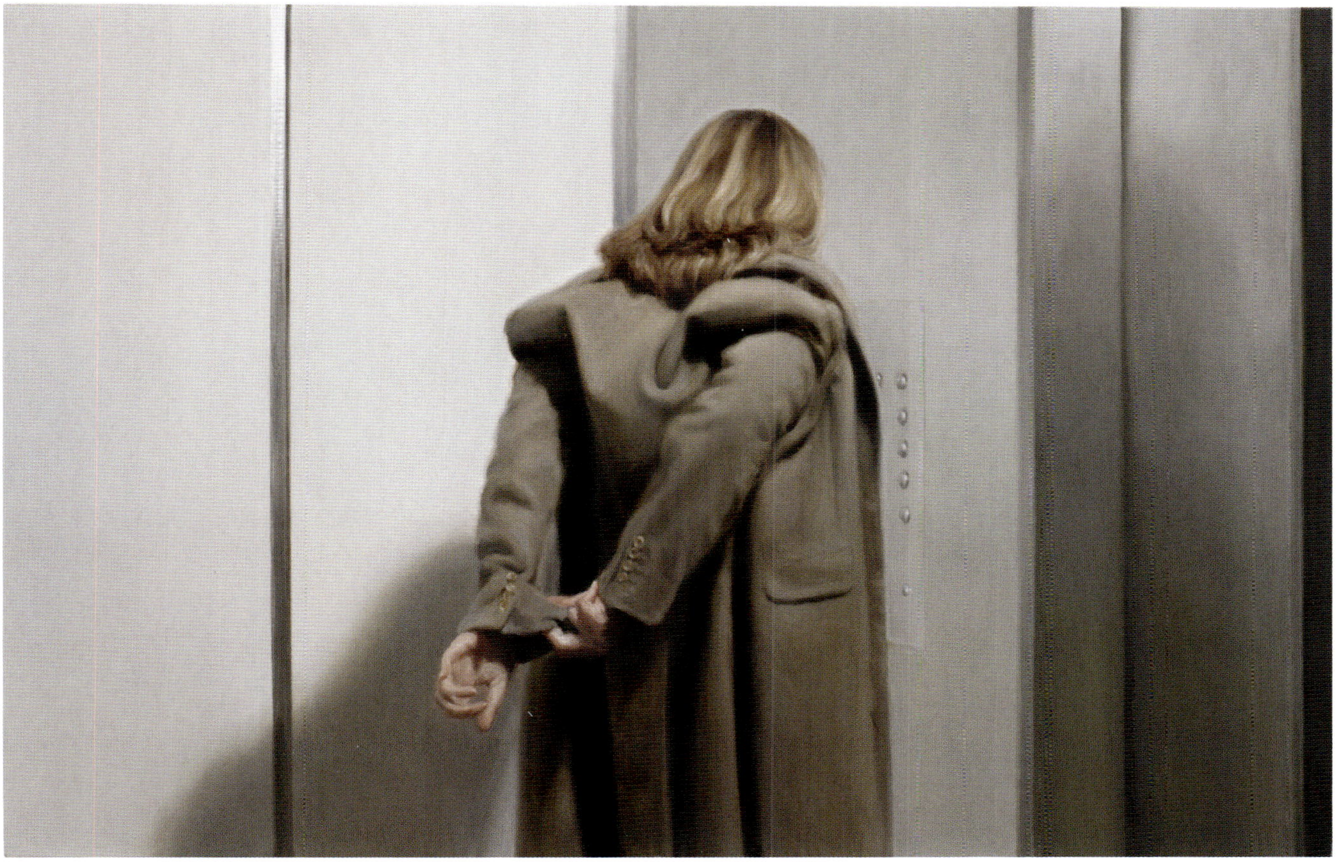

Another Hotel #4
2011, oil and varnish on aluminium
in perspex box frame, 135 × 155 cm
(53 × 61 in).

James White
Born: 1967, Tiverton (UK)
Lives: London

James White's paintings capture the everyday and the overlooked in the way that Weegee's crime-scene photographs captured violence. The British painter has compared his work to film noir, but another parallel that comes to mind is the work of 'hard-boiled' genre writers such as Raymond Chandler, Jim Thompson and Ross McDonald, who refused literary mannerisms to create a form that was much closer to their materialistic and savagely capitalistic environment. Refusing common painterly tricks such as showy brushstrokes, characters, juxtapositions of subject matter and even colour, these pictures dissect moments in their stark presentation, creating possible narratives and building up suspense. White graduated from the Royal College of Art with an MA in 1991.

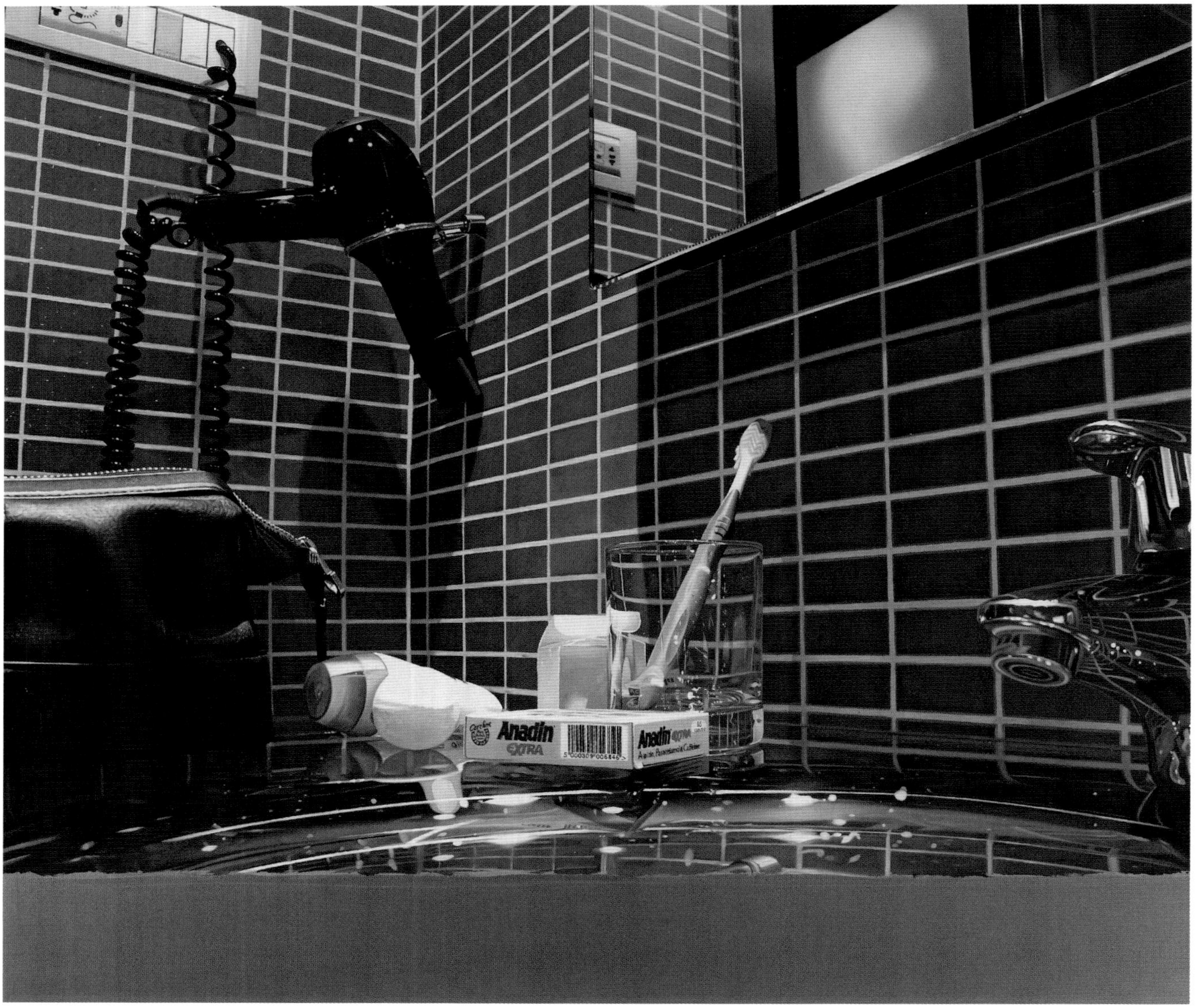

Style

The function of the act of painting in itself is significant in the sense that it serves to introduce a layer of time to a given moment. It focuses the gaze and lends the objects/scenes an intensity that would be missing if they were to remain as a photographic snapshot. It's important that the paintings aren't undermined or infected by any kind of artistic flourish; the style has to be as anonymous as possible for the images to resonate in the way I want them to. It did take a couple of years for me to feel that the paintings were doing what I wanted them to do both conceptually and technically.

Working on plywood and aluminium

I've never really worked on canvas, not even at art school. It just seemed wrong, I didn't want the texture of the canvas to be an issue and I certainly don't want to spend hours laying down coat after coat of gesso to remove that texture – the paintings themselves take long enough. My paintings aren't large and to get what I feel is the right ratio of detail to scale, a hard, smooth surface seems to work best. The choice of materials for the support, combined with the vitrine-like acrylic cases I use to enclose the panels, give the paintings a sculptural quality, a kind of 'objecthood'. As a result of this, hopefully there's a density to the work, which just wouldn't be present if the paintings were on canvas.

The still life tradition

I think it would be hard to deny a relationship to the still life tradition: much of my work does focus on the familiar objects we all use everyday and they are paintings after all. But in my case it's essential for them to appear as I find them, so there's more of a voyeuristic feel to the image. The images need to have that accidental quality that you don't really get with true still life. The objects are a focal point but they're not the subject matter – in this sense you could say that my work has more to do with Stephen Shore's road-trip photographs of the 1970s than it does with Pieter Claesz.

On the relationship with film and photography

The work does have a strong cinematic connection, there's a parallel with the 'cut-away' shot in film – the paintings function as a pause within a wider narrative. I've been thinking about this recently, especially in the new paintings: the image as a film still. Ed Ruscha's paintings and drawings titled *The End* are important for me, there are various different versions, but particularly those where the painting is cut in half by the division between each frame. There is a particular relationship [in my work] with photography, far more so than with painting really. They work best when it looks like I've released the shutter by accident – in order for the scenes in the paintings to resonate they need to have an incidental, throwaway quality to them, not composed at all. For the paintings to work in the way I want them to, the images have to contain anti-subject matter. There's nothing special about a folded newspaper on a table, or a half-finished cup of tea, but when seen within the context of a crime-scene photograph then that's another matter. There are certain things to which I keep returning, like hotel rooms, and I've made a few paintings recently that take a view up or down a staircase or ladder. With the newer paintings there's a stronger psychological element, a kind of Hitchcockian sense of ambient dread.

What painting does that photography, film and digital media can never do is allow the viewer direct access to the work itself, and when I say work I mean the actual physical evidence of artistic labour, to connect with the author, to occupy the same space in front of the work as the person who created it. When I'm in a museum with my nose up as close to that special painting as is allowed, I'm sharing that engagement with the work, with its maker – we all know the feeling.

The Sink
2008, oil and varnish on birch-ply
in perspex box frame, 75 × 100 cm
(29½ × 39 in).

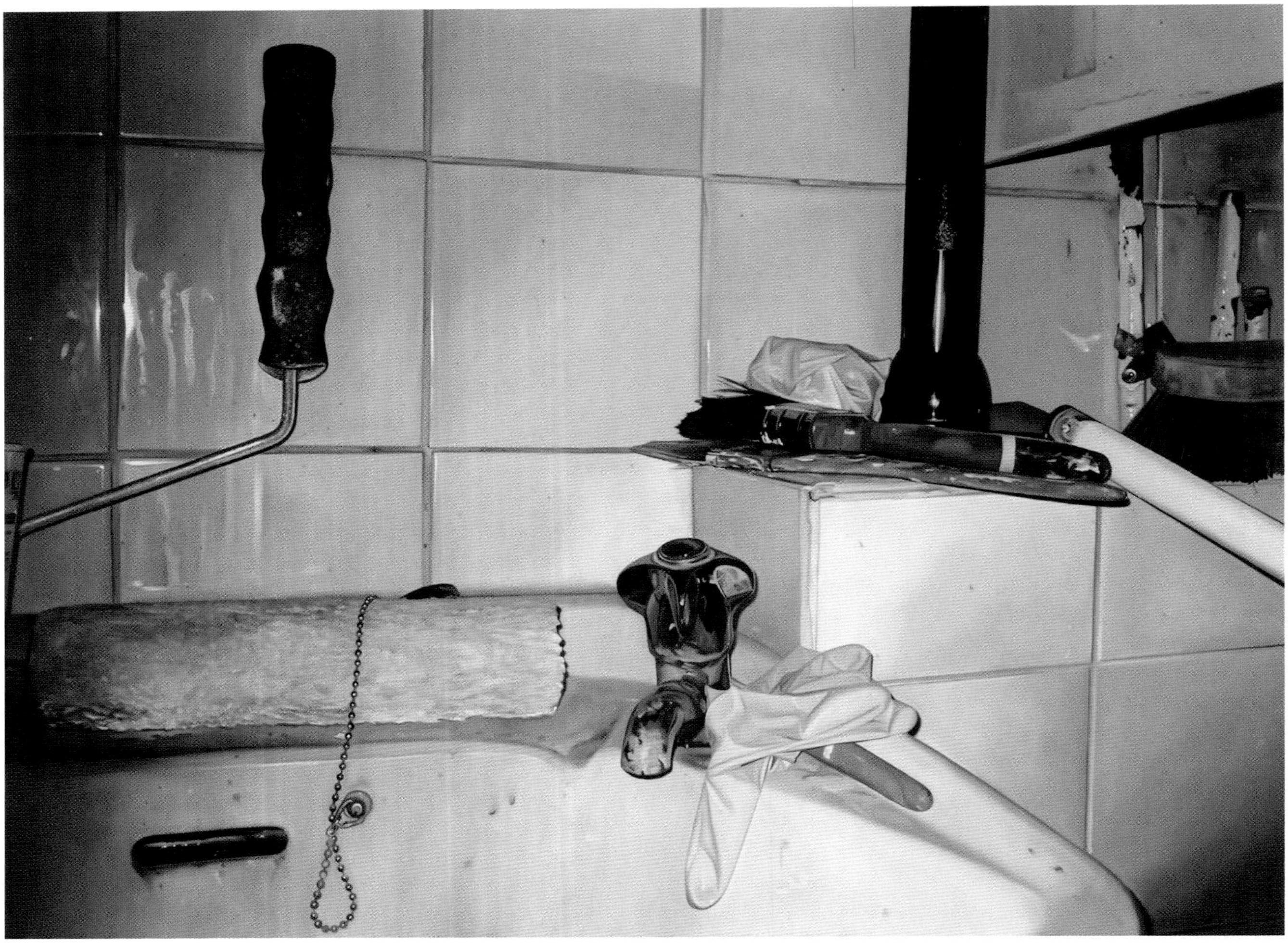

Burger Box
2010, oil and varnish on birch-ply
in perspex box frame, 103 × 123 cm
(41 × 48 in).

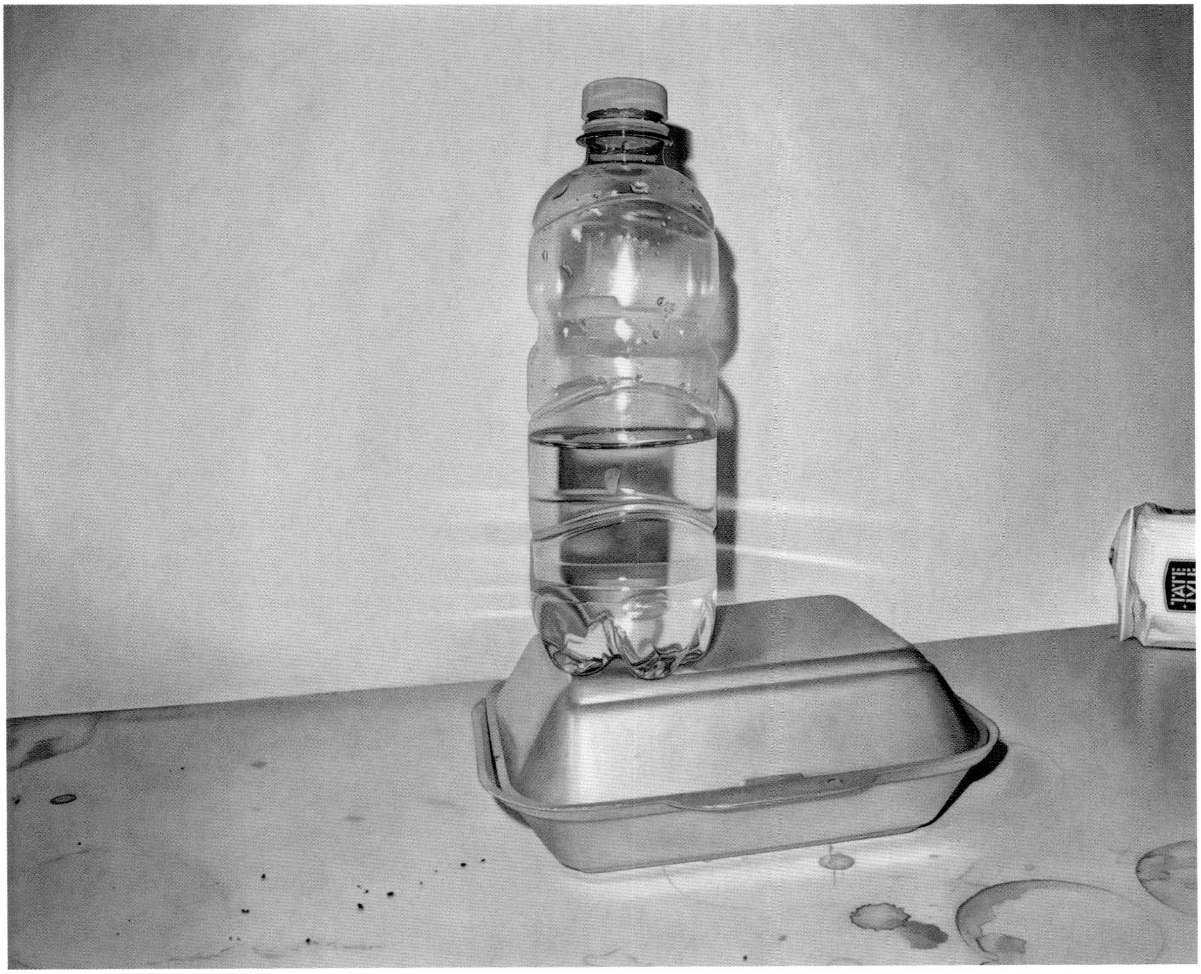

R six four double seven one
2007, oil and varnish on birch-ply in
perspex box frame, 130 × 100 cm
(51 × 39 in).

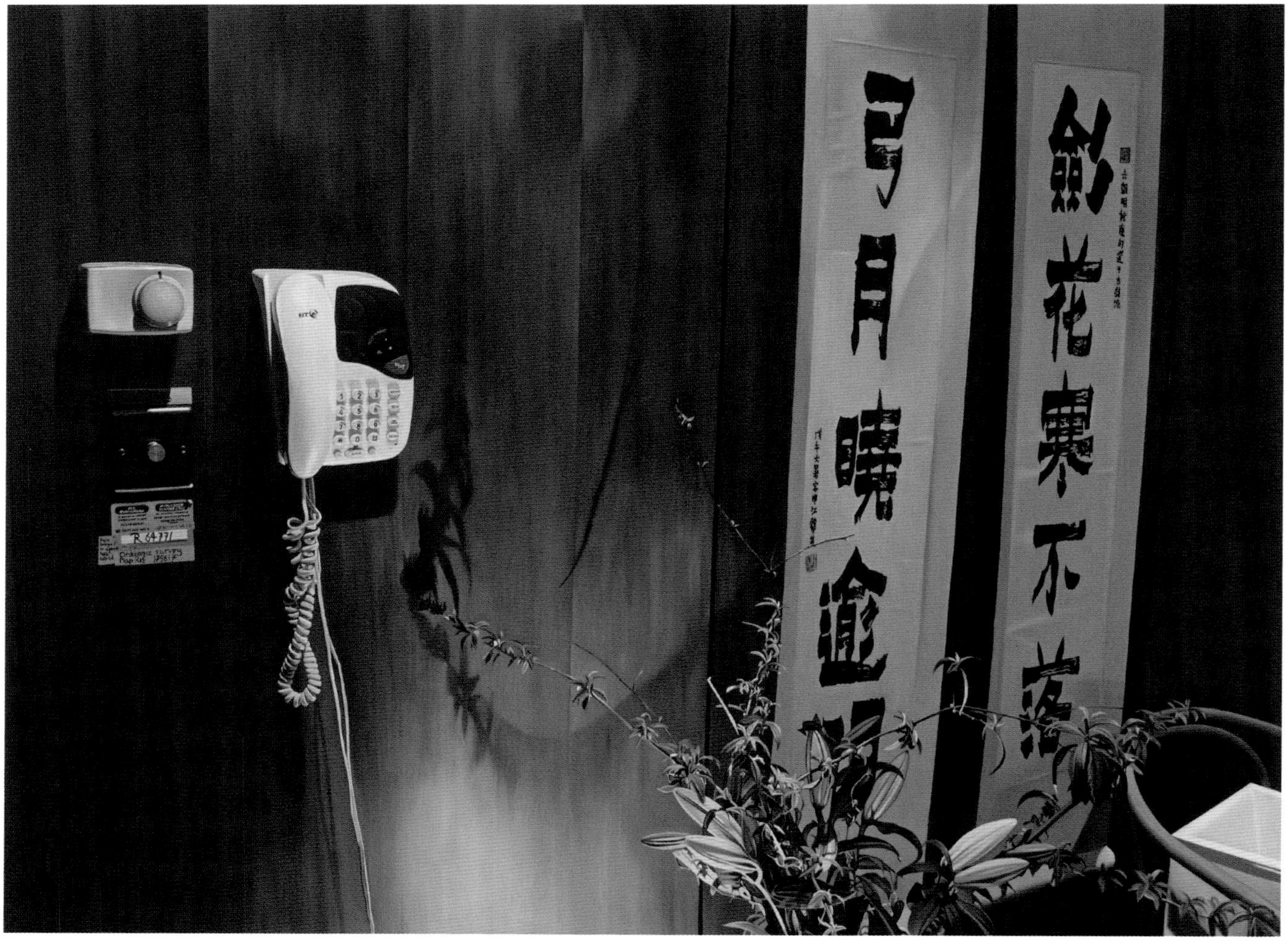

The Door (Ajar)
2012, oil and varnish on aluminium panel
in perspex box frame, 124 × 124 cm
(50 × 50 in).

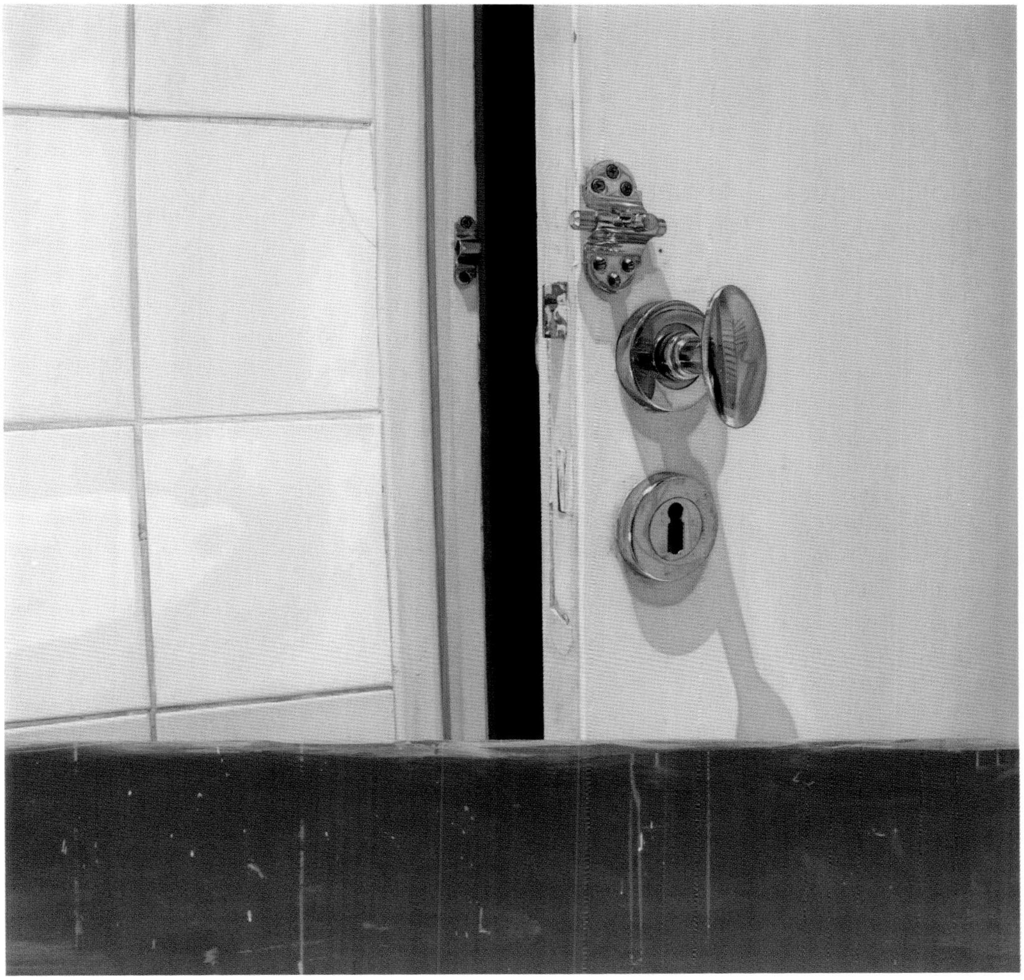

Mother with Child
2007, oil on canvas, 55 × 50 cm
(21⅝ × 19¾ in).

Uwe Wittwer
Born: 1954, Zurich
Lives: Zurich

Uwe Wittwer plucks images seemingly at random, like memory would do, from the labyrinth of the Internet. He traces the trajectory of each through time, patiently uncovering the feelings latent within them: violence, loss or moments of happiness (the paintings often seem to glow in reddish spots like hot embers). The painter's careful exploration of visual codes (from celluloid effects to clothes and poses) brings these elements back to life through his brushwork, in tantalizing visions that are neither of the past nor present but reside somewhere in between. It might be tempting to mention ghosts, but the subjects in Wittwer's paintings, even if at times removed or seen through a number of layers, still feel poignantly and physically alive.

Process
Most [of my] works are based on photographs found on the Internet. The memory plays an essential part – reflecting on how we remember things is central to a lot of my work. My mind is full of the works I've seen in museums over the years. Usually I [begin with a] sketch on the computer, be that for [producing a] painting, watercolour or inkjet.

The writer and critic Brian Dillon mentioned the 'state of reverie' – this reflects well my method of looking for images on the Internet. That and the above-mentioned images from museums for the referential works (appropriation). I make images, a practice of finding and remixing images as a Postmodernist proposition.

Subjects
There has to be something in an image that attracts my attention and that has something to do with my work as a whole. You can find a few threads in my work, around which this evolves: icyll/family albums; references to Old Masters; violence in different social forms. There are themes that run through my work over many years. Some subjects might lie dormant for a while and can be picked up again. Even though the subject is important, it is more about where the final work takes the observer, what happens from then on.

Location
Swiss light is not as intense as [the light] in southern England or northern Germany, where the land is more flat and the light so different, which is better for painting.

Influences
Without the classical painters I would not be doing what I do; they're a big influence. In the process of painting I'm confronted with some of the same questions they were – and the materials haven't changed much.

The role of painting in contemporary culture
The privilege of a painted image is that it can demand to be seen in real life, rather than reproduction. Another privilege is the slow process of creating the artwork. Obviously today painting does not play the same role as it did in the time of, say, Picasso. But a painted work has a material sensuality that is lacking in photography, for example. In painting you have to make decisions constantly: this is a cultural experience and I think this rubs off on the observer too. In fact, all this raises the question not so much of the role of painting, but whether art in general still has an impact on contemporary culture.

Advice to younger painters
My advice would be: put meaning into your work, not just beauty. Keep a high standard – formally and in terms of subject matter. Find a system for quality control over the years, look for feedback and criticism from others. Be aware of what's happening in the art world, but find your own language. Keeping a fixed work rhythm can help. The reality of an artist's life will most likely be less romantic than you'd expect. Be aware that the role of an artist is that of a creator but also that of an entrepreneur. Keep an inventory of your work. You can be friends with folks at galleries, but don't forget it's a working relationship and your work may need to come first when you part ways.

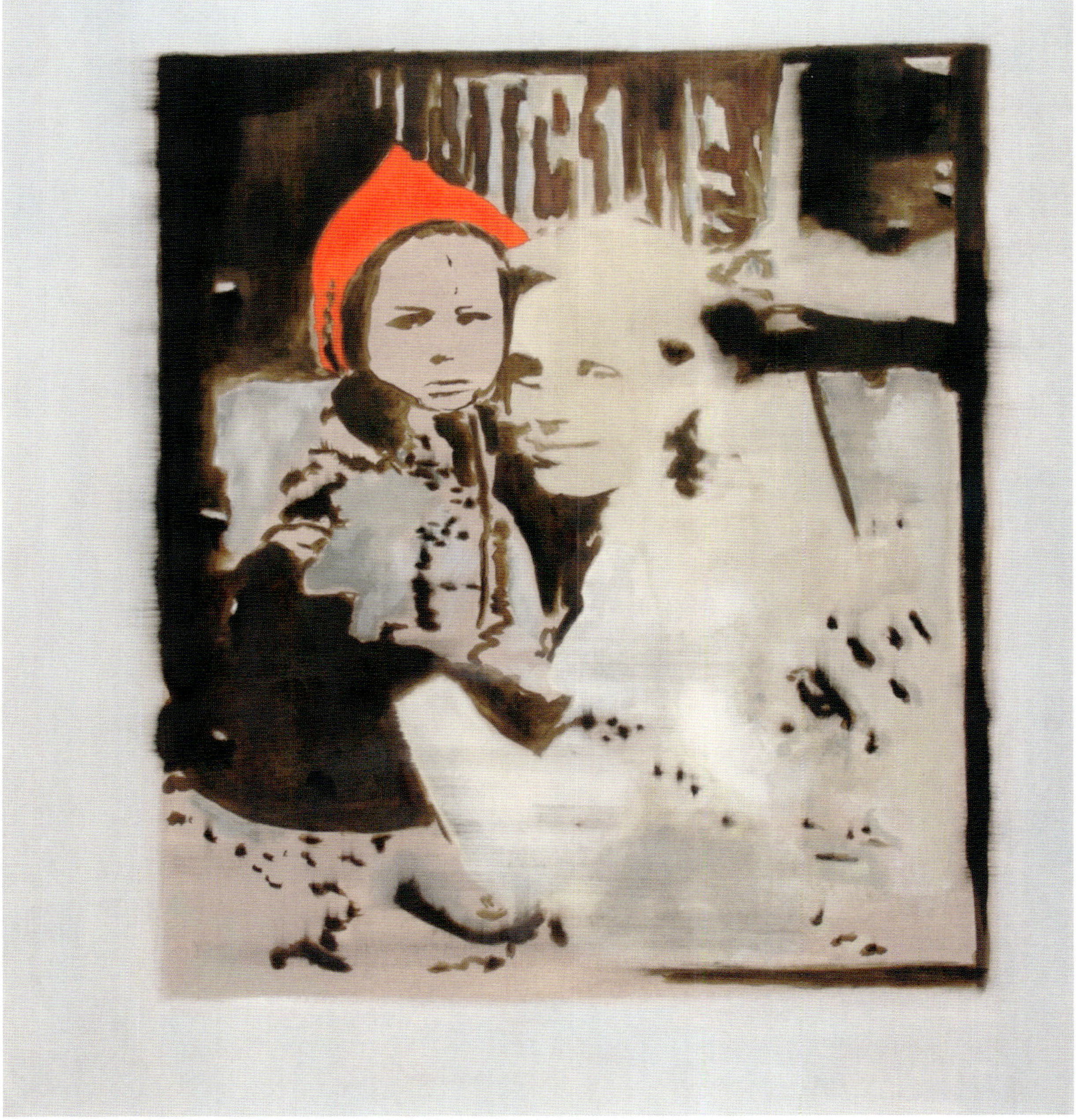

Watchtower Negative, Camp
2009, inkjet, 180 × 150 cm
(71 × 59 in).

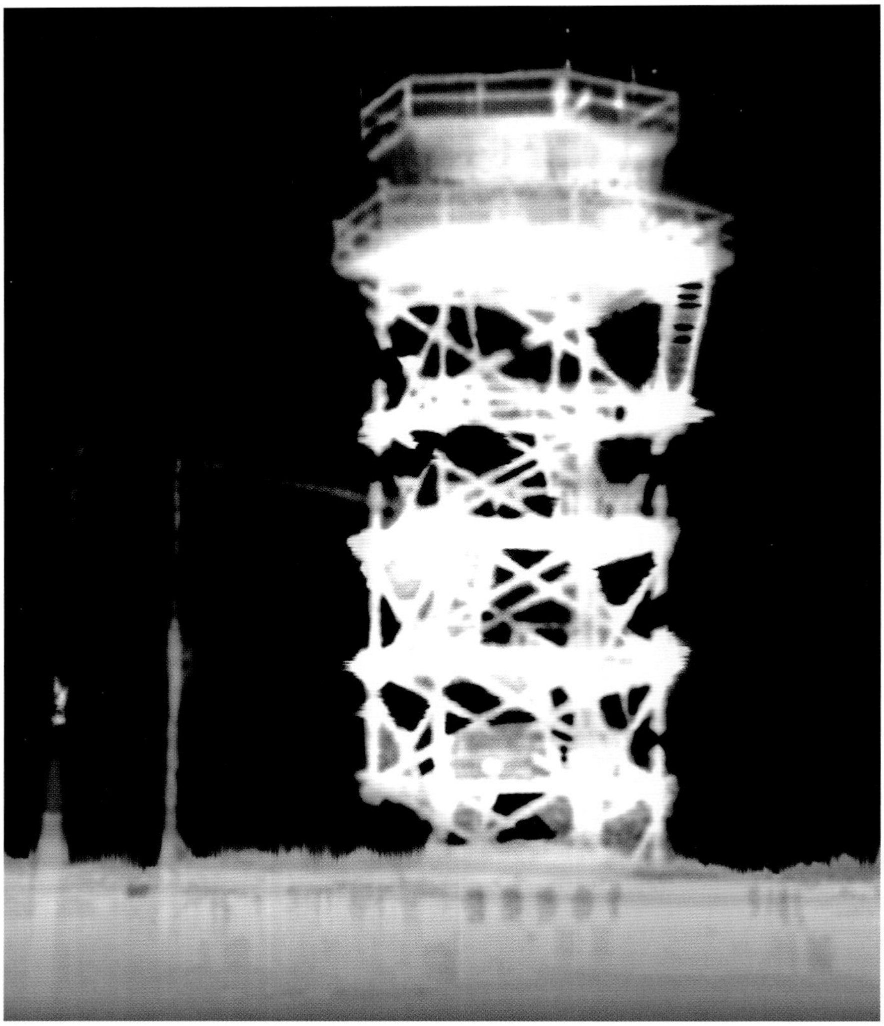

Three Sisters
2009, inkjet, 180 × 150 cm
(71 × 59 in).

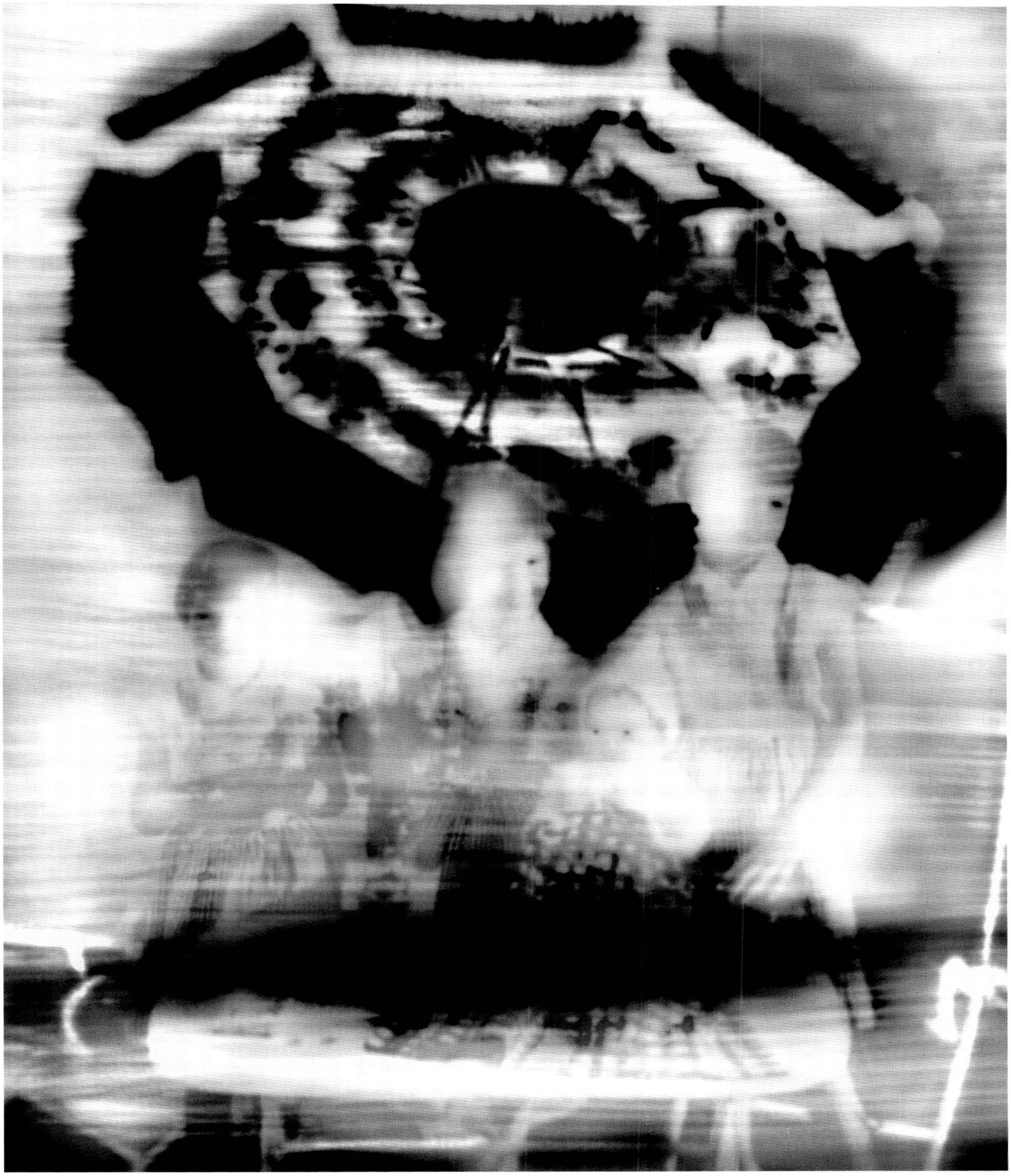

Hunt
2007, oil on canvas, 55 × 50 cm
(21⅝ × 19¾ in).

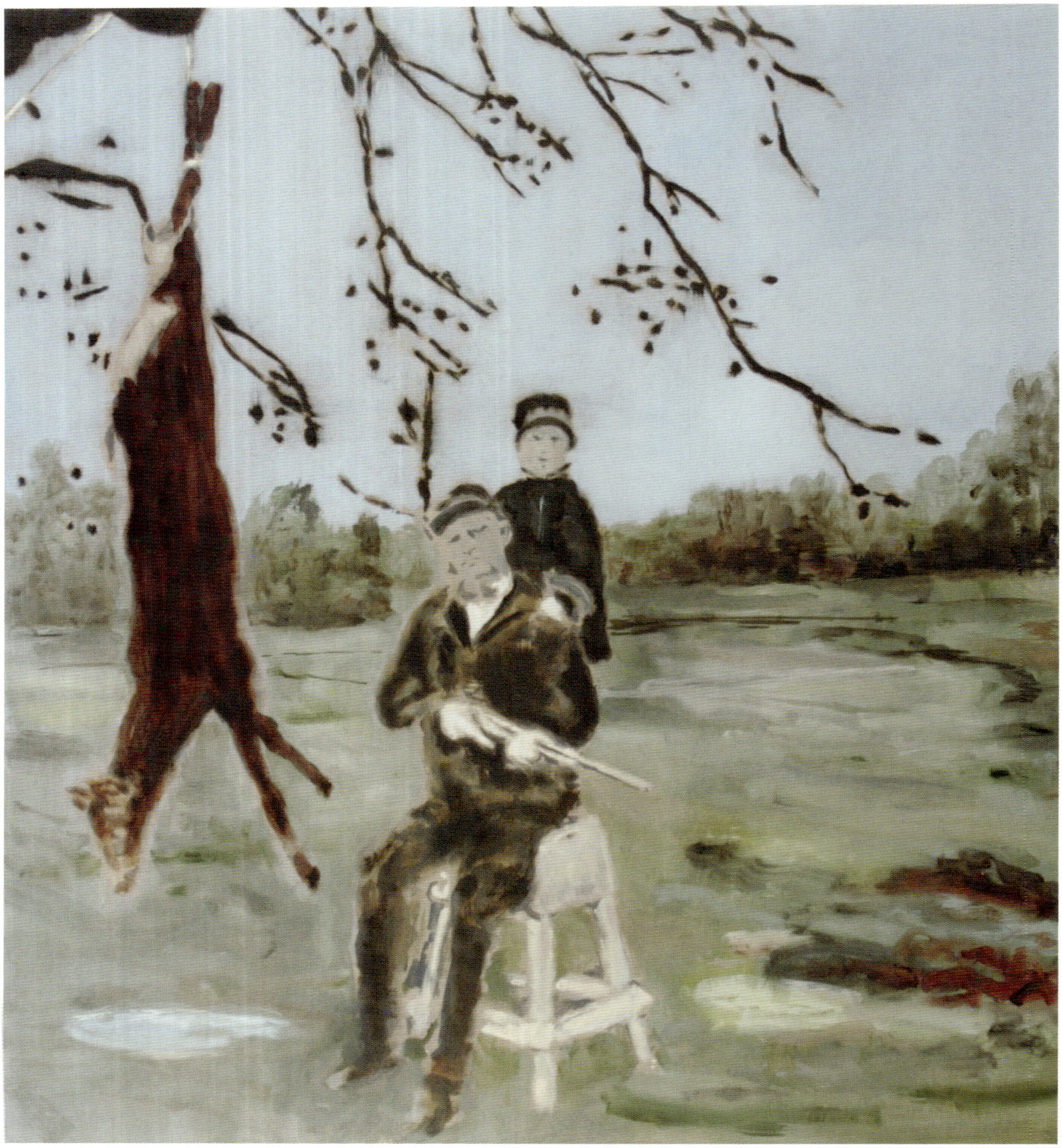

Three Sisters
2009, oil on canvas, 110 × 100 cm
(43 × 39 in).

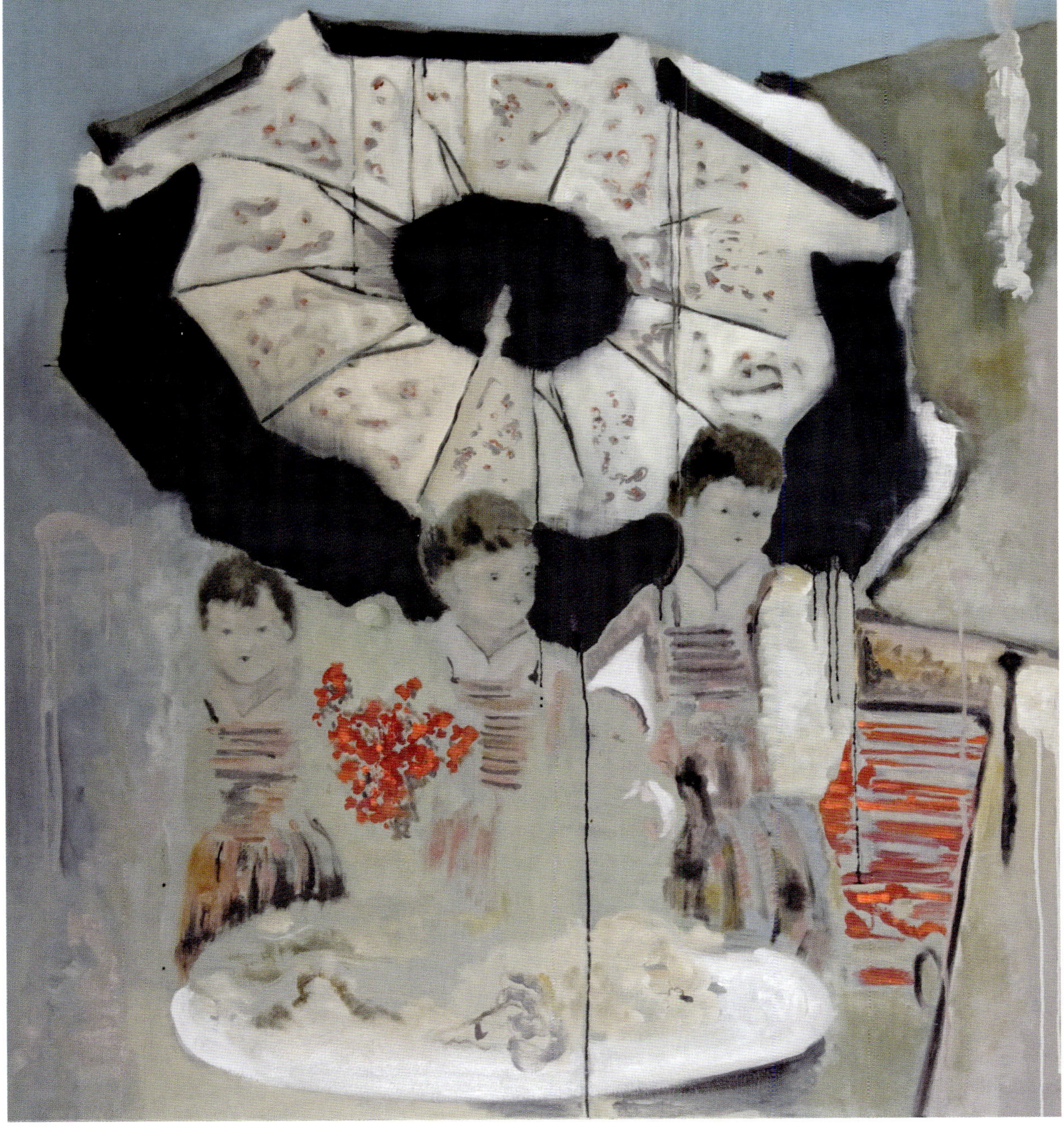

Hyper- and hypo-individualism, the post-Facebook portrait, the post image-capture still life, humanizing the feel of now, painting as a political act, recapturing presence

Part 2:
Unstill Lives

Faced with a unique and unforgettable moment, the natural reflex of our contemporaries is to take up a mobile phone or a camera and snap a picture (to then send it out into the digital stratosphere). No key moment goes by without a blink towards social-media posterity. We are never completely *there*, while not being completely somewhere else either.

So, to put it mildly, the notion of *presence* has become problematic, and for most of us the present has become a battlefield of information fighting for our semi-comatose attention. 'This form of existential boredom and pain is what we depict,' we are told by artists Muntean and Rosenblum. 'Sometimes it seems that making and sharing such photographs replaces the actual experience.' Their paintings question if there is still a coherent structure to the self and, if that is so, 'how can we recapture it?'

For other painters, their first impulse is to take a step back and observe the interplay between presence and absence. Today, we are never far away from the gaze of cameras and this near ubiquity has created a (not entirely unjustified) sense that we are all constantly under surveillance. The idea of 'presence' includes this third person, this ominous observer. We are always looking over our shoulders, thinking: is someone filming this? This soft and all-pervasive paranoia is, for example, particularly acute in the work of Caroline Walker. In her London interiors, the Scottish painter finds the perfect oblique standpoint from which to measure the lives of their stage-managed occupants, observing her subjects from a precise middle distance between the intimacy portrayed and the intrusion of the artist, while we, the viewers, are left hanging in the balance.

Is there an escape from this labyrinth of reflections? This is one of the key questions facing the portrait painters of the post-Lucian Freud generation. If there is, perhaps it will be found through painting, a medium that – from the act of sitting to that of touching a wet surface and leaving a mark, to the considered response of looking it inspires – is all about sharing presence. Creating and capturing a shared presence in space and time, in the here and now, or the there and then: this is what the best portraits, landscapes and still lifes can still do. Alessandro Raho describes the ability of [portrait] painting 'to humanize the feel of now'; looking at Oda Jaune's portraits, we might be tempted to rephrase this as 'to flesh out the feel of now'.

Raho's idea assumes a different dimension in the paintings of Ronald Ophuis. The Dutch artist goes to great lengths to distance himself from normal journalistic procedures and look at the most atrocious acts, not just squarely in the face, but with precisely that humanizing gaze. The truth his scrutiny reveals is that these barbaric acts are committed by human beings, more often than not sane human beings, people like you and me. There is also a particularly human poignancy, something more difficult to glean from media images (whether in photographic or film form), in Tim Eitel's paintings of those on the edges of society, or Ayman Baalbaki's depictions of his homeland.

The post-Facebook portrait and the post-image capture still life are complex affairs, a game of hide and seek with presence. Like an archaeologist, the contemporary painter sieves through piles of media rubble, while constantly gauging the distortion of mediated distance and degenerated light.

Ayman Baalbaki
Born: 1975, Ras-El-Dekwayneh (Lebanon)
Lives: Beirut

Ayman Baalbaki was born in Lebanon in 1975 at the outbreak of the civil war that affected his country for 15 years. Officially ended in 1990, that war has left Lebanon in a state of constant turmoil and with social and political consequences that are still dramatically present. Baalbaki's painting practice stems from his need to understand and define the complicated circumstances surrounding him. His passionate commitment to contemporary reality emerges not only in the subjects represented (soldiers, militants and urban landscapes) but also in the use of a thick, vibrant brushstroke. In this way the artist allows the physicality of his gesture to become the most immediately powerful vehicle of representation.

Background
Painting was always present in my daily life. I was born into an artistic family (my father and uncle were both painters), and other than the artistic background, literature, politics and history were always present. I graduated in painting and sculpture from the Lebanese Institute of Fine Arts. I also attended the spatial art course at the École nationale supérieure des Arts Décoratifs (EnsAD) in Paris and I have a DEA [MFA equivalent] in Art of Images and Contemporary Art from the Université Paris 8. For me the school in Beirut was not useful, I would even say it was bad; there, my father's knowledge was more helpful. On the contrary, studying in Paris, as I have noticed since, was a key to filtrating my memory, to stepping directly towards the act of painting, and towards the things that move me most.

Subject matter
I express my fixations, trying to define what surrounds me and to reflect that in a personal language. I work on socio-political subjects because I live in a region of conflict. Wars and politics have always been present, since before I was born, and I can't run away from such reality. Starting from my local history and life in Lebanon and its surroundings, ideas become a conducting thread – one leads to another. Lately I have found a relationship between my principal themes and the general structure of Arabic pre-Islamic poetry, which deals with issues of loss, wandering and identity.

Process
A lot of work has gone into the process of developing my personal language, but I don't think that I have undergone harsh difficulties. I consider the wrong turns I made to have been necessary: all of this made me feel that my approach was produced naturally. Maybe because I was raised in an artistic household. In general, I stop painting a piece when I feel that my painting is mature and warm, and many times I rework a painting all over again because I decide to interfere when something feels incomplete.

On the social and political role of painting
While in Western culture the image is very important, Arabic and Semitic cultures give higher status to text, at the expense of the image. Painting still plays a part within the wider artistic scene, although this may vary from one civilization to another; this role is maintained if the painting is an attempt to express the urgency and complexity of the real. And this belief in the power of painting comes from my confidence in a human being's capacity for expression, whatever his means are.

On painting and digital technology
Despite the speed of technology, the presence of painting is still strongly established. Digital art lacks the physical approach of painting, and thus loses matter and sensibility, even though Photoshop is very effective for many artists.

Al Mulatham
2010, acrylic on printed fabric laid on canvas, 200 × 150 cm (79 × 59 in).

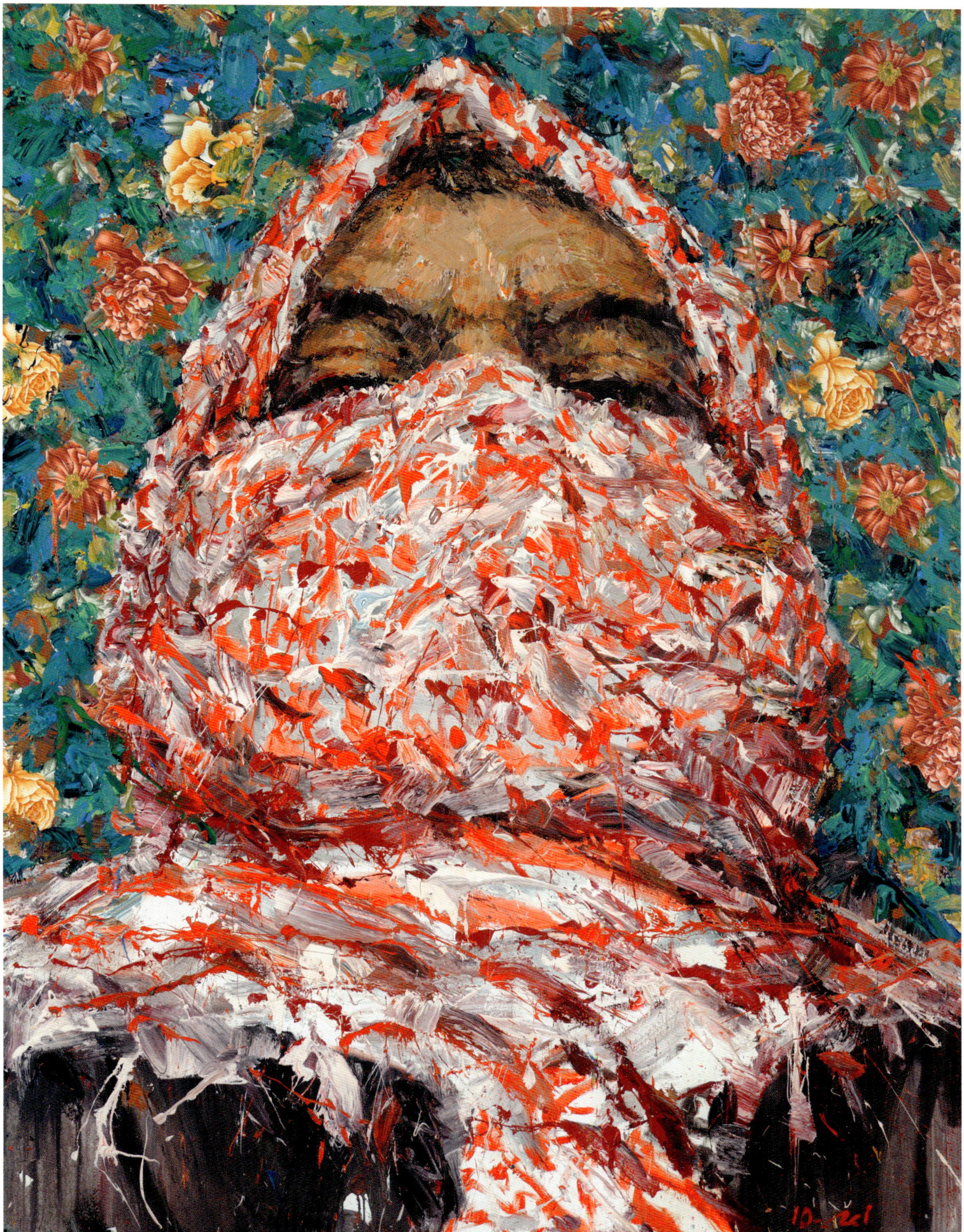

Al Mulatham
2002, acrylic and ink on paper,
160 × 110 cm (63 × 43 in).

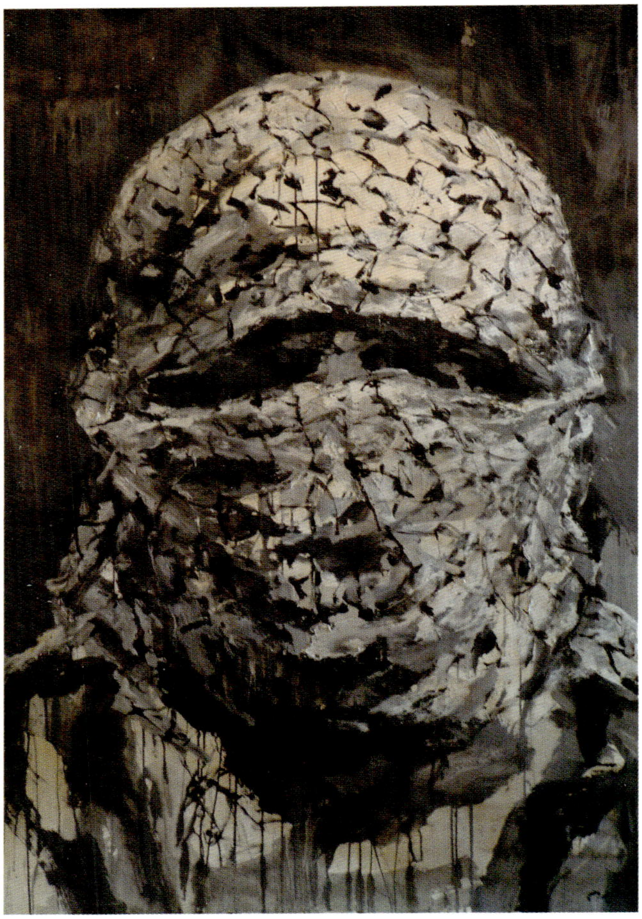

Al Mulatham
2005, acrylic on canvas,
200 × 160 cm (79 × 63 in).

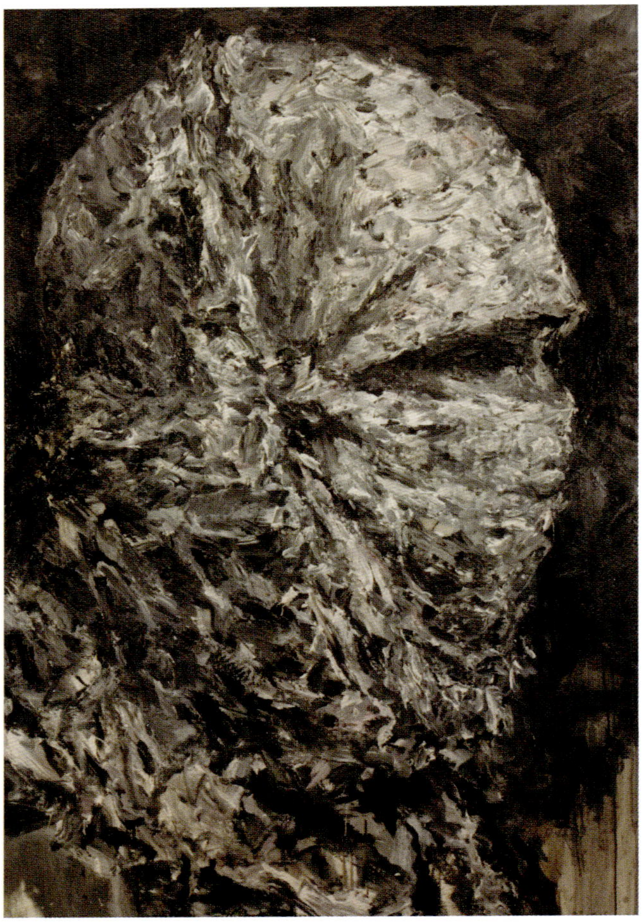

Merkabah (Vendor's Cart)
2009, mixed-media installation,
234 × 252 × 88 cm (92 × 99 × 35 in).

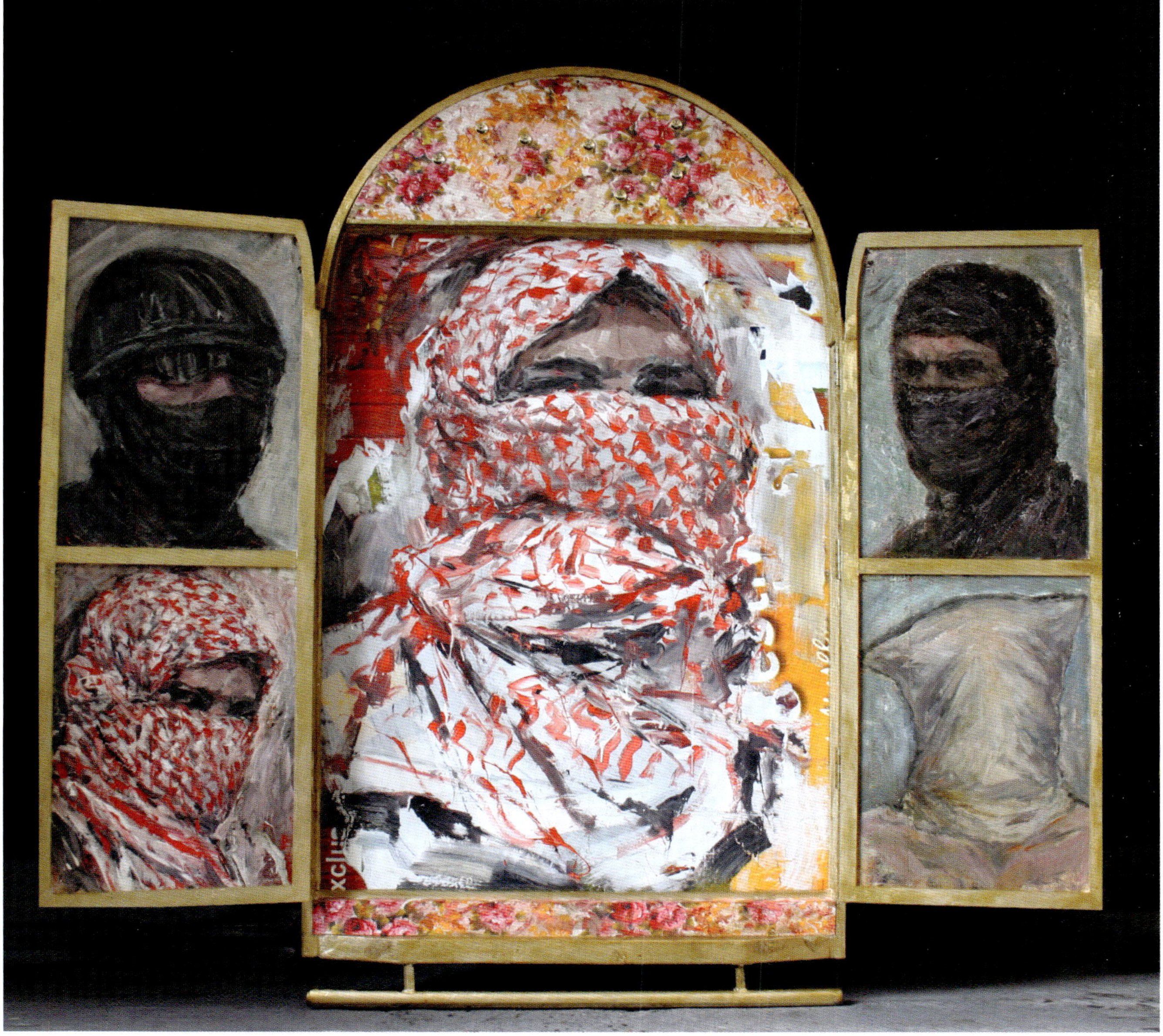

Burj El Murr
2011, acrylic on fabric laid on
canvas, 150 × 200 cm (59 × 79 in).

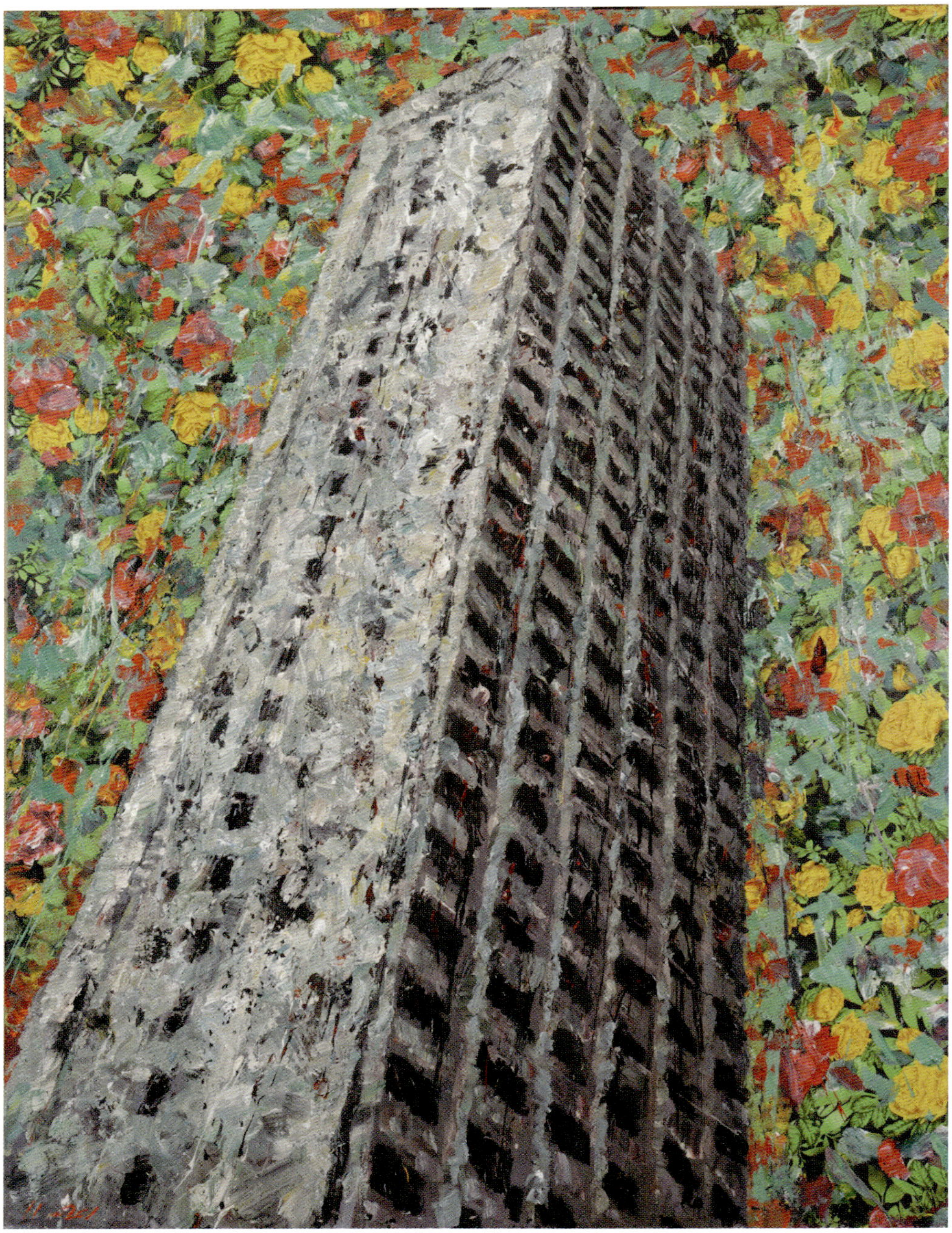

Untitled
2010, mixed media on canvas,
144 × 206 cm (56¾ × 81 in).

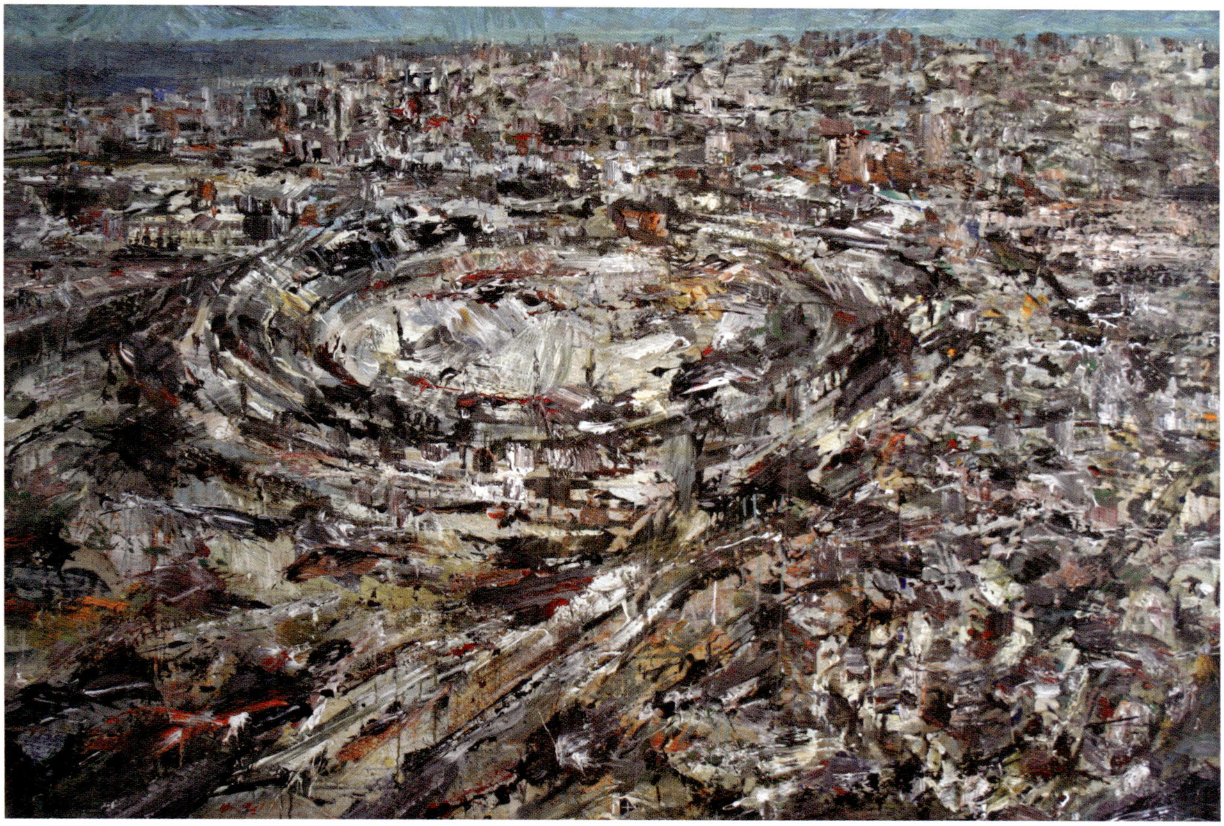

La Croix (The Cross)
2012, oil on canvas, 195 × 140 cm
(76¾ × 55 in).

François Bard
Born: 1959, Lille (France)
Lives: Paris and Burgundy

Parisian François Bard's paintings speak the language of the street, still somewhat rare in his chosen medium of classical oil painting. His subjects do not stand in the sober and reflective poses of traditional portraiture, but rather seem to be waiting for a bus, about to go into a meeting, smoking a cigarette on a balcony – or else to have come out of an action movie. Bard's attention to clothes and accessories is equally revealing: the painter makes polo shirts, tracksuits and trainers speak. His characters are not the traditional well-behaved painterly subjects either, and a strong undercurrent of threat is brought to the fore by perfectly captured clashes of light, colour and texture.

Background
There was no artist in the family. I always wanted to live and work as an artist. I think I was 7 or 8 when I saw a dusk scene by Renoir in a book at the library in Troyes and thought I wanted to be an artist [Bard graduated from the École nationale supérieure des Beaux-Arts in Paris, in 1980].

On creating a personal style
Work, work and work: through work I could gradually find a way to express my artistic intentions. I tend to be suspicious of styles. I try to remain as instinctive as I can. Style is too often confused with a personal technique, which is a big mistake.

Process
It takes me approximately a week to paint a portrait, with a model who sits for me three hours every afternoon. I also use these moments to take photographs of the models. Usually I pick my models from everyday life. Initially, their own stories don't interest me. But the more I work with a model, the more I get to know them. They all have their own history and past, which eventually shows in the way they behave with me. At some point, whether I want it or not, this dimension, this human 'effect', appears in the paintings. This [the life of those around me] is the true source of inspiration. The point is to sublimate the routine [commonplace], to create a sort of contemporary icon – starting not from the divine but, on the contrary, from the real, simple basic facts of life and, gradually, growing toward a more mystical dimension.

Latent violence
I am interested in the dual nature of violence. It brings out the dark and more often unspoken part of man. To me, it has to do with the balance (or lack of balance) between life and death, light and shadow. As far as men are concerned, I am always a bit suspicious of the idea of beauty. I am instead interested in what each one has experienced in his life. This gives much more depth and reality to the painted characters.

The language of street fashion
I feel very attuned to street codes. They are the most honest reflection of today's world. I like logos, signs. And this does not specifically speak just about now, it is timeless.

Figurative painting today
Figurative painting is definitely back. I would say that it never disappeared. It was maybe just less visible, less fashionable. Painting this way is, to me, a way to go further, deeper into the search. But first, there must be a project, an intention. Painting can still capture the feeling of being alive today. It is a way of stopping time and thus becoming eternal. It goes beyond mere everyday life. To me, in a more conceptual way, it aims to speak to the soul. It might sound presumptuous, but I find icons in everyday life; I aim to 'lift up', to sublimate the prosaic.... The road is infinite and existential. It takes a lifetime ... and more!

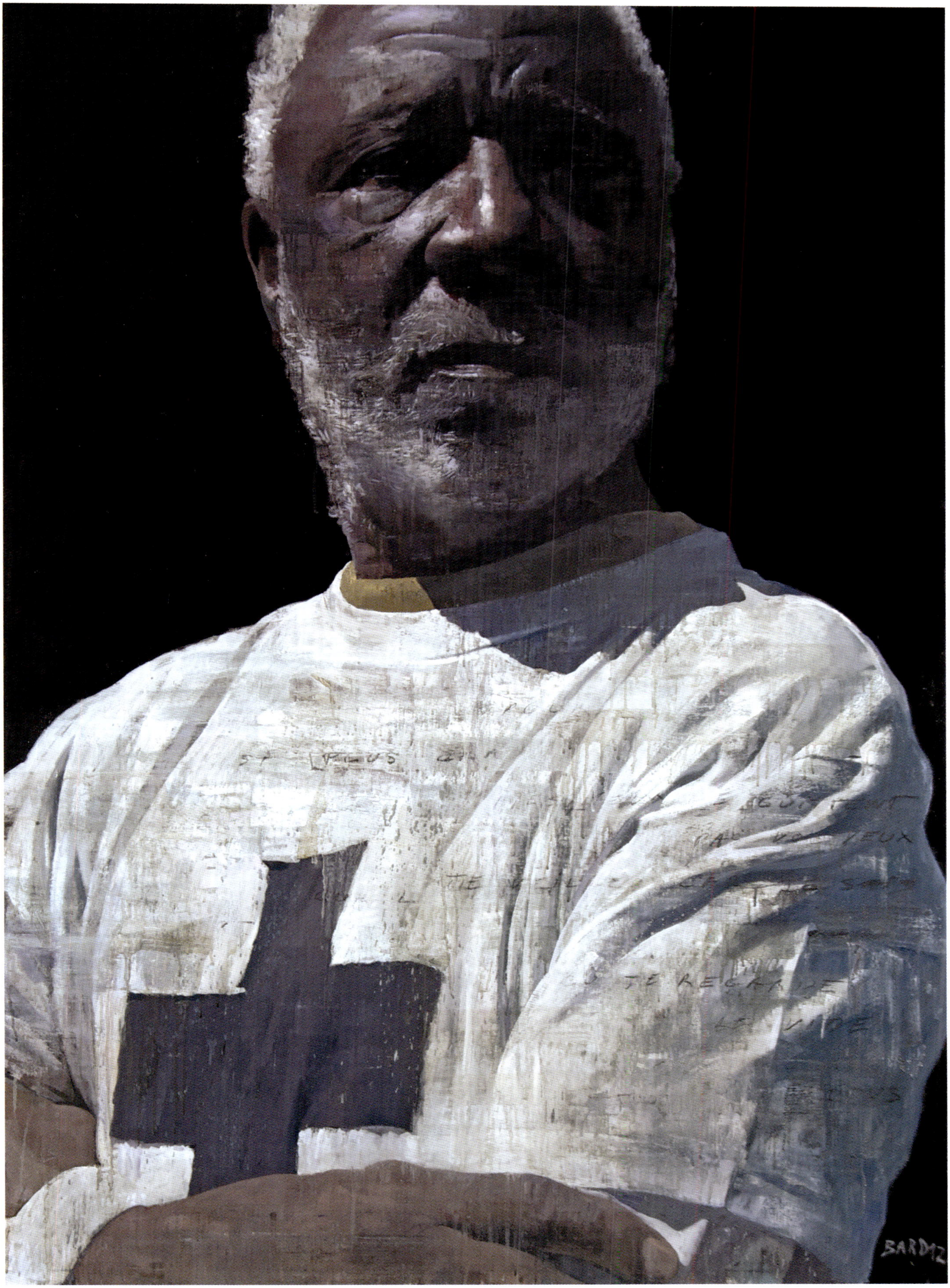
BARD12

L'hôtesse (The Hostess)
2011, oil on canvas, 160 × 160cm
(63 × 63 in).

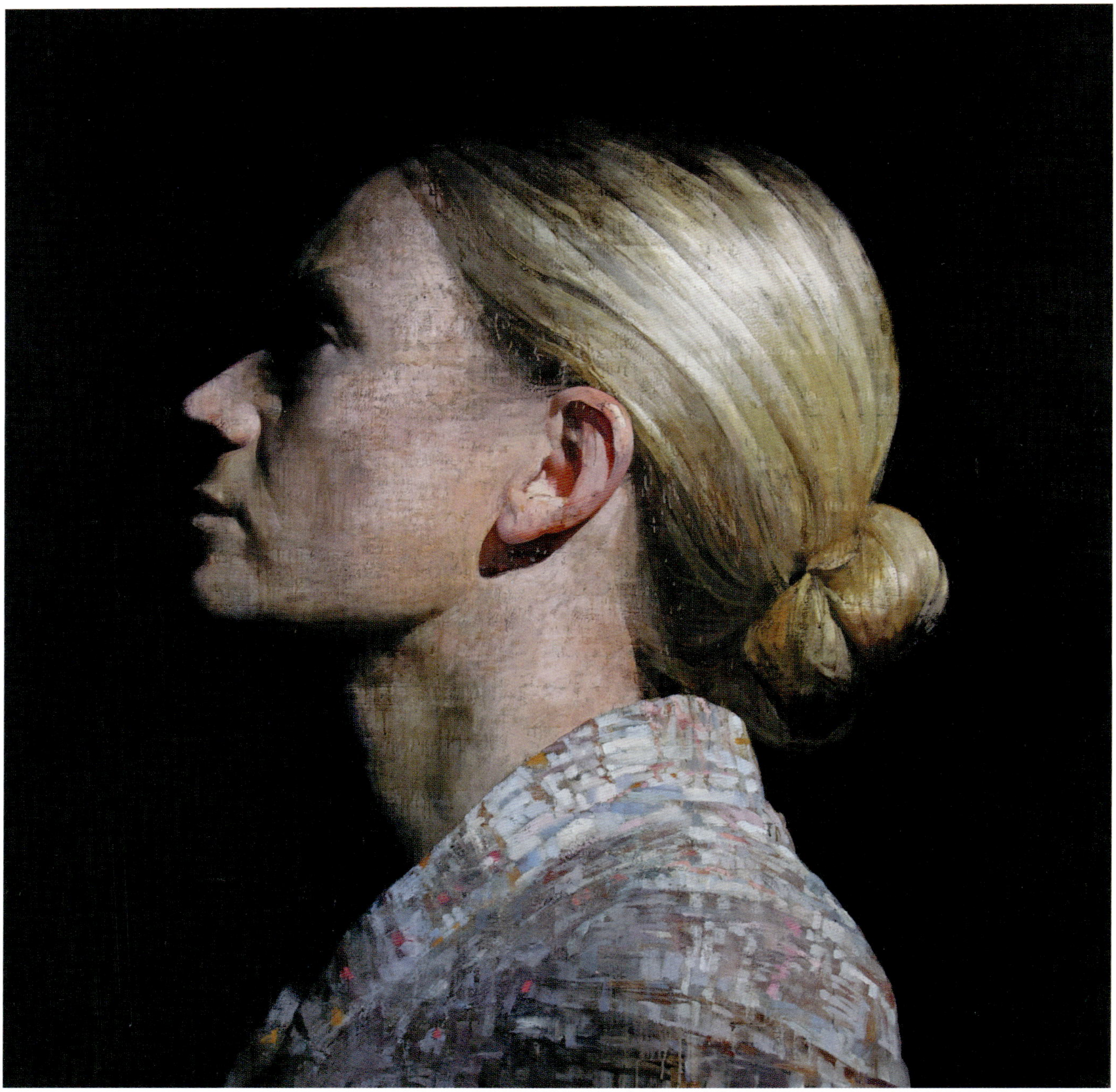

Contre-nuit (Counter-night)
2012, oil on canvas, 130 × 110cm
(51 × 43 in).

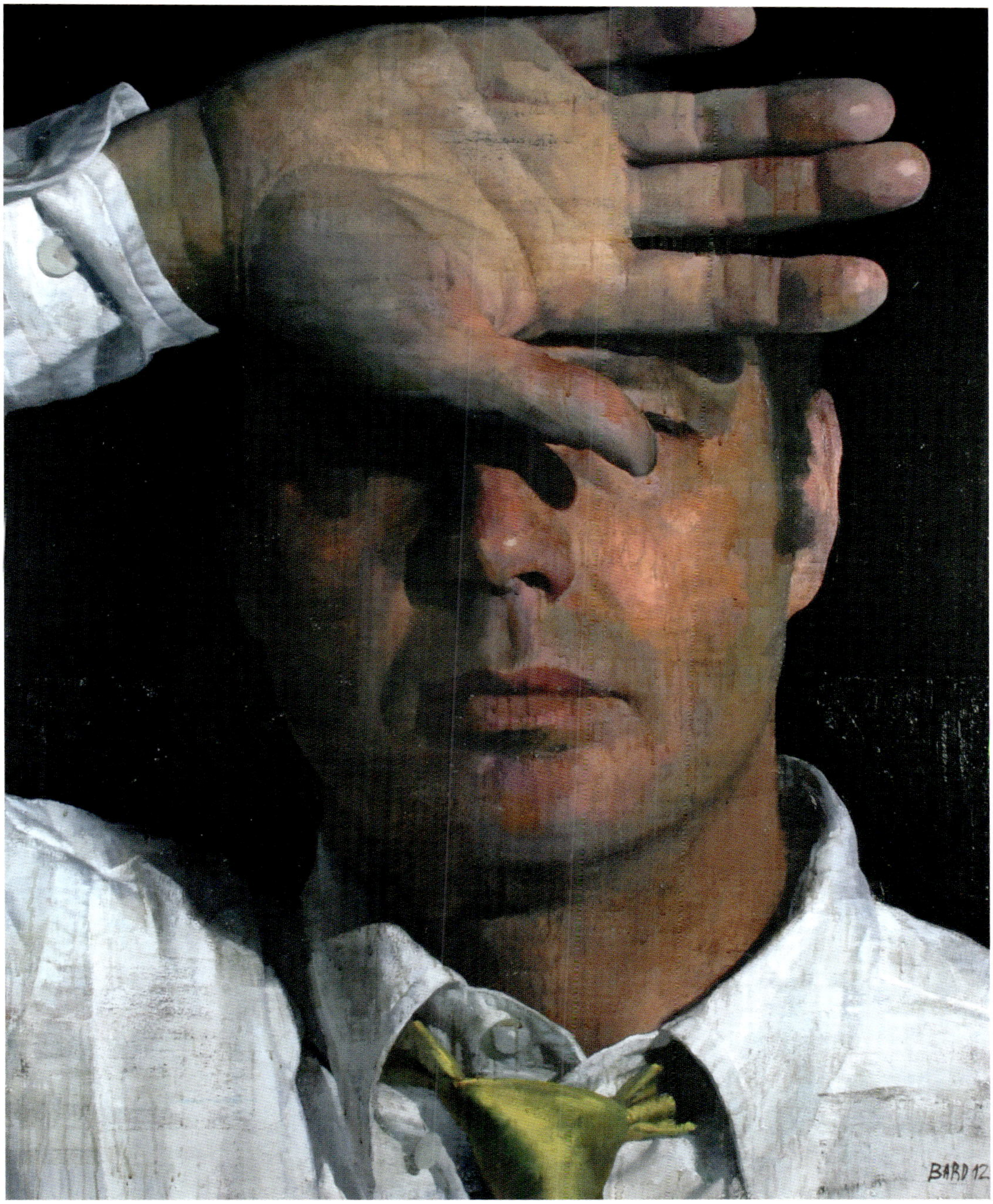

Vertige (Vertigo)
2012, oil on canvas, 130 × 170cm
(51 × 67 in).

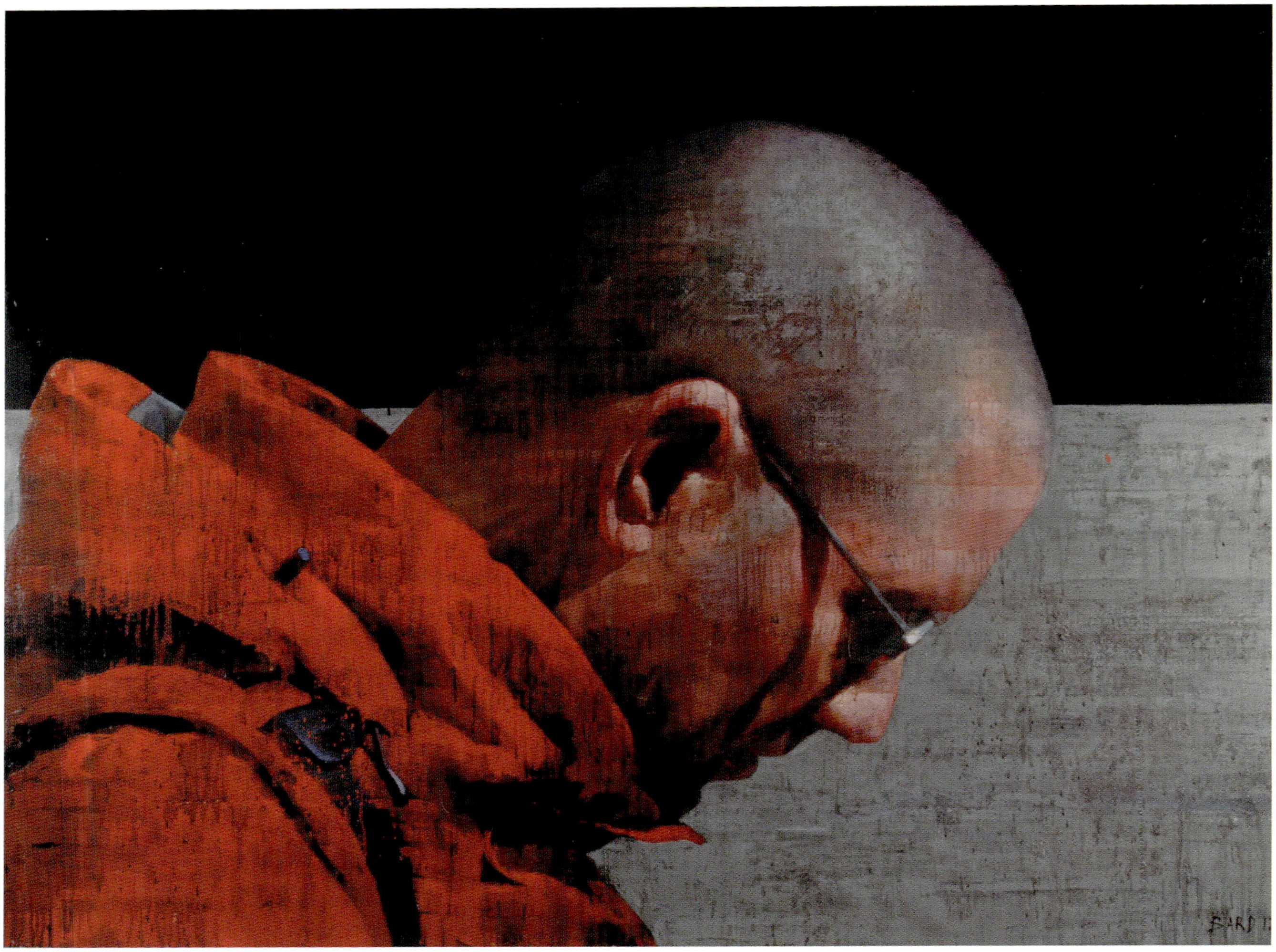

Contact
2012, oil on canvas, 130 × 170 cm
(51 × 67 in).

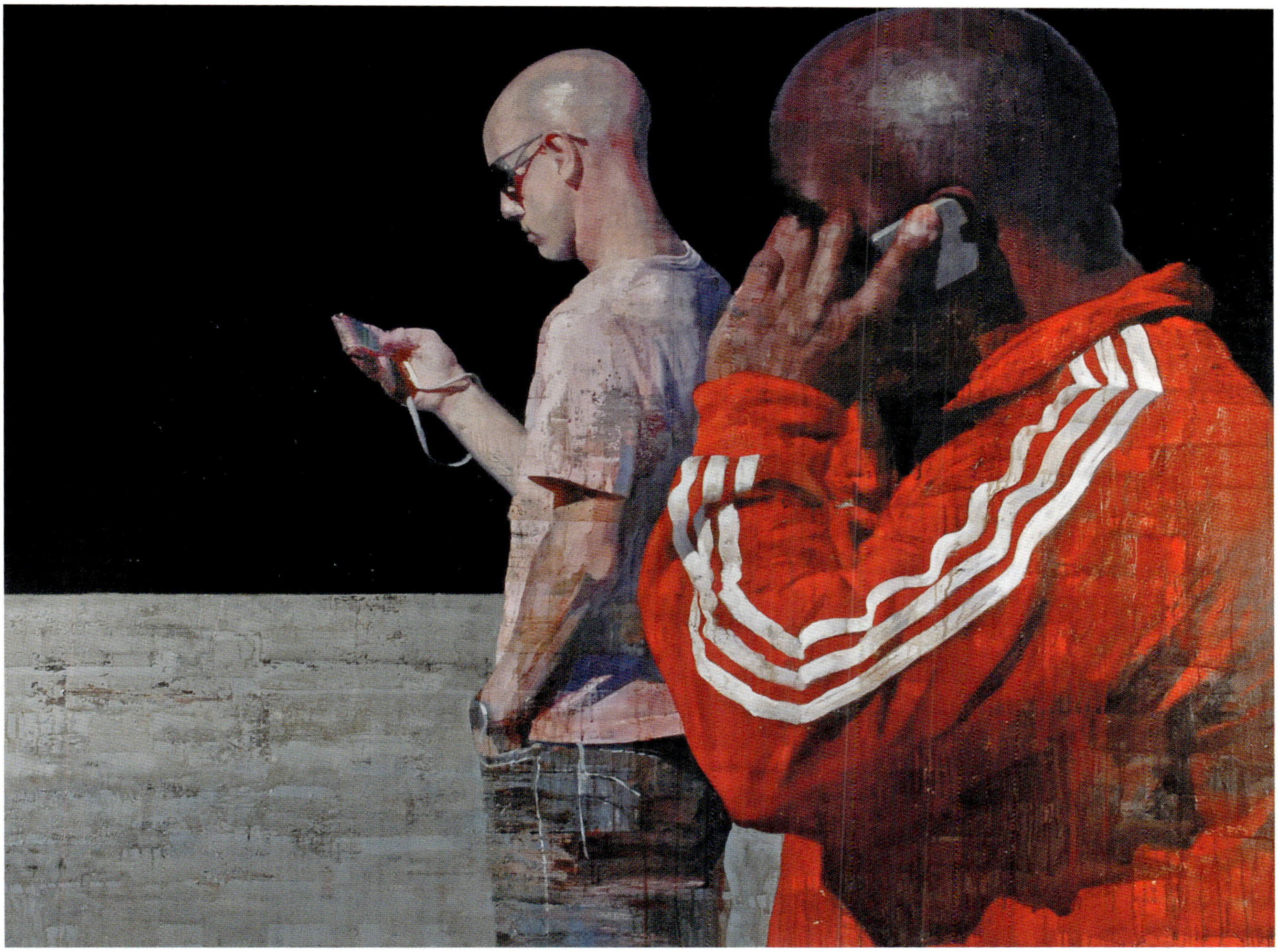

Charcoal (with blue bench)
2011, charcoal on paper, 108 × 150 cm
(43 × 59 in).

Kevin Cosgrove
Born: 1984, Navan (Ireland)
Lives: Dublin

The art of Kevin Cosgrove is a heartfelt meditation on the value of physical labour. His paintings make visible and palpable the concept behind his artistic practice, depicting workspaces filled with tools but deprived of any human presence. Furthermore, through the materiality of painting as a process and as a craft, Cosgrove – the son of a draughtsman-turned-miner – transforms into concrete action his belief in the merit inherent in working with humble dedication and passion.

Background
I am from a non-artistic background. There was an appreciation for the arts but also a distance from that world of galleries and museums. This was probably typical for most people who lived outside the cities at the time. My father worked as a draughtsman at the beginning of his working life. His job also involved cartography and surveys for the mine he worked for. You could say what he did was a two-dimensional activity that was directly related to work carried out. It was both a utilitarian process and a craft for him. He engendered an appreciation for practical knowledge and honour in labour.

Becoming an artist
It was an ambition that built up momentum from a young age. I was quite disorientated in the school system. This led me to look outside school and normal career paths. I felt that there was a different form of logic besides formal education. Although I didn't really understand what an artist was at the time, I felt more capable in that field.

Art college was very positive for me [Cosgrove attended the Dún Laoghaire Institute of Art Design and Technology and the National College of Art and Design, in Dublin]. While still an institution it [the National College] was very liberating from my perspective. We were left largely to our own devices and, if we wished, we were free to dip into one discipline or another. Most of my activities were centred around painting. I spent some time working non-figuratively, developing my understanding of paint; figure – ground relationships, colour, form and composition, as well as investigating supports and presentation.

Subject matter
My paintings often depict depopulated workspaces. The motif of the workshop relates to my philosophy on the value of work and manual know-how. I had always found workshops interesting, mysterious and romantic as a child. This respect for manual logic had a special emphasis in my relationships with my father and brother. The motif also satisfied more literal themes that I wanted to address, questions I had about painting being a 'proper job'. Part of my initial impetus towards these spaces was the technical challenge they presented. I wanted to apply my trade to the best of my abilities, and the workshops provide a broad variety of objects and references to work with. This kind of reflexive approach felt like the most honest path from which to work.

Ideal masters
I look regularly for cues from historical painters, such as Velázquez, Rembrandt, Goya, Corot, Courbet and Manet. I see these painters as links in a long chain of artists who had an intuitive understanding of the medium and the language of paint. When painting I tend to seek out things like light gleaming off metal tools, or the contours and folds in a pair of discarded overalls. When rendering such details I get a sense of connection or participation in the historical tropes of painting. This practice of looking back also corresponds with my interest in the transference of skill and techniques in general.

Process
I work mainly from photographs. Sometimes I add elements from previous paintings or photographs, or, occasionally, from art history. If I need a tree I like to borrow something

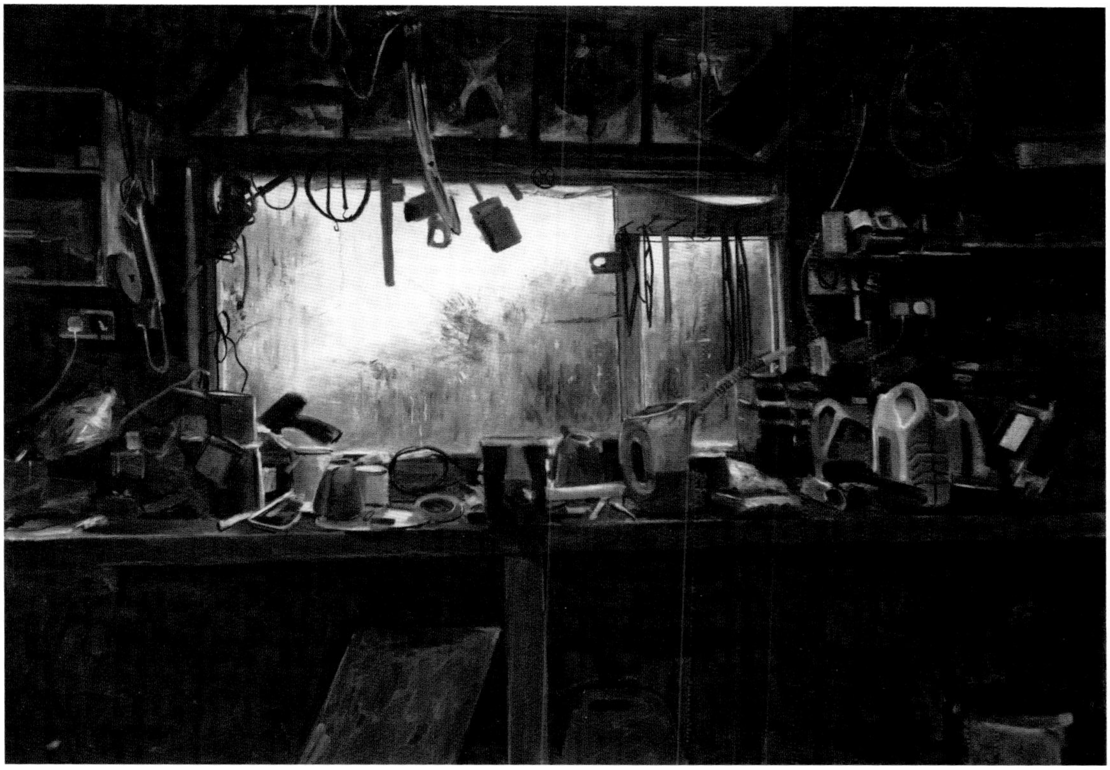

from Corot. I am very fond of his wispy, tangling birches. I like to embellish certain aspects of my photographic sources to draw out the narrative, composition or colour.

For some projects I like to make two paintings from the same image. This is a great way to work as it frees [me from] the need to follow the source. I move objects around or focus on different areas. When showing two paintings drawn from the same source people tend to look more closely at the quality of the application and the differences between them. They consider the painting before them and seldom refer their interest back to a 'photographic source'. That is liberating for me as it becomes more about paint.

When painting the first work, you get to resolve the difficult or problematic parts of the composition. You go to the next version with that experience. Sometimes you get beaten twice and that's fine too. For me the practice has always been about the consistency and success of methodologies or understanding through doing. In a way, making two similar paintings brings the methodology to the fore rather than the emphasis being on a finished work.

Developing technique

I have always had an interest in painters with natural ability, who are often considered painters' painters. I felt that, if that facility was there, it was important to use it. I started out by making a lot of works. This helped me to develop a casual, laid-back approach that was still skilful. I went for loose strokes that also provided a maximum economy for description. The only problem with this was it made it difficult to linger on parts of the painting I liked. I began to feel like I was passing by really interesting opportunities for paint technique or execution, which could develop colour, composition and narrative. I felt I had to slow down. I suppose I settled into the motif I was using and wanted to opt for a more mature interpretation of my source material.

In making the faster works it was more about the sense of space and the off-beat positioning of machines, or a ladder etc. I feel that with the slower works I took more control and considered how objects were arranged, exploring their individual and social significance. The slower works look in and around the figurative space, whereas the faster paintings are more about surface, more autonomous. It was exciting to make that transition. I started to spend a day or two on an area that had previously taken a few hours to paint. While the results took longer, it was very rewarding to see a final work.

The vocabulary of the brushwork

The elements of materiality and craft inform both the application and execution as well as the conceptual understanding of a work. I like the paintings to be placed out of step with how everyday images are consumed. I accept that in some ways paintings are outmoded by nature. The vocabulary of the brushwork tells a story particular to paint, the history of art and its language. This is often suggestive of time. The narrative of my work has a similar pace, as many of the workshops are depopulated and the eye has to wander without knowing where to go.

Car Lift
2011, oil on linen, 100 × 130 cm
(39 × 51 in).

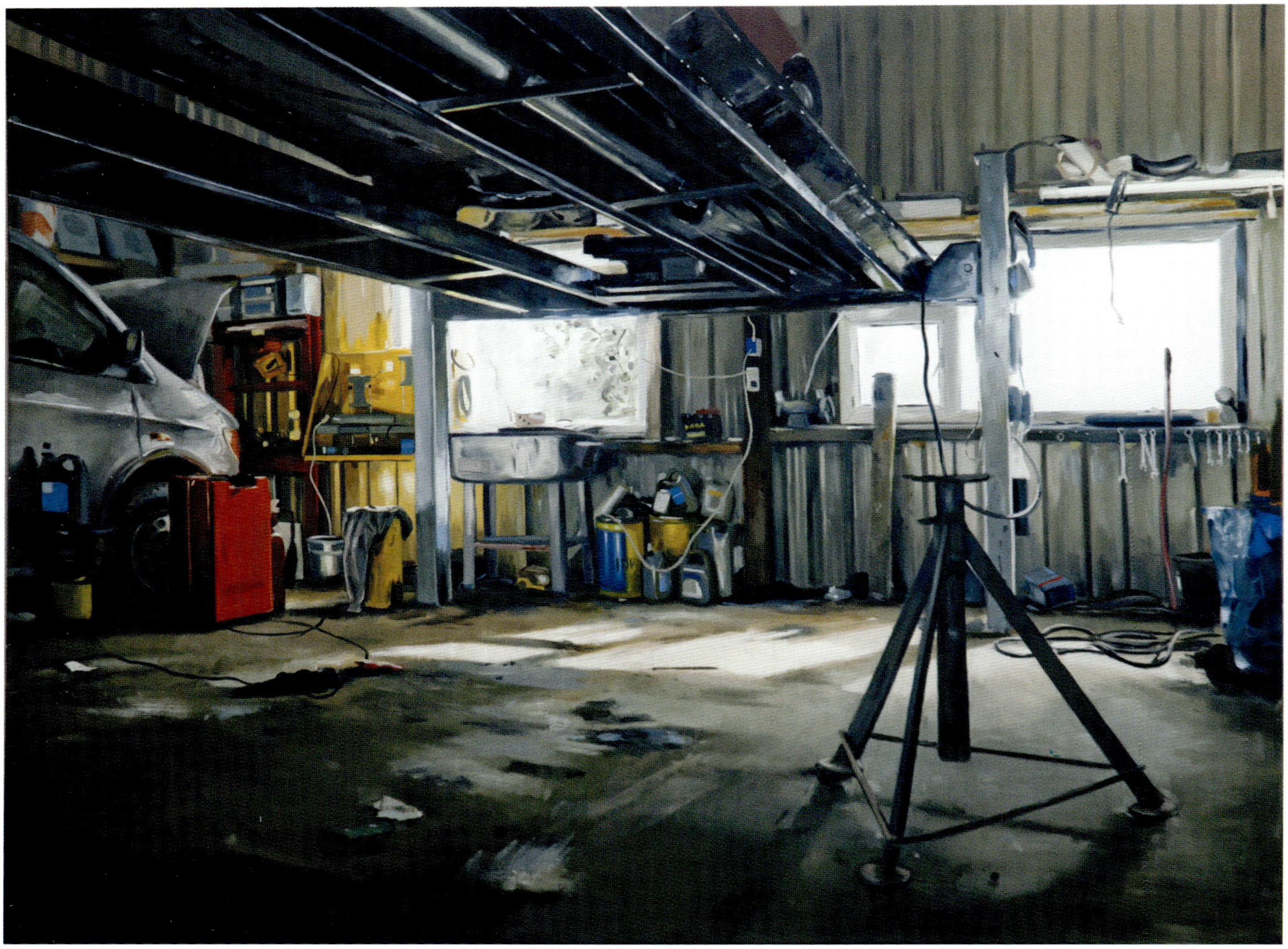

Museum Workshop
2011, oil on canvas, 50 × 60 cm
(19¾ × 23⅝ in).

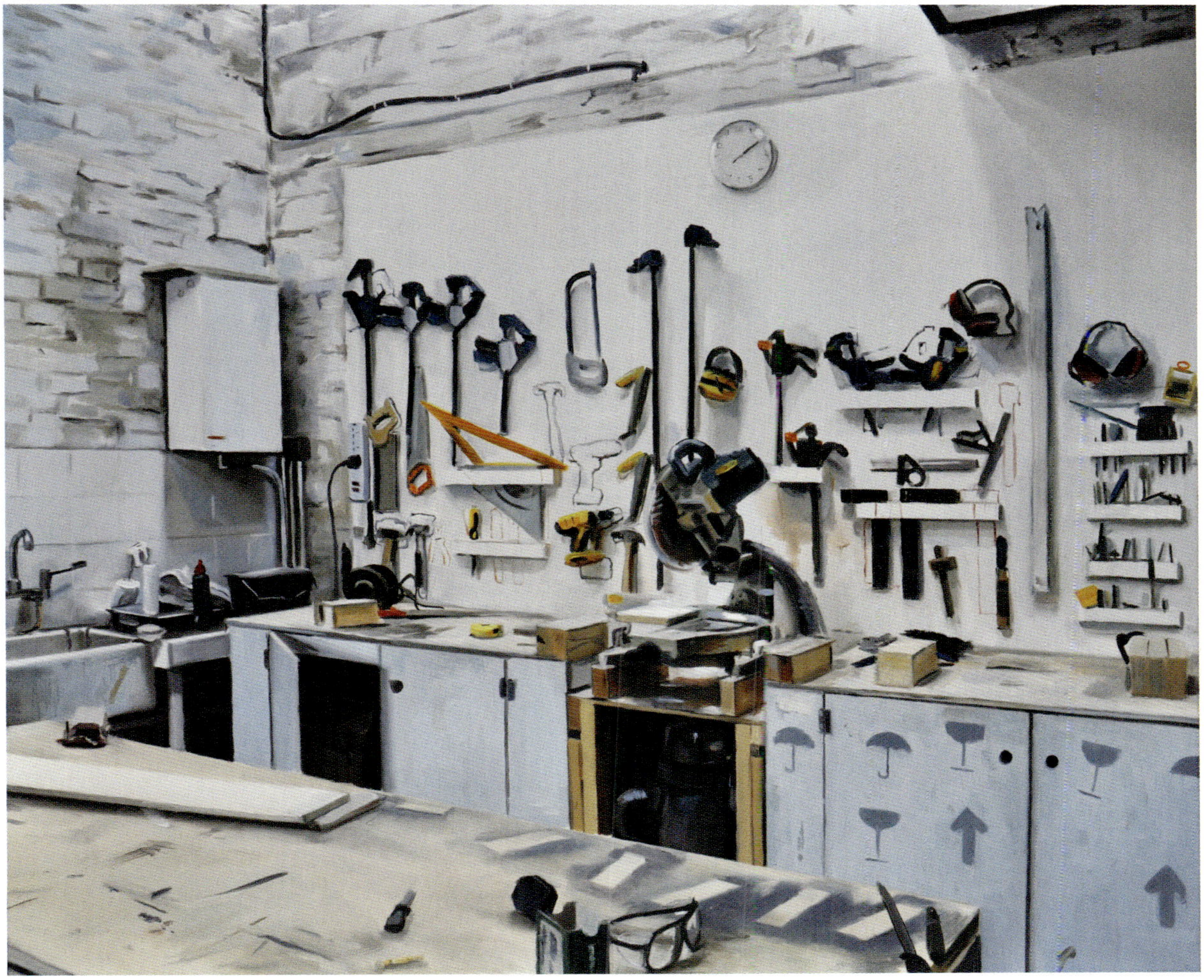

Taxi on Lift
2011, oil on linen, 35 × 45 cm
(13¾ × 17¾ in).

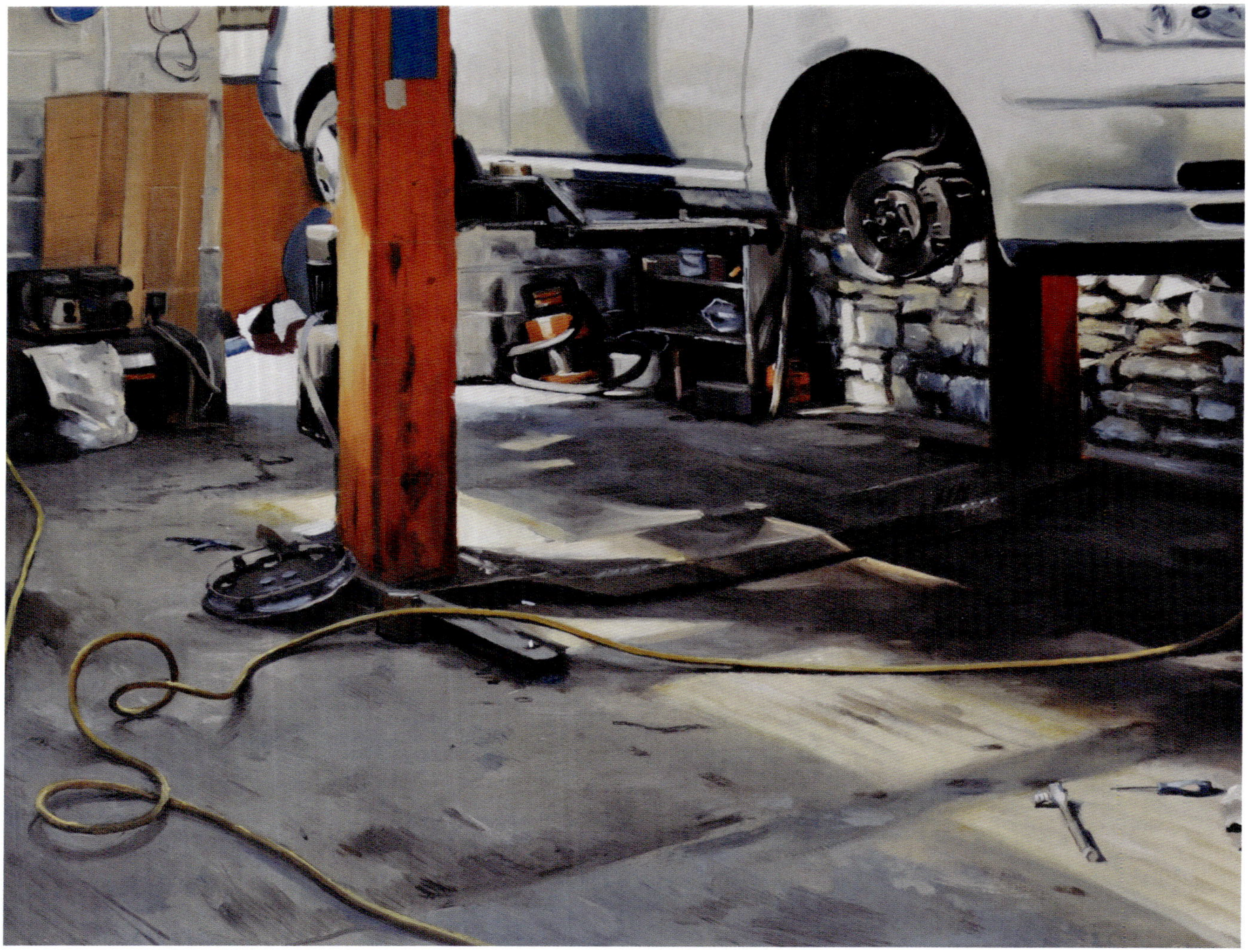

Workshop with Car Door
2012, oil on linen, 40 × 50 cm
(15¾ × 19¾ in).

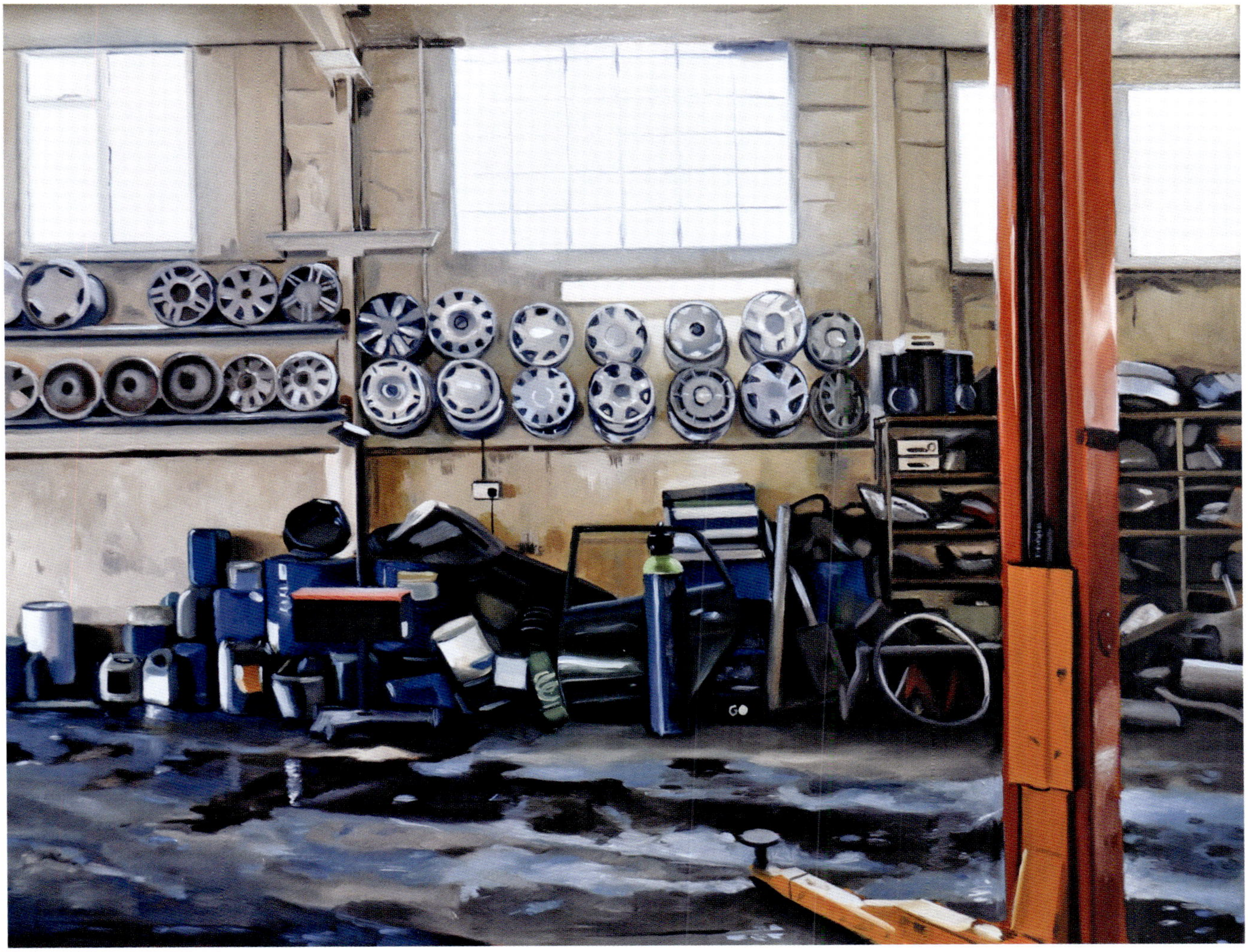

Any window, any morning, any evening, any day (installation view), 2012, oil on linen.

Cynthia Daignault
Born: 1978, Baltimore, Maryland
Lives: New York

Brooklyn-based painter Cynthia Daignault was a few years into her professional career when she went on an artist's residency and spent three months alone in the woods with her work. She describes the experience as 'incredibly intense. I would be lying if I said I didn't cry and drink through the first bit of it, but when I emerged I knew without doubt that painting is my life's vocation.' This intensity has remained in her works. These often transcend the two-dimensional, single-canvas model, but do so without losing any accuracy or compositional rigour. Daignault refutes the usual labels: 'I am not a conceptual painter, nor is anyone, for the term implies that there is a type of painting that is non-conceptual. The very act of rendering anything in paint is conceptual. I am not a figurative painter, nor is anyone, for the term implies that the act of figuration isn't at its core an act of abstraction. I endeavour to dismantle these binaries with which we talk about painting (alive, dead, figurative, abstract, conceptual, expressionist) to explore the liminal spaces between polarities in order to expand the meaning and relevance of painting in contemporary art and life.' Her subjects, she says, are simply 'light and colour, ideas and things'.

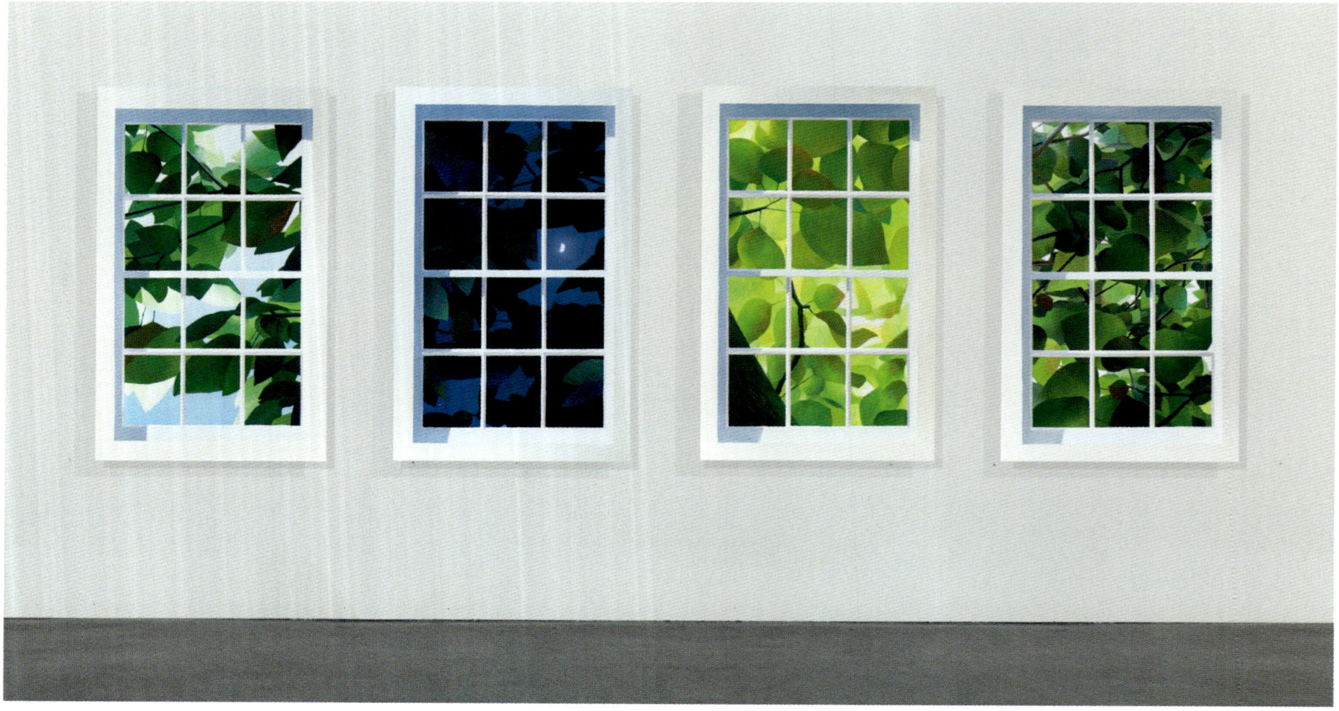

Training

I did not pursue a graduate degree in art. I fully respect that there are infinite paths to becoming a painter. Yet I chose a path based around a traditional model of mentorship in which I moved to the city and hung around a lot of older and more established painters. That was a wonderful decision. I wish more young painters felt empowered to forgo the professionalism of the modern MFA to explore more non-conventional paths.

References

Often I will use photographs, objects and memory to create drawings from which I paint. Overall, I try to use photography and life as little as possible. Though it is more difficult and uncomfortable, I continue to force myself to try to invent, imagine and remember as much as possible because I don't want the works to be about photography or realism; I want them to be about feelings and concepts, memories and ideas, to look real enough to be plausible, but unreal enough to reference something outside of the physical world.

Materials

One of the best things about being a painter is being on a continuum with a long, unbroken history of human production that stretches back thousands of years. I use very traditional materials: oil on lead-primed linen and a classical palette. This is one of the ways I reach back to all those painters who preceded this moment. As we enter a post-industrialist age many materials, which have been in use for many hundreds of years, are already unavailable; there is no doubt that in my lifetime, many of the traditional materials of figurative painting will no longer be available (the specific linen, lead white, pigments, etc.). In many ways, I find it incredibly moving that I may be among the last generation of painters who even has the option of working in the same materials as Velázquez, Courbet, Goya, Manet, Titian or Tiepolo.

Subjects

I paint light and time, both central to the traditional conceptual frameworks of all painting. I literalize and bring these to the forefront. I paint objects that I think of as still lifes. To me, they are like concrete word poetry. Objects are conceptual, poetic and metaphorical, and as subjects they encompass what is framed within the object and its associations, as well as what is left out. I want the object in my work to be Platonic (non-specific), universal and open-ended (like Morandi's empty vessels). A sense of 'placelessness' is important: universal contexts locate the objects inside the mind.

When to stop

There is a moment when I just can't work on a painting any more. I will be thinking, 'I have so much to do (I need to fix that green, repaint that shadow ...)', but then all of a sudden, I just can't do it. No doubt this ennui is a defence mechanism that prevents me from tweaking a painting forever. I describe it as the tipping point when I have more to lose than to gain.

Photoshop

I find Photoshop to be a great tool – if I want to test something out (say adjust the colour of something). I don't see it as any detraction: I still have to make the paintings and nothing I can do digitally can replace or prepare me for what happens when I'm actually moving the paint around the canvas. Photoshop is merely an abstract idea-making machine, like drawing or photography; I can get ideas for a painting from within it, but at the end of the day I still end up shifting coloured mud around some fabric.

On the role of painting

In this era of late capitalism, probably only consumer products have any role in shaping contemporary culture. In that, paintings are still commodities: they have a cultural effect relative to their market, which is smaller in scale than the iPhone, but larger in scale than alpaca socks.

CCTV Monitor (installation view)
2012, oil on linen.

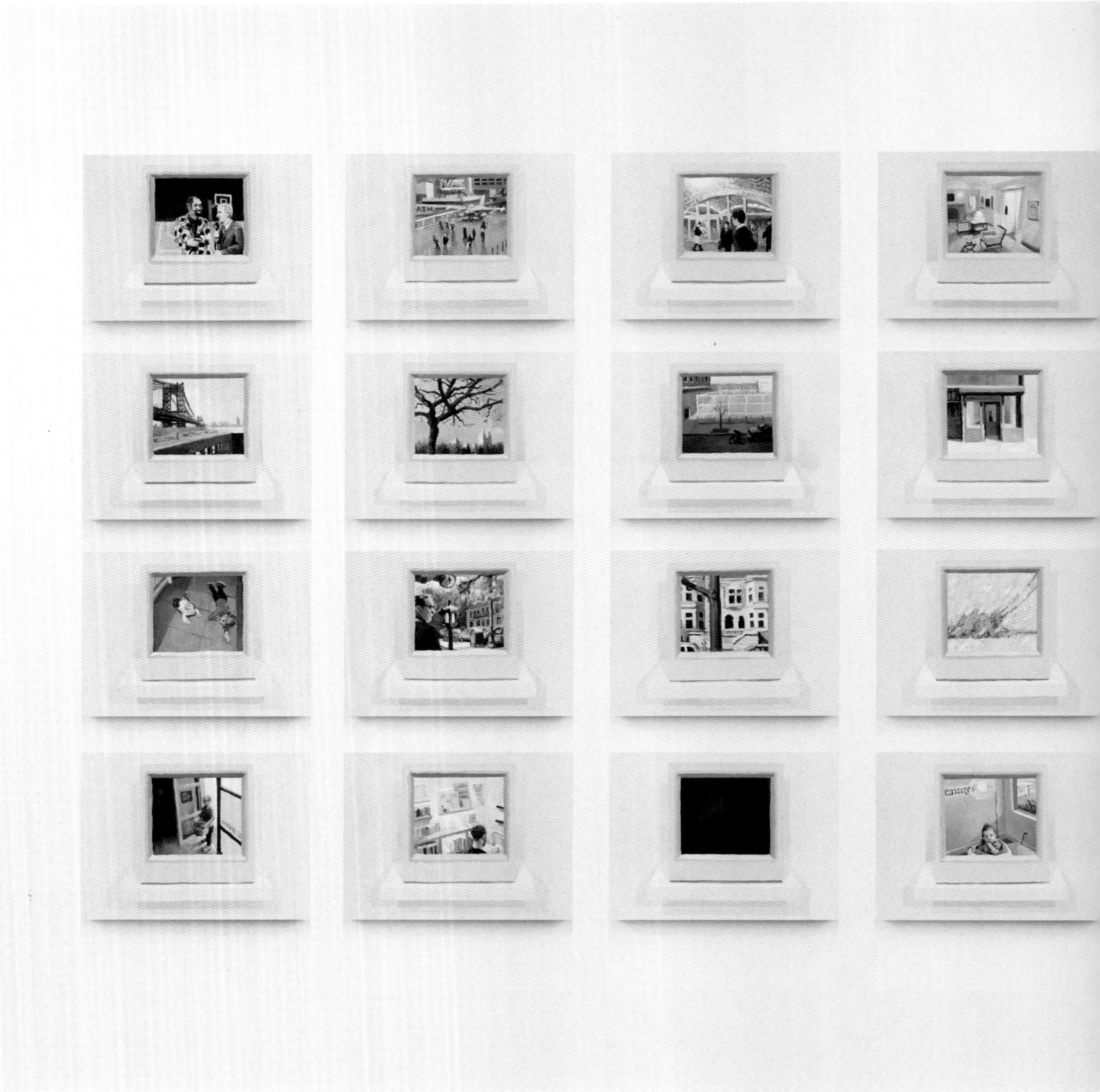

CCTV Monitor
2012, oil on linen, 30 × 41 cm
(11¾ × 16 in)

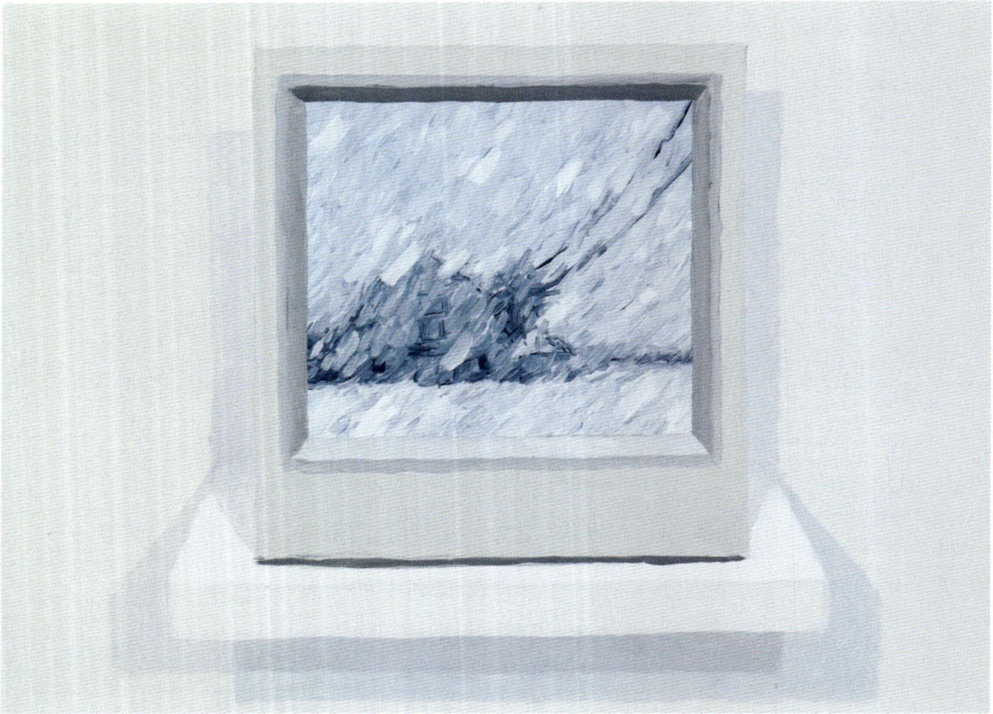

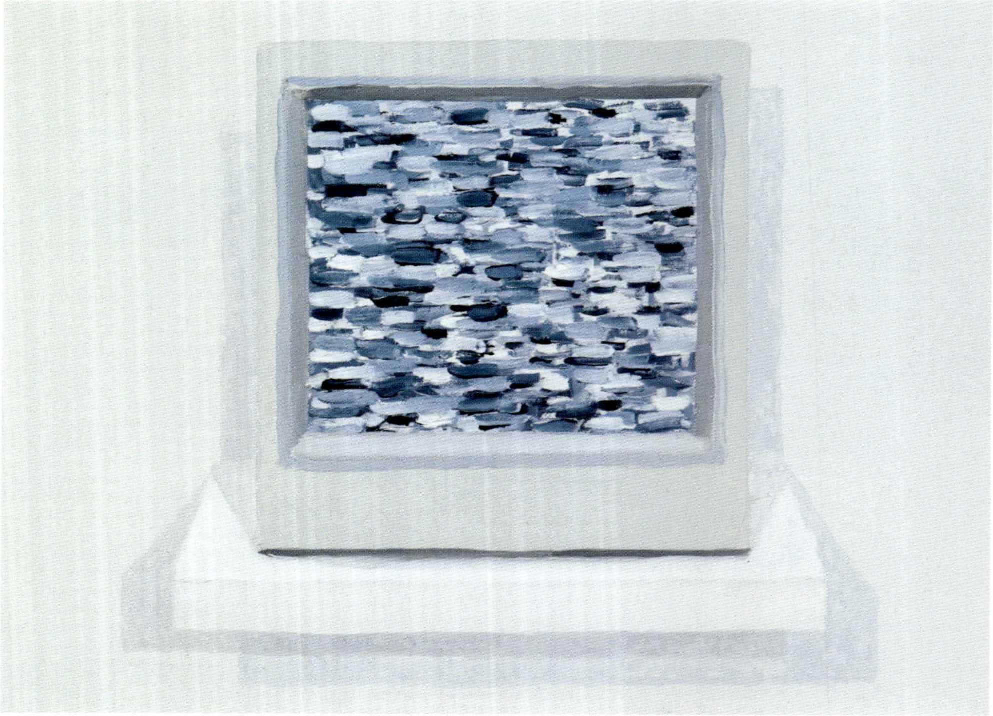

Below: I think of the Big Sky, and nothing matters much to me (detail)
2011, oil on linen; two parts: 61 × 86 cm (24 × 34 in) and 107 × 244 cm (42 × 96 in).

Bottom: Black LCD (Off)
2011, oil on linen, 61 × 86 cm (24 × 34 in).

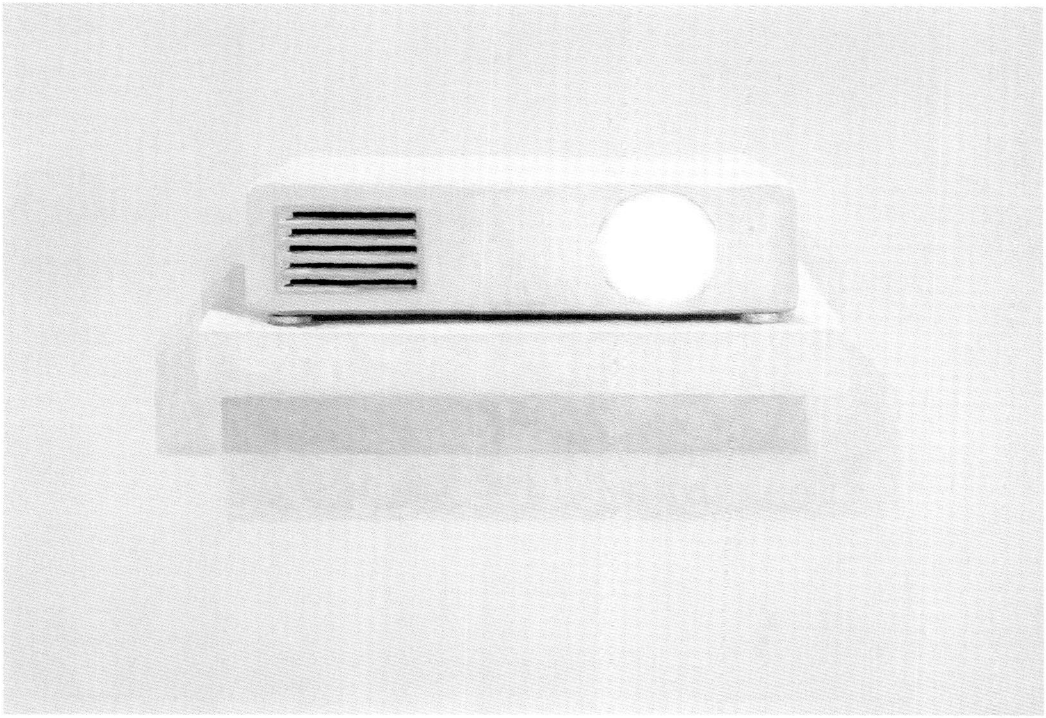

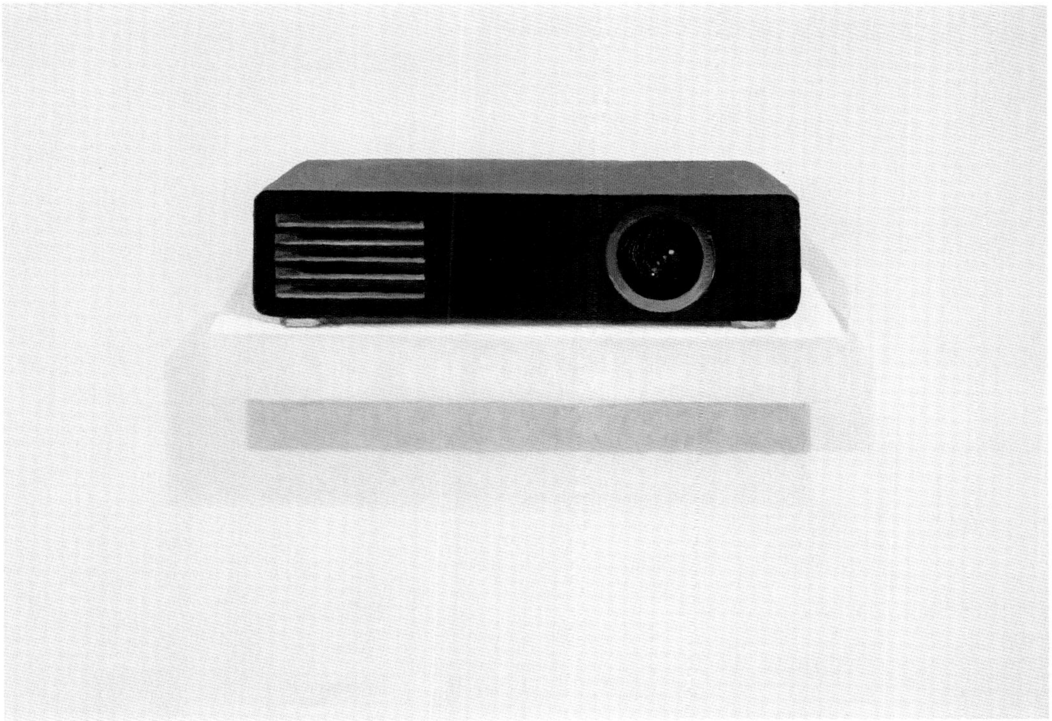

Tauben
2007, oil on canvas, 274 × 206 cm
(108 × 81 in).

Tim Eitel
Born: 1971, Leonberg (Germany)
Lives: Berlin

While touching upon such strong subjects as homelessness, protests or the security apparatus, Tim Eitel's paintings succeed in 'keeping their secret'. Based on the artist's own photographs of streets, people and situations (a Tamil protester on hunger strike in Paris, for example), they remain mysterious while being almost aggressively expressive and striking in their compositional force. Poignant, they never veer into sentimentality. Backgrounds often seem about to drift into abstraction, yet hold back, never letting go of their grip on the physical reality of the world. It is a virtuosic act of painting: Eitel treats heavy subjects with deftness and a light touch, while avoiding shallowness, provocation or facile interpretation. One could almost say ('almost' could be a leitmotif for this style) that his clearly heartfelt concern for those existing on the margins of society is reflected in the way the subjects in his paintings exist on the margins of realism. With great care and precision, and while using a pared-down Minimalist language (attenuated and brought under control), Eitel's paintings express how reality itself can be both familiar and yet thoroughly alien.

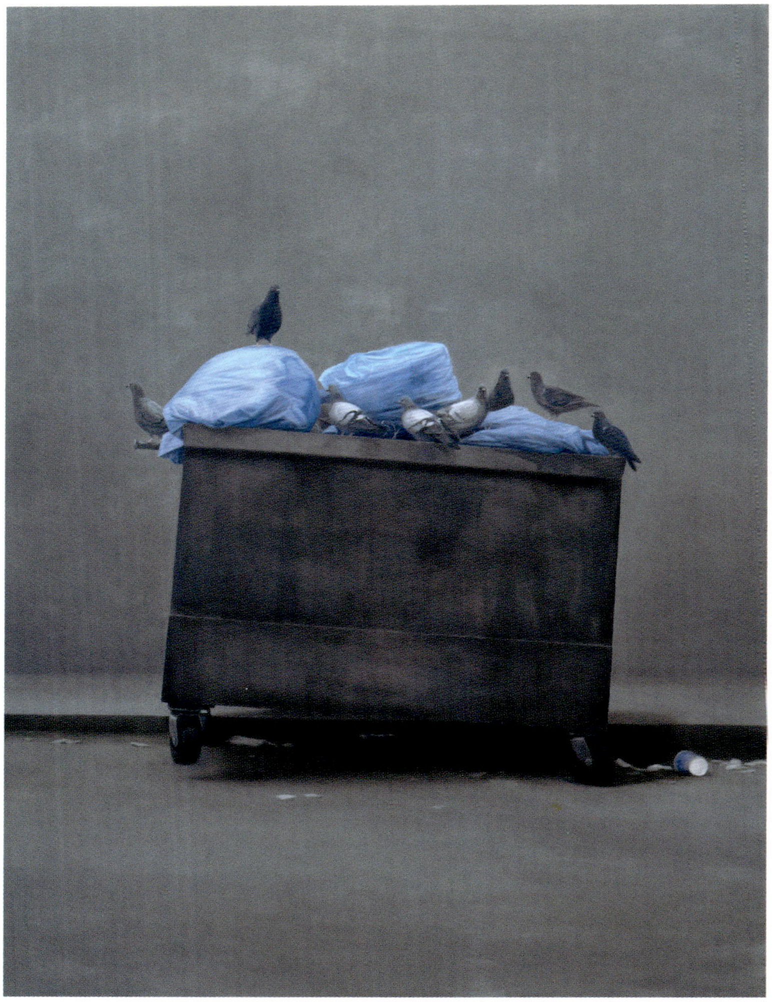

Key influences and themes
[I decided I wanted to be an artist] when I saw a Francis Bacon retrospective in Stuttgart (my hometown) in the mid-1980s. I was floored by the energy his paintings exuded. Looking at his work made me want to paint [Eitel studied painting under Arno Rink at HGB, the Academy of Visual Arts in Leipzig].

My work feeds off the places I'm in: situations I see in the street, figures, objects, gestures that strike a nerve in me are the starting point for my paintings. In truth, when I'm doing a painting a lot of things influence the work: movies, photographs in newspapers, things that cross my path, but they never do so in a direct way. I definitely feel a lot of attraction to certain movies, like *Deserto Rosso* by Antonioni, and books, like Strindberg's *Inferno*, but how this informs my work I couldn't tell.

And I look at all painting. One never knows where one will find a nice little trick to steal.

Other media
I'm a child of the media age. Images in all kinds of media are a source of inspiration to me; they shape the way I see things. Isn't it almost two decades now since everything was ruled by a videoclip aesthetic – fast cuts, etc.? Everything seems to have slowed down since then. It's a pity, really.

Will a movie ever be like a sculpture?
Hopefully not! But, one day, cyberspace will have much more physical presence than a painting.

Narrative
Each work contains multiple narratives. The first of these is the fact that it's a painting and I thought it had to be done and so I made it, and I want you to look at it. And you'll see it as a painting and see where it fits within your conceptions of that. I don't see any kind of underlying storyline [in the paintings] myself. Of course there is a lot of great art that tells stories we already know so you can pack a lot of action from the before and after into one pregnant moment.... But my interest is more in situations, in constellations [alignments of chance], in what meaning there is [left] when you strip them of all narrative.

It seems that when I work on a certain theme, I begin to see it everywhere, and I start to become obsessed about it. When this happens I know it's time for a break.

Process
I use my own photographs as material. Not in a literal way, as I am not at all interested in copying a photograph, but as one would use sketches, I use this fragment and that fragment to build a new image. But I don't do preparatory sketches. I feel like this would spoil the fun. I like the unexpected to happen. To finish a painting can take quite some time: up to a year. I know that it is finished when I experience the work as if somebody else had painted it.

Routine
I go in the studio every day after lunch, even if I'm in a terrible mood and have no idea what to do. I feel terribly lazy when I skip a day.

Realism
My work definitely is not 'realistic'. It is *synthetic*. It is the construction of images that in one way or another relate to the perception of the real. My paintings are not documentary but constructed. They derive from multiple sources and analogies. They don't depict reality but constitute something that could only come alive as a painting.

Painting and politics
Art is usually seen as political when it tells you what to think. I want my work to be much more open, not least because I do not know the answers myself. Still, while I don't see my painting as political, I do present a *Menschenbild* (I don't think you can translate that really – images of humanity, human themes), so the response can never be purely aesthetic.

Öffnung
2006, oil on canvas, 274 × 220 cm
(108 × 87 in).

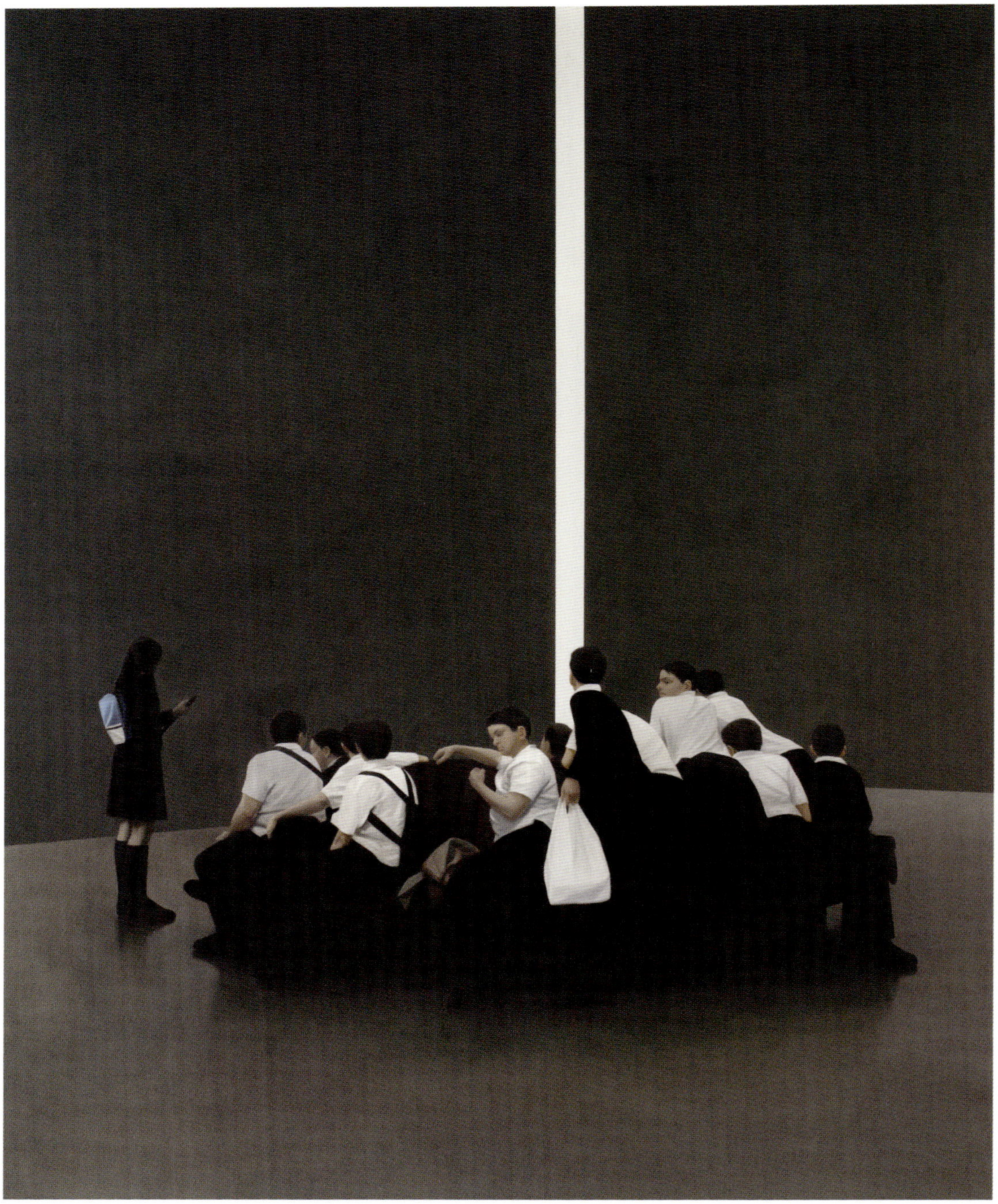

Boot
2004, oil on canvas, 250 × 210 cm
(98 × 83 in).

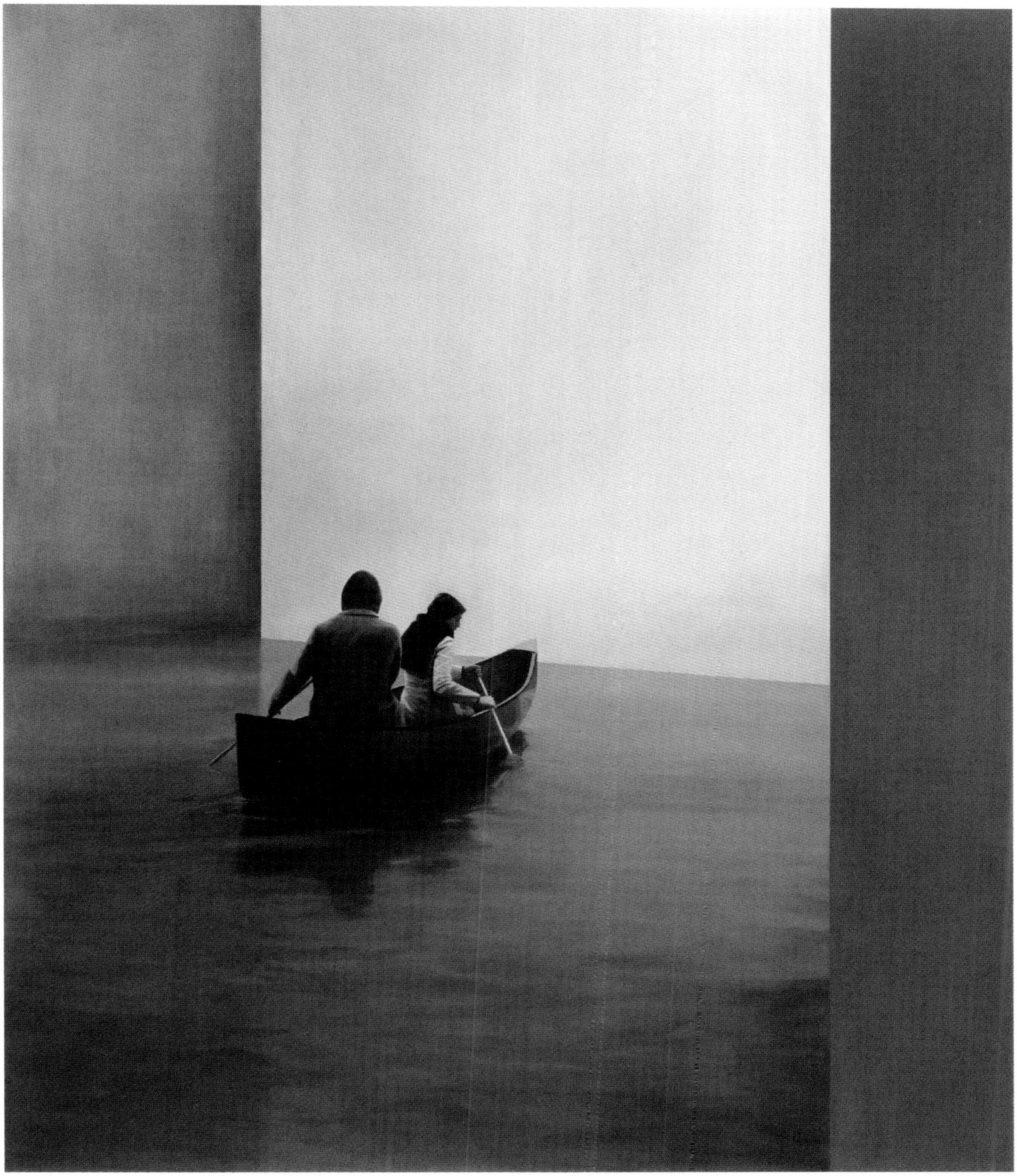

Besucher
2009, oil on canvas, 226 × 257 cm
(89 × 101 in).

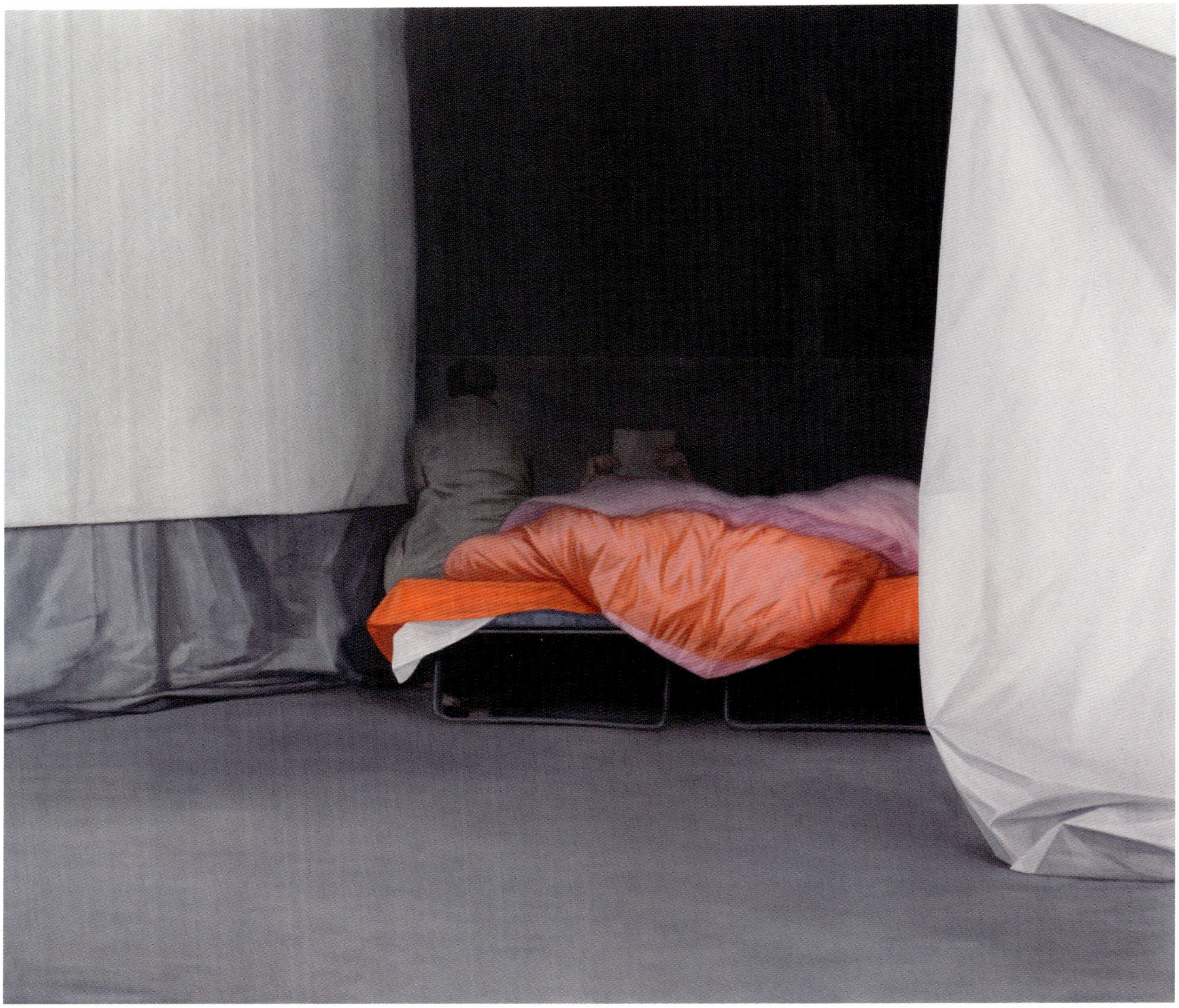

Architect
2012, oil on canvas, 210 × 250 cm
(83 × 98 in).

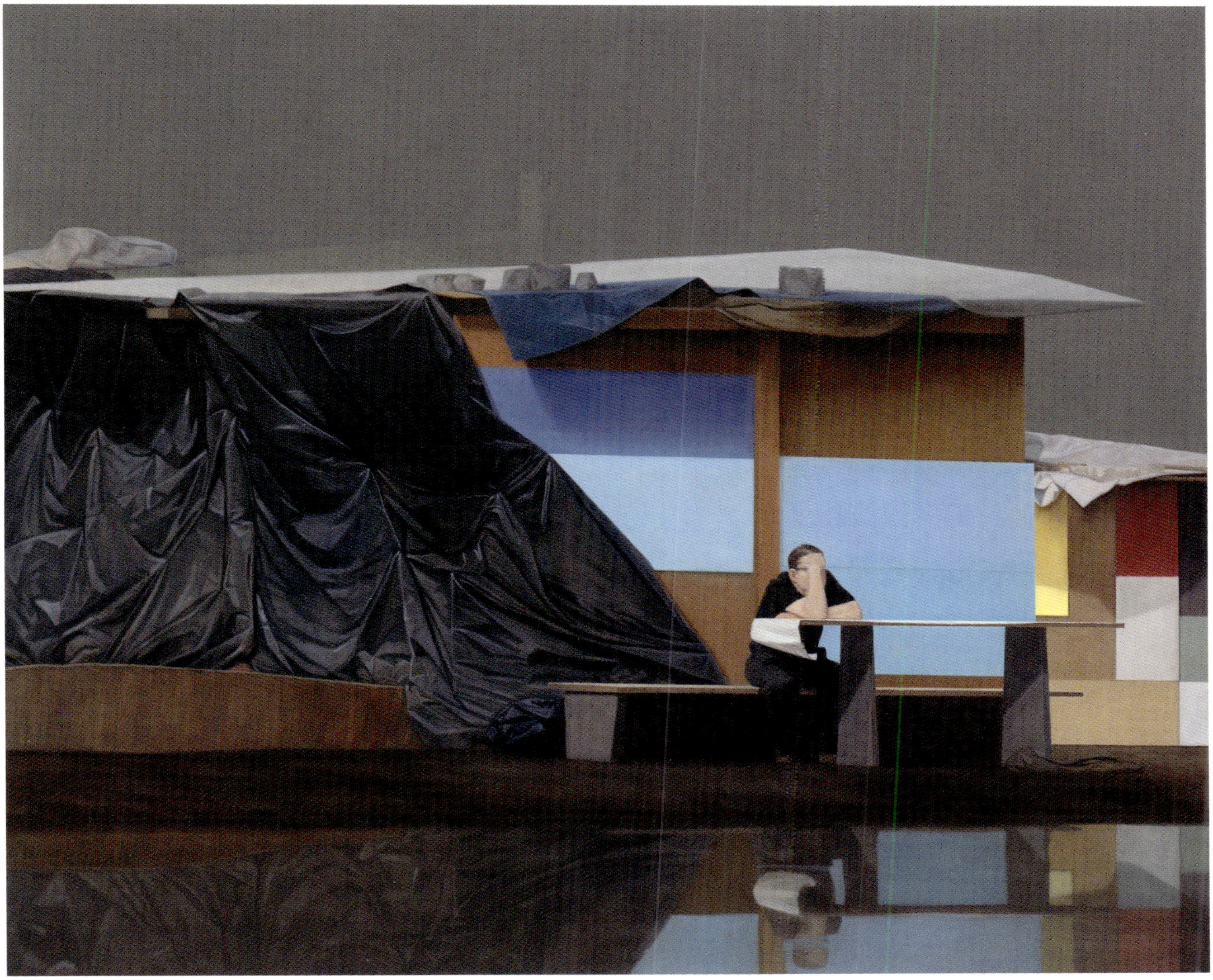

Open and Closed Space Painting
(installation view, Kochi-Muziris
Biennale, Kochi, India)
2012, watercolour on wall.

Zhang Enli
Born: 1965, Jilin Province (China)
Lives: Shangai

Zhang Enli was born in Jilin, northern China, in 1965, and now lives and works in Shanghai. His paintings communicate in the most simple and direct manner, focusing on mundane objects rendered in a sober, almost 'transparent' fashion: the interplay of balls (a football and a basketball) in a net, the shapes and loops of the actual net, the tension of branches in the air, the strength of a table or a chair, the depth of a bucket. It would be tempting to connect this to the universe of his materially deprived childhood, but every one of these works is like a masterclass in the form, showing how figurative painting, when so perfectly pitched, has a capacity to convey lived experience and memory with devastating effectiveness, going to places and reaching perceptual corners that words could only dream of reaching.

Background
My main childhood memory is still that of a life in material poverty: the desire to eat a meal of meat and the satisfaction (the happiness) of being able to eat a piece of meat – it could be one of the happiest things for a child.

Some changes and the formation of simple concepts began to take shape at university [Arts & Design Institute of Wuxi Technical University, China]. In 1985 it was already possible to find books on various Western artists as well as American art magazines. At the same time, books about old Chinese art and literature were almost invisible. For someone who wanted to become an artist, the main difficulty was not being able to see more exhibitions of artists from other countries.

Art school
I studied design. It was an important step in my development; many of my personal views were formed at this time. Design is a profession of 'fuzzy and unimaginable boundaries'. At the time, 'design and real life' were independent of one another, unrelated, as material conditions in China at that point were too simple to meet even basic living requirements. Design was therefore based on abstract concepts built in the mind, not on their actual application. This knowledge helped me break away from what is, and what is not, the concept of the oil painting. This was a very important period for me.

Then the best way I found to develop was by gradually becoming more introverted and peaceful/plain, so my vision of painting became closer to reality, and the way of painting got closer to transparent watercolour painting. My use of thin and blank paints takes elements from traditional Chinese paintings. I had practised Chinese painting for many years before I went to university.

Process
My works are painted from life and memory, and from photographic references for some details.

Style
I have gone through a long period of transformation and growth. A person is like a container. Gradually you remove other people's things from this container and what is left, finally, is you – or it may also be nothing, just empty.

Tradition
I like to look for starting points in the works of earlier painters. Like the perspective in Paolo Uccello's works, which allowed me to really study perspective, painting a series of works regarding perspective, exploring the relationship between perspective and painting; perspective and people's psychology.

The politics of painting
The significance of painting is that it can impact very directly on people. The frailty of painting is just an appearance: a real painting allows for the understanding of people, as well as the fragility and transience of life.

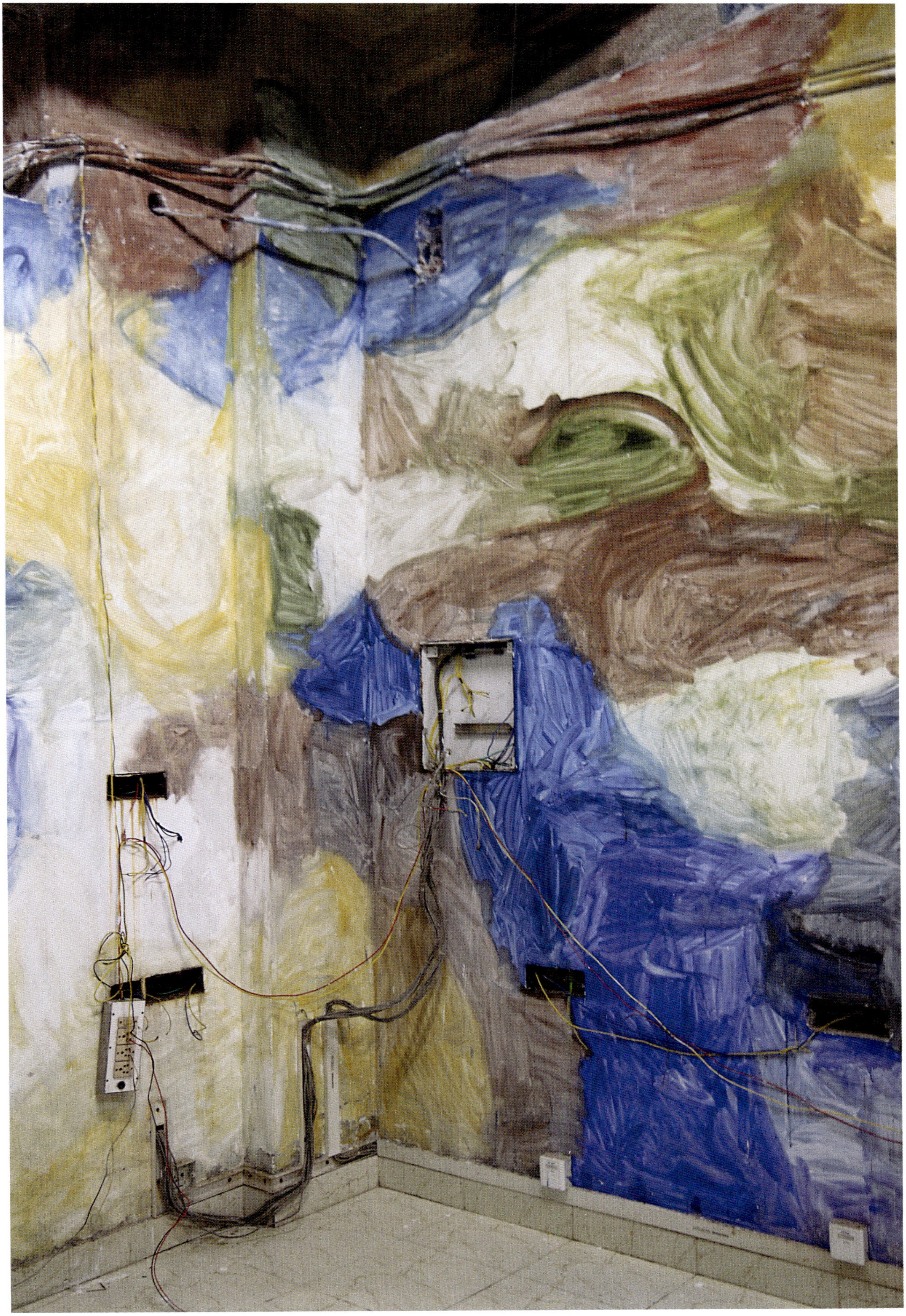

Studio (installation view, Minsheng Art Museum, Shanghai), 2010, watercolour on wall.

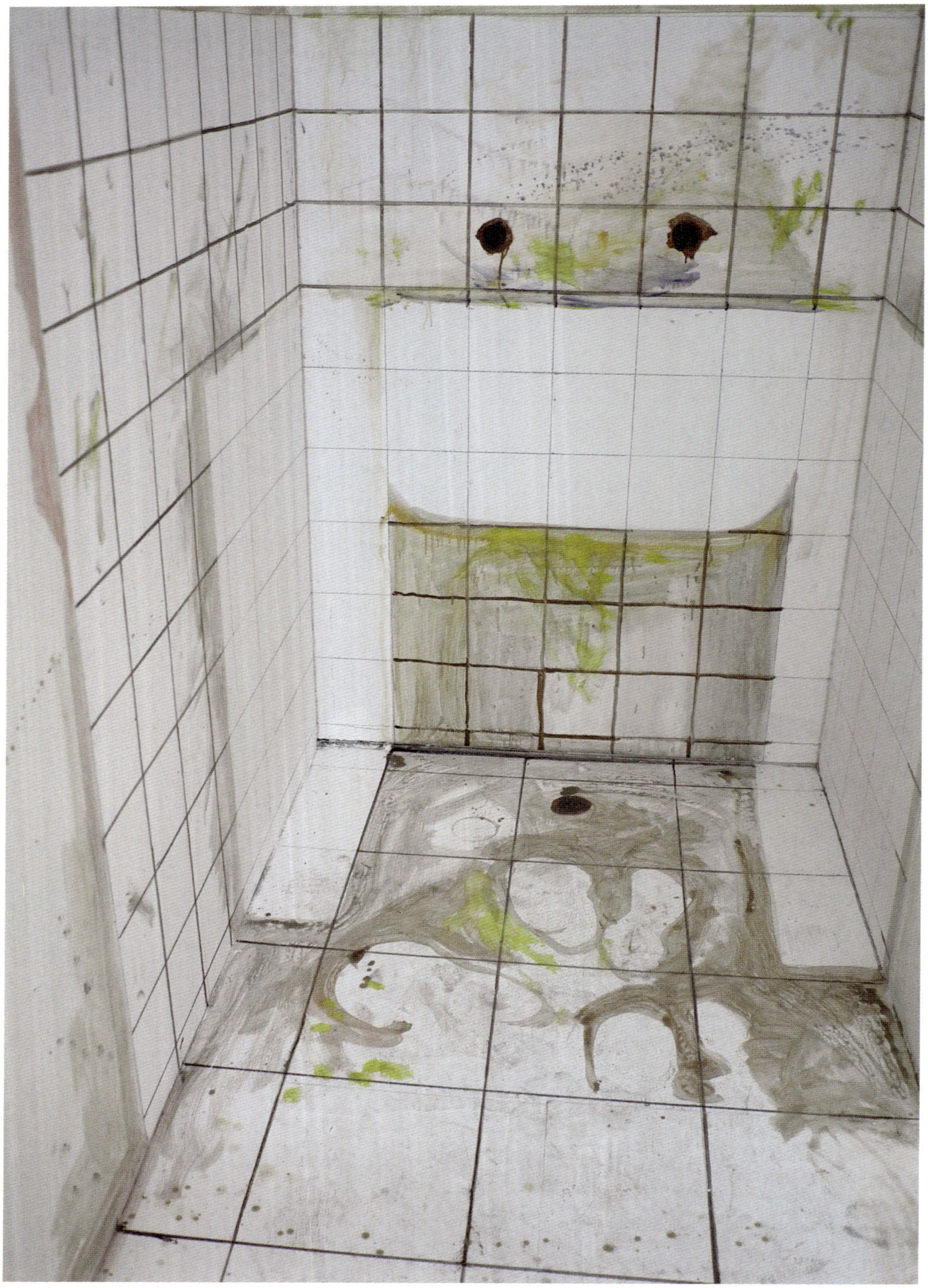

Circulez! Il n'y a rien à voir
(with Moshekwa Langa, installation view,
objectif_exhibitions, Antwerpen, Belgium
2007), watercolour on wall.

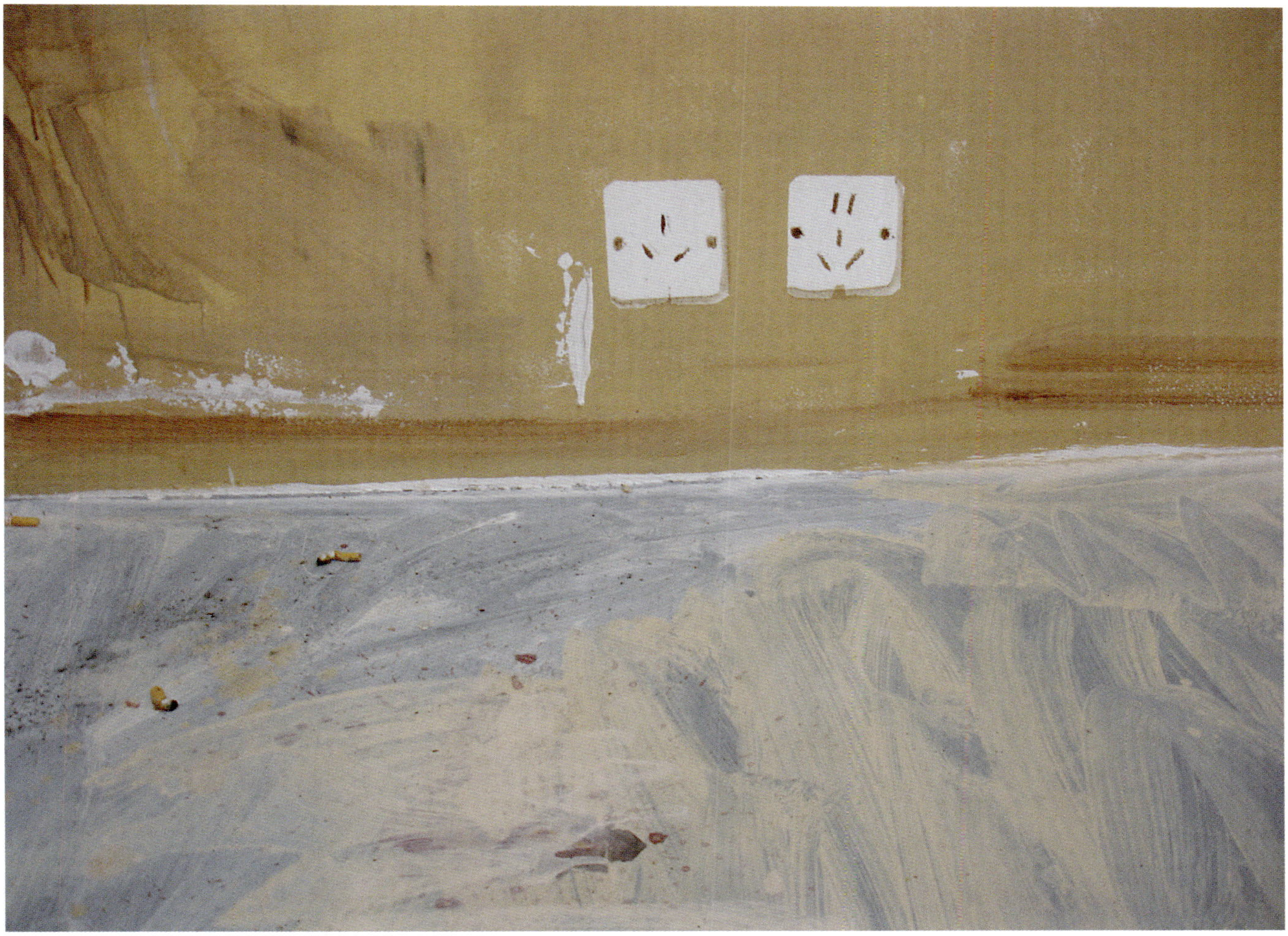

Studio
2011, watercolour on wall.
(installation view), the 6th Curitiba
Biennale, Museu Alfredo Andersen,
Curitiba, Brazil.

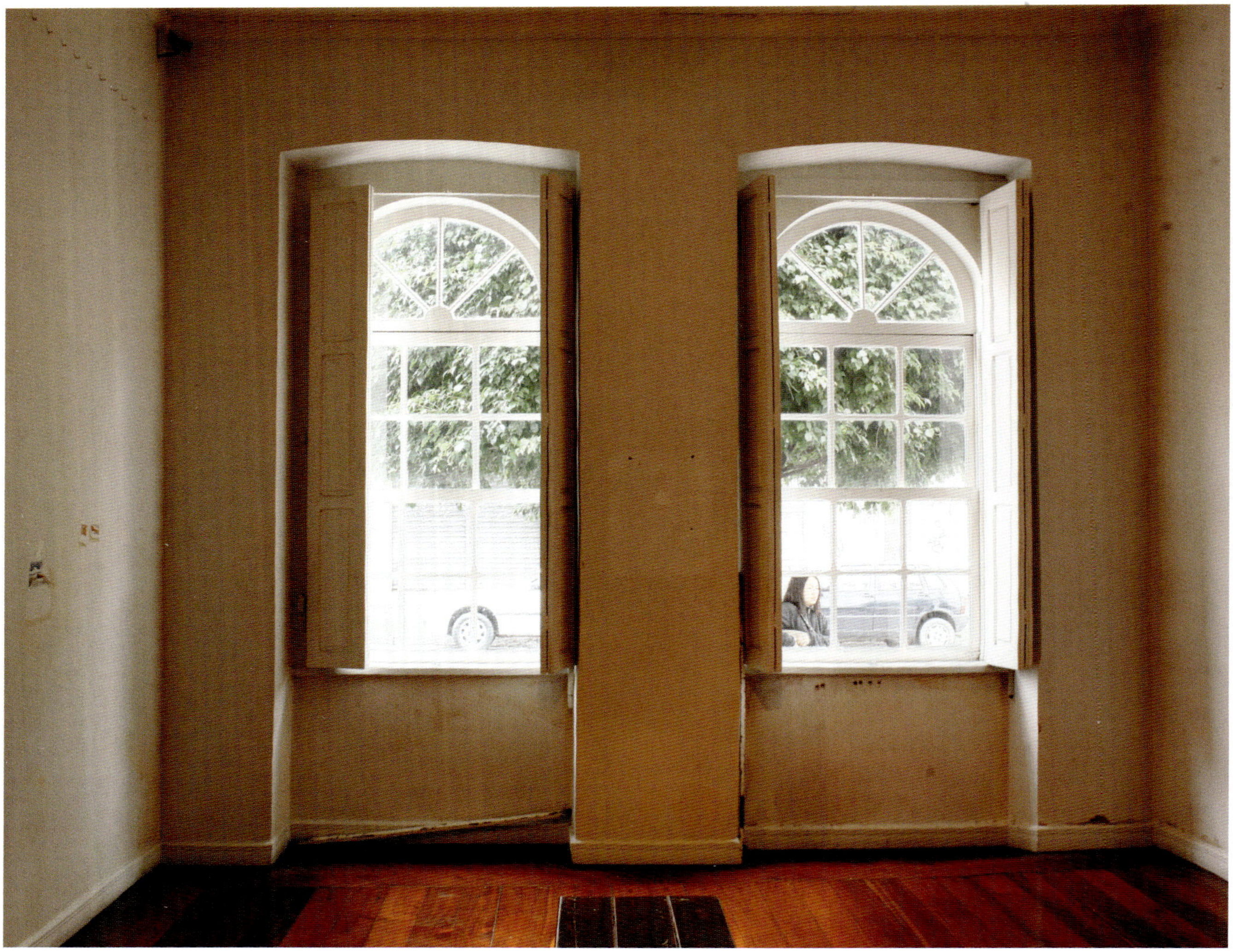

Space Painting
2010, watercolour on wall.
(installation view), Gwangju
Biennale, South Korea.

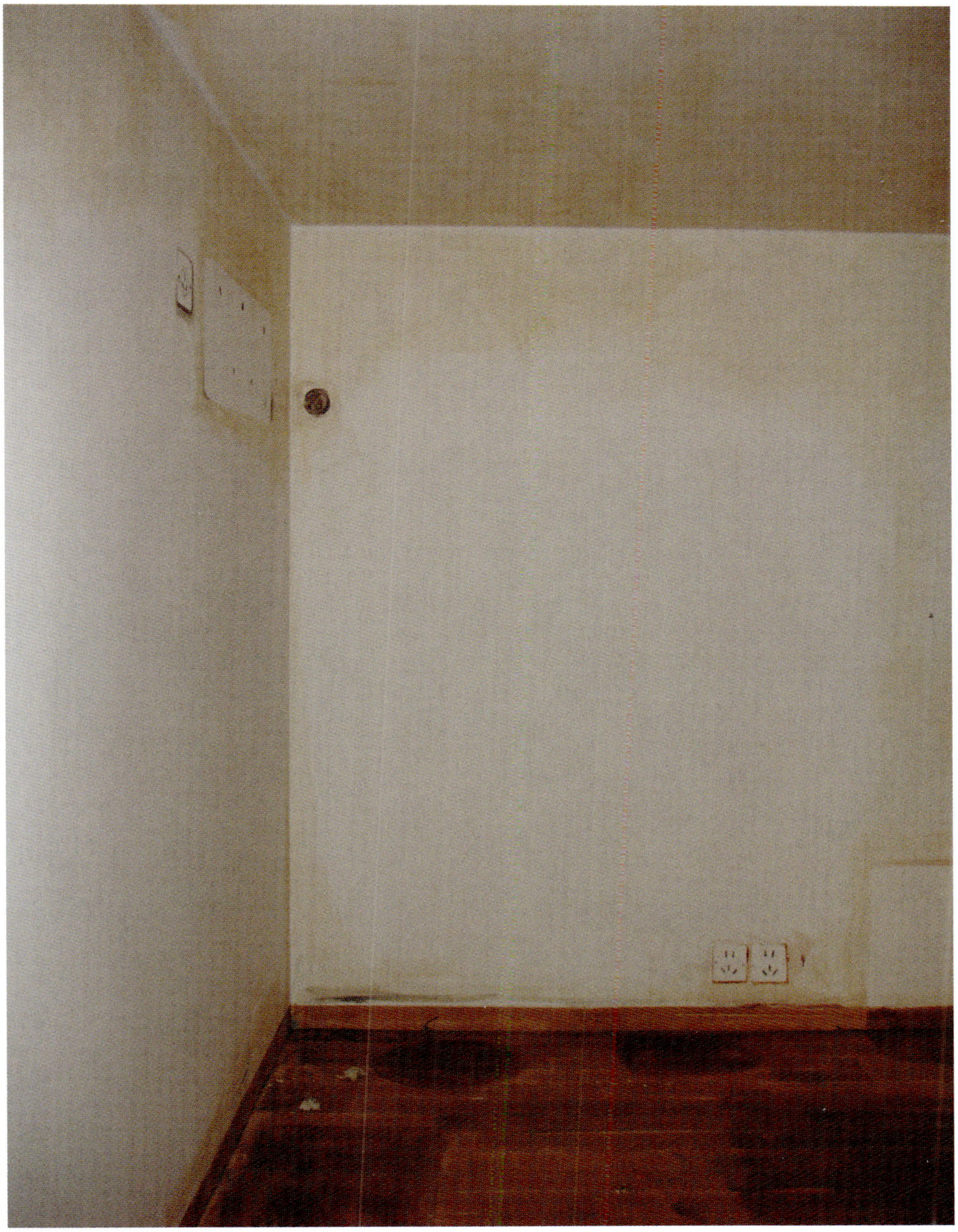

Maya Gold
Born: 1978, Jerusalem
Lives: Tel Aviv

Israeli artist Maya Gold began her experience as an artist almost by chance. She treasures her initial 'artistic ignorance' as a key factor that allowed her to develop a personal visual language. In her 'human landscapes' an apparently motionless perfection reveals a disquieting suspension of everyday life. This subverted natural order is reflected in her painting technique, where shadows come before the objects.

Background

I was born in Jerusalem and raised in Beit Shemesh, a small town between Jerusalem and Tel Aviv. The decision to apply for the Bezalel Academy of Art and Design was quite arbitrary. I started there right after I finished my mandatory military service. Contrary to most of the students in the art department, I had no knowledge of art history or contemporary art. I was introduced to artists like Duchamp and Warhol and to new ideas and concepts. This was a period of new revelations and excitement. I see the time I spent at Bezalel as one of the crucial points of my life. I think that this 'artistic ignorance' enabled me to develop individual ideas, and something of that still stays with me.

Beyond politics

I feel that as an Israeli artist I am always expected to refer to the complex political situation and to the occupation. This expectation can be tiring. I am sure one can find the influence of living in this reality in my paintings. Yet I wouldn't like the discourse around them to be political. For me, art is beyond politics. My work deals with the connection between art and daily life, with the unique ability of art to be a part of daily life but yet to be 'unusual' at the same time. My paintings depict ordinary moments that, through pictorial actions, such as changing the point of view or the perspective, lose their balance and thus are excluded from the pre-existing order.

Technical inversion

Sometimes I draw little sketches or notes on coffee-shop napkins, but it's hard for me to take a sketch seriously, I need the 'real thing'.... Some of the works require technical preparations. It's important for me to know where I want to locate the figure or object, since technically the shadow is painted in the same paint layer that indicates the ground and the sky, and before the object. The paintings are actually painted from the end to the beginning. Sometimes I stage situations and photograph them or make objects especially for them.

Painterly 'mishap'

The pictorial space is often not a specific site and that's why it is characterized by atmospheric colours such as blue or grey, which portray only seasons, or hours of the day. Even when the ground is depicted, it functions as a background. The interruption of order, or the 'mishap' that occurs in the paintings, is as important to me as the pictorial gestures, even though it is all carried out on a stretched canvas and by pictorial means.

Scale and point of view

The first time I used the above-ground point of view was towards the end of my MA. This piece was constructed of 2,500 cake-decoration figurines of soccer players, painted in brown and ochre and attached vertically to the wall. Since then I have been exploring this point of view. I am still using it in order to create the changes that occur in the viewer's eye when they see from afar abstract geometric shapes, or colour spots, the meaning of which only becomes clear through a closer view. This point of view also dictates the need for using large colour areas.

Usually, if there is a human figure involved, the pictorial space will be large-scale. This is in order to reinforce the feeling of detachment, that 'nowhere' feeling. The figure is small enough to act in this new space.

Untitled
2009, oil on canvas, 147 × 175 cm
(58 × 69 in).

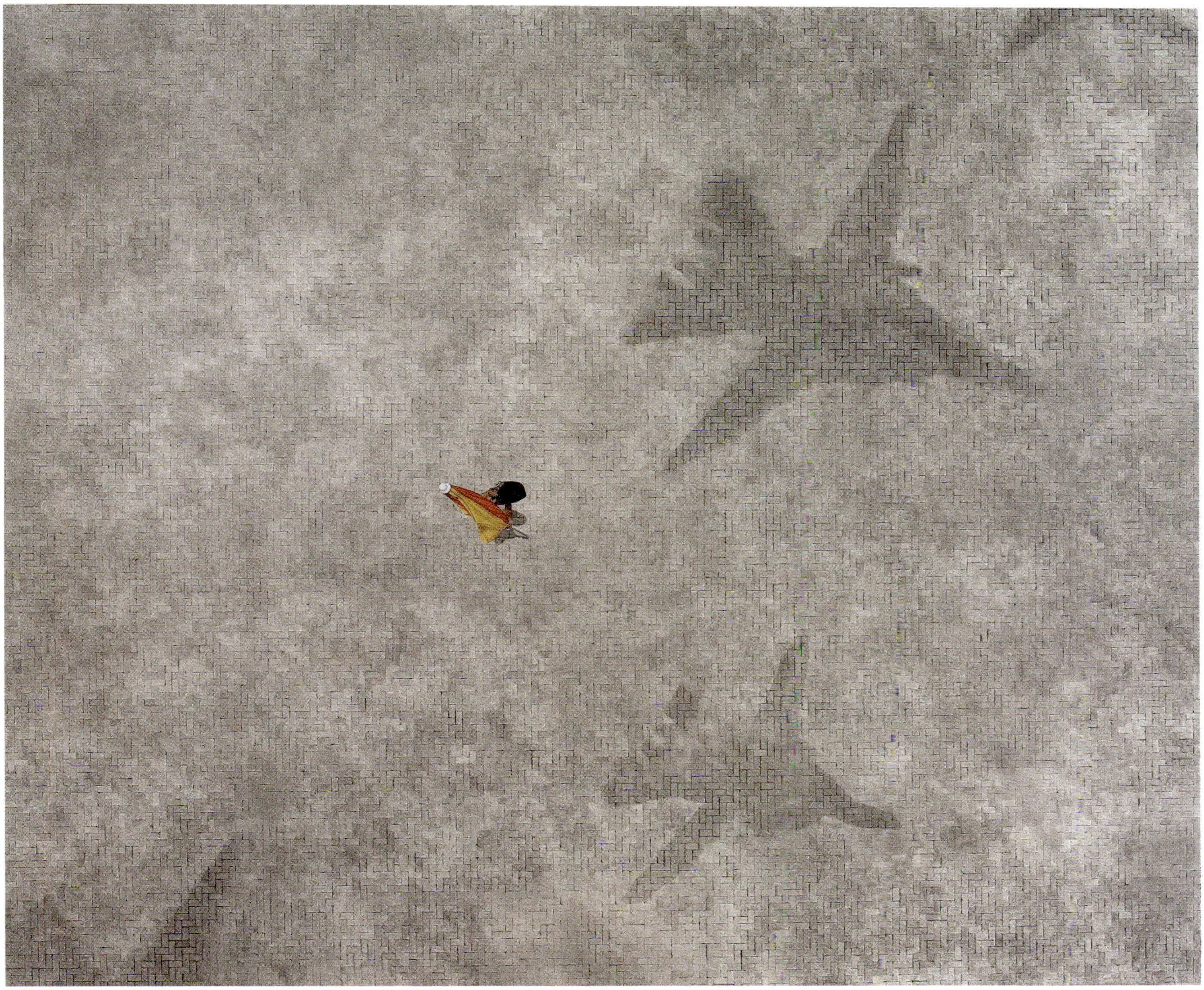

Echo
2010, oil on canvas, 110 × 192 cm
(43 × 76 in).

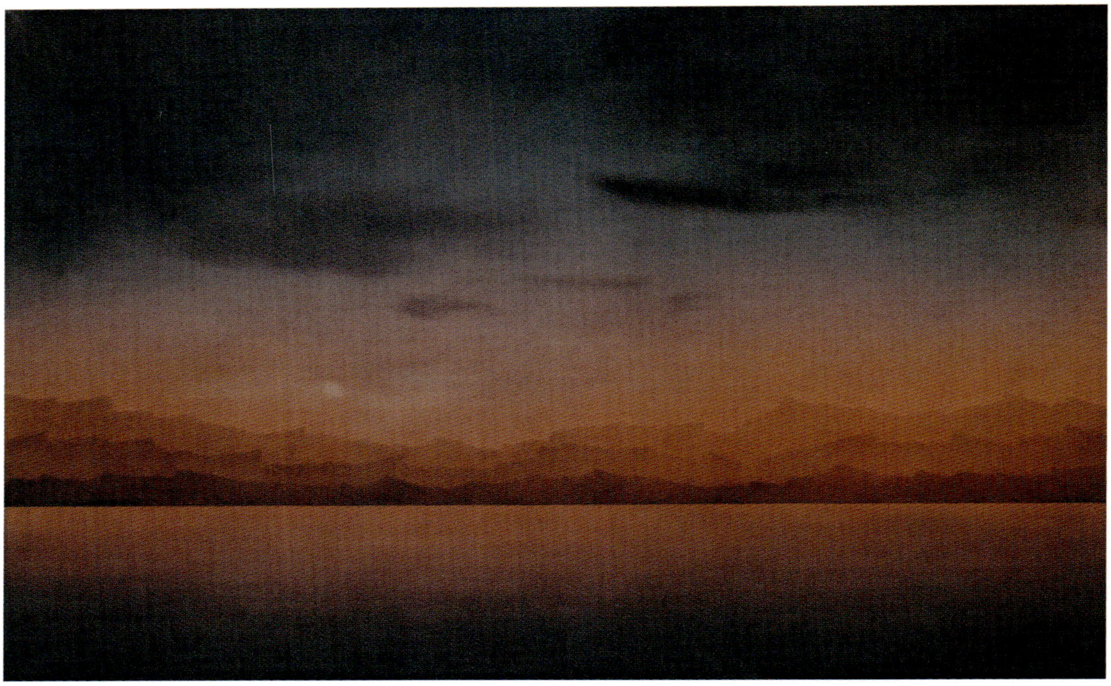

Maritime
2008, oil on canvas, 127 × 172 cm
(50 × 68 in).

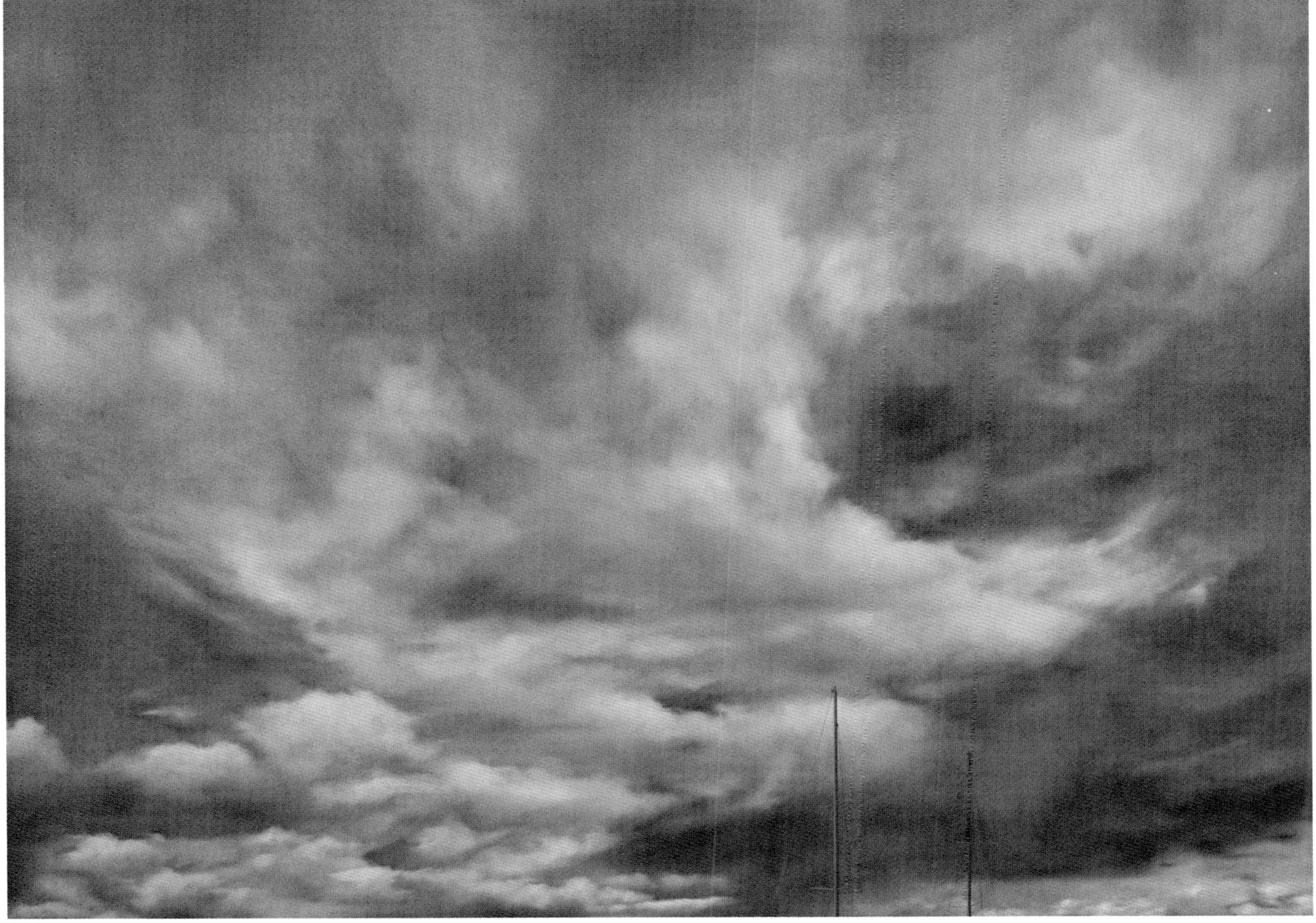

Once in a Blue Moon
2010, oil on canvas, 165 × 130 cm
(65 × 51 in).

Oda Jaune
Born: 1979, Sofia
Lives: Paris

The expression 'to see a painting in the flesh' could not find a better embodiment than in Oda Jaune's paintings. With generous brushstrokes the Bulgarian painter builds odd bodies characterized by impossible anatomies. The artist assigns a fleshy form to inner reality and the subconscious, at a time when reality is often interpreted only through objective data and external appearances. In spite of a certain proximity to the visual universe of Surrealism, the humanish creatures depicted by Jaune respond to a uniquely mysterious mixture of passionate sensuality and spiritual tenderness, leaving no space for the grotesque, or violence. Layer upon layer, she gives form to dreamlike scenarios, suspended between dream and nightmare. A big leg attached to a torso, clusters of organs instead of the head, a vagina in place of the mouth: in the hands of this sensitive painter the canvas functions like a mirror and the improbable displacement of limbs and organs turn out to be visible traces of the invisible human soul.

Background
My father is a graphic designer and my sister is a painter. It was clear from the beginning that I would spend my life painting and drawing. I started drawing and painting as a child. I never asked myself the question 'what shall I do in life?' I just knew. I feel like I was born into painting.

Art school
It was fun [Jaune attended the Kunstakademie in Düsseldorf]. I learnt a lot because I had great teachers. Obviously I did not always agree with everything that I was told, but one learns also through disagreeing. I attended life-drawing classes, yes, and loved it! I have always loved the human body.

Subject matter
I don't have a favourite subject. My motives change with each painting. However, I do choose to paint human beings and put them into the desired context to express what is on my mind and what I feel. Painting is my language for things that I cannot put into words or speak of.

Inner portraiture
I don't see myself as a portrait painter. In fact I rarely paint a portrait of somebody that I know. I paint emotions, struggles, power structures and inner feelings. If a face works as an effective subject for me to express what I want, I will paint that face but I do not consider this a portrait.

A magical process
My approach to painting is entirely instinctive. The painting evolves as I work on it. My technique evolved naturally over the years, through working hard, and it keeps developing. But I don't think there is a specific technical aspect or effect I am trying to achieve. The truth is that I forget technique when I paint. I paint from memories and imagination – all kinds of sources and inspirations.

Sometimes I find images on the Internet or use old photographs that I discover, but these usually serve as fragments of the whole painting. For example, I can come across an advertisement in a magazine and part of that image could end up as the background of one of my paintings. My decisions are subconscious and there is no recipe. There is a unique magic in painting that cannot be put into words and that no other media can convey.

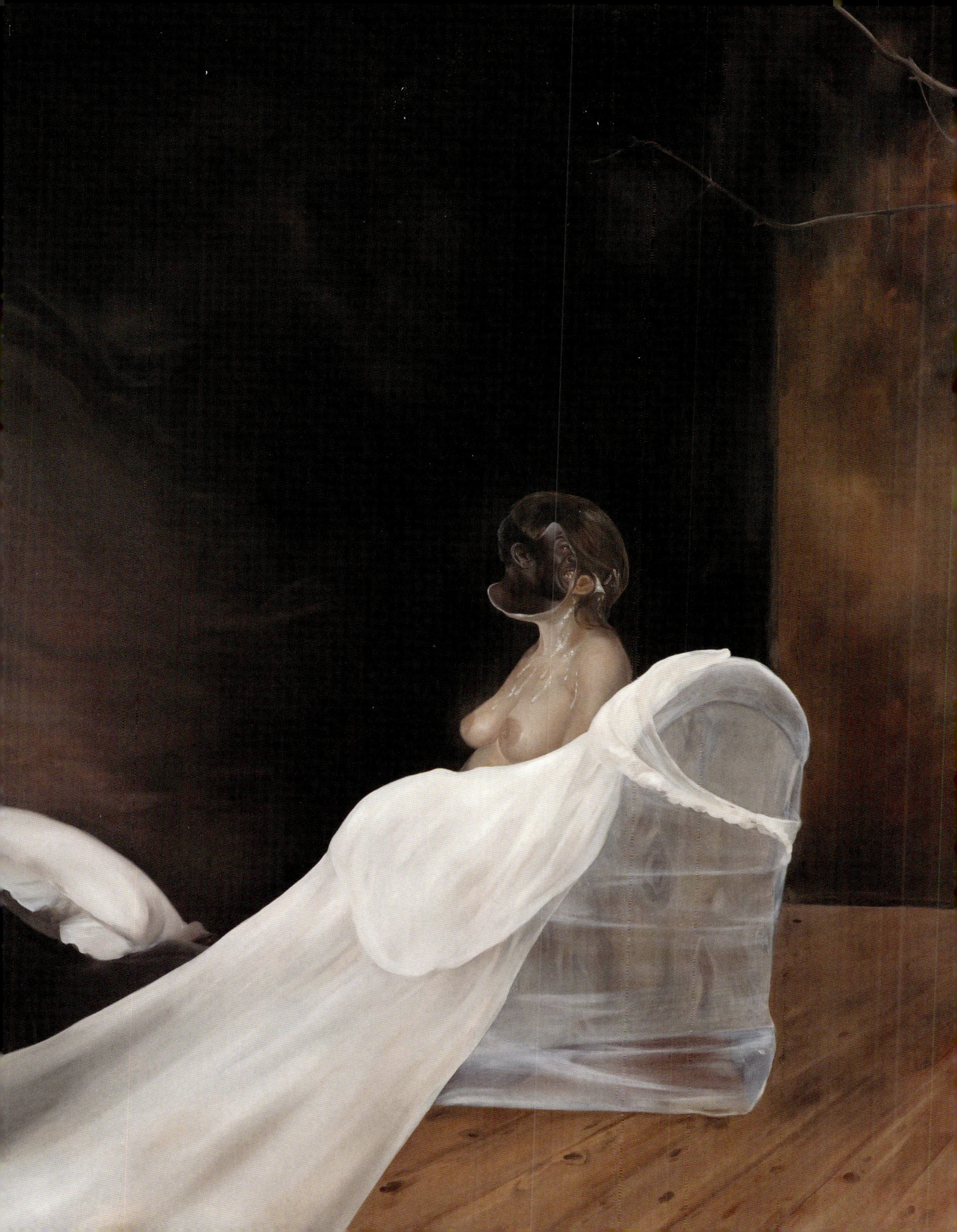

White Paper
2009, oil on canvas, 73 × 60 cm
(28¾ × 23⅝ in).

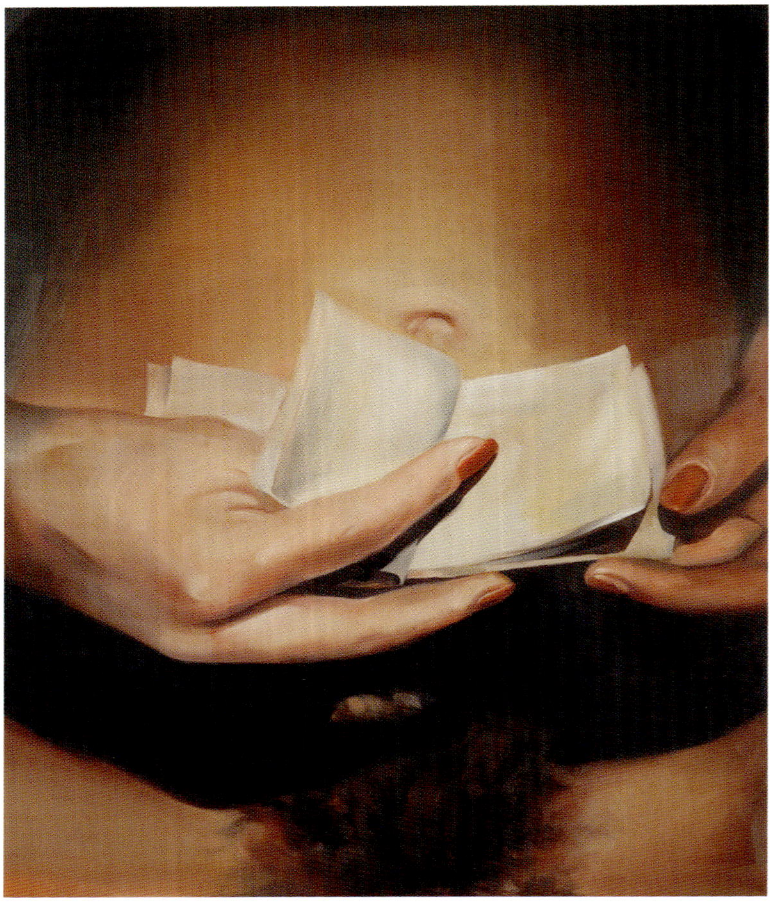

Dissolved Girl
2010, oil on canvas, 195 × 130 cm
(76¾ × 51 in).

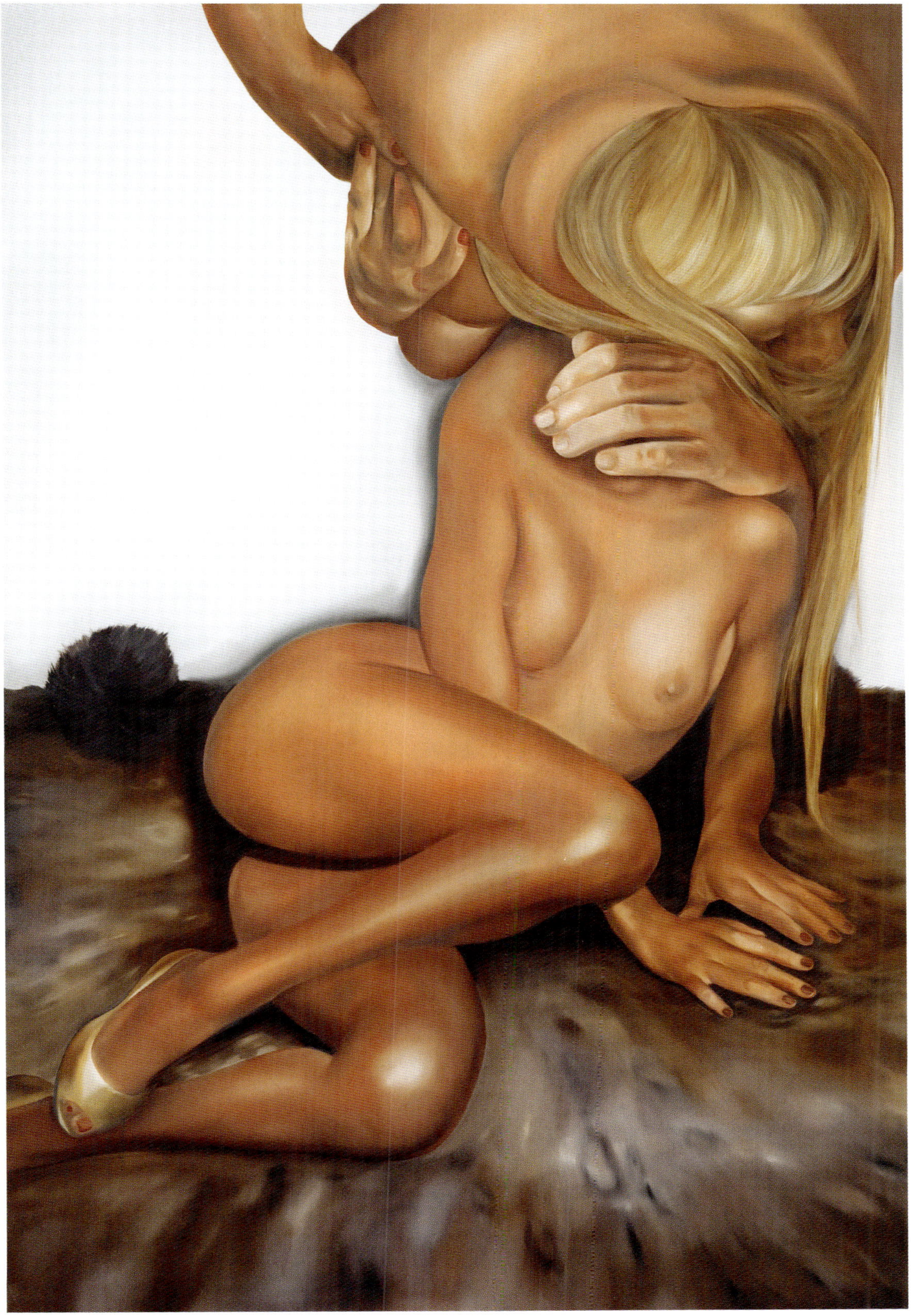

Tear Drop
2010, oil on canvas 65 × 54 cm
(25⅝ × 21¼ in).

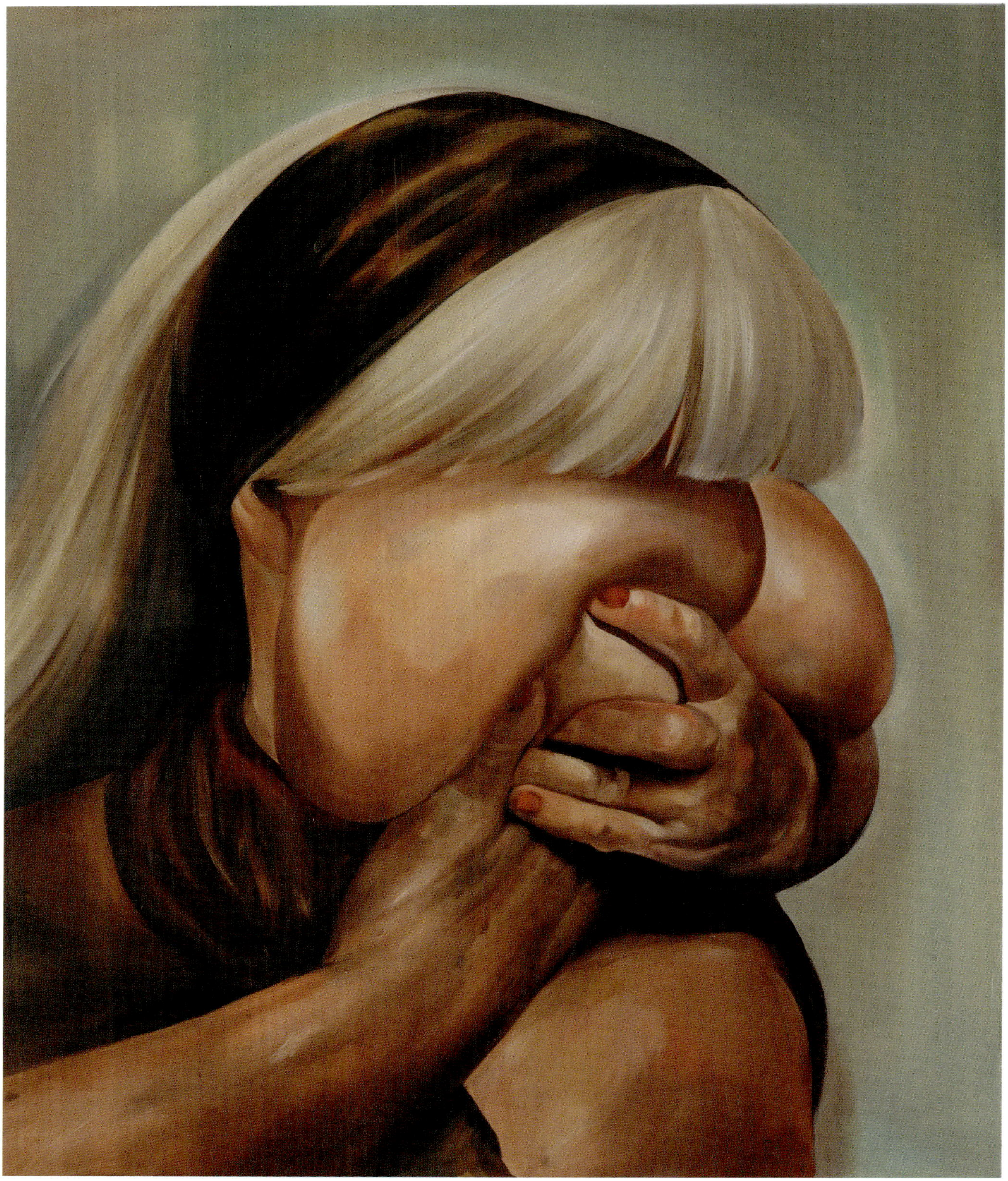

Twosome
2012, oil on canvas, 190 × 280 cm
(75 × 110 in).

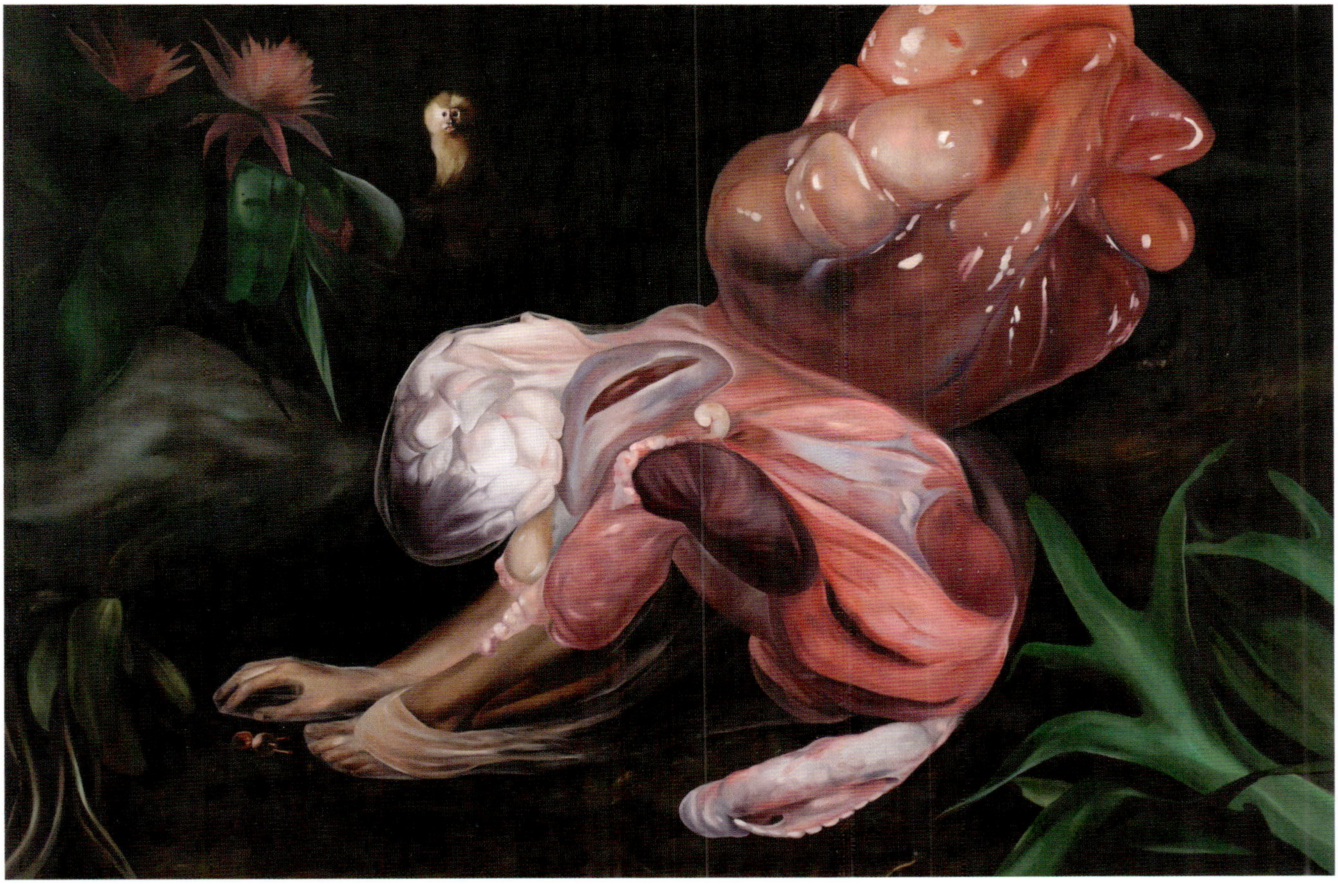

Grasshopper
2009, oil on board, 244 × 183 cm
(96 × 72 in).

Chantal Joffe
Born: 1969, St. Albans, Vermont
Lives: London

If Paint were ever to become a person, and were Paint to start hanging around London, making friends and taking pictures, these pictures would probably look like Chantal Joffe's. Her work is characterized by a passionate relationship with the medium (she likens it to a religion), which has allowed her – like every great love affair – to preserve a sense of spontaneous discovery, of innocence, which she explores at length and in depth with each new encounter with both medium and subject matter.

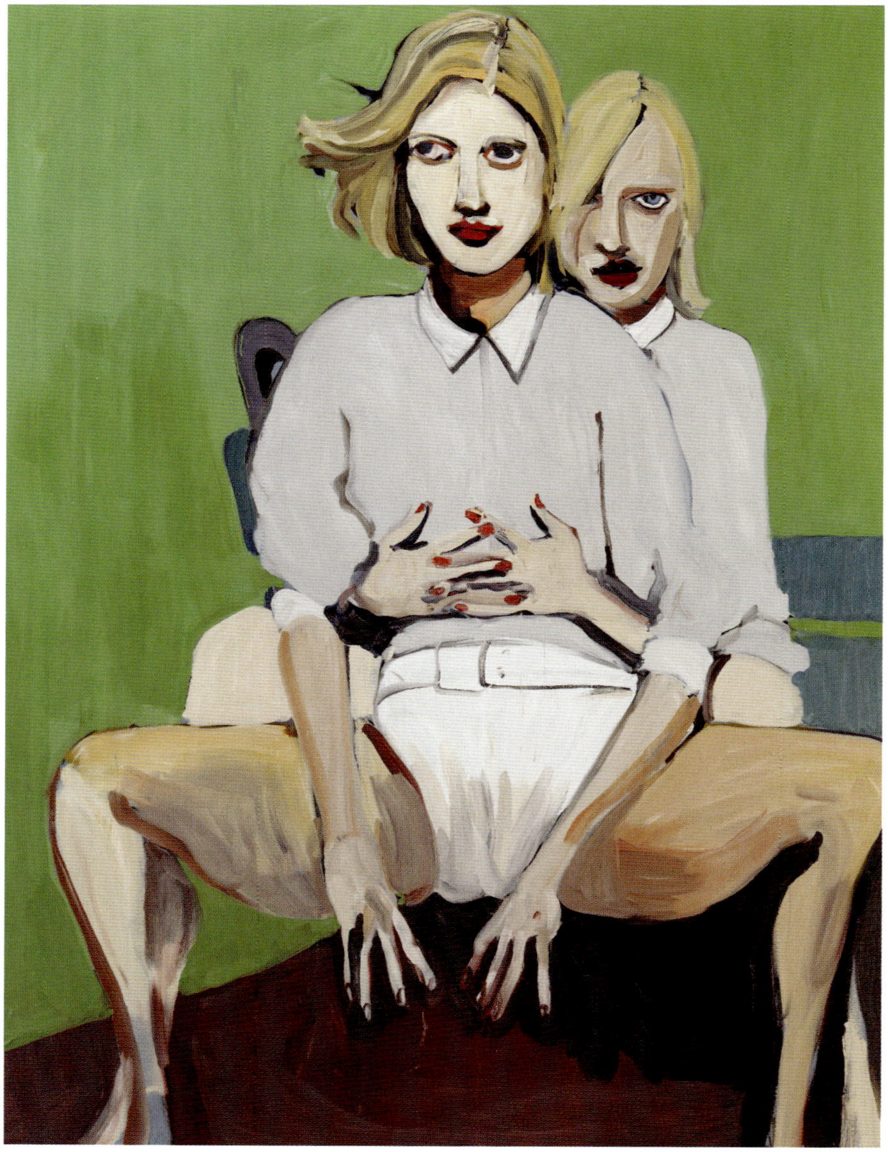

Background

My mother is a painter but she never took us to museums or galleries. The first big show I ever saw was the Renoir show at the Hayward [1985], when I was 15. I couldn't believe it, it was a good feeling to feel I was discovering it for myself. My first sketchbooks (when I was about 7) were [filled with] head-and-shoulder portraits of people: a bearded man with glasses and so on. I only ever really liked painting people.

Art school

I couldn't believe how wonderful it was when I got to Camberwell. I didn't ever want to leave, even when it closed at nine o'clock at night. I would make my way home on the tube black with charcoal. I couldn't wait to get there in the morning. I tried to go to college the day after the hurricane in 1987!
Art school was a revelation to me.

Painting v. Conceptual Art:

I don't think I ever wavered from my conviction that some painters were gods and that painting was the best thing you could do. I am not someone who cares what others think, particularly. I was at Glasgow with Jonathan Monk, David Shrigley, Simon Starling, Toby Webster; and I knew them as friends, but it never struck me that what they were doing was more interesting than what I was. It's funny how you can be quite monomaniacal! Either you fall in love with painting and believe in it or you don't. It's a bit like a religion in that way; you can doubt it, or believe it. It's a belief structure and Conceptual Art is like that as well. Not to say that I am not interested in Conceptual Art, it's just not the way I work.

Subjects

I like to look at people in the street, on buses. London is a great place to look at people. My favourite model, Megan, I first saw dropping her son off at nursery school; when I asked her to sit for me she thought I wanted her to babysit. I find it difficult to ask people to sit though. And you have this impression of someone, you read their body and you invent a life and a personality for them. It's distracting when they come and sit for you and you find out that they are an entirely different person. You have to start again and reformulate your approach to them. It interferes with what I am trying to do. It reminds me of Munch and his wish to get back to the original feeling or view. That is what I am trying to do, get back to the original version or view of that person. Too much socializing with them gets in the way of that!

On painting men

I am certainly less interested [in painting men]. I've painted a man recently as part of a pair and I've really struggled to make it look like he was ever alive or existed in any place.
I think my brain is limited in that I can't empathize with men. I can paint women because I empathize with them, I can think of how they feel. My boyfriend would agree....

Beauty

I'm not sure that I think about beauty explicitly. I'm drawn to different people. My earliest consciousness of that is looking intently at people on buses, particularly people's legs, the line and shape of them. When I was a teenager that was the first thing that I looked at! I spent a lot of time at school looking at other people. There was this trend, when I was at school, to wear a bun [a type of hairstyle] that was held by a plastic cage with a spike through it. It was the worst thing that I have ever seen but also formally fascinating. I have always been interested in looking at other people in a real 'teenage girl' way. There are people, bodies, faces that I am really drawn to and there are those that don't draw me in at all. I love the way models will appear in different guises in different images, but you can identify the good ones no matter how they are presented or styled; they have a special quality. I don't know if I think of 'beauty' in any specific way but rather as what your eye likes to rest on.

Red Head on Ochre
2012, giclee on paper, 40 × 33 cm
(15¾ × 13 in).

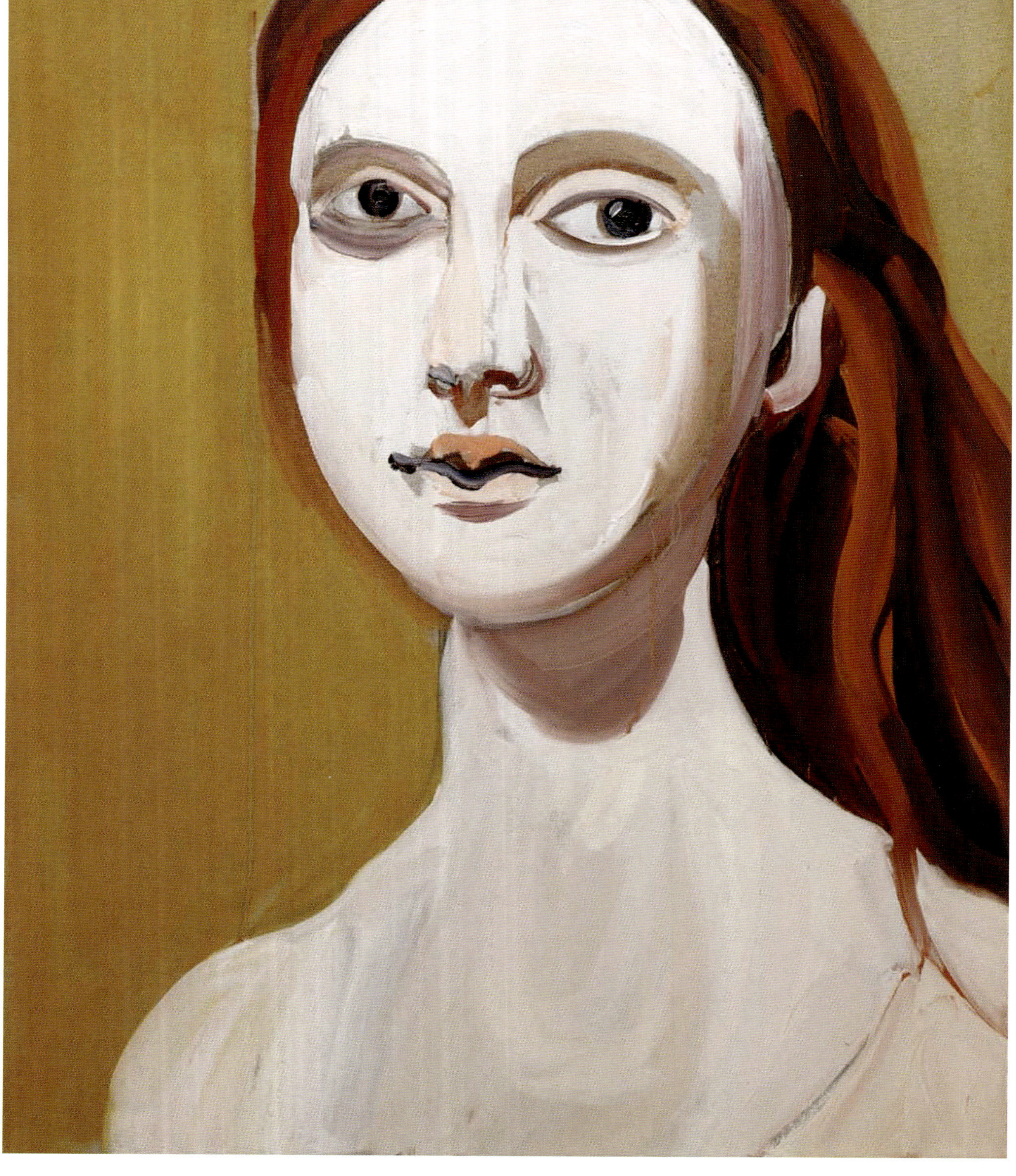

Untitled (Susan)
2010, oil on board, 138 × 184 cm
(54 × 72 in).

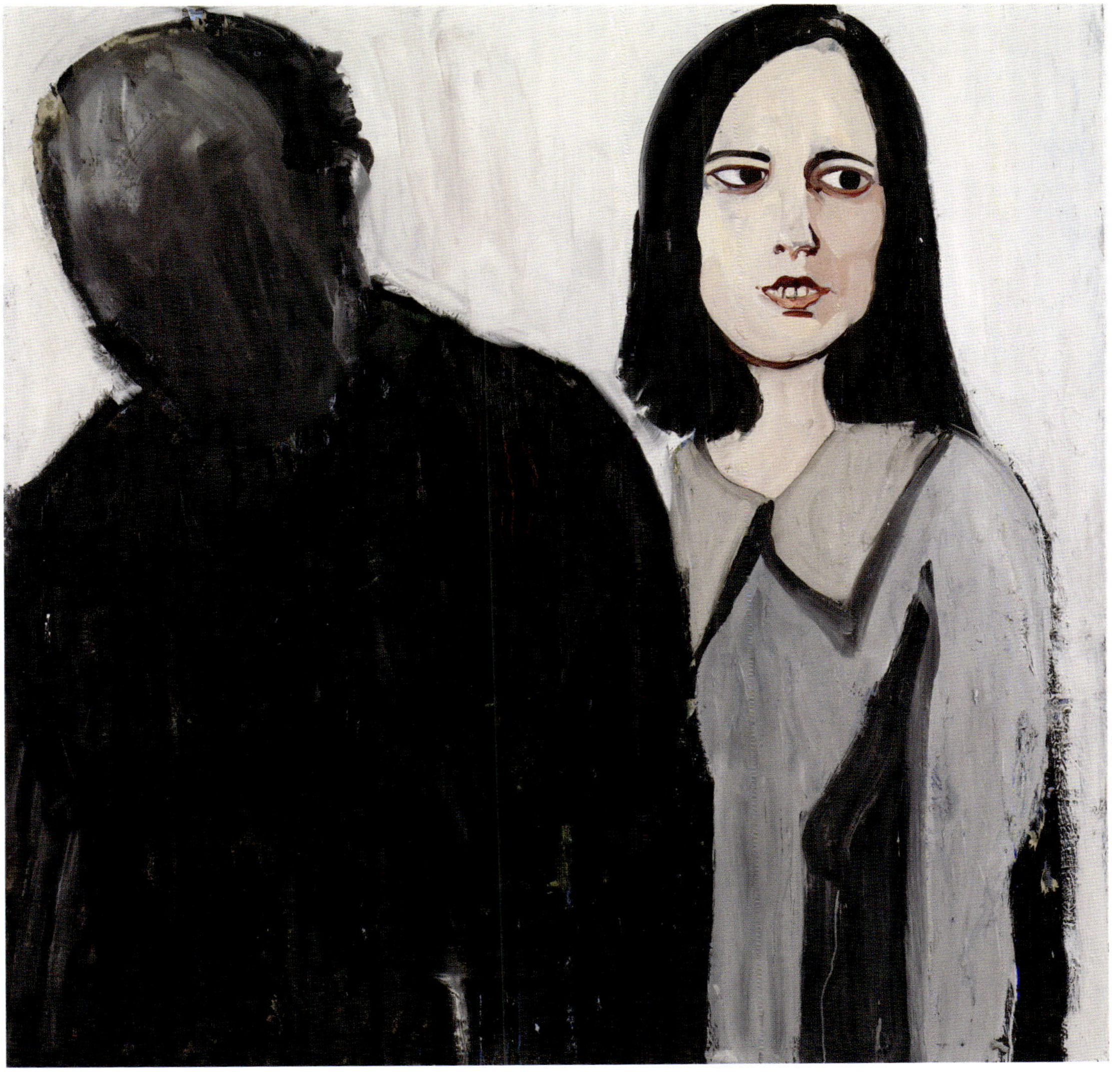

Isabella in a Blue Dress
2010, oil on canvas, 80 × 40 cm
(31½ × 15¾ in).

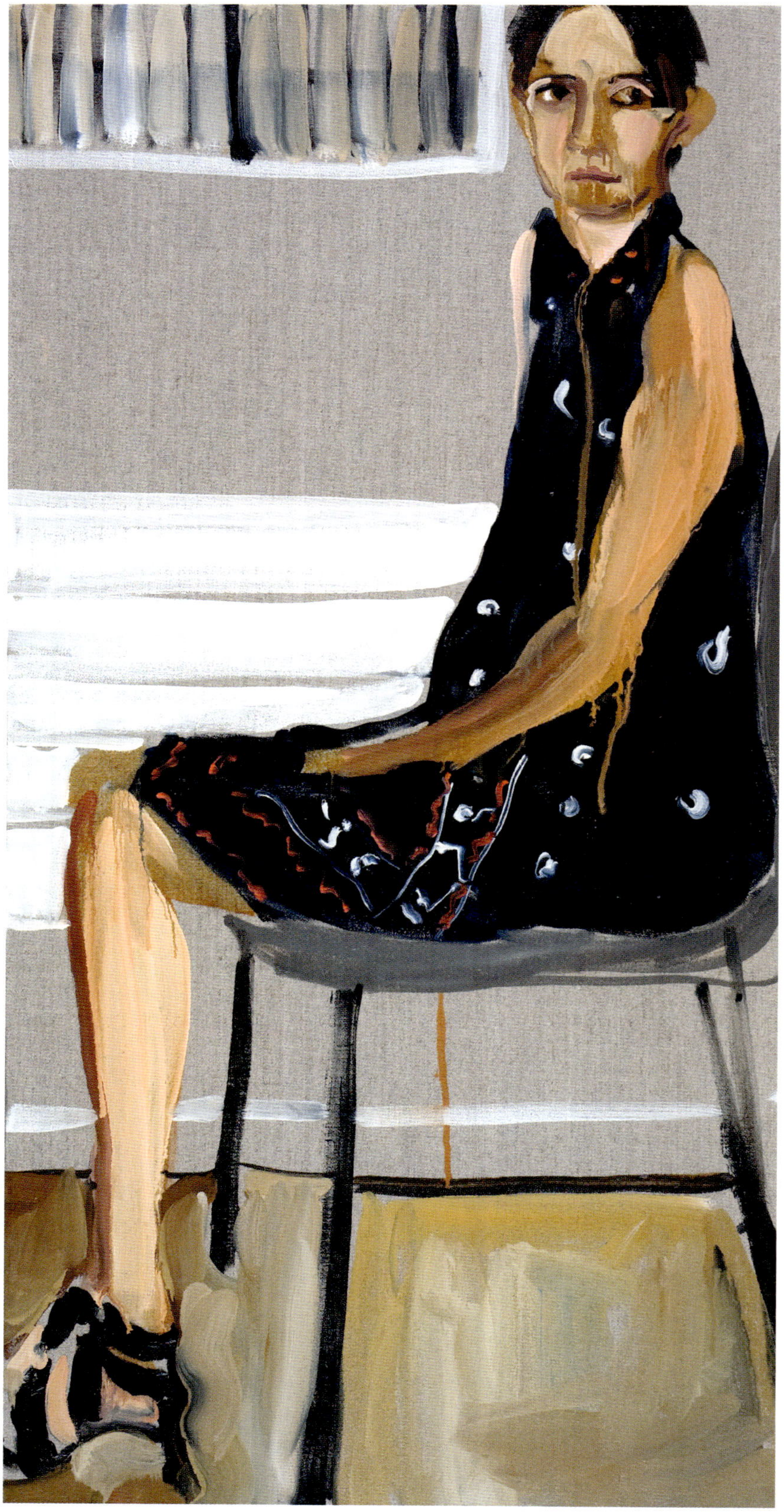

Dan Eating a Banana
2012, oil on board, 40 × 30 cm
(15¾ × 11¾ in).

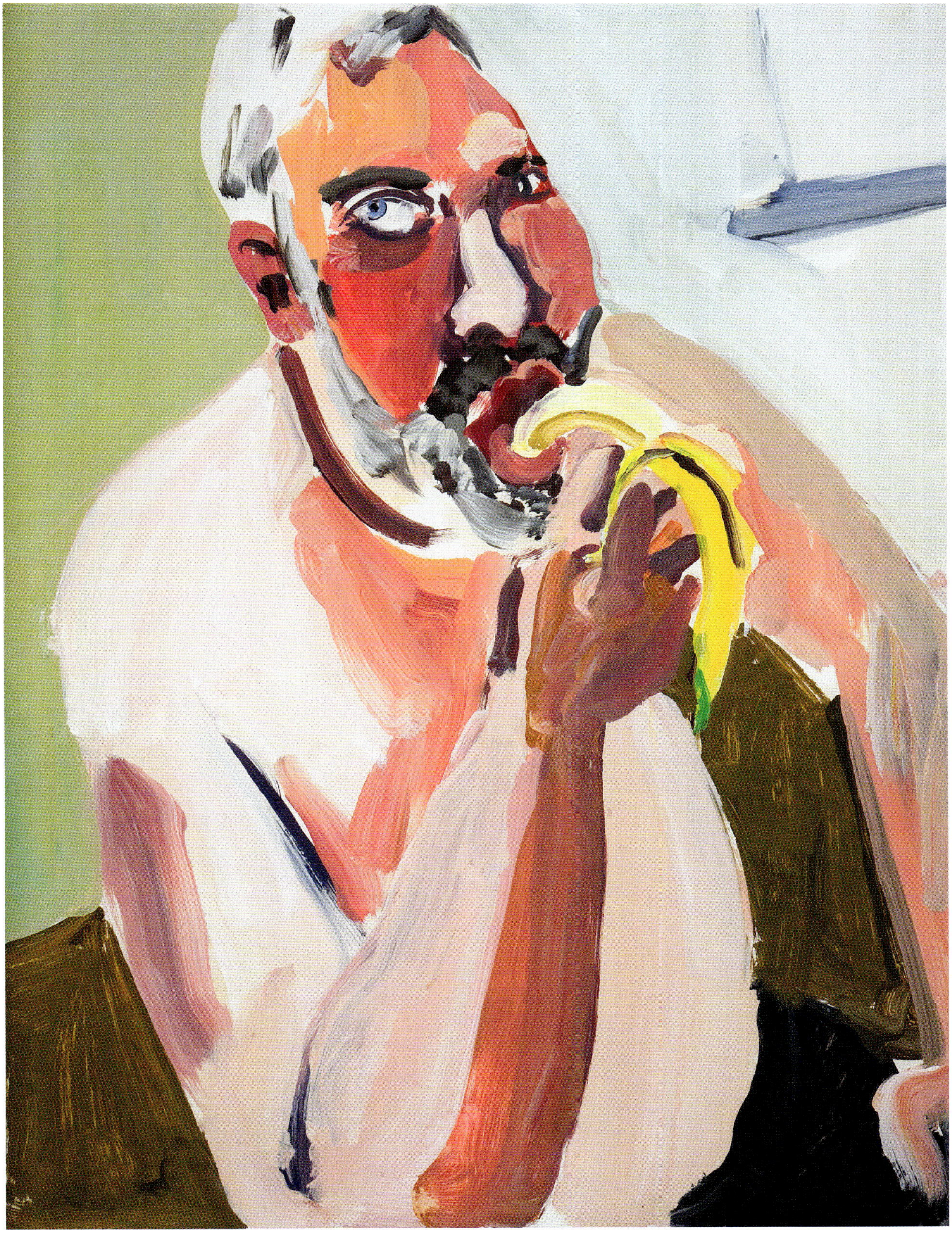

Wegweiser
2012, oil on canvas, 117 × 115 cm
(46 × 45 in).

Thoralf Knobloch
Born: 1972, Bautzen (Germany)
Lives: Berlin

With very broad strokes, you could draw a parallel between the fine and often fuzzy line separating figuration and abstraction, and that separating reality and our perception of it. This path has guided a whole generation of German painters from the so-called Leipzig and Dresden schools (the heirs of Richter, Kiefer and Kippenberger). A perfect example of that would be Ebehard Havekost, who will sometimes veer one way, sometimes the other. Berlin-based artist Thoralf Knobloch, on the other hand, has always resisted the drift towards lyrical blurriness. His is a robust brand of Realism, in which the element of abstraction is added as an extra layer, or rather, an extra dimension.

Art schools, style and technique
During our two-year foundation course we did a lot of drawing and painting of nudes. In the years that followed there was a great deal of emphasis placed on that area in specialist classes too. I'm convinced it was important and useful for me. But at the end of the 1990s I began to take photographs instead of drawing from nature.

While I was studying at the Dresden Academy, painting from photographs would have been frowned upon, but in the 1990s there were a lot of painters working from photographs, and I tried it too. I finished my studies at the Academy in 1994. My first exhibition was held in 2002. In the intervening eight years I tried out various methods until I achieved results that I found acceptable to some degree. I don't feel like I belong to any particular German school of painting, but the Dresden painting and drawing tradition has certainly influenced my work.

Process
For me, it was never about painting photo-like surfaces; rather the photographs replaced the sketches as an aid to my memory. The execution on the canvas then takes place in the traditional way: preliminary drawing, various types of colour application, then balancing out the colours, surfaces and lines.

My pictures are painted from my own photographs; sometimes I research a subject thoroughly, even over a long period of time; sometimes I just use snapshots. The process always starts with photographic research in my area or surroundings. Then I have to make choices, firstly on the screen and then from the paper copies. When I finally decide on a subject, it will be for reasons of both form and content, but intuition also plays an important role. I don't do any landscape research in the traditional sense. I paint objects in a space; landscape is often just defined by a horizon line or colour field.

Any amount of time can pass between the individual steps of the process from selecting the subject to the final coat of colour – that's why some pictures are finished in a week and others only after two years. On average I need two to three weeks to finish a painting.

Narrative
I link the things I paint to tell stories, even speculatively. But as I'm painting they are less important to me than the formal aspects of the subject. Those observing my pictures sometimes then perceive these as a narrative, but the stories they connect with can be very different from my own.

In some of my paintings there are objects and places that create a sense of deterioration, or things that are not in use any more. It's possible that this is nostalgia.

Capturing reality
Reality is always complex and an individual work of art, regardless of the technique used, can never capture everything. Realism is a starting point for alienation and abstraction.

I paint objectively, not Photo-Realistically. In my painting I distance myself from the object to concentrate on form and abstracts. I try to create something new every time, and to make sense of the chaos.

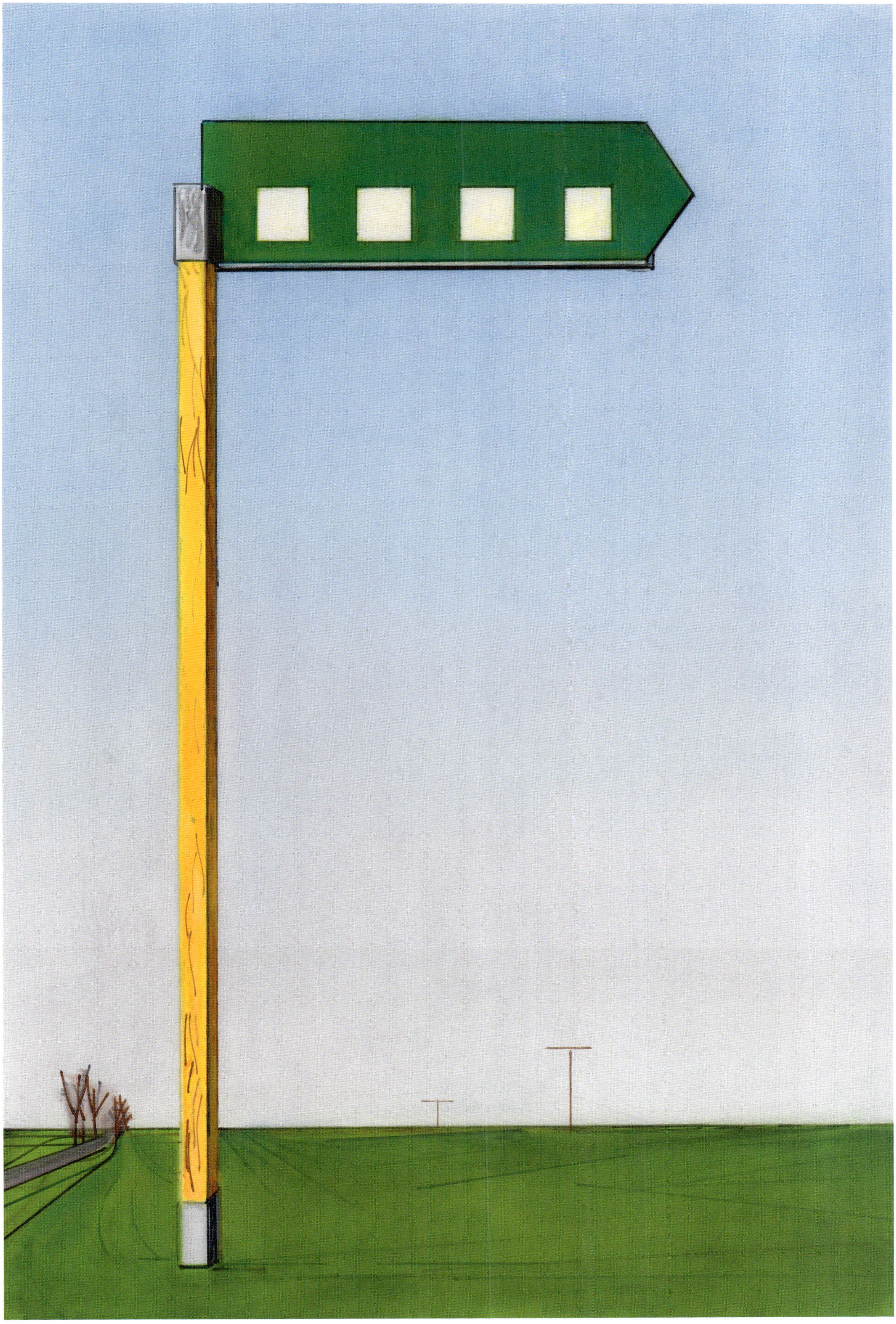

Tankstelle, Nachts
2011–2012, oil on canvas,
180 × 120 cm (71 × 47 in).

Bahnkreutz
2012, oil on canvas, 165 × 110 cm
(65 × 43 in).

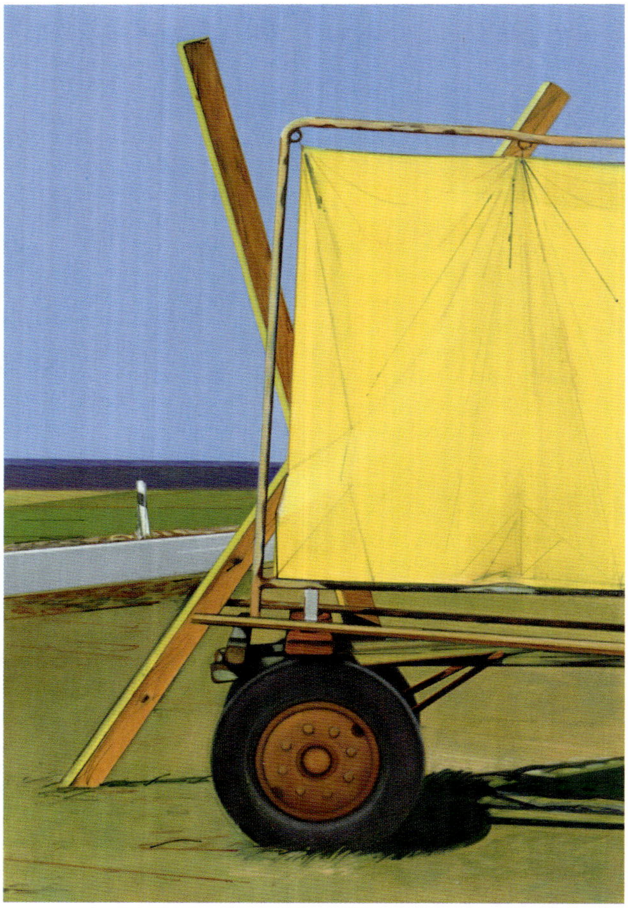

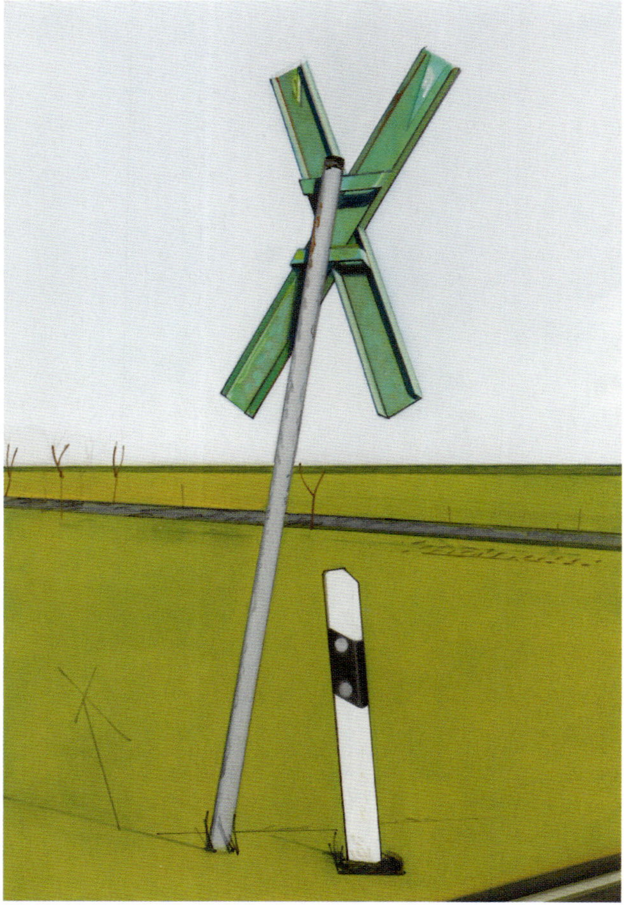

X, Sommer
2012, oil on canvas, 180 × 120 cm
(71 × 47 in).

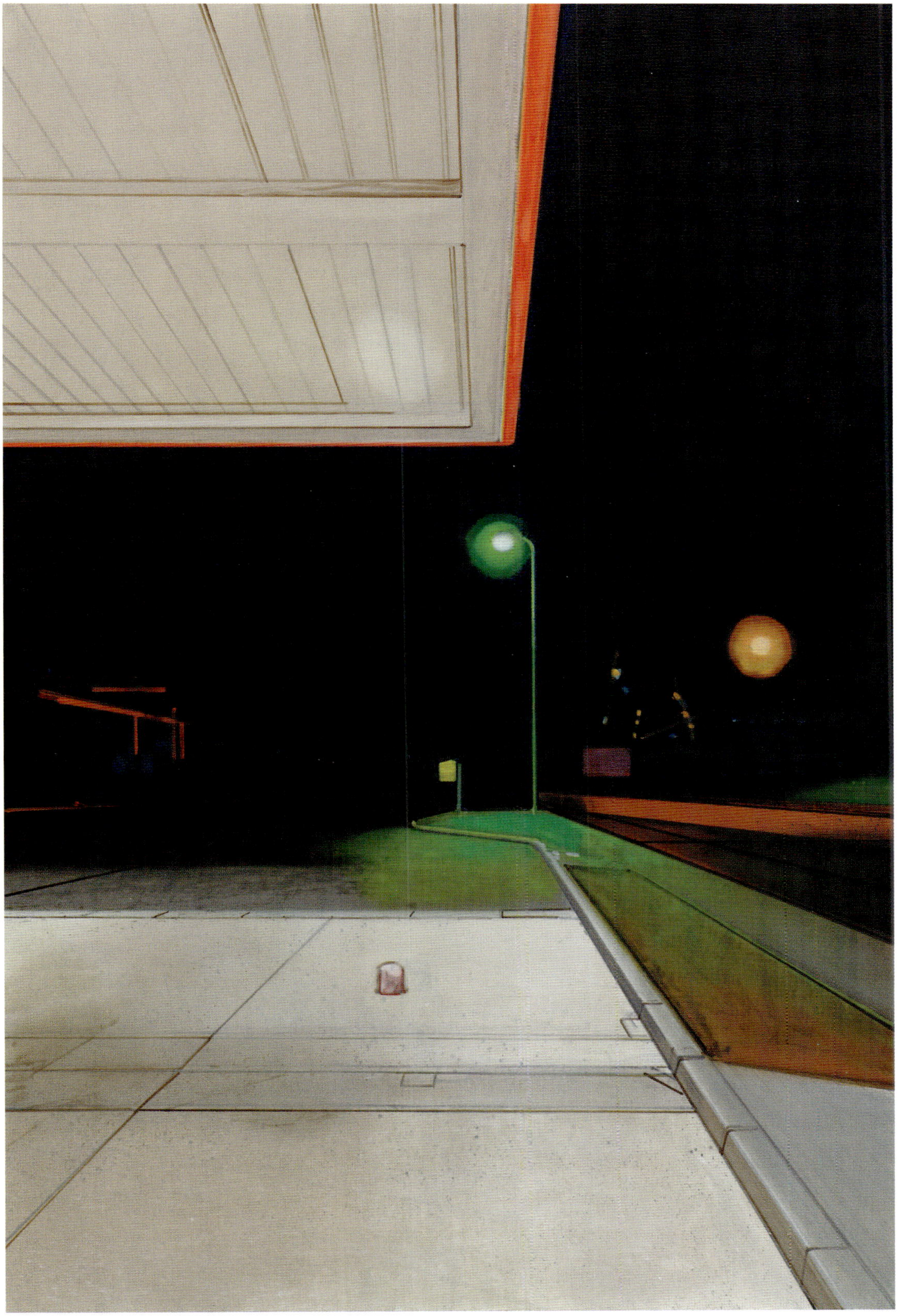

Boot im Eis, Kieloben
2011–2012, oil on canvas,
140 × 210 cm (55 × 83 in).

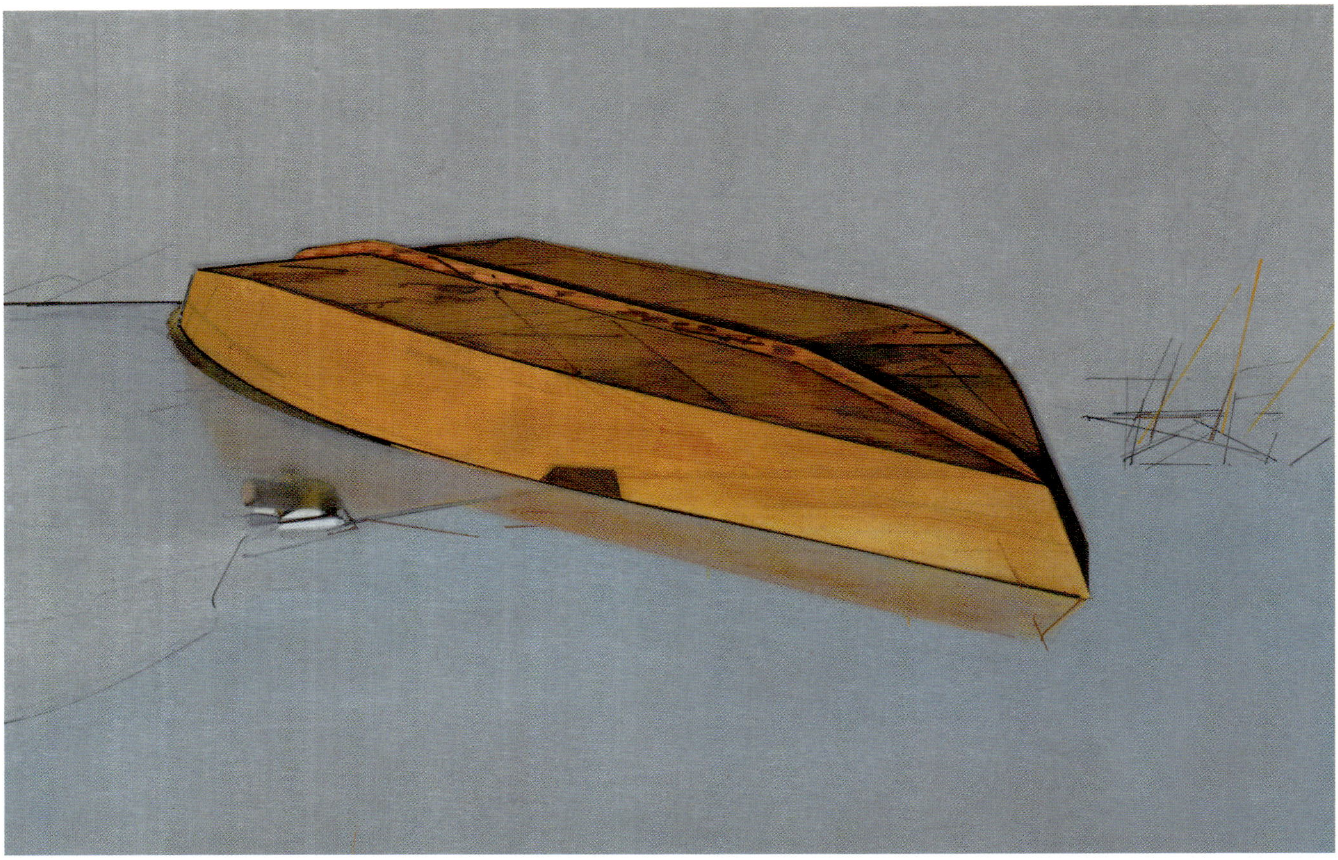

Rettungsgerät
2012, oil on canvas, 150 × 100 cm
(59 × 39 in).

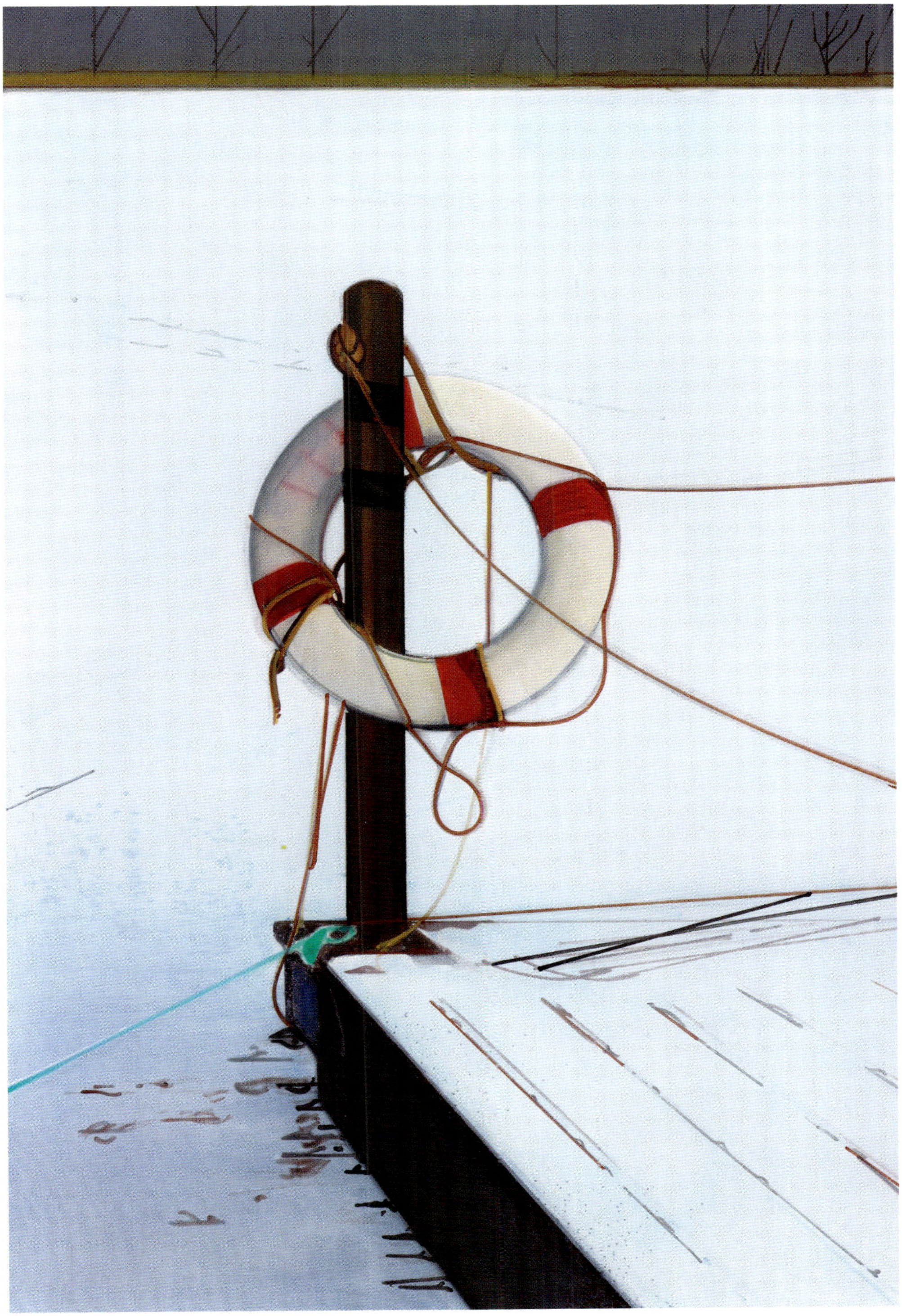

The Bet, Boy or Girl, Sierra Leone 2001
2012, oil on canvas, 340 × 540 cm
(134 × 213 in).

Ronald Ophuis
Born: 1968, Hengelo (Netherlands)
Lives: Amsterdam

A pregnant woman is held up in the air by three soldiers, a fourth stands in between her legs holding a knife to her belly. 'It is all part of a bet,' Dutch artist Ronald Ophuis explains in the softest possible tone, waving at the cinema screen-sized canvas covering one whole wall of his studio, and on which a typical African street is depicted. 'When I was in Sierra Leone, I was told about this game the boys [the child soldiers fighting in the civil war] used to play whenever they came across a pregnant woman. It was called "Boy or Girl". They would bet on what it would be, then use a knife to improvise a primitive Caesarean, like cutting a pig open. It was a recurrent story. I checked it with the other guys. They all recognized it.' Perhaps more than any other painter of his generation, Ronald Ophuis asks the question of just how far painting can go, and what its role is in our image-saturated world.

Controversy
Confused viewers did break into galleries showing my work in order to destroy it. A group has even brought the work to court on the basis of child abuse. A painting is less objective than a photograph, and if certain people don't like it, they can find fault with the fact that someone actively wanted to paint this.

Influences
I was raised as a Catholic. There was this great fresco painting in the church of my grandmother. It was a crucifixion and, as a child, it was always a sensational visit. I try to recapture that sensation ... I have left the Catholic religion and the focus is on the suffering of normal people, under extreme circumstances.

There was a visit to the Louvre and the paintings of Eugène Delacroix and Théodore Géricault, particularly *The Raft of the Medusa*. When I saw that painting, I thought, that's what I want to do: it was also partly based on real stories.

The ethics of painting
I find it more interesting when the violence has a human root, when people don't move around and the violence bursts out in a land close to where they were born, instead of something like the Iraq invasion. I am more interested in identifying myself with that perpetrator: how far would you go yourself if you were in that position? It is not so easy to condemn a perpetrator when you are really looking into it. Take the case of the Sierra Leone child soldiers. They did cruel things, but they were on drugs, they were forced to be part of these armies, often enslaved when they were kids with no possibility of real love. They knew that a normal return to society would be very difficult for them. When they saw a happy pregnant woman, there was something there they couldn't reach. Once you identify yourself with the child soldiers, you can't judge them anymore. I want to work without morality. Unlike journalism, a work of art gives you the opportunity to identify with another person, both victim and offender. I try not to work with a set of morals: your frame of mind will stay within a confined area and the impact of the work will diminish.

In the beginning, I couldn't help asking myself about why I was jumping from genocide to genocide. But the work is really more about mankind than about war.

Child soldiers
In Sierra Leone I would go out in the morning to these car-washing areas. They had buckets of water and their fingers were all bent as they had done so much shooting. I had a guide with me. I would take them with me to a bar on the beach and explain to them who I was and what I was doing. Getting the stories out of former child soldiers was easy. But they would speak about what 'we' did – always 'we did this or that', never 'I'. It was always told like a bad movie, or a comic strip. Most of them were sleeping rough, or had a very low position in their families and houses. The war was like a school for them. There was one guy who was highly intelligent and I asked him what he was planning to do. He replied that he was trying to get a driving licence, because in that way he could re-enter the army, then he could be sent as a UN soldier to other wars. Quite a few of these war 'veterans' are now being hired as guards in foreign compounds.

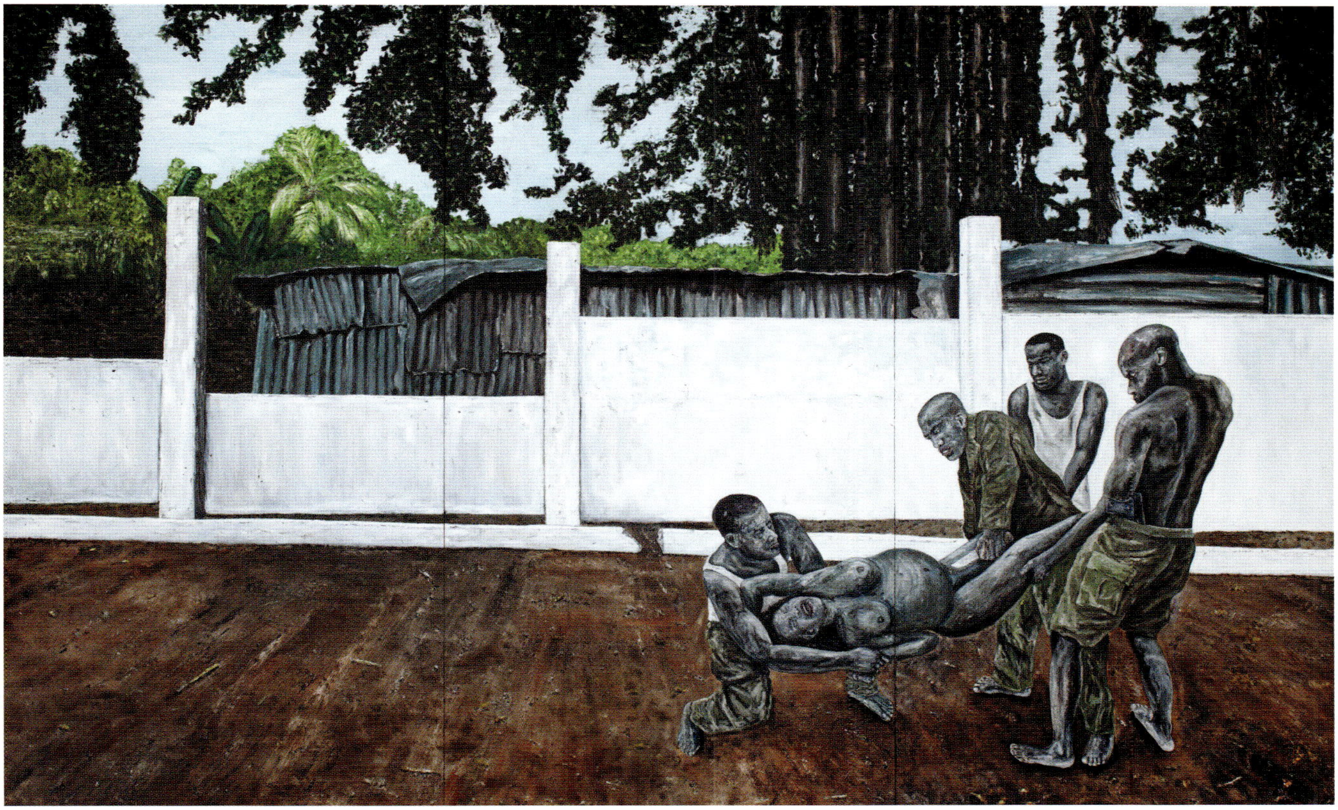

Process
I start by reading all kinds of books on a subject. I build an image archive. Then I visit the places. I always go to a place only once the war is finished. I am not a war photographer. I want to collect the stories, and it is better to wait. These stories I collect by interviewing people. I then create re-enactments with actors.

In Sarajevo and Srebrenica I was amazed at how much had been destroyed. Even the smallest barn on a dead-end street would be shot through. I took pictures of the locations where those traumatic events happened, and interviewed people. In former Yugoslavia it was much harder to talk to the perpetrators of atrocities as they were afraid that what they said could be used against them in courts later. But one of them told me about how he felt there was this unspoken dialogue between perpetrator and victim. Most of the victims who knew that they were going to be killed didn't protest. Perpetrator and victim were connected to death, as a kind of godly experience. Back then [as a child at church] I couldn't suppress the sensation: what would it feel like to be hanging from that cross, to endure those tortures, hearing the death sentence, being pure? – but also the sensation of how it would feel to speak a death sentence, to nail someone to a cross.

Painting, photography, film
There are not so many differences between news photographs of various wars: all you see is a lot of dead bodies. Superficially, photographic images and painted images may cover the same content. But they are completely different. How would Jeff Wall paint? What would a Lucian Freud photograph look like? As soon as you ask yourself these questions, you feel the enormous distance between these two media. I always work on this scale. It is important as people can look at the scenery or notice details and have time for contemplation and for getting into the painting. And the paintings need to be roughed up a little bit. They shouldn't be too photorealistic.

It is hard to remember a painting With a movie it's different. You can recall the feeling quite easily. But a painting is this one individual image to which you need to come back again and again. Journalism will inform you, but at the same time it gives you very little of the suffering, the confusion, the deprivation or the fear. Journalism is much more superficial and does not appeal to beauty or style. Even if it does not reflect the fantasies of the spectator, the experience of a painting will be physical and less easy to ignore. A painting claims more time, and if you're moved by the work you will take more time to read it. Not only the depiction, but also the way it has been painted claims your attention.

Gacaca. 4 Hutu prisoners during
Their Trial, Rwanda 2004
2010 oil on canvas, 300 × 400 cm
(118 × 158 in).

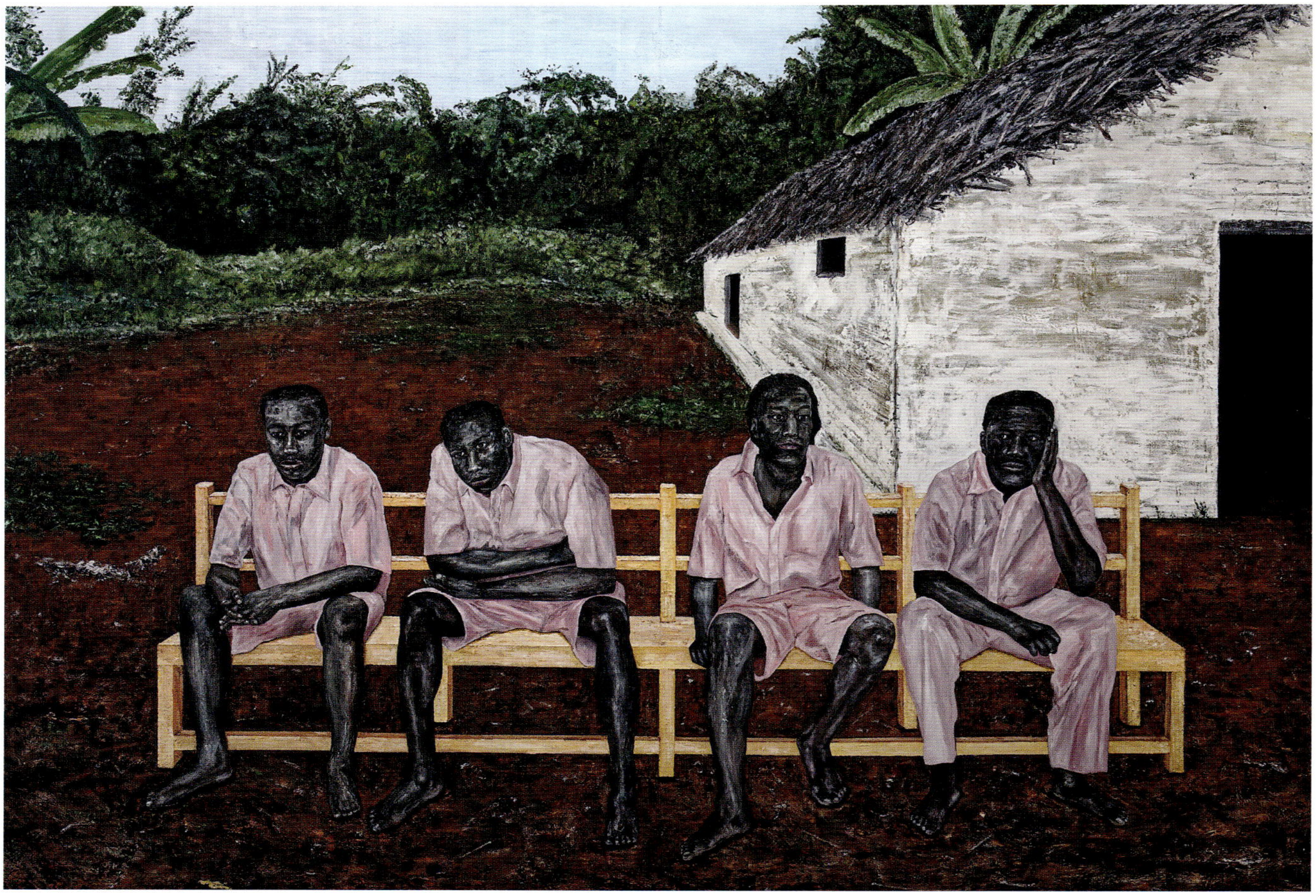

Wounded Man
2010, oil on canvas, 190 × 130 cm
(75 × 51 in).

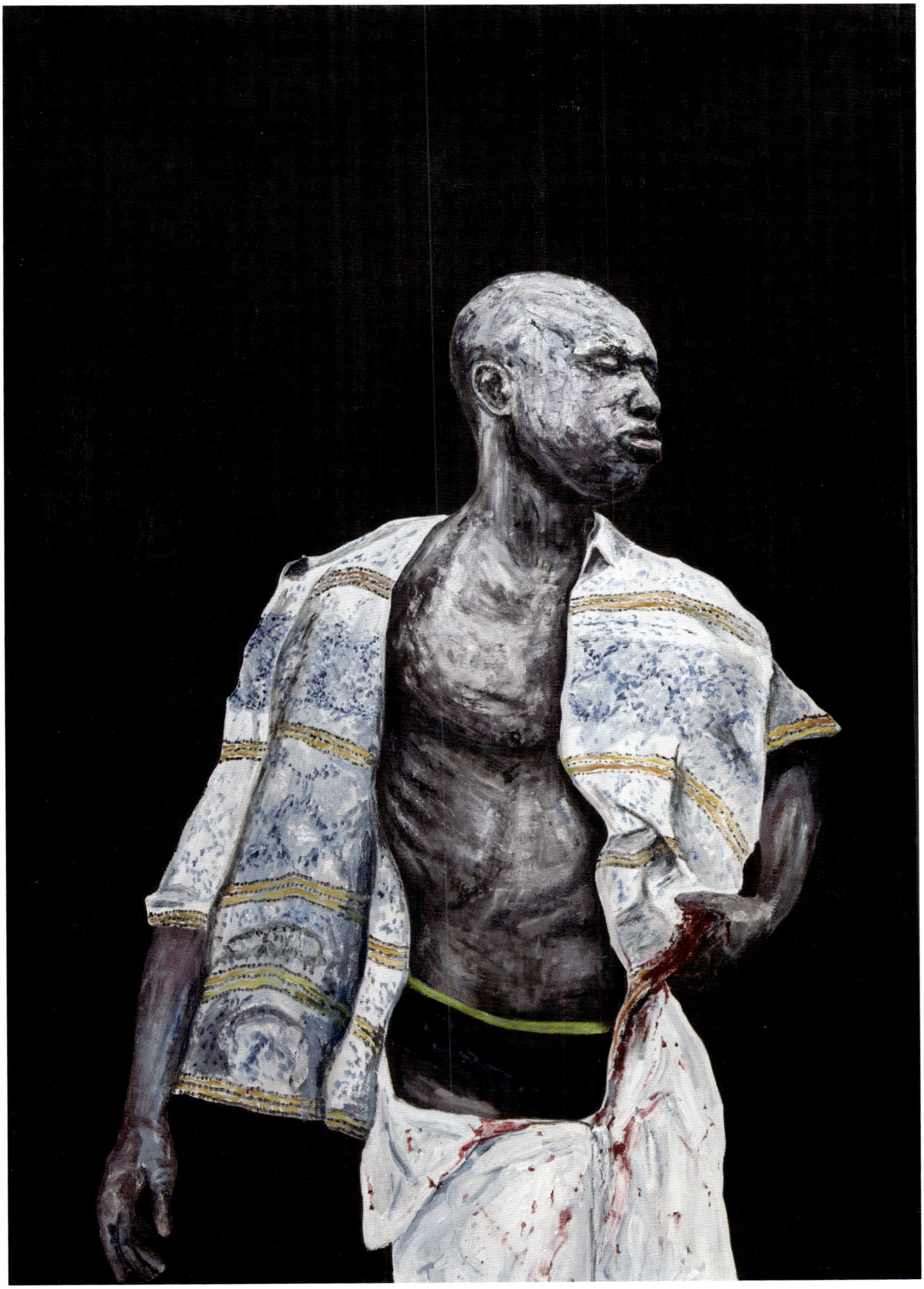

Marches Funebres. Girl with Gun
2011, oil on canvas, 200 × 340 cm
(79 × 134 in).

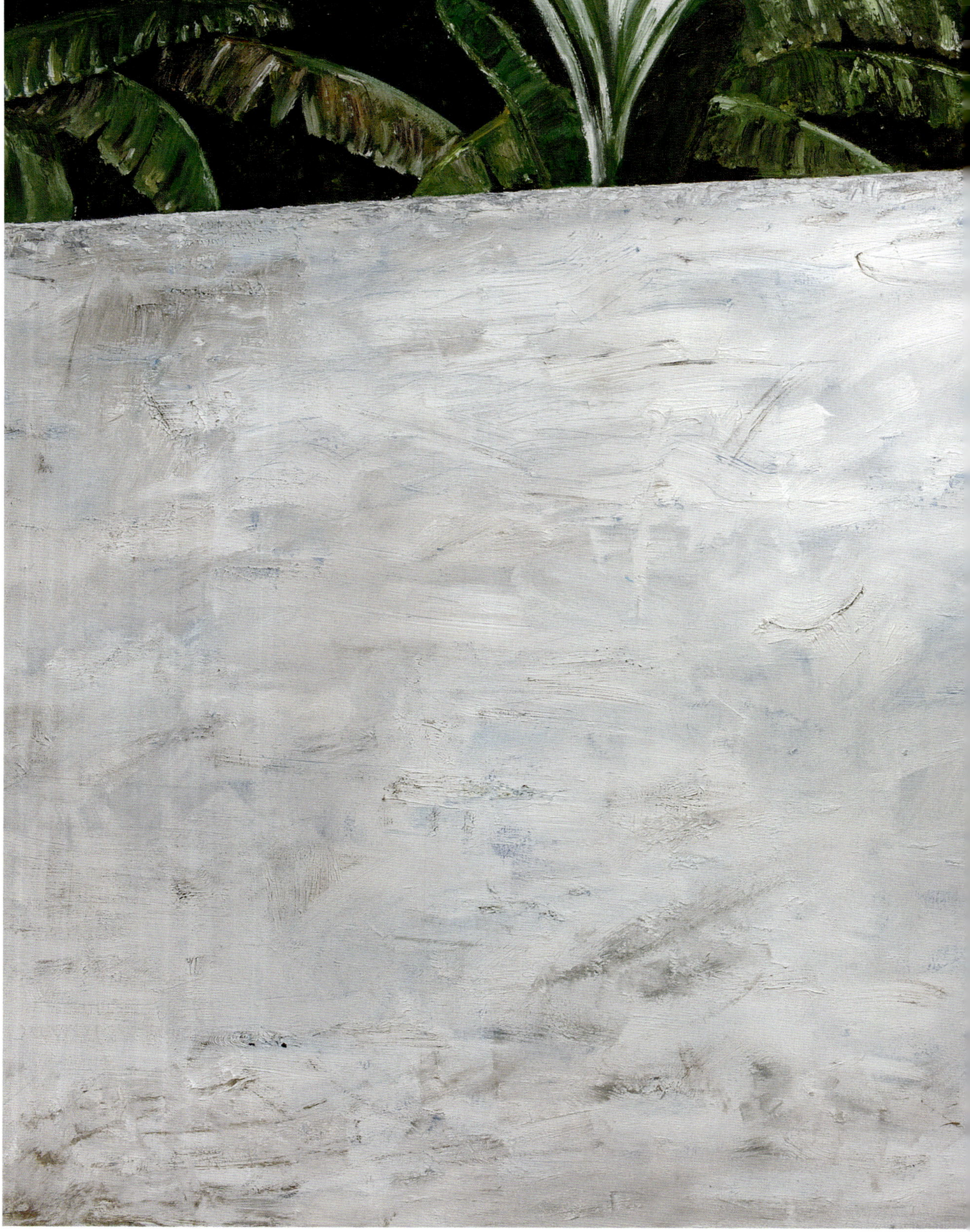

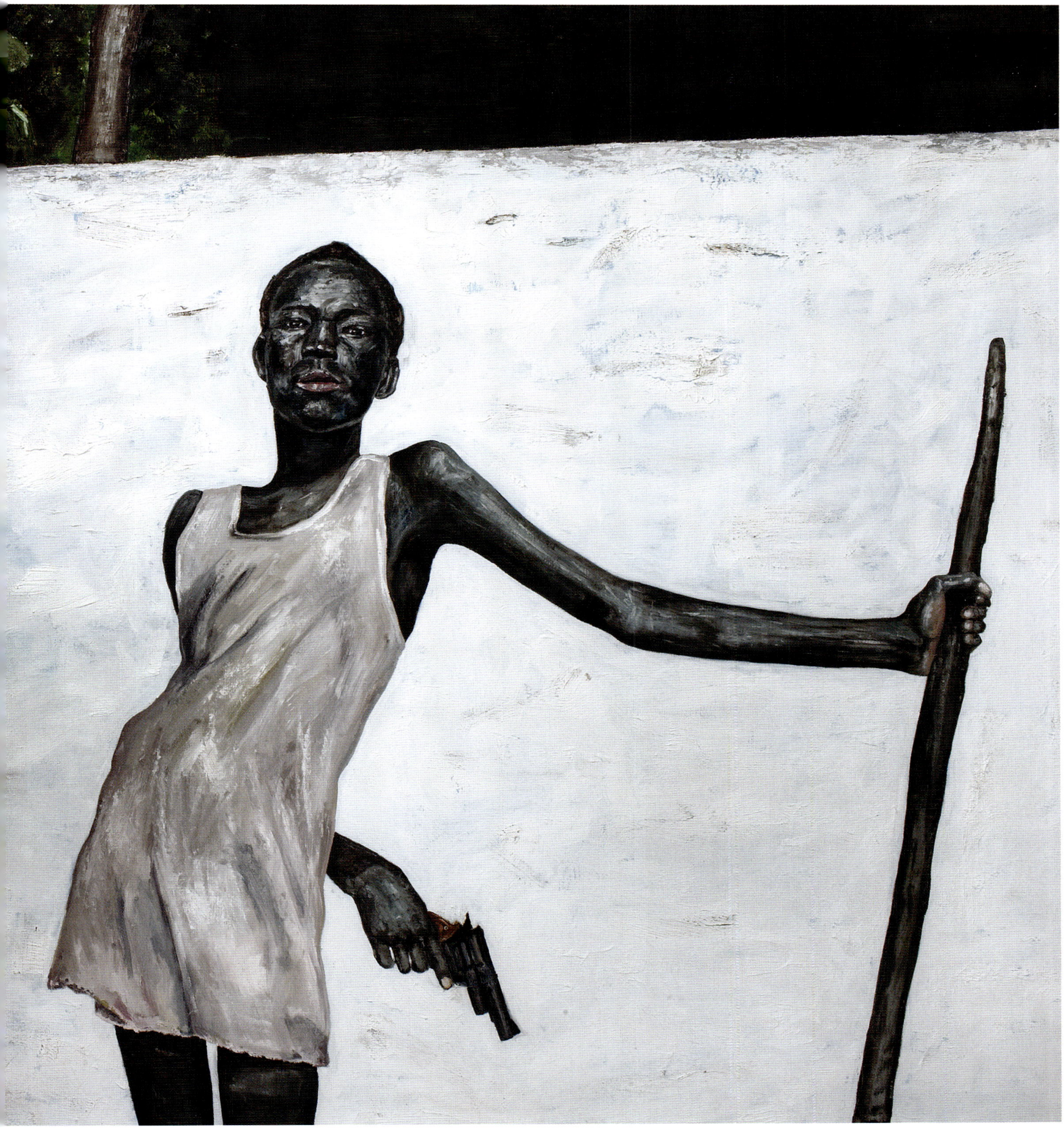

War Story Teller, Small Soldier
2012, oil on paper, 60 × 60 cm
(23⅝ × 23⅝ in).

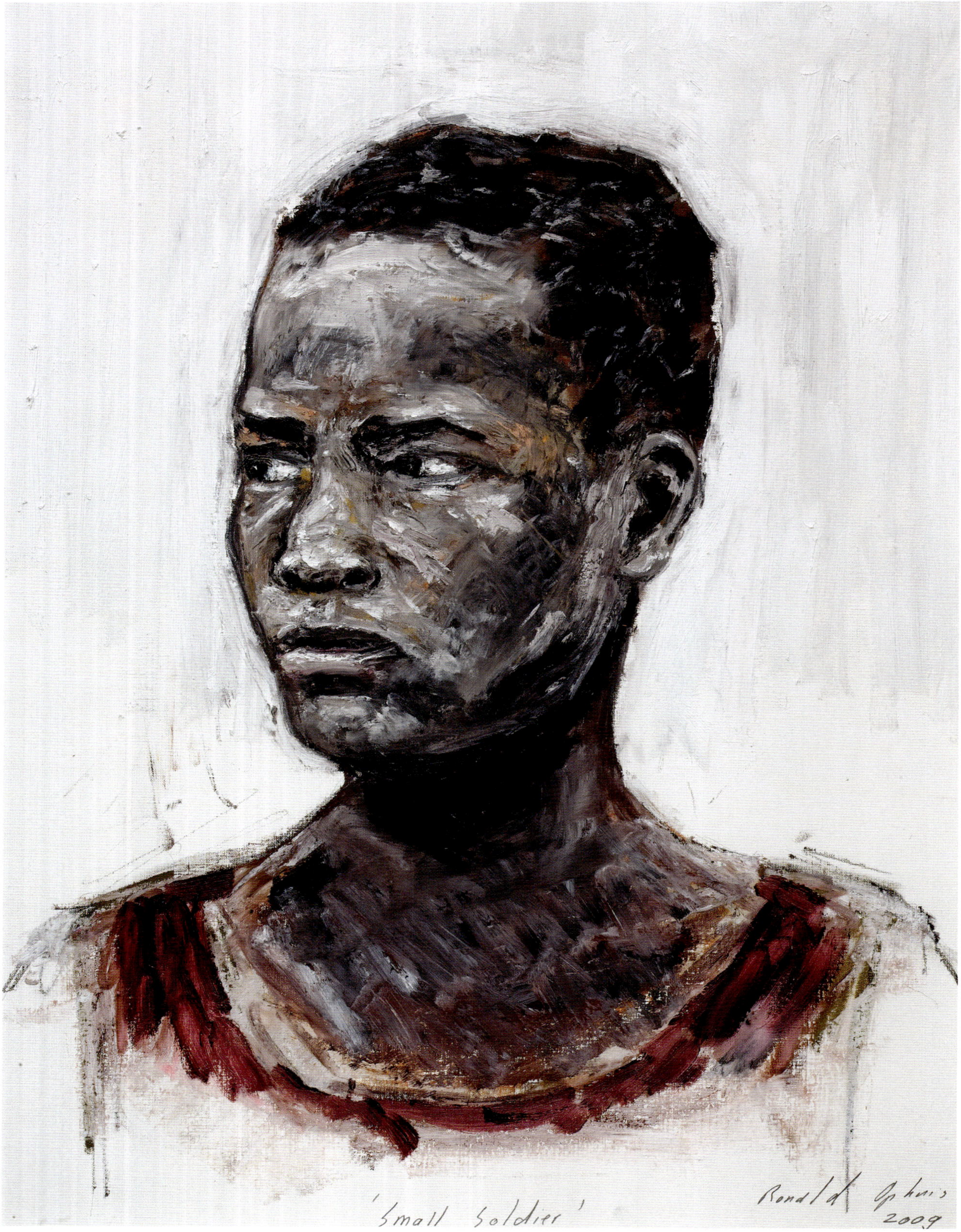

War Story Teller, Sierra Leone 2010 nr. 2
2011, oil and oil pastel on prepared
paper, 65 × 50 cm
(25⅝ × 19¾ in).

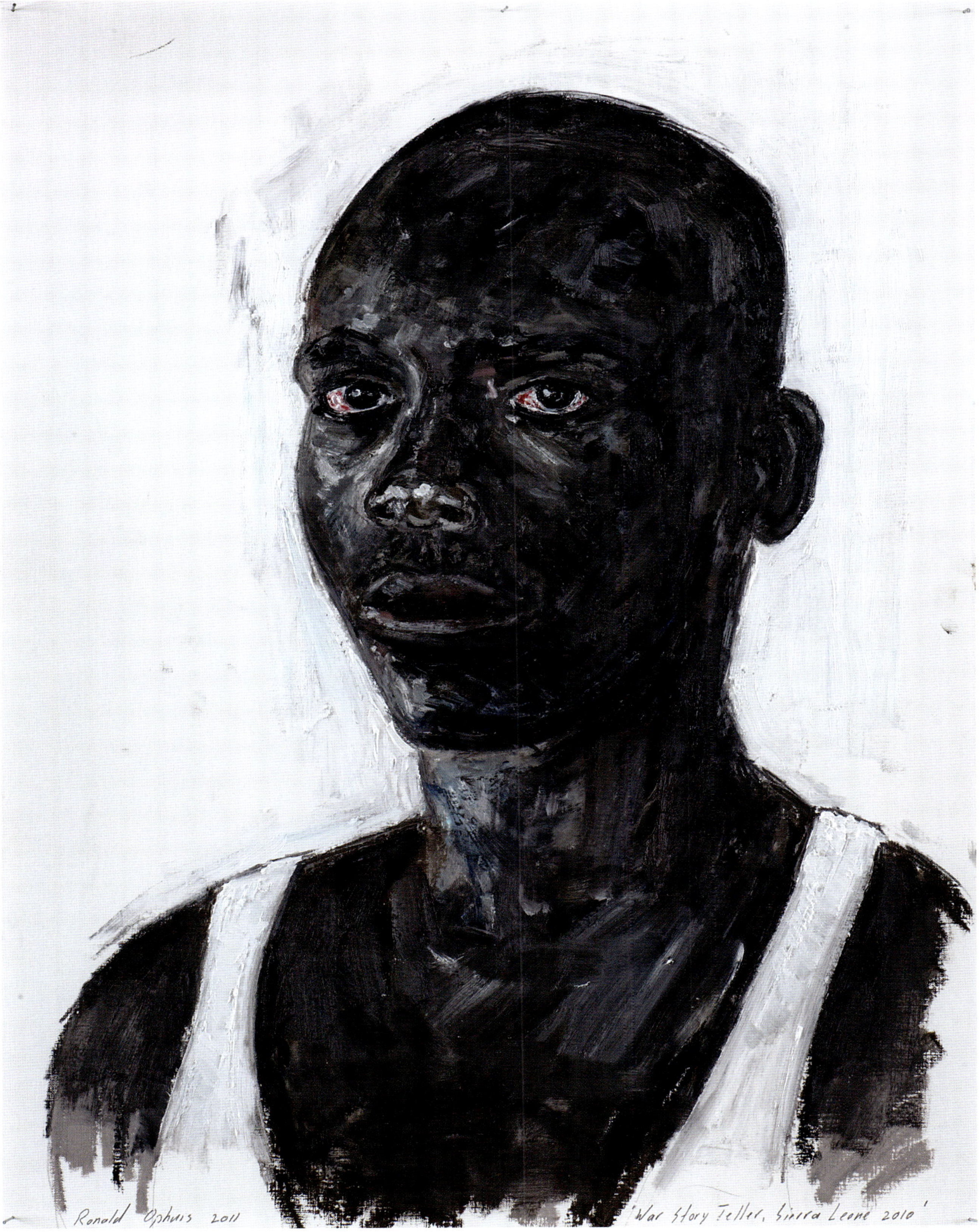

Packing and Checking 02
2012, oil on canvas, 180 × 250 cm
(71 × 98 in).

Jina Park
Born: 1974, New York
Lives: Seoul

'Fleeting moments' is a much-abused expression, but in the case of Korean artist Jina Park it is hard to avoid it. Students say goodbye to one another at the end of a day at school; museum workers take an inventory of paintings at a warehouse; people queue at the airport; or they sit or lie down on a sunny though completely unremarkable day: Park's subjects reflect her obsession with capturing time, scrutinizing moments in the way a scientist might work on a molecular structure, putting daily life and its mysterious processes under a microscope. But if the above description makes her work sound stern and lifeless, it is anything but that. Her choices – whether subject matter or point of view – reveal an acute intelligence at work, as well as a refreshing sense of humour.

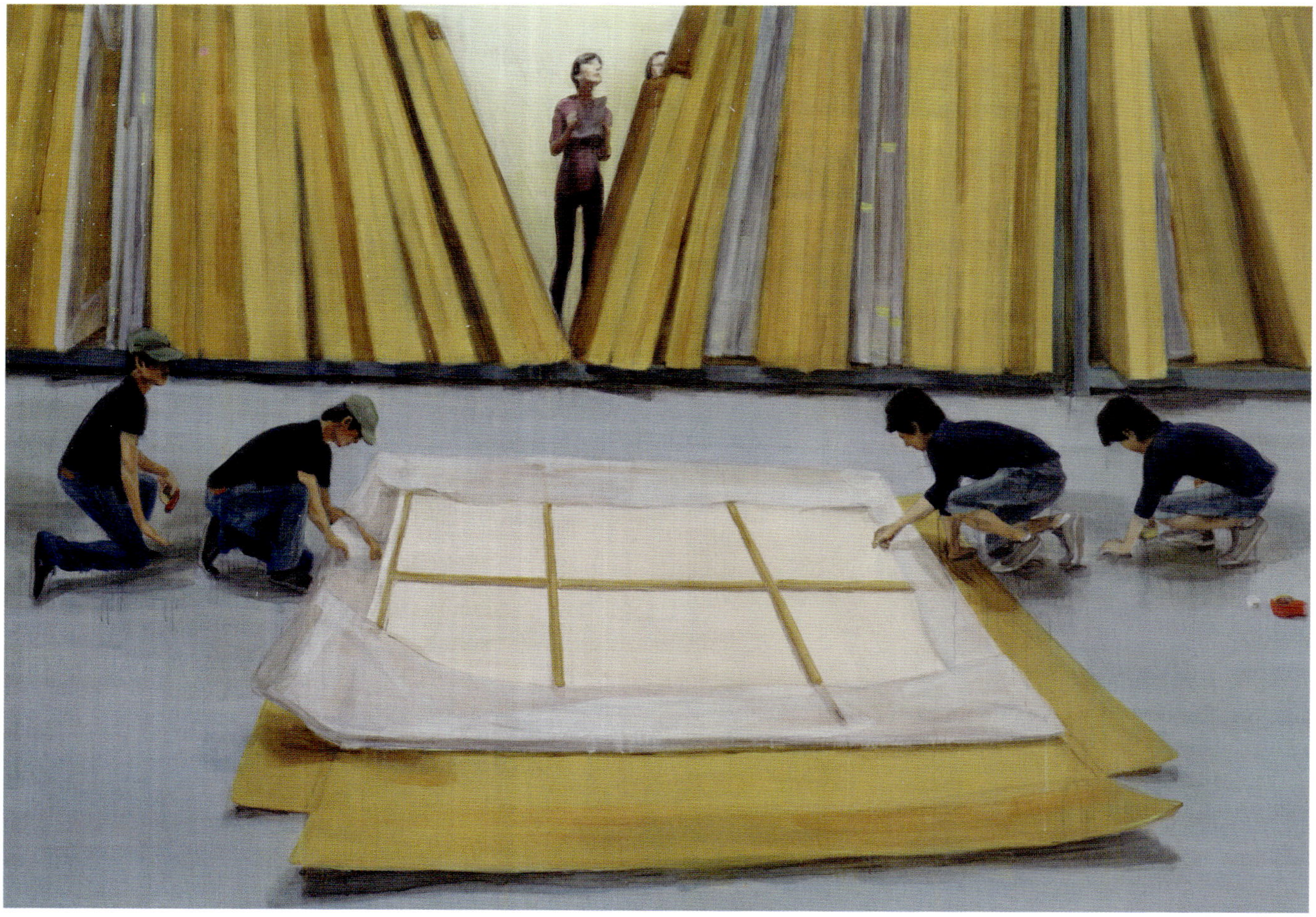

Subjects and process

Mostly I paint from casual snapshots. I take photographs of people and events around me and use them as sketches: the daily life of those around me is my main interest and subject. The places in my paintings exist, as places I have been. However, they are not described in a concrete way, but just so that they appear as real spaces in a contemporary urban surrounding. I have a tendency to be drawn to places that have a neutral quality and look somewhat like a void.

I work with oils, sometimes watercolours and gouache. I stop when there is nothing left to be painted. It takes rather a long time for me to make the final decision, and I often stare at an almost-finished picture hung on the wall for days before I decide to stop. Usually I don't go back to the painting once I have made a decision to finish, because the decision is part of that painting at that moment, like subjects, technique or composition. I like to keep some momentary freshness in it.

Technology and references

I don't know what the role of figurative painting is exactly, but I do think it is considerably influenced by computer graphic (CG) images. I know several painters who use Photoshop to make an image to which they refer to later. In my case, I did series of paintings in which a figure is doubled, with some time differences. The idea came up naturally in the process of composing a picture out of several photographs, but it could have been partially influenced by all the CG images out there with multiplied figures.

Photography has a key role in my paintings. I like the casual, momentary and accidental qualities of snapshot photography, and try to convey these in my paintings. Sometimes when I see a scene or a small event around me, a visual idea strikes me, so I take pictures with my camera or mobile phone to document them. But scenes from films tend to linger in my mind and appear throughout my painting. Nowadays, I often get a strong impression from contemporary dance performances, so this could influence me as well. I would say it [my style] has built up naturally over years. But there could be a moment in the future when I will need to make a rather abrupt change.

Influences

If I have to choose only one influence that would be Edouard Manet.

The role of painting

That role may be smaller than it used to be, but that is not necessarily a bad thing, as it could mean that you are freer to move in different directions. And I think it wouldn't be a problem even if painting had no more role at all. Many things can exist without a role.

Figurative painting

The narrative in [my] paintings is brief and transient, so one might read no narrative at all. I hope it is open and the viewer can see their own narrative in the work. I believe that painting can convey quite successfully the feeling of being alive today. I see and realize something – I cannot tell exactly what it is – which I then try to identify and show through painting.

Realist painting can still move people who look at it. Even just in terms of technique: people are awed by it and want to figure out how it is done. Sometimes I wonder if this is an instinctive reaction, something we are born with. One thing that I think painting is able to achieve comparably well (whether through a realistic mode or not) is that in its finished condition it can still show the process of being painted. It works instantly as an image and is very physical at the same time.

A Man Ironing in a Round Gallery
2010, oil on canvas, 230 × 155 cm
(91 × 61 in).

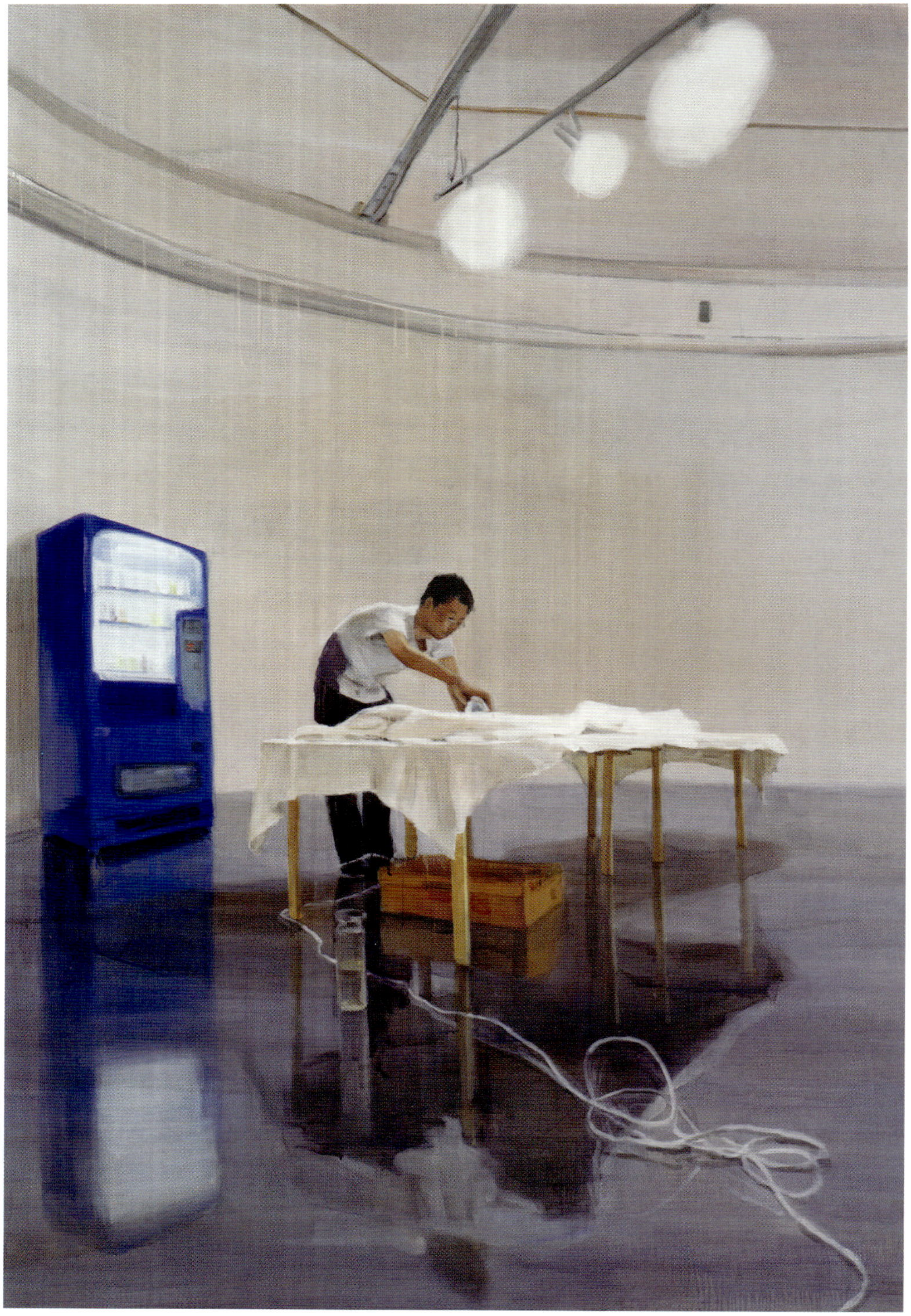

Ladder 02
2010, oil on canvas, 230 × 170 cm
(91 × 67 in).

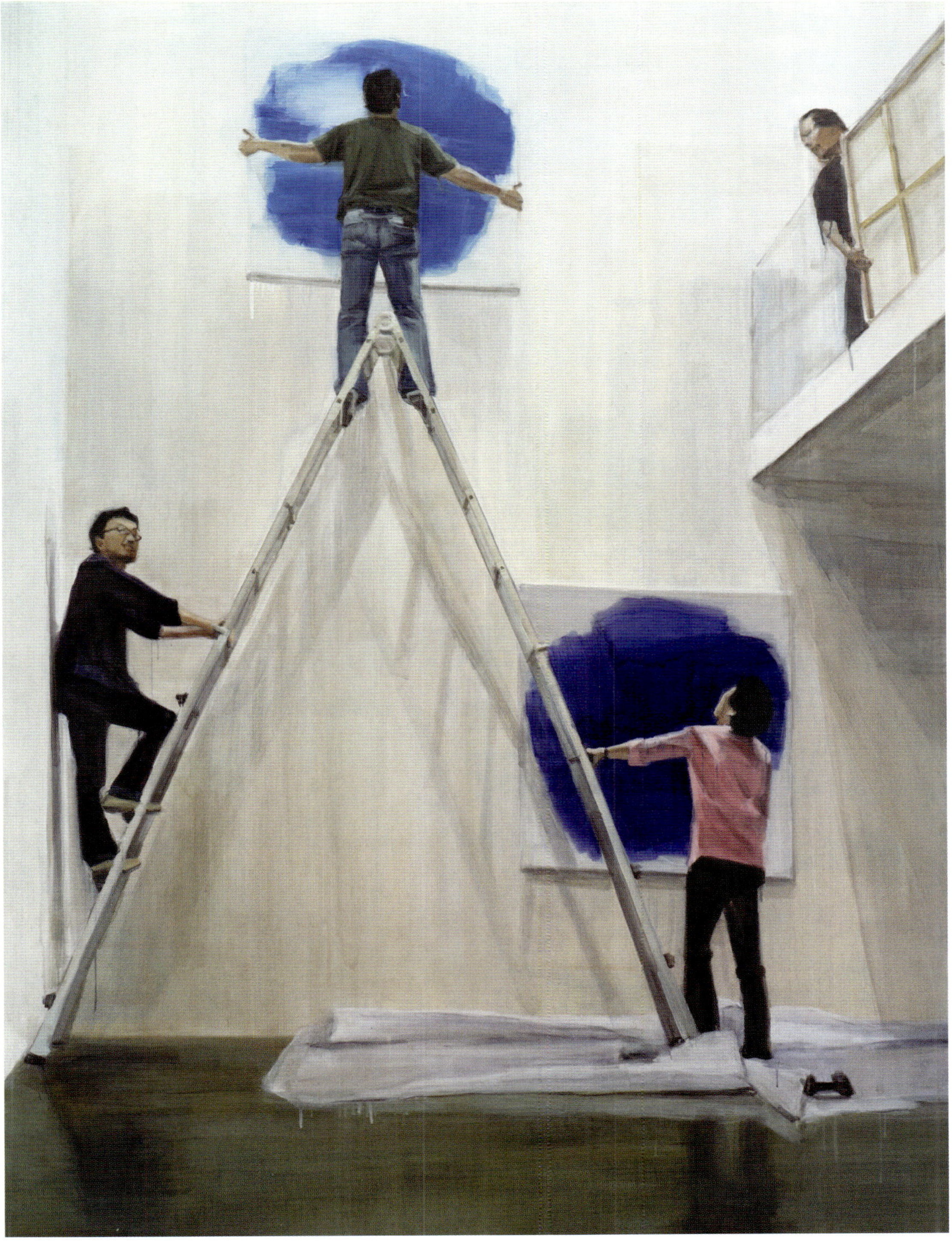

Good-bye
2012, oil on canvas, 154 × 154 cm
(61 × 61 in).

Waiting for Screening 01 (Parreno
Installation, Centre Pompidou)
2010, oil on canvas, 260 × 200 cm
(102 × 79 in).

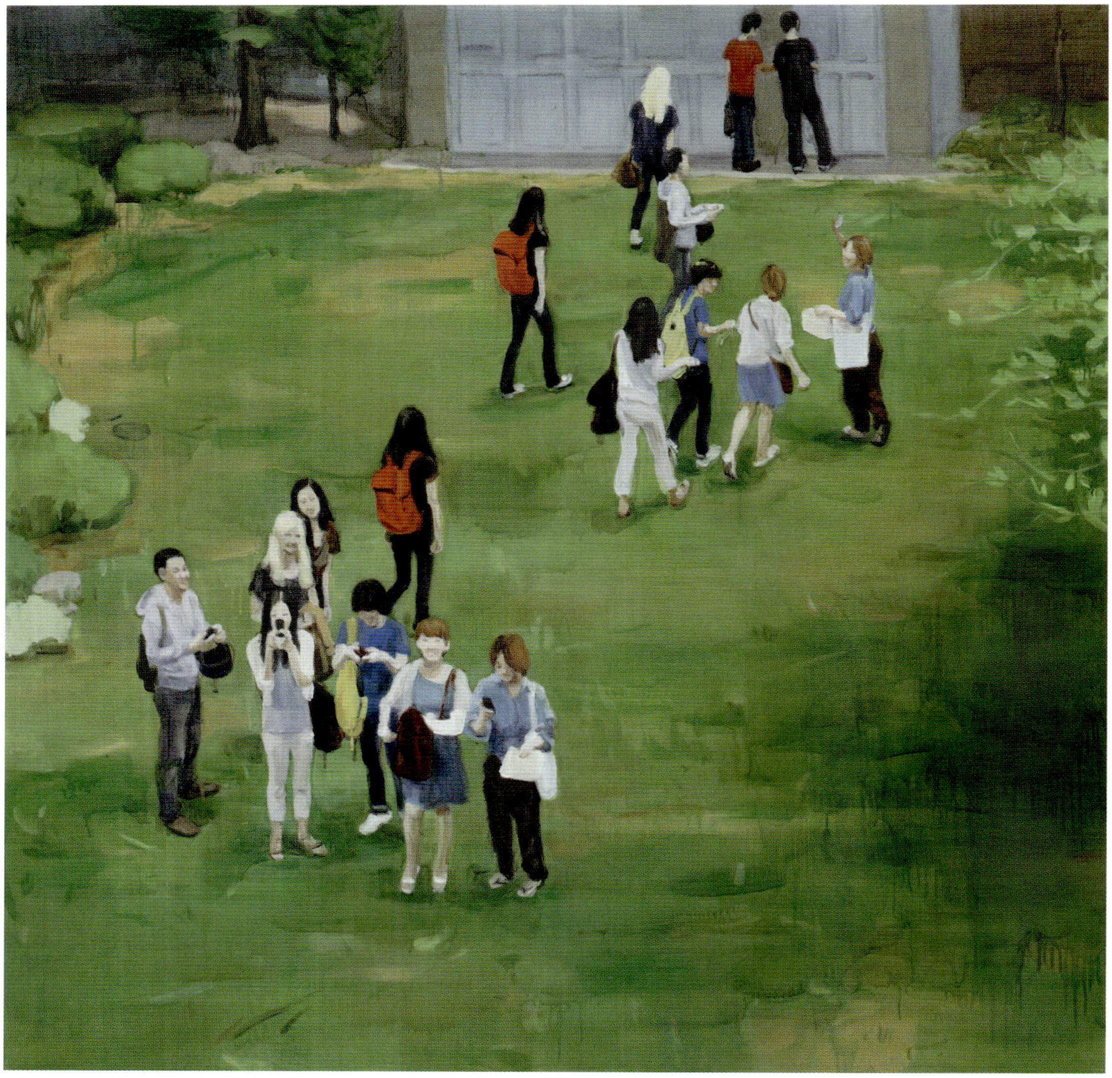

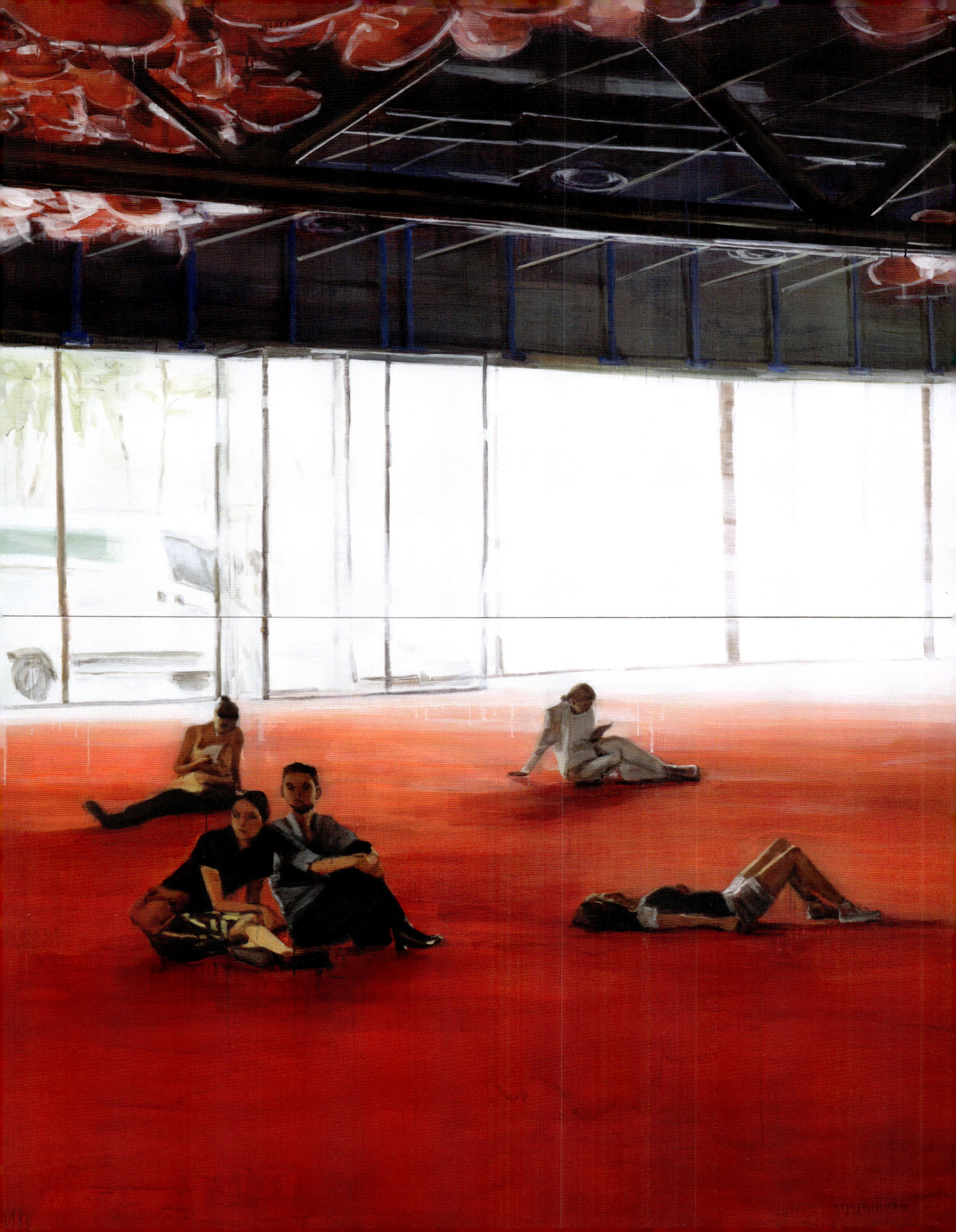

Till Rabus
Born: 1975, Neuchâtel (Switzerland)
Lives: Neuchâtel

The outstanding precision of Till Rabus's painting technique may have something to do with the fact that he studied art in a school founded by master watchmakers (L'École supérieure des Beaux-Arts de la Chaux-de-Fonds). Inspired by the apparently meaningless scenes of everyday life, he transposes them on to canvases as magnified details, working with obsessive repetition and an always cheerful undertone. The hyperrealism of his painterly renditions is accompanied by a strong streak of humour, which makes his work delicate even when the subject represented is – in some cases – disgusting.

Background
My father is a painter and my mother works with embroidery. They have an artistic temperament and they passed it on to me and my brother. I attended an art school created and financed by watchmakers in Neuchâtel. It is a very academic school where I learnt to be conscientious and precise.

Influences
I have been fascinated by the art world since I discovered the Young British Artists in the 1990s and the first of the two Venice Biennales curated by Harald Szeemann [in 1999]. Other spectacular exhibitions by Swiss artists touched me deeply, such as Fischli/Weiss, Roman Signer, Urs Fischer. Their different ways of perceiving the contemporary world with humour, mockery, absurdity and poetry convinced me that I had to throw myself into artistic expression.

Multimedia artists and sculptors generally inspire me more than other painters. But recently I have discovered very beautiful things in contemporary painting, especially through artists like Johannes Kahrs, Michaël Borremans and Adrian Ghenie.

Inspiration
The view of a used condom in the public toilets at the end of a night out, chewing gum mashed into a bus stop, or even my neighbour taking apart tyres all day and storing them in the back of my house – all are small images belonging to the banality of the everyday that also reveal a society from which I try to diverge.

I am contemplative and I often gaze at the 'not big things'. My attention focuses on meaningless details. I try to question the place of objects around us, and I try to produce shapes, an order and subjects starting from the shapeless, the disorder and the anonymous.

Usually I work in small series of three or four canvases. In this way I can plunge for a long time into a subject that I feel the need to approach.

Process and technique
I spend a lot of time working out my installations and then I take pictures of them. When I find the picture that works in composition, lighting and perspective I start a painting. I made different attempts before finding a technique that suited me and this has happened little by little over the years. I work in two successive layers of painting. The first layer, a quick and diluted acrylic, constitutes the support base. After, I apply a second layer with oil painting, spending more time and refining the details.

The role of painting
I think that in a world increasingly mechanized, industrialized and computerized, the human gesture will keep on making sense, especially when it is elaborated and mastered. Maybe the role of the artist in our society is to find new ways of looking at things and to play with codes that lead us to reflection.

Patchwork Hotel n°1
2012, oil on canvas, 190 × 170 cm
(75 × 67 in).

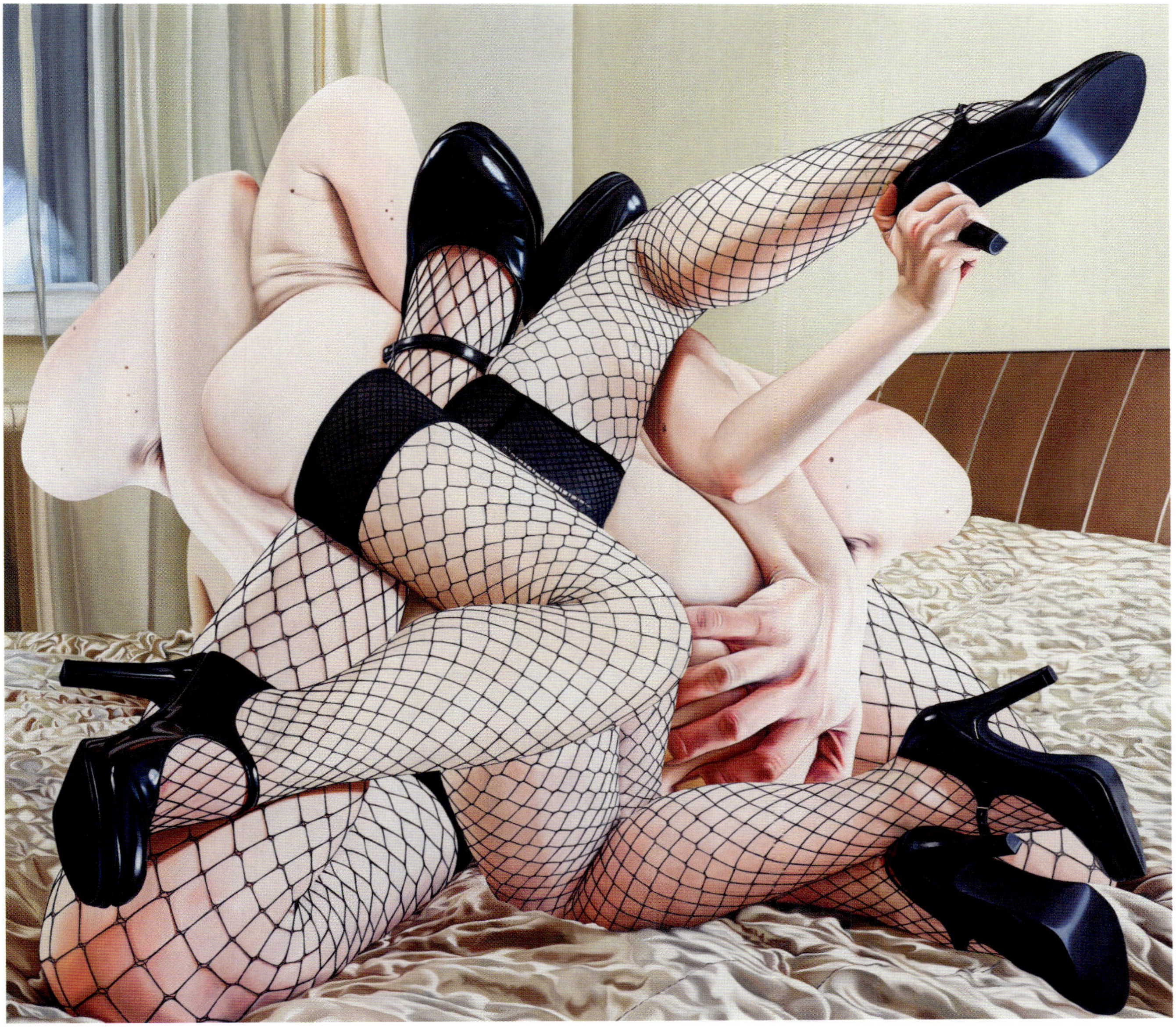

Voodoo n°1
2012, oil on canvas, 190 × 180 cm
(75 × 71 in).

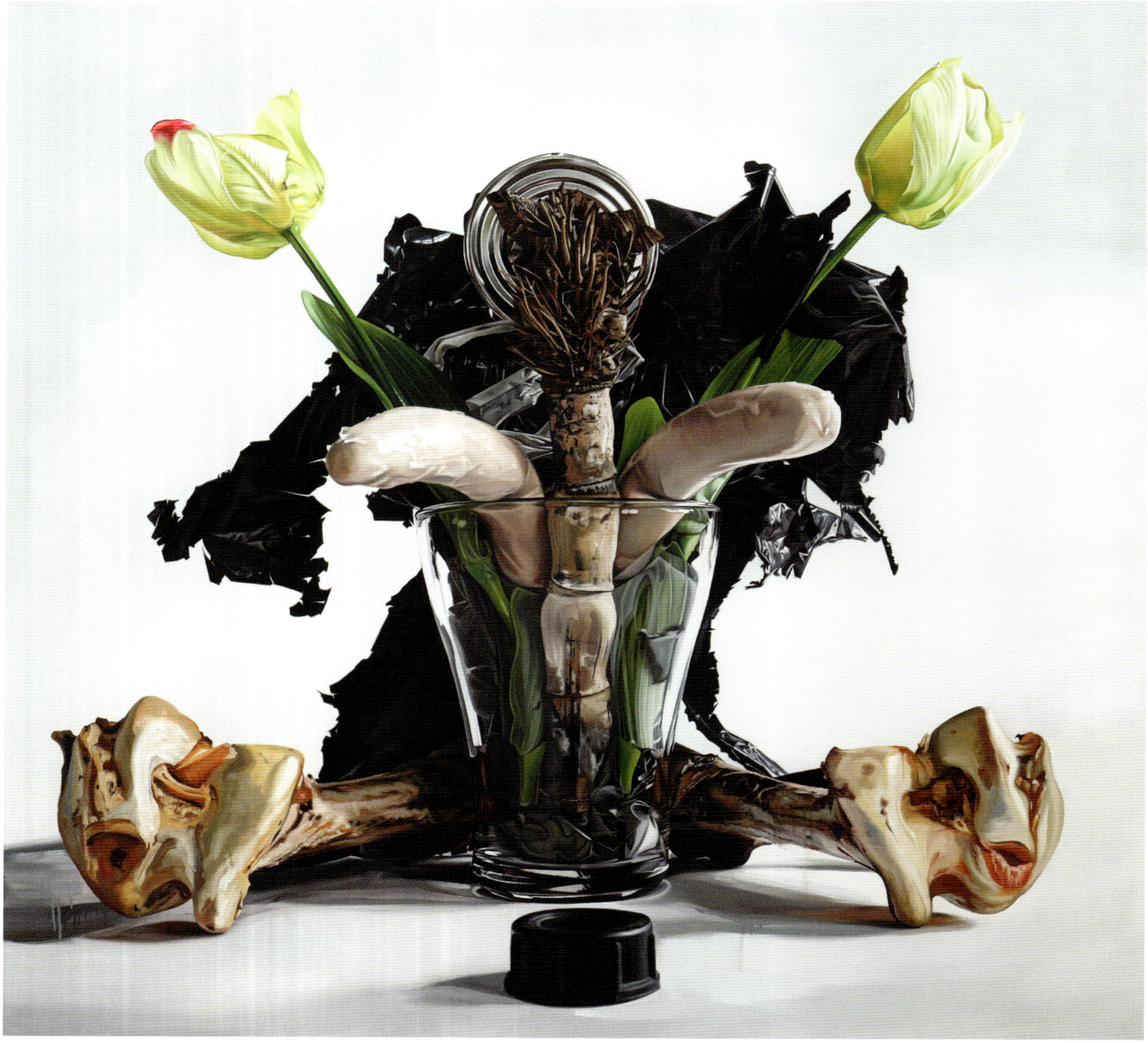

Composition Picturale n°2
2011, oil on canvas, 190 × 250 cm
(75 × 98 in).

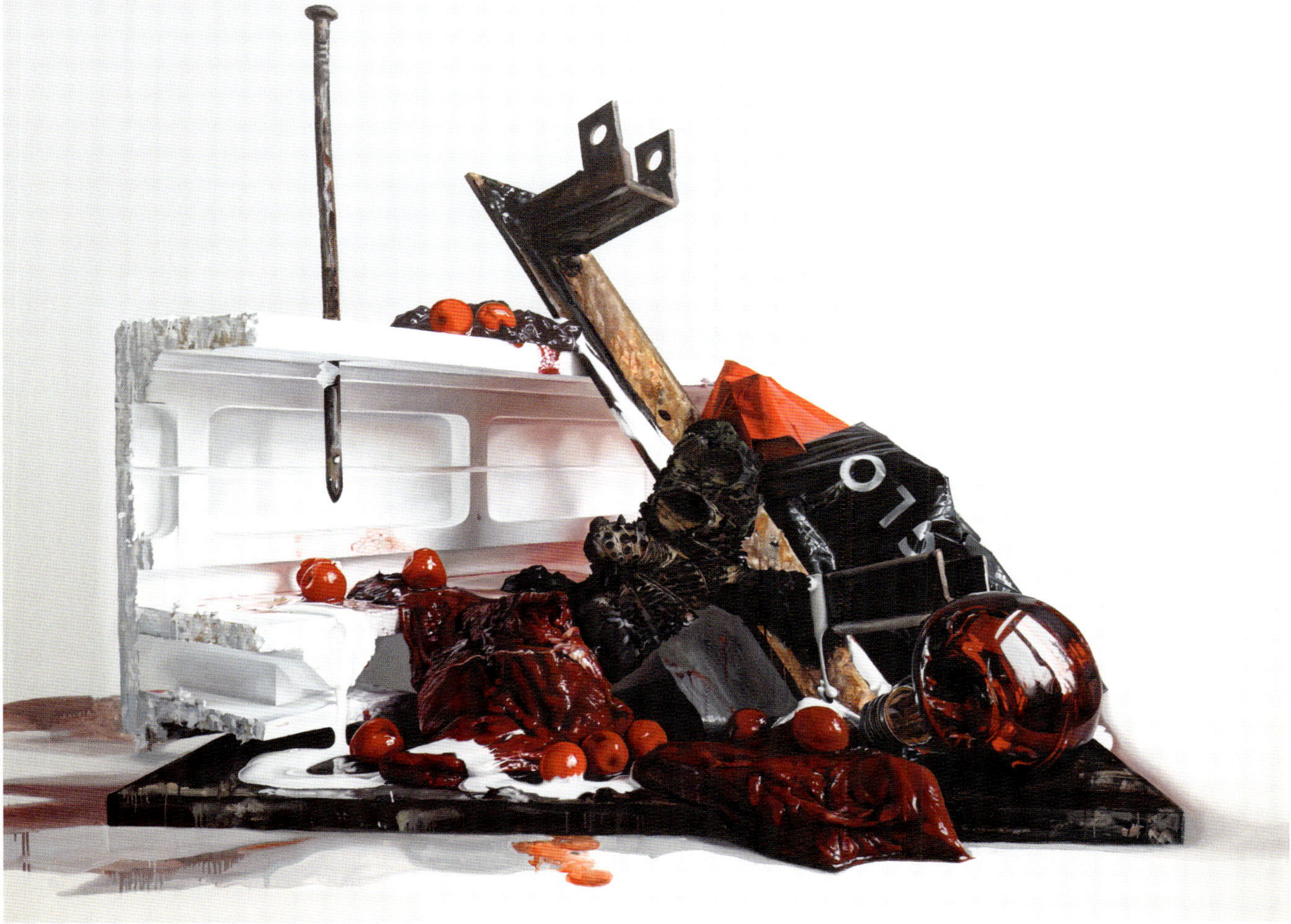

Epouvantail n°4
2011, oil on canvas, 230 × 160 cm
(91 × 63 in).

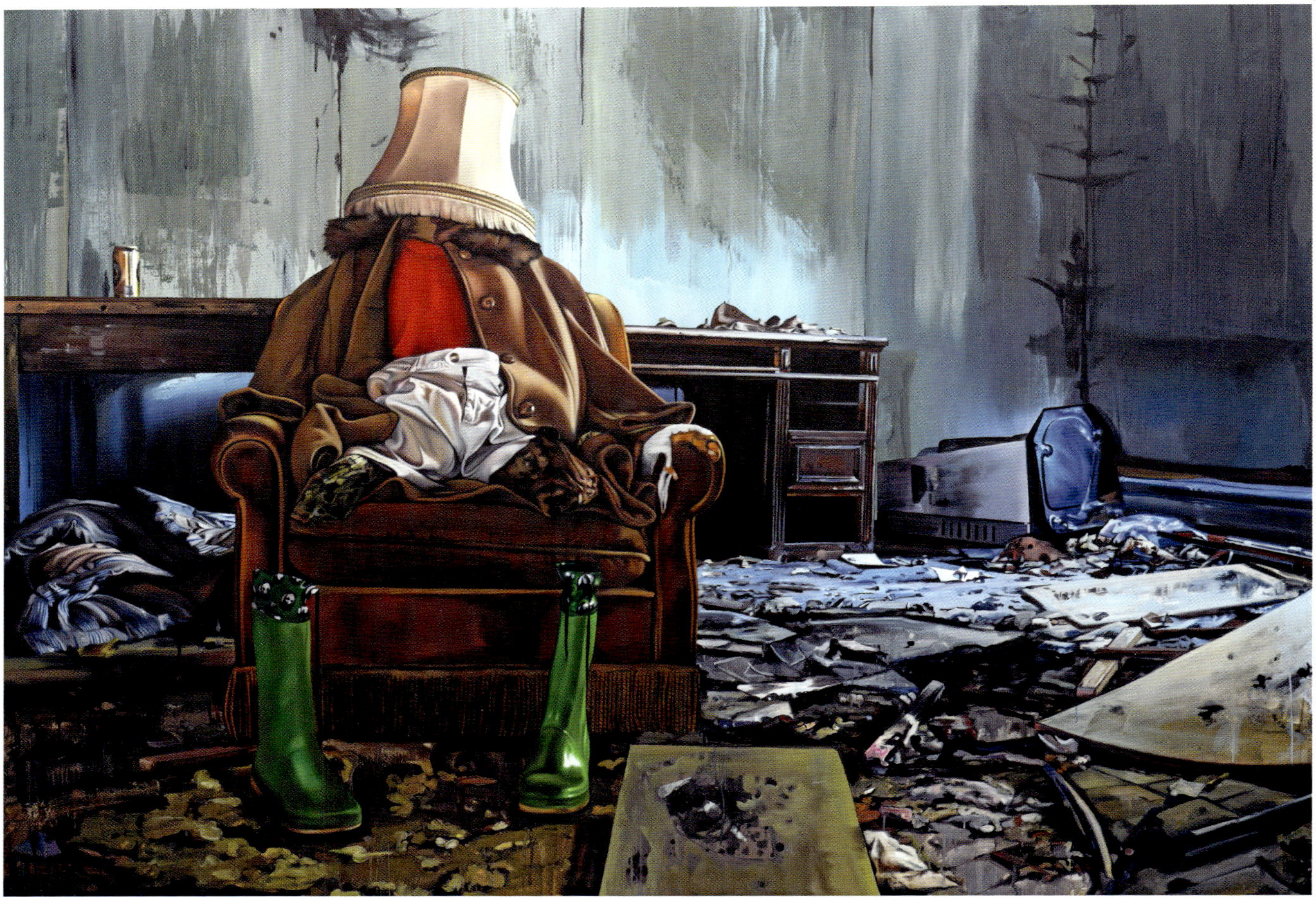

Capotes dans WC Publique
2009, oil on canvas, 160 × 230 cm
(63 × 91 in).

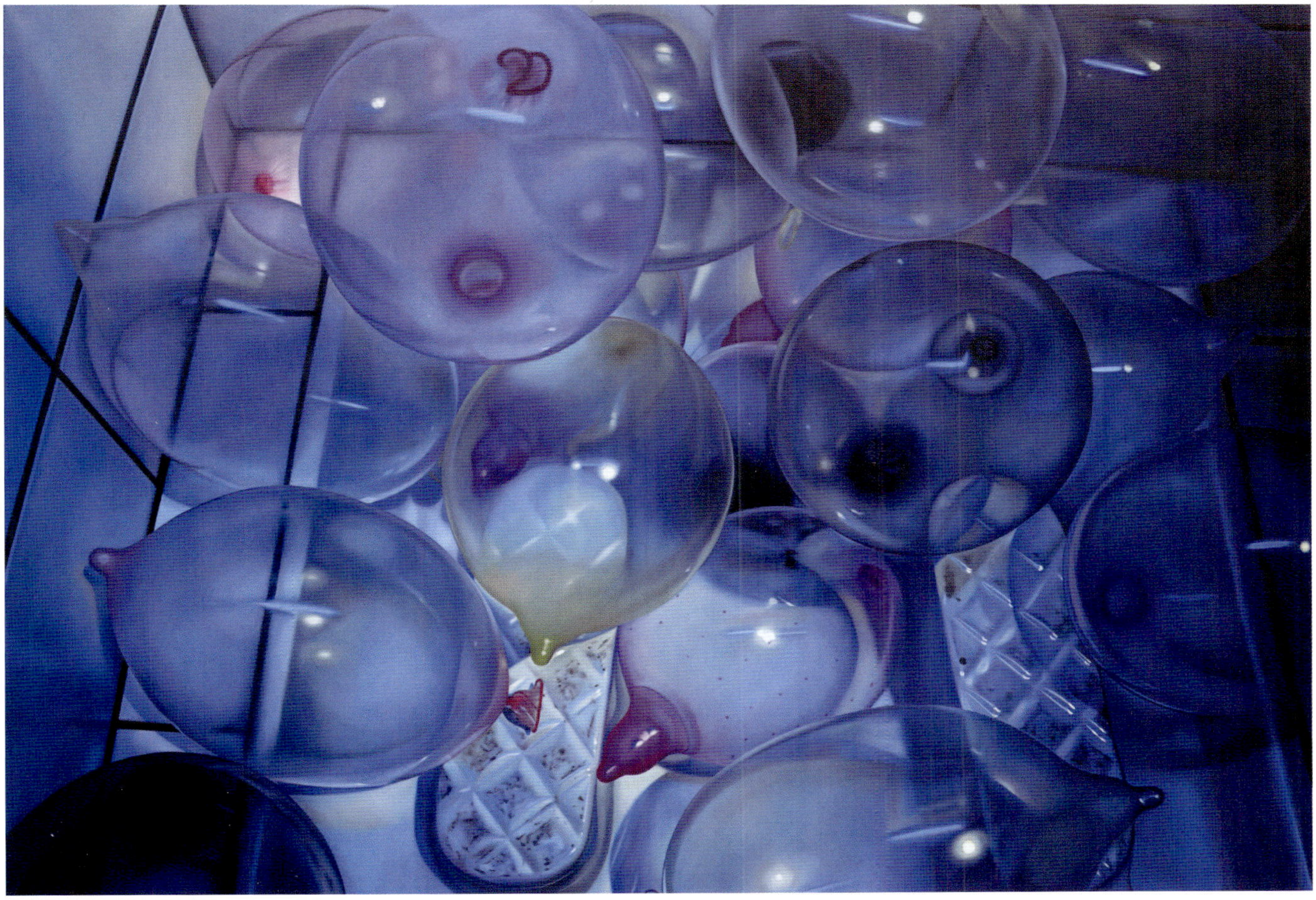

Alessandro Raho
Born: 1971, Nassau (Bahamas)
Lives: London

By playing on the clash between classical representation and urban iconography – what would Velázquez have done if his sitter were wearing a Disney T-shirt or a YSL dress? – Alessandro Raho's portraits are capable of catching tantalizing glimpses of life, from the mystery of a weary look to the charm of a button popping out of Michael Craig-Martin's cardigan. His work treads a thin line between observational accuracy and the undeniable fact of the fading of both subject and object – the interplay of colour, form and texture suggesting that at any minute these canvases could disintegrate into dust.

Background
My mum told me when we came to London [from Nassau] I was a bit sad: any 4-year-old would rather be in the Bahamas. The bright colours had left their mark. I had photos of us all at the beach with palm trees in the background and bright sun, and on a cold, grey day in south London I'm sure my relationship to pictures was shaped partly by feeling a sense of loss looking at these (not just emotionally, as my parents separated, but aesthetically too).

Development
Something I got from Goldsmiths was the idea of trying to make paintings that looked like 'our time'. I was frustrated with my paintings looking out of sync with things that moved me. I had been endlessly using portraiture in many forms, but I had the epiphany that joining it with the 'photographic' would give it the final modern feel. Photorealism wasn't what I was after, but the big influences on me – TV, film, etc. – had all been photographic. That was the common denominator; I had to bring that into my paintings. But I didn't feel a slave to making the painting look 'photographic': I just wanted to use the basic concepts of its realism to stop a kind of stylized figure appearing.

Process
I take photographs in the studio and then work from these. I have a set-up like a photography studio, which is an important part of the process. Trying out poses and different clothes is as much part of the art as the actual painting.

Subjects
I'm really not sure why some people feel right for the pictures: wounded beauty, defiance, strength, there are so many things. One of the qualities of painting someone's portrait is that it isn't necessarily endorsing or being critical of its subject, it's usually just describing the way they look.

I think it's more a look I'm after, an emotional feeling rather than a type of person. I remember reading *Crime and Punishment* on the train on my way to the studio, when I was younger. There was a brilliant description of a charged meeting between two characters, the man trying to force the woman into marriage using his wealth and power. It captured the way you could look with desire at something [or someone] denied to you. That same dynamic was at work in a lot of 1980s pop videos: George Michael in 'Careless Whisper' begging you, the viewer, not to leave him, looking 'through' the picture plane at you (in a reversal, the desired pop star was desiring you). Many of these dynamics take place with the painted portrait. I like the painting to have an emotional effect and appear fabricated at the same time.

Portraits today
I think that part of their effect is to humanize the feel of now. There is something about the effect of painting that does this. While I'm attracted and addicted to the media maelstrom of images, I'm also seeking something to hold on to – a physical object (an act of redemption?) and a way of coping with my feelings towards these images.

Influences
Peter Doig gave me a tutorial. He asked me if I had heard of Alex Katz (I hadn't), and said that I should go to the library and check him out. I hadn't seen anyone so comfortable with painting their family life. It was a pretty conservative subject matter, but the paintings blew me away. It made me feel I didn't have to try so hard to be interesting. Other artists inspired me: David Sims's photos for Gap; Manet; Caravaggio. I remember thinking I wanted to redo Richard Avedon as Frans Hals at one point. Things come from everywhere. The attention Almodóvar pays to clothes in a scene, a jacket one of my friends is wearing...

Michael Craig-Martin
Michael had a way of giving good practical advice. I remember we once had a tutorial about the edges in my painting, how a figure 'met' the background, and how I could improve it. I felt, right, that's resolved, now, next problem! It made you feel you could progress, which is important because an art degree can feel like a very groundless experience.

Clothes
I've been getting more specific, finding clothes that help me portray feelings I'm after. The world that shaped my aesthetic preferences, which was the 1980s, was a world in which clothes took on a symbolic meaning, the Ferré suits in [TV show] *Miami Vice* having as much impact as (really more than) the stories. The feelings conveyed by these aesthetics had a big effect on me. So much was contrived and artifice, but I was deeply moved by it (not in an ironic intellectual way, I was too young).

As I found the specifics of clothes and faces from our time, I felt I found my way. Clothes allow all sorts of games too. I painted a Mickey Mouse T-shirt on [the model] Jessica, and the two levels of realism, the 'realistic' face of Jessica and the cartoon face of Mickey, enabled me to get across some particular feelings I had. Patterns and stripes are giving me a way to paint abstract paintings embedded within figurative works.

I like the idea that in the particular is contained the universal. I have found recently that the landscape paintings I have done and the still lifes seem to be already contained in the portraits, sometimes by a motif in a T-shirt, or in a more elusive way.

Photoshop
Photoshop has come so close to painting in some ways: I've made prints where I've spent so much time adjusting every colour value, just like painting. In one key aspect though it is very different: it doesn't adjust the surface of the print in a three-dimensional way – that avenue of expression is still reached only by painting. With painting you are always aware of its surface and image, and they [painting and digital art] are completely different ways of describing images. The lovely and demanding quality of painting, moulding the surface to create an image, is still something that appeals to me. Working purely on the image doesn't excite me as much, that's more the area of photography.

When I paint someone's head, and describe its appearance and the illusion of the perception of it, something is added by the surface of the paint itself mimicking the flesh. It's the painting equivalent of the word 'onomatopoeia'. Also, the speed at which you work is perceptible in the paint; all these things have a meaning, for example, is the hair painted quickly or slowly, with intensity or casually? These decisions convey a feeling that is very attractive to someone who is trying to describe the emotional feeling of looking at something, not just the actual retinal image perceived.

Job description
I like to record the people around me, just as a primal act; I like to draw people I know and record them, like the cave painters. I want to cut all the extraneous content and get to something essential. I'm trying to make internal feelings external. With a painting you are bringing different thoughts and ideas to one place so it's hard to describe what you do. Certain people will take away the image as the idea of the piece, others may look at the way it's painted. But how does one describe why a brush-mark appears right and satisfies?

Young Kim
2013, oil on canvas, 120 × 90 cm
(46¼ × 35⅜ in).

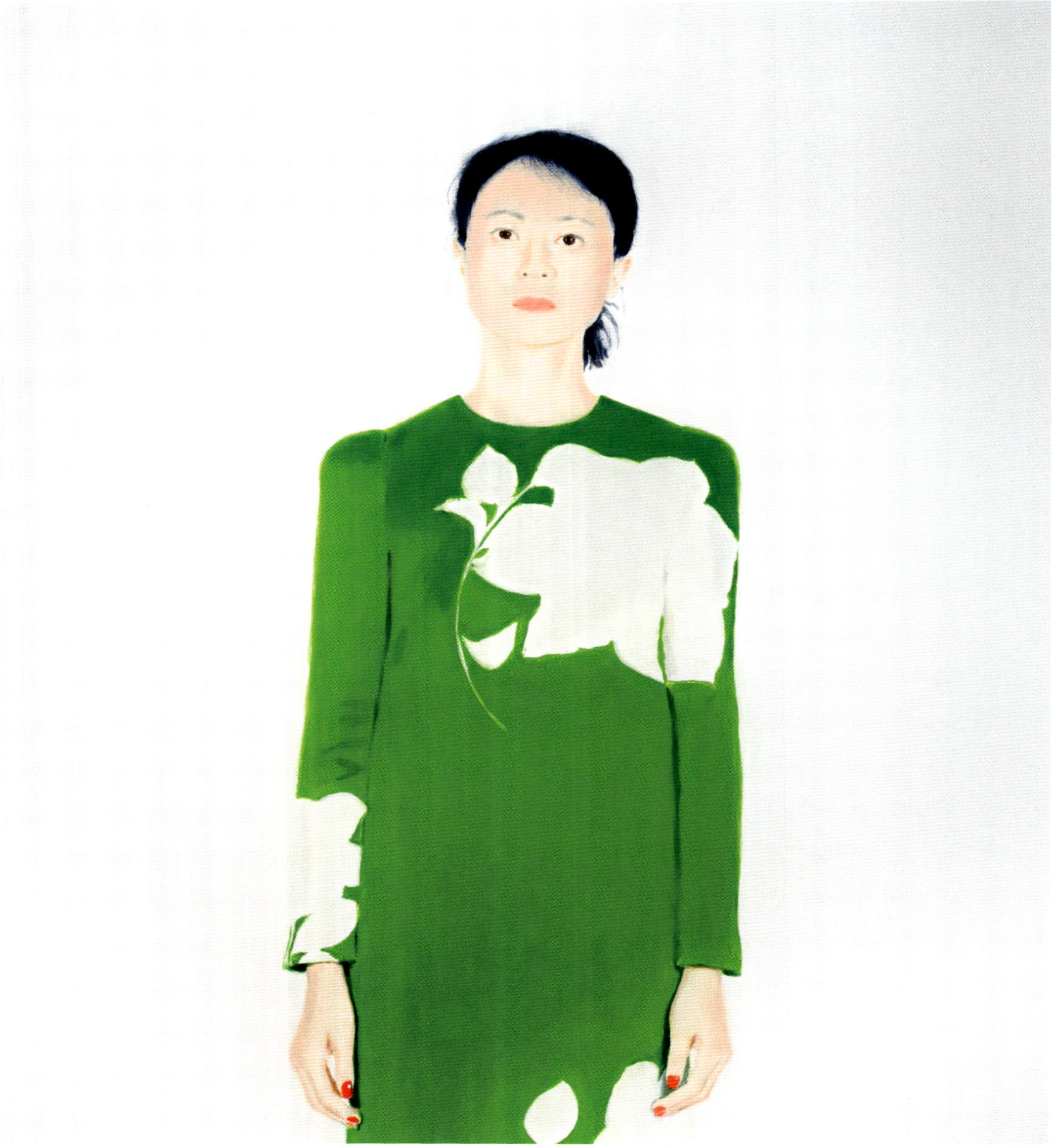

Young Kim
2013, oil on canvas, 91 × 73 cm
(35⅞ × 28¾ in).

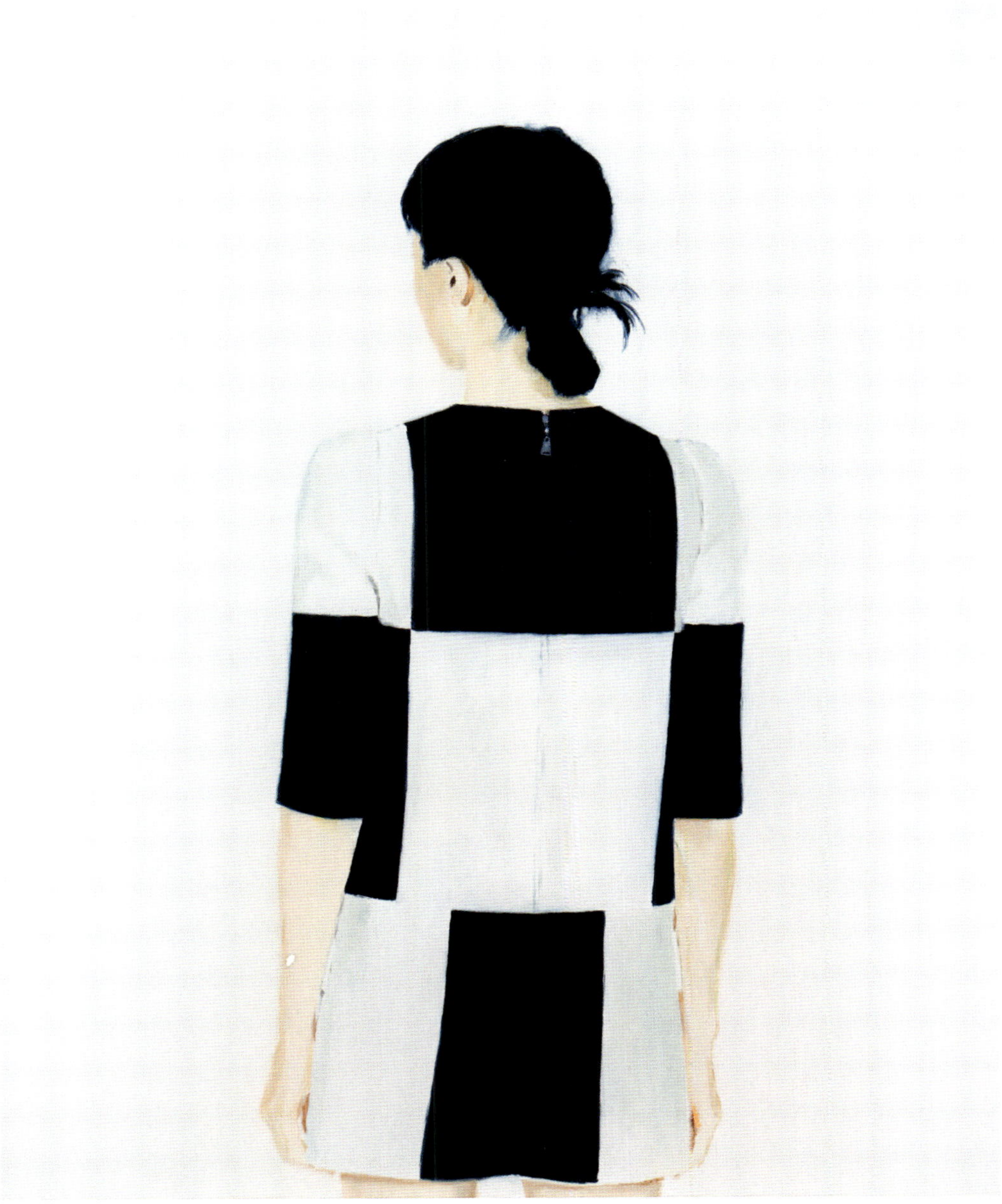

Lizzy Disney
2011, oil on canvas, 247 × 170 cm
(97 × 67 in).

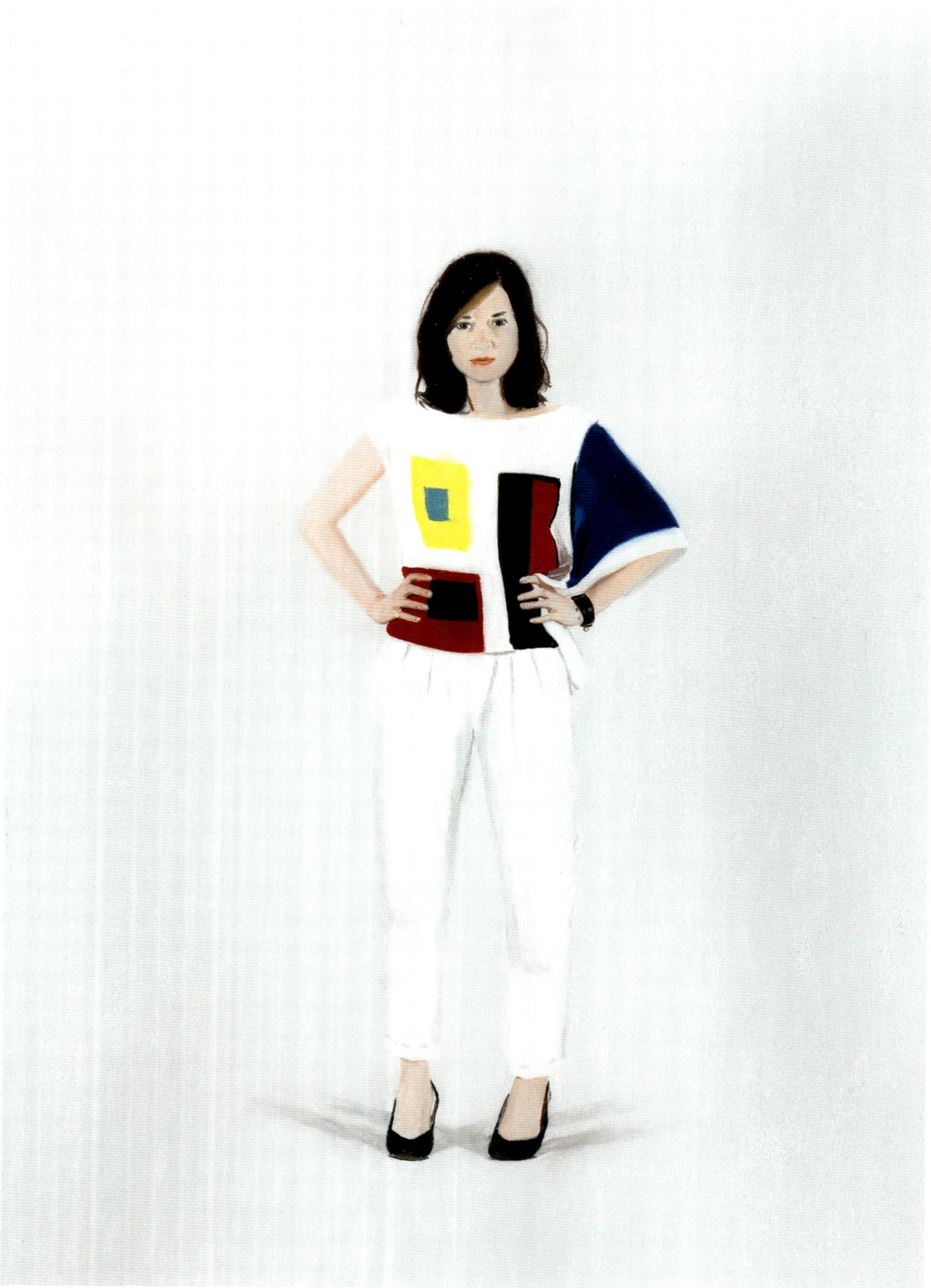

Jessica
2013, oil on canvas, 54 × 37 cm
(21¼ × 14⅝ in).

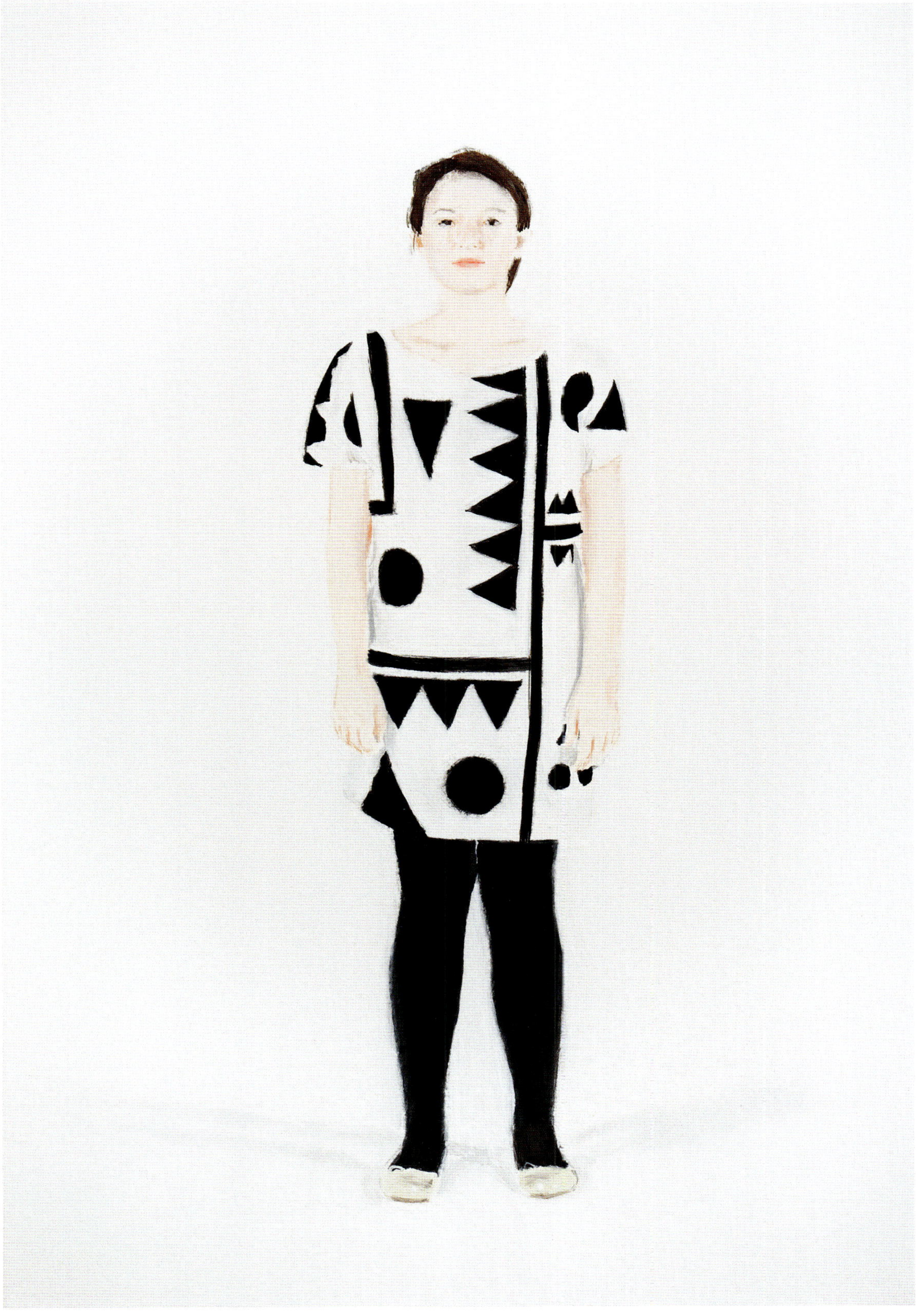

Ben
2013, oil on canvas, 123 × 112 cm
(48 × 45 in).

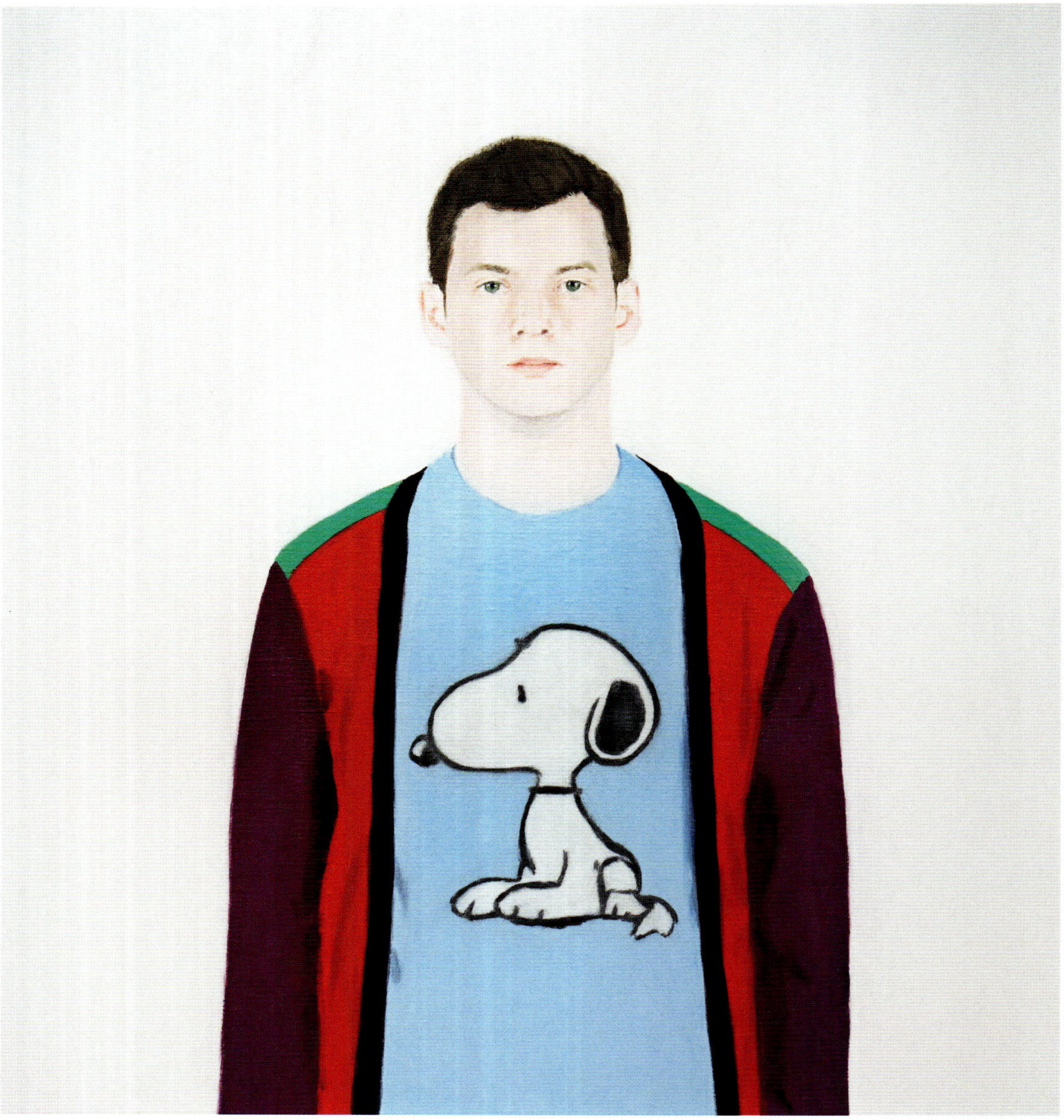

Alex Katz
2013, oil on canvas, 124 × 89 cm
(49 × 35 in).

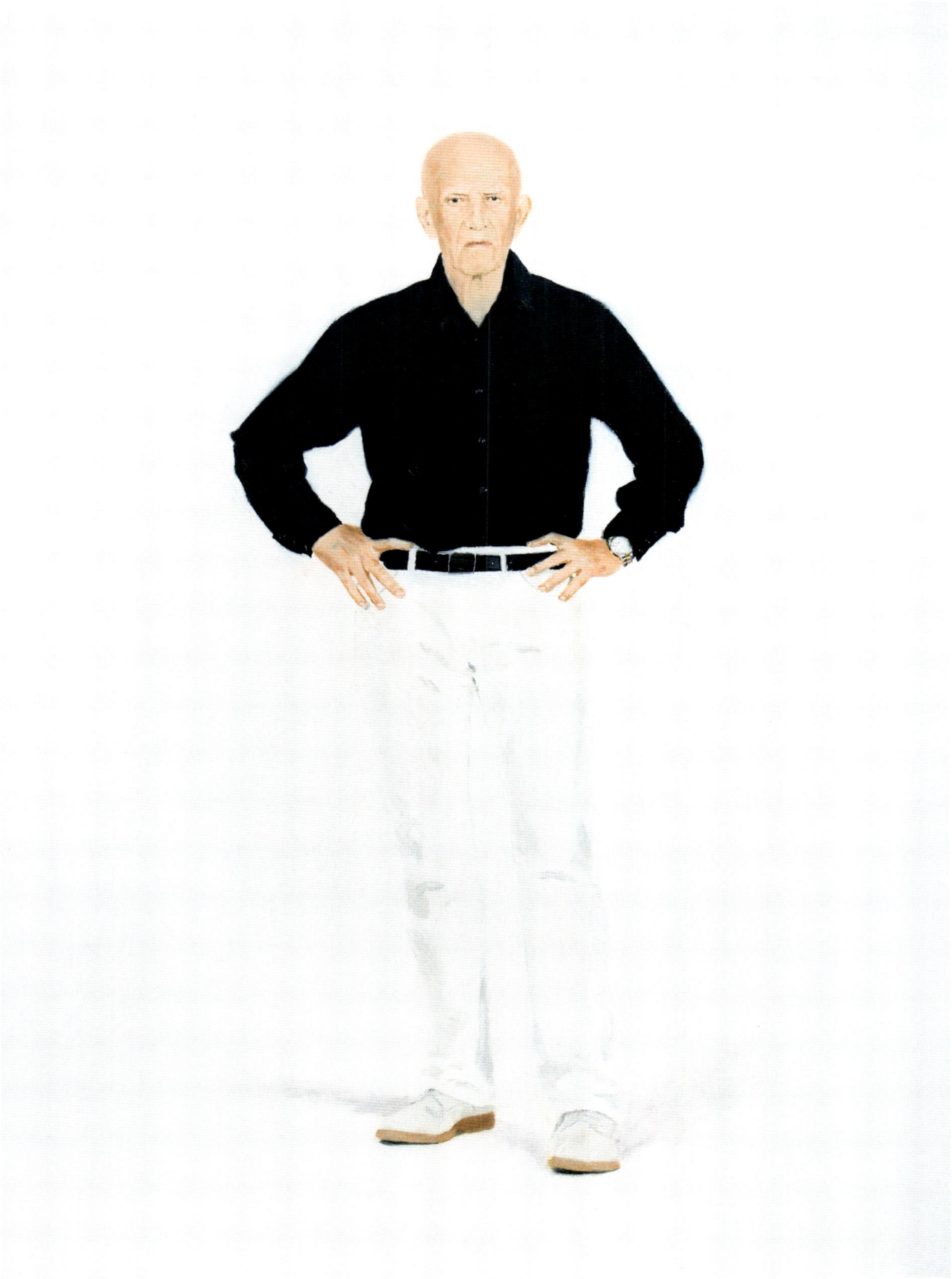

New Apartment
2011, oil on canvas, 74 × 58 cm
(29⅛ × 22⅞ in).

Serban Savu
Born: 1978, Sighisoara (Romania)
Lives: Cluj (Romania)

Serban Savu often paints his subjects from a slightly raised point in the distance, a viewpoint reminiscent of that of an omniscient narrator in a Realist novel. The painter calls this 'distant empathy'. We never see the faces of his characters, but this only increases our curiosity and the poignant sense that they belong to a certain deprived socio-economic group. It would be tempting to make comparisons with Brueghel or to Hopper, or to mention what has become known as 'the Cluj school of painting' (according to the artist, 'just a label artificially created in order to name a wave of painters from Cluj'), but the truth is that Savu's project is a highly personal and timely one, anchored in his memories of growing up in Socialist Romania as well as his analysis of the realities of his homeland today. 'I am trying to create the "perfect painting", including all my thoughts about the world I live in.'

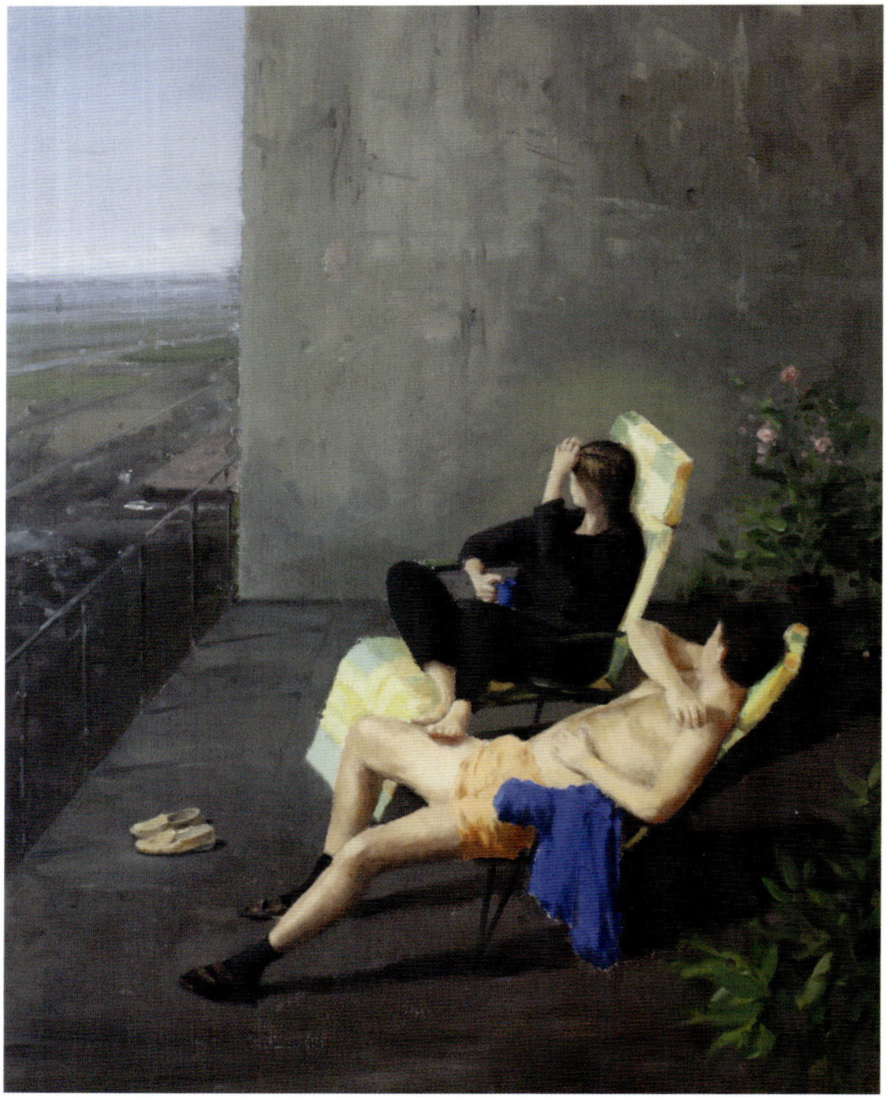

Background

I always knew that I would be a painter and have no explanation for this. When I was in kindergarten my teacher asked me what I wanted to do when I grew up and my answer was that I wanted to be a painter. My family encouraged me, so it was a natural choice to go to art school and afterwards to the University of Art and Design in Cluj-Napoca (UADC). The most important thing during my studies was meeting my artist friends Adrian Ghenie and Victor Man, with whom I've spent a lot of time and had long conversations about art. The theoretical courses at the University provided us with solid information on the history of art up to the historical avant-garde, but nothing on the contemporary period. Back then, in the mid-1990s, the vibe at the painting department was towards Neo-expressionism and abstraction, but my colleagues and I were interested more in figurative painting and were left to do the research on our own.

After I graduated I was totally clueless about what was going on in the real world (the Internet was just developing). I won a government grant to go to Venice, in Italy, for two years and that was the breakthrough. Besides falling in love with Titian and the whole Venetian painting school, I had the chance to see the 2003 Venice Biennale many times. At that edition of the Biennale, [Francesco] Bonami organized the show about painting at the Museo Correr – 'Pittura/Painting? From Rauschenberg to Murakami 1964–2003'. This was my artistic education.

Romania's Socialist past

When the Communist regime fell I was just 11 years old. For me that period means childhood, a very happy period. I was affected only by the direct effects of the regime like the lack of heat, hot water, electric power or food, but we were having fun during the blackouts, or picking up mushrooms in the forest because we couldn't find anything to eat in the stores. Today my position is that of an observer: I want to understand more of what happened and what is happening today.

Socio-political realities

When I came back from Italy in 2004 I started to see more clearly the reality around me. I was able to compare two cultures in a more complex way. That was the moment when I found my way: suddenly I knew it, it was like taking a veil off things. Actually since my adolescence I have been preoccupied with social realities and I have always tried to find reasons and causes, but I didn't imagine that I could paint these things. The Italian experience was the wake-up moment for me.

Process and subject matter

Usually there is an idea that has been preoccupying me for some time, but really it starts with a scene or a place. Then I use my own photographic archive or I go 'location-hunting', or searching the Internet for scenes or images that might inspire me. I use Photoshop to create the 'sketch' for the painting, putting together different scenes, moving the characters around or even 'painting' with the mouse. When all these boring preparations are through I can start painting. The result is similar to the sketch but also very different. It's similar in terms of composition or colour, but very different in terms of language. The whole process might take from one week to one month, depending on the size of the painting or the rhythm each painting requires. Each image has a maximum potential at a certain size and my aim is to find that size. Painting in a large format is very different from painting in a small one. Some paintings need a lot of energy and freshness, others require a more rational approach. These differences can be translated into different perceptions of time.

The landscape is important: it acts like a character, defining the other characters and giving meaning to the whole scene. I deliberately choose a raised and distant point of view in order to have a better perception of the landscape. When I see a place in reality (I prefer to call it a place, not a landscape) I act like an X-ray machine, trying to understand why it looks like this, and I have to dig a little bit into recent history. Such a place often is a catalyst for a painting; I try to figure out what people do in a place like that. I follow that place from time to time to check out what's going on there.

Narrative and empathy

I feel like a puppeteer moving the characters around. But I don't think the narrative is important: it is more important for a painting to provoke a narrative in the imagination of the viewer.

My characters are anonymous but somehow representative. There is the paradox of the 'distant empathy' (as I like to call it) in my works. I empathize with the people I paint, but I want to be in the observer's distant position. I have the feeling that I know exactly who the people I paint are because I know the codes of the reality around me. Sometimes I have no idea what they are doing and that intrigues me, and I try to imagine their lives. You could say I am a voyeur, spying on people that I am interested in without being seen.

The language of painting

I use painting as a tool in order to express some ideas, without neglecting the language of this medium. I try not to be bound to a formal approach – that's why some of my works look almost Impressionistic, while others are more Realist. The aim is to find the right voice for each painting. I do not intend to innovate the language of painting; my goal is to talk about the society I live in.

The Tunnel
2010, oil on canvas, 78 × 110 cm
(30¾ × 43 in).

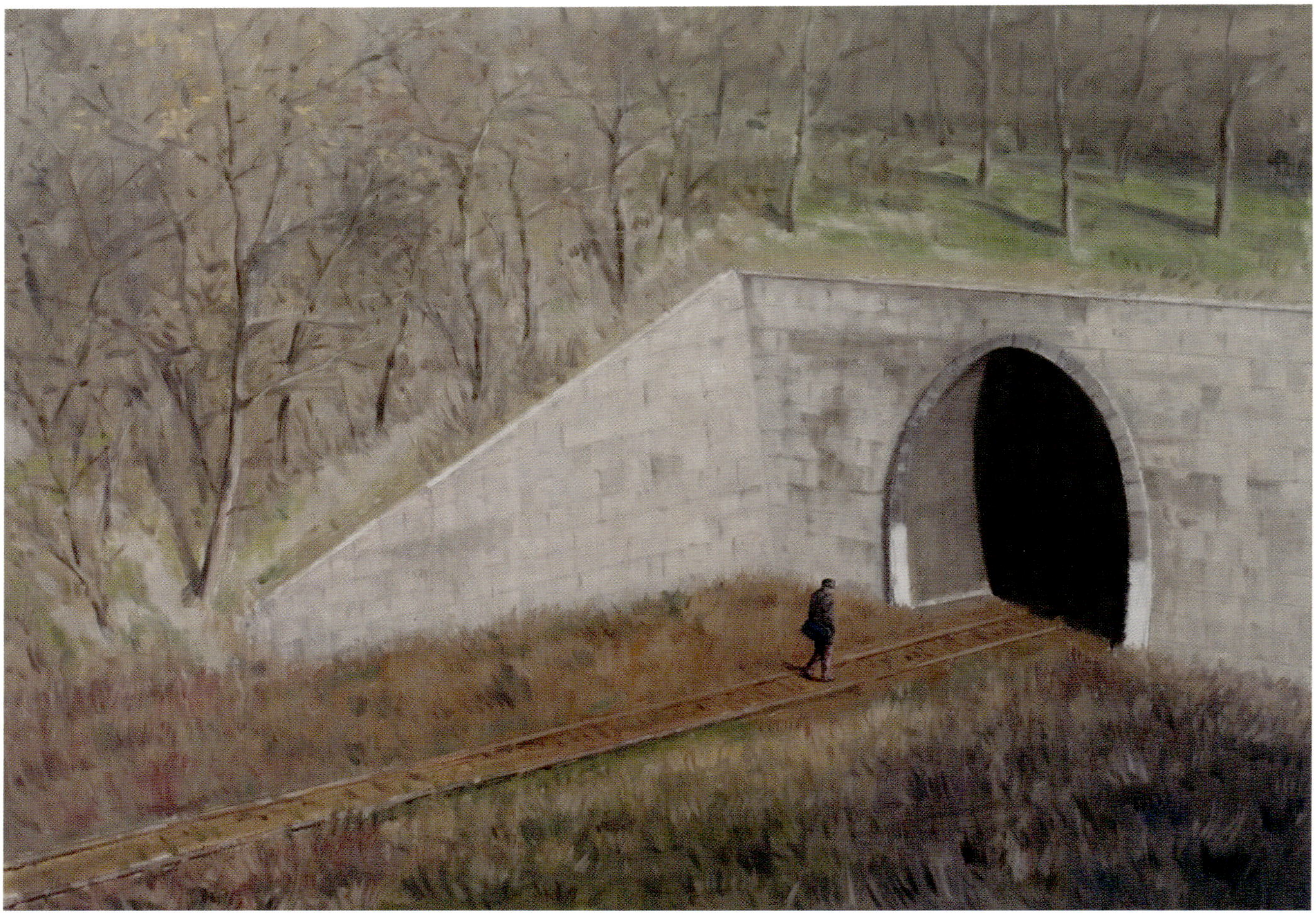

Landscape with Clerk
2013, oil on canvas, 144 × 190 cm
(56¾ × 75 in).

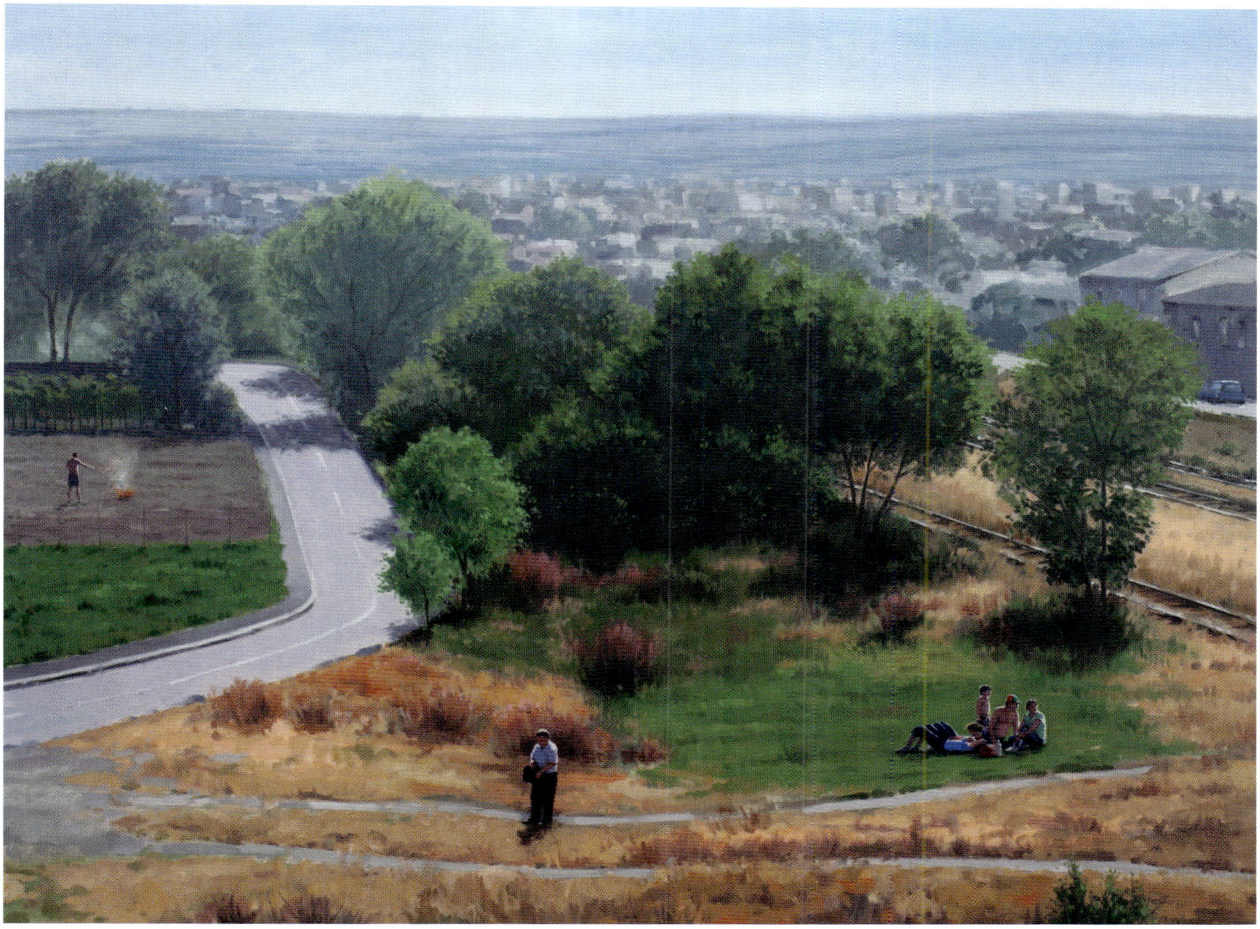

The Owner, His Right Hand and the Workers
2012, oil on canvas, 135 × 190 cm
(53 × 75 in).

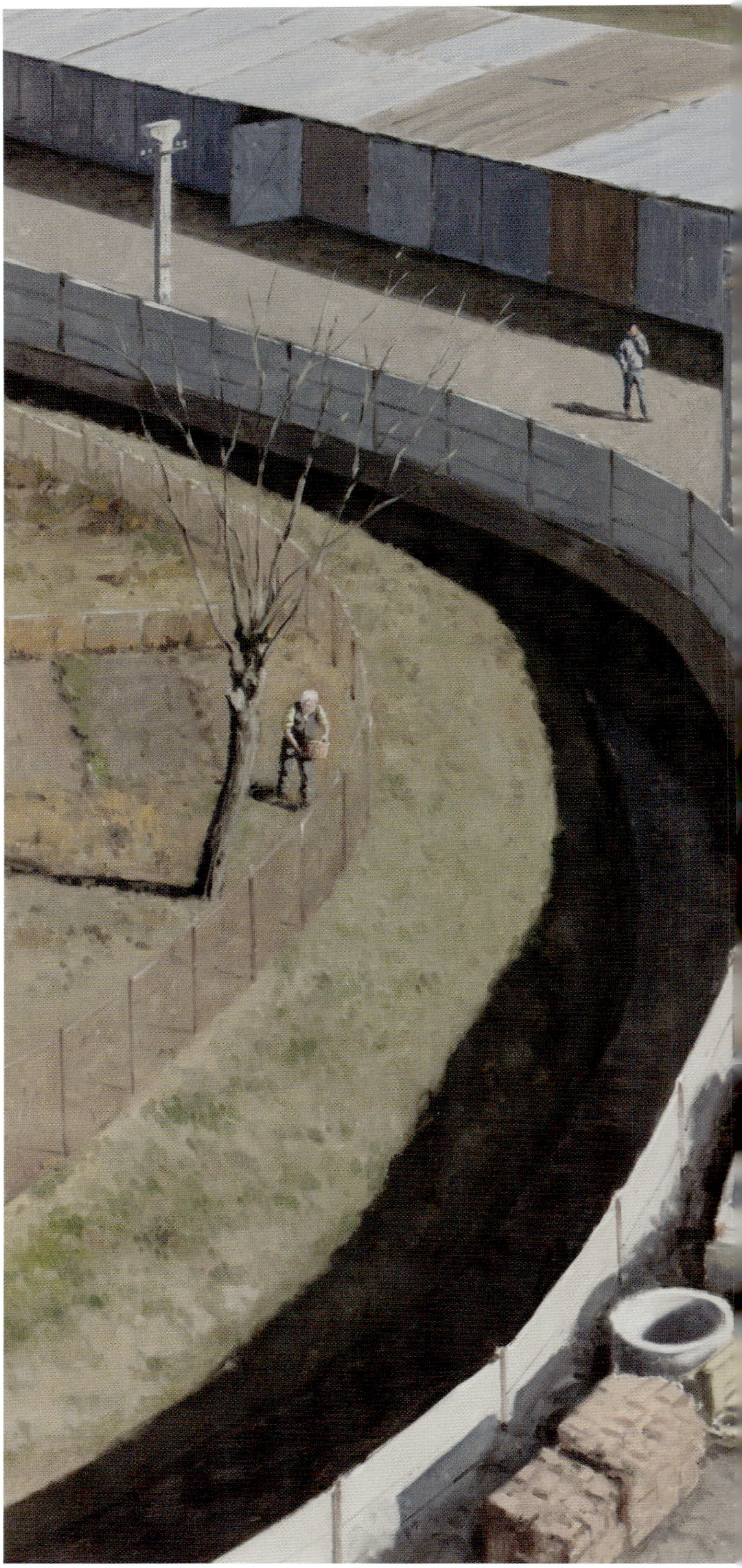

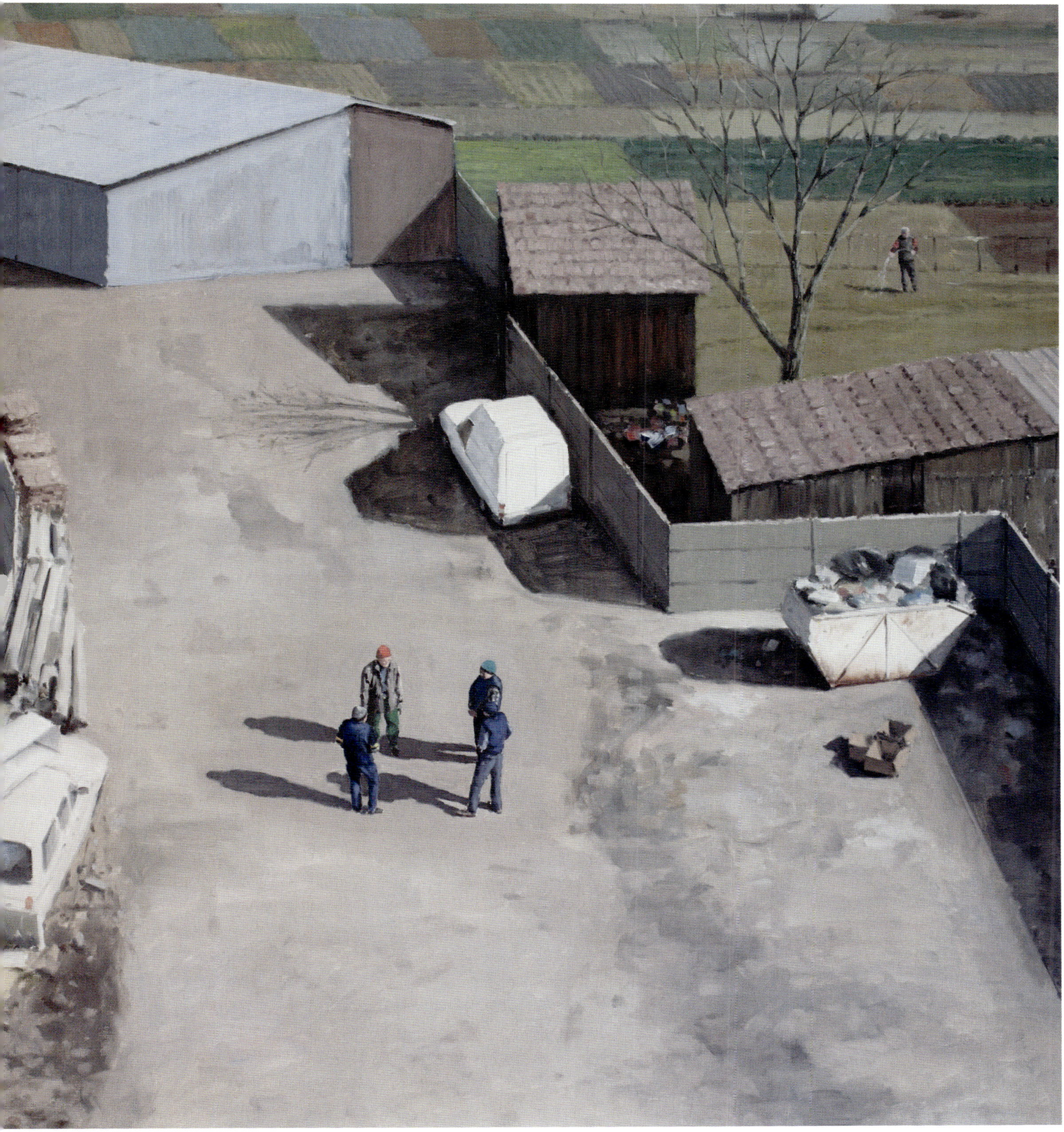

Depot
2010, oil on canvas, 83 × 130 cm
(32¾ × 51 in).

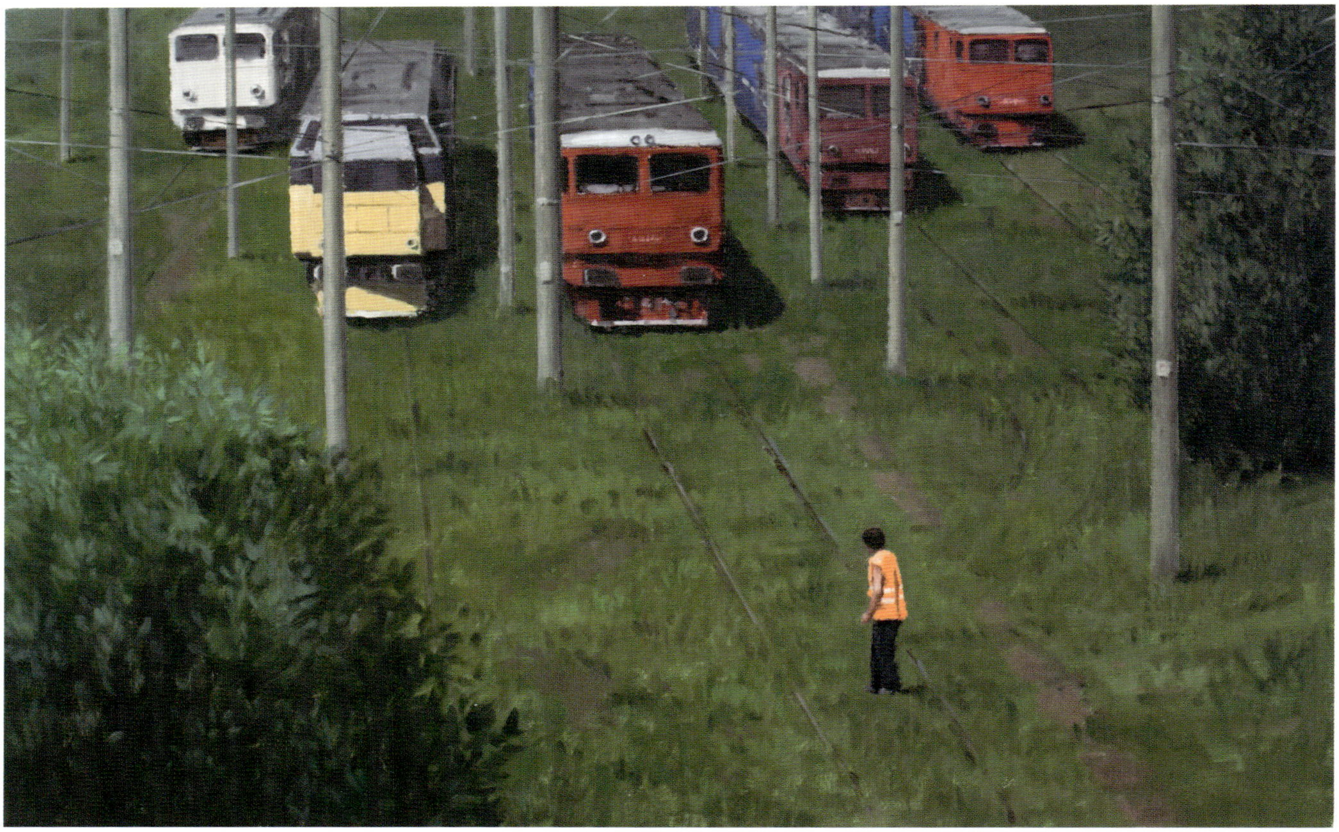

Holy Week
2013, oil on canvas, 170 × 143 cm
(67 × 56 in).

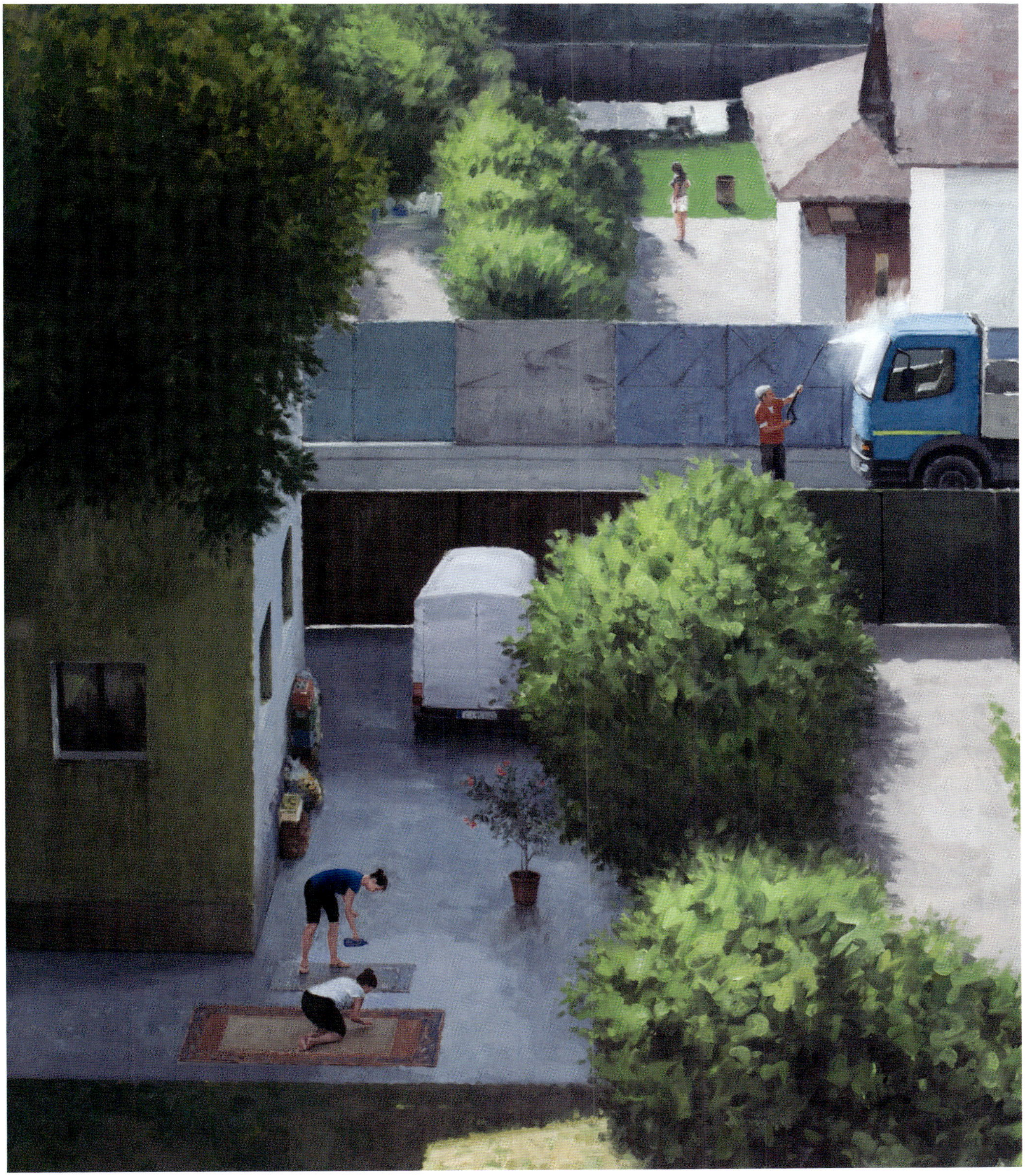

6am Wednesday
2009, oil on canvas, 200 × 130 cm
(79 × 51 in).

Lynette Yiadom-Boakye
Born: 1977, London
Lives: London

Do not try to recognize anyone in the paintings of British-Ghanaian artist Lynette Yiadom-Boakye. Even if they are representations of people, these are not portraits. The various characters (mainly British-Ghanaian) populating her canvases are figments of her imagination. The artist does not even make use of models for them. However, she is well aware of the history of Western portraiture painting and she is very fond of Degas, Monet and Sickert. 'They weren't formally perfect but there was a kind of violence around them that they made clear,' she has said. Yiadom-Boakye's own style is fast-executed, vibrant and not always correct in anatomical detail. The undefined backgrounds are built up with large, quick brushstrokes. But it is exactly in this way that she creates unsettling atmospheres and infuses these fictional, apparently ordinary characters with indecipherable, captivating gestures and moods.

Art school
I learnt a lot in art school. Then I had to unlearn about a fifth of what I'd learnt. But that's useful [Yiadom-Boakye attended Falmouth College and the Royal Academy Schools].

Drawing
Drawing is incredibly important. Everyone should do it. It's not just about learning how to draw. It's about learning how to look, how to see in line, how to see in light, how to see in tone, etc. It's about understanding space, colour and movement.

On painting people
One could draw anything, but the human figure makes the most sense as it is the one subject we all recognize immediately, that we all know or think we know. This makes it both the most difficult and the easiest subject to work from. The people in the paintings are not anyone I know, they are composites of life drawing, photographs and imaginings: fiction. Thus, I'm probably less interested in real people than I am in painted people. In many ways, I would find it distracting to think about, or aim to depict, real people. My method affords me the freedom to invent a world and re-order it.

Developing technique
It has been a slow process but a prolific one. There are wrong turns every week. I don't have a failsafe method. But this is important: I learn from my mistakes. That's part of the process. I work quickly. I feel that I have a better understanding of what I do now than ever before but that's not to say I don't make mistakes. I'm very rarely completely satisfied with anything.

On Photoshop and painting
I can't see a natural connection between the two. I've never used Photoshop for my work. Personally, the idea makes me feel ill, perhaps because I don't enjoy using computers and they are not relevant to my idea of what painting is or should be. I have no interest in finding a connection. Which is probably why I paint. There are people who use Photoshop. There are people who paint. There are people who like to use the two together. If your painterly intention necessitates one of those three then so be it.

On inspirations
There are a lot of [painters who inspired me] – some because I liked the work, some because I really didn't like the work but needed to understand why. That helped me to get a sense of what was important to me about painting itself, how best to fulfil my intentions (and what those intentions are), some kind of personal belief system to help me judge what doesn't work and why.

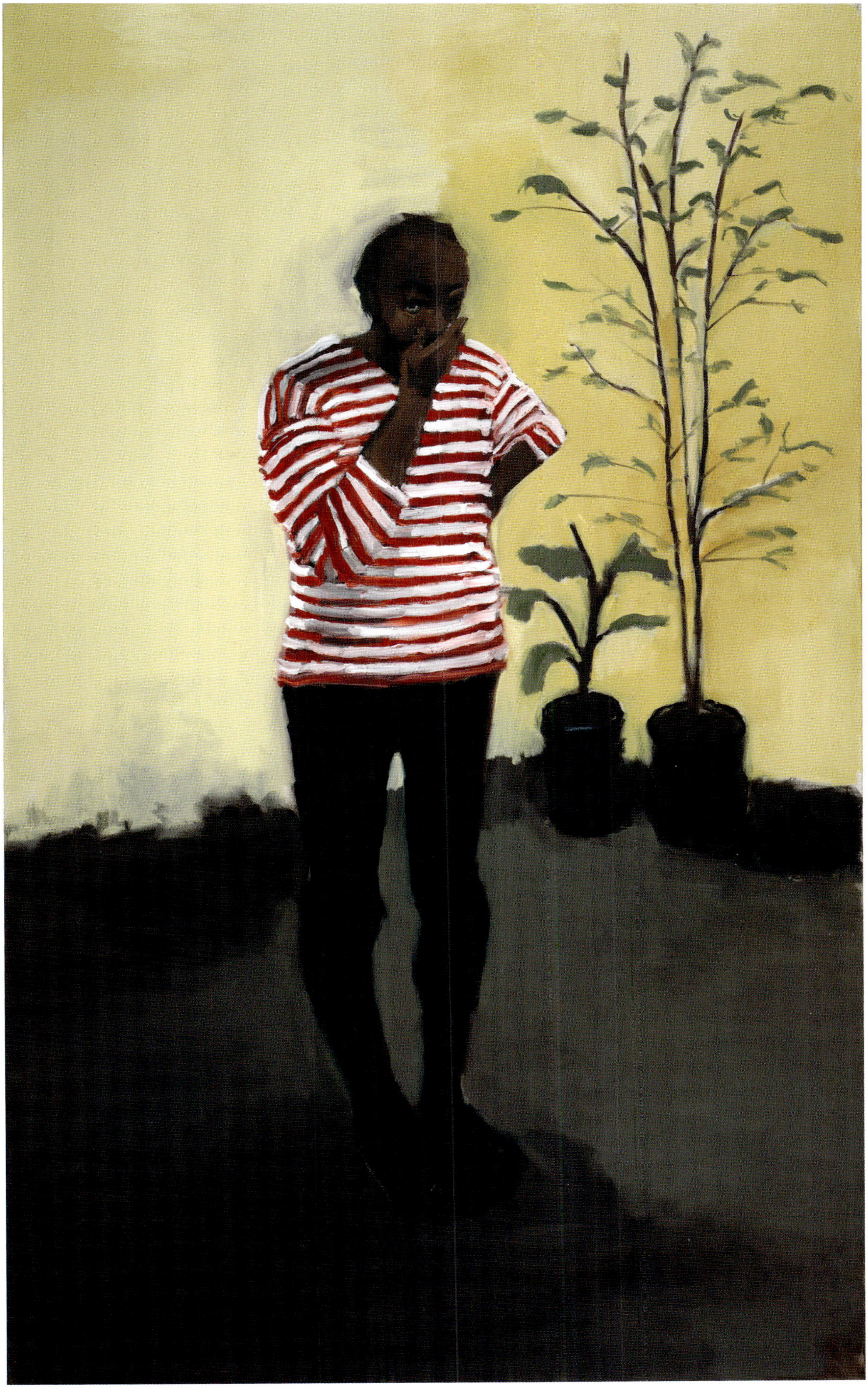

An Authority
2011, oil on canvas, 55 × 45 cm
(21⅝ × 17¾ in).

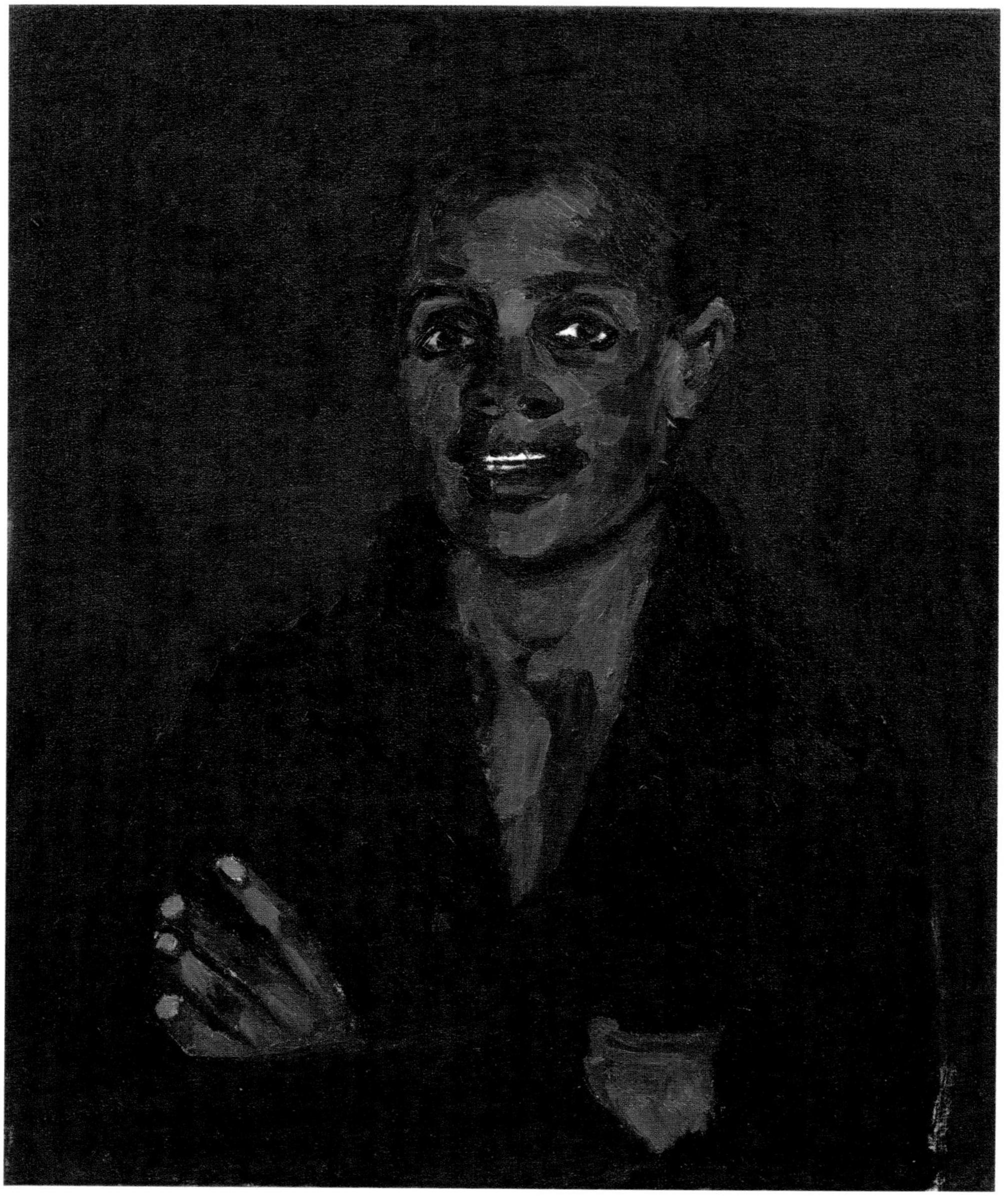

11pm Friday
2010, oil on canvas, 200 × 130 cm
(79 × 51 in).

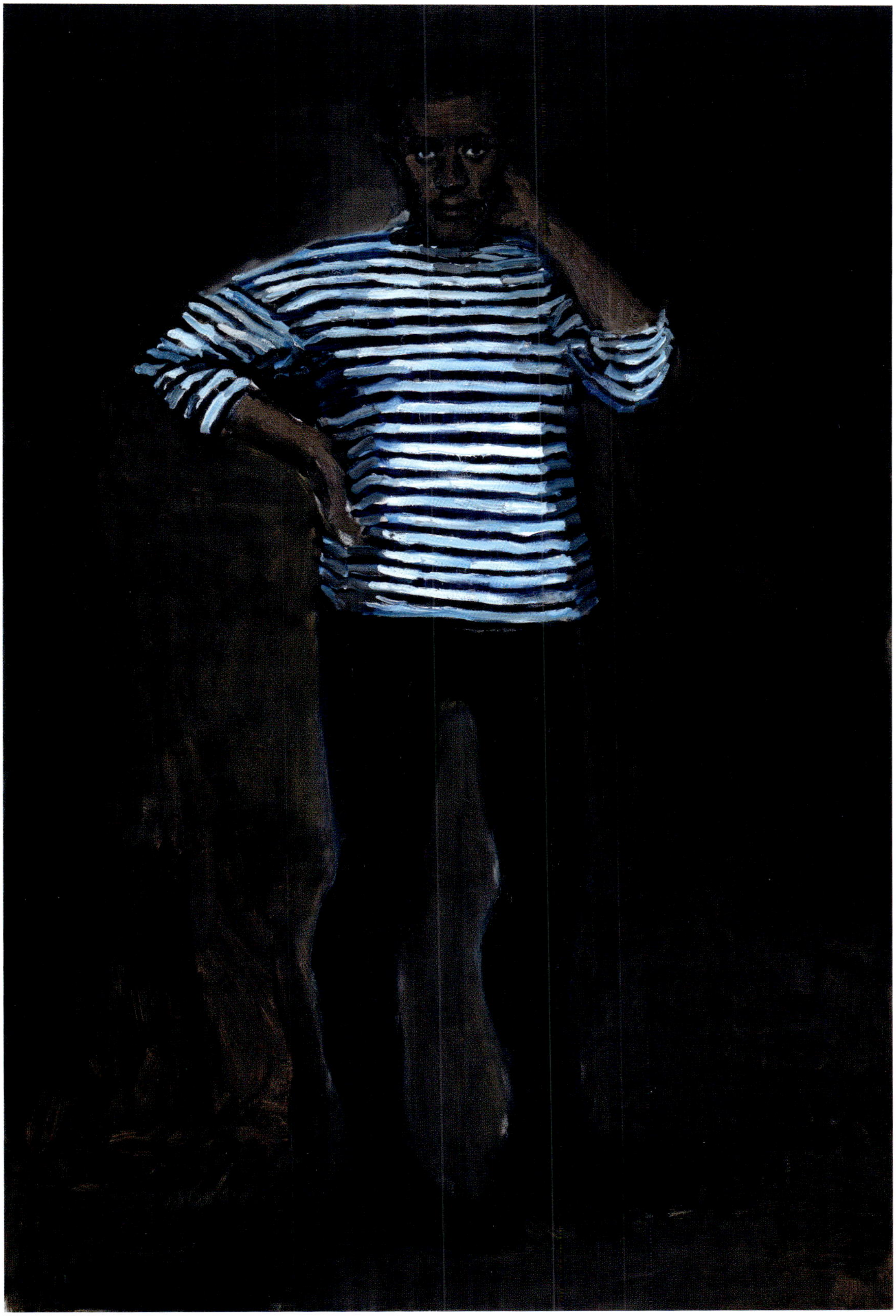

A Bounty Left Unpaid
2011, oil on canvas, 200 × 160 cm
(79 × 63 in).

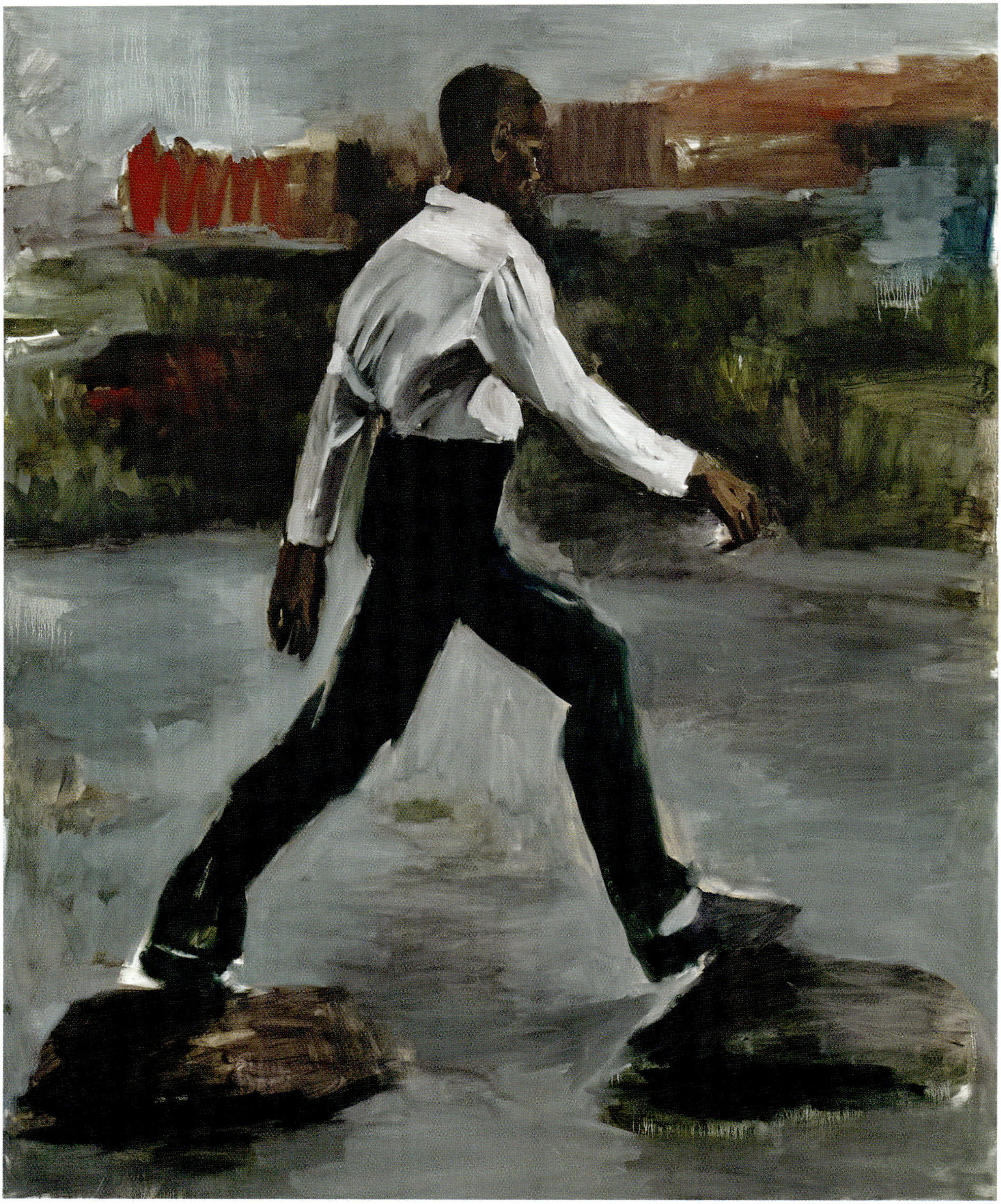

A Toast to the Health Of
2011, oil on canvas, 200 × 250 cm
(79 × 98 in).

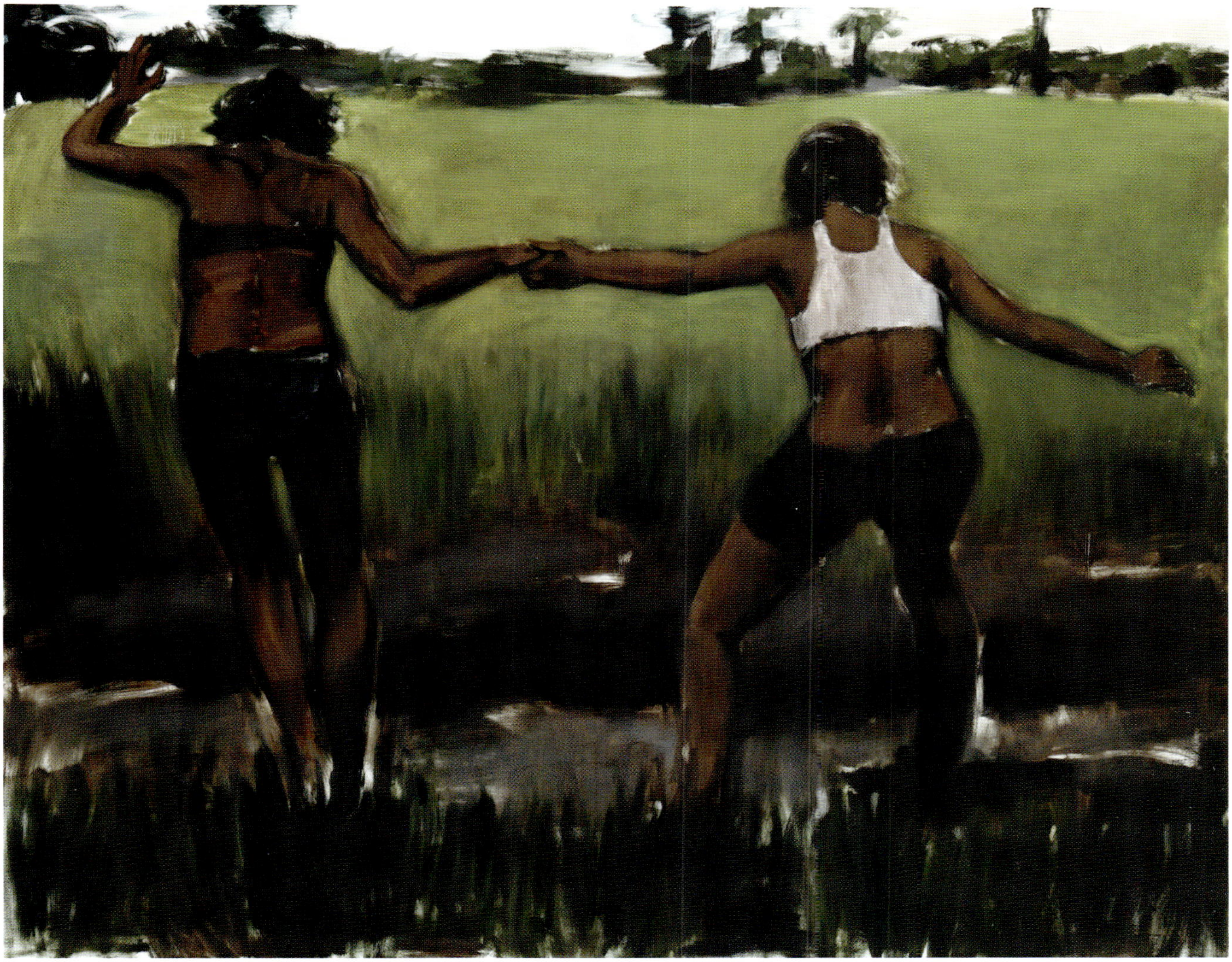

Liu Xiadong
Born: 1963, Liaoning (China)
Lives: Beijing

Liu Xiadong knew that he wanted to be an artist from the day he enrolled at the Central Academy of Fine Arts (CAFA) in Beijing. His work cherishes and reinterprets the strong education in figurative painting that he received. Inspired by the troubles and complexities of everyday life, Liu Xiadong chooses normal people as the subjects for his paintings. In their faces and gestures he sees the most representative embodiment of the many different difficulties of contemporary times.

Drawing
Throughout my eight years of art education I had drawing classes almost every day. I think they are incredibly useful to help an artist in determining proportions of space as well as accurate use of colour. Of course, painting, according to painters, is a completely different story!

Life painting
A lot of my work is painting from life. Painting from life plays a significant role in shaping my use of colour and space. I find that through the use of oil paints, I am able to articulate and express my thoughts accurately. After painting a large number of works, slowly but surely my own artistic style started to develop. In recent years, I have been painting out in the field. In these cases, I often build and use a temporary painting studio.

Art history
Painters are like art history's 'rings', like the links connecting the chain. All painters in the very long history of art have impacted on my work. Regardless of whether I like it or hate it, they are all my natural resources. I cannot pick and choose any one of them. It is the [combined] impact of the 'ring'.

Painting is like eating
As a painter, I am born hungry and I want to eat everything I can see. Painting anything makes me happy. It is like eating: eat until you are full. But of course, eating until you're 80 per cent full is often better than not stopping.

Painting nostalgia
In the era of Photoshop, paintings seem more demanding visual items because they require a real engagement. A painting is not just an image, but more like a collection of feelings and traces that have been left behind. It is the nostalgia for this world that causes me to engage in figurative painting. When one attempts to respond rapidly and forcefully to the fast changes of contemporary life, there is the risk of a loss of culture.

Against style
Painting is the oldest form of contemporary art, regardless of which artistic media can better reveal the truth. The history of painters is merely the history of forming one's own style. But once a style is formed, it is difficult to reflect directly and effectively on contemporary society. To reveal the truth, painters must undermine their own style at any given time. This is the hardest problem for an artist to handle.

H's Family
2009, oil on canvas, 290 × 259 cm
(114 × 102 in).

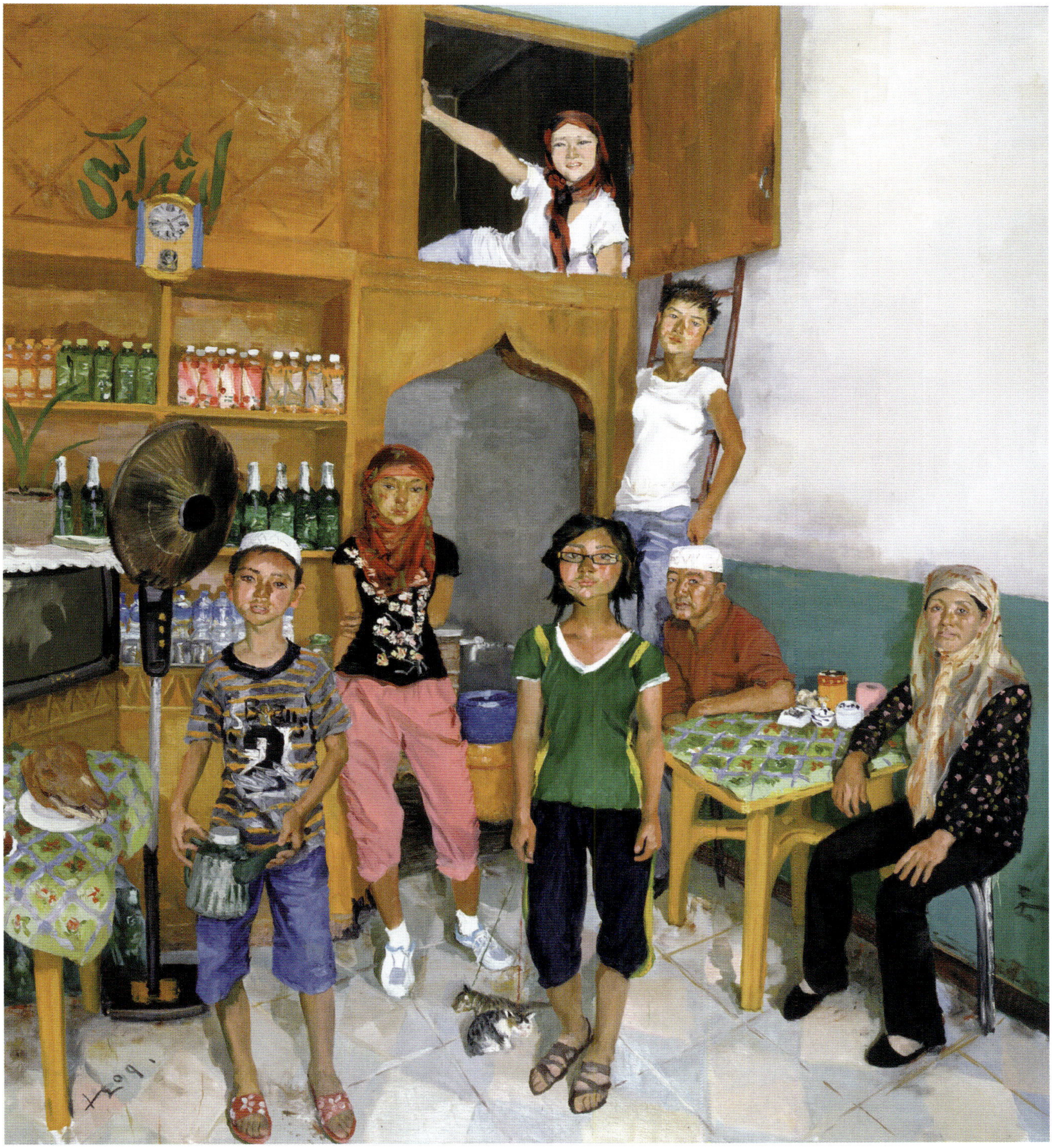

Jincheng Airport
2010, oil on canvas, 300 × 400 cm
(118 × 158 in).

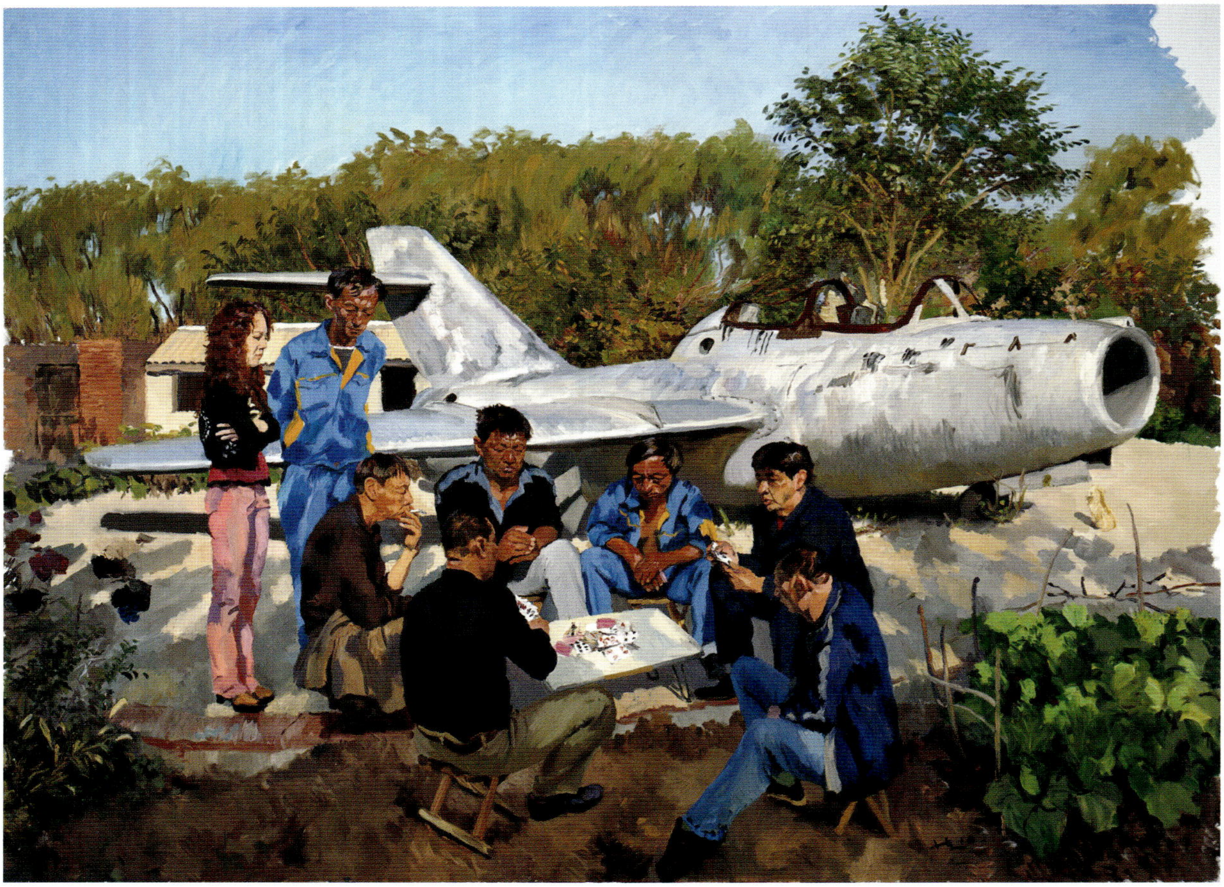

My Egypt
2010, oil on canvas, 300 × 400 cm
(118 × 158 in).

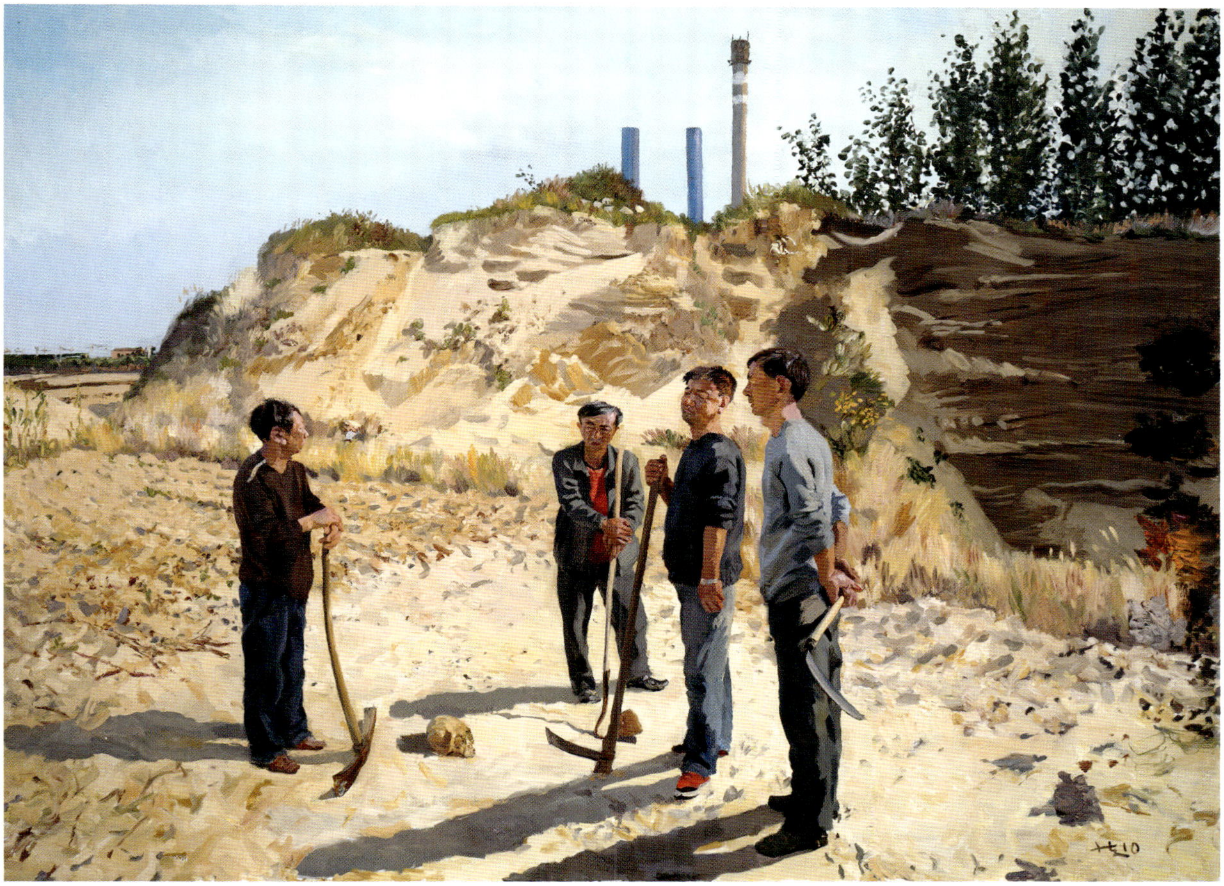

Blonde Ambition
2012, oil on board, 45 × 55 cm
(17¾ × 21⅝ in).

Caroline Walker
Born: 1982, Dunfermline (UK)
Lives: London

'It was always painting for me, right from the start; painting was always the medium I enjoyed looking at most, and that I find the most exciting and direct to work with.' A natural painter, Caroline Walker grew up in Scotland and remembers forming a relationship with the collections in Edinburgh's National Galleries. She highlights painting's 'mimetic and expressive qualities (the way it can remind you of the tactility of a particular material)' as well as the 'visceral quality of paint itself'. With simplicity and clarity, and by carefully studying and arranging the subtleties of movement within domestic environments, her work captures the relationships between human beings and defined psychological spaces.

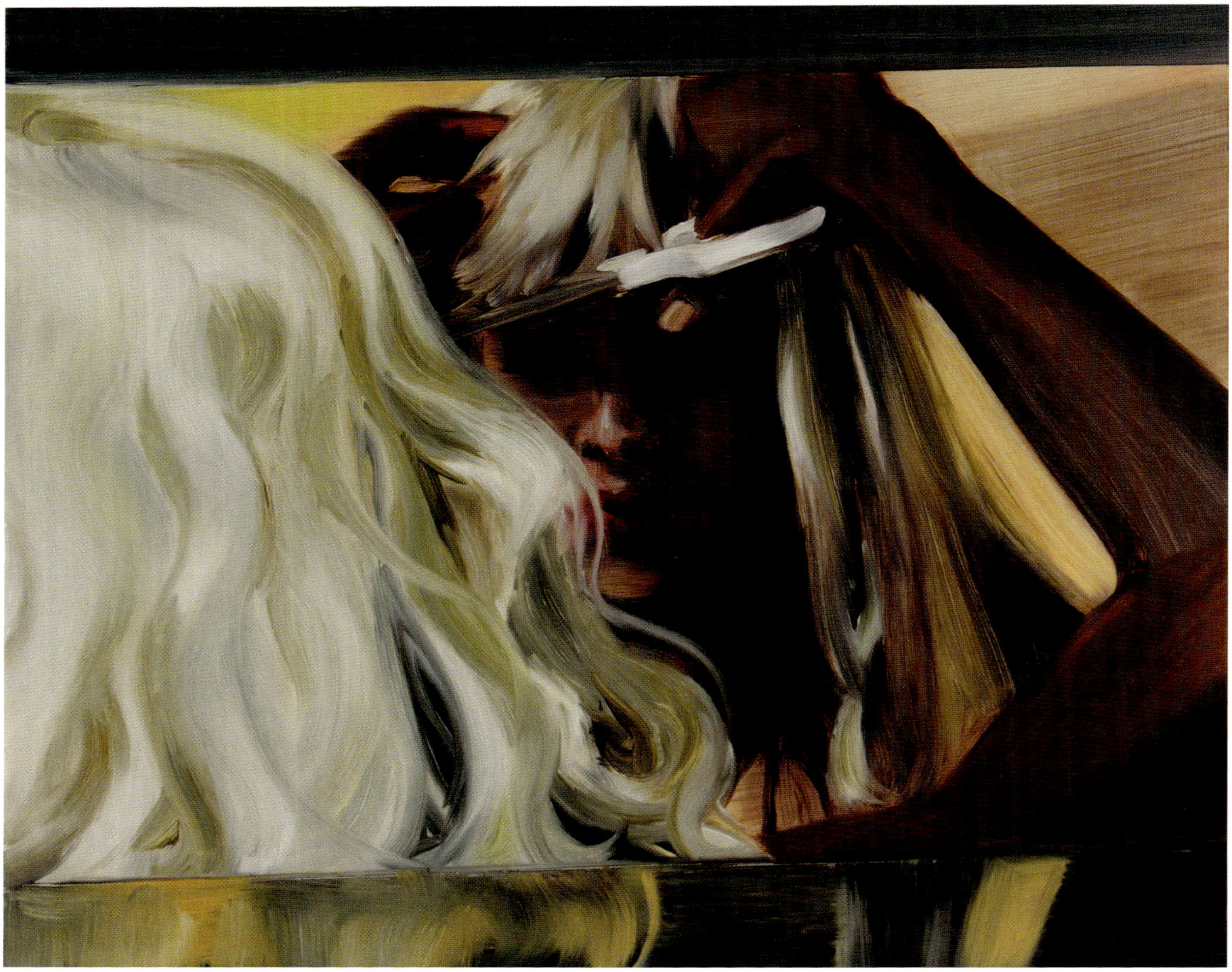

Why painting today

We always talk about how our generation lives in an image-saturated culture where we consume and discard images with little pause for thought, and this seems to have given painting a new agency as a slower medium. It can ask a viewer to reassess how they look at the world in a very direct and personal way. It can communicate something subjective or imaginative that is very particular to how direct the process of making a painting is.

Process

For several years, I was either inventing the interiors and the people that inhabited them, or relying on friends and family and their houses. It wasn't until I started my MA that I began picking apart what I was interested in and thinking about who this person was and where they were. I started working with a model who was a sitter for dogs and cats in different houses around London. Every time I worked with her she'd be in a different house, and it was interesting for me that this wasn't 'home' for either of us but somewhere that could be treated like a 'set' for exploring a narrative.

After I finished at the RCA (Royal College of Art) I began being more selective about the houses in which I located the figure. Previously they had always been Victorian period houses with fairly traditional décor, so I wanted to change this completely and started looking at very contemporary neo-modernist homes and the concept of the 'Grand Design' as the ultimate made-to-measure house: a place completely designed inside and out for its inhabitants, and which dictates how one might live in it. I've always been interested in an undercurrent of something more sinister in the banal. The aspirational space of these luxury homes seems like the ideal platform to explore the idea of the public appearance of a lifestyle belying the reality of what goes on behind closed doors. The architectural setting for the figure is now always the starting point for developing a series of work.

Firstly, I locate a house I want to use for a photo shoot, so far through people I know that know someone else.... Although there is a connection in this way, they're never places that I've been to before. When the location is set I start loosely planning a narrative – maybe the women are at a strange pool party, doing domestic chores, or something altogether more ritualistic or unexplained. While these ideas are coming together, I start sourcing models/actors and getting props and clothing for them. Once the location, models and props are all decided, I spend a day at the house directing the women in these different scenarios while I photograph and film them.

I take hundreds of photographs and though there are these loose narrative themes that help me to direct the models on the day, these are really just a starting point, and often the unplanned material can lead to the most successful paintings. I make lots of sketches and then oil studies and measured drawings to work out what material I will use to make big paintings and the exact scale of these works. The scale is dictated by designing a space that the viewer feels they are already in, could walk into, or are surreptitiously spying on.

In terms of my painting itself, I start by making an acrylic underpainting in quite saturated colours, using the paint almost like washes of watercolour. This helps me build a very vibrant ground on which to work with the oil paint on top. Using the acrylics and then the oils like this, it's effectively like a glazing technique that gives the dark colours real depth and adds luminosity to the brighter areas. This technique has been particularly effective in my latest series of works, with its sun-drenched scenes around an outdoor swimming pool.

How we live today

I use painting to reflect on how we live our lives in private spaces and how the domestic can become a stage for the performance of archetypes of femininity. What I set up, in the elaborate staging of my subject matter, makes painting the ideal medium as it is itself already a space of construction and illusion, so the process of painting just seems to compound this fiction. Though I take lots of photographs, these don't seem to hold the same emotional charge and odd atmosphere that the resulting paintings do. Perhaps it's something to do with the time spent working with a particular image and deciding what you want from it, then transforming it and manipulating it into something completely different – this is something that I only discover through the process of painting.

On women as subject

I paint women because in some ways I am always painting myself, and my own experiences or anxieties, but from a distanced, objective position that I hope can also reflect how we all encounter the world.

I use painting to explore the psychological space of home, and particularly how this relates to women, from a social, cultural and political perspective but also from an art-historical standpoint, reflecting on and drawing from the proliferation of images of women throughout a long history of Western painting, and reassessing this in a contemporary context and through a female gaze.

Illuminations
2012, oil on linen, 240 × 305 cm
(95 × 120 in).

Recreation Pavilion
2013, oil on linen, 280 × 190 cm
(110 × 75 in).

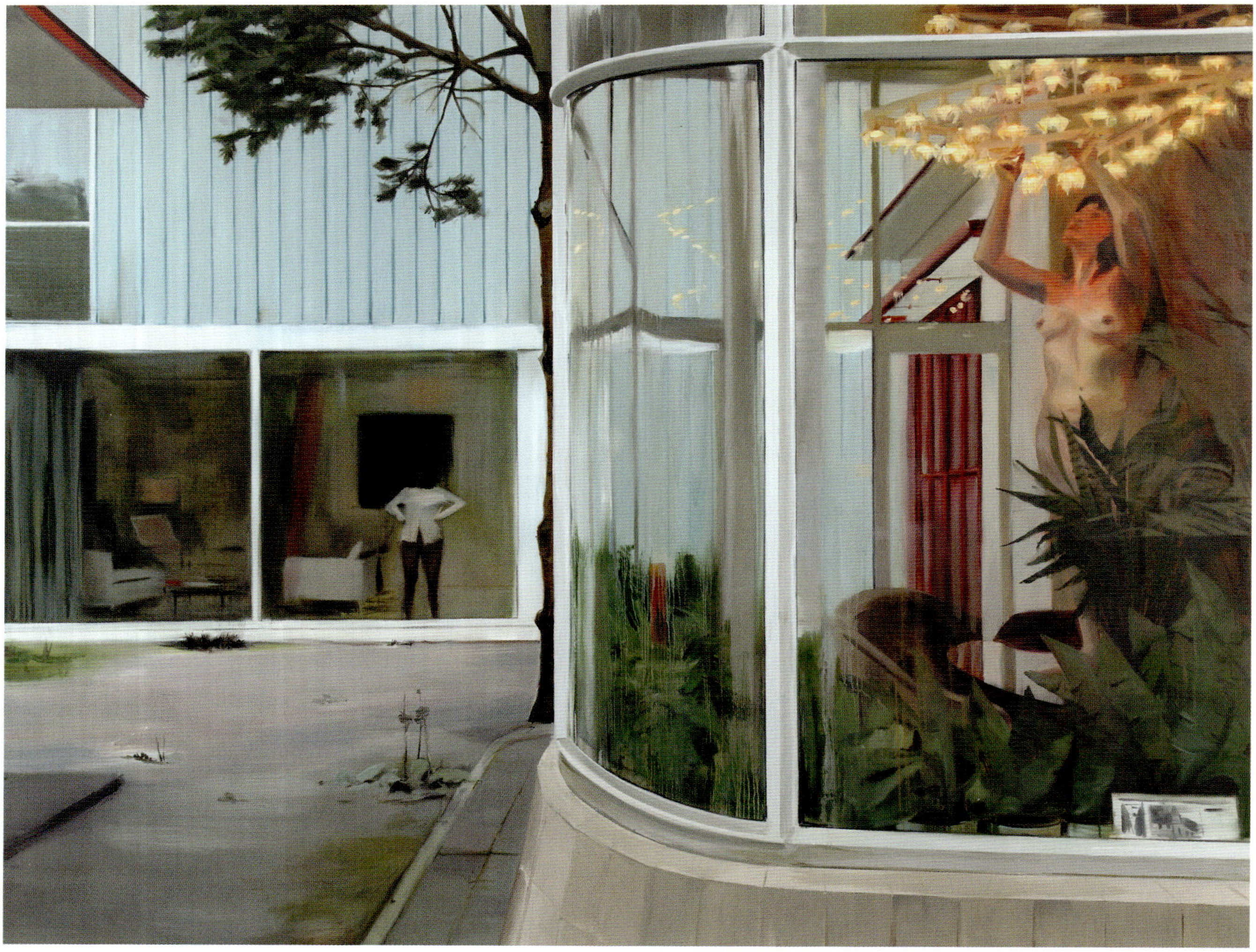

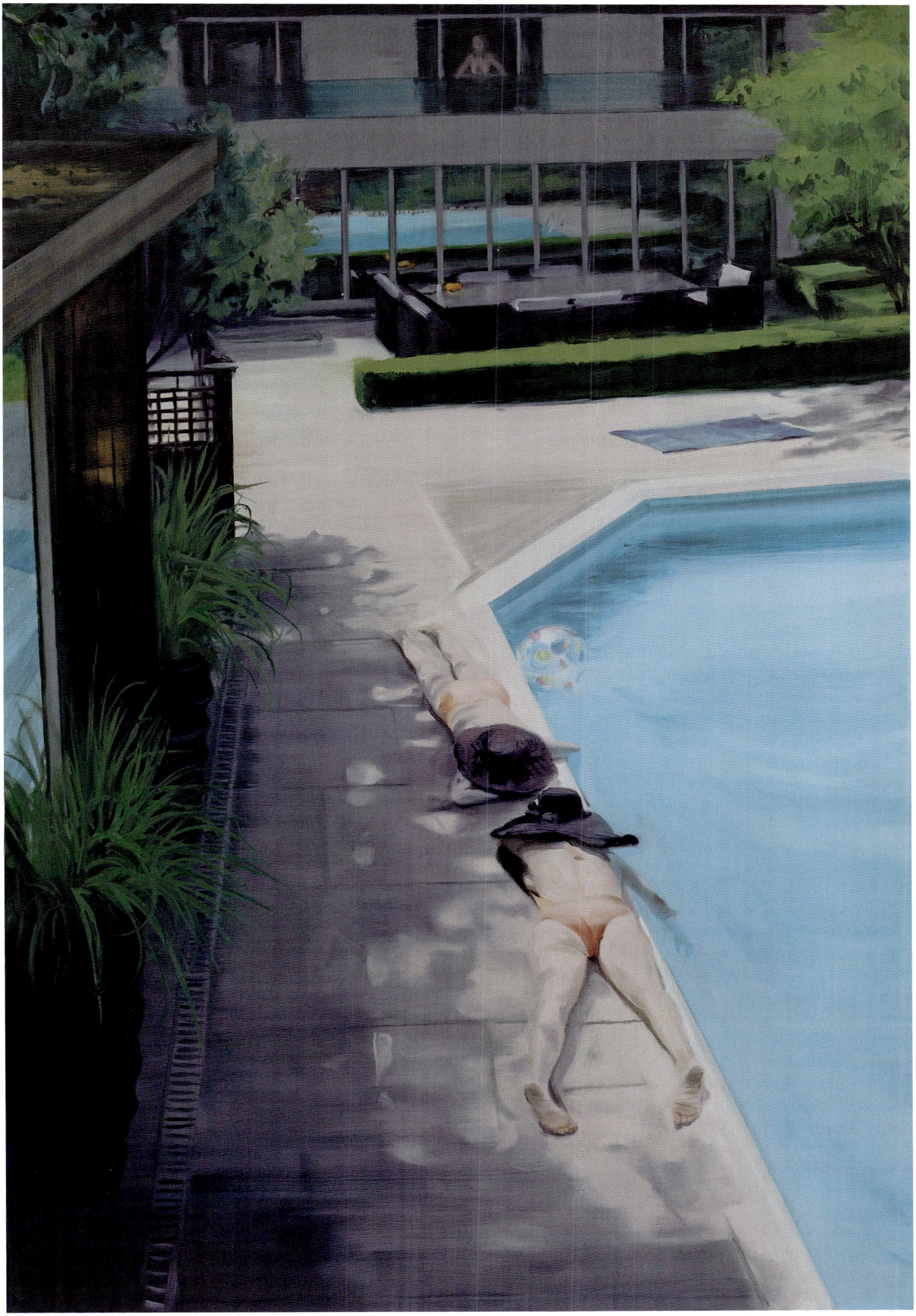

Pool Party
2012, oil on linen, 167 × 240 cm
(66 × 95 in).

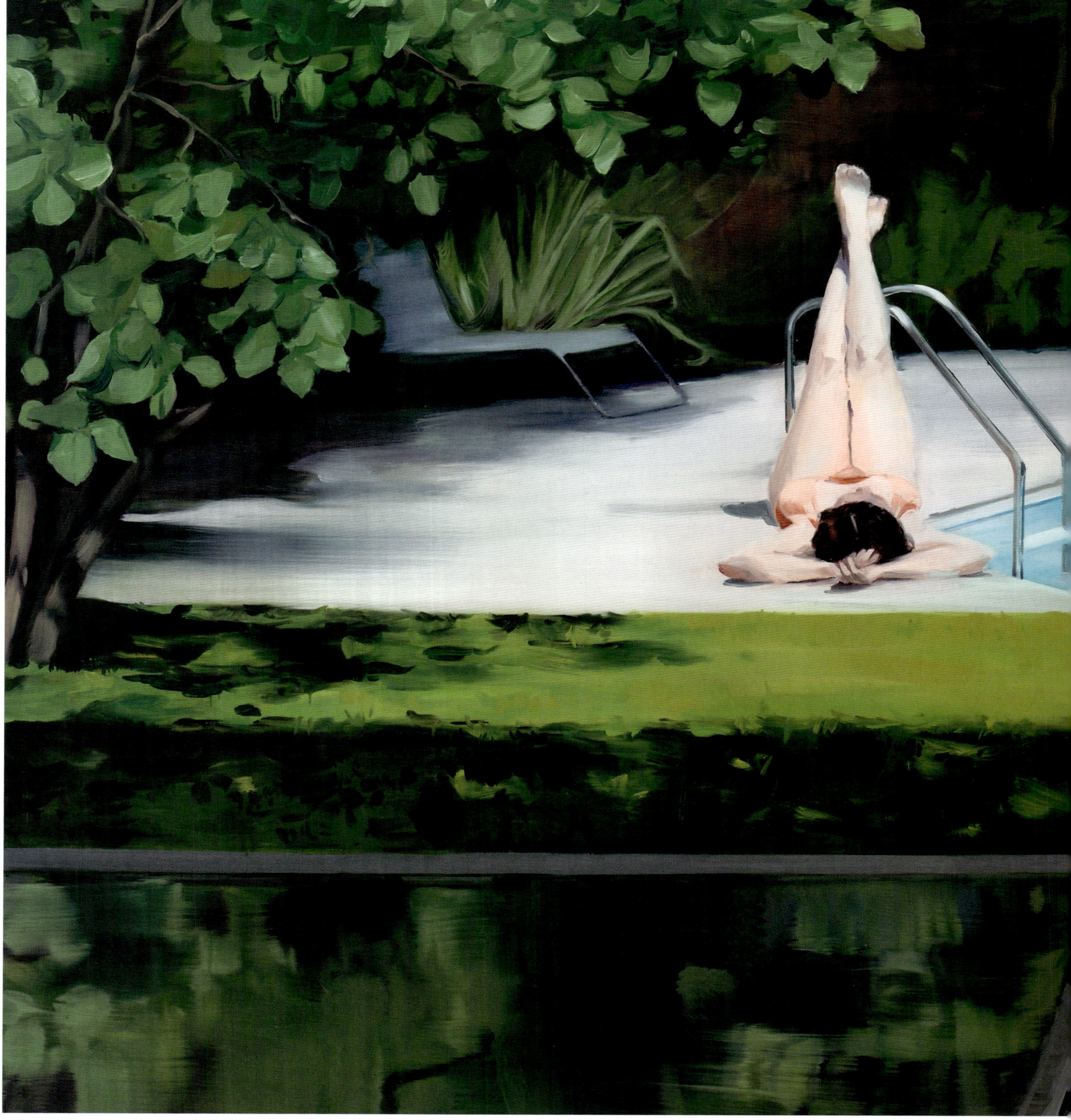

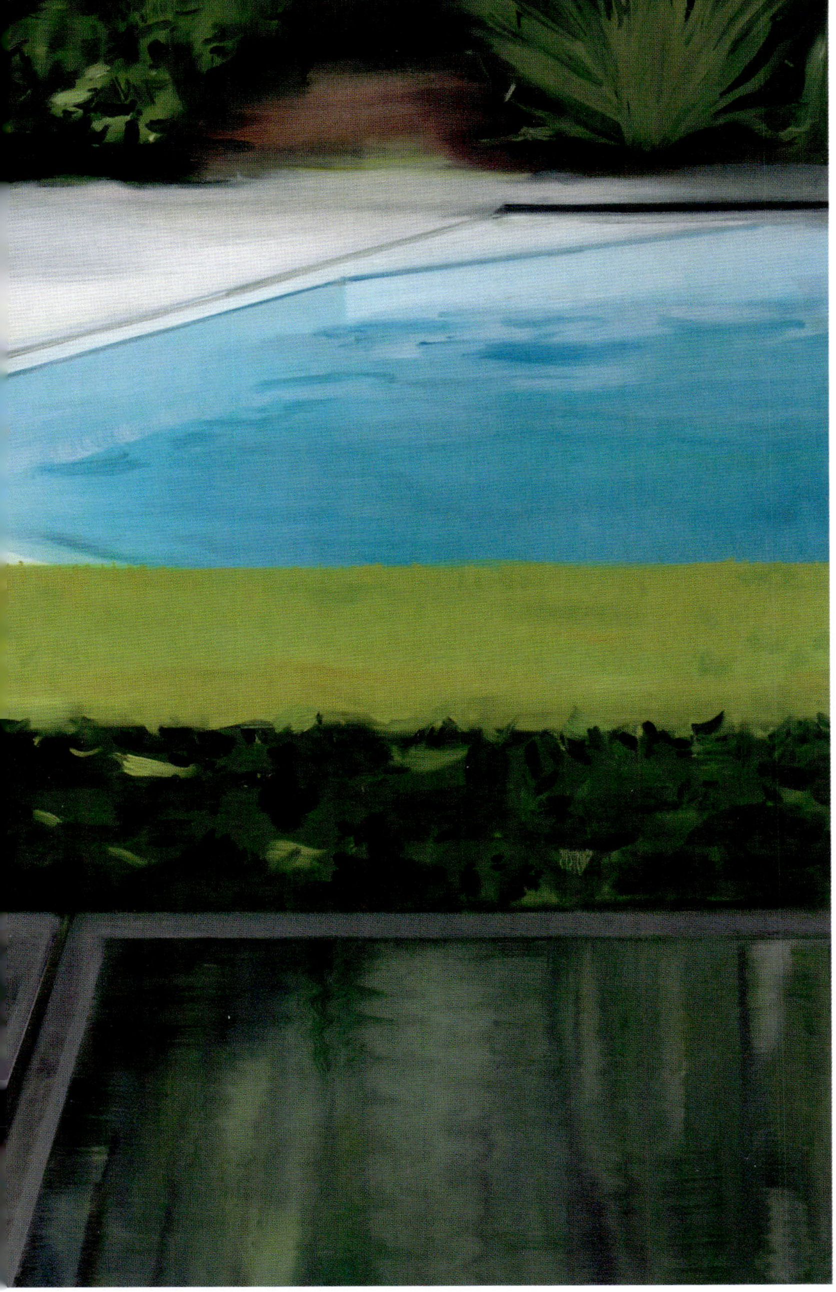

The Masquerade
2012, oil on linen, 180 × 240 cm
(71 × 95 in).

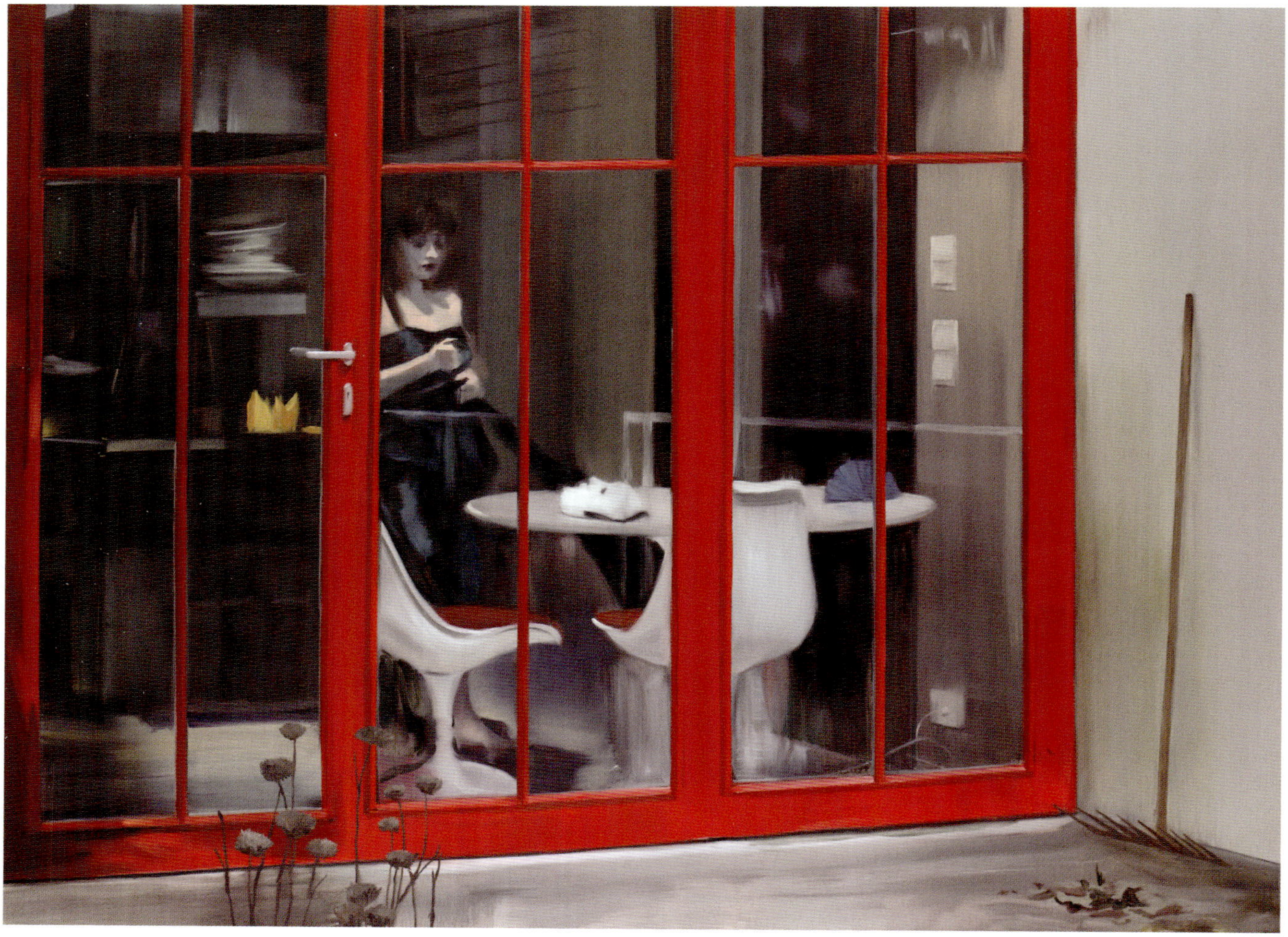

Vantage Point
2010, oil on canvas, 211 × 182 cm
(83 × 72 in).

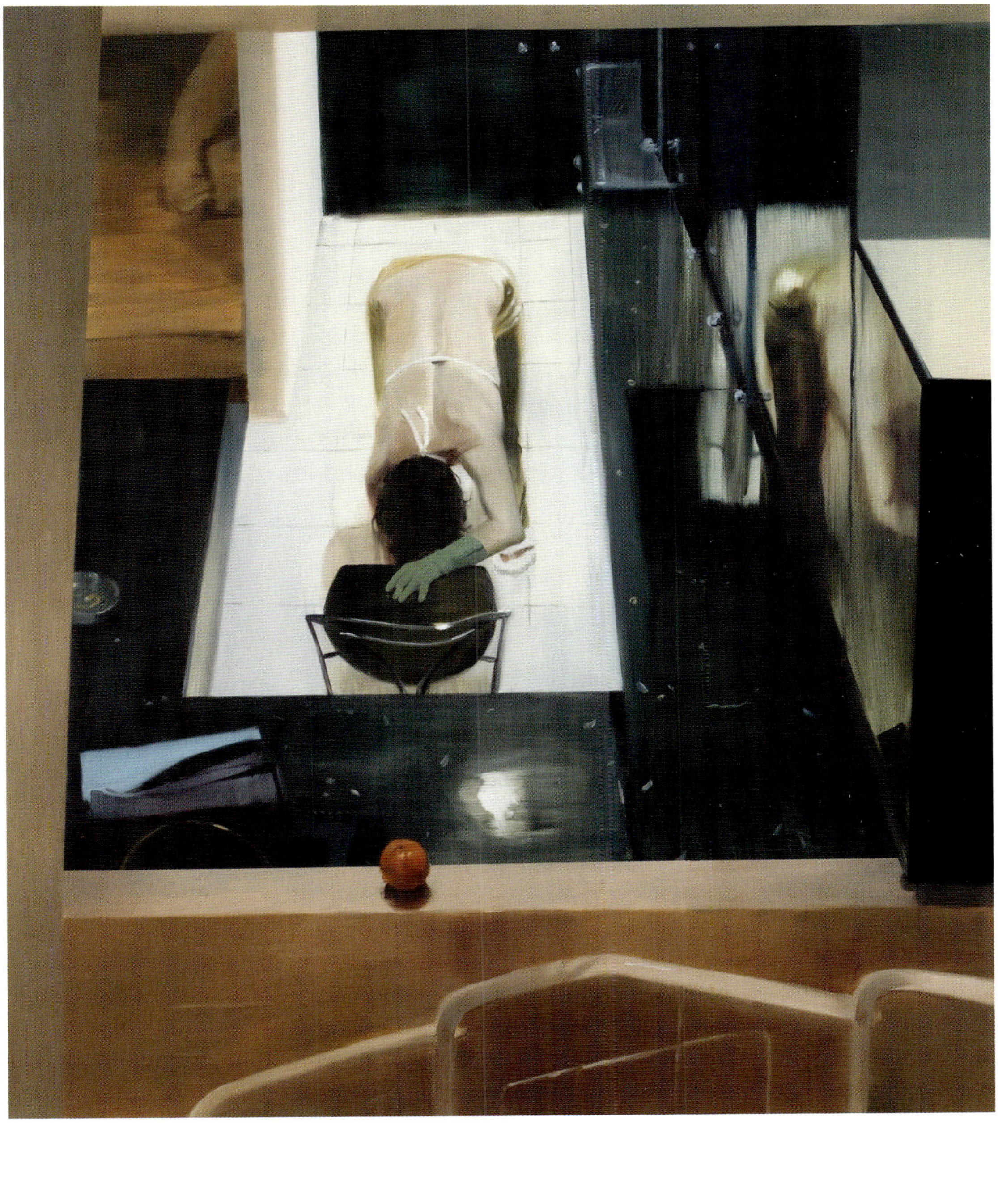

Natalie Grocery
2007, oil and digital media on canvas, 102 × 147 cm (40 × 58 in).

Dan Witz
Born: 1957, Chicago, Illinois
Lives: New York

Brooklyn-based artist Dan Witz is not your usual fine art painter: he alternates the discipline of painting in his studio (often working for weeks or months on a single large-scale canvas) with the freedom and the immediacy of going out and making street art. He was attracted to painting by the physical intensity of Old Master paintings – something that reminded him of his days as a punk rocker. Indeed, his series of paintings, 'Mosh Pits', reaches to the limits of what can be achieved with a painted surface in terms of presence and energy.

Background
I was born in Chicago in 1957, and grew up there and in the suburbs. I moved to New York City in 1978 to go to art school (Cooper Union). After a brief career in music I settled down to making art. I didn't have a happy time at art school. Most of my time was spent on the streets of the Lower East Side and playing in punk bands. Being a Realist painter I wasn't really accepted by the Neo-expressionists dominating the painting department at the time. Looking back, I can see how important an education this was.

Influences
I've always been mesmerized by Old Master paintings. Not so much the imagery, but the presence, that brief miraculous moment of transferral to the painting's space – when you're there, you suspend disbelief and surrender yourself to the painting's universe. This is what has always excited me about art – that crazy moment when you leave your body and go down the artist's rabbit hole.

Early in my education I discovered that disciplined figurative study was the common starting point for artists I admired. The usual path is to use this classical education as a jumping-off point to more expressive, or less literal, approaches to making art. I stuck with Realism though. I've never got past how cool it is to make space and light and time occur on a flat surface.

These days, it's about trying to make my stuff even more realistic – past the point of what's been possible in the past. I mean, isn't that what we're supposed to be doing – pushing on to new forms? To this end, I use whatever digital and photographic aids I can; I experiment with new technologies and blend them with Old Master techniques.

Street art v. painting
My big easel paintings can take months to complete so it can be a relief for me to get out of the house and do some street art. I used to work on street art in the warmer months and paint in the studio when I couldn't be outside. But now I keep both activities going at once.

I'm aware that some people assume the studio work funds the street art, and [that] that's why I do it, but that's not the case. I love painting. Part of me would be content just to be a traditional painter, maybe teach, live somewhere leafy, have a quiet, focused life. But there's another part of me that's perpetually restless and dissatisfied – self-destructive and always at war with wherever I am. I've tried concentrating solely on street art, which with the travel and meeting new people and all the media attention can be very exciting, but it's too up and down, and at the end of the day leaves me either impatient, or burnt out and depleted. Each side has benefited from the other.

Technology
Some technical innovations, like using digital media to make stickers, I've adapted for studio use. Most of my paintings now start from digital photos as *grisaille* under-paintings. As I said, the idea is to push on to new forms. There's a tool in Photoshop called Free Transform – for me it's really opened up fundamental new possibilities for composing. I don't think it's what Adobe had in mind when they named it, but it has completely freed and transformed my way of working. I have

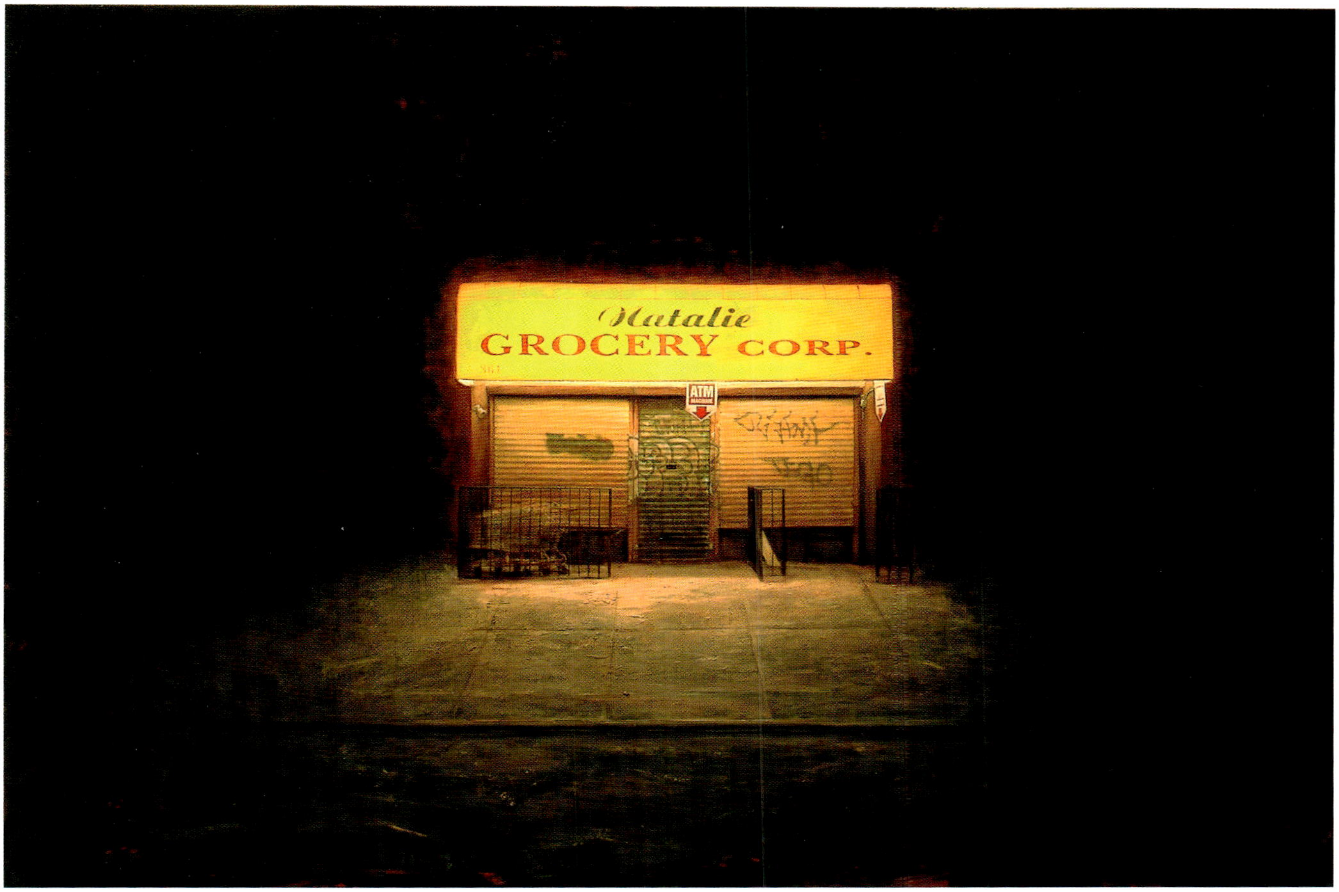

to admit, when I first caught wind of the full possibilities of Photoshop, it was so exciting I briefly considered losing my brushes and becoming a digital artist. I'd always thought that if something purely digital would satisfy my expressive needs I'd gladly use that and be done forever with the heartache and endless labour of figurative painting. Clearly this hasn't happened. I guess I'm stuck with being a painter. For better or worse I need to add something handmade and human, I need to tweak the image with some expression and depth or my stuff just doesn't come to life.

Realism

I suspect the enduring appeal of Realism is in its accessibility. People in the new, more egalitarian, art world are tired of art that looks down on them – art that's so opaque it repels all attempts to decode it without a PhD in art-speak.

'Mosh Pits' paintings

They're a bitch to create. They're driving me out of the studio to do street art. A lot of my themes have come from my early experiences living in downtown NYC and playing in art-punk bands. The group figure paintings come from that and a lifelong interest in Baroque forms – how a flat composition of shapes and colours can evoke such physicality and presence.

Back in my early twenties, as my brief career as a punk rocker was closing down, I knew that I'd really miss the physical intensity of performing. But I began to discover in my museum wanderings that painting actually had plenty of potential for the intensity I needed. The action, especially in the large set pieces, can literally knock you off balance; sometimes it even manages to reach an almost punk-rock level of threat and adrenalin.

After photographing in the mosh pits for a while I became familiar with patterns in the music. I could sense the moment coming when things would totally go berserk. I had the camera on a pole, so, while insinuating myself into the action, I'd hit the timer, count down with the music and lift the camera over the crowd hoping the shutter would click at the optimum moment. It was mostly luck but when I nailed one it was as satisfying as performing. And being tossed around in the mosh pit definitely satisfied my need for an art form that involved risk. After that it is a question of spending crazy hours at the computer, editing, Free Transforming and composing – trying to recreate and organize the chaos.

Sapphire Lounge (square)
2008, oil and mixed media on
canvas, 124 × 124 cm (49 × 49 in).

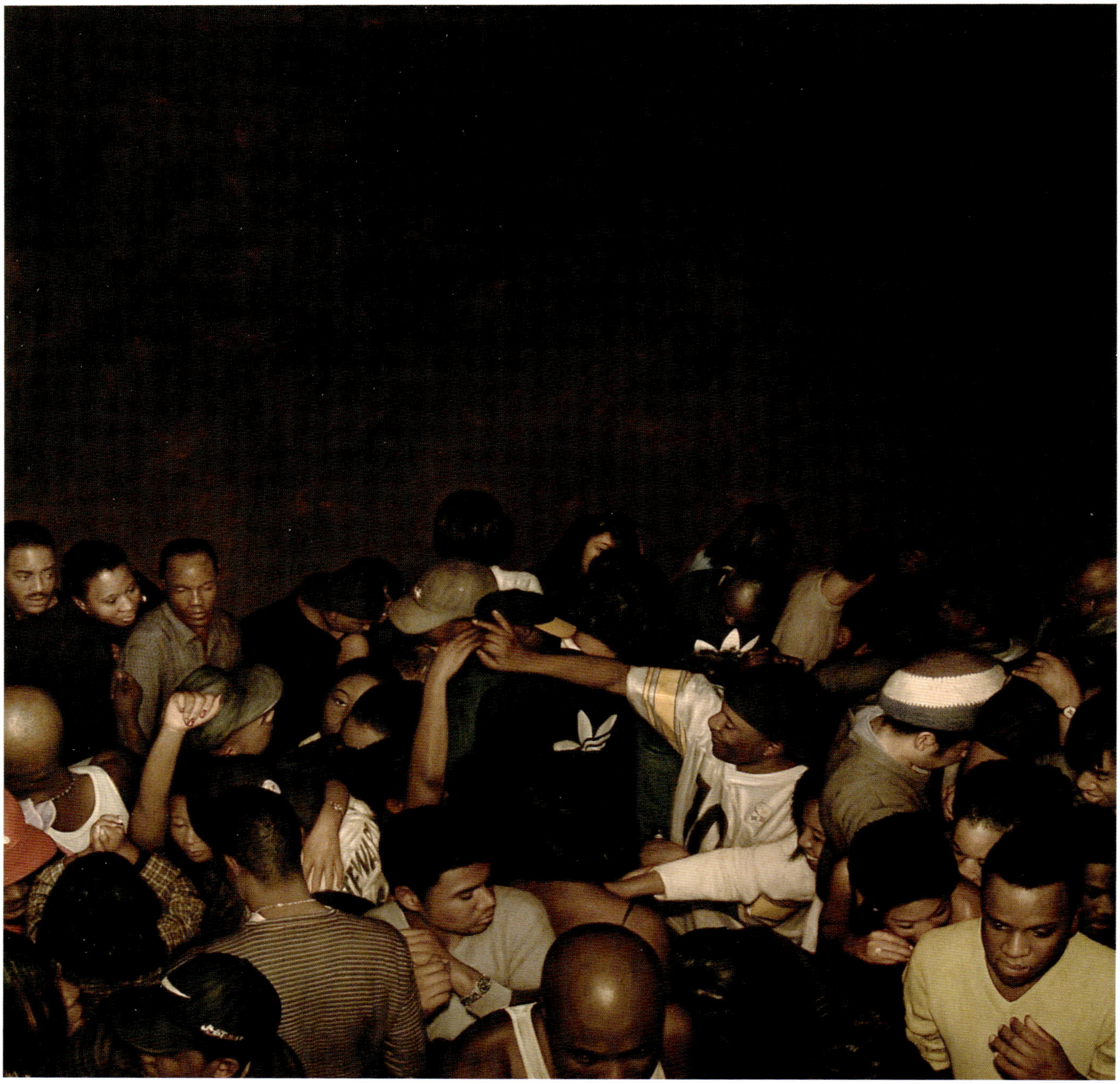

70 Commercial Street
2010, oil and digital media on
canvas, 102 × 137 cm (40 × 54 in).

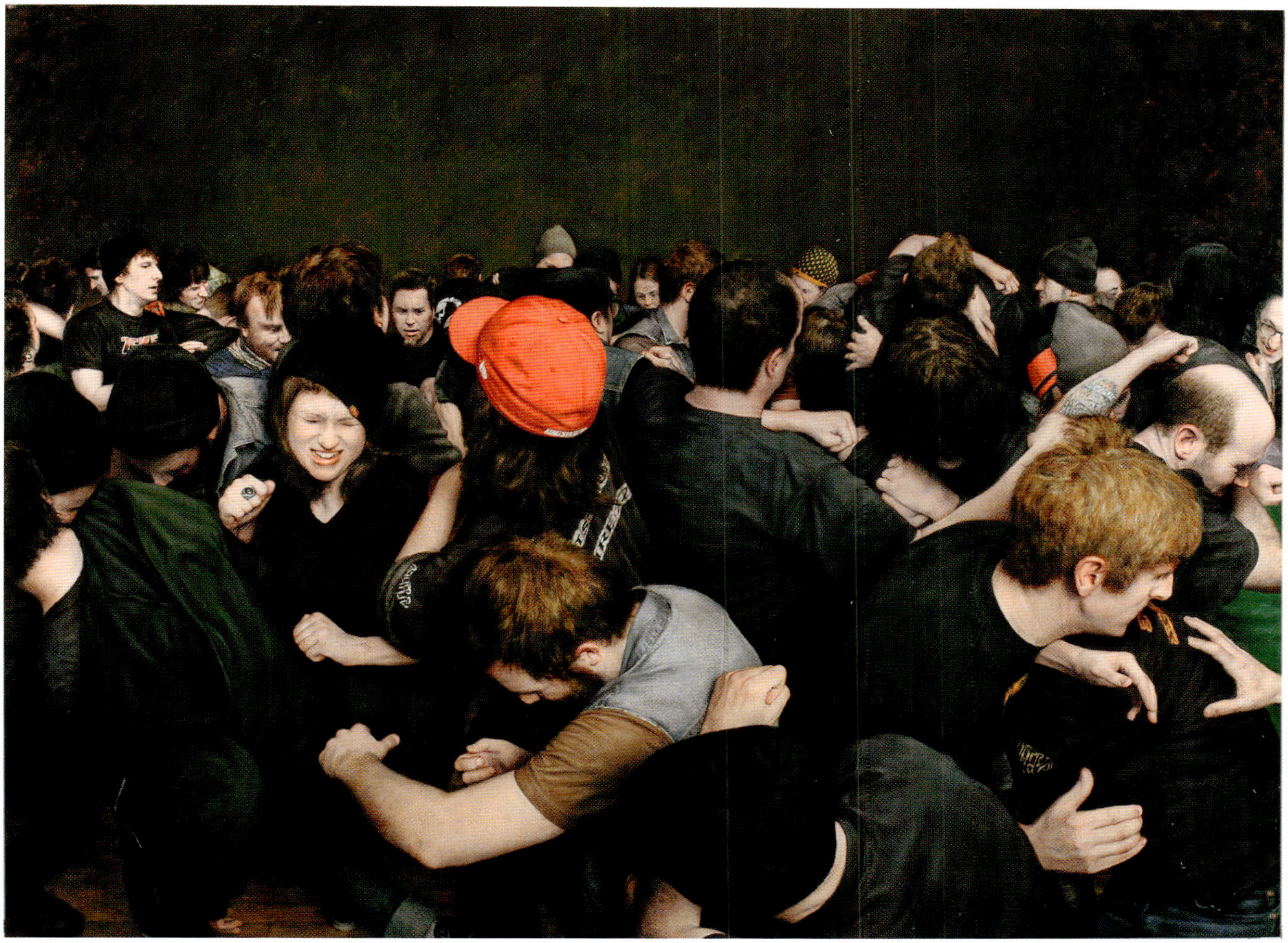

Grand Central Station
2007, oil and digital media on canvas, 102 × 213 cm (40 × 84 in).

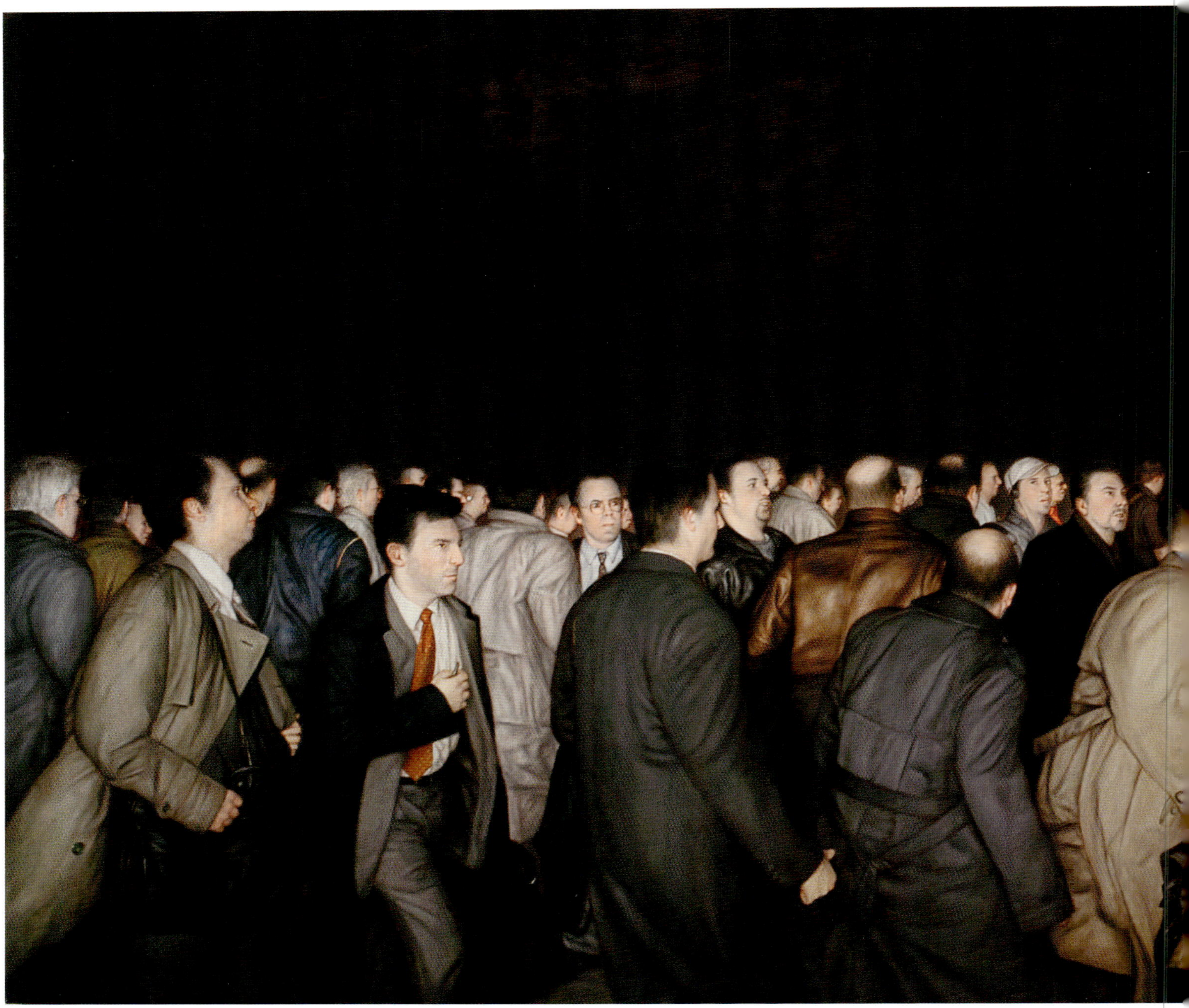

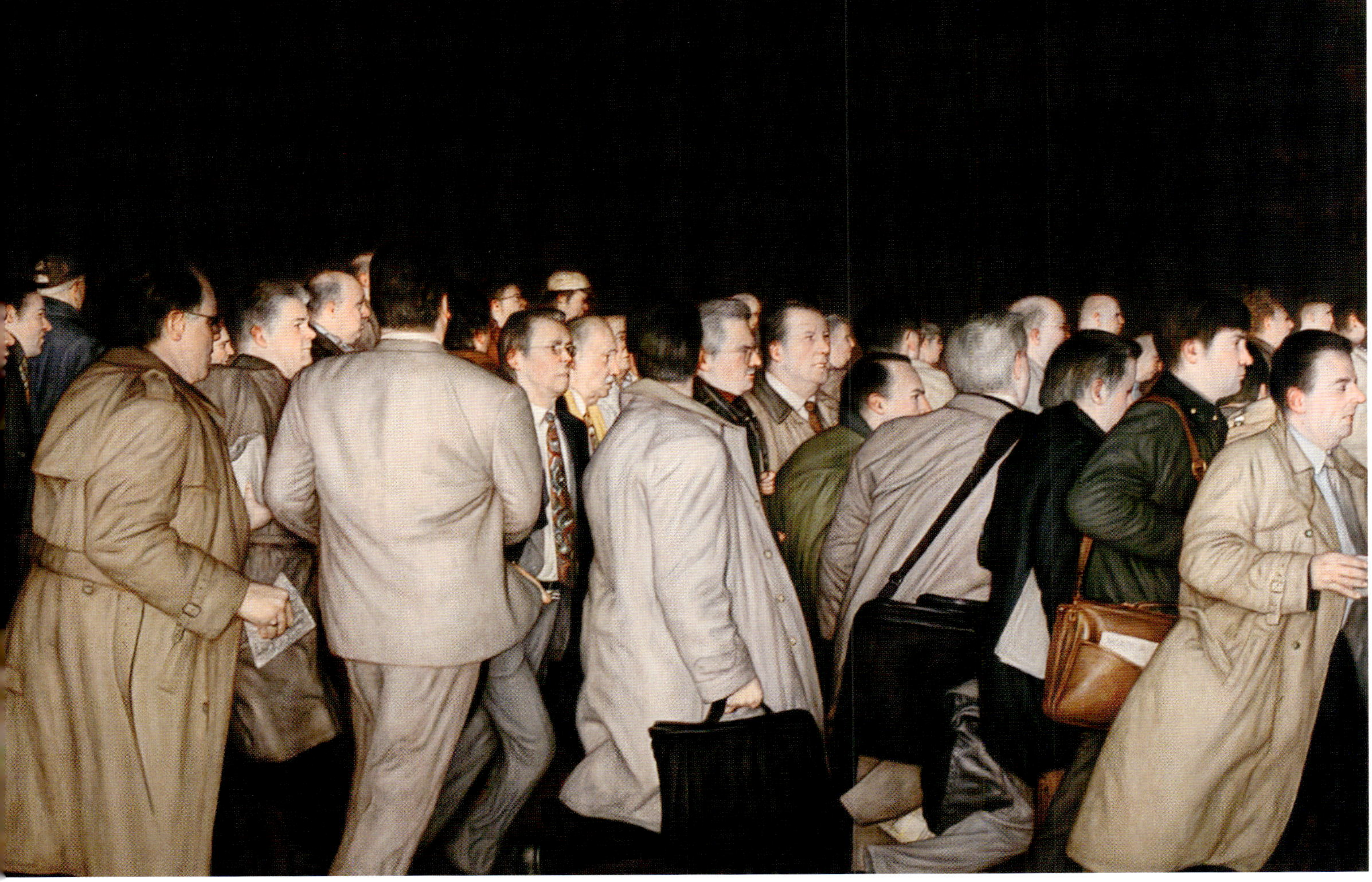

Brent (Jumpsuit)
2012, oil and digital media on canvas, 127 × 102 cm (50 × 40 in).

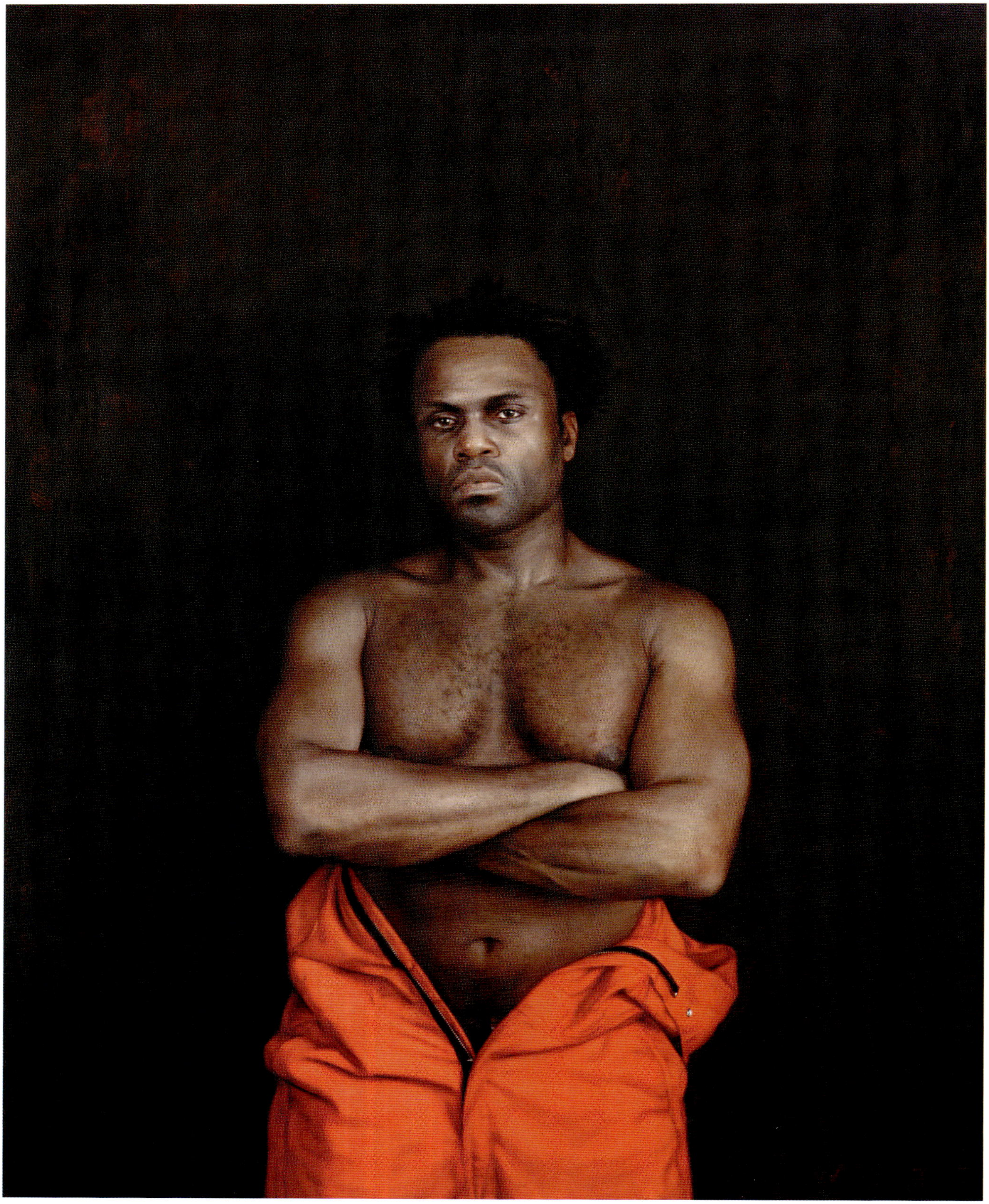

Raquel
2012, oil and digital media on canvas,
51 × 38 cm (20 × 15 in).

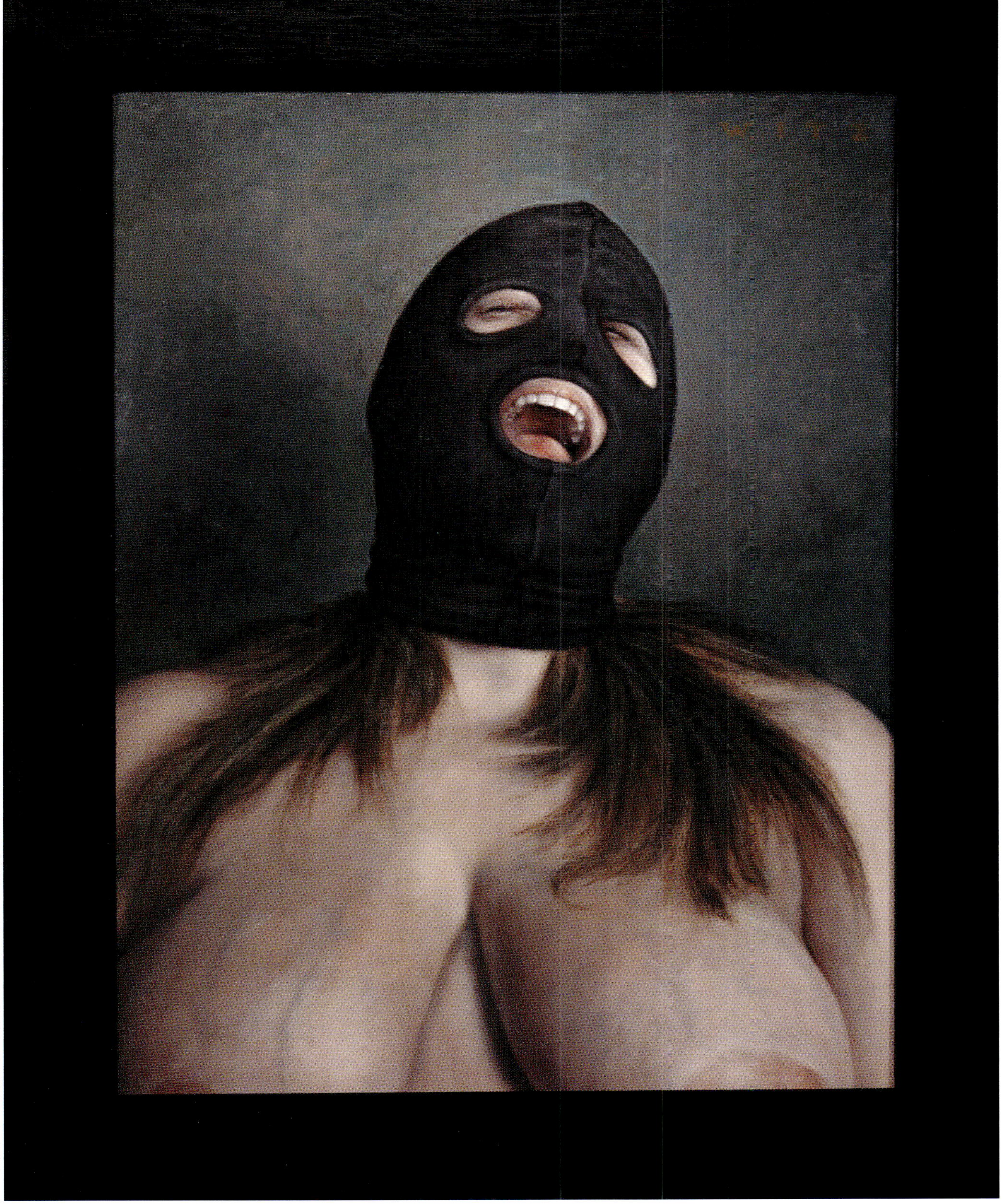

Neo-traditionalism, looking at the past or the future, thought systems, imaginary scenarios, Utopias, dreams

Part 3:
New Pastorals and Other Imagined Realities

Every step forward into modernity carries with it a look back: the regret for what used to be, the feeling of a certain loss of innocence, a more or less acute sense of nostalgia. This is by no means a new phenomenon, but in a world that keeps changing faster and faster, it is impossible to ignore this other, hidden part of the modern dream – even if a large part of contemporary culture and advertising tries to repress this feeling.

In an era dominated by new technologies, mass-media images, an unforeseen acceleration in all aspects of life and the seemingly irreversible process of urbanization, painting a natural landscape may seem like nostalgia for a past as idyllic as it is irrecoverable. And yet, listening to the artists' words and looking closely at their works in Part 3, you discover that their choice, this Neo-traditionalism, could not be more contemporary. We should remember that, as Sigrid Holmwood points out, the pastoral genre was born at the same time as the first stock market was founded. Originally, idealized landscapes were painted for urbanites: people who lived in the city and had lost touch with the restful and meditative power of nature. These paintings allowed them to imagine some continued contact with the land without renouncing the frantic rhythm of city life. Even more, they functioned as a reminder of the basic human need for inner peace. In this light, rather than thinking of landscape painting today as a nostalgic genre, its production can be seen as a very contemporary response to the many contradictions brought about by the unstoppable race of capitalism.

Holmwood effectively summarizes the timely aspect of her practice when comparing the idea of 'Slow Paint' with the Slow Food movement. For her peasant scenes, she produces her own painting materials (from pigments to papers) using natural ingredients, in a renewed celebration of handmade labour that involves not only the subject represented but also the artistic process. Influenced by the visual language of movies, TV and digital images (their vivid colours and lights), Toshimitsu Baba addresses the ungraspable nature of perception and the slipperiness of contemporary images. He translates the inner accumulation of memories and sensations derived from nature into his ideal landscapes, using gradations of colour and weight.

From the hippie experiences of Jules de Balincourt to David Brian Smith's upbringing in a family of shepherds, for many contemporary painters their art is not only about transferring familiar landscapes and environments on to canvas. The experience of the natural landscape and its evocation in art also serve as an investigation of their inner lives, of memories and the need to preserve a simple and direct contact with the basic needs of the soul. Today's painters are also using implied narrative within landscape to explore this less tangible, spiritual or psychological element of what it means to depict a scene. Kent Dorn's interest in the hippie Utopia is balanced by a second strand of work that screams horror-movie location; the haunted houses in Nicholas McLeod's ethereal paintings leave the mind with unanswered questions: 'if you leave something implied, the image has a much more powerful effect'. We must see the construction in idealized landscape, in the choice of composition, which only the painter's hand and marks can make more evident.

As declared by Smith, the condition of the artist resembles that of a shepherd or peasant in its loneliness and isolation. But this is not a negative or anti-contemporary status, if we trust Masakatsu Kondo when he says: 'I feel some isolation, but I've become comfortable with the situation; in fact, I feel liberated and my sorrow becomes a faint freedom.'

Landscape in Blue 2
2012, oil on aluminium, 91 × 148 cm
(35⅞ × 58 in).

Toshimitsu Baba
Born: 1981, Nagano (Japan)
Lives: Tokyo

In Toshimitsu Baba's works the romantic ideal of transcendence through landscape painting is re-examined and reinvented for the digital age. There are nods towards *Ukiyo-e* and traditional Japanese art, but also echoes of Seurat and the almost scientific manner in which the painter developed his methods. The resulting works are precise renderings of remembered landscapes, reflected in the visual cortex, fading and shimmering in the back of a mind used to digital screens and the vivid colours of contemporary Japanese culture. These landscapes are also anonymous, classified simply in terms of colours and numbers – another gesture alluding to the passing and ungraspable nature of perception.

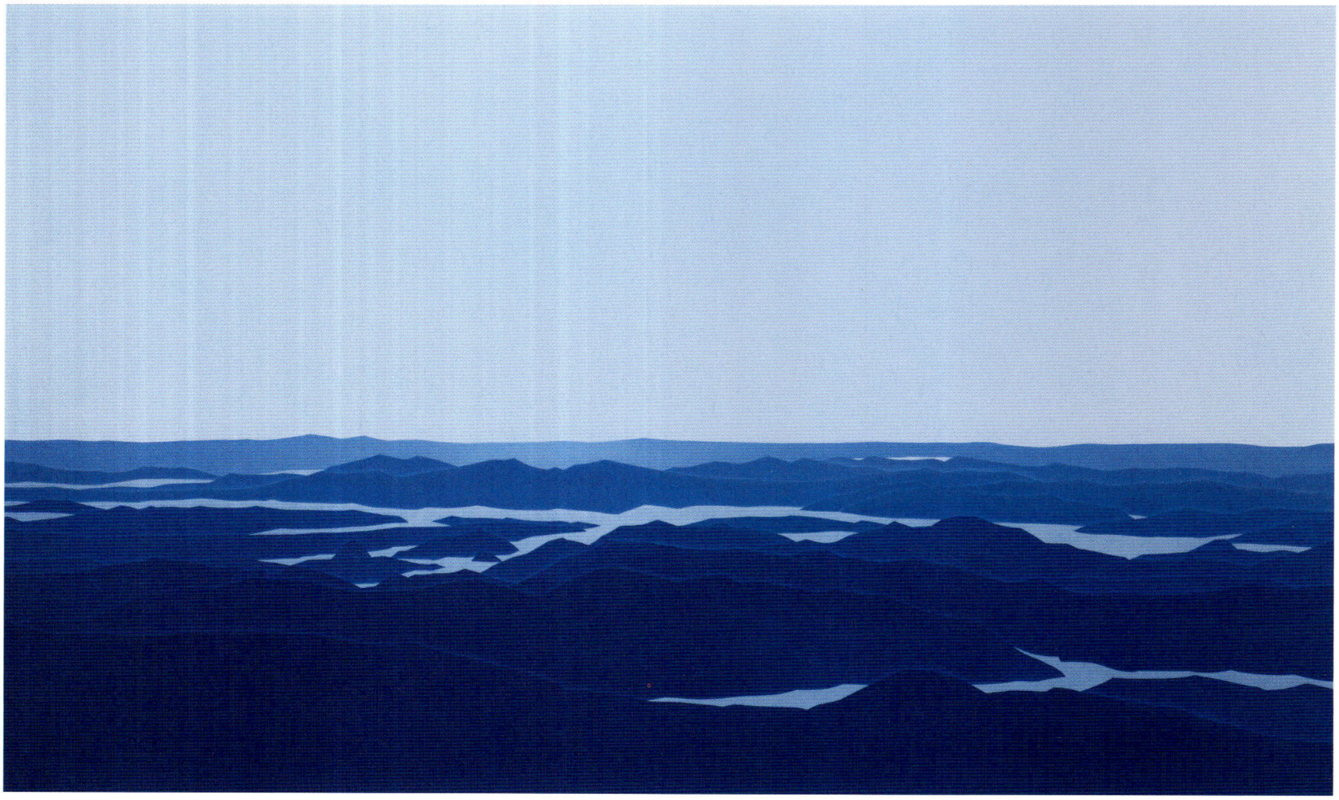

Background

My parents worked in the medical services and, since the workplace of my parents was a hospital, the idea of death is something I have always been familiar with. Now I feel that this is one of the reasons I decided to be an artist.

I wanted to be an artist, but thought I could not make a decent living out of it. I decided to study architecture, but I dropped out after finishing my first year. My drawing technique was still amateurish, so I went to Tama Art University. I kept drawing during my undergraduate and graduate schools, a total of six years. I think these years were fruitful. I really improved my technique in terms of how to understand space and depth, contrasting density and thicknesses of colour. This training, and judging things in monochrome, perhaps has something to do with the region where I was born and raised. During winter, the snowy world in front of me was just like a monochrome world. I might be trying to reproduce a world that feels familiar.

Style and technique

I have always thought about how to express what I feel through the texture of things. During my first year of university, I did oil painting as a concrete depiction, like photorealism. I was painting in controlled colour. During my second year, I drew and painted in more detail and the colours became more vivid. I began to draw and paint the landscape with the concept of gradation of colour. I thought that I should not use outlines, so that I could get closer to the landscapes in my memory. In a real landscape, of course, there are no outlines. By placing multiple layers of colour side by side, the natural scene of the landscape emerges.

The concept of outlines, which I discovered during the fourth year, is something I learned by doing lots of drawings of nudes. It evolved up to the point where I was comfortable with what I chose as the object and the way I drew it. It was like sorting out my own rule. I ended up finding something that has a lot in common with Japanese *Ukiyo-e* and traditional Japanese painting, but was derived from my own continuous research and work.

Tradition

In traditional Japanese art, each motif is divided by the outlines, then coloured evenly. If you look at a motif, it does not seem to be a tri-dimensional object with any weight. However, when combined, these appear tri-dimensional in the context of the whole image. I thought this method could be applied in my ideal landscape painting.

In traditional Japanese painting, the surface dries very fast and it is difficult to create contrasting densities since a special glue is used. The surface of oil paintings dries slowly so it is easier to create rich contrasts. I use oil in order to create the weight of the colours: for the distant views I tend to use more white and faint colours; neutral colours for middle distances; and highly coloured for the nearer views. As a result, the whole image is composed of a gradation of colour and weight. This is what I always keep in my mind and I try to improve the quality day by day.

I did a lot of research on how oil painting looks, depending on the support medium and I picked up the aluminium panel instead of canvas or wood panel. Aluminium is not so influenced by humidity and changes of temperature. I do not have to polish the surface, and the strokes of the brush don't show so much when I paint. In addition to oil, I have started using watercolour lately. I tried to avoid watercolour in the past, since the borders can bleed. But after some research I found the solution. I use Fabriano Extra White as the support medium. I use an airbrush so I also need masking tape, a sheet and so on.

Technology

I use software for rectifying photographs since it saves time. But drawing with a computer means that the image is first input, then the information is transferred to the printer, and the image is printed out on the support medium. During this process the images fall apart. In order for me to carry down the image directly, from my mind to the support (I wish I could do that with technology!), I have to rely on my hand skills: figurative painting still plays an important role when it comes to transmitting an accurate and precise image.

Influences

I feel the influence of the vivid colours and lights from PCs, movies and TV. These clear and vivid images remain in the back of my mind. I should also mention Japanese manga and animation. What's distinctive about manga is that all the items, including human figures, tools, interiors, landscapes and nature, are simplified, reduced to the minimum amount of information, and I think this idea can be applied when it comes to my work. I think manga is a great textbook in terms of finding this balance.

Subjects

I prefer to paint landscapes with which I am familiar. It has been more than ten years since I left my hometown. It appears in my dreams as a nostalgic scene, surrounded by rivers and mountains; the peach field gives out a sweet scent in summer; rice ears burn in the sunset in the autumn. It is better to know more than just the closed visual information from, say, a photograph. It is important to know the scent of the wind, the humidity surrounding the place and the altitude of high sky.

On painting

It is difficult to say where I am located exactly in the map of painting.... I aim at the fusion [point] between Japanese *Ukiyo-e* and manga and the volume and perspective of traditional Western painting. What I would like to paint is something like 'what I see in my dream'. Not Surrealism, but something accumulated deep in my heart, memorable, the environment I grew up with or the scene of a turning point in my life. For these landscapes, I do not need any concrete and specific information.

Landscape in Sepia 4
2011, oil on aluminium, 70 × 113 cm
(27⅝ × 45 in).

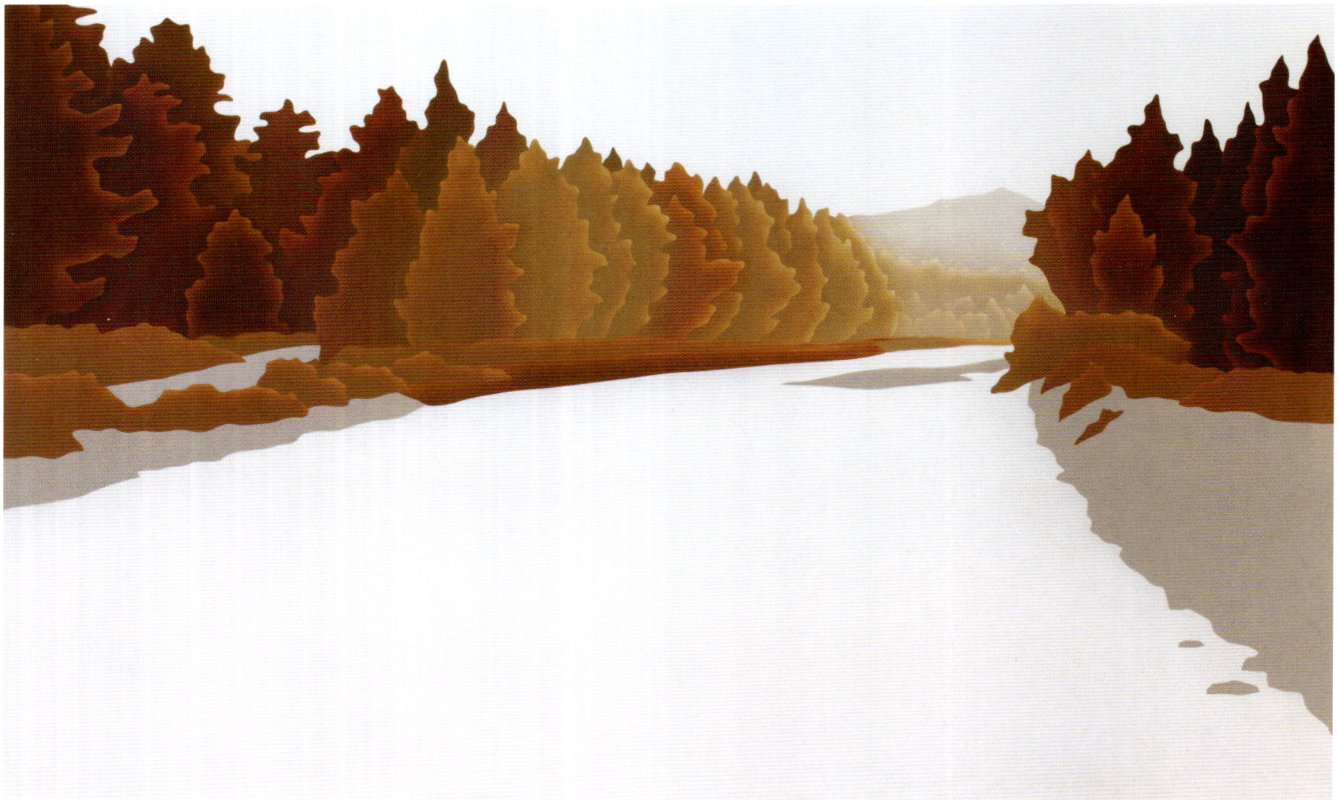

Landscape in Green 2
2010, oil on aluminium, 113 × 70 cm
(45 × 27⅝ in).

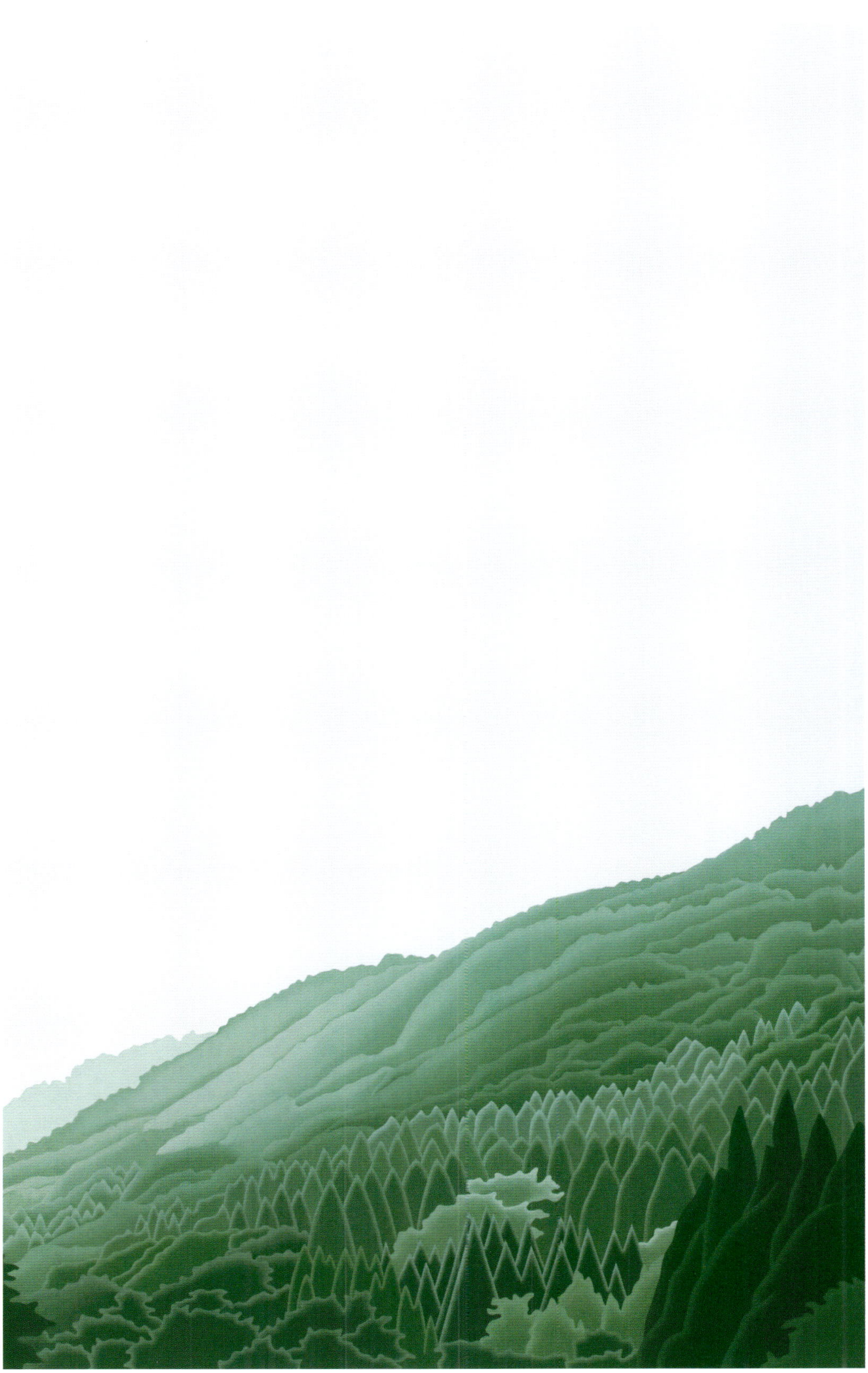

Landscape in Sepia 3
2010, oil on aluminium, 22 × 19 cm
(8¾ × 7½ in).

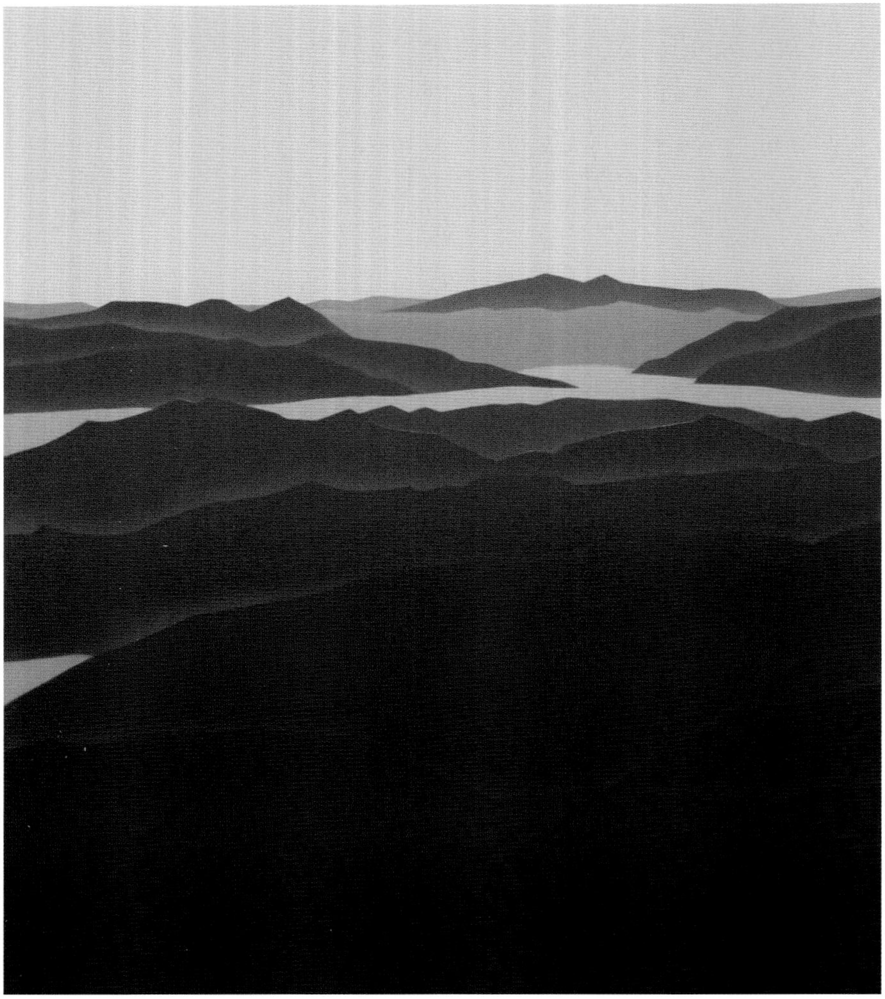

Landscape in Green 6, 2010, oil on aluminium, 58 × 49 cm (22⅞ × 19⅜ in).

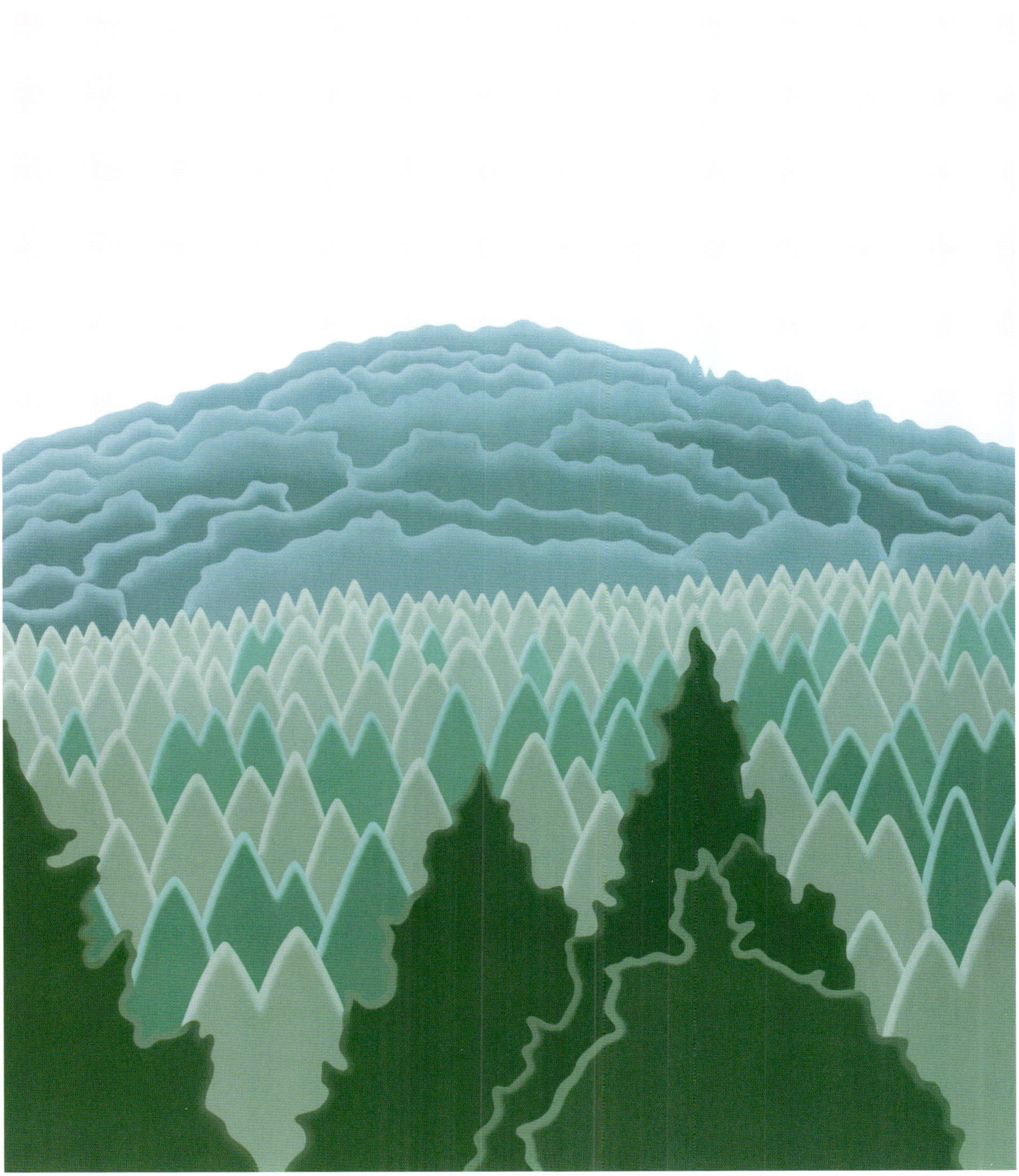

Itinerant Ones
2012, oil on panel, 43 × 33 cm
(17 × 13 in).

Jules de Balincourt
Born: 1972, Paris
Lives: New York

De Balincourt has said that he doesn't 'feel at all connected to the *Artforum* art world. I never studied painting; I really only started doing it when I moved to New York...'. But the art world doesn't seem to feel the same way and his spontaneous, sensual, freestyle paintings have had a great impact. The painter started his New York career delivering art to the houses and studios of such artists as Jasper Johns and Philip Johnson (which, he says, allowed him to cease thinking of New York as an 'impenetrable fortress'), but he enters by the front door these days. With a personal biography that is as restless and multicoloured as his paintings, he can now joke that he is feeling 'jaded' and wouldn't mind 'leaving for the tropics. I could definitely see myself having the Gauguin experience – without the sexually transmitted diseases or young women.'

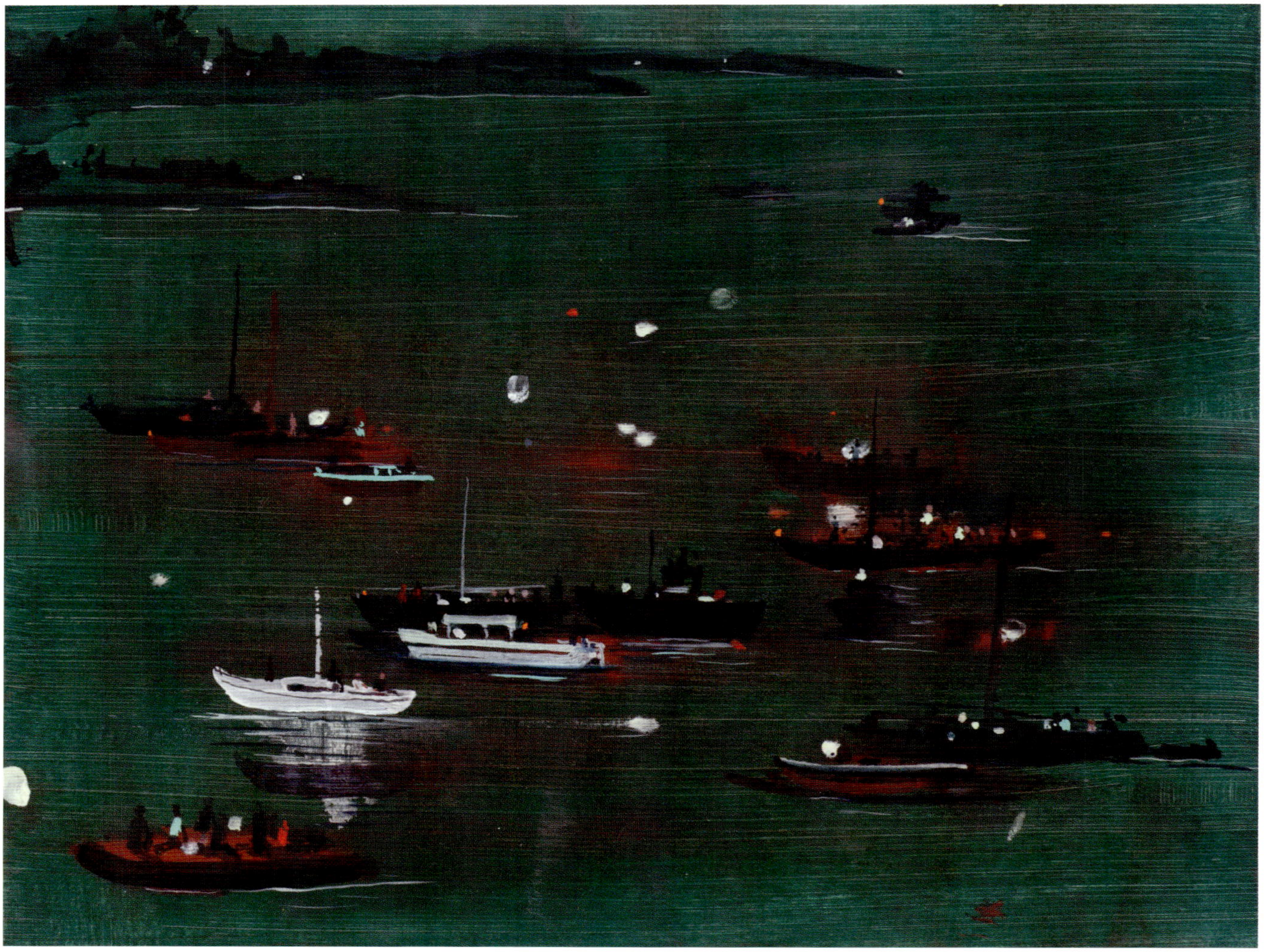

Background

I was born and raised in Paris in the early 1970s with brief one-year stints living in Ibiza, in Zurich, and travelling in a VW bus in Mexico before finally settling in Southern California with my sister and mother. My father stayed in Paris, which always kept me connected to Europe. In a sense, I always had this experience [of being] a perpetual nomad/tourist, never settling in one place for more than a year until I was about 10 years old, always having an 'outsider gaze', looking in on a foreign culture.

I went to art school [an MFA from Hunter College in 2005], but most importantly at an early age I went to Waldorf schools in Paris and LA, which I believe had a big influence on me and my art. We were not really dealing with language or numbers, it was really about a hands-on approach to learning: working in clay, knitting, drawing, cooking, dancing.... It was wonderful until finally I went to an American public school, where I had a harsh reality check.

Process

I will start a painting by just putting some marks down until something appears within the painting.... At other times, I'll be inspired by something I read.... It's a daunting, mysterious search most of the time.

Primarily I paint from my imagination; sometimes I will use a photographic reference, though I prefer working intuitively. Usually I start one painting and make the next painting as a response or partner to a previous painting, working on up to ten paintings simultaneously. As I am beginning one painting I am finishing others I started months prior. I like to think of the paintings as having relationships: every king needs a queen.

Abstraction v. figuration

I think there's a tension in my paintings between figuration and abstraction. I'm often tempted to bring in a figurative element, to insert a recognizable reality into my paintings, but that would be too easy, wouldn't it? The question is: how do you make an abstract painting that also communicates something outside of its own inner workings as an abstract painting? I'm not interested in lines and shapes alone, in patterns, colours or beauty. I'm interested in the way those things build up to the ideas I want to convey. I want to make abstract painting that has the energy of figurative work, and the same kind of anxiety, angst or complexity. Then again, even a figurative painting is an abstract painting. You might feel you recognize an image in a figurative work, but it's also made of abstract shapes and lines.

Primitivism

When I was 19, 20 years old, I was a young surfer, a hippie, living off the tailcoats of Grateful Dead concerts. I was making ceramic and goatskin drums and selling them at concerts, following the band on tour. It was a big thing, then: the Rainbow Gatherings, the Dead concerts. They had a whole village of people following them. I had my pickup truck with a little bed. We would all drive down to Mexico and camp out anywhere we wanted. I can't believe I did that, but we were just living out the idea of being young, romantic and free. There's something laughable about all of it, now. Post-hippie culture comes off as a bit pathetic that way.

Personal style

In this day and age where everything is becoming more and more homogenized and globalized I hope that personality and character can still resonate.

I see myself as a sort of cultural sieve, processing media, culture, socio-political events and then transforming them into the most primary, elementary form of painting, transferring the information as cavemen did with sticks, with animal hair and pigments from the earth on to a wooden panel ... a contemporary anthropological alchemy of sorts.

Malpais (Bad Lands)
2008, oil on panel, 203 × 178 cm
(80 × 70 in).

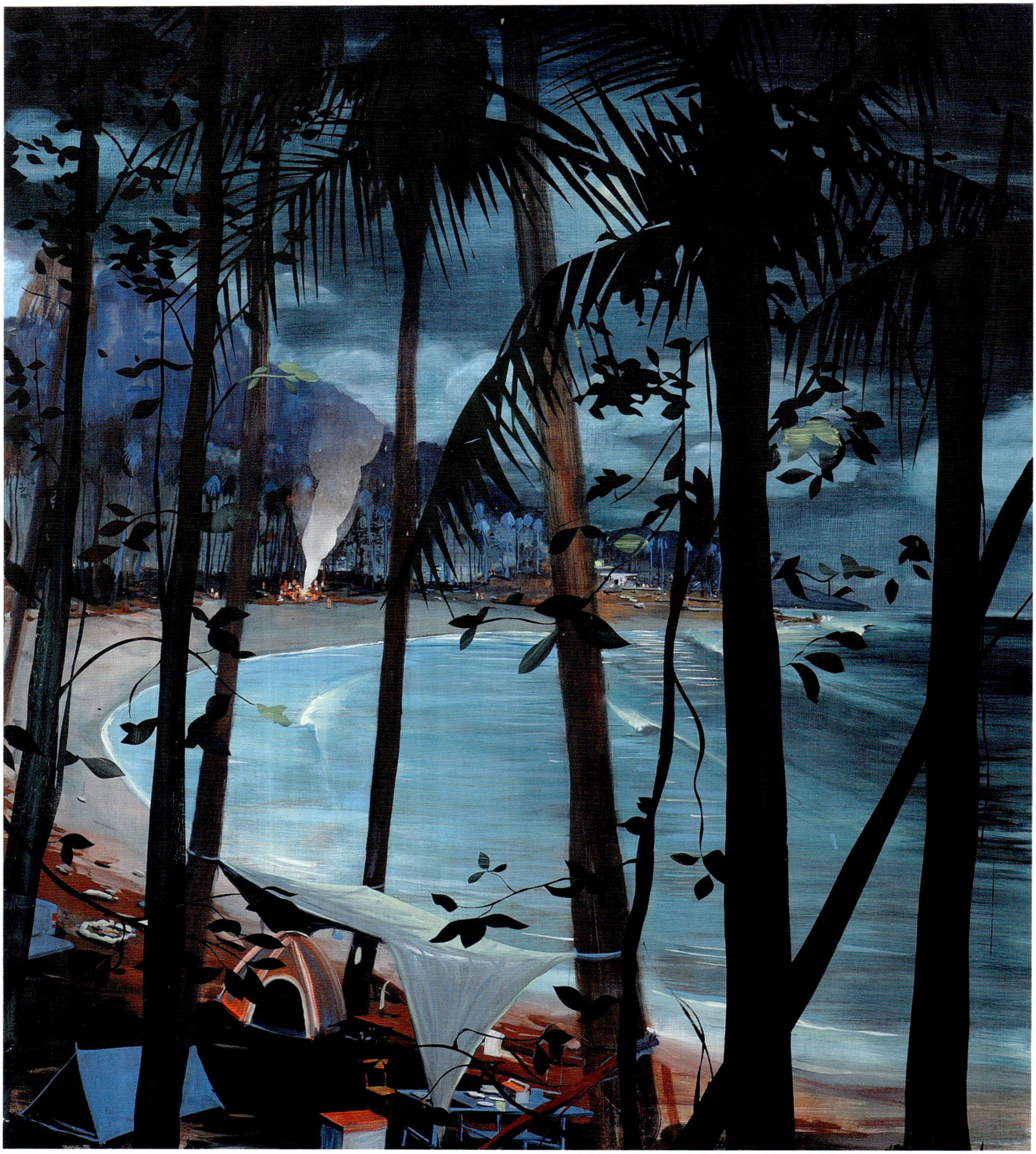

Idol Hands
2012, oil on panel, 193 × 167 cm
(76 × 66 in).

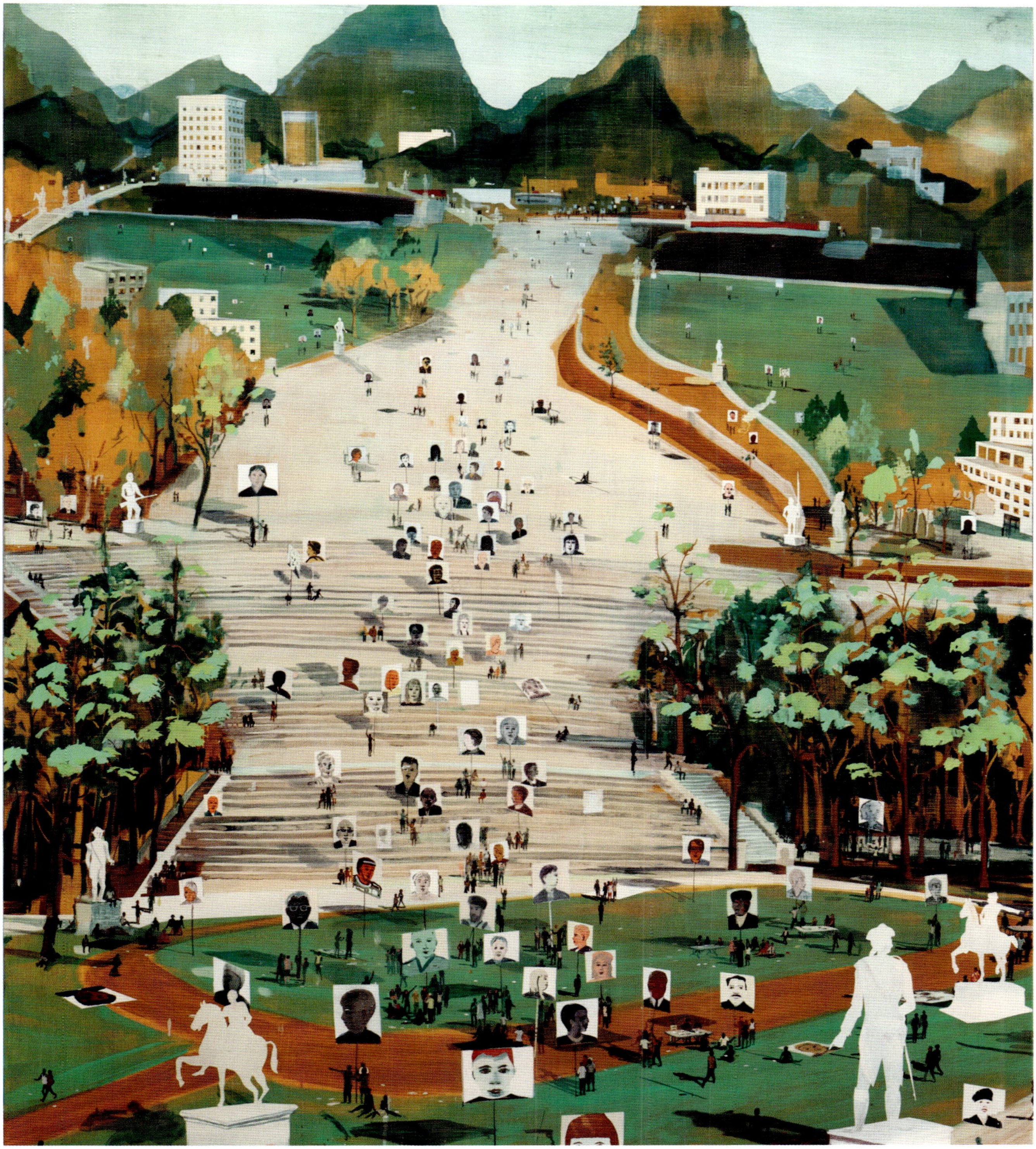

Neither Day or Night
2011, oil on panel, 243 × 335 cm
(96 × 132 in).

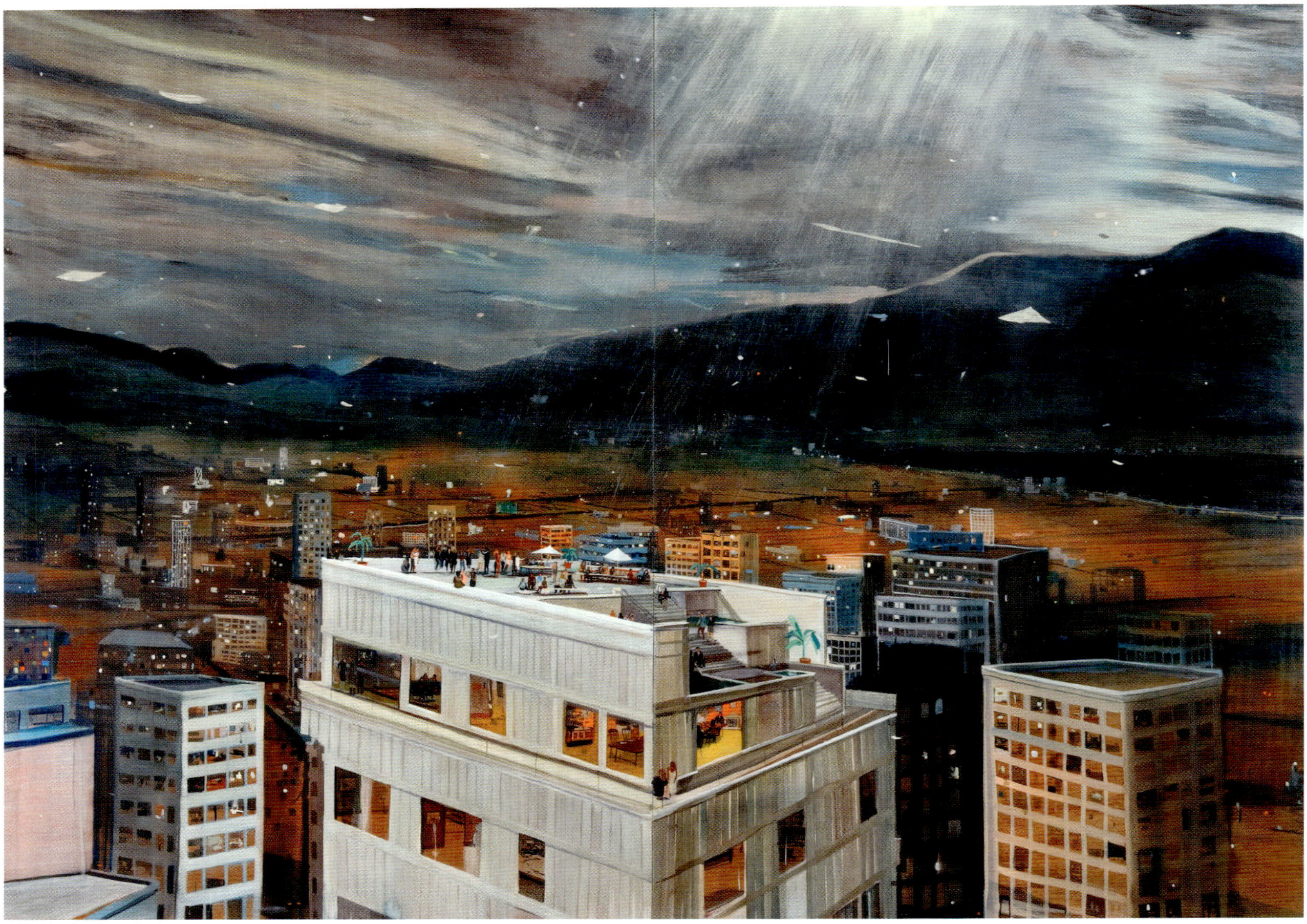

Utopie Tyrannique
2010, oil on panel, 122 × 147 cm
(48 × 58 in).

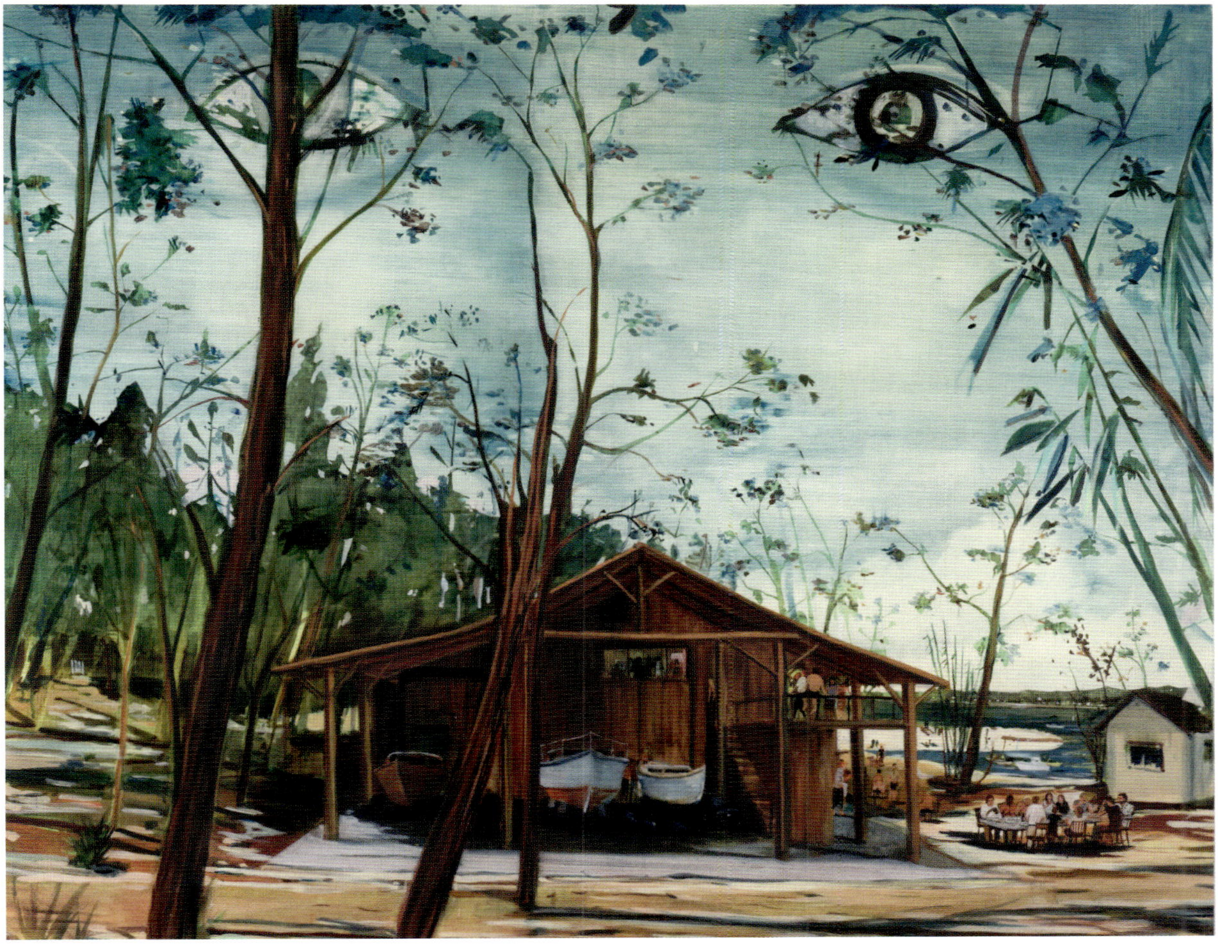

Untitled (Fireworks)
2012, oil, acrylic and enamel on panel, 193 × 168 cm (76 × 66 in).

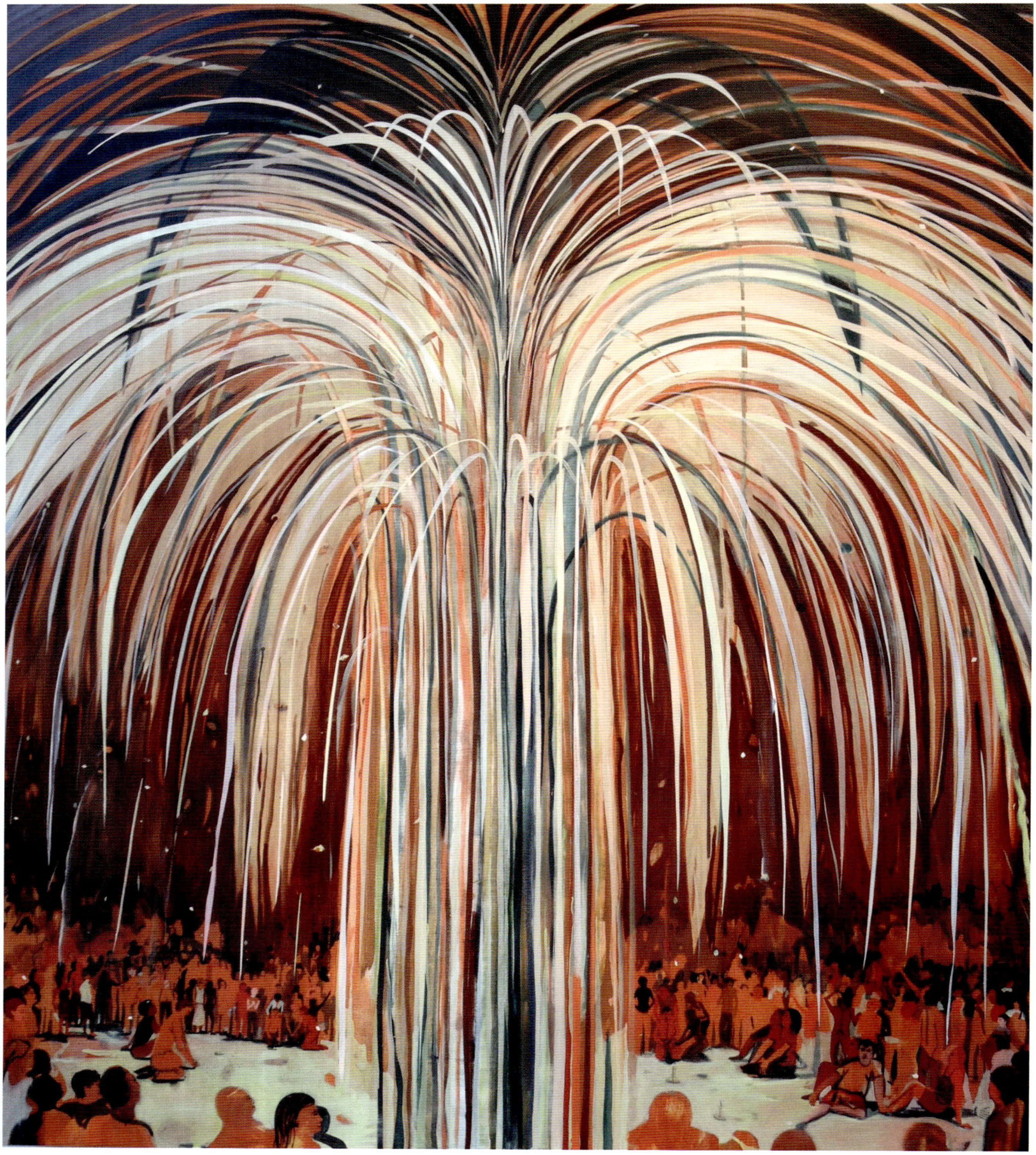

Think Globally, Act Locally
2007, oil on panel, 244 × 335 cm
(96 × 132 in).

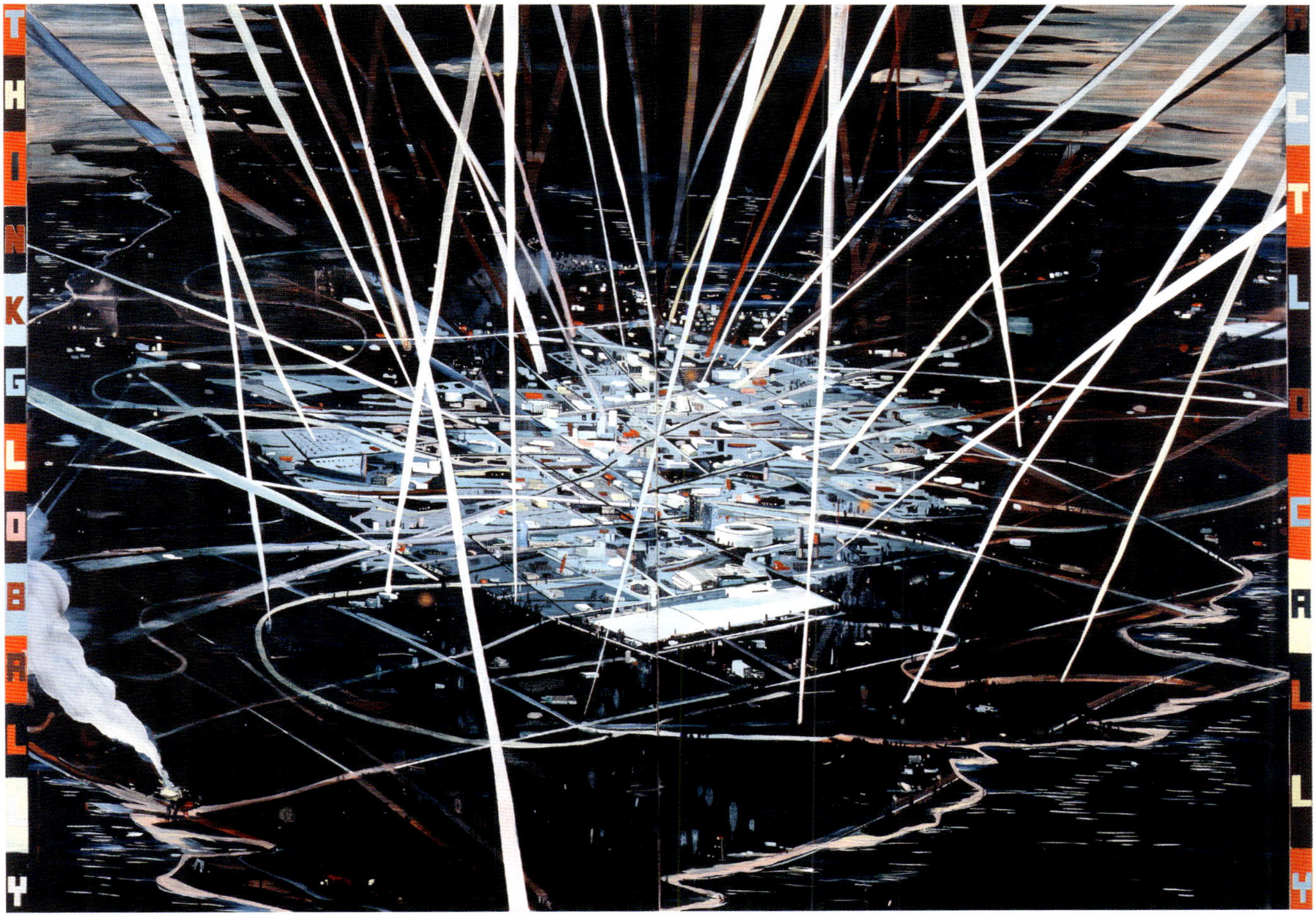

Drifters
2009, oil on panel, 12.5 × 18 cm
(5 × 7 in).

Amy Bennett
Born: 1977, Portland, Maine
Lives: New York

Amy Bennett infuses her paintings with a sense of impending drama, conjuring up a mood that recalls the mysterious unsolved crimes typical of small, semi-rural communities. Not only does she create meticulous paintings on a small scale, but she also builds 3-D sets that serve as models for her scenes, complete in every detail. Inspired by Hitchcock, the Coen brothers and David Lynch, for her personal painted stories Bennett works like a director, setting scenes and creating atmospheres filled with suspense.

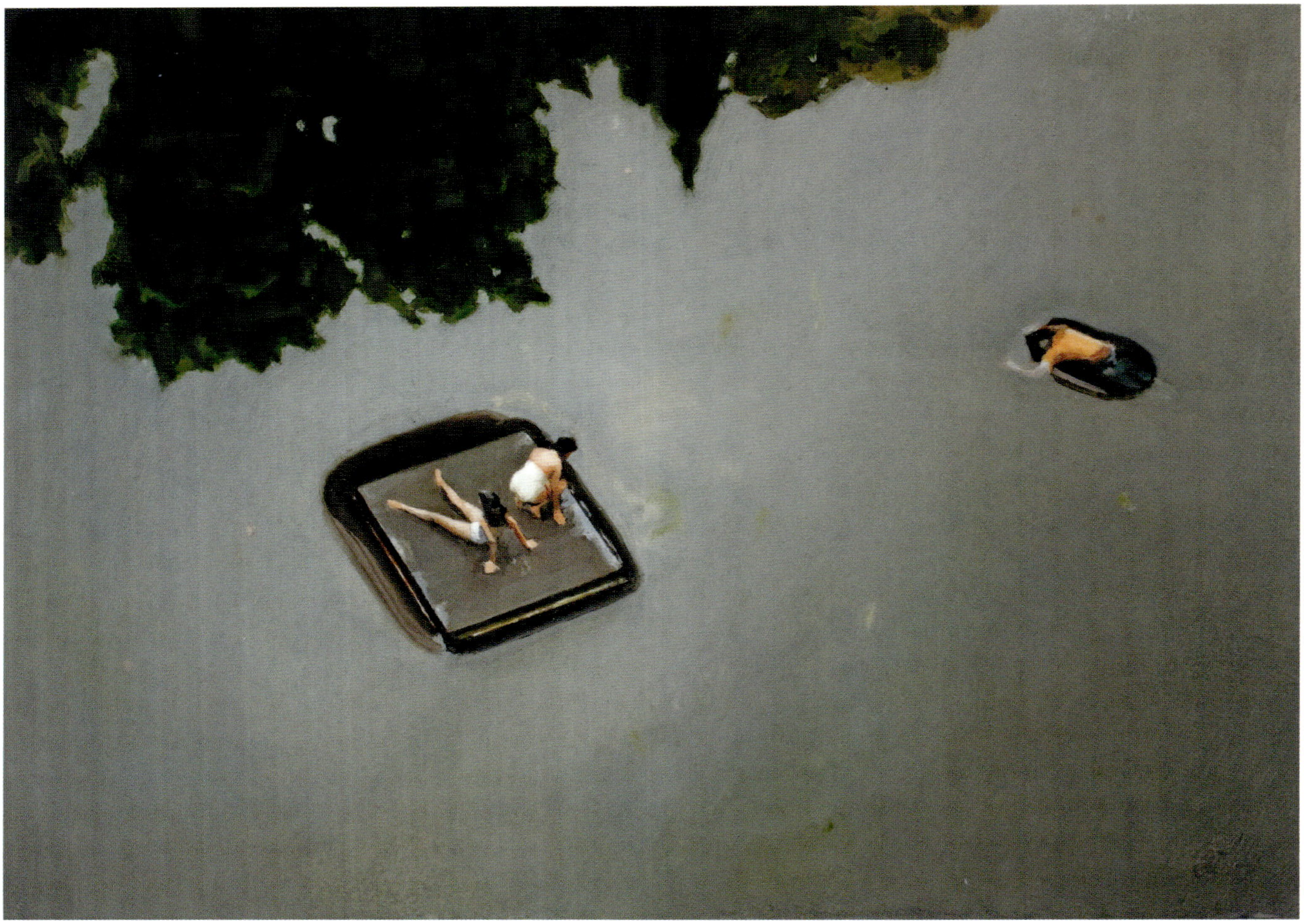

Narrative painting
I create 3-D models that serve as still lifes for my narrative paintings. They are depictions of fictional worlds that I create and light to explore themes of isolation, transition and loss, as well as the awkwardness of people trying to coexist and relate to one another. Throughout each series there are incomplete stories told over time via repeating characters and locations, creating a sense of history. The paintings capture moments that hopefully elicit specific feelings and provoke the viewer to consider the moment before or after the one presented.

Welcome to the dollhouse
I had just seen Hitchcock's *Rear Window*, was reading a lot of short stories, and was overhearing a lot of drama from my neighbours in my apartment building of 300-plus units, so I had the idea of looking down into apartments to describe the dramas of residents living in close proximity. Using walls of foam core and cardboard, I set up interiors using doll's-house furniture. I wired the arrangements with tiny lights and painted from [these scenes], having to invent the figures. Of course the figures were painted a little differently from the rest of the setting, which I was able to observe, so I was delighted to discover the much smaller HO-scale miniatures most commonly used for model railways. At that time, I also drastically reduced the scale of my paintings, so 4- or 5-inch (10 – 12-centimetre) figures shrank to 1 inch (2.5 centimetres). Details such as facial expressions and specific clothing styles became obscured, but the subtleties of poses and the meanings of gestures still translated.

Lighting
I did not study lighting or photography – I just wing it. It's an exciting part of the process because the lighting usually brings the diorama to life. I have a variety of hardware-store bulbs in my studio and a pile of gels that I rarely use. I still use doll's-house lights from time to time for their ability to spotlight tiny things.

Painter v. director
Movie-makers are also creating a world that they can control and light specifically to achieve a dramatic effect. Painting has the added challenge of compressing time, or finding the crux of the moment to depict. For me, this moment usually conveys the feeling that something is about to happen or has just happened. Plus, the act of building the model triggers my imagination, to picture what exactly might be going on in this place I'm creating. The act of translating three dimensions to two is a very meditative process and forces you to be very present. At the same time, I have used photographic reference in combination with the model when I physically can't paint in the conditions required for what I want to depict, such as in a night scene.

Shooting from the easel
I play with the model, experimenting with lighting, and usually use a camera to document my play. Looking through the snapshots helps me to consider which arrangement is most interesting and to determine the size of the panel I'll be painting on. Once I have the scene finally arranged and lit, I begin developing the painting through several layers while observing my diorama as a still life, a process that typically takes one month. I try to paint the scenes in such a way that they feel like a believable world, but an alternative world. After the painting has dried, I brush on a varnish that I sand manually to a high polish. I intend for the detail and smooth finish to intensify an artificial effect. Hopefully [my paintings] are like the kind of dream that feels almost disturbingly real and sticks around with you all day. There is never anything supernatural or impossible in my paintings, but since they are realistic scenes depicted in a phony world, there is usually something a bit 'off' to signify that they are constructions of the imagination.

Coincidence
2007, oil on panel, 51 × 51 cm
(20 × 20 in).

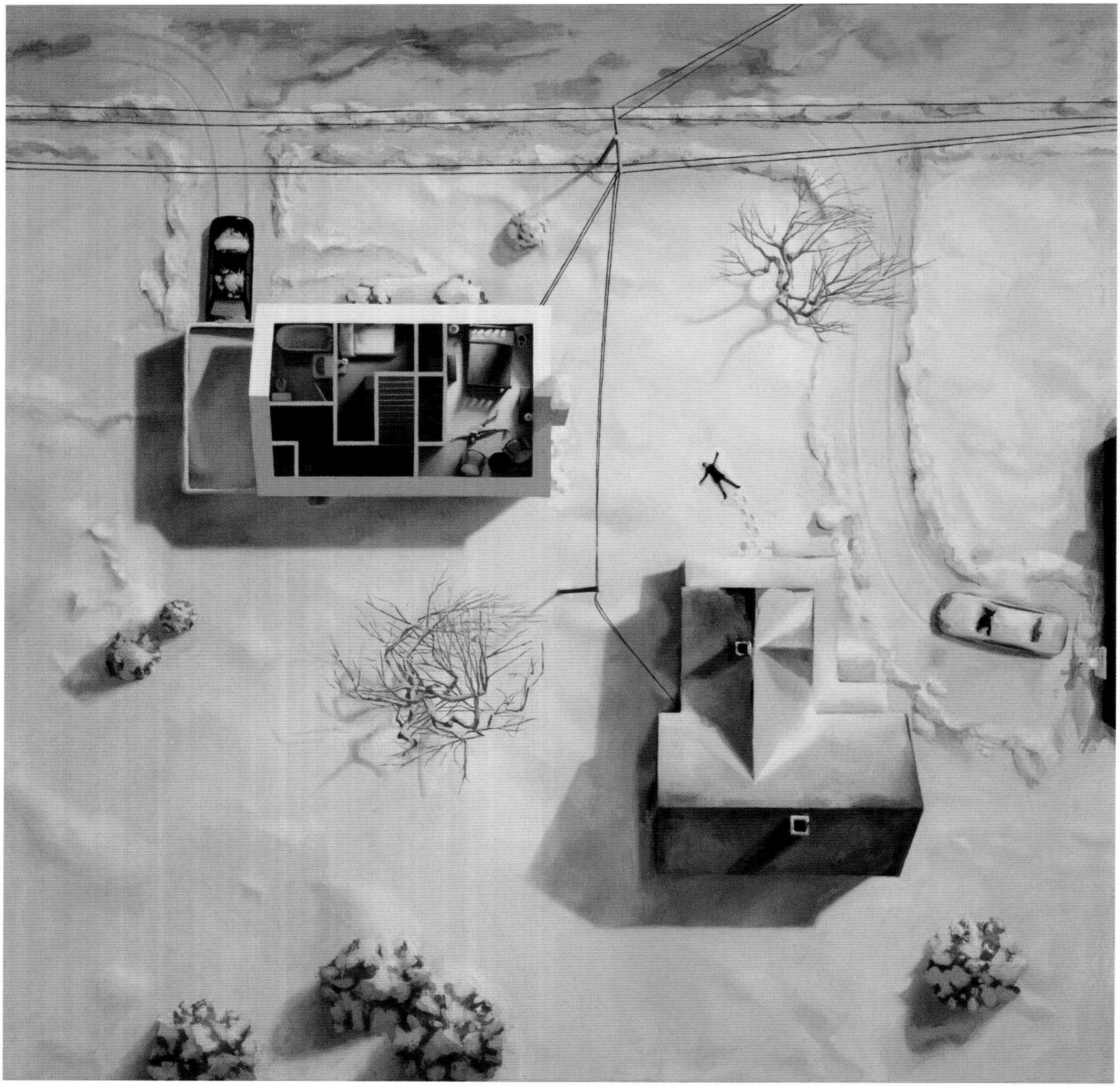

Losing Heart
2009, oil on panel, 56 × 56 cm
(22 × 22 in).

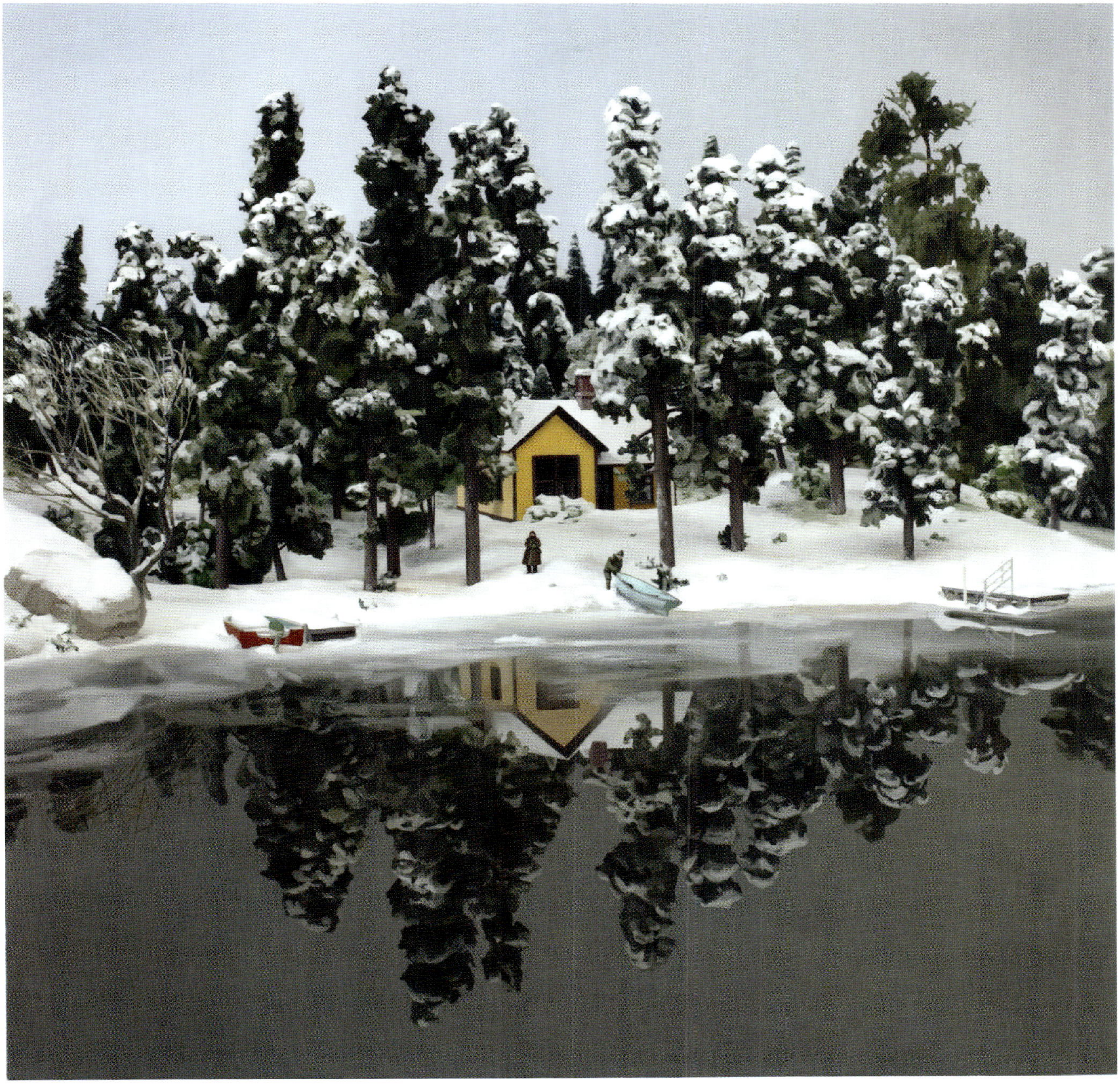

Into the Woods
2008, oil on panel, 35.5 × 45.75 cm
(14 × 18 in).

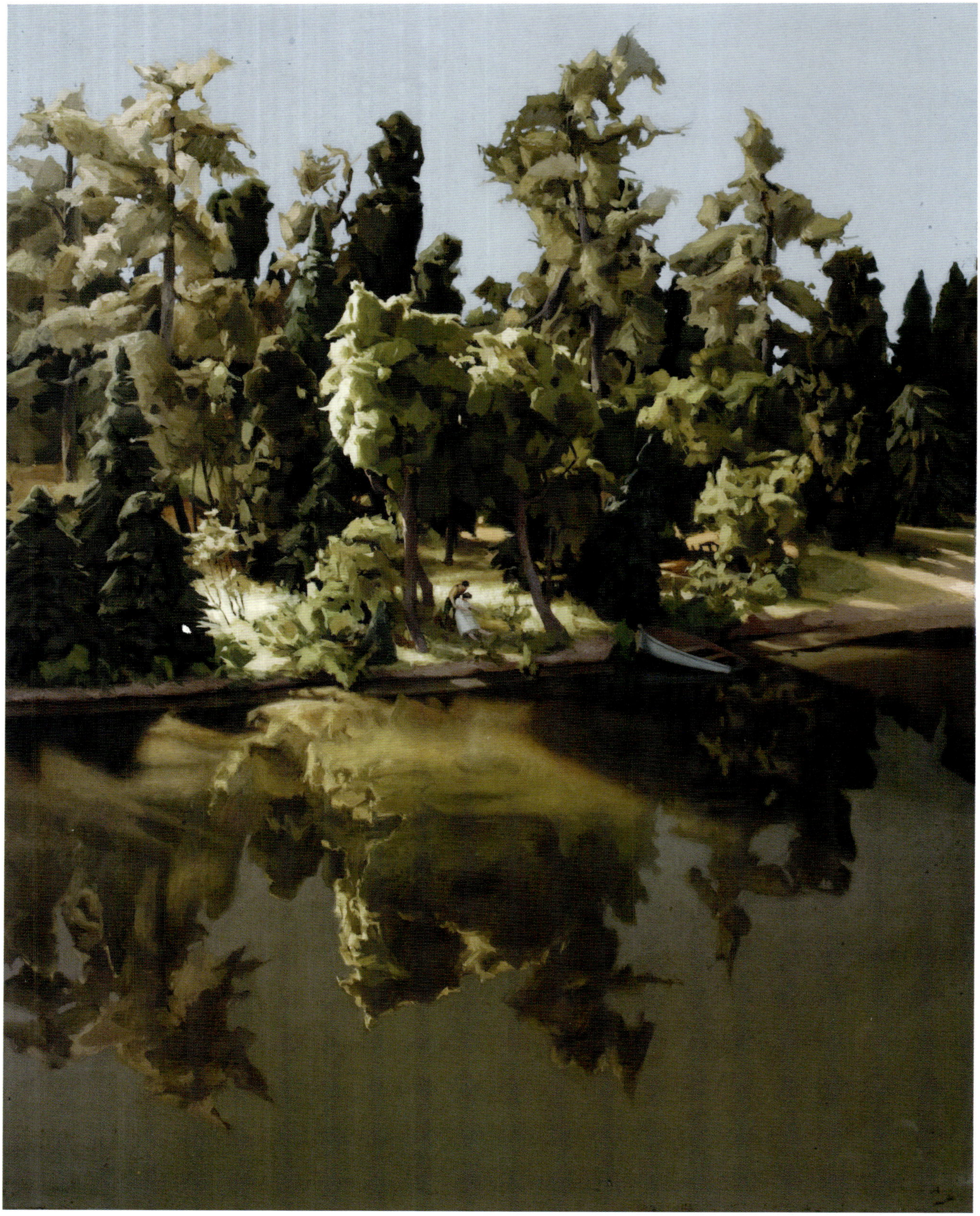

Taking Arms
2008, oil on panel, 45.75 × 61 cm
(18 × 24 in).

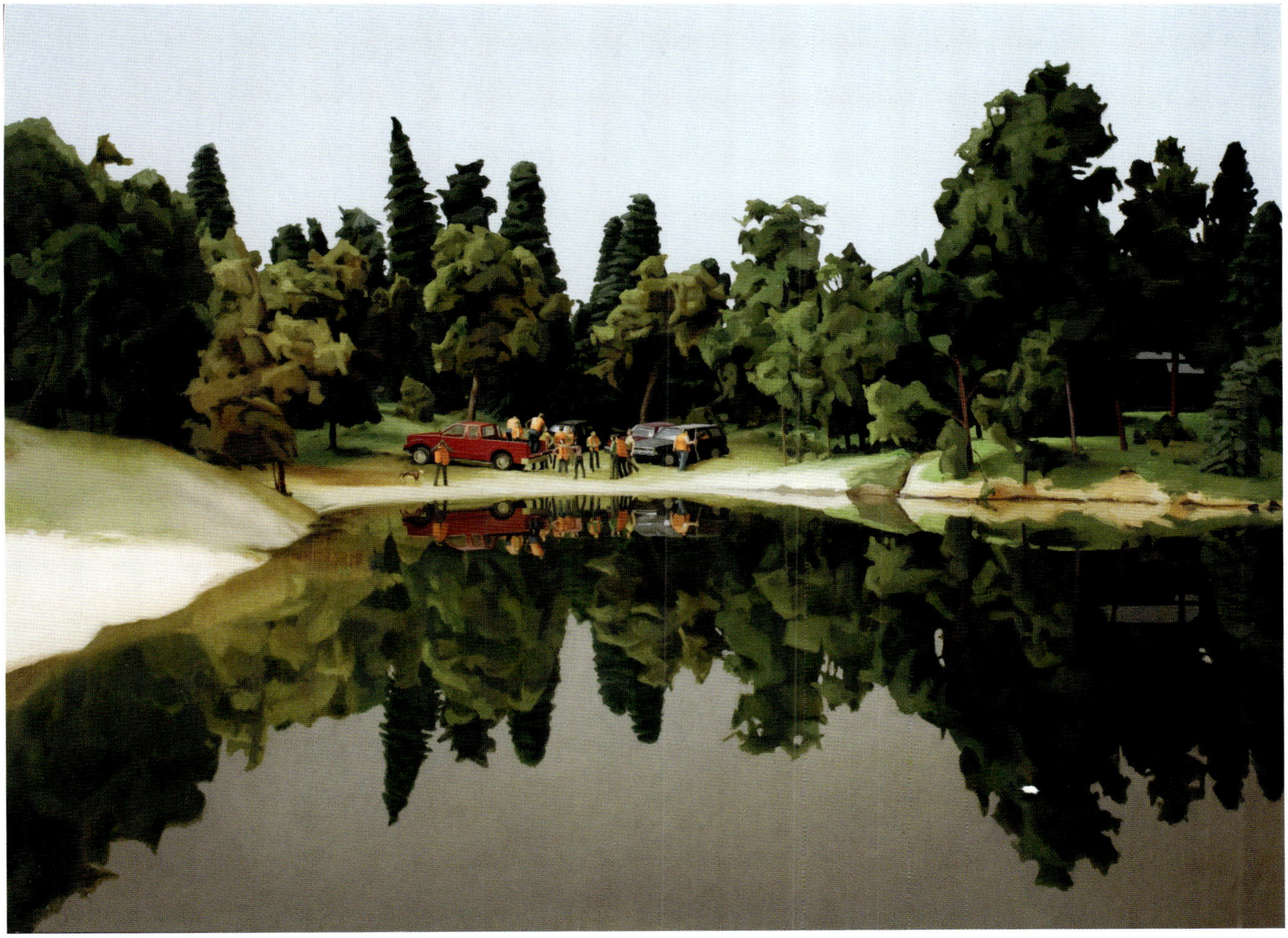

Great Expectations – We Were Silhouettes
2011, oil on linen, 180 × 300 cm (71 × 118 in).

David Brian Smith
Born: 1981, Wolverhampton (UK)
Lives: London

The landscape paintings of David Brian Smith originate from his personal memories, often starting with photographs. With his masterful use of varied materials (including bitumen and gold leaf) and a remarkable dedication to the very craft of painting, the artist transforms the original images into dreamlike scenes. Their timeless quality places them beyond notions of temporality, the traditional and the contemporary.

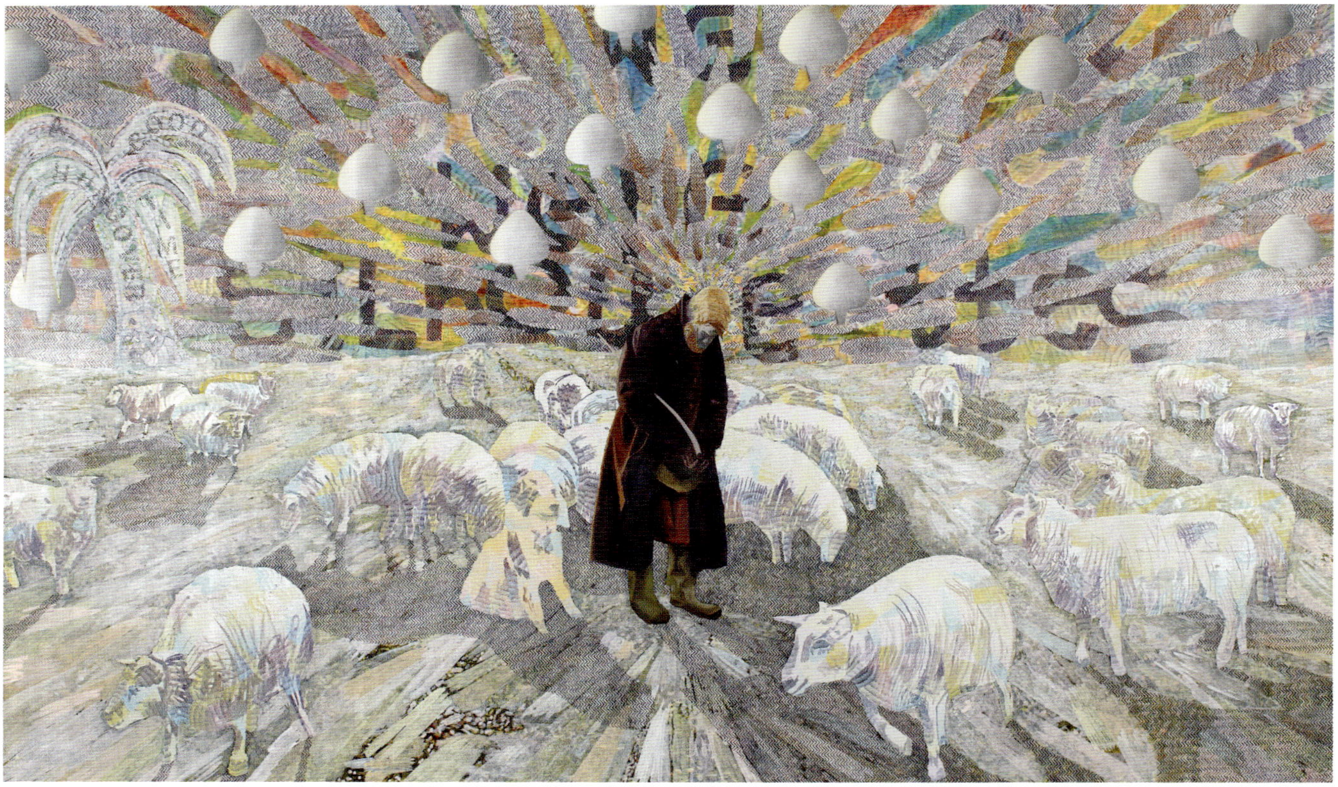

Background
I went to Wolverhampton University, in the late 1990s. It was one of the last undergraduate painting courses in the country and I had a fabulous time. We just painted for three years, didn't really question things and were very prolific. We were like monkeys with brushes; nothing was precious apart from our naïvety. After that I had a studio for three years in the city, before moving to London to attend Chelsea College of Art, where I made many good friends and collaborators.

Inspiring people
Many of my early inspirations no longer paint or make art. Andy Warhol and William Blake come to my mind. I generally admire hard work. Blake's interest in painting and poetry is something I share and Warhol's desire to get an audience to listen is something to which I relate.

Materials and process
I work with different materials: oil paint, gold and silver leaf, pigments (fluorescent mainly), bitumen, herringbone linen, rabbit glue, staples, wood, spray-paint, varnishes, turpentine. Through years of playing and painting, I'm always looking for new ways to apply and manipulate the materials. Painting is easy when a piece obviously needs a lot of work and you can see the problems. In that case, I know what needs to be done. When a painting is already good, things are much more difficult and sometimes you have to sacrifice and rework previously finished, precious areas to make it better.

Composition
Sometimes I use a black-and-white photograph to paint in a simple composition. Like, for example, a large ant-hill with a figure on top and a figure standing on the ground. Three components, no detail and no suggestion of colour: I interpret this as a simple composition. Thereafter the painting begins and often the initial composition will be painted out. Memory plays a role in it, in the sense that you can't stop it, things will come into your mind and you can't block them before it's too late!

Subject matter
It takes time to find an image, make a successful painting from it, trust and understand the source and develop a sense of ownership. An image has to transcend its specificity and relate to an audience when it leaves an artist's studio in a reworked form. How will a figurative painting be perceived or read? The original idea for my shepherd works was to make 100 paintings, all in the same size, with text on them telling people how fucked off I was at the time. The series was titled 'Great Expectations': I was thinking about an artist's expectations and how these are often unfulfilled and quashed. The series is ongoing, the text has become more about life and less about how bad it can be. I started to look at iconic film posters, particularly the *Rocky* poster where he [the eponymous hero, played by Sylvester Stallone] is punching the air with his back towards us. This image has been replicated millions of times, yet still it gives a feel-good sense of hope and achievement every time I see it. The shepherd and my great grandfather, Fred Goodwill, on top of the ant-hill are my Rocky Balboa.

Narrative and text
I place text in my paintings and use a sketchbook to write poems and aphorisms. My paintings are often autobiographical. I want to create a specific narrative throughout a body of paintings. It is a work in progress or perhaps is already happening, but I can't see it yet.

The shepherd theme
I grew up on a farm in Shropshire. My father being a shepherd and my mother a shepherdess, I grew up with the sound of bleating sheep outside my bedroom window. Abandoned lambs would be living in cardboard boxes in our kitchen during the lambing season. I make landscape paintings in my Hackney studio, in London. A current theme in my work is a shepherd surrounded by a flock of sheep. I guess the subject of landscape brings me closer to what has gone, it's not all sweet. Being an artist is as lonely as being a shepherd.

Great Expectations II
2010, oil on linen, 180 × 150 cm
(71 × 59 in).

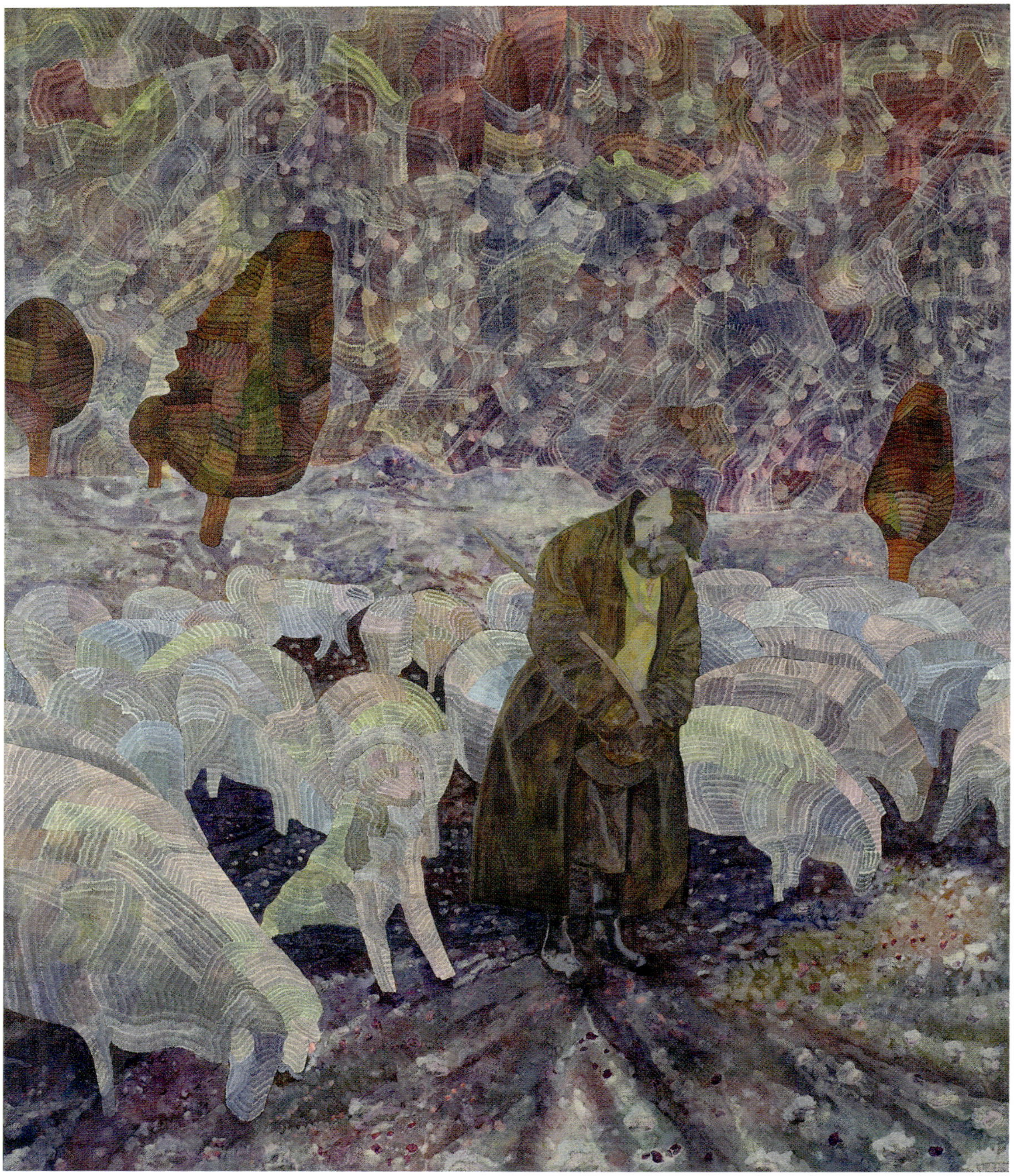

Great Expectations – Witty Man
2012, oil and gold leaf on
herringbone linen, 180 × 150 cm
(71 × 59 in).

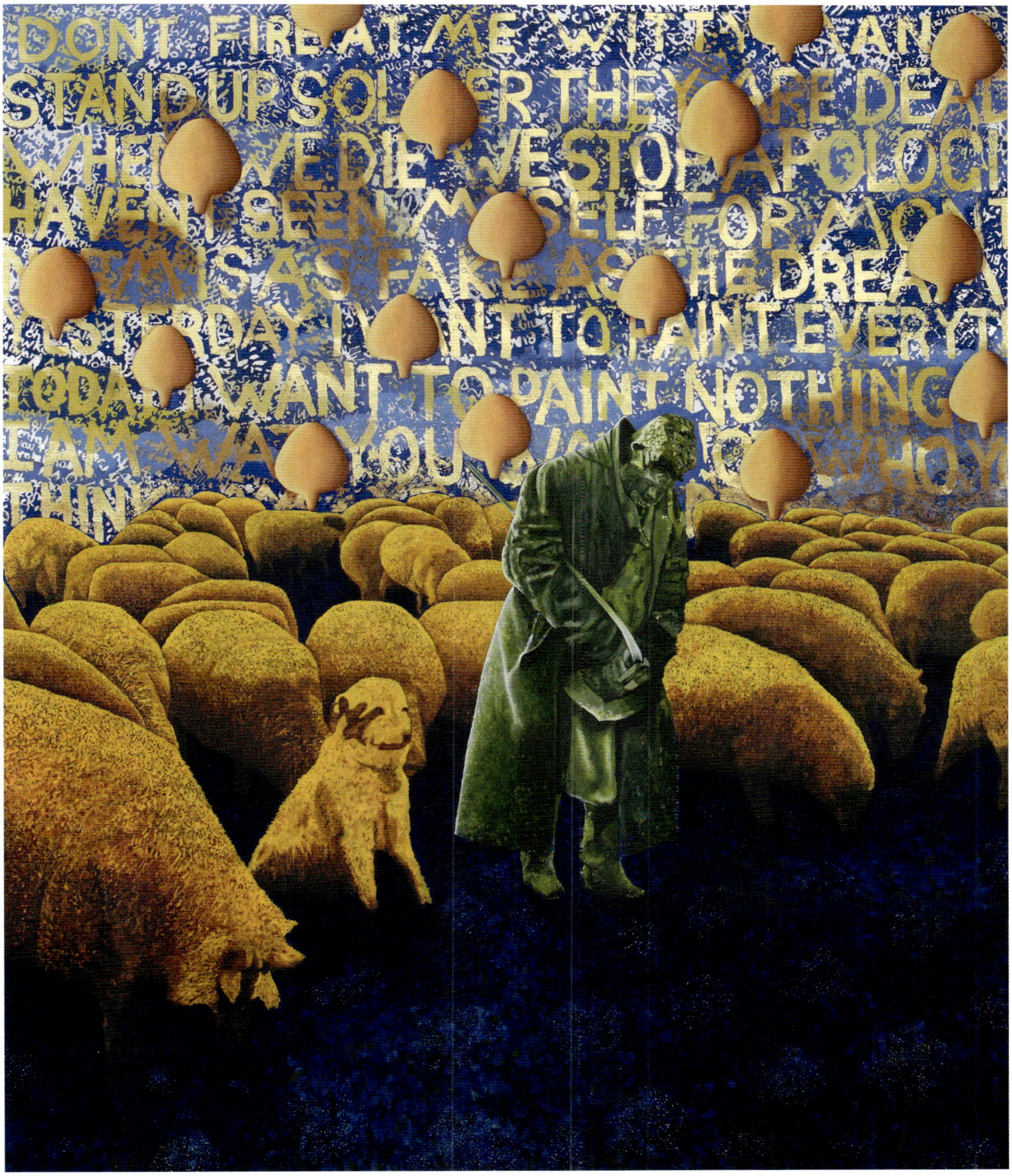

Headland
2010, oil on herringbone
linen 180 × 150 cm (71 × 59 in).

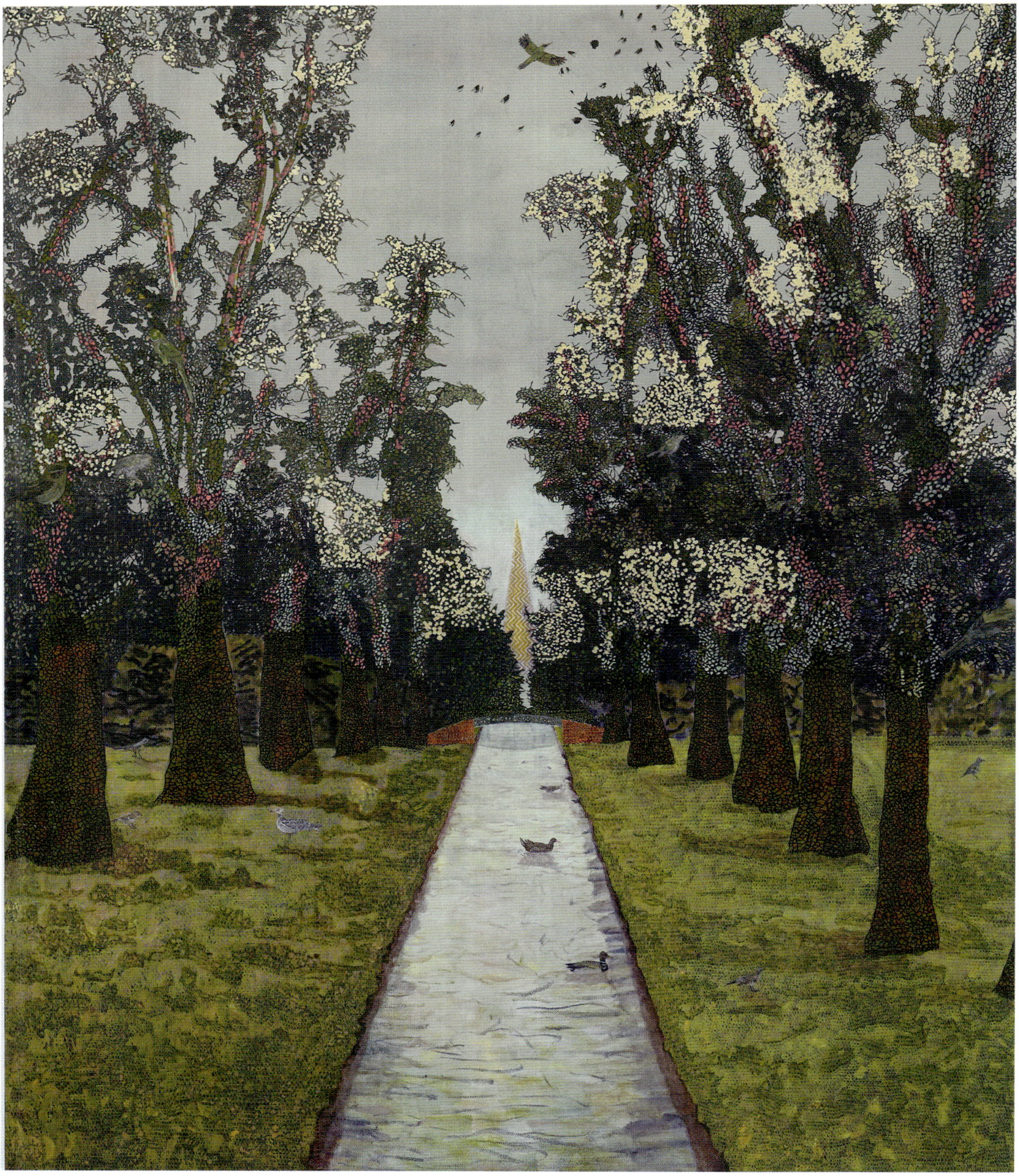

Forteen Drunken Nights
2010, oil on herringbone linen,
180 × 150 cm (71 × 59 in).

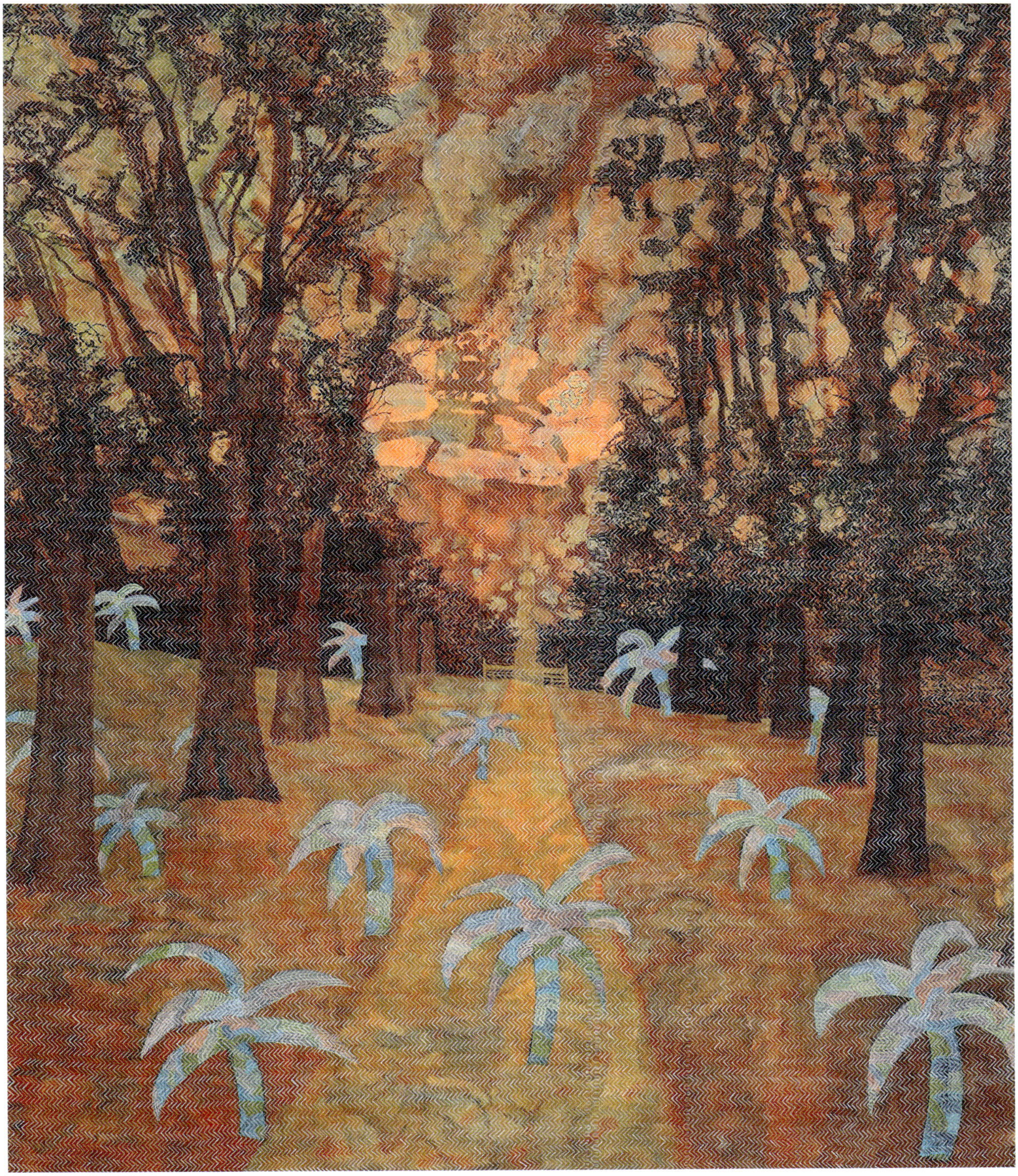

Jonas Burgert
Born: 1969, Berlin (Germany)
Lives: Berlin

The work of German painter Jonas Burgert seems to attract comparisons with other media – from theatre and dance to computer games. Unable to resist the temptation, we might juxtapose it to comics, drawing yet another comparison in the way these images grip your attention and create a strange sense of expectation: it is as if you enter a gigantic graphic novel and turn the volume of detail up to the maximum. But the truth is that his work stands as a perfect demonstration of the specificity of figurative painting. The painter has said that he values in particular the ability to reinvent his 'pictorial language every day – there is a vast spectrum of illusion. The affective work of painting stands in contrast to the construction of the digital image, where a concept is carried out and runs the risk of becoming illustrative. One brushstroke can alter an entire picture.'

Background
'I spent my childhood in West Berlin, which was a kind of island from where I could not get away so easily. At that time, Paris or Munich, or some other European city was naturally closer to me and easier to get to than East Berlin. Then the wall came down and all at once we were at the centre of things again, my city became twice as big and interesting, and the whole world came here' (from an interview with Claudia Stockhausen).

Art is one great story
'As an 18- to 20-year-old I used to read a lot. Then I suddenly stopped. I had so many stories and narratives in my head that literature tended to block me rather than act as a positive inspiration. More than from literature, I gain my inspiration from the street, or from the bar of a corner pub. I feel it's a place where the entire range of dramatic expression of an individual's psychology can be observed: loneliness, hate, the desire to impress, revenge, addiction, excess. For me everything plays itself out directly before our eyes, and literature seems to be a detour rather than a direct route.... It is not so much the actual story, or literature per se, that interests me, but the fundamental human concerns and actions – love, hate, envy, jealousy, euphoria and fear – intrinsic to literature that contribute to my work. That's perhaps why the observer may draw so many literary allusions and associations' (from an interview with Claudia Stockhausen).

Process
'I don't really make many sketches before I start painting. I am much too impatient for that. For me, the thoughts I entertain before I start painting are much more important than a sketch or any preliminary practical work. In fact, the thought activity is the most laborious and electrifying process of them all because it determines the painting and the composition of the whole at a theoretical level. As soon as that is completed, I simply start to paint. The basic composition is naturally decisive, especially in my large-format paintings, so I start by painting spatial lines, the long diagonals and so on. And then I merely have to react artistically to these first steps. So there's lots of room for spontaneity. I have never yet painted a picture whose final state resembled what I had previously thought out.... My work is an ongoing process of wrestling with the painting, a constant and lengthy conversation with it' (from an interview with Claudia Stockhausen).

Against Minimalism
'I understand the qualitative principle of reduction, and esteem quite highly some of the works of art to which it has given rise, but there is a danger of thereby excessively shortening the path to the picture. I am not against reduction and simplicity, but on the other side are mass, chaos, complexity and abundance. Simplicity tries to find one sign for our communication. But the world is cynical. A single sign is not enough. Sometimes less is in fact less. Notwithstanding, during my student days this reduction was propagated as a standard of value. Fidelity to a concept makes you defensive; I wanted to work offensively.... Our present era is characterized by inundation. We experience overflowing structures, sheer mass and chaos. We live with sand and poison. Why shouldn't all that be painted? The quality of a picture should be evaluated independently of dogmas' (in conversation with Heinrich Dietz).

Schwinde
2013, oil on canvas, 90 × 80 cm
(35½ × 31½ in).

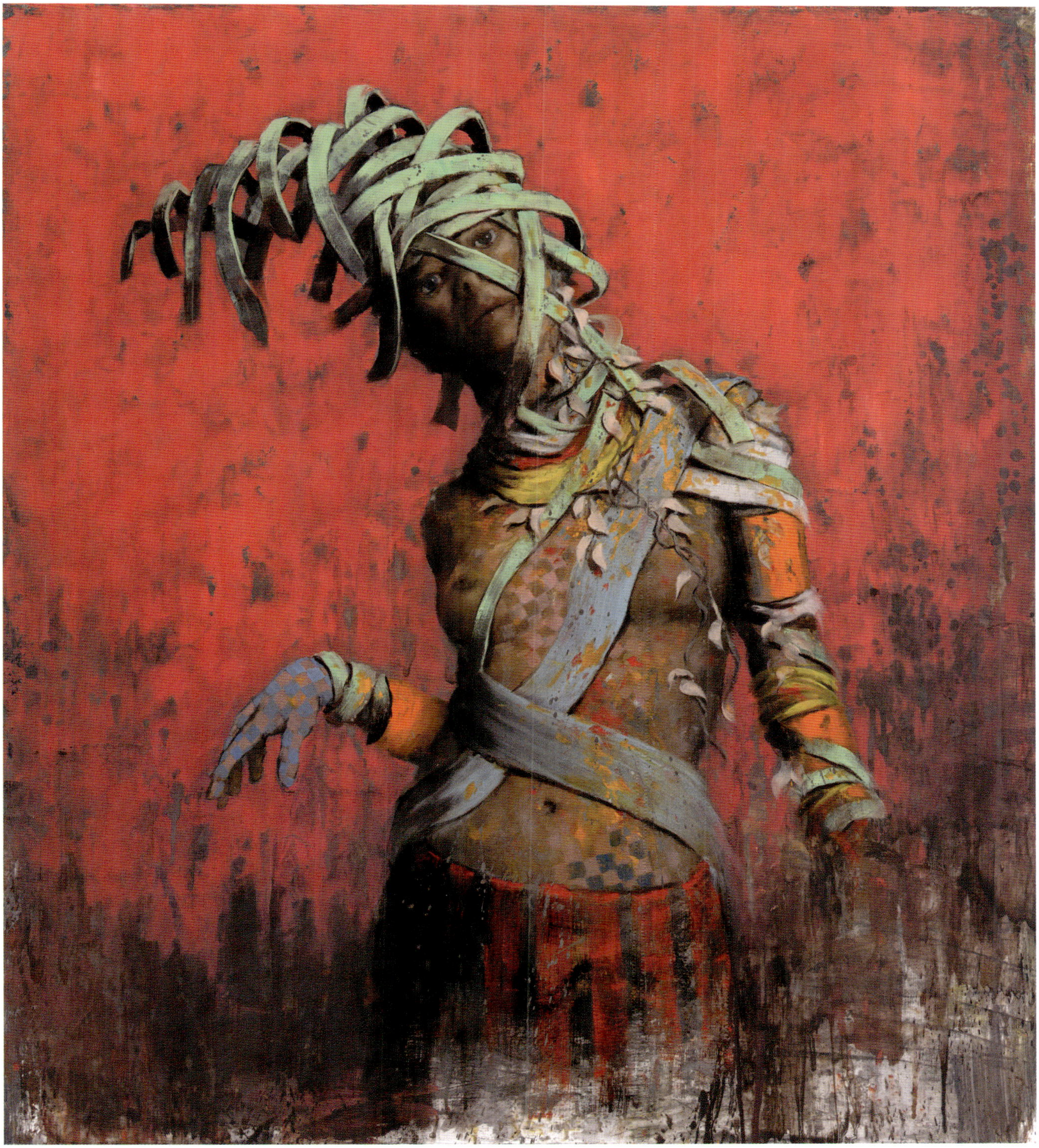

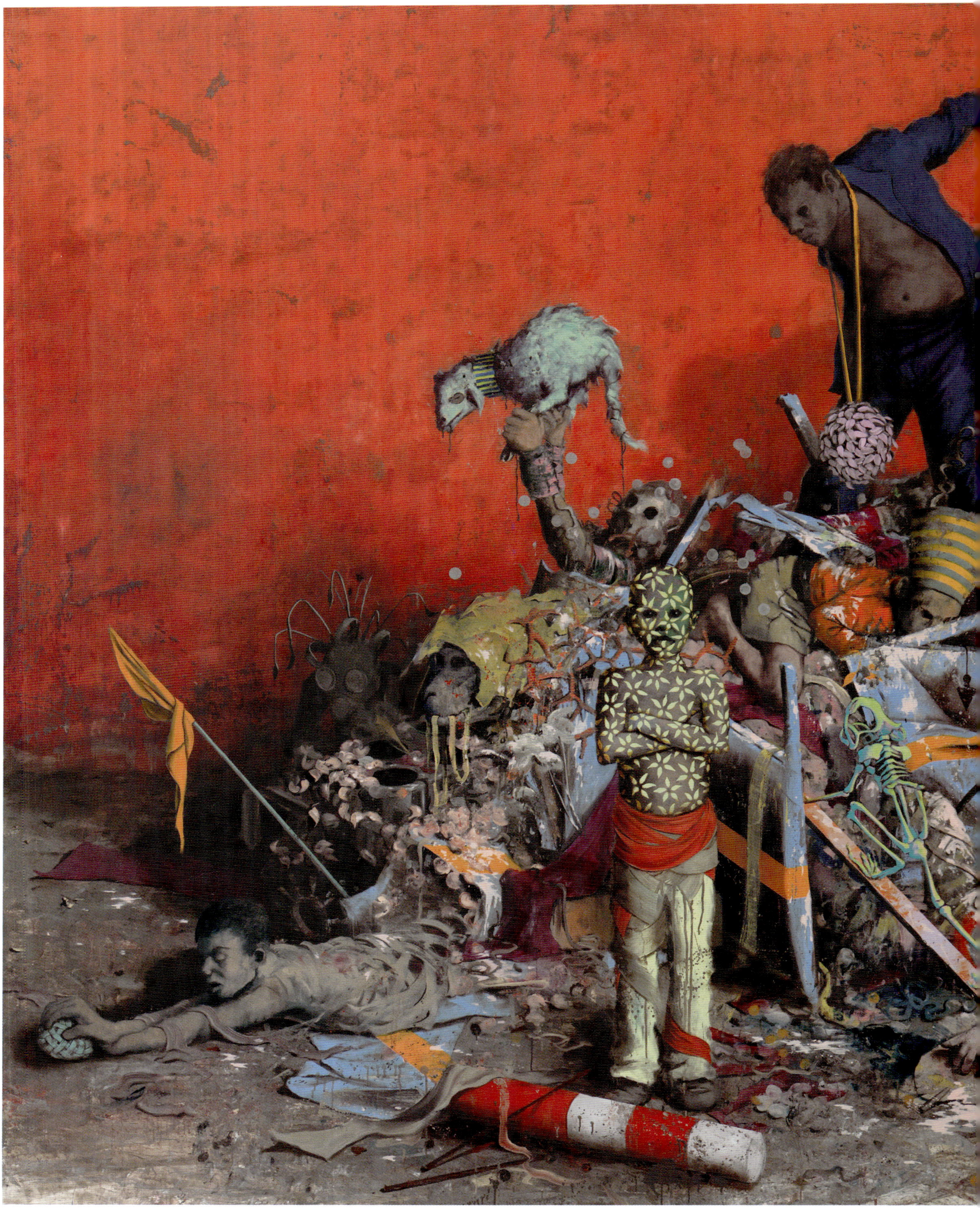

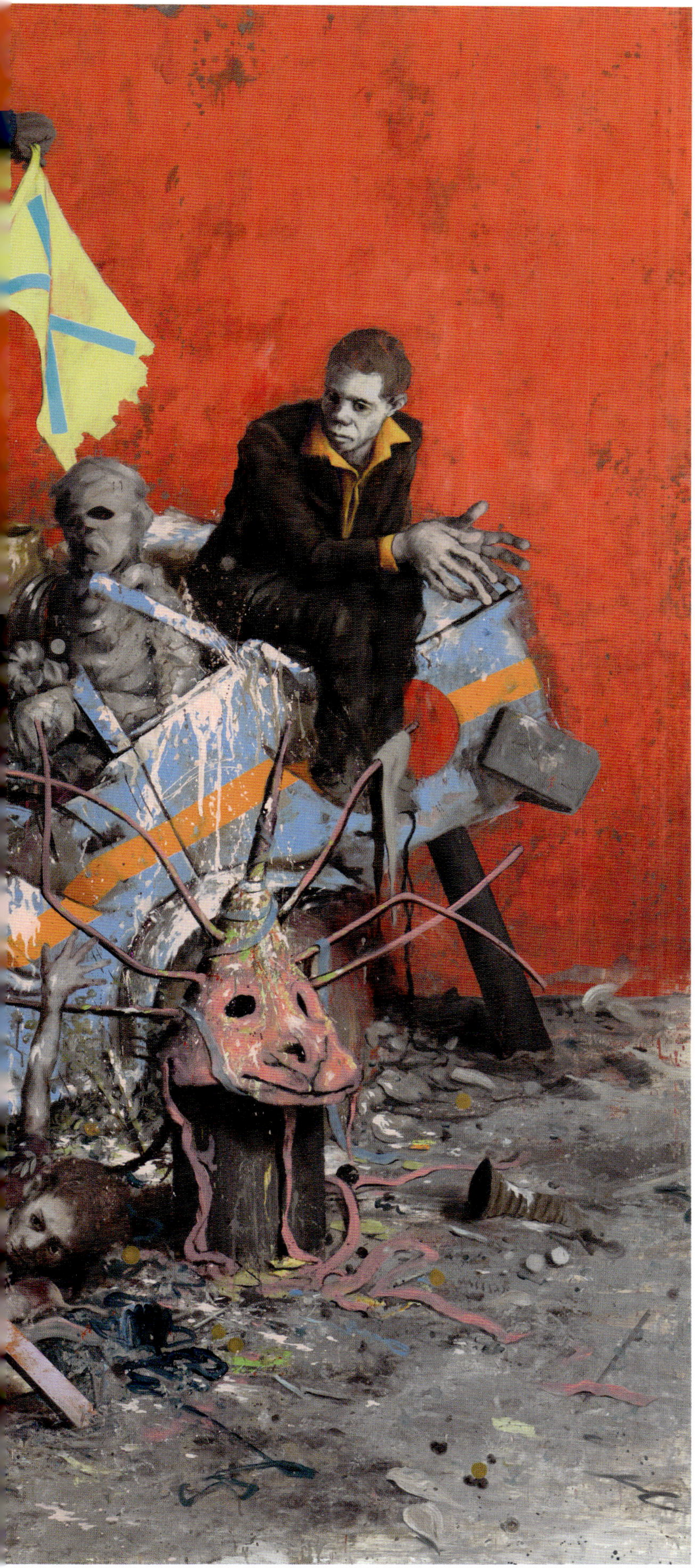

Stückfrass
2013, oil on canvas, 240 × 300 cm
(95 × 118 in).

Feinschaft
2012, oil on canvas, 120 × 100 cm
(47 × 39 in).

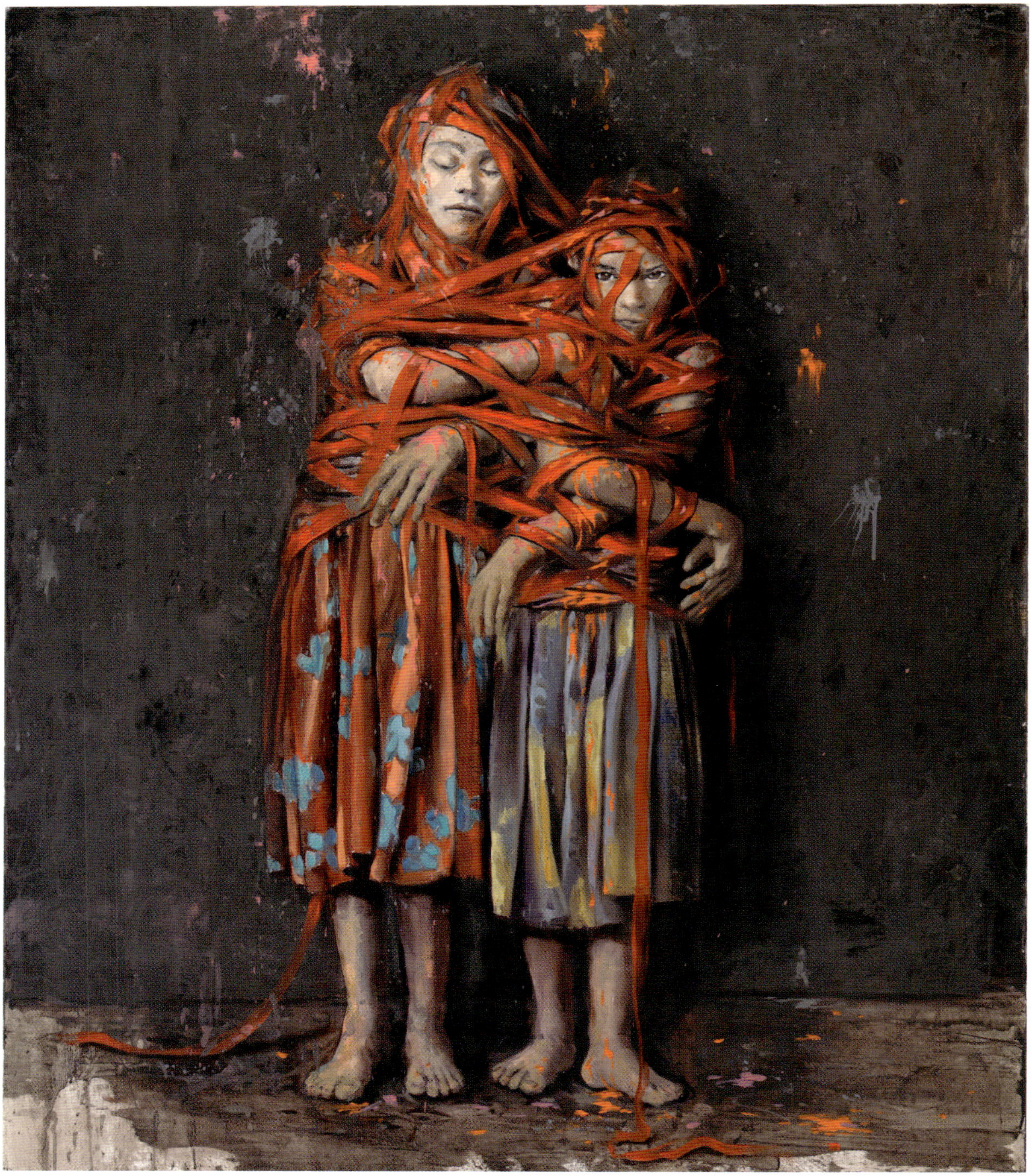

Kleiner Mut
2010–2011, oil on canvas, 90 × 80 cm
(35½ × 31½ in).

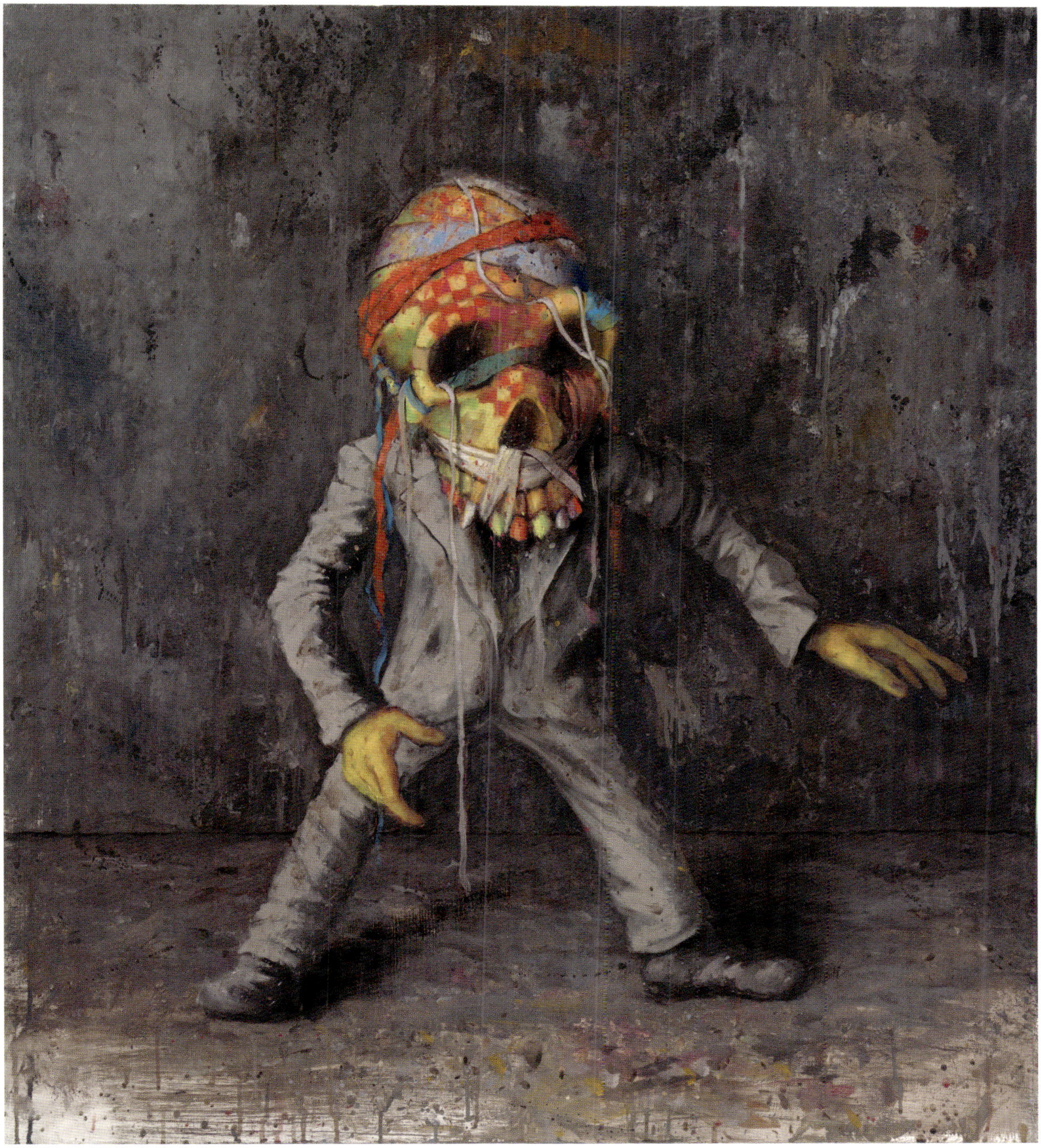

Dead End (Water's Edge)
2012, mixed media on canvas,
114 × 175 cm (45 × 69 in).

Kent Dorn
Born: 1977, Greer, South Carolina
Lives: Houston, Texas

There is a distinctive, tactile quality to the paintings of American Kent Dorn. In retrospect, it is not surprising that graphic design, the discipline in which he intially enrolled at college, never suited his artistic search. His scenes are a personal interpretation of the sublime, evoked through idyllic rural landscapes and populated by characters that seem to belong to the hippie era or to a horror movie from the 1980s. But Dorn's artistic practice cannot be confined to a celebration of his unusual references. His choice of subjects and his style serve as metaphors for a subtle meditation on the medium of painting and the role of the painter.

Art education
I attended a small liberal arts college in South Carolina. Fortunately I had a phenomenal painting instructor, Peter Kaniaris, who mentored me along the way.

One of the unique things about my art education is that it was, unlike most contemporary art programmes, very structured and rigorous, perhaps even old-fashioned. When it came to technical instruction, the curriculm was skewed heavily toward traditional approaches to drawing and painting.

From design to painting
From the outset I had struggled with the dry, technical details of the graphic design studio. In particular I remember a 'Print and Production' class in which we studied the weight and finish of paper; it was as dull as it sounds. Before long, I found myself working long nights in the painting studio and avoiding design work, so I dropped out of design and devoted all my time to painting.

Inspiration
I'm a sucker for artists with an existential bent, so I've looked to painters like Lucian Freud and Francis Bacon, or, from a little further back in history, William Blake and Caspar David Friedrich, for cues. I also find outsiders like Charles Burchfield, Henry Darger and Joseph Yoakum just as relevant as any of the Old Masters. But Philip Guston has been the single most influential artist for me. Not because of his supposed bad painting or his renunciation of abstraction; I'm taken by how he used painting and his life as a painter as his subject.

There's always music playing in my studio and I listen to a lot of cinematic, instrumental music [by groups] like Earth, Zombi, Tangerine Dream, Klaus Schulze – music that could serve as a soundtrack for the end times. And I really love 1970s and 1980s horror movies. I grew up on those films and they're largely what I watch today. My paintings are a product of conflating the foreboding ambience of that music and those films with art-historical tropes in a way that addresses my situation as a painter.

Subject matter
The recurrent subjects in my paintings are wastelands, drifters and seekers. Most of my subjects are informed by places I've been or things I've seen, particularly the landscape of the rural South [in the United States]. There are some things that I've taken directly from horror films – settings, or even the grotesque – but I think the thing that has proved most captivating is suspense. Injecting the idyllic with an air of unease or uncertainty seems pretty loaded to me.

I'm interested in the hippie counterculture because it's emblematic of a failed Utopia. I'm intrigued by the extremes to which people will go in an attempt to conjure something outside of themselves. In that way I find it to be a useful metaphor.

I am working with an overarching narrative, but for each individual painting it's not so much a story that I have in mind, but a moment or incident. I never really know what a painting is going to be before making it, and I wouldn't want to. For me, that is the point of painting – the unknown.

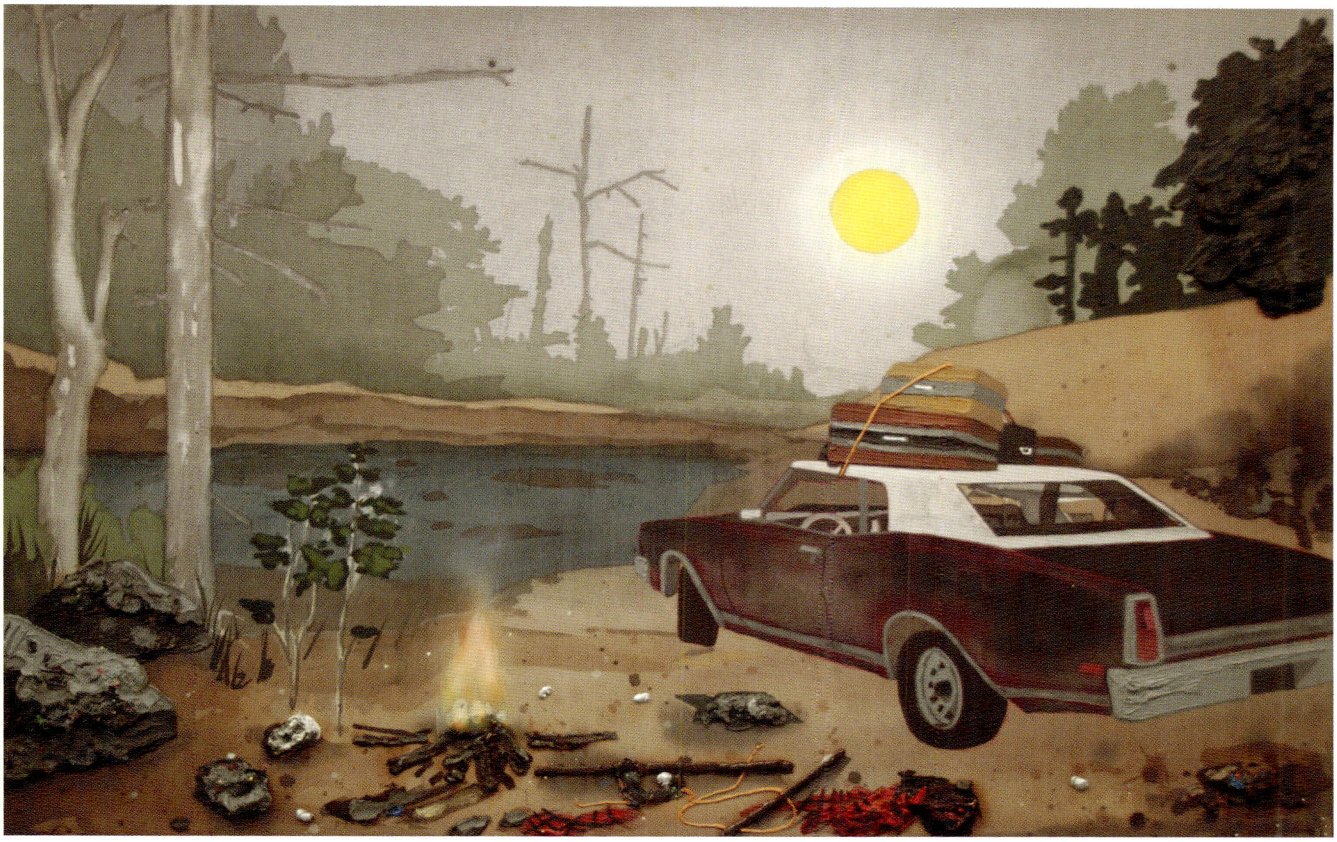

Technique

For the last eight years I've made paintings using a combination of watercolour, a waxy concoction of oil paint, and my palette scrapings. When I first started painting, I was incredibly naïve about what a painting could be or do, and for years I assumed it was possible to invoke some sort of sublime or metaphysical experience. After years of frustrated attempts, I found myself in a bit of a dilemma. While working around those aforementioned questions about painting I had begun making collages. The way that I finally decided to reintroduce paint was by attaching dried scrapings from my palette to the collages with pins, in the same treatment as fabric, photographs or anything else I was using at that time. I then started to paint over and around those dried mounds in order to integrate them loosely into the painting/composition. For a time I left the pins because I liked the way they introduced an element of time and a sense of precariousness, with the paint being merely pinned to the surface. I've since done away with the pins, but I'm still working with absurd juxtapostions of surface, interrupting delicately stained watercolour backdrops with necrotic globs of paint – there's an abjectness there, a disruption of the idyllic.

Oddly, my subjects and the decision to paint thickly came about simultaneously. What I wanted my paintings to articulate was a sort of baffled romanticism. In order to accomplish this I decided to use the tactile reality of the paint's surface as a foil to the unreality of the escapist space depicted.

On the physicality of painting

I don't know if materiality is painting's principle area of innovation but I do think it's the thing that sets paintings apart from other types of images and why painting continues to be a viable and perplexing medium.

Paintings are physical things – objects – and the particulars of how an image is [made] manifest with paint is what makes it more than a picture. Furthermore, making a painting is an attempt to take something fleeting and make it eternal, so on a very basic level all paintings strive to become monuments. This is something I addressed specifically with my portraits of 'Mystics' and 'Fugitives'. In those paintings I saw the figure/portrait as a metaphor for the medium of painting itself, as I questioned the sort of faith and the general superstition that can go hand in hand with making a painting. What I sought was a bit of a paradox, a portrayal of eternal temporality.

Fall
2010, mixed media on canvas,
114 × 81 cm (45 × 31⅞ in).

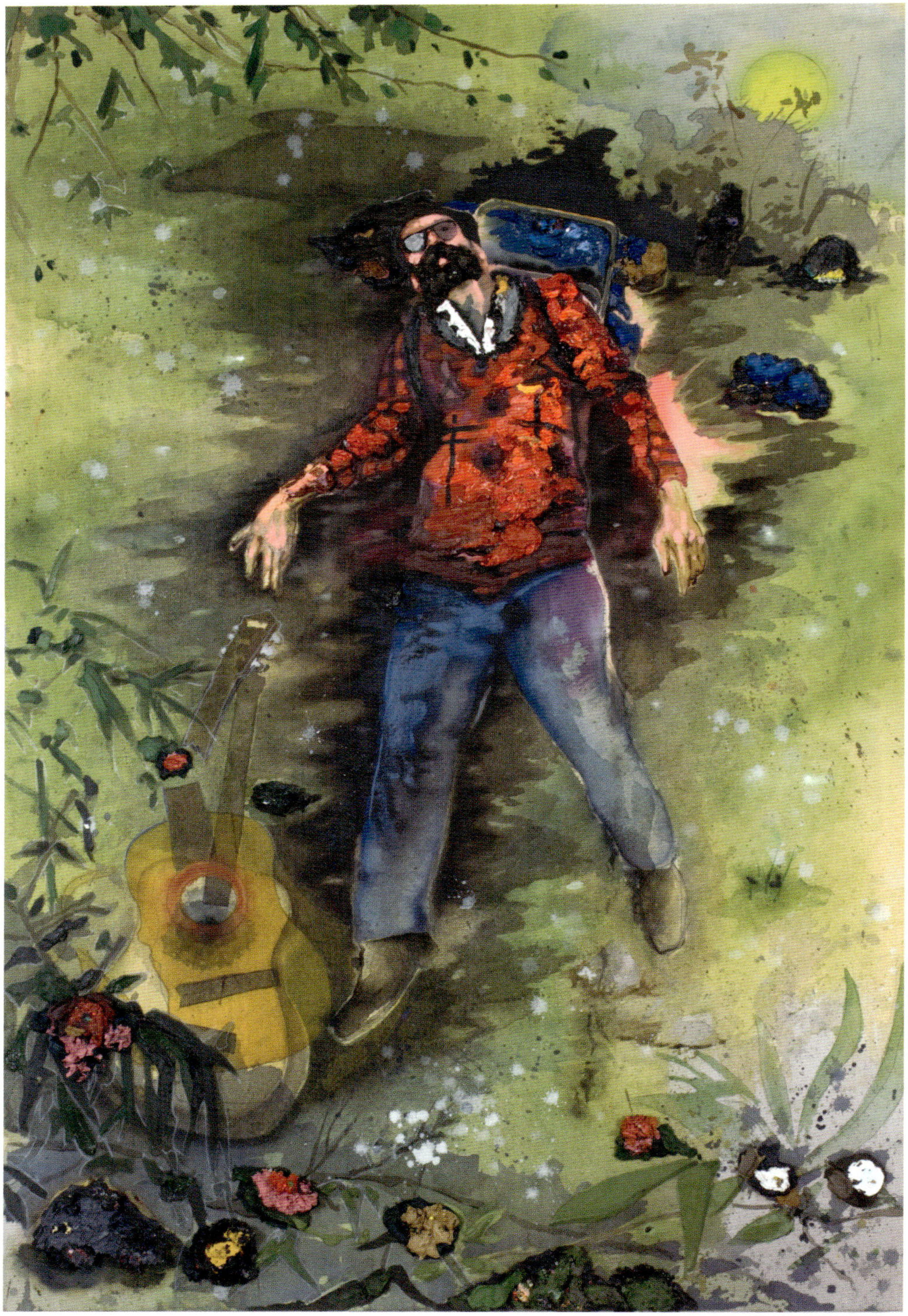

Untitled (Van)
2010, mixed media on canvas,
114 × 152 cm (45 × 60 in).

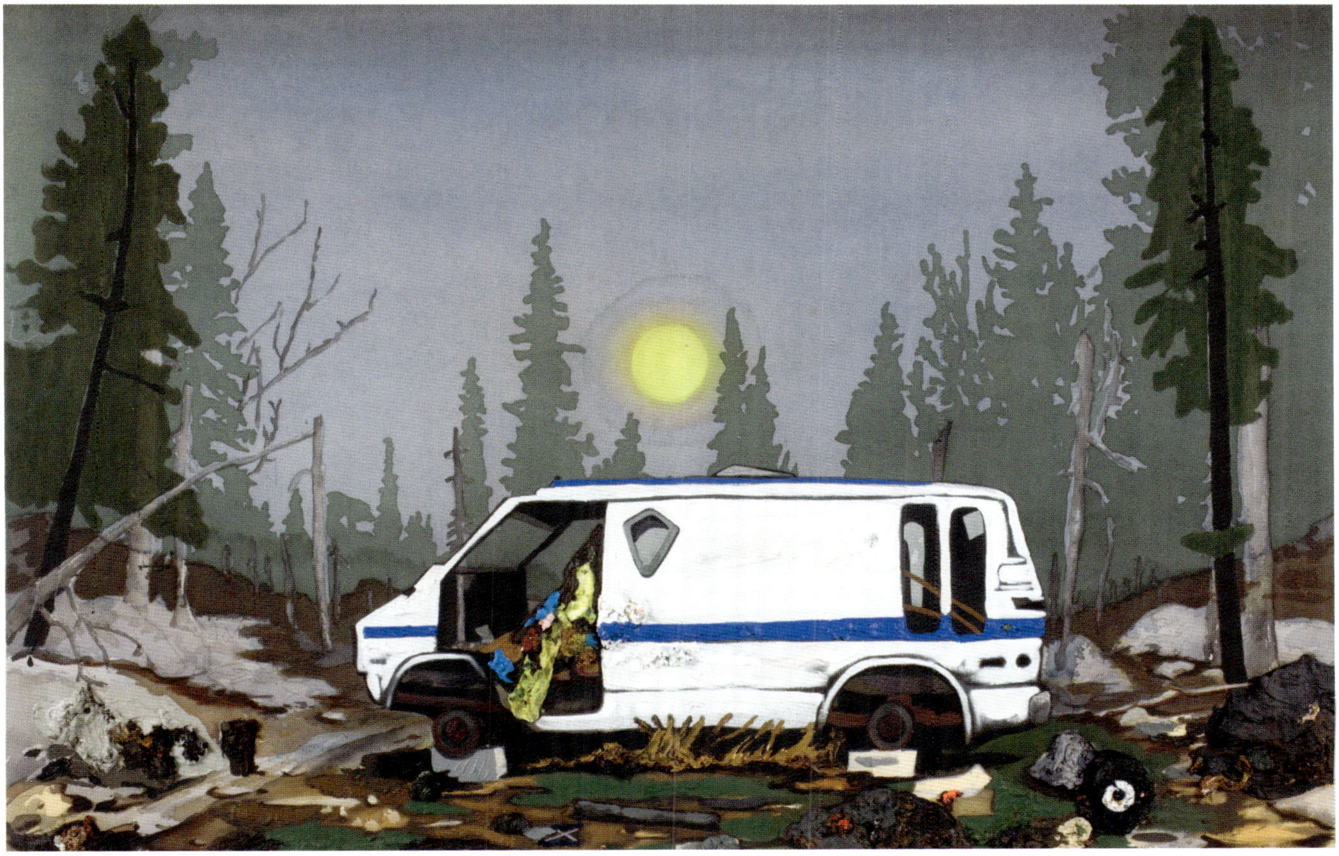

In Progress
2010, oil on canvas, 70 × 100 cm
(27⅝ × 39 in).

Joyce Ho
Born: 1983, Taiwan
Lives: Taipei and Los Angeles

Joyce Ho left Taiwan when she was 14 and says that the experience of being transplanted from home, family and culture had a huge impact on her work. While it was liberating to raise herself with her two sisters in the US, there was also something unsettling about this sudden sense of dislocation. After graduating from college in California, she moved back 'home' to Taiwan, but over the course of eight 'short' years, found that she no longer fitted in to her own culture. She says that this sense of 'liminality', of not feeling Taiwanese while at the same time being unable not to be Taiwanese, plays a huge role in her artwork. In 2008, Ho started working with the Taiwanese avant-garde theatre company Riverbed Theatre; eventually she moved back to the US and completed an MA in 2010.

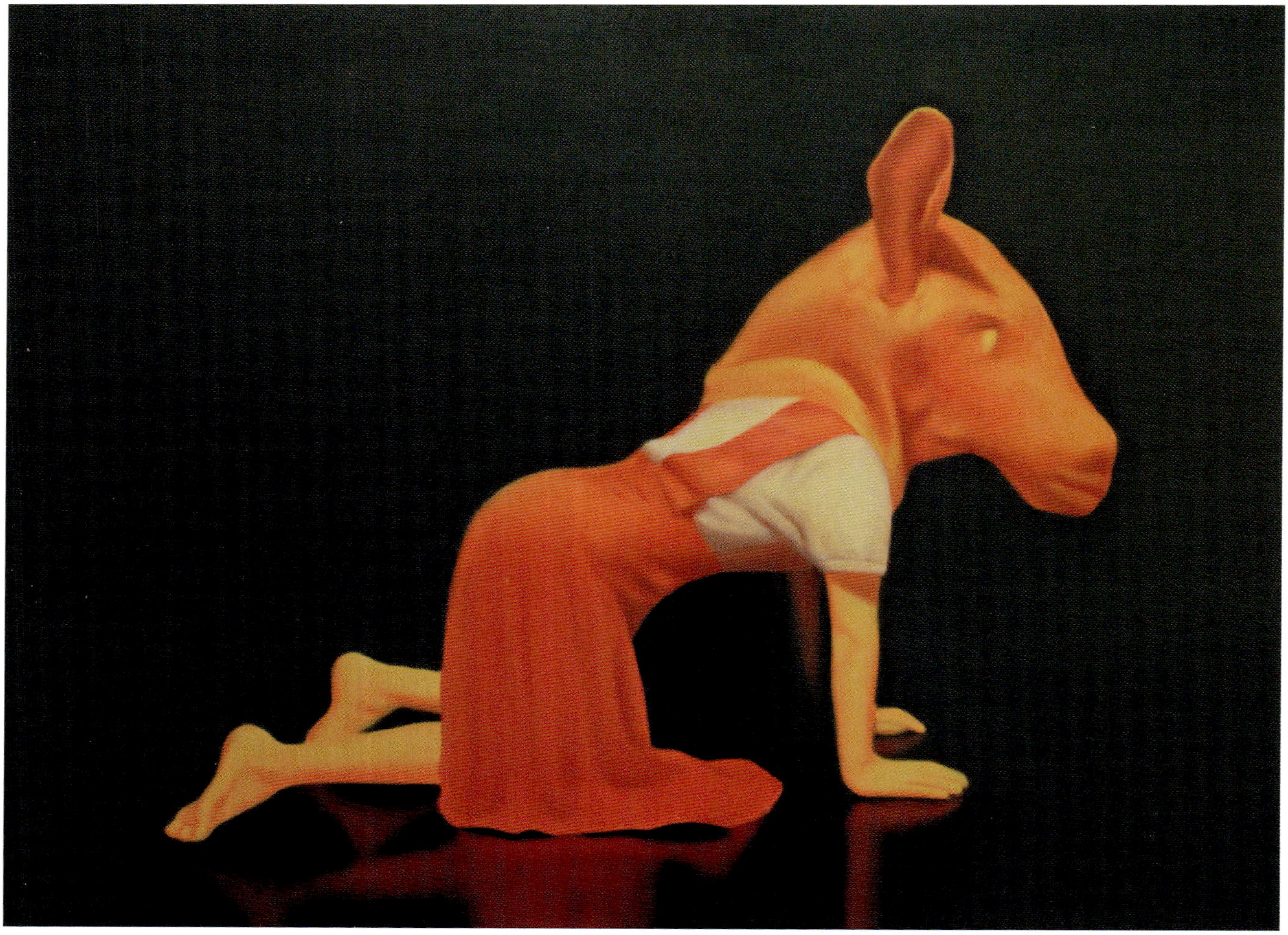

Influences
Many of my early paintings were based on performances from Riverbed Theatre productions. The company had staged a number of works inspired by visual artists ranging from Magritte to Francis Bacon, and there was something exciting about adding a final stage to this transformative process from fine art to theatre and then back to fine art. The company's artistic director Craig Quintero encouraged this process and started to incorporate my paintings back into the performances. I created two-dimensional masks that could be used in the productions. Craig often mentions Robert Wilson's aphorism, 'I don't create meaning. I create images,' and there is something about this that resonates with me. As an artist I am not interested in telling one story or communicating one meaning but in creating a series of questions.

Setting up scenes
I started composing my own images often using my father or my sister as models, and using my parents' home as the 'set'. There is something exciting about transplanting the actors from the theatre into our apartment and merging these two worlds. I spend a few months developing a series of images and then, over the course of an evening take a number of photographs and experiment with different compositions and lighting. I choose rooms with more angular architecture and multiple lighting sources. There is something cold and inhuman about many of the new high-rise apartments in Taipei, with their cold, reflective marble floors, fluorescent lights and long corridors. These apartments seem more like conference rooms or hotels. For my last painting, I convinced my sister to be the model. I had her put her head into a huge cotton ball while resting her head on a table at a very uncomfortable angle. I had to stop shooting every three minutes, because she was afraid of suffocating. The process did not go very smoothly. I have always been against the cliché of artists having to 'suffer for their artwork'. I prefer having my sister suffer!

Effects
The images I paint all have some disturbing quality, whether it's the angle of the character's head or the awkwardness of the distorted bodies. But in order to complicate these unsettling images, I use strong yellow hues to create a warm overall lighting that emanates throughout the entire space. I like this idea of 'peaceful violence', of seducing the viewer with bright colours, while simultaneously confronting them with the damaged characters.

Narrative
I am very interested in the narrative quality of painting – that paintings, like theatre, have the ability to draw spectators into the world of the work. I try to seduce the spectators, to engage with my painting and finish its story. I view my work as a starting point for the audience instead of a conclusion.

Film and theatre
I watch a lot of films and have many favourite directors, but my use of lighting, perspective and space is drawn more from my work with theatrical space. I think like a director of the stage and often use theatrical metaphors to describe my work.

The role of painting today
In this era of mimetic excess, of mass production and cloning, there is something endearing about the honesty and frailty of the human traces that resonate through something as simple as a brushstroke.

Survival Instinct
2012, oil on canvas, 45 × 60 cm
(17¾ × 23⅝ in).

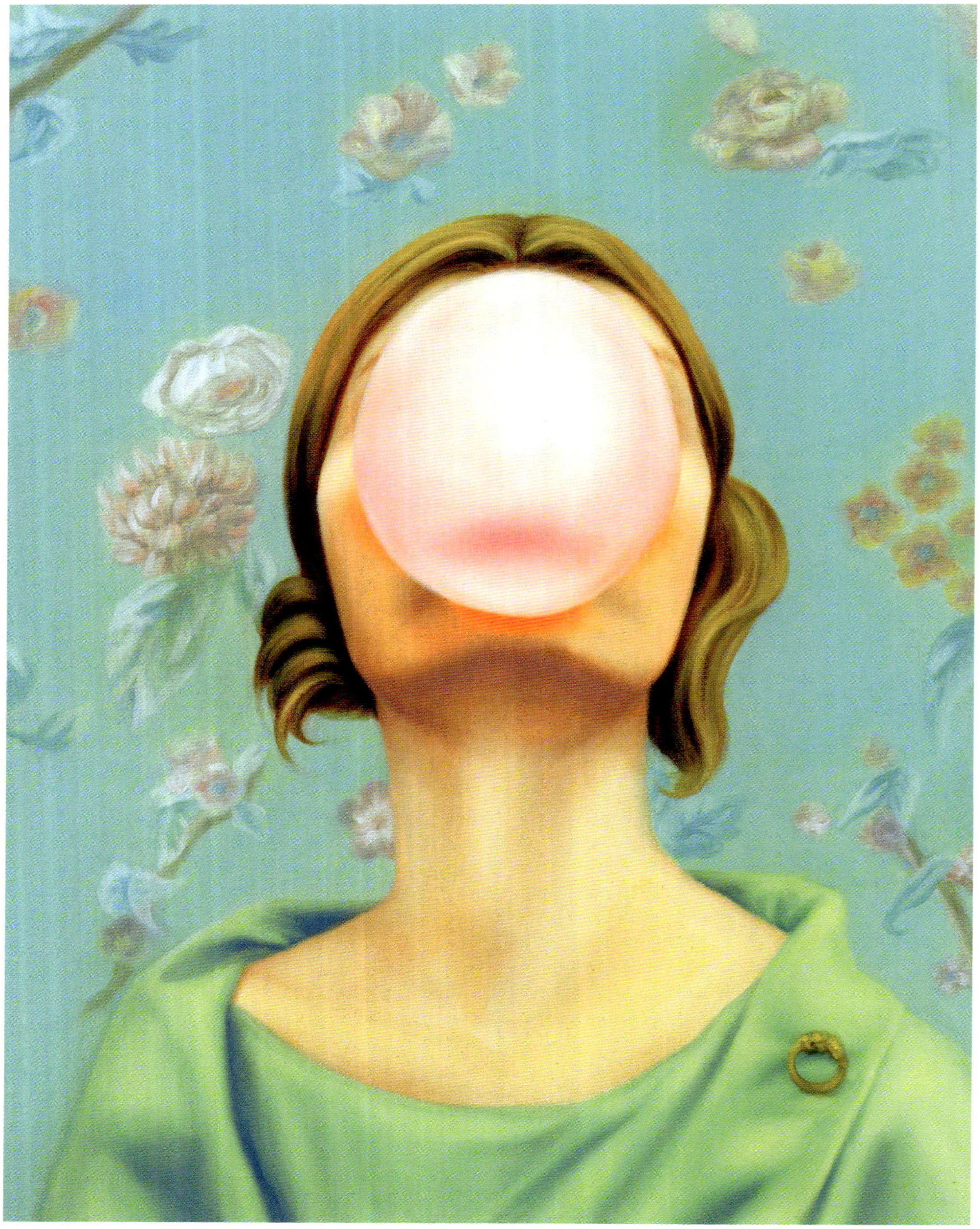

Finale
2012, oil on canvas, 46 × 61 cm
(18⅛ × 24 in).

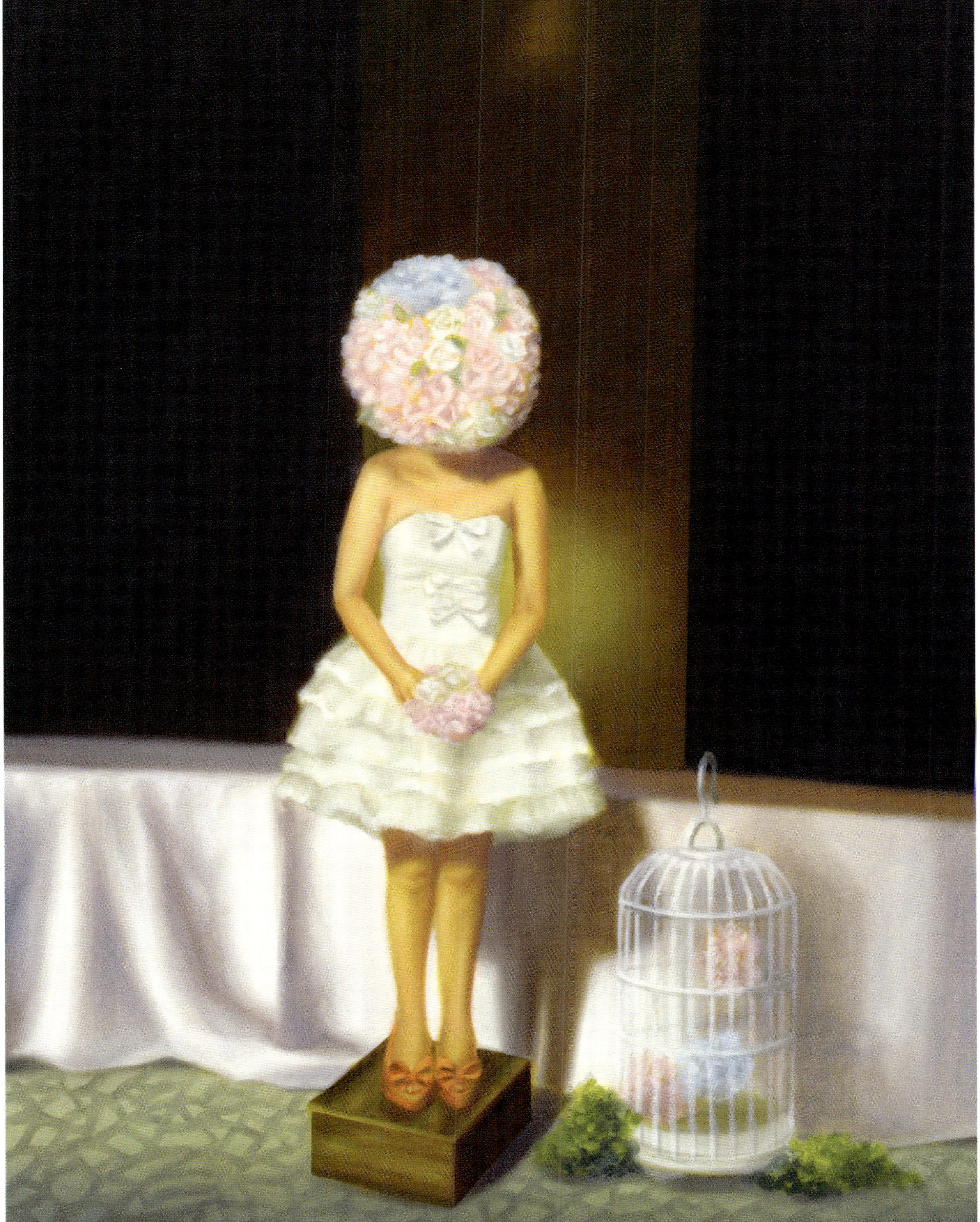

Things in Common
2010, oil on canvas, 91 × 117 cm
(35⅞ × 46 in).

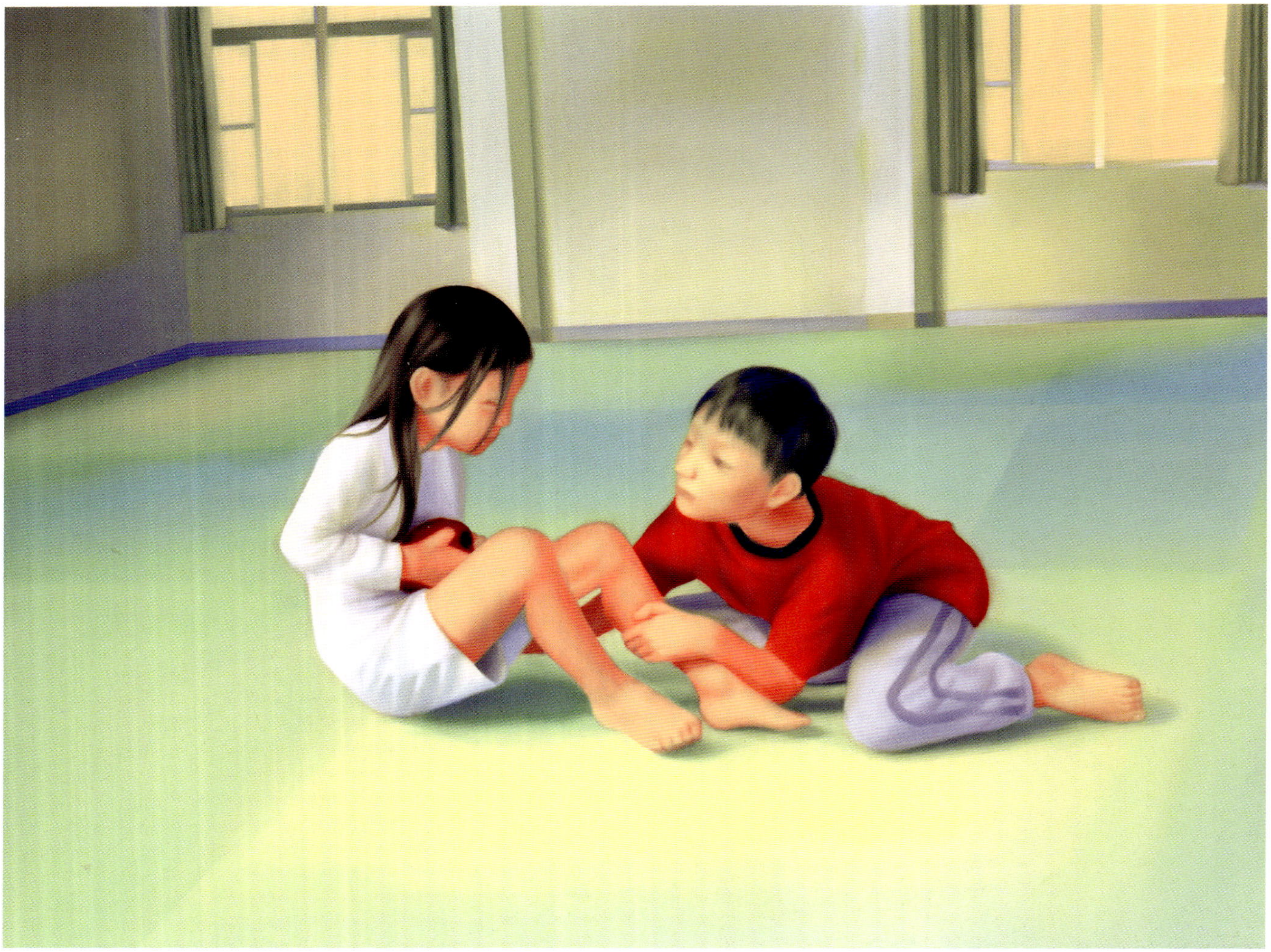

Comings and Goings
2010, oil on canvas, 70 × 100 cm
(27⅝ × 39 in).

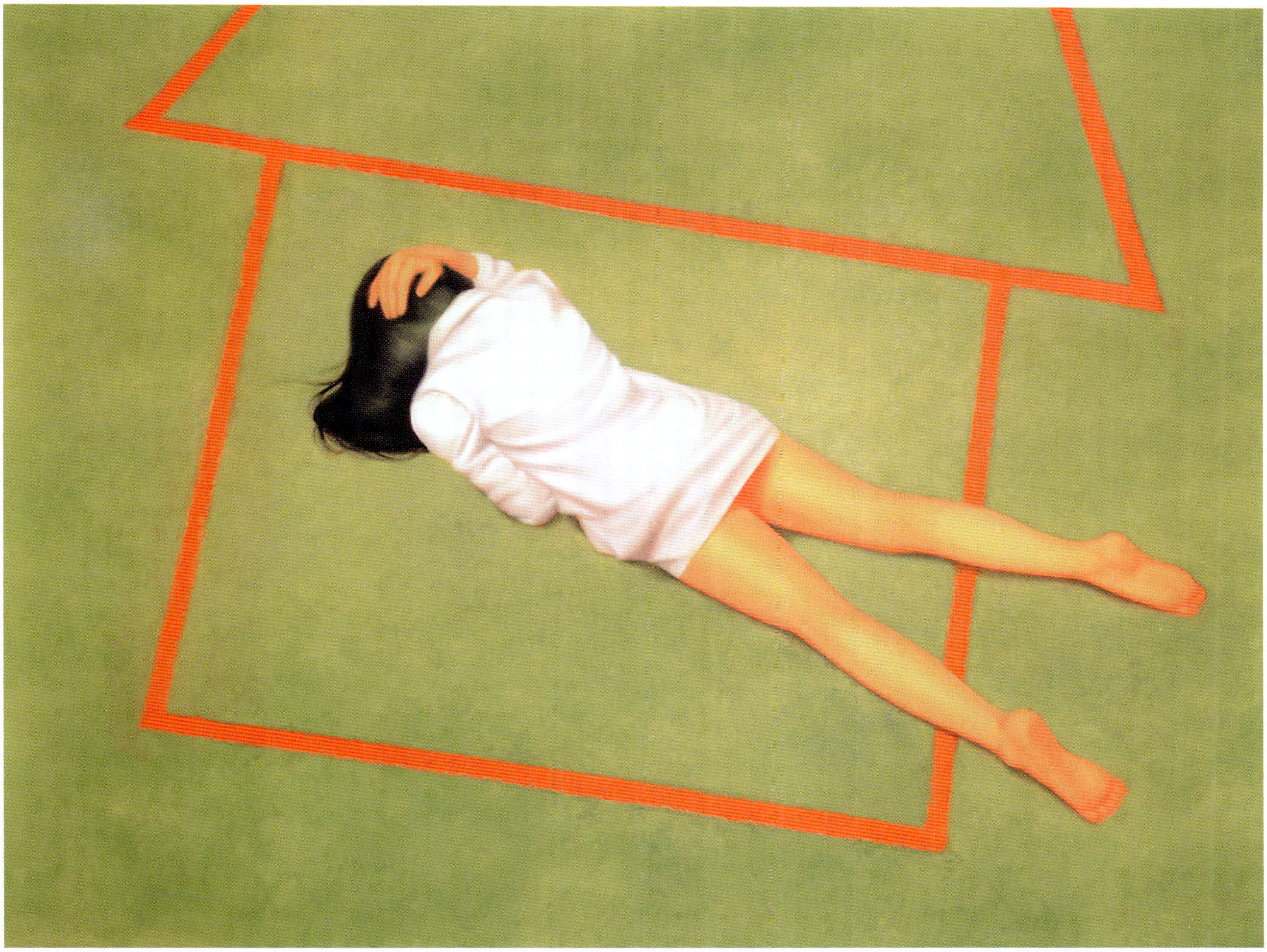

Sigrid Holmwood
Born: 1978, Hobart (Australia)
Lives: London

These paintings by London-based artist Sigrid Holmwood, made with traditional techniques involving handmade paper, old recipes for pigments and paints, and often focusing on historical re-enactments, should not look so new. Yet they do, and are, according to the artist, very much about today. 'My work is about the experience of contemporary life. It is a common contemporary fantasy to wish one could somehow grow one's own food, weave one's own clothes. I use archive photographs, old paintings and my imagination to weave together a world that isn't exactly the past, but rather a parallel world. How we interpret history is always about our society more than about the past.' She connects some of this to 'anxieties about the alienated existence of post-industrial life. We seek a greater union with the material and natural world, and the knowledge needed for basic survival. My paintings of "peasant life" made with handmade paints reflect these contemporary fantasies. Just as there is the "Slow Food" movement promoting an attention to the ingredients and cultural meanings of food in opposition to multinational fast food, my paintings can be seen as a "Slow Paint" movement.'

The tradition of peasant painting
I consider myself to be part of the history of peasant-painters that began with [Pieter] Brueghel [the Elder] in the sixteenth century and continued with nineteenth-century artists such as Millet and Van Gogh. What marks out these peasant-painters is that they not only painted peasants, but also dressed and performed as peasants in order to get closer to their subject matter (think of Van Gogh's self-portrait with a straw hat). I too have my own hand-sewn sixteenth-century clothes and there is a strong performative element to my work.

The art market
It is important to remember that the emergence of peasant scenes and landscapes as genre within Western art happened around the same time, and place, as the emergence of the first stockmarket in Antwerp. The first open art market, where you could buy ready-made paintings (rather than commissioning, as had previously been done) was close to the Bourse there. The explosion of genres at this time reflected artists trying to find their niche with the new bourgeois collectors. Tracing the history of peasant-painting is really tracing the history of the art market and capitalism.

Tradition
I am very interested in this concept of tradition, as well as its basic meaning – passing on elements of culture from one generation to the next. When I stayed with the ethnic minority Naxi Dongba shamans in the Yulong mountains of China in 2011 (for a project with Vitamin Creative Space), I encountered a people in the process of defining their tradition in order to create a sense of a nation of people within China. The shamans were researching their own culture and rediscovering elements, such as papermaking, that had been lost during the upheavals of the twentieth century.

Materials and subjects
[My materials include] plants, berries, mushrooms, insects, natural earths, semi-precious stones and other pigments made by alchemy. I use binders such as eggs, cheese, soured milk, glue made from parchment clippings and linseed oil.

The idea of making my own paint came through two different routes. On the one hand it was a practical solution as I simply couldn't get shop-bought paint to behave the way I wanted it to. The kind of paint I needed was not available in tubes; so I made it. At the same time, I realized that it was a response to the common criticism that painting is not relevant in a contemporary world of mass-produced, machine-made, perfect surfaces. I always felt that the attraction of painting is that it is handmade, so making every aspect of it by hand seemed a good way to emphasize my position.

The place of craft
The idea of craft was quite denigrated when I was at art school [Holmwood attended Ruskin School of Drawing and Fine Art, Oxford, and graduated from the Royal College of Art in London in 2002], but now, in a post-financial-crash world it is becoming increasingly pertinent as something that has its value inscribed through the tangible human labour involved in making it. Furthermore, an intimate interaction with materials allows for the generation of ideas, through the acquired sensitivity for the individual character and stories behind the pigments.

Alchemy

I develop the recipes for my paint from a number of sources. I read old medieval and early modern treatises on painting, which include recipes for pigments, and I also read a lot of conservation reports, especially those with microscopic cross-sections and reconstructed recipes. The reports help me to determine which of the old recipes were most common. The pleasure – and pain – of reading the old painting treatises is that the recipes have symbolic and philosophical meanings as well as practical ones, and some are much more symbolic than practical. For instance, there is a classic recipe for Spanish Gold from the twelfth-century monk, Theophilus, which involves a complicated process including persuading two male cockerels to mate and lay eggs. The eggs are subsequently incubated and hatched by toads, and chicks with serpents' tails emerge. These are burnt alive and mixed with additives such as the blood of a red-haired man. Clearly, this recipe only works in a philosophical world. On the other hand, a seemingly fanciful recipe for red pigment that involves pouring mercury into an egg and burying it in horse manure for 40 days and 40 nights is in fact a subtle way of telling you the real process for making vermillion, or mercury sulphide. The egg is the symbol of transformation – in this case the transformation of mercury and sulphur through roasting. Sulphur is represented by the yolk of the egg and the heat of a kiln by the horse manure. Mercury and sulphur themselves had important cultural meanings as some believed their combination resulted in the 'Red King', otherwise known as the Philosopher's Stone. The practical-sounding recipes are just as philosophical in their meanings as the overtly symbolic ones.

Meaning in materials

With this in mind, I evolve my own meanings for the pigments that I make. Many are not actually historical ones, but use historical methods to make pigments from dyestuffs that would not have been used in the past. For instance, the body of work that I made after my journey to China was done entirely on handmade paper that I made from fabric that I had first dyed with healing plants that are part of Chinese medicine. I am now working on a show in response to the peasant–painters of the region of Halland, Sweden, and making pigments from mushrooms by adapting recipes for dyeing wool with fungi. The use of mushrooms for dyes has only been around since the 1980s in Sweden because of the mycophobia of the local peasant culture. Mushrooms are very evocative of the wild forest, spirits and hallucinations, which is probably why they were shunned in the first place. These magical and healing associations act as conveyors of meaning within my paintings.

On a deeper level, I often work with images that refer back to the materials I am using and manual labour. Sometimes this is very obvious, such as an image of papermaking, and sometimes it is more subtle, for instance an image of harvesting flax is an image of the materials of oil painting being made – linseed oil and linen canvas. Other images I choose make more metaphorical reference to the practice of painting, such as a shaman, a witch, a magical toad or a horse with an erection.

The practice of painting

It is hard not to go too far [when working on a particular painting]; it is important to stop when it is already saying what you want it to say. If I go too far then the brush-marks start to be obscured and lose their freshness. A fresh and confident brush-mark is something I admire in peasants' painting.

When asked to describe what I do, I generally say 'I make my own paints and paint peasants', then I leave it hanging there in all its ridiculousness.

Three Women Working Wool
2013, mushroom pigment made from blood red webcaps (cortinarius sanguineus), plant pigment made from yarrow (achillea millefolium), chalk, chrome yellow, red lead, woad, red earth and zinc white bound in egg on hand-woven linen, 112 × 152 cm (44 × 60 in).

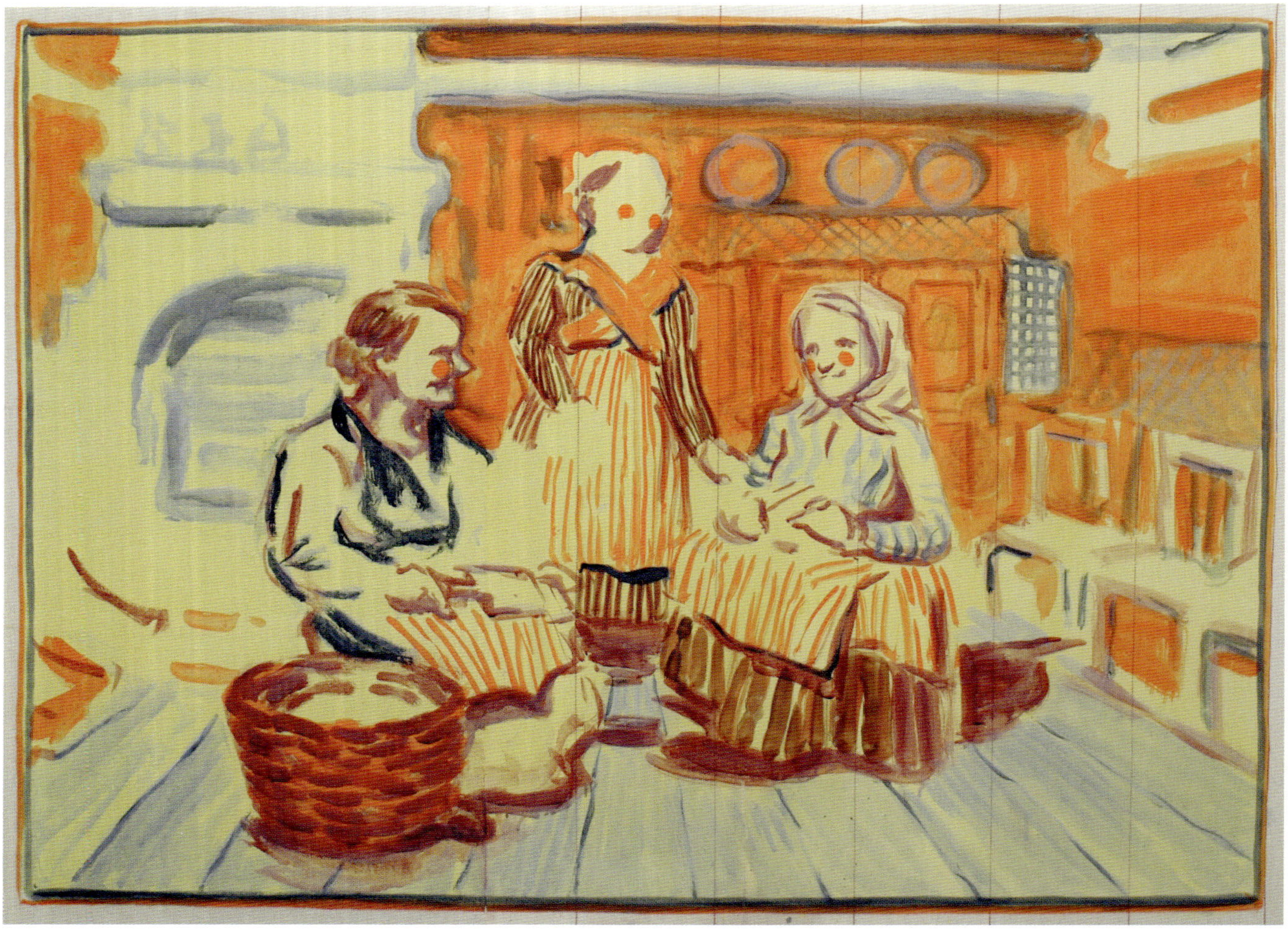

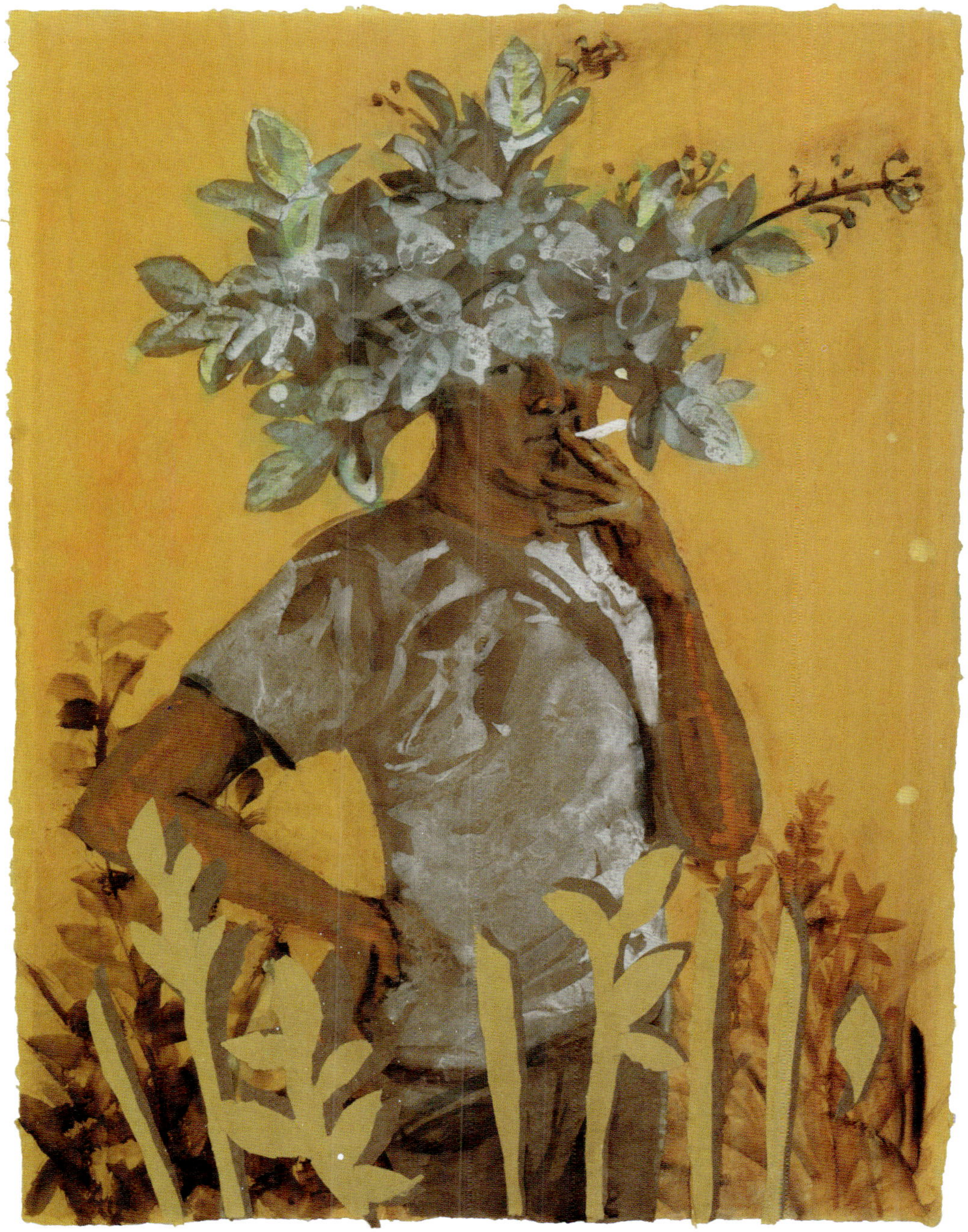

He Jie Xian as Pan Smoking 2012, yellow paper made from denim dyed with pomegranate rinds and pagoda tree flowers, purple paper made from denim dyed with madder roots and iron, painted with oyster shell white, malachite, caput mortuum, ochre and gamboge bound with parchment clipping glue, 98 × 75 cm (38½ × 29½ in).

Leaping Hogs Acre Boundary Ditch
2009, fluorescent golden yellow, lead antimonate, lead-tin yellow, green earth, smalt, gamboge in free-range egg tempera on board, 122 × 142 cm (48 × 56 in).

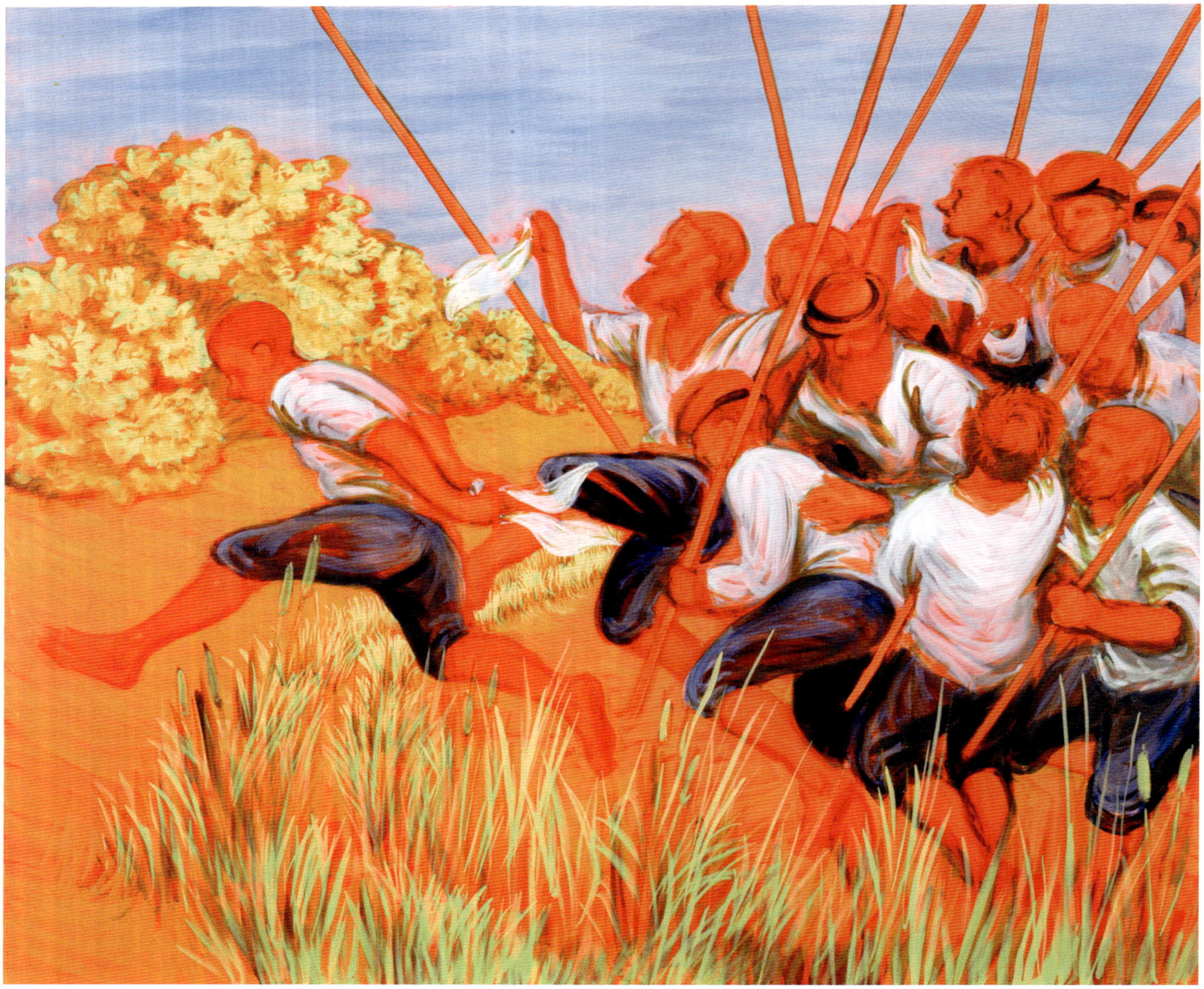

Path from St George's Hill
2009, fluorescent orange yellow egg/oil emulsion; burnt sienna, lead antimonate, verdigris, smalt, lead white, and schiet yellow in oils on canvas, 92 × 93cm (36¼ × 36⅝ in).

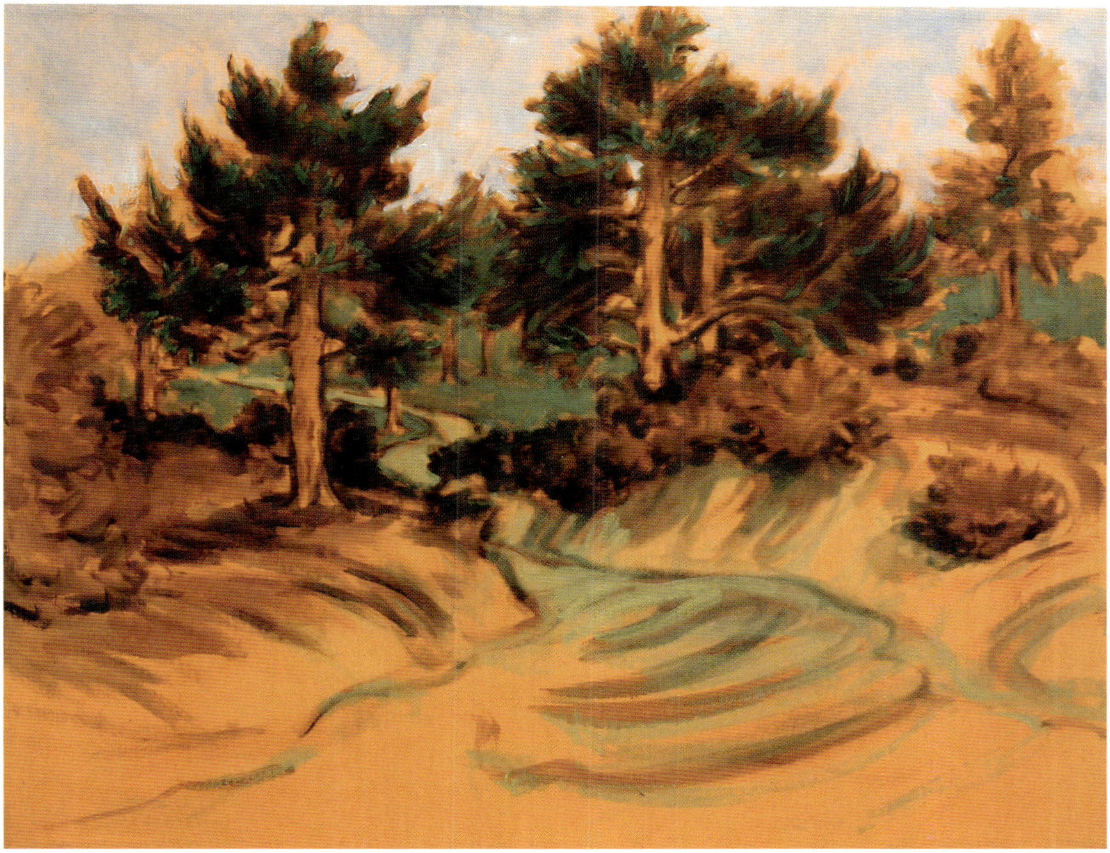

The Scream
2010, acrylic on canvas, 82 × 65 cm
(32⅜ × 25⅝ in).

Josephine King
Born: 1965, London
Lives: London

Are these self-portraits? And if so, what self are we talking about? The sexually-assertive artist inspired by other female artists? The aggressively colourful, ranting *MODERN WOMAN (TRICKED + TRAPPED. STARING INTO THE ABYSS OF MISERY)*? The lonely, self-destructive Art Deco harlequin, or the angry and ostracized *SELFISH BITCH* female artist, her 'unused womb bleeding paint'? The benumbed patient of a psychiatric ward surrounded by grey and black patches, the grief-stricken owner of a deceased dog, or the bipolar doll being surgically unstitched over a blood red background? Always executed as frontal full-length self-portraits, these paintings mix a graphic directness with a subtle and broad set of references – visual, structural, textural and linguistic. This is the modern self in all its levels and colours. Typically, a work will present nods to Ancient Egyptian art, classical painting and Art Nouveau while making abrupt and highly personal allusions to the traumas of bipolar disorder. King's visual virtuosity combines itself with a cruelly self-analytical mind to create powerful statements of what it is to be a woman, or just a highly complex individual, today.

Background
I had artistic parents who both went to art school. My childhood was full of music and museum visits. There was a great sense of youthfulness and freedom from the 1960s. We travelled – I remember MoMA in New York, and Picasso's goat [*She-Goat*, 1950], which I loved. The Tutankhamun exhibition in London [British Museum, 1972] impressed me deeply. The Boar and Bear Hunt tapestry in London's V&A fascinated me. From the age of 10, I lived in Amsterdam. I went to the Rudolph Steiner school there. Art was a pleasure. At 23, I went to art school but it was only when I was 26 that I knew I wanted to be a painter. I went to the Gerrit Rietveld Academie in Amsterdam and did my postgrad in Lisbon.

Process
I try to get the most intense colours possible. All my colour choices are instinctive. And because I use inks a lot, paper is the best support.

I have a vast body of gathered material in the form of sketchbooks – hundreds of them. This is one source; another is looking at past masters. And finally, yet another source is the desire to express something elusive.

In reply to what comes first, words or images
The words come first, and writing is something I do every day.

Influences
I'm not trying to execute a life-like form. The paintings are 'of the mind'. I cover the surface in a patterned, abstract way; it is the interplay of pattern and colour that excites me. And, yes, the Egyptians, Duccio and so many others have been an influence. I'm interested in the sense of mystery.

On her relationship to the tradition of portraiture
I don't do portraits. But my self-portraits are in the tradition of all self-portraits. I am exposing myself to the viewer as truthfully as I know how. With my self-portraits, I try to get my deepest self out. In this I have no fear. Examples [of painters working] in this tradition are Rembrandt, who painted himself as a tired old man, and Alice Neel, who painted herself completely naked.

In painting Modern Woman I am looking outside of myself rather than just looking within. Showing myself naked in both mind and body depicts how it feels for me to be going against the grain of society. As a woman painter, I have nothing to lose.

Depression
I would argue that my work goes far beyond the portrayal of depression. Recently exposed works (the self-portraits) have brought that to a wider audience but that is only a small part of my work. It's certainly not depression that stimulates my work. I suffer from both mania and depression and I paint through both these states.

Discipline
I do aspire to the discipline of hard work. I live among people who work hard and I could say that is a certain inspiration. The ideal conditions for me to be working are: in my own studio; quiet, familiar conditions.

I would say that what I do is indefinable concerning painting. But I get up and paint every day and it is exhausting.

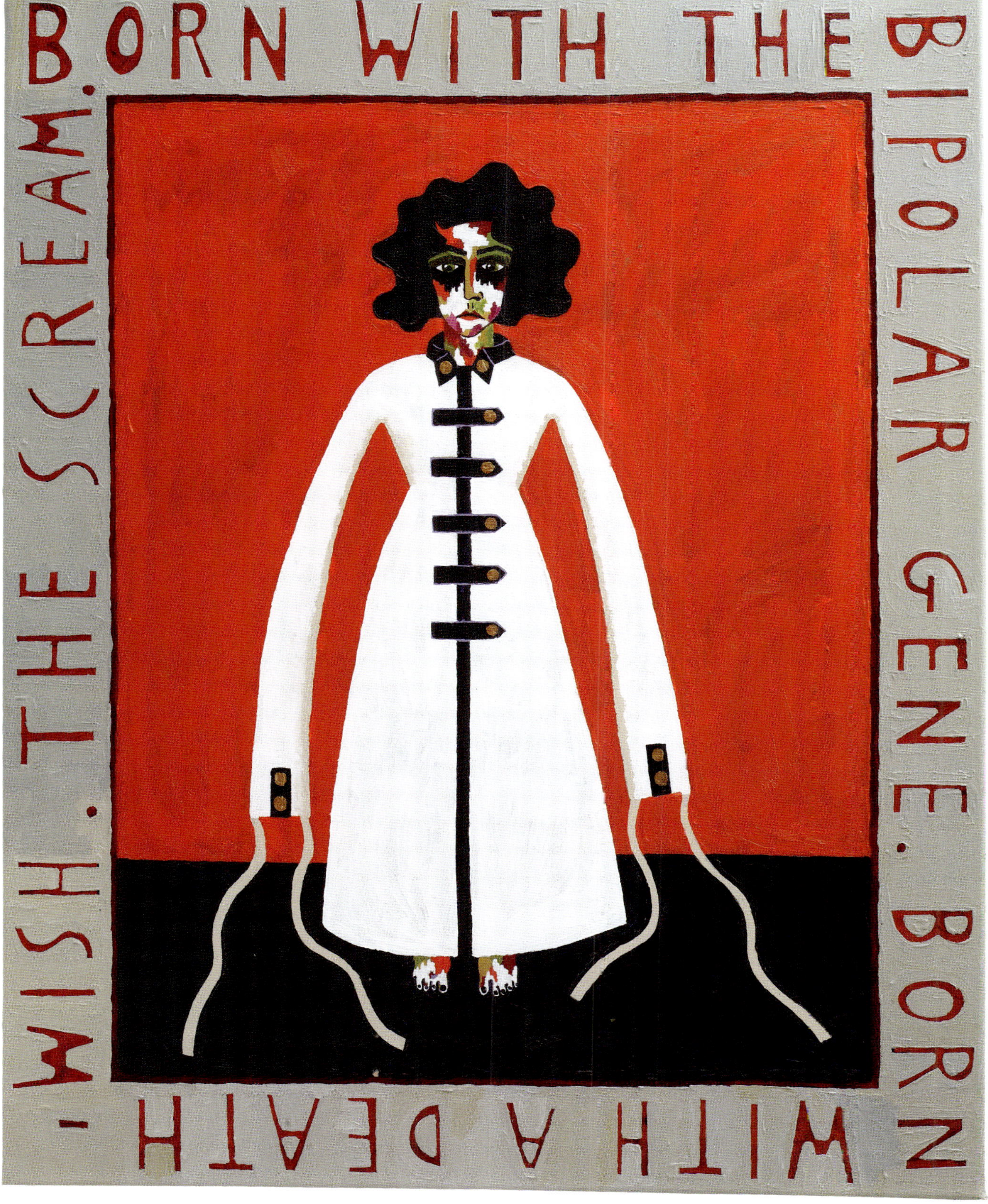
BORN WITH THE BIPOLAR GENE. BORN WITH A DEATH-WISH. THE SCREAM.

No Title
2009 acrylic on canvas, 100 × 70 cm
(39 × 27⅝ in).

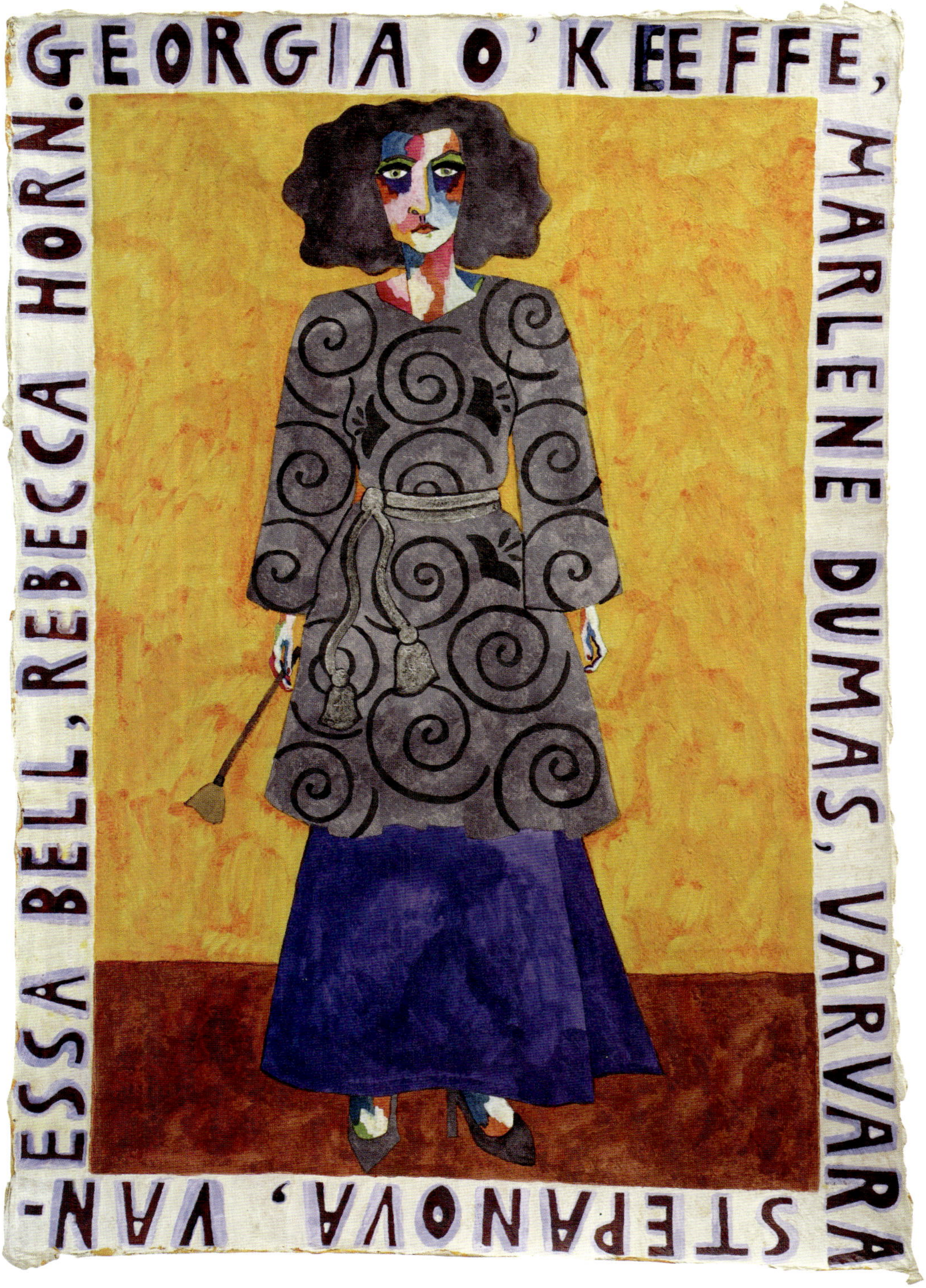

Bipolar Made Me
2009, ink on paper, 100 × 70 cm
(39 × 27⅝ in).

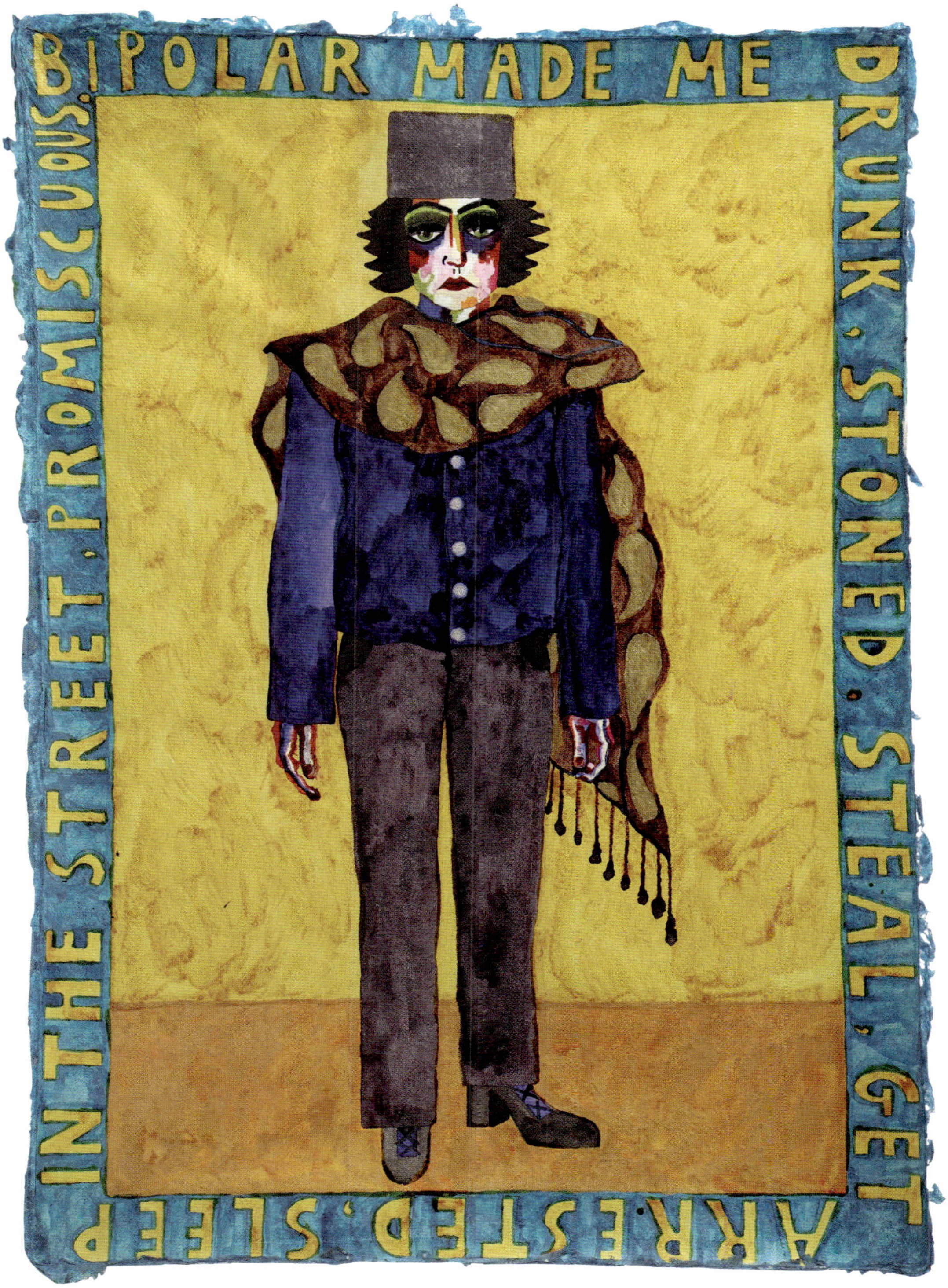

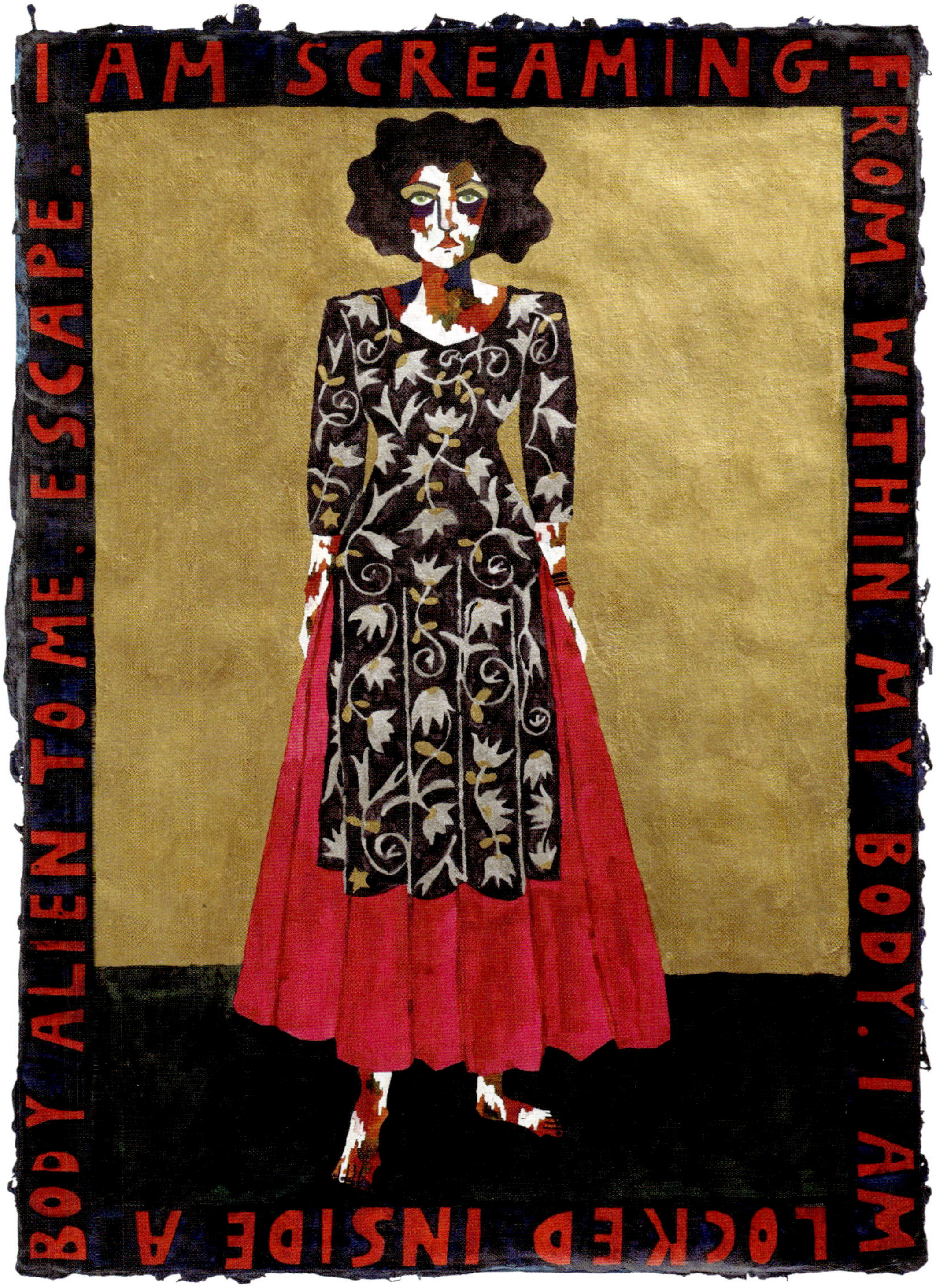

Manic Depression
2009, ink on paper, 100 × 70 cm
(39 × 27⅝ in).

Suicide
2010, ink on paper, 100 × 70 cm
(39 × 27⅝ in).

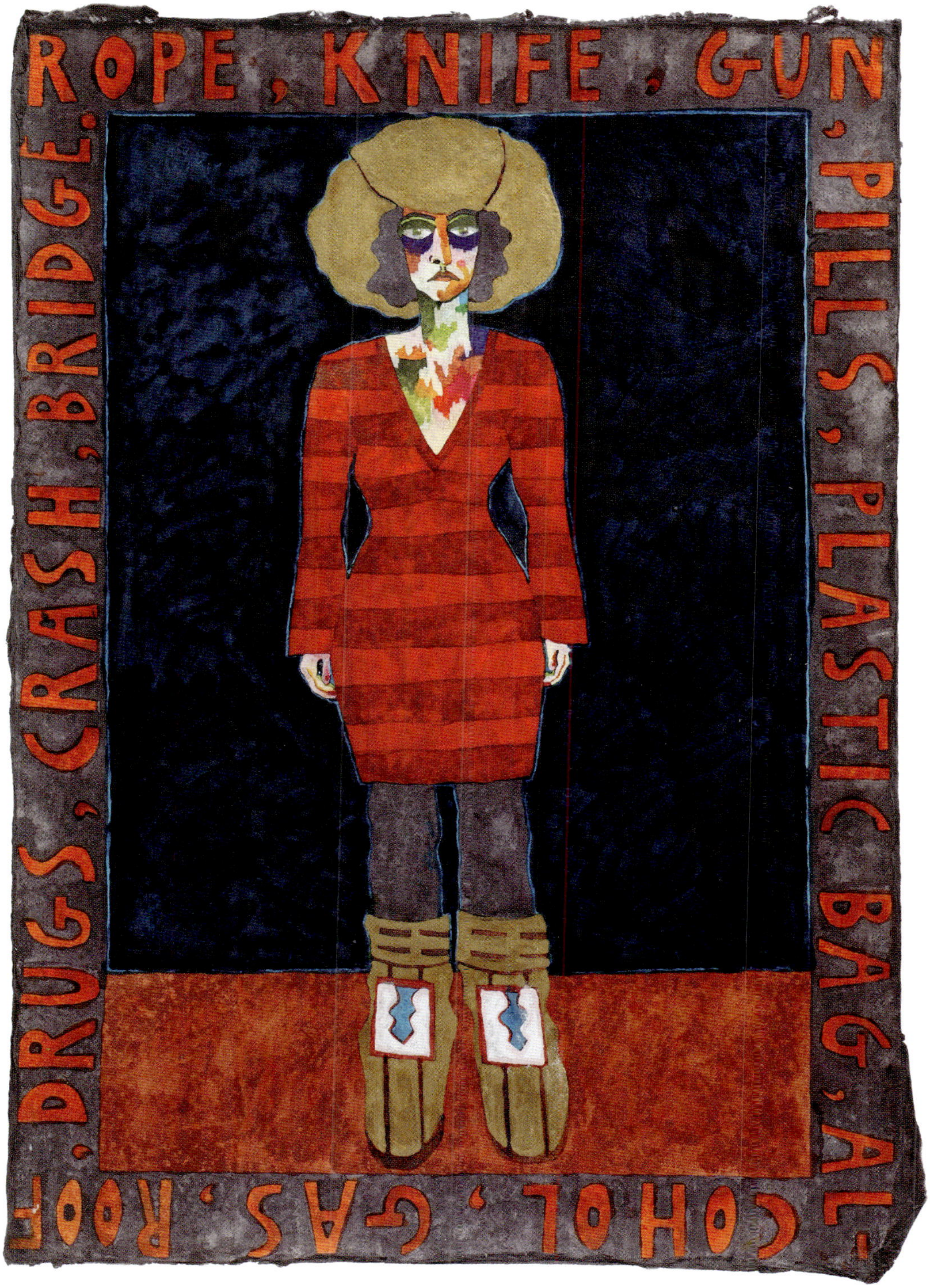

Mountain F
1997, acrylic on canvas, 219 × 240cm
(86 × 95 in).

Masakatsu Kondo
Born: 1962, Nagoya (Japan)
Lives: London

When asked to define what he does, the Japanese painter tells us that 'painting is my statement when I am silent'. Painting is by its very nature a contemplative medium – a rare thing in our over-saturated, media-soaked cities – and this is clearly central to Kondo's work. Living in London, which he describes as being, among other things, 'rampant with crime', the painter says he works more from his own states of mind and is not particularly interested in art as a socio-political medium. Nature and spirituality are clearly important to the artist (as is his background). He defines the role of painting today as 'shaping up the individual soul and spirit in the moment'.

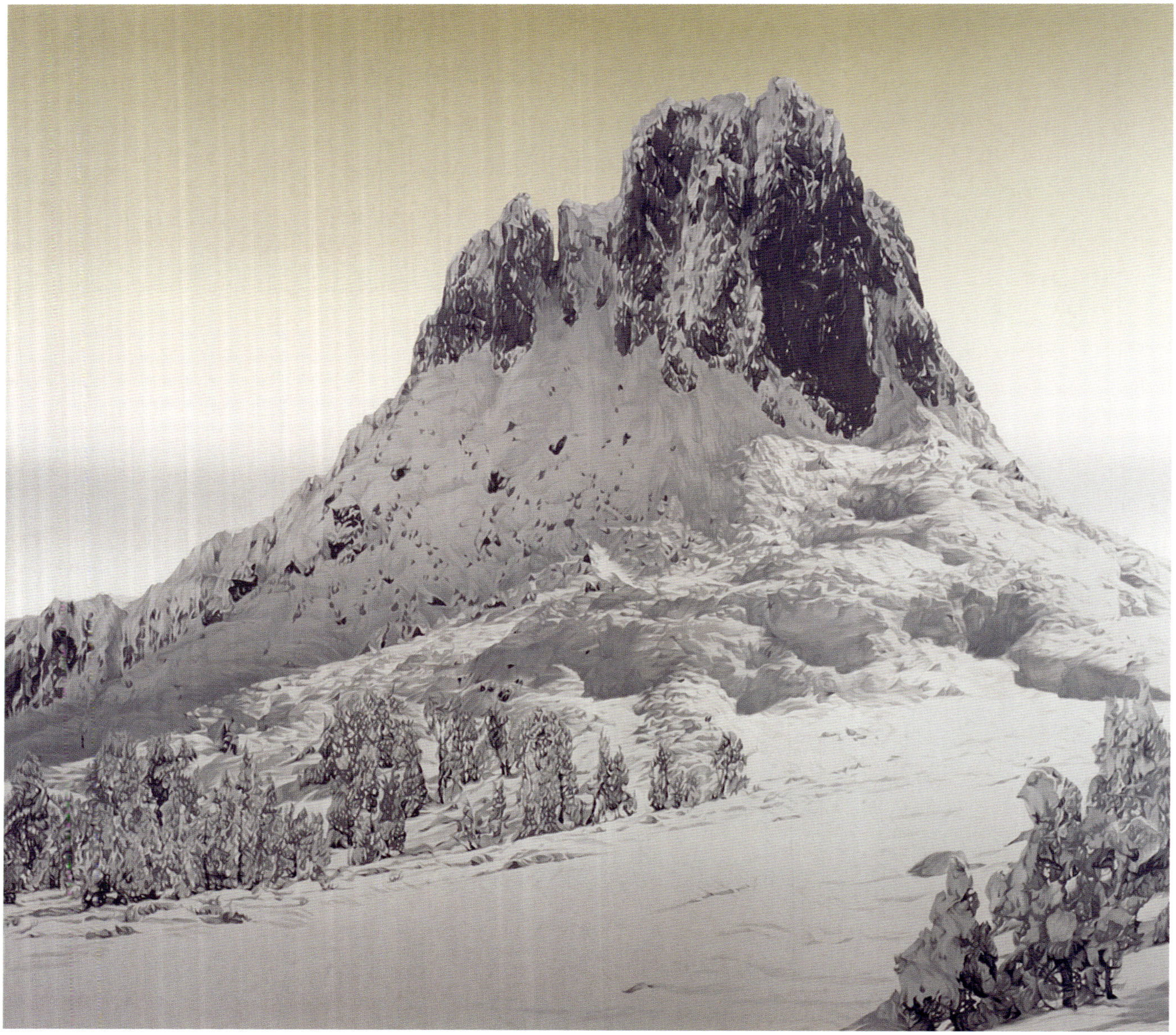

Background
As a child I grew up in a farmer's family. I used to run around fields and scenic mountains. I was lost in the fascination of nature, looking at animals, trees and catching insects and I would run home when it got dark. There are lots of animistic stories based on Shintoism and Buddhism, and these have urged me to gain a deeper relationship with nature.

I wrote a statement for my painting *Mountain F*, which I think neatly summarizes the relationship between my background and my paintings: 'When I grew up as a child in Japan, on a clear winter day, one could see the mountains called Sanage-yama to the east and Ibuki-yama to the west. And just north of our town, there was a small hill with three black boulders, one of which had a footprint-like indentation. The local legends had it that a mythical goblin called Tengu used this as a stepping-stone to jump across from Ibuki-yama to Sanage-yama. As a child I knew this to be a made-up story but I remember pondering over the legend from time to time when I gazed upon these mountains as I played.

The work is based on an actual mountain in Tasmania but the image in my painting is affected by how I see those mountains in my mind.'

Traditional Japanese art
I am very interested in the way Noh (Japanese traditional theatre) expresses mythological stories in codified form with symbolic masks and costumes, especially in describing the passage between reality and the afterlife. Something that excites me is the way Noh reconfigures abstract events.

I have great admiration for Hokusai; I hope I can live to 90 [years old] and keep progressing like him. I feel his language of simplified subjects and strong compositions manages to summarize a certain perception of reality, and his way of stripping down his choice of colour is always fascinating. Yet somehow the element of life is still breathing within his visualization.

Scene
Having lived more than 20 years in London, I feel I do not belong to any particular scene. I feel some isolation, but I've become comfortable with the situation; in fact, I feel liberated and my sorrow becomes a faint freedom Maybe this has become the central element of my identity.

Process, subject matter and style
Many paintings are based on my own memories but I look for clues in actual photographs (a photograph that matches my own memory). I hope I am not confined to one style: I prefer to work through a certain mood and feeling instead of being focused on one style. Technique is constantly developing with each painting. Different subjects will function as triggers for the evolution of technique and style I sometimes find interesting results from unexpected material events. In order to obtain this, I have moments of hard negotiation or painful failure. All this process is very important for every painting I work on.

The choice of subject matter is drawn from a metaphysical plot, or idea, while its realization is mostly the product of chance or fate. In this abstract conversation I find clues in books (often encyclopedias), films, TV ... I can then project my feelings on to these images and play around with the drawings I make of them. It becomes a subject when it changes itself from a strong impression into a reality. But really the image is only crystallized in the daily practice of painting on the canvas.

Painting as a journey
A big painting can take about a month or two, but it is never a routine. Each painting has its own journey. I am willing to take the risk of experimenting and accepting the displacement of material accidents on canvas. Through instantaneous decisions, failures, emotional pain, verifications, I will progressively get closer to the abstract objects in my mind that I have been holding on to as the subject. Contemplation of nature plays an important part.

I hope my paintings are never a conclusion, and that they just open up a space. They consist of layers of consciousness and unconsciousness, events and phenomena recurring behind my eyes.

On the role of painting
Art is never hemmed-in by a subject, it is an opportunity for travelling into images. I keep visiting the gallery to look at them intensely to confirm what's there ... what I can feel instead of what I can read. Paintings force you to have a physical relationship in space as well as involving you, forcing you to check details, layers and senses.

Rooted Blue Boat
2008, oil on canvas, 190 × 270cm
(75 × 106 in).

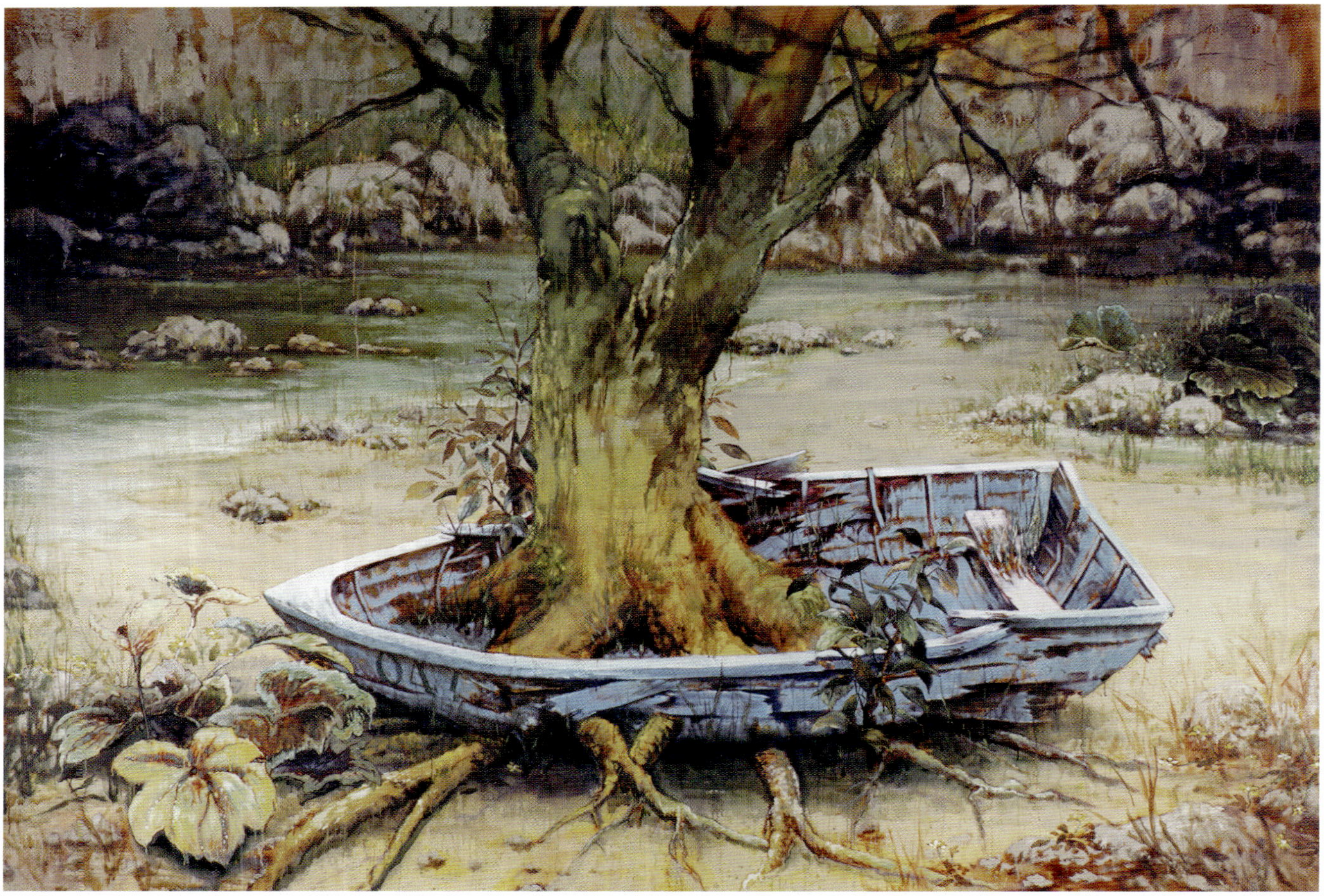

Old Nest
2012, oil on canvas, 270 × 195cm
(106 × 77 in).

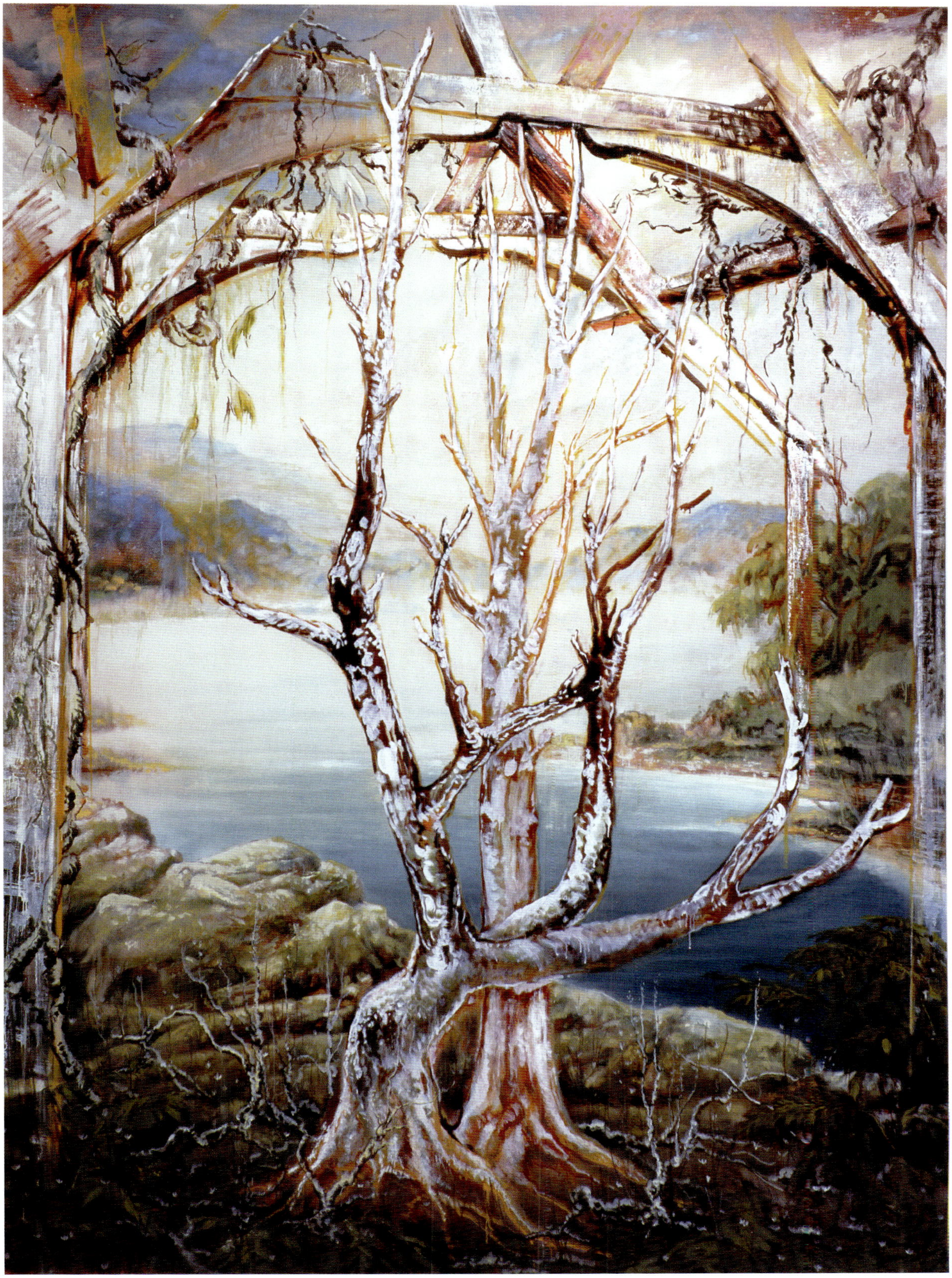

Long Snake Moan
2011, acrylic and oil on board,
122 × 140 cm (48 × 55 in).

Nicholas McLeod
Born: 1982, Norfolk (UK)
Lives: London

Nicholas McLeod moved from his native Norfolk to London in search of the excitement of the big city. After a period spent in random jobs and travelling around the world, he decided to study Fine Art Painting at City and Guilds of London Art School, graduating in 2009. McLeod has developed a refined painting technique, with which he is constantly experimenting, for the subject matter to which he returns obsessively and almost exclusively. In remote, disused and haunting places he recognizes a space where the banal and the momentous meet.

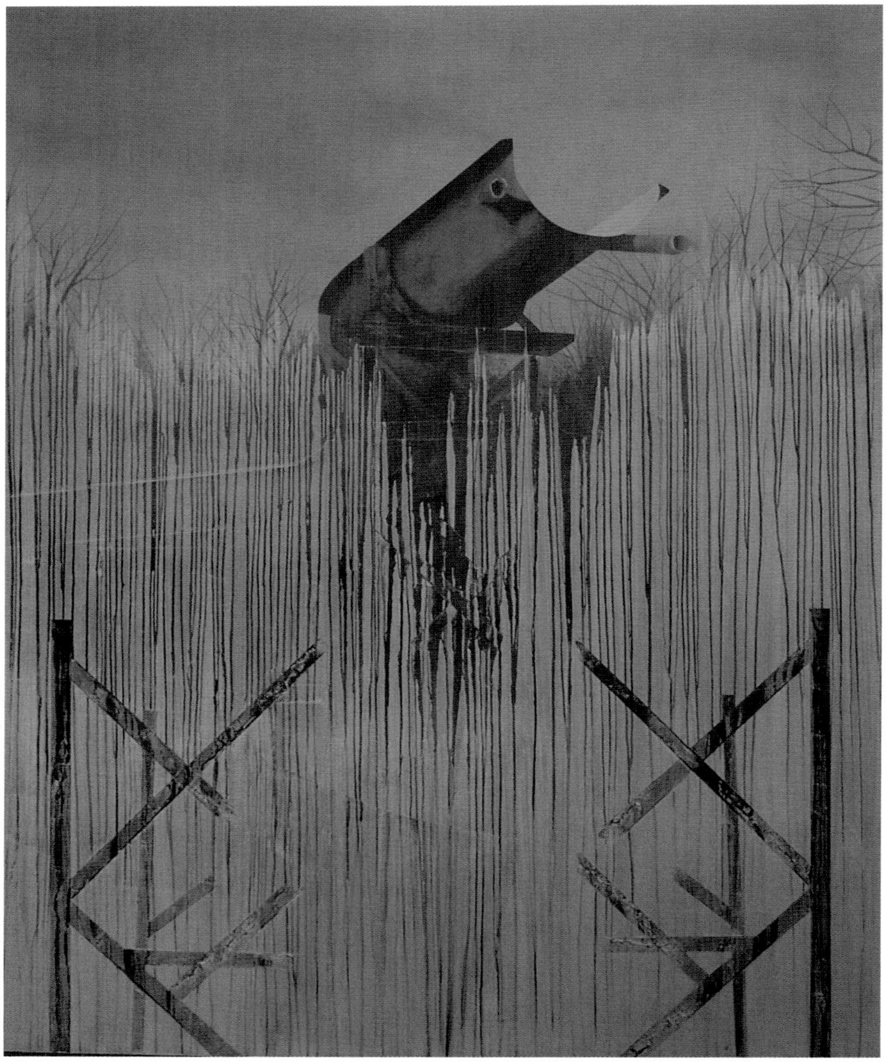

Inspiration

I used to type words like 'haunted house' or 'horror house' into web search engines and look at the images that would come up. I am interested in the psychological effect such environments have on us. The dual notions of the familiar/unfamiliar, intrigue/repulsion, beauty/horror, are themes that I attempt to deal with through my practice. The choice of the subjects was a very instinctive process: even before printing the image out, I would already be thinking in terms of painterly execution. I also like the static and the distortions produced by old VHS players on the surface of the screen. When I took a photograph of the screen, the effect was even more distorted. I started working on techniques for replicating those visual distortions. In some of my paintings, a thin layer of paint comes down [across the surface] and the way the pigment is almost dissolving looks like static on the TV screen.

I also look at old 'true crime' magazines. For me, their images instantly sum up everything that I am trying to capture in my work. In the 1950s the photographic and printing technologies weren't so advanced, but I think those kinds of images hold much more power and energy than the contemporary ones. In my work, I try to capture that strange artificial light and the creepy details.

Subject matter

I've always been fascinated by [the film] *Psycho* and when I was at art school, I started painting the house from it and from *The Amityville Horror* and similar films. This kind of visual imagery has been overdone and can easily border on cliché. But when I went to see a show of Michael Raedecker's work, I saw that he was creating quite haunting images in a really subtle way. It had a profound effect on me. I understood that if you leave something implied, the image has a much more powerful effect. From that moment, I have always tried not to be too specific or didactic. I think that the job of the artist is to lead the viewers to a certain thing and then just let them go with it in their own personal way.

Process

I guess there is a whole mystique around the artist and the idea of the studio. Painting is a strange occupation: I lock myself in my studio for 14 hours a day, not talking to anyone and not answering the phone. Spending so much time trying to make work in a confined space is quite a brutal thing. But I believe that if you want to improve and get better at it, the only way is just to keep working as much as possible. I tend to make several paintings of the same image and some of them can take me two or three weeks. You have to be pretty obsessed with one image to keep repeating it over and over. The reason why I do it is that I want to capture the feeling that they evoke in me. It is a long process of trial and error and you can only figure out how to use certain techniques and how to employ them by trying them out – through applying paint on the canvas and seeing what happens. My work consists of figuring out how you can articulate your concerns in the most concise way.

Technique

Part of what inspires me to use the medium of paint for this is that it can be so many things at the same time, from immediate to slow, powdery to slick, thick to thin, delineated to evanescent. It is these inherent contradictions that I exploit in order to bring me close to the unease I wish to convey.

Speaking about Hitchcock's film *The Birds*, the philosopher Slavoj Žižek describes the moment they attack as, 'a foreign dimension intruding upon the domestic space ripping apart the sense of reality'. He goes on to state that, 'when our proper dwelling within a symbolic space is disturbed, reality disintegrates'. I see the poured paint or the areas of impasto within my own paintings operating in a similar way. These techniques are employed to intrude upon the figurative elements of my work. They are an attempt to disrupt and destabilize the image and to try to articulate the emotional response that I have towards my source material. Essentially I want my work to oscillate between the accurate representation of a subject and the complete annihilation of it.

The speed of painting

I hope that when people look at my paintings they see something new and fresh. I want people to think: 'I've never seen something like this. How has he made it? How has he created that effect?' That is what interests me in painting. I am one of those people who looks at a painting wondering what colour glaze has been used and what colour has been used before the one on top. I used to be a real geek, look at Constable's paintings in Tate Britain and make notes on how I thought he had done things. And this informs the way I paint now, working with contrasts and layers upon the surface. I've always been interested in different speeds of painting, the slow and more detailed one combined with the speed of poured paint that washes down the thick paint. There is always something of interest going on, on the surface of the painting.

Lingering (Version 2)
2012, acrylic and oil on canvas,
100 × 122 cm (39 × 48 in).

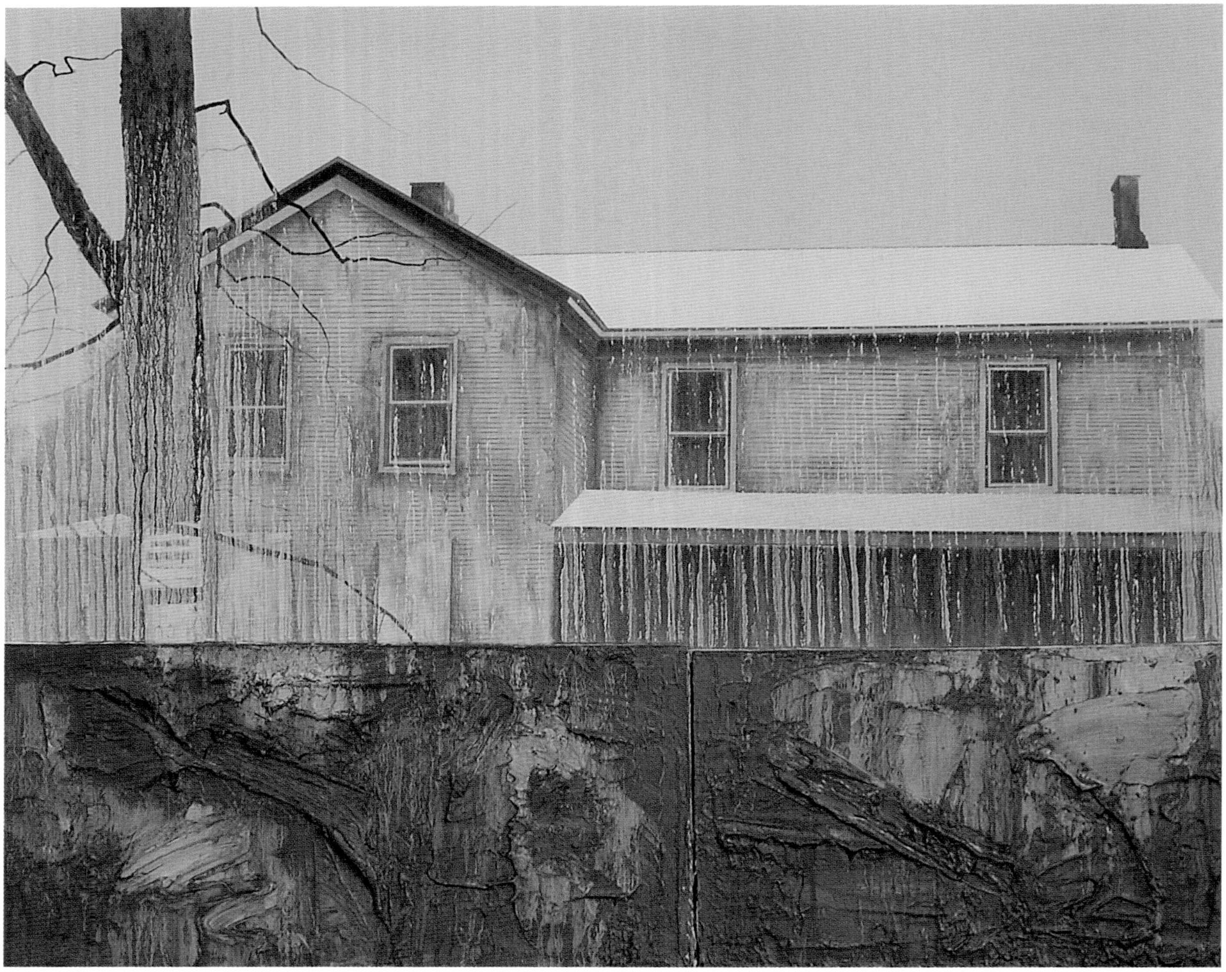

Old Appetites
2011, acrylic and oil on board,
122 × 154 cm (48 × 61 in).

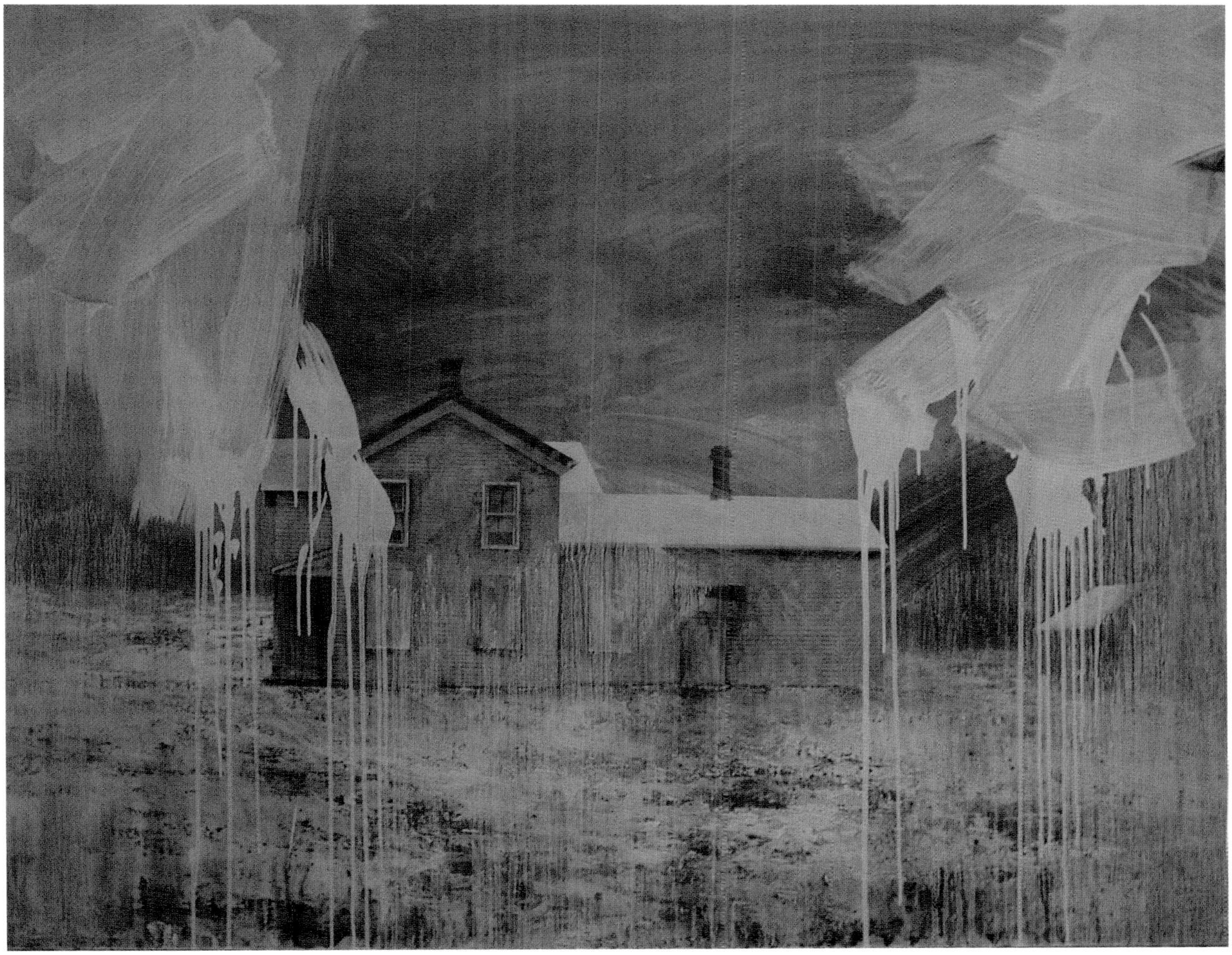

Freedom under Flag
2011, acrylic on canvas, 200 × 150 cm
(79 × 59 in).

Hesam Rahmanian
Born: 1980, Knoxville, Tennessee
Lives: Dubai

Hesam Rahmanian describes himself as being like an ant building a world around him. Growing up surrounded by animals, his first dream was to become a veterinarian. When he realized that art, as a process of creation, is the closest thing to nature he opted for painting instead. Since then, animals have been the main subject of his art. But in 2009 Rhamanian created a series of works reflecting on the elections and subsequent protests in Iran. Apart from this specific choice to depict events, for him the political nature of painting lies in its inherent ability to challenge and propel contemporary culture.

Art school
At art school I was required to take life-drawing classes and the only benefit was the big studio space, of which I took advantage. What they teach in art school is formal training, but the same skills can be developed in a more natural progression and in a more firmly anchored way when self-taught.

Ideal masters
From childhood I was fascinated by the spontaneity in the works of Francis Bacon and always considered David Hockney a master of drawing and colour. Gerhard Richter and Luc Tuymans are certainly the leading painters today; Wilhelm Sasnal's fluid use of paint and simple suggestions of form are a great inspiration to me.

Inspiration
Whatever the source of inspiration, it is always challenged through the process of creating an artwork. The process, or decomposing period, between life and death, and back round to life, is very important to me. I'm interested in how this process leads to creation, in a way that is similar to the process of creating art and painting.

Process
I pursue my instinctive interests, obsessions and dreams. Rather than becoming bored of a routine approach, I evolve my work. All of my work is the result of the path of explorations behind it. When I work I think about painting. I think about the subject I am painting. I let myself enjoy and discover new things. The discovery of new things leads into other discoveries; sometimes the new discoveries are related to the previous work and sometimes not.

Technology
Photoshop and digital media alike are just another medium. If they facilitate the artist's ambitions or enhance their developments, then why not use them, as David Hockney did. This being said, no medium can ever replace another – technical or technological progressions are not used exclusively over older methods.

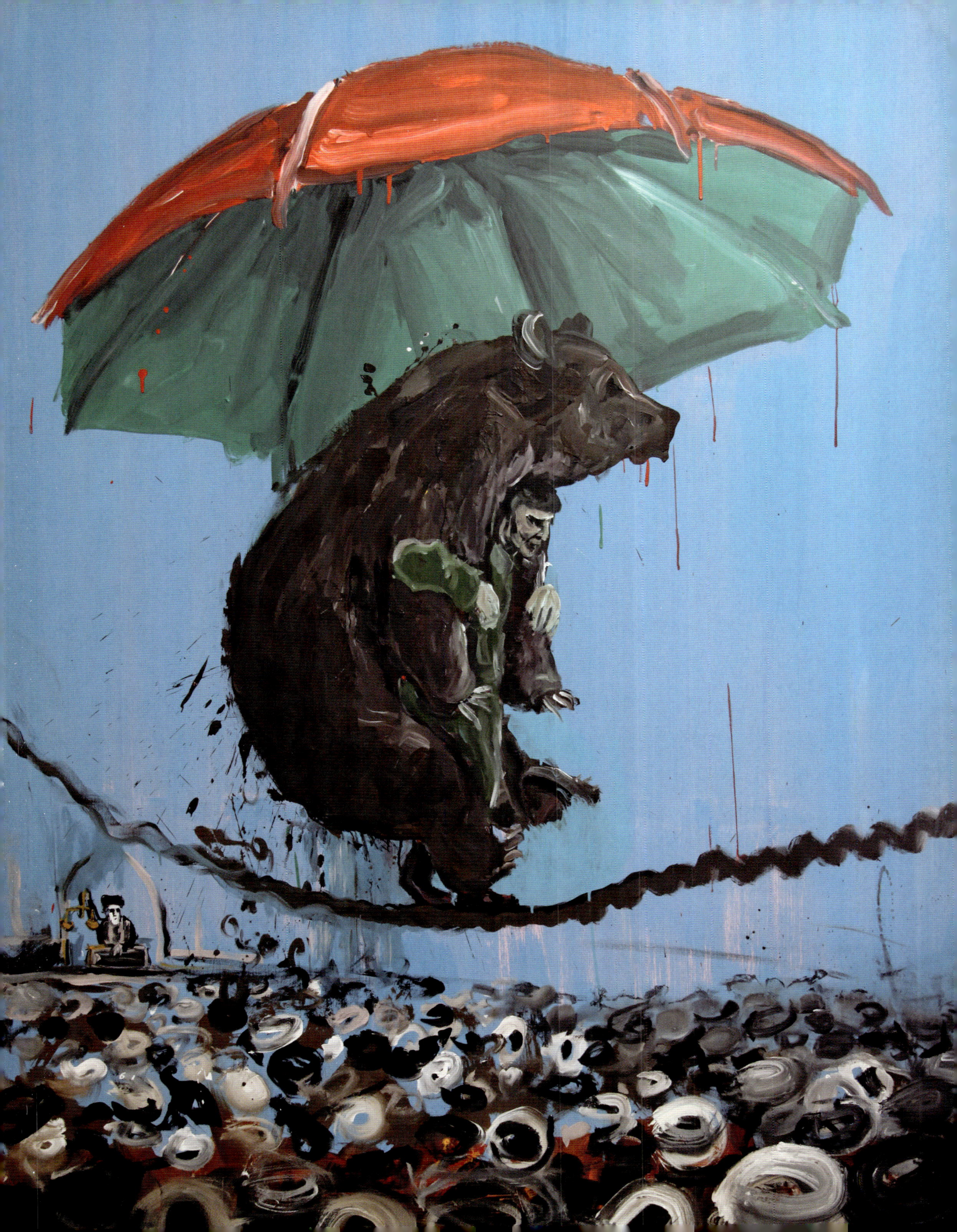

Old but Eager
2012, acrylic on canvas, 70 × 50 cm
(27⅝ × 19¾ in).

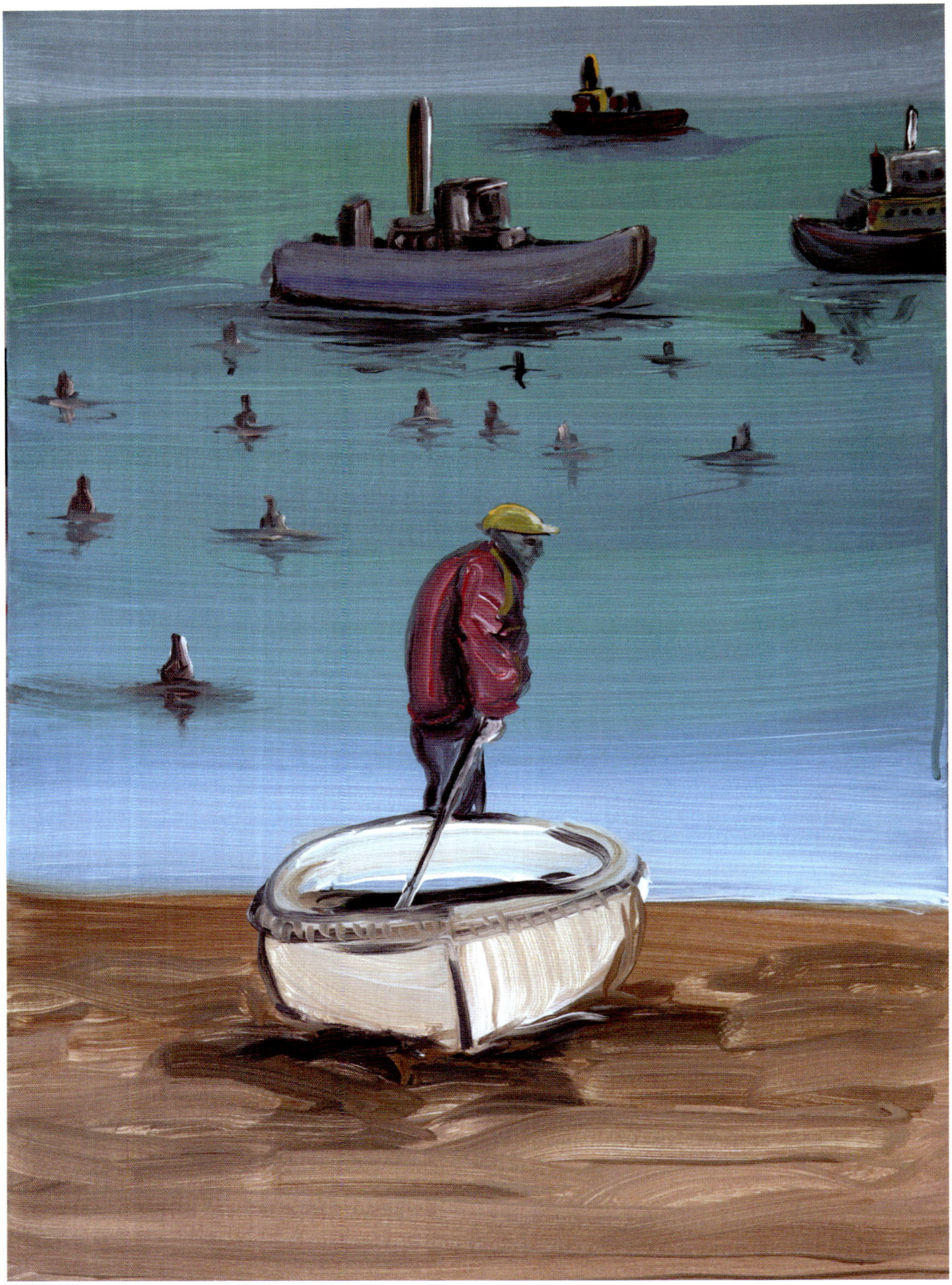

The President is Dead (IV)
2011, acrylic on canvas, 120 × 150 cm
(47 × 59 in).

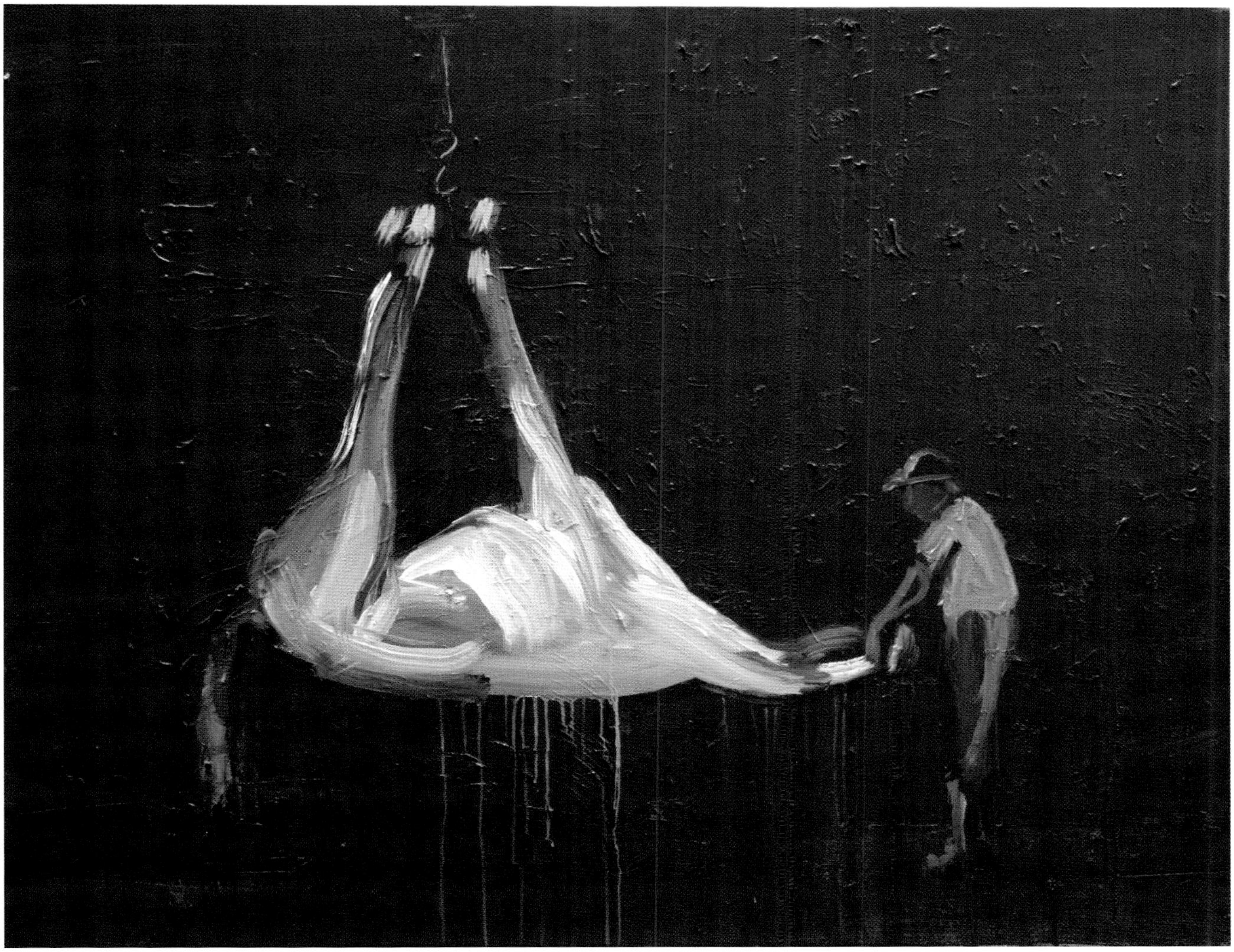

Long Hard Road out of Hell
2011, acrylic on canvas 150 × 194 cm
(59 × 76 in).

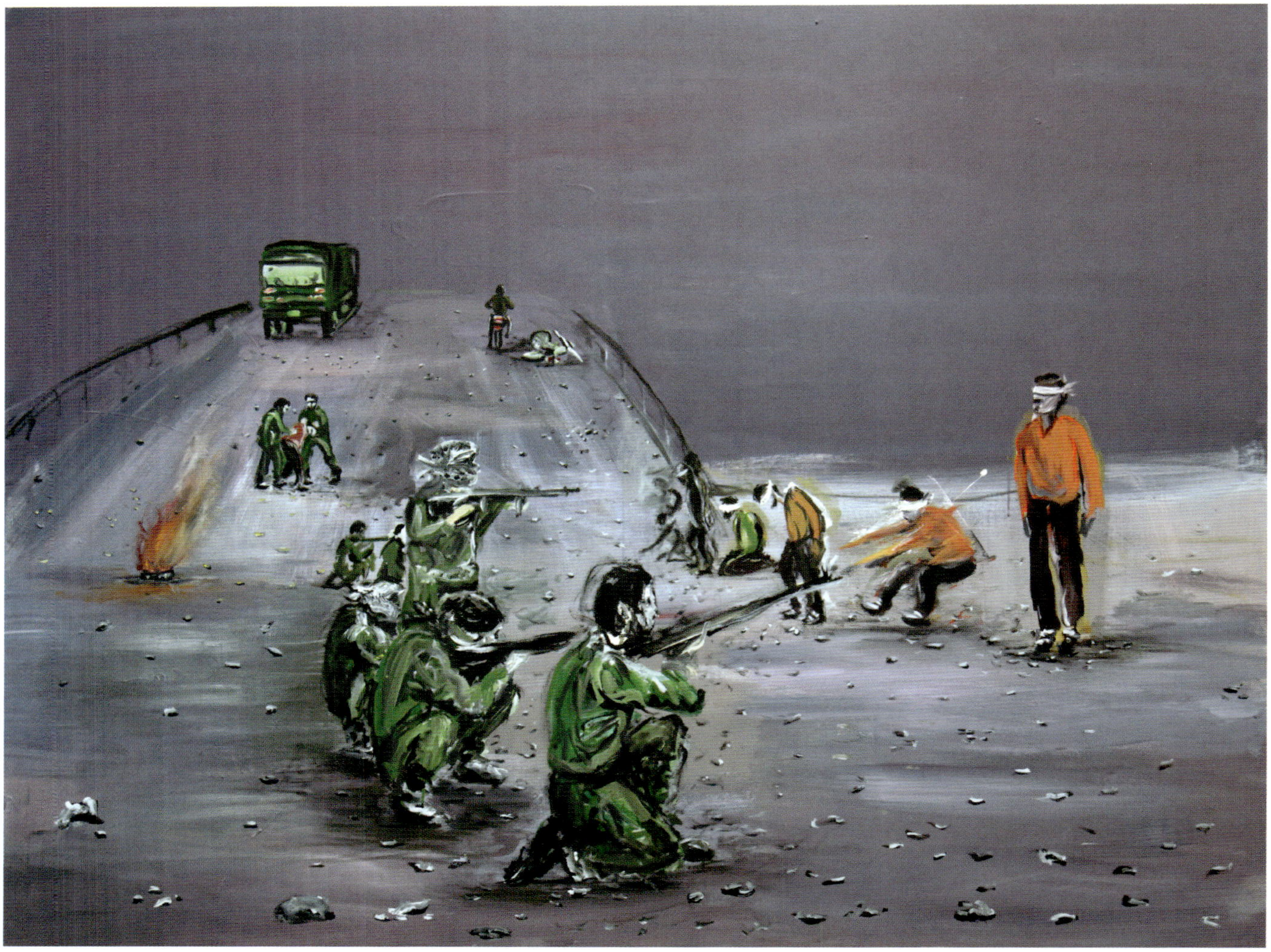

Follow the Leader (I)
2010, acrylic on canvas, 180 × 145 cm
(71 × 57 in).

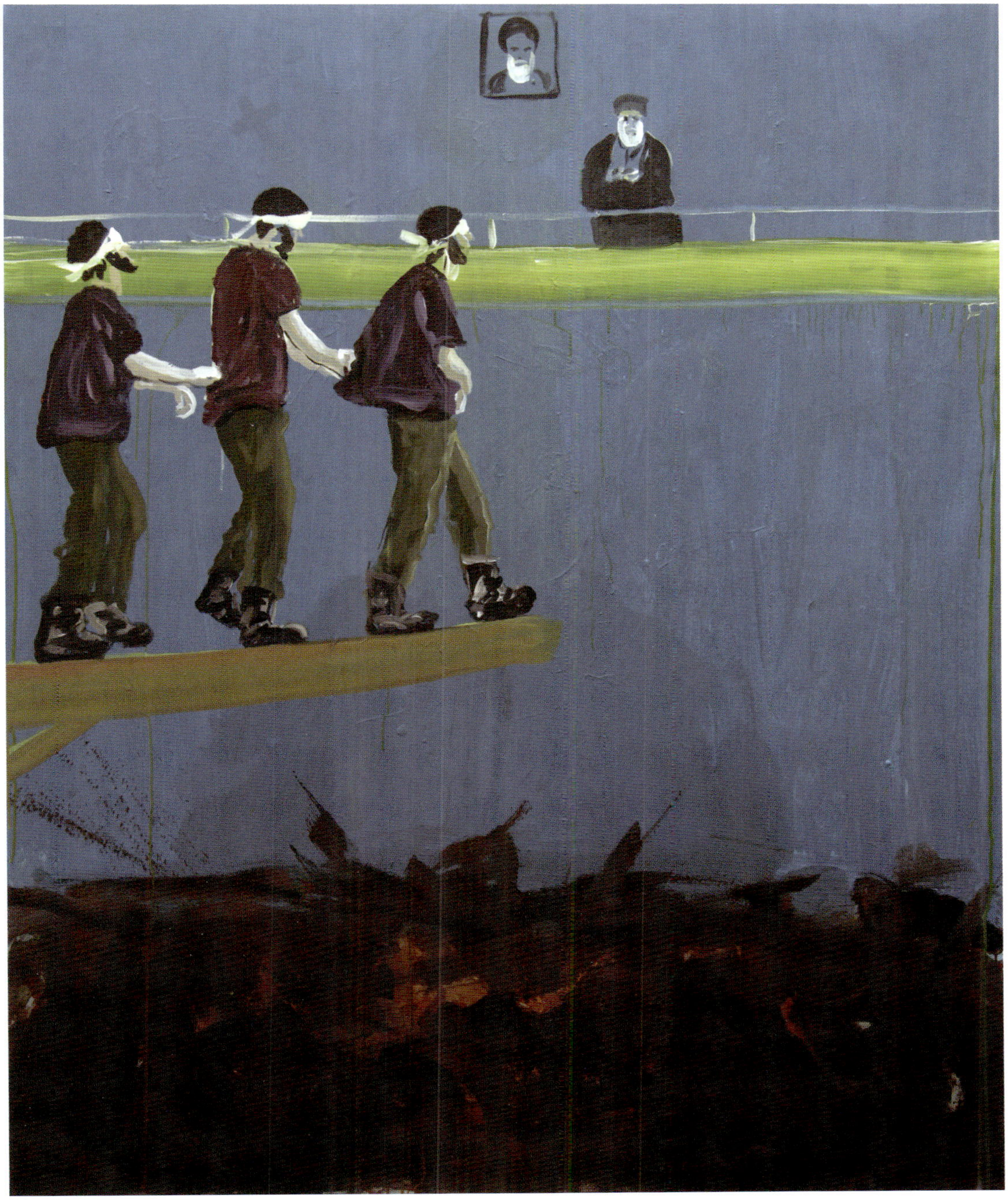

That Which Makes Me (3)
2010, watercolour and acrylic on paper, 28 × 28cm (11 × 11 in).

Simon Willems
Born: 1971, Shoreham-by-Sea (UK)
Lives: London

The art of Simon Willems wrestles with the perceptive distinction between the real and the imaginary, especially in reference to forgotten or denied systems of belief. Images from the Internet, news, history and cinema, as well as those depicting some of Willem's own experiences, become metaphors for the many let downs that affect contemporary existence. In his canvases characters from *Star Wars* and fast-food culture icons inhabit scenarios extracted from real documentaries of the Nazi era, religious symbols are interwoven with leisure destinations in snow globes and solitary landscapes inspired by art history shelter contemporary hermits. The apparently incongruous universes of reality and fiction merge with a consistency made possible only by painting.

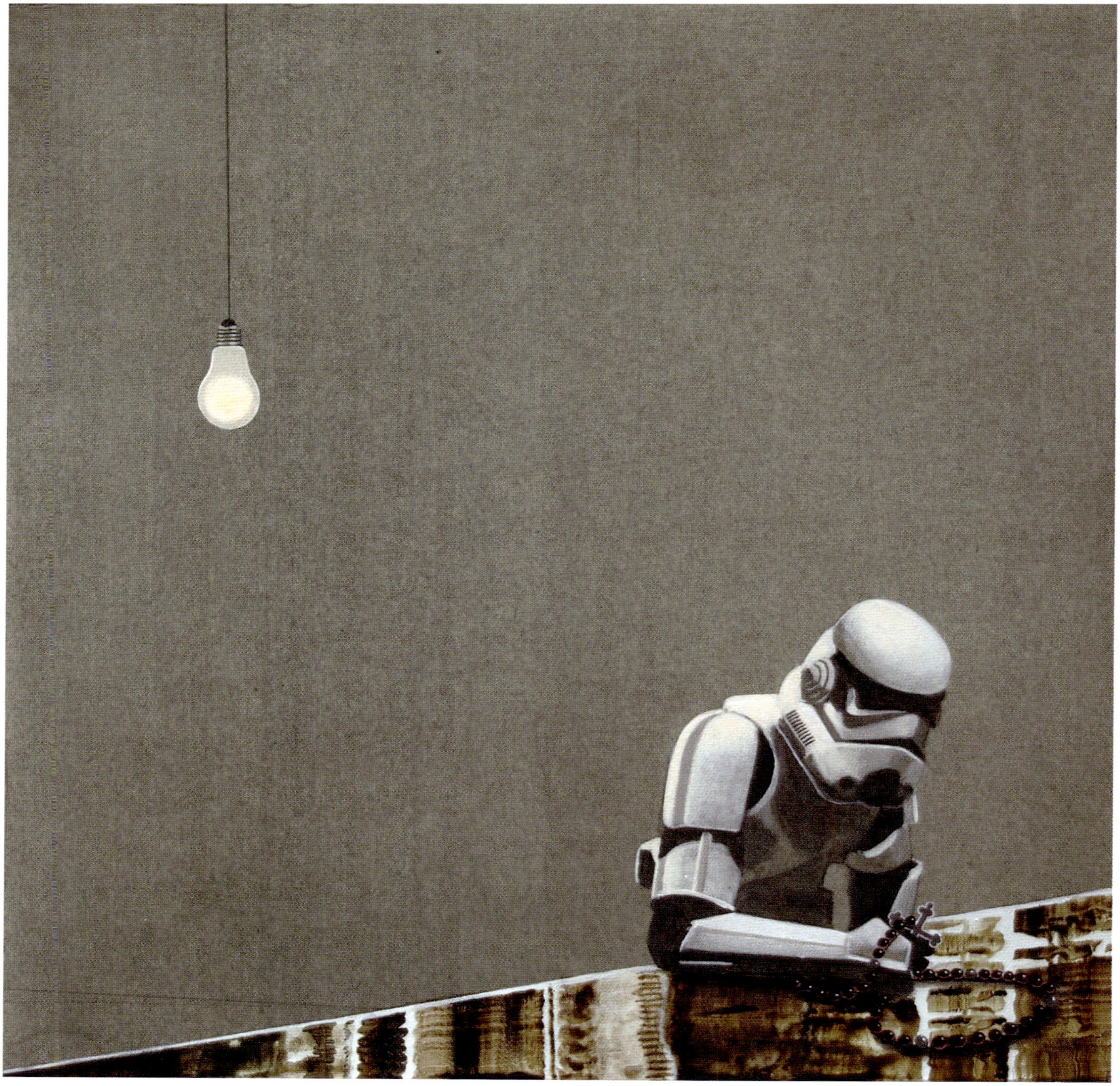

Ideas
My work develops from anecdotal, documentary as well as imagined sources. I tend to be drawn to images and ideas that deal with themes of alienation, withdrawal and denial.
My thinking tends to stem from the recognition of incongruous contexts that refer to specific places and people, fictitious and real. I am drawn to narratives where history, denial and belief become interchangeable. The work can be drawn as much from a news article or actual experience as it might from a found image or piece of art history. My project 'All Things For All People' was conceived in response to the unexpected discovery of a mountainside religious cult, which I became aware of, oddly, through a pair of binoculars from a pedalo, while in France in 2009. The event in this sense became the catalyst for the project.

Preparation
Most of the time I'll stew over an image or idea for several months before I start. Within this period I'll assess the possibilities – in terms of how I understand what I'm interested in and how its context makes sense to me. This develops into a body of reference made up of drawings and notes that enables me to move forward.

Process
I've normally got any number of paintings on the go at any one time and they'll all make different demands on me. Some pieces can take a matter of hours to resolve, whereas others can take up to a couple of years. Critically the terms of a painting can change dramatically during its making and it's often the recognition of that which takes the time. Sometimes I don't know if a painting is finished – it's far from an exact science.

Cinematic and pre-cinematic
I guess my most direct reference to films is *Star Wars*, but even then it was more to do with the idea of humanizing fictitious icons to force real emotions in the viewer, than it was specifically about *Star Wars*. Some of the thinking for the 'Stormtrooper Mourning the Loss of his Mother' series for instance was inspired by Oliver Hirschbiegel's film (2004) *Der Untergang* (*Downfall*) about Hitler's last few days in the bunker. In a more archival way I sometimes photograph film-stills in order to record and refer to formal atmospheric details. I'm very interested in those pre-cinematic painters whose work anticipated the advent of film – like Albert Bierstadt.

Realism
Realism is a fraught and pluralistic term. In the more generic sense, Realism lends itself to our culture of 'image' and images. This affords us a certain scope to reflect, anthropologically and politically, in how we understand those terms. In an age of instantaneity and faceless production, Realism in painting offers us the possibility of the individual voice. This should be cherished.

The role of painting
Painting as an activity is an anachronism in the twenty-first century. Yet it's important to recognize that anachronism is not synonymous with defunction. Painting is not mutually exclusive from that which followed it historically, and in our age of endless images, painting can, among other things, be image too. However unlike other contemporary methods of image production, painting is achieved through a slowness, what some have termed a belatedness. Image as an object and as a representation of compressed time in this sense is painting's key difference and its opportunity.

Meal Deal Archive (2)
2010, oil and acrylic on linen,
35 × 30 cm (13¾ × 11¾ in).

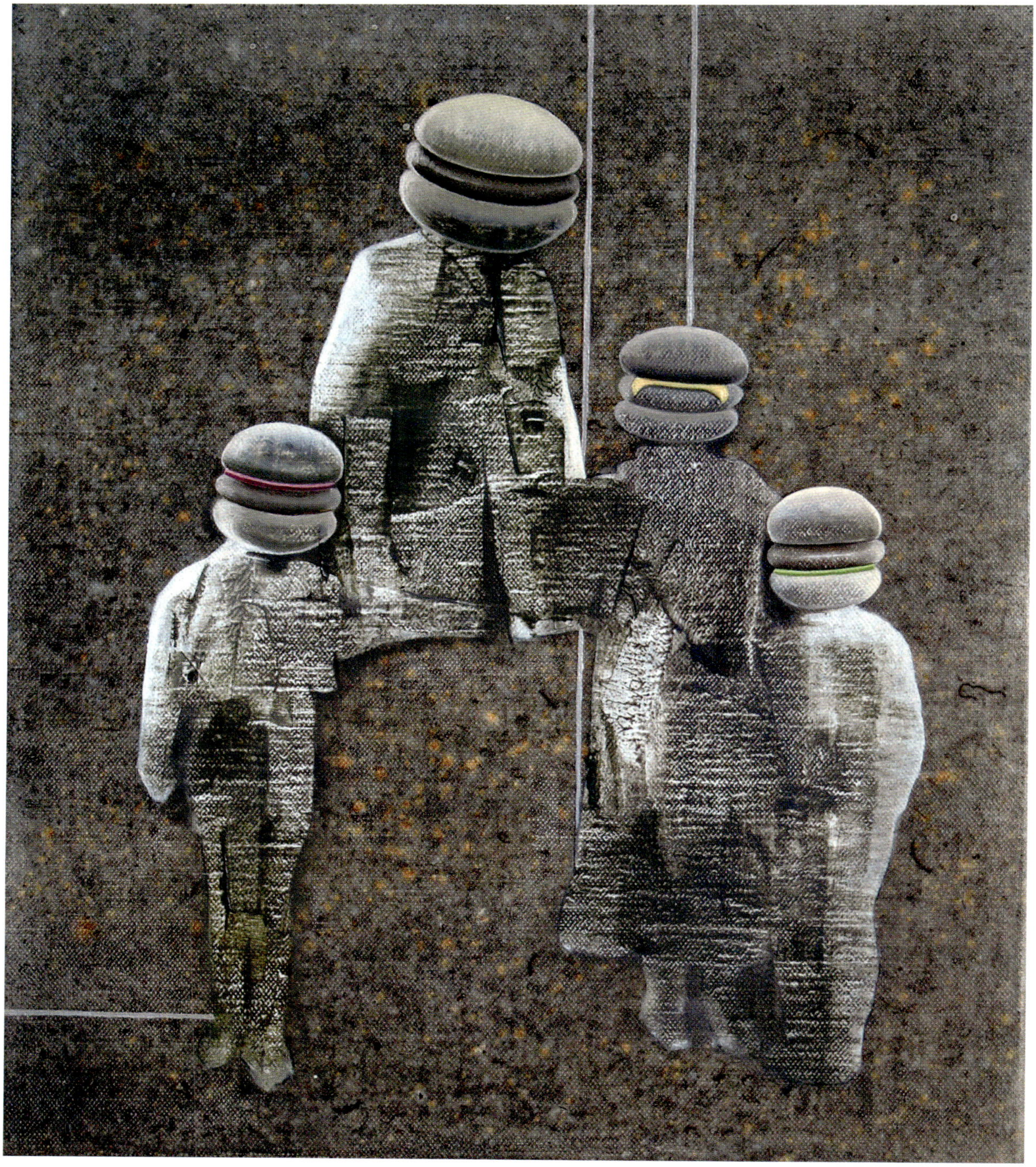

You Do Not Want to Believe
2013, oil and acrylic on linen,
90 × 70cm (35½ × 27⅝ in).

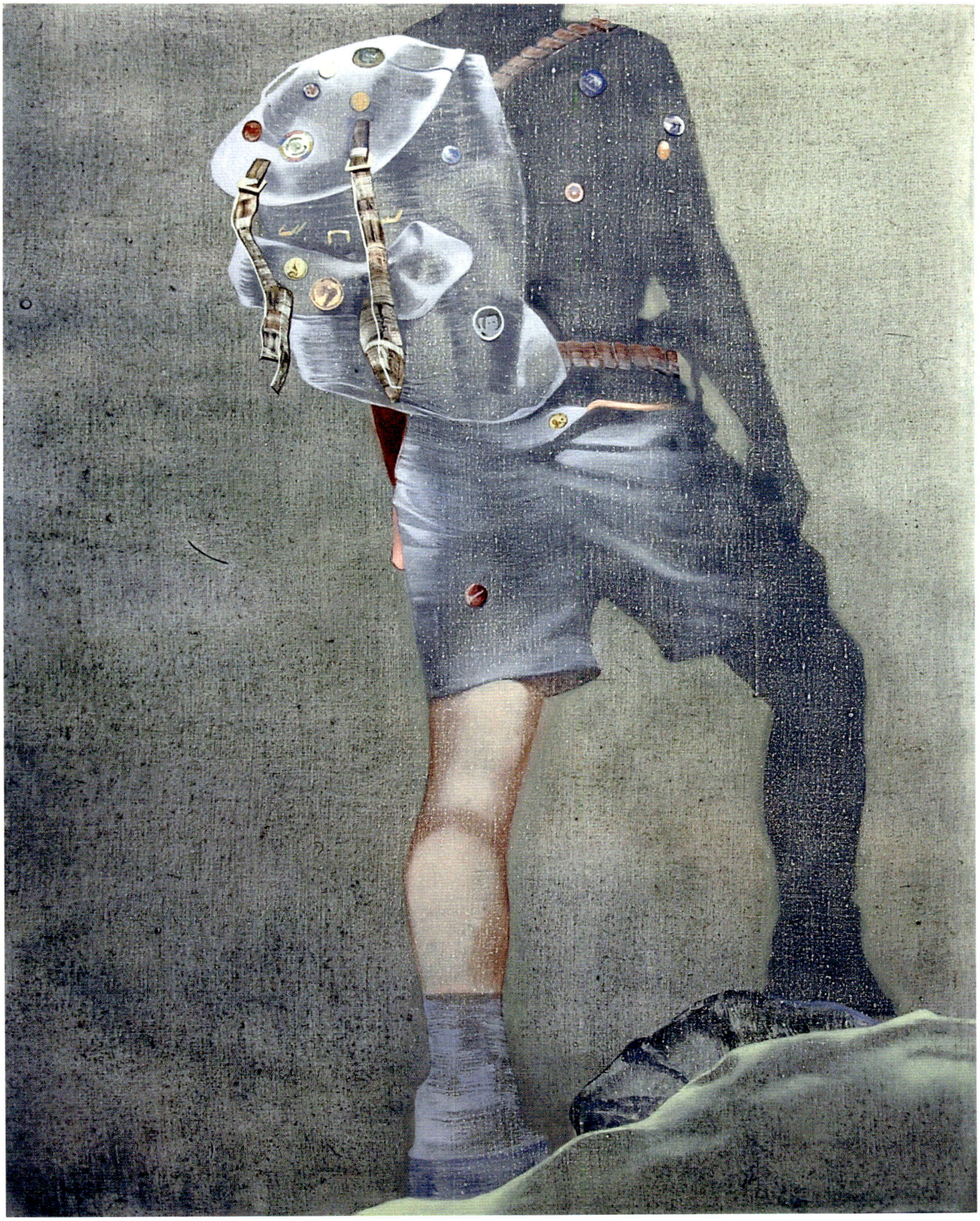

Marc Valli is the founder of the retail and bookselling company Magma as well as the magazines *Graphic* and *Elephant*. His books include *RGB: Reviewing Graphics in Britain*, *Walk the Line* and *Microworlds* (also with Margherita Dessanay).

Margherita Dessanay studied Contemporary Art Theory at Goldsmith's, University of London and writes regularly for *Elephant* magazine. She has co-written a number of books, including *It's A Stick Up!* and *Stencil Republic*.

Eduardo Berliner
Woman with Dog and CPR, photo: Eduardo Berliner
Little Pig and Tubing, photo: Edouard Fraipont
Handsaw, photo: Andrea Capella

Anna Bjerger
Man with Light, photo: Peter Tijhuis. Courtesy of the artist, David Risley Gallery, Copenhagen and Galerie Gabriel Rolt, Amsterdam
Film Still, Swimmers, Abyss, Camouflage and Wood Anemones, courtesy of the artist, David Risley Gallery, Copenhagen and Paradise Row Gallery, London

Guillaume Bresson
All images, courtesy of Galerie Nathalie Obadia Paris/Bruxelles

Andy Denzler
All images, courtesy of the artist

Jeremy Geddes
All images, courtesy of the artist

Luka Kurashvili
All images, © Luka Kurashvili. Courtesy of Ten Haaf Projects Amsterdam

Jerome Lagarrigue
All images, courtesy of Galerie Olivier Waltman Paris/Miami

Ulrich Lamsfuss
Dirk Hasskarl, Michel Houellebecq (Qvest Sept./Okt. 2006), photo: B. Huet/Tutti. Courtesy of Gallery Daniel Templon
Fergus Greer, Leigh Bowery, 14/ August 1990, Session III (Looks), photo: Jörg von Bruchhausen. Courtesy of Rennie Collection, Vancouver
Holger Niehaus/Ulrich Lamsfuß, Arbeiterbild, Fließbandarbeiterin (Sophie Rois), photo: Jörg von Bruchhausen. Private Collection. Courtesy of Galerie Hammelehle und Ahrens, Cologne
Heike Ollerz/Ulrich Lamsfuß, African Torso, Dual Sex (3B scientific, Made in Germany III), photo: Tamara Lorenz. Courtesy of Galerie Hammelehle und Ahrens, Cologne

Marcin Majewoski
All images, courtesy of the artist

Harding Meyer
All images, courtesy of Galerie Voss, Düsseldorf

Justin Mortimer
All images, courtesy of the artist

Muntean and Rosenblum
All images, courtesy of Georg Kargl, Vienna, Team Gallery New York, Mario Sequeira, Portugal

Benjamin Rubloff
All images, courtesy of the artist

Wilhelm Sasnal
Roy Orbison, Kacper and Untitled (2012), copyright Wilhelm Sasnal, courtesy of Sadie Coles HQ, London
Kodak, Untitled (2010), Untitled (Andrzej and Adam) and Untitled (Anka), courtesy of Anton Kern Gallery, New York

Li Songsong
All images, © Li Songsong, courtesy of Pace Beijing

Wayne Toepp
All images, courtesy of the artist

Jonathan Wateridge:
All images, copyright Jonathan Wateridge
Inter, Glass Doors, Boy on Wall, Lift I, Lift II, photo: Frederik Nilsen. Courtesy of L&M Arts, Los Angeles
Matinee and Swimming holes, photo: Tessa Angus. Courtesy of All Visual Arts, London

James White
All images, courtesy of Max Wigram Gallery, London

Uwe Wittwer
All images, © photo Atelier Uwe Wittwer. Courtesy of Atelier Uwe Wittwer

Ayman Baalbaki
All images, courtesy of Agial Art Gallery, Beirut

François Bard
All images, courtesy of Galerie Olivier Waltman, Paris/Miami

Kevin Cosgrove
All images, photo: mother's tankstation Dublin. Courtesy of mother's tankstation, Dublin
Charcoal (with blue bench), private collection, Ireland
Car lift, private collection, Marc and Livia Straus
Museum Workshop, private collection, Ali Adler
Taxi on lift, private collection, South Korea
Workshop with Car Door, private collection, London

Cynthia Daignault
All images, courtesy of Cynthia Daignault and Lisa Cooley, New York

Tim Eitel
All images, © Tim Eitel, courtesy Galerie EIGEN+ART Leipzig/Berlin and Pace Wildenstein/DACS, 2013
Tauben, photo: Uwe Walter, Berlin. Collection Essl Foundation, Klosterneuburg/Vienna
Öffnung, photo: Kerry Ryan McFate. Private collection
Boot, photo: Uwe Walter, Berlin. Staatliche Museum Berlin, National Gallery, Collection Marx
Besucher, photo: Uwe Walter, Berlin. Collection of George and Margot Greig
Architect, photo: Uwe Walter, Berlin. Private Collection, Rheinland-Pfalz

Zhang Enli
All images © Zhang Enli. Courtesy of the artist and Hauser & Wirth/ ShanghART
Circulez! Il n'y a rien à voir (with Moshekwa Langa), © congo bleu. objectif-exhibitions

Maya Gold
All images, courtesy of Alon Segev Gallery, Tel Aviv
Echo and Maritime, photo: Meidad Suchowolski

Oda Jaune
All images, photo: B.Huet/Tutti. Courtesy of the artist and Daniel Templon Gallery

Chantal Joffe
All images, courtesy of the artist and Victoria Miro Gallery, London
© Chantal Joffe

Thoralf Knobloch
Tankstelle, nachts, Boot im Eis, kieloben and Rettungsgerät, photo: Jörg von Bruchhausen. Courtesy the artist and Galerie Gebr. Lehmann, Berlin | Dresden
Wegweiser and Bahnkreutz, photo: Werner Lieberknecht, Dresden. Courtesy of the artist and Galerie Gebr. Lehmann, Dresden/Berlin and Wilkinson Gallery London
X, Sommer, photo: Jörg von Bruchhausen, Berlin. Courtesy of the artist, Galerie Gebr. Lehmann, Dresden/Berlin and Galleri Flach, Stockholm

Ronald Ophuis
Wounded Man and Marches Funebres, Girl with Gun, courtesy of Galerie Bernard Ceysson
The Bet, Boy or Girl, Sierra Leone 2001, courtesy of Aeroplastics Contemporary Brussels and Galerie Bernard Ceysson
Gacaca, 4 Hutu prisoners during their Trial, Rwanda 2004 and War Story Teller, Sierra Leone 2010 nr. 2, courtesy of Upstream Gallery, Amsterdam
War Story Teller (portrait), courtesy of Aeroplastics Contemporary Brussels

Jina Park
Packing and Checking 02 and Ladder 02, private collection
Good-bye, collect on of Mongin Art Space

Till Rabus
All images, courtesy of the artist
Capotes dans WC publique, courtesy of Aeroplastics Contemporary Brussels
Voodoo n°1 and Composition picturale n°2 and Epouvantail n°4, private collection

Alessandro Raho
All images, courtesy of the artist and Alison Jacques Gallery, London
All images, photo: © Michael Brzezinski except Lizzy Disney, photo: © Todd White

Serban Savu
New Apartment, Landscape With Clerk and Holy Week, courtesy of the artist and Plan B Gallery, Cluj/Berlin
The Tunnel and The Owner, His Right Hand and the Workers, courtesy of the artist and Nicodim Gallery, Los Angeles
Depot, courtesy of Galerie Hussenot, Paris

Lynette Yadom-Boakye
All images, courtesy of the artist, Corvi-Mora, London and Jack Shainman Gallery, New York

Liu Xiadong
All images, © Liu Xiadong. Courtesy of Mary Boone Gallery, New York

Caroline Walker
All images, courtesy of the artist

Dan Witz
All images, courtesy of the artist

Toshimitu Baba
All images, courtesy of Toshimitsu Baba and BASE GALLERY, Tokyo

Jules de Balincourt
Itinerant Ones and Idol Hands, courtesy of Salon 94, New York
Malpais (Bad Lands), Neither Day or Night, Utopie Tyrannique, Untitled (Fireworks) and Think Globally, Act Locally, courtesy of Galerie Thaddaeus Ropac, Paris

Amy Bennett
All images, courtesy of the artist

David Brian Smith
All images, courtesy of David Brian Smith and Carl Freedman Gallery, London

Jonas Burgert
All images, courtesy of the artist and Blain|Southern. Photo: Lepkowski Studios

Kent Dorn
All images, courtesy of the artist

Joyce Ho
All images, courtesy of the artist

Sigrid Holmwood
All images, courtesy of the artist

Josephine King
All images, copyright Josephine King

Masakatsu Kondo
All images, courtesy of the artist

Nicholas McLeod
All images, courtesy of the artist

Hesham Rahmanian
All images, courtesy of the artist and Gallery Isabelle van den Eynde

Simon Willems
All images, courtesy of the artist

Published in 2014 by
Laurence King Publishing Ltd
361–373 City Road
London EC1V 1LR
United Kingdom
email: enquiries@laurenceking.com
www.laurenceking.com

A catalogue record for this book is available from the British Library.

ISBN: 978 178067 2830

Design: Matt Willey

Cover image: *Grand Central Station 2007*, Dan Witz

Printed in China